Criminal Law

First published	September, 1965
Reprinted with corrections	September, 1966
Reprinted	June, 1967
Second edition	May, 1969
Reprinted with corrections	February, 1970
Reprinted	November, 1970

Criminal Law

by

J. C. SMITH, M.A., LL.B.

of Lincoln's Inn, Barrister-at-Law;
Professor of Common Law and Head of
the Department of Law, University of Nottingham

and

BRIAN HOGAN, LL.B.

of Gray's Inn, Barrister-at-Law;
Professor of Law, University of Leeds

SECOND EDITION

LONDON
BUTTERWORTHS
1969

ENGLAND:	BUTTERWORTH & CO. (PUBLISHERS) LTD. LONDON: 88 KINGSWAY, W.C.2
AUSTRALIA:	BUTTERWORTH & CO. (AUSTRALIA) LTD. SYDNEY: 20 LOFTUS STREET MELBOURNE: 343 LITTLE COLLINS STREET BRISBANE: 240 QUEEN STREET
CANADA:	BUTTERWORTH & CO. (CANADA) LTD. TORONTO: 14 CURITY AVENUE, 16
NEW ZEALAND:	BUTTERWORTH & CO. (NEW ZEALAND) LTD. WELLINGTON: 49/51 BALLANCE STREET AUCKLAND: 35 HIGH STREET
SOUTH AFRICA:	BUTTERWORTH & CO. (SOUTH AFRICA) LTD. DURBAN: 33/35 BEACH GROVE

A/345.42

Standard Book Number—Casebound: 406 65802 1
Limp: 406 65803 X

Made and printed in Great Britain by
William Clowes and Sons Limited, London, Beccles and Colchester

Preface to the Second Edition

The past four years have seen far-reaching changes in the criminal law. The Criminal Law, Criminal Justice, Sexual Offences and Abortion Acts of 1967 and, above all, the Theft Act 1968 have effected major reforms in the substantive law. There have been many other statutory changes and a considerable amount of case law. We have attempted to take account of all these developments in this new edition. The whole of the text has been carefully reconsidered in the light of the many constructive comments made by reviewers and our own thoughts on the subject since the first edition. The discussion of general principles has been somewhat expanded but the general plan of the book remains unchanged. The utility of a book which examines the substantive law in some detail seems to have been amply demonstrated by the kind reception accorded to the first edition.

Our thanks are due to Mr. Ian Hooker of the University of Nottingham who has read the proofs and to all those—who include judges, students and policemen—who have helped us by their criticism and comment. The responsibility for any errors which remain is ours.

We have endeavoured to state the law in force on February 1, 1969.

J. C. SMITH
BRIAN HOGAN

1 February, 1969

Preface to the First Edition

It is thought that university teachers and undergraduates will require no explanation or apology for the production of a new text-book on the substantive law of crime. Criminal Law has not received the same detailed and critical examination in university text-books as have other fields of the common law, for example, Contract and Tort. In the university law schools Kenny's *Outlines of Criminal Law* has long held almost unchallenged sway but it is now sixty-three years since the first edition of that classic work appeared. An immense amount of work has been done on the Criminal Law in the meantime, not least by the present learned editor of Kenny, Dr. J. W. C. Turner. There may now be something to be said for a book which makes a completely fresh start. Cross and Jones's *Introduction to Criminal Law*, on the other hand, may be thought too brief for the needs of the undergraduate—though we are full of admiration for the amount of information and learning which those authors have packed into so small a space. Moreover, both of these books deal in a single volume not only with the substantive law but also with Criminal Procedure and Evidence. Dr. Glanville Williams's great work, *Criminal Law: The General Part*, covers only general principles, while other books covering the whole field do not face up to the problems with which the undergraduate is expected to grapple.

We have endeavoured to provide the undergraduate with as complete an exposition of the substantive Criminal Law as he has to guide him in other fields of study. We have excluded Procedure and Evidence from consideration except in so far as these are necessary for an understanding of the law. Only by so doing could we give our subject the kind of treatment we think it demands. Moreover, Evidence is now commonly regarded as a worthy subject of academic study in its own right; and Criminal Procedure is by no means always part of a Criminal Law course.

All the more important crimes are examined. Few courses, in or out of universities, perhaps cover so much ground; but the book allows scope for selection. In making the book reasonably comprehensive, we have not been unmindful of the fact that the practitioner commonly, and increasingly, finds assistance in the solution of problems in books designed primarily for students; and the citation of authorities is, therefore, more extensive than the needs of the undergraduate alone would have required. We have drawn freely on the published researches of scholars in the Criminal Law, not only in Britain but also in the Commonwealth and United States. In particular, we would acknowledge our debt, which will be apparent in almost every chapter, to the writings of Dr. Glanville Williams.

We have derived great assistance from many discussions with our colleagues and students at Nottingham and elsewhere; and our thanks are particularly due to Mr. P. R. H. Webb who read the whole of the manuscript. Tribute is also due to the helpfulness and, particularly, the patience of our publishers who waited a long time, without complaint, for the manuscript. Even their tolerance, however, is hardly in the same class as that of our wives, particularly throughout a recent long vacation during which we almost lived in the law library.

The book began as the work of only the first-named author, but the task proved greater than expected and a large proportion of the text has been contributed by the second. It has been revised in common and we each accept responsibility for the whole. We have endeavoured to state the law as at April 30, 1965.

J. C. SMITH
BRIAN HOGAN

Contents

PART I

General Principles

CHAPTER 1.   CRIME AND SENTENCE

CHAPTER 2.   THE DEFINITION OF A CRIME

CHAPTER 3.   THE CLASSIFICATION OF OFFENCES

CHAPTER 10. INCITEMENT, CONSPIRACY AND ATTEMPT

PART II

Particular Crimes

CHAPTER 11. HOMICIDE

CHAPTER 12. NON-FATAL OFFENCES AGAINST THE PERSON

CHAPTER 13. SEXUAL OFFENCES

CHAPTER 14. ROAD TRAFFIC OFFENCES

CHAPTER 15. OFFENCES AGAINST PROPERTY INVOLVING FRAUD

CHAPTER 16. OFFENCES AGAINST PROPERTY INVOLVING MALICE

CHAPTER 17. OFFENCES AGAINST PUBLIC MORALS

CHAPTER 18. OFFENCES RELATING TO THE ADMINISTRATION OF JUSTICE

INDEX

Abbreviations

The following are the abbreviations used for the principal text-books and legal journals cited in this book.   References are to the latest editions, as shown below, unless it is specifically stated otherwise. The particulars of other works referred to in the text are set out in the relevant footnotes.

Archbold	*Criminal Pleading, Evidence and Practice*, by John Frederick Archbold. 36th ed. (1966) by T. R. Fitzwalter Butler and Marston Garsia.
Blackstone, *Commentaries*, i	*Commentaries on the Laws of England*, by Sir William Blackstone, Vol. 1 [4 Vols.]. 17th ed. (1830) by E. Christian.
C.L.J.	Cambridge Law Journal.
Can. Bar Rev.	Canadian Bar Review.
Co. 1 Inst.	*Institutes of the Laws of England*, by Sir Edward Coke, Vol. 1 [4 vols.] (1797).
Col. L.R.	Columbia Law Review.
Crim. L.R.	Criminal Law Review.
C.L.P.	Current Legal Problems.
East, 1 P.C.	*A Treatise of the Pleas of the Crown*, by Edward Hyde East, Vol. 1 [2 vols.] (1803).
Edwards, *Mens Rea*	*Mens Rea in Statutory Offences*, by J. Ll. J. Edwards (1955).
Foster	*A Report on Crown Cases and Discourses on the Crown Law*, by Sir Michael Foster. 3rd ed. (1792) by M. Dodson.
Hale, 1 P.C.	*The History of the Pleas of the Crown*, by Sir Matthew Hale, Vol. 1 [2 vols.] (1682).
Hall, *General Principles*	*General Principles of Criminal Law*, by Jerome Hall (2nd ed., 1960).
Halsbury	*The Laws of England*, by the Earl of Halsbury and other lawyers. 3rd ed. (1952–64) by Lord Simonds [43 vols.].
Harv. L.R.	Harvard Law Review.
Hawkins, 1 P.C.	*A Treatise of the Pleas of the Crown*, by W. Hawkins, Vol. 1 [2 vols.]. 8th ed. (1795) by J. Curwood.
Holdsworth, 1 H.E.L.	*A History of English Law*, by Sir William Holdsworth, Vol. 1 [14 vols.] (1923–64).
J. Cr. L.	Journal of Criminal Law (English).
J. Cr. L. & Cr.	Journal of Criminal Law and Criminology (U.S.A.).

Kenny, *Outlines* *Outlines of Criminal Law*, by C. S. Kenny. 19th ed. (1965) by J. W. C. Turner.

L.Q.R. Law Quarterly Review.

M.A.C.L. *The Modern Approach to Criminal Law*, ed. by L. Radzinowicz and J. W. C. Turner (1948).

Med. Sci. & L. Medicine, Science and the Law.

M.L.R. Modern Law Review.

Pollock and Maitland, 1 H.E.L. *The History of English Law before the Time of Edward I*, by Sir Frederick Pollock and F. W. Maitland, Vol. 1 [2 vols.] 2nd ed.

R.C.C.P. Report of the Royal Commission on Capital Punishment, 1953, Cmd. 8932.

Russell *Crime*, by Sir W. O. Russell. 12th ed. (1964) by J. W. C. Turner [2 vols.].

Stephen, *Digest* *A Digest of the Criminal Law*, by Sir James Fitzjames Stephen. 9th ed. (1950) by L. F. Sturge.

Stephen, 1 H.C.L. *A History of the Criminal Law of England*, by Sir James Fitzjames Stephen, Vol. 1 [3 vols.] (1883).

Street, *Torts* *The Law of Torts*, by H. Street (4th ed., 1968).

U. Pa. Law Rev. University of Pennsylvania Law Review.

Webb and Bevan, *Source Book* *Source Book of Family Law*, by P. R. H. Webb and H. K. Bevan (1964).

Williams, C.L.G.P. *Criminal Law: The General Part*, by Glanville L. Williams (2nd ed., 1961).

Y.L.J. Yale Law Journal.

Table of Statutes

References to *Stats.* are to Halsbury's Statutes (2nd Edn.) showing the volume and page at which the annotated text of the Act will be found.

Table of Cases

NOTE. In the following Table references are given where applicable to the English and Empire Digest where a digest of the case will be found.
Cases are listed under the name of the accused whenever the usual method of citation would cause them to be preceded by the abbreviation "R v." signifying that the prosecution was undertaken by the Crown.

A

PAGE

2*

X

Y

Z

PART I

General Principles

CHAPTER 1

Crime and Sentence

This book is about the substantive law of crime. That is, it attempts to state and to discuss the law which determines whether any act is a crime or not. The book is not about the procedure by which the law is enforced or the evidence by which criminal offences are proved, except in so far as these matters are inseparable from the discussion of the substantive law. Procedure and evidence are subjects of equal importance which are admirably discussed in other books.[1]

The criminal law is no more an end in itself than the law of procedure and evidence through which it is enforced. Our criminal law has grown up over many centuries and the purposes of those who have framed it, and of those who have enforced it, have undoubtedly been many and various. Consequently, it is not easy to state confidently what are the aims of the criminal law at the present day. The authors of a completely new code of criminal law are, however, in a position to state their objectives at the outset. "The general purposes of the provisions governing the definition of offences" in the American Law Institute's Model Penal Code[2] might be taken as a statement of the proper objectives of the substantive law of crime in a modern legal system. The purposes are:

> "(a) to forbid and prevent conduct that unjustifiably and inexcusably inflicts or threatens substantial harm to individual or public interests;
> (b) to subject to public control persons whose conduct indicates that they are disposed to commit crimes;
> (c) to safeguard conduct that is without fault from condemnation as criminal;
> (d) to give fair warning of the nature of the conduct declared to be an offense;
> (e) to differentiate on reasonable grounds between serious and minor offenses."

---

[1] See R. M. Jackson, *Enforcing the Law*; Harris, *Criminal Law* (21st ed. by Anthony Hooper) Part V; Cross, *Evidence* (3rd ed.); McClean and Wood, *Criminal Justice and the Treatment of Offenders*.
[2] Proposed Official Draft, Art. 1 1.02 (1). *Cf.* Walker, *The Aims of a Penal System*.

The reader will judge for himself how far these purposes are fulfilled by English criminal law as he studies the general principles and particular offences discussed in the succeeding chapters. For example, whether our law is confined to forbidding conduct that is "inexcusable", whether it adequately safeguards conduct that is without fault from condemnation as criminal, are matters which are particularly considered in the chapter on "strict liability",[3] but which constantly arise elsewhere.

While the definition of offences can adequately *forbid* unjustifiable and inexcusable conduct, it cannot prevent it. The fact that an act is known to be forbidden by the criminal law may, for many persons, be sufficient to ensure that they will not commit such an act. For others, however, this will not be enough. Hence our need for a law of criminal procedure, of evidence—and of sentencing. The mere fact of conviction, being a public condemnation[4] of the conduct in question, has some value in the prevention of crime, but it is far from being sufficient. Some, at least, of the purposes for which the criminal law exists can be fulfilled only through the imposition of sentences. It is therefore desirable at the outset to enquire to what ends sentences are directed—or professedly directed—by those who impose them.[5] When a sentence is to be imposed, the first decision to be made should be as to the object to be achieved by it.[6] Is the aim simply to mete out an appropriate punishment to a wrongdoer? Or is it to deter the wrongdoer and others from committing such offences in the future? Or to protect the public by shutting the offender away? Or is it the reform of the offender? When this first decision has been made, a second decision—what measure is most appropriate to achieve the desired objective?—must follow. It is only with the first decision that we are concerned in this chapter.

1   RETRIBUTION AND MORAL BLAMEWORTHINESS

The traditional attitude of the common lawyers is that a crime is essentially a moral wrong.[7] The doctrine of *mens rea* is based on the assumption that some kind of blameworthy intention is required.[8] Thus DENNING, L.J., wrote that, ever since the time of Henry I

> "in order that an act should be punishable it must be morally blameworthy. It must be a sin."[9]

---

[3] Below, p. 59.

[4] Below, p. 22.

[5] Judges, unlike juries, are generally required to give reasons for their decisions; but they need give no reasons when imposing sentence. For a cogent argument that judges ought to be required to give reasons, see D. A. Thomas, [1963] Crim. L.R. 243. In fact, judges often do give reasons; and, of course, the Court of Appeal does so when dealing with appeals against the sentence.

[6] See D. A. Thomas, "Sentencing, The Basic Principles", [1967] Crim. L.R. 455 and 503.

[7] Below, p. 18.

[8] Though, as will appear below, in many offences in the modern law, *mens rea* does not imply an intention which is blameworthy in any moral sense; and *mens rea* is sometimes dispensed with.

[9] *The Changing Law*, 112.

For Blackstone, the *first* requirement of crime is that there must be a vicious will:

> "In all temporal jurisdictions an overt act or some evidence of an intended crime is necessary in order to demonstrate the depravity of the will, before the man is liable to punishment. And, as a vicious will without a vicious act is no civil crime, so, on the other hand, an unwarrantable act without a vicious will is no crime at all. So that to constitute a crime against human laws, there must be, first a vicious will; and, secondly, an unlawful act consequent upon such vicious will."[10]

The criminal law assumes, in the absence of evidence to the contrary, that people have it in their power to choose whether to do criminal acts or not, and that he who chooses to do such an act is responsible for the resulting evil. The law further assumes that the evil which might result from particular crimes can be nicely measured and graded, so that we have an elaborate scale of permissible punishments, varying from life imprisonment[11] to a mere fine. But it is also recognised that the imperfections of definition are such that an act which is within the definition of the crime may be morally blameless and deserving of no punishment. Thus it is the almost invariable practice of Parliament to fix a maximum but no minimum punishment and to leave it to the judge or magistrate to fix a sentence, varying from an absolute discharge to the statutory maximum. The only significant exception to this rule is murder, where the court is required to impose a sentence of life imprisonment.

The traditional attitude of the common law and of Parliament to crime has, not unnaturally, been reflected in the sentencing practice of the courts. A scale of punishment being provided, varying with the potential moral wickedness of the offence and its danger to society, the court, until recent times, generally saw its task as one of fitting the penalty to the particular degree of iniquity and dangerousness evinced by the particular defendant. Where there is a statutory maximum,[12] it should be reserved for the very worst type of offence falling within the definition of the crime, and a sentence which does not allow for this is wrong in principle.[13] The judge should ask himself, "what proportion does the crime before me bear to the greatest possible crime coming under the same name?"[14] "Steering by the maximum", as this process has been called, is, of course, possible only when the statutory maximum is not altogether out of proportion to contemporary attitudes to the crime in question, and today many maxima are altogether out of proportion.[15] Thus, the normal punishment for malicious damage to property is two years' imprisonment.[16] For malicious damage to hopbinds, it is fourteen years. This severe punishment is obviously aimed at a social problem which is no longer urgent and one would not expect the judge to attach any importance to it today. But where the statute is a modern one,

---

[10] *Commentaries*, iv, 20.
[11] The death penalty may still be imposed for treason, piracy with violence and setting fire to Her Majesty's ships; but it has, in effect, been eliminated as a penalty in peace-time.
[12] In the case of common law misdemeanours (other than attempts (see Criminal Law Act 1967, s. 7 (2), below, p. 163)), there is no maximum.
[13] *Edwards* (1910), 4 Cr. App. Rep. 280; *Austin*, [1961] Crim. L.R. 416; *Da Silva*, [1964] Crim. L.R. 68.
[14] FRY, J., in (1902), 52 *Nineteenth Century*, 848. See also BRAMPTON, B., at 852.
[15] See the *Justice* Report, "Legal Penalties: The Need for Revaluation", [1959] Crim. L.R. at 394.
[16] Below, p. 455.

"it is inevitable and indeed right that a judge or bench of magistrates in considering sentence should pay some regard to the statutory maximum (apart from the obligation not to exceed it)."[17]

If punishment is assessed in accordance with the degree of moral blameworthiness, it seems to follow that it is imposed *because* of the moral blameworthiness. No further justification is needed:

". . . . there is a mystic bond between wrong and punishment . . . Hegel . . . . puts it, in his quasi-mathematical form, that wrong being the negation of right, punishment is the negation of that negation, or retribution. Thus the punishment must be equal, in the sense of proportionate to the crime, because its only function is to destroy it. Others, without this logical apparatus, are content to rely upon a felt necessity that suffering should follow wrongdoing."[18]

The most forceful judicial statement of the retributive attitude to punishment is that of STEPHEN, J.:

"I am . . . of opinion that this close alliance between criminal law and moral sentiment is in all ways healthy and advantageous to the community. I think it highly desirable that criminals should be hated, that the punishments inflicted upon them should be so contrived as to give expression to that hatred, and to justify it so far as the provision of means for expressing and gratifying a healthy and natural sentiment can justify and encourage it."[19]

It is unlikely that any judge would put forward views in these terms today. But it would be a mistake to assume that the attitude is dead. It is often argued today that retribution is a relic of barbarism and has no proper place in the assessment of punishment. It is clear that this is not the view of the judges. Such a theory, said ASQUITH, L.J.,

"runs counter to one of the cardinal principles of justice—that punishment should be proportioned to guilt."[20]

The judge's task, after all, is to do justice; and how is punishment to be related to justice, except by asking whether it is deserved or not?[1] If punishment were to be based purely on theories of deterrence and reformation and the question of what the accused deserved were to be eliminated, would not the concept of justice be eliminated too?[2] Certainly, as a matter of fact, the courts constantly act on the assumption that the punishment must be proportioned to moral guilt; and the Court of Appeal will interfere where it is satisfied that there is a disproportion.[3]

The question then arises, by what standards is the judge to estimate what punishment is deserved? The judicial answer seems to be, by the degree of revulsion felt by the law-abiding members of the community for the particular criminal act in question. Thus DENNING, L.J., said:

"The punishment inflicted for grave crimes should adequately reflect the revulsion felt by the great majority of citizens for them. It is a mistake to

---

[17] *Justice* Report (above, footnote 15) at 397.
[18] Holmes, *The Common Law*, 42. For Holmes's criticisms of this theory, see pp. 45–46.
[19] 2 H.C.L. 81–82.
[20] "Problems of Punishment", *The Listener*, XLIII at 821 (May 11, 1950).
[1] See C. S. Lewis (1953), 6 *Res Judicatae*, 224 at 225.
[2] See Morris and Howard, *Studies in Criminal Law*, 147 at 174.
[3] To take a few cases decided in 1959 as an example, one finds that "a comparatively trivial offence did not merit three years corrective training": *Watkins*, [1959] Crim. L.R. 138; "The sentence was out of proportion to the offence": *Smidt*, [1959] Crim. L.R. 219; *Parr*, [1959] Crim. L.R. 299; "The sentence was out of proportion to the gravity of the crime": *Redmond*, [1959] Crim. L.R. 374; "Seven years for stealing property to the value of 50s. seemed altogether out of proportion": *Gould*, [1959] Crim. L.R. 597.

consider the objects of punishment as being deterrent or reformative or preventive and nothing else. . . . The ultimate justification of any punishment
is not that it is a deterrent, but that it is the emphatic denunciation by the
community of a crime. . . ."[4]

In the appeal against the sentences imposed on those convicted of the "Great
Train Robbery", LAWTON, J., in rebutting counsel's argument that it was wrong
to impose a retributive sentence, is reported to have said that it was the duty of
the courts to show public revulsion at a particular type of crime by the punishment imposed.[5] Severe sentences have been upheld in recent years expressly on
the ground that the sentence must mark public revulsion.[6] It is in fact a constant theme in judicial pronouncements about punishment that, while the judge
must not be influenced by public hysteria, he must take into account the general
attitude of responsible members of the public, if respect for the law is to be
upheld. The criminal law, said BIRKETT, J.,

> "must represent a remarkably high average of the population's views with
> regard to penalties; and the law abiding citizen must feel that the law is
> effective in protecting him from infractions of his liberty by wrongdoers."[7]

Closely associated with the notion of proportioning the punishment to the
public's view of the moral culpability of the offender is another idea: that it is
necessary to satisfy, by a sufficient punishment, a public desire for vengeance
against the wrongdoer.[8] Thus Sir John Barry of the Supreme Court of Victoria
recently wrote:

> "It is . . . true beyond question that in the reality of the social process an
> important end of the criminal law is to reinforce and uphold the moral senti-
> ments of the community that favour the promotion of virtue and discourage
> the pursuit of evildoing, and in practical affairs this is done by gratifying the
> desire for retaliation which a crime arouses, and by way of deterrent ex-
> ample."[9]

There is evidence in judicial pronouncements that this is a factor which
weighs with English courts in fixing sentences, at least in some types of case,
particularly sexual offences.[10] So in a case of rape at Nottingham Assizes the
judge said:

> "Unless the courts take steps to protect children and young women, we
> shall find members of the public taking the law into their own hands."

One sixteen-year-old and two eighteen-year-old boys were sent to prison for
three years.[11]

---

[4] R.C.C.P. (1953), Cmd. 8932, p. 18.
[5] (1964), *The Times*, July 9. For criticism of this judicial attitude, see J. D. Morton
(1959), 1 *Osgoode Hall Law School Journal*, 95, commenting particularly on *Willaert*
(1953), 105 Can. Crim. Cas. 172.
[6] *Davies*, [1965] Crim. L.R. 251; *Mitchell*, [1965] Crim. L.R. 319.
[7] Eighth Clarke Hall Lecture, "The Problems of Punishment", 10; *Cf.* Lummus, *The
Trial Judge*, 56; HAWKINS, J., *Reminiscences*, 2, 228; Sir John Barry, *op. cit.*, footnote 9,
infra, at xxiv.
[8] "The thirst for vengeance is a very real, even if it be a hideous thing; and states may
not ignore it till humanity has been raised to greater heights than any that has yet been
scaled in all the long ages of struggle and ascent": CARDOZO, J., *Selected Writings*, 378.
[9] Introduction to Morris and Howard, *Studies in Criminal Law* at xxv. The learned
judge adds that the objective should be "to confine the elements of vindictive retribution
within the narrowest possible limits . . .".
[10] See *Sexual Offences* (Report of the Cambridge Department of Criminal Science),
186, n.1.
[11] *The Nottingham Evening Post*, November 26, 1961. And see *Read* (1060), *The
Times*, July 28.

2 RETRIBUTION AND THE HARM DONE

So far it has been assumed that retribution means that the convicted person should receive punishment proportioned to his moral guilt. It must now be noticed that there is another measure of retribution which is very much alive: that the punishment should be proportionate to the harm done. This may be illustrated by the attitude of the courts to attempts to commit crimes.[12]

An attempt to commit a crime is a common law misdemeanour and, as such, until 1967 was punishable with fine and imprisonment at the discretion of the court and without limit, provided only that the sentence was not an inordinate one.[13] Thus, it was theoretically possible to punish an attempt to commit any crime which was not punishable with life imprisonment more severely than the same crime when completed. It was, however, held to be improper to pass a sentence greater than that which could be imposed for the completed offence[14]; and this principle is now embodied in the Criminal Law Act 1967.[15] But the point of present interest is that it is the usual practice of the courts to punish an attempt to commit a crime *less* severely than if the attempt were successful.[16] Yet the moral guilt of him who attempts and fails is just as great as that of him who attempts and succeeds. Indeed, as will appear,[17] by a curious anomaly it is frequently necessary to prove a more blameworthy state of mind in order to procure a conviction for an attempt than for the corresponding complete crime. Failure to complete the offence by no means necessarily shows that the offender is the less dangerous; he may have been merely unlucky. Yet failure appears to be a mitigating factor. This is true not only of the judicial but also of the legislative attitude. So when Parliament provides a statutory punishment it is usually less than for the complete crime—for example, rape is punishable with life imprisonment, attempted rape with seven years. Nor is this attitude confined to attempts. According to the Departmental Committee on Persistent Offenders:

> "... if a persistent office-breaker breaks into a railway booking office with intent to steal large sums of money and for some reason or other only manages to obtain a few trifling articles, the court will probably consider appropriate a very much lighter sentence than if he had succeeded in his object."[18]

In such cases it seems that the punishment is being proportioned to the harm done. A similar theory seems to be implicit in some rules of the substantive law. If D assaults P, occasioning him actual bodily harm, D is liable to five years imprisonment.[19] Now suppose P dies. D is guilty of manslaughter[20] and liable to life imprisonment. Yet his act and his moral blameworthiness are the same in both cases. Here too the judicial attitude reflects that of the legislature —and perhaps of us all? If D drives his car dangerously, he is liable to two

---

[12] Below, p. 163. *Cf.* Criminal Law Act 1967, s. 4 (3), below, p. 521.

[13] *Morris*, [1951] 1 K.B. 394; [1950] 2 All E.R. 965.

[14] *Pearce*, [1953] 1 Q.B. 30; [1952] 2 All E.R. 718; *Verrier* v. *D.P.P.*, [1966] 3 All E.R. 568 at p. 575.

[15] Section 7 (2) below, p. 163.

[16] See, *e.g. Rankin* (1960), *The Times*, March 30.

[17] Below, p. 163.

[18] Report (Cmd. 4090, 1932), 9. See the discussion of this example by Cross, "Paradoxes in Prison Sentences" (1965), 81 L.Q.R. 205.

[19] Offences against the Person Act 1861, s. 47; below, p. 263.

[20] Below, p. 216.

years' imprisonment whether he injures anyone or not;[1] but if he drives in exactly the same way with exactly the same state of mind and kills P he is liable to five years' imprisonment.[2]

These examples seem, on the face of them, to show that there is at work "a crude retaliation theory".[3] Professors Wechsler and Michael,[4] however, discussing the particular case of homicide, offer two reasons to justify a more severe punishment in the case where death is caused than in an otherwise exactly similar case where death is not caused:

> "In the first place, popular indignation is inevitably aroused by the actual occurrence of a wrong, with the result that death and other very severe penalties are more likely to be tolerated when homicidal behaviour has resulted fatally than when it has not. In the second place, the deterrent efficacy of a body of criminal law is not greatly lessened by making the discrimination. Men who may act in order to kill will hope for and contemplate success rather than failure. Consequently if the prospect of being punished severely if they succeed will not deter them from acting, the prospect of being punished just as severely if they fail is unlikely to do so."

The theory is (i) that the judge (and the legislator) may properly take account of public sentiment without necessarily approving of it. Thus he may, for example, impose a greater sentence in the case of the consummated crime than the attempt, not because he thinks it worse, but because he thinks public opinion either demands or will tolerate, a severe sentence, which it would not demand or tolerate in the case of an attempt. The same reasoning presumably applies to the case of the thief who only gets away with a small fraction of what he hopes to get away with. And (ii) the potential offender, weighing up the pros and cons of committing the offence, will have the punishment for the complete offence in mind.

Professor Cross,[5] on the other hand, finds the best justification for sentencing more severely where the offender has succeeded than where he has not in the words used by Edmund DAVIES, J., in sentencing one of the main participants in "The Great Train Robbery":

> "It would be an affront if you were to be at liberty in the near future to enjoy these ill-gotten gains. I propose to ensure that such an opportunity will be denied you for a very long time."[6]

Such "deterrence by deprivation of fruits" is in point where the offender has made a profit by his crime; but it has no application where the harm done does not bring a benefit to him.

3 THE SENTENCE TO FIT THE CRIME

In *Director of Public Prosecutions* v. *Ottewell*[7] Lord REID said:

> "It was rather tentatively suggested by the learned Attorney General that there is a 'tariff' for each kind of offence which is varied upwards or downwards according to the circumstances of the offence and the character of the

---

[1] Road Traffic Act 1960, s. 2; below, pp. 332–333.
[2] Road Traffic Act 1960, s. 1; below, p. 337
[3] Williams, C.L.G.P. 136.
[4] (1937), 37 Col. L. Rev. 1294–1295.
[5] (1965), 81 L.Q.R. at 218.
[6] *The Times*, April 18, 1964.
[7] [1968] 3 All E.R. 153 at 155.

accused. Offences of a particular kind vary so vastly, however, in gravity that there cannot and should not be any 'normal' sentence, and there is no workable standard by which to judge whether any particular standard is extended beyond what is 'normal'".

While it is clear that there is no single sentence which is normal for a particular category of crime[8]—for example, rape—there is certainly a range within which a sentence will be regarded as normal for that category and outside of which it will be regarded as abnormal. Moreover, many of the principles of sentencing are explicable only on the assumption that there is a punishment appropriate to the circumstances of the particular offence before the court. Thus, it is wrong to increase the sentence because the accused has insisted on pleading not guilty or conducted his defence in a particular way[9]; but the sentence may be reduced on the ground that he pleaded guilty.[10] The sentence may be reduced because D informed against his co-prisoner; it should not be increased because D did not inform.[11] D's good record may be a ground for mitigating the sentence; but his bad record must not be allowed to aggravate it.[12] These rules are meaningful only if there is an appropriate sentence for the offence, from which the appropriate subtractions can be made. This appropriate sentence is based on notions of retribution and deterrence and the principles discussed in this paragraph do not necessarily apply where the court is thinking in terms of a preventive or reformative sentence.

4 JUSTICE AND EQUALITY[13]

The judge seeks to do justice by imposing the sentence the criminal deserves. But he also strives to be just in another and sometimes conflicting way—that is, by treating the criminal before him equally with others who have an equal degree of moral guilt. Here the judge may impose a sentence greater or less than he thinks the criminal deserves in order to comply with the norm. Thus an American judge writes:

> "If in the district in which a judge sits his fellow judges have established and insist on following, a pattern for dealing with offenders of a particular type, it is his responsibility either to get them to change or to come close to their standard."[14]

The Court of Appeal attaches the greatest importance to this principle of equality and constantly interferes with sentences in order to implement it. It is thought more important that sentences should be proportionate to one another than that they should be proportionate to guilt. Thus the court declared that D deserved the sentence of four years imposed on her but they reduced it to three because her co-prisoner, who was not appealing, had received only two

---

[8] But *cf.* the "Judges' Memorandum of 1901 on Normal Punishments", Appendix V, p. 250 of Jackson, *Enforcing the Law*. Professor Cross's view is that there can and should be a statement of the normal punishment for offences: (1965), 81 L.Q.R. at 213.
[9] *Regan*, [1959] Crim. L.R. 529; *Harper*, [1967] Crim. L.R. 714.
[10] *De Haan*, [1967] 3 All E.R. 618.
[11] *James and Sharman* (1913), 9 Cr. App. Rep. 142.
[12] *Boardman*, [1958] Crim. L.R. 626.
[13] D. A. Thomas, "Sentencing Co-Defendants. When is Uniform Treatment Necessary?", [1964] Crim. L.R. 22.
[14] Judge WYZANSKI, U.S. District Judge (1952), 65 Harv. L. Rev. 1281 at 1292.

years and the disparity was too great.[15] Where the degree of responsibility of two accused is different, the principle of equality requires that they should receive different sentences.[16]

But it is recognised that the severity of the sentence may vary with the locality in which the offence is committed. Thus two persons with the same moral guilt but acting in different places may properly receive different sentences; the principle of equality gives way to the necessity for protecting the public. So severe penalties have been upheld for sexual offences against young girls[17] and for using a knife to wound,[18] where the court knew, or was advised, that offences of the type in question were prevalent in the locality. Local conditions other than the prevalence of offences may cause an offence to be regarded as more serious than if it were committed elsewhere. If there is, for example, a group of goods depots in the area, dishonesty by employees may be regarded as particularly detrimental to the public interest. Sheep-stealing in Westmorland, though not a prevalent offence is very serious because it strikes at the root of trust necessary between neighbouring farmers in an area where sheep graze unfenced.[19]

The Court of Criminal Appeal has confirmed that the prevalence of a particular crime in a locality is a proper consideration,

> "so long as it does not result in a convicted man being made the scapegoat of other people who have committed similar crimes but have not been caught and convicted."[20]

5 THE PROTECTION OF THE PUBLIC

The considerations so far examined all give way in judicial thought to what, as EDMUND DAVIES, J., said recently, is the prime object of the criminal law—the protection of the public by the maintenance of law and order. Addressing the Magistrates' Association, the judge said:

> "It seems to me that accordingly every court sentence should primarily be surveyed in the light of one test: is that the best thing to do in the interest of the community?—always remembering, of course, that the convicted person, despite his wrongdoing remains a member of the community."[1]

There can be little doubt that this is the predominant judicial view.[2]

It is the deterrent aspect of punishment which is prominent here; and there is no doubt that judges do believe in the value of punishment both as a deterrent to the person sentenced and to others. From time to time examples are quoted to illustrate the effect of severe sentences: a wave of post office frauds, which subsided after the Court of Criminal Appeal had laid down that the minimum sentence should be three years' penal servitude; and an epidemic of lead stealing,

---

[15] *Richards (No. 2)*, [1956] Crim. L.R. 127. See also *Dermody*, [1959] Crim. L.R. 63; *Appleby*, [1960] Crim. L.R. 712.
[16] *Bold*, [1962] Crim. L.R. 58.
[17] *Cargill* (1913), 8 Cr. App. Rep. 224; *Nolan* (1960), *The Times*, March 30.
[18] *Lee*, [1962] Crim. L.R. 500.
[19] *Graham*, [1964] Crim L.R. 486.
[20] *Withers* (1935), 25 Cr. App. Rep. 53 at p. 54; *Murphy* (1963), *The Times*, December 3.
[1] (1963), 19 *The Magistrate*, 183.
[2] *Cf.* BIRKETT J., 8th Clarke Hall Lecture at 27; SALMON, J., [1960] C.L.J. at 45; Lord GODDARD, C.J., below, p. 14.

which declined after the judges began to impose stiff sentences.[3] But it is impossible to be certain that the crimes stopped *because* of the sentences.

> ". . . in concrete terms we are almost totally ignorant of the deterrent effect on potential offenders attributable to particular sentences".[4]

But, even if the judge is himself sceptical of the deterrent effect of punishment, the general belief in it is so strong that it is a factor he may not ignore. An American judge[5] points out that:

> "So far as is known, nobody has devised nor even attempted to devise any method of testing its validity, certainly not in any measurable or quantitative manner. It is so subjective a factor that it is almost impossible to conceive of any method by which to test it. Yet it would seem to be one of those social realities which is real because the 'common sense' of society tells us that it is real; and the sentencing judge cannot afford to overlook it."

There may be a conflict here with the principle that the punishment should be proportionate to guilt; and, when this happens, it is very probable that that principle will have to give way. ASQUITH, L.J., makes the point very clearly:[6]

> "Everyone has heard of an 'exemplary' sentence: and nearly everyone agrees that at times such sentences are justified. But it is not always observed that an exemplary sentence is unjust; and unjust to the precise extent that it is exemplary. Assume a particular crime is becoming dangerously frequent. In normal times the appropriate sentence would be, say, two years. The judge awards three; he awards the third year entirely to deter others. This may be expedient; it may even be imperative. But one thing it is not; it is not just. The guilt of the man who commits a crime when it happens to be on the increase is no greater than that of another man who commits the same crime when it is on the wane. The truth is that in such cases the judge is not administering strict justice but choosing the lesser of two practical evils. He decides that a moderate injustice to the criminal is a lesser evil than the consequences to the public of a further rise in the crime-wave".

It is common for the courts to do "injustice" of this sort for exemplary sentences are regularly upheld by the Court of Appeal.[7]

In 1958 SALMON, J., sentenced to four years' imprisonment each of nine youths convicted of assaults and wounding offences on coloured men; their appeal was dismissed by the Court of Criminal Appeal.[8] These young men had no previous convictions, and it is probable that, if their offence had not been committed in a period of race riots which greatly disturbed the public, they would have been much more leniently dealt with. As it was, the Court of Criminal Appeal thought "the time had certainly come for the courts to put down offences such as these with a heavy hand".[9] Subsequently SALMON, J., extra-judicially expressed his views on the right treatment of crimes of violence:

> "Nothing is more effective to stamp out crime than a long term of imprisonment. That may sound harsh, but we have to remember the twelve thousand

---

[3] Lord GODDARD, C.J.: see (1956), 120 J.P.N. 691.

[4] Wootton, *Crime and the Criminal Law*, 101.

[5] Judge Joseph N. ULMAN of the Supreme Bench, Maryland, "The Trial Judge's Dilemma: A Judge's View", in *Probation and Criminal Justice* (edited by S. Glueck) at 115.

[6] *The Listener*, XLIII at 821.

[7] *E.g.*, Cargill (1913), 8 Cr. App. Rep. 224; *Rhodes*, [1959] Crim. L.R. 138; *Kent* [1959] Crim. L.R. 468; *Machin*, [1961] Crim. L.R. 844; *Musk and Reynalds*, [1963] Crim. L.R. 63; *Eminson*, [1963] Crim. L.R. 584; *Smith*, [1963] Crim. L.R. 526.

[8] *Hunt* (1958), *The Times*, November 26.

[9] *Ibid.*

or so of ordinary people who last year were the victims of crimes of violence. They, and their like, must be protected. And in these circumstances it does not wring my withers at all to be told how awful it is that a comparatively young man should be shut up for a long time."[10]

Like the principles of justice, other ethical considerations are put aside in the interests of protecting the public. To quote a South African judge:

"The punishment of A in order to deter B, C and D from crime may be open to moral objections. In theory it conflicts with the principle that a human being must be treated as an end in himself and not as a means to the benefiting of other persons. But it provides a practical justification for punishment that few persons of common sense would, on reflection, reject."[11]

When the court speaks of protecting society, it generally means protection by the deterrence of others. Society may also be protected by incarcerating the individual offender for a long period. Here, however, the principle of the just punishment comes into its own again. The courts are generally unwilling to increase a sentence beyond what is "deserved" simply to protect the public from the particular offender. Thus, while a blameless record may induce the court to impose a lower sentence than the crime "merits", a bad record will not usually be considered grounds for imposing a higher.[12] This would savour of punishing the offender for his past crimes for which he has already paid. In sentencing to preventive detention[13] the courts adopted a different principle on the basis that preventive detention was not a punishment. Paradoxically, the Court of Criminal Appeal has quashed sentences of imprisonment as being too severe and then substituted a longer sentence of preventive detention.[14]

Preventive detention has now been abolished, but the court has been given instead a power to impose an "extended term of imprisonment", where the conditions specified in the Act are fulfilled and the court is satisfied, by reason of the offender's previous conduct and the likelihood of his committing further offences, that it is expedient to protect the public from him for a substantial time.[15] The extended term may exceed the statutory maximum for the offence of which D has been convicted; but the sentence may be an "extended term" within the meaning of the Act, though it is less than the statutory maximum. The expression means extended beyond the term which would have been imposed if the new power had not been given.[16] The significance of the term being certified to be an extended one is that, instead of being granted remission, the person so sentenced may be released on licence at any time on or after the day on which he could have been discharged from prison if remission had been granted.

This emphasises the importance of the judge's decision as to his purpose in imposing sentence. If a man, convicted of an offence for which the appropriate *punishment* is one year's imprisonment, is sentenced to five years, the sentence

---

[10] [1960] C.L.J. 45, 48. Whether the sentences in fact had any deterrent effect is questionable. See R. M. Jackson, *Enforcing the Law*, 209.
[11] SCHREINER, J., "The Prisoner in Court" (1945), 12 *Race Relations*, 51 at 58.
[12] Above, p. 10.
[13] See Williams, "The Courts and Persistent Offenders", [1963] Crim. L.R. at 730.
[14] *Kenny* (1962), *The Times*, January 23; four years an "excessive sentence" for larceny of a wallet; five years' P.D. substituted (39 previous convictions); *Caine*, [1963] Crim. L.R. 63; sentence of five years' imprisonment for embezzlement of £21 on one day quashed. Two years would have been the maximum appropriate sentence of imprisonment. Seven years' P.D. substituted.
[15] Criminal Justice Act 1967, s. 37.
[16] *D.P.P.* v. *Ottewell*, [1968] 3 All E.R. 153.

will clearly be excessive, unless it is intended to protect the public and not simply intended to punish. The judge now declares his purpose by issuing a certificate that the sentence is an extended term. We may therefore still have the Court of Appeal saying that a sentence, imposed as a punishment, is excessive; but that it is upheld, or even increased, on the ground that an extended term is called for to protect the public.

In dealing with preventive detention, the courts did not by any means disregard the doctrine that the punishment should fit the crime. Even in the early case of *Churchill*,[17] where the Court of Criminal Appeal laid it down that, when preventive detention was imposed, there was no question of punishment, it was recognised that the seriousness of the offence which has brought the offender before the court cannot be ignored. Though the court was not consistent in the matter, it not infrequently quashed sentences of preventive detention because of the relative triviality of the latest offence.[18] There is no reason to suppose that this principle will not apply to extended term sentences under the Criminal Justice Act 1967. The "inadequate" offender who commits repeated trivial offences is now more likely to be put on probation with a condition of residence in a hostel.[19]

6 THE REFORM OF THE OFFENDER

There are many writers today who maintain that the reformation of the offender should be the main,[20] if not the only object of sentencing. It is clear that this is not the general view of the judges. Lord GODDARD, C.J., is reported to have said that:

> "The function of the criminal law is deterrence, not reform. As law, it was not concerned with the reform of the criminal. That was a matter for those persons and societies who, to their honour, were trying to do something about it."[1]

The pre-eminence given by the courts to their duty to protect the public necessarily implies that, whenever there is a conflict—as there frequently must be—between deterrence and reform, it is probably reform that will have to give way.

Thus in *Stewart*,[2] a sentence of three years' imprisonment on a boy of sixteen for robbery with violence was upheld. The court was prepared to accept the view that the boy was unlikely to commit a similar offence again. The best course from his point of view would be to continue his education and receive some disciplinary training. But a substantial period of imprisonment was thought to be the only appropriate penalty to show young men they could not commit this offence with impunity.

---

[17] [1952] 2 Q.B. 637.
[18] *Ashworth*, [1959] Crim. L.R. 867 (present offence unpremeditated); *Kavanagh*, [1959] Crim. L.R. 62 (latest offence merely the stealing of a raincoat); *Naughton*, [1961] Crim. L.R. 187 (theft of offertory box worth £1.); *Greenacre*, [1959] Crim. L.R. 374 (present offence—stealing cakes and jellies—"not a very serious one"). But in *Lyne-Ley*, [1965] Crim. L.R. 121, seven years imprisonment was upheld on a man who repeatedly committed trivial offences and was a public nuisance. And see *Harpur*, [1965] Crim. L.R. 251.
[19] D. A. Thomas, "The Criminal Justice Bill: New Issues in Sentencing Policy", [1967] Crim. L.R. 277 at 281.
[20] See especially Wootton, *Crime and the Criminal Law*, Ch. 4.
[1] (1958), 122 J.P.N. at 479.
[2] [1961] Crim. L.R. 844.

More recently, the Court of Criminal Appeal has said that, in the case of a young offender, there can rarely be any conflict between his interest and that of the public; for the public have no greater interest than that he should be a good citizen.[3] But this does not alter the attitude of the court when it finds that there is a conflict.

Just as the principle that the punishment should fit the crime might conflict with the objective of prevention, so too it might conflict with the objective of reformation. Corrective training (now abolished by the Criminal Justice Act 1967) was a sentence which was intended to be reformatory; but the courts were unwilling to impose it unless the offence which brought the accused before the court merited the period of detention involved.[4] The courts might be expected to be similarly reluctant to extend a sentence of imprisonment beyond what they think to be deserved, so that the offender may be reformed; though in *Greedy*[5] a sentence was increased from three to five years "to give time for the treatment to be effective."[6]

All this is not to say that the courts are not interested in the reform of the criminal. It is clear that they are concerned, and increasingly concerned, with the reformation of the individual. As the Streatfeild Committee said:

"... the courts have always had in mind the need to protect society from the persistent offender, to deter potential offenders and to deter or reform the individual offender. But in general it was thought that the 'tariff system'[7] took these other objectives in its stride. Giving an offender the punishment he deserved was thought to be the best way of deterring him and others and of protecting society.

Over the last few decades, these other objectives have received increased attention. The development has been most obvious in the increased weight which the courts give to the needs of the offender as a person. It is realised that whatever punishment is imposed, he will eventually return to society, and sentences are increasingly passed with the deterrence or reform of the offender as the principal objective; and in assessing the offender's culpability his social and domestic background is more closely examined."[8]

But, while the judges are not entirely consistent, it would seem that, generally, the reformation of the offender is still only something they aim at in so far as it is compatible with what they regard as their main functions of protecting the public and doing justice.

---

[3] *Smith*, [1964] Crim. L.R. 70.
[4] *McCarthy*, [1955] 2 All E.R. 927.
[5] [1964] Crim. L.R. 669.
[6] *Cf*. Morris and Howard, *Studies in Criminal Law* at 175: " ... power over a criminal's life should not be taken in excess of that which would be taken were his reform not considered as one of our purposes."
[7] *I.e.*, giving a sentence proportionate to the offender's culpability.
[8] (1961), Cmd. 1289, at 76.

CHAPTER 2

The Definition of
a Crime[1]

It is now rather unfashionable to begin law books with definitions. One reason for this is the difficulty frequently encountered in defining the subject-matter of a particular branch of the law; and nowhere has this been more greatly felt than in the criminal law. But a book about crimes which does not tell the reader what a crime is allows him to proceed with his own preconceived notions in the matter; and it is well recognised that there is a popular meaning of crime which is different from and narrower than, the legal meaning. A law book must be concerned with the legal meaning of crime; and the reader is entitled to know what it is, or at least why it is so difficult to tell him.

An attempt to define *a crime* at once encounters a serious difficulty. If the definition is a true one, it should enable us to recognise any *act* (or *omission*) as a crime, or not a crime, by seeing whether it contains all the ingredients of the definition. But a moment's reflection will suffice to show that this is impossible. When Parliament enacts that a particular act shall become a crime or that an act which is now criminal shall cease to be so, the act does not change in nature in any respect other than that of legal classification. All its observable characteristics are precisely the same before as after the statute comes into force. Any attempt at definition of a crime will thus either include the act at a time when it is not a crime, or exclude it when it is. Suicide was a crime until August 3, 1961, when, by the Suicide Act 1961,[2] it became perfectly lawful to kill oneself. Homosexual acts committed by adult male persons in private were offences until July 27, 1967, when by the Sexual Offences Act 1967,[3] such acts became permissible. The nature of the acts in question, their morality or immorality and their consequences do not change overnight; but their legal nature does.

---

[1] Kenny, *Outlines of Criminal Law* (15th ed.) Ch. 1; C. K. Allen, "The Nature of a Crime", *Journal of Society of Comparative Legislation*, February, 1931, reprinted in *Legal Duties*, 221; Winfield, *Province of the Law of Tort*, Ch. VIII; Williams, "The Definition of Crime" (1955), 8 C.L.P. 107; Hughes, "The Concept of Crime: An American View", [1959] Crim. L.R. 239 and 331.
[2] Below, pp. 237–238.
[3] Below, p. 320.

1 CHARACTERISTICS OF A CRIME

1 A Public Wrong

It is, of course, possible to point to certain characteristics which are generally found in acts which are crimes. They are generally acts which have a particularly harmful effect on the public and do more than interfere with merely private rights. Sir Carleton Allen writes:

> "Crime is crime because it consists in wrongdoing which directly and in serious degree threatens the security or well being of society, and because it is not safe to leave it redressable only by compensation of the party injured."[4]

This explains why acts have been made crimes either by judicial decision or by legislation, and it does not necessarily accurately represent the present state of affairs. A crime may remain a crime long after it has ceased to be a threat to the security or well-being of society.[5] Thus Allen's proposition tells us what—as he thinks—ought to be criminal rather than what is criminal.

The public nature of crimes is evidenced by the contrast between the rules of civil and criminal procedure. Any citizen can, as a general rule and in the absence of some provision to the contrary, bring a criminal prosecution, whether or not he has suffered any special harm over and above other members of the public. As a member of the public he has an interest in the enforcement of the criminal law. D steals P's watch. P may prosecute him—so may Q, R, S, T or any other citizen. In practice, of course, the vast majority of prosecutions are carried on by police or other public officers who have no personal interest in the outcome. The individual who starts a prosecution may not discontinue it at will,[6] for it is not only his concern but that of every citizen. The Crown, however, through the entry of a *nolle prosequi* by the Attorney-General, may stay the proceedings at any time[7] without the consent of the prosecutor. If the prosecution succeeds and a sentence is imposed by the court, the instigator of the prosecution has no power to pardon the offender. This belongs to the Crown, representing the public interest in the matter.

All this contrasts sharply with civil wrongs—torts and breaches of contract. There, only the person injured may sue. He (and only he) may freely discontinue the proceedings at any time and, if he succeeds and an award of damages is made in his favour, he may, at his entire discretion, forgive the defendant and terminate his liability.

Crimes, then, are wrongs which the judges have held, or Parliament has from time to time laid down, are sufficiently injurious to the public to warrant the application of criminal procedure to deal with them. Of course this does not enable us to recognise an act as a crime when we see one. Some acts are so obviously harmful to the public that *anyone* would say they should be criminal—and such acts almost certainly are—but there are many others about which opinions may differ widely. When a citizen is heard urging that, "There ought to be a law against it . . .", he is expressing his personal conviction that some variety of act is so harmful to society that it ought to be discouraged by being

---

[4] *Legal Duties*, at 233–234.
[5] Williams, 8 C.L.P. at 126–127.
[6] *Wood* (1832), 3 B. & Ad. 657.
[7] After the indictment has been signed: *Wylie* (1919), 83 J.P. 295.

made the subject of criminal proceedings. There will almost invariably be a body of opinion which disagrees. But even if *everyone* agreed with him, the act in question would not thereby become a crime. Public condemnation is ineffective without the endorsement of an Act of Parliament or a decision of the court.

2 A Moral Wrong

The second characteristic of crimes which is usually emphasised is that they are acts which are morally wrong. As seen above, the traditional attitude of the common law has been that crimes are essentially immoral acts deserving of punishment. In the early days of the law, when the number of crimes was relatively few and only the most outrageous acts were prohibited—murder, robbery, rape, etc.—this was, no doubt, true. But now many acts are prohibited on the grounds of social expediency and not because of their immoral nature. Especially is this so in the field of summary offences—and summary offences are crimes.[8] Moreover many acts which are regarded as immoral—for example, adultery—are not crimes. Thus the test of immorality is not a very helpful one.

Whether an act ought to be a crime simply on the ground of its immoral nature has been the subject of vigorous debate in recent years. This sprang from the view of the Wolfenden Committee on Homosexual Offences and Prostitution that the enforcement of morality is not a proper object of the criminal law. The function of the criminal law, as they saw it is:

". . . to preserve public order and decency, to protect the citizen from what is offensive or injurious, and to provide sufficient safeguards against exploitation and corruption of others, particularly those who are specially vulnerable . . .

"It is not . . . the function of the law to intervene in the private lives of citizens, or to seek to enforce any particular pattern of behaviour, further than is necessary to carry out the purposes we have outlined."

This view was challenged by Lord DEVLIN,[9] who argued that there is a public morality which is an essential part of the bondage which keeps society together; and that society may use the criminal law to preserve morality in the same way that it uses it to preserve anything else that is essential to its existence. The standard of morality is that of "the man in the jury box", based on the "mass of continuous experience half-consciously or unconsciously accumulated and embodied in the morality of common sense".

To this it has been answered[10] that it is not proper for the state to enforce the general morality without asking whether it is based on ignorance, superstition or misunderstanding; that it is not a sufficient ground for prohibiting an act that "the thought of it makes the man on the Clapham omnibus sick". But if we are not to base criminal law on the general morality, does not this imply that "our law making is or should be controlled by independent Gods of Pure Reason, installed somewhere in our political systems and endowed with power to determine such questions for society, free of the prejudices to which lesser men are subject?"[11] "A free society is as much offended by the dictates of an intellectual oligarchy as by those of an autocrat."[12]

---

[8] Williams (1955), 8 C.L.P. at 110.

[9] The Maccabaean Lecture, "The Enforcement of Morals" (1959), 45 *Proc. of British Academy*, 129 reprinted in *The Enforcement of Morals* (1965), p. 1.

[10] H. L. A. Hart, *The Listener*, July 30, 1959, p. 162.

[11] Rostow, "The Enforcement of Morals", [1960] C.L.J. 174 at 189.

[12] Devlin, "Law, Democracy and Morality" (1962), 110 U. Pa. Law Rev. 635 at 642 reprinted in *The Enforcement of Morals* (1965), p. 86.

In the midst of this controversy was decided the case of *Shaw* v. *Director of Public Prosecutions*,[13] in which Lord SIMONDS asserted that

> "there remains in the courts of law a residual power to enforce the supreme and fundamental purpose of the law, to conserve not only the safety and order *but also the moral welfare of the state*";

and that the King's Bench was the *custos morum* of the people and had the superintendency of offences *contra bonos mores*.

> "*Shaw*'s case", concludes Lord DEVLIN, "settles for the purpose of the law that morality in England means what twelve men and women think it means—in other words it is to be ascertained as a question of fact."[14]

Subsequently, however, the particular rule of law that caused the Wolfenden Committee to formulate its general principle[15]—that homosexual conduct between consenting male adults is an offence—has been repealed by the Sexual Offences Act 1967. The enforcement of morality, as such, by the criminal law is losing ground.

2 CRIMINAL PROCEEDINGS

Because of the impossibility of defining the criminal quality of an act, most writers—and the courts—have been driven to turn to the nature of the proceedings which may follow from its commission.

> "The criminal quality of an act cannot be discerned by intuition; nor can it be discovered by reference to any standard but one: is the act prohibited with penal consequences?"[16]

The problem then becomes one of distinguishing criminal proceedings from civil proceedings. Any attempt to distinguish between crimes and torts comes up against the same kind of difficulty encountered in defining crimes generally: that most torts are crimes as well, though some torts are not crimes and some crimes are not torts. It is not in the nature of the act, but in the nature of the proceedings that the distinction consists; and generally[17] both types of proceeding may follow where an act is both a crime and a tort.

Kenny,[18] in the most celebrated of all attempts to define a crime, directed his attention to ascertaining the essential distinction between civil and criminal procedure. He rejected any distinction based on (i) the degree of activity manifested by the State in the two types of proceeding; for though the "contrast is a genuine and vivid one", it was incapable of being applied with precision;[19] (ii)

---

[13] [1962] A.C. 220; [1961] 2 All E.R. 446; below, p. 160.

[14] 110 U. Pa. Law. Rev. at 648. See also H. L. A. Hart, *Law, Liberty and Morality*; Hughes, "Morals and the Criminal Law" (1962), 71 Y.L.J. 662. For an excellent discussion of the whole controversy, see Basil Mitchell, *Law, Morality and Religion in a Secular Society* (1967).

[15] Above, p. 16.

[16] *Proprietary Articles Trade Association* v. *A.G. for Canada*, [1931] A.C. 310 at p. 324, *per* Lord ATKIN.

[17] Assault is an exception: Offences against the Person Act 1861, ss. 44 and 45; and see Howard, [1958] Crim. L. R. 33.

[18] *Outlines of Criminal Law* (15th ed.), Ch. 1.

[19] Kenny was greatly troubled at several points in his analysis by the anomalous form of proceeding known as a penal action. This was a civil action which might be brought by any member of the public—a common informer—but its object was the punishment of the defendant; and the successful plaintiff was enriched by the penalty imposed. By the Common Informers Act 1951 such procedure is abolished and any offence formerly punishable by common informer procedure is made punishable on summary conviction by a fine not exceeding £100.

The penal action was in no case the *sole* objection Kenny found to any of the rejected definitions; so he would presumably have reached the same result, even if these proceedings had already been abolished.

the tribunals; for both civil and criminal cases may be heard in the magistrates' courts and the House of Lords; (iii) the object of the proceedings; for, while "the object of criminal procedure is always *Punishment*", the award of exemplary damages in civil actions is also punitive; (iv) the nature of the sanctions; for, while criminal sanctions never enrich any individual, it was not true to say that all civil actions do, since some civil actions for penalties could be brought only by the Crown.

Kenny finally seized upon the degree of control exercised over the two types of proceeding by the Crown[20] as the criterion, and defined "crimes" as

> "wrongs whose sanction is punitive and is in no way remissible by any private person, but is remissible by the Crown alone, *if remissible at all.*"[1]

He thought it necessary to bring in the element of punishment only to exclude actions for the recovery of the Crown's debts or other civil rights; and the italicised words were included so as not to exclude certain crimes which cannot be pardoned.[2]

Kenny's definition has been much criticised. Winfield[3] thought it led to a vicious circle:

> "What is a crime? Something that the Crown alone can pardon. What is it that the Crown alone can pardon? A crime."[4]

Winfield thought it advisable not to accept this part of Kenny's definition; and he concentrated on the question, what is punishment? The answer he arrived at is that: "The essence of punishment is its inevitability . . . no option is left to the offender as to whether he shall endure it or not"; whereas, in a civil case, "he can always compromise or get rid of his liability with the assent of the injured party".[5] Thus we seem to arrive back at the just rejected test of who can remit the sanction.

More substantial is the point made by Williams.[6] If we are going to define crime by reference to procedure, we ought to make use of the whole law of procedure, not just one item of it—the power to remit the sanction. If a court has to decide whether a particular act which has been prohibited by Parliament is a crime, it may be guided by a reference in the statute to any element which exists only in civil, or only in criminal, procedure as the case may be. A crime is:

> "an act that is capable of being followed by criminal proceedings, having one of the types of outcome (punishment, etc.) known to follow these proceedings."[7]

This definition is by no means so unhelpful as at first sight may appear; for there are many points of distinction between civil and criminal procedure, and the specification in a statute of any one procedural feature which is peculiar either to the civil or the criminal law will therefore point to the nature of the wrong. The question in issue may well be whether a rule of criminal, or a rule

---

[20] Above, p. 17.
[1] *Op. cit.*, at 16.
[2] A public nuisance while still unabated and offences under Habeas Corpus Act 1679, s. 11.
[3] *Province of the Law of Tort*, Ch. VIII.
[4] *Ibid.*, at 197.
[5] *Ibid.*, at 200.
[6] 8 C.L.P. 107 at 128.
[7] *Ibid.*, at 123.

of civil, procedure should be followed.[8] While it may be that no statute or decision gives guidance on this precise point, the procedure test may yet supply the answer if a statute or decision indicates, as the appropriate procedure, some other rule which is peculiar either to civil or to criminal proceedings. Of course, the definition tells us nothing about what acts *ought* to be crimes, but that is not its purpose. Writers who set out to define a crime by reference to the nature of the act, on the other hand, inevitably end by telling us, not what a crime is, but what the writer thinks it ought to be; and that is not a definition of a crime.

3 THE PRACTICAL TEST

From time to time the courts have found it necessary to determine whether a proceeding is criminal or not. Before the Criminal Evidence Act 1898, the defendant could not give evidence on oath on his own behalf in a criminal case whereas (since the Evidence Act 1851) he had been able to do so in a civil action. If he wished to give evidence the nature of the proceeding had to be ascertained.[9] The same problem could arise today if it were sought to *compel* the defendant to give evidence.[10] But much the most fruitful source of this problem has been the Judicature Act 1873, s. 47, and its successor, the Judicature Act 1925, s. 31(1) (*a*), which provides that no appeal should lie to the Court of Appeal "in any criminal cause or matter". The question whether a particular proceeding is a criminal cause or matter has frequently come before the Court of Appeal and the House of Lords. In these cases the test which has regularly been applied is whether the proceeding may result in the punishment of the offender. If it may, then it is a criminal proceeding.[11] As a practical test, this seems to work well enough; but it must always be remembered that it is a rule with exceptions; for some actions for penalties are undoubtedly civil actions, and yet they have the punishment of the offender as their objective; and for this reason the test of punishment is jurisprudentially unsatisfactory.[12]

The meaning of punishment itself is not easy to ascertain; for the defendant in a civil case, who is ordered to pay damages by way of compensation, may well feel that he has been punished. It has been suggested[13] that:

> "What distinguishes a criminal from a civil sanction and all that distinguishes it . . . is the judgment of community condemnation which accompanies and justifies its imposition."

According to this view it is the condemnation, plus the consequences of the sentence—fine or imprisonment, etc.—which together constitute the

---

[8] *Cf.* P. J. Fitzgerald, "A Concept of Crime", [1960] Crim. L.R. 257 at 259–260.

[9] *Cattel* v. *Ireson* (1858), E.B. & E. 91; *Parker* v. *Green* (1862), 2 B. & S. 299.

[10] He is compellable in a civil but not in a criminal case.

[11] *E.g.*, *Mellor* v. *Denham* (1880), 5 Q.B.D. 467; *Seaman* v. *Burley*, [1896] 2 Q.B. 344; *Robson* v. *Biggar*, [1908] 1 K.B. 672; *Re Clifford and O'Sullivan*, [1921] 2 A.C. 570; *Amand* v. *Home Secretary and Minister of Defence of the Royal Netherlands Government*, [1943] A.C. 147.

[12] It is thought not to be a substantial objection that exemplary damages may be awarded in some civil cases; for this is merely ancillary to the main object and the occasions for their award are now much restricted: *Rookes* v. *Barnard*, [1964] A.C. 1129, at p. 1221; [1964] 1 All E.R. 367, at p. 407.

[13] By H. M. Hart, "The Aims of the Criminal Law" (1958), 23 *Law and Contemporary Problems*, 401, 404.

punishment; but the condemnation is the essential feature. From this, it is argued that "we can say readily enough what a 'crime' is":

> "It is not simply anything which the legislature chooses to call a 'crime'. It is not simply anti-social conduct which public officers are given a responsibility to suppress. It is not simply any conduct to which a legislature chooses to attach a 'criminal' penalty. It is conduct which, if duly shown to have taken place, will incur a formal and solemn pronouncement of the moral condemnation of the community."[14]

But if "the formal and solemn pronouncement" means the judgment of a criminal court (and what else can it mean?) we are driven back to ascertaining whether the proceeding is criminal or not. How is the judge to know whether to make "a solemn and formal pronouncement of condemnation" or to give judgment as in a civil action? Surely, only by ascertaining whether the legislature (or the courts in the case of a common law crime) have prescribed that the proceeding shall be criminal; and this must depend, primarily, upon whether it is intended to be punitive.

---

[14] H. M. Hart, "The Aims of the Criminal Law" (1958), 23 *Law and Contemporary Problems*, 405.

CHAPTER 3

The Classification
of Offences

1 TREASONS, FELONIES AND MISDEMEANOURS: ARRESTABLE OFFENCES

At common law a crime might be classified either as treason, felony or misdemeanour. Originally the distinction between felony and misdemeanour was a distinction between serious and minor offences (the former involving penalties of a different order from the latter)[1] but over the years this distinction, though always broadly discernible, became blurred. The practical importance of the distinction came to lie in certain consequences which turned upon whether the offence was felony or misdemeanour. For example, the general power of arrest without warrant was available only in respect of felonies; only in felonies was the distinction drawn between principals and accessories to the crime; and it was an offence to conceal (misprision), or to agree not to prosecute (compound), a felony, though it was not an offence to conceal a misdemeanour and probably not an offence to compound one.

But now, by s. 1 of the Criminal Law Act 1967, all distinctions between felony and misdemeanour are abolished and, on all matters on which a distinction has previously been drawn, the law is assimilated to that applicable to misdemeanour at the commencement of the Act. Consequently there is no distinction of substance between the former felonies, whether created at common law or by statute, and misdemeanours and all may be conveniently called "offences".

It will be appreciated, however, that for some purposes, and especially for the purposes of the law of arrest without warrant, it is necessary to maintain a distinction between those (serious) offences in respect of which it is necessary that there should be a power of arrest without warrant and those (minor) offences in respect of which there is no general need for such a power. The Criminal Law Act, s. 2, accordingly introduces the new concept of the arrestable offence,

---

[1] See generally, Pollock and Maitland, 2 H.E.L., Cap. VIII, s. 2.

which is defined as any offence "for which the sentence is fixed by law[2] or for which a person (not previously convicted) may under or by virtue of any enactment[3] be sentenced for a term of five years, and to attempts to commit any such offence."

Moreover, the Criminal Law Act 1967 creates offences in relation to arrestable offences which cannot be committed in respect of other offences. Under s. 4 (1) it is an offence to assist a person guilty of an arrestable offence,[4] and s. 5 (1) creates an offence of agreeing for gain to conceal information relating to an arrestable offence.[5] These offences had their counterparts in the earlier law; the first closely resembles the former offence of being an accessory after the fact to felony, and the latter has features—though very emaciated features—of the former offences of misprision and compounding.

The modern classification of arrestable and "non-arrestable"[6] offences has superseded the former classification of felonies and misdemeanours. No doubt it would simplify things if it were possible to dispense altogether with any mention of felony and misdemeanour, but this is not possible. The terms appear regularly in pre-1968 cases and the student must know to what they refer. Most of these cases remain unaffected by the abolition of the distinctions between felony and misdemeanour since the law is, in the main, the same for both. And even cases which raise the peculiarities of felony may remain authoritative in other respects. For example, although it is no longer necessary to draw the elaborate distinctions relating to degrees of participation in felony, the cases may remain authoritative as showing the limits of criminal participation in an offence.[7]

The Criminal Law Act 1967 does not affect the substantive law of treason,[8] and consequently the law of accessories, misprision and compounding in relation to treason remains unaltered. These topics do not receive extended treatment in this book[9] since they are not of any great significance. Curiously, cases on misprision and compounding of felony may remain relevant in determining the scope of these offences in relation to treason.

2 INDICTABLE AND SUMMARY OFFENCES

For procedural purposes crimes are classified as indictable and summary offences. Summary offences are offences which may be tried by courts having summary jurisdiction and the trial is conducted by magistrates without a jury; a trial on

---

[2] These are murder (Murder (Abolition of Death Penalty) Act 1965, s. 1 (1)); treason (Treason Act 1814, s. 1); piracy with violence (Piracy Act 1837, s. 2); and setting fire to Her Majesty's ships, stores etc. (Dockyards Protection Act 1772, s. 1).

[3] The requirement that the offence be one which "by virtue of any enactment" carries five years' imprisonment excludes common law misdemeanours, see above, p. 5, footnote 12, from the definition of arrestable offence.

[4] See further below, p. 517.

[5] See further below, p. 521.

[6] *I.e.*, offences for which no *general* power of arrest without warrant exists under s. 2 of the Act. There are numerous particular powers of arrest without warrant under statutes (see Devlin J. D., *Police Procedure, Administration & Organisation*, 1966, pp. 308–327 for a comprehensive list) in respect of offences which would not otherwise satisfy the definition of arrestable offence.

[7] See further below, pp. 80–81.

[8] Section 12 (6).

[9] But as to misprision of treason, see below, p. 557.

indictment always takes place with a jury before assizes, the Central Criminal Court, the Crown Courts, or quarter sessions.[10] For practical purposes it is the question of trial with or without a jury which is the important distinction between trial on indictment and summary trial.[11] In other respects the course and conduct of the trial is very much the same.

The classification of offences as indictable and summary broadly reflects a distinction between serious and minor crimes. Some offences are so obviously serious that they are triable only on indictment, and some offences are so obviously minor that they can be tried only summarily. But there are very many crimes the gravity of which turns upon the particular circumstances of the case. Recognising this, Parliament has from time to time provided that offences which were originally triable only on indictment may also be tried summarily, and in certain cases offences have been made both indictable and summary. In so doing Parliament has been careful to safeguard the right to trial by jury, and the result is that a simple classification of offences as indictable only, or summary only, is no longer possible. The classification now adopted is as follows.

1 Offences which are Indictable only

The offences which fall within this group include any offence punishable by death or by imprisonment for life on first conviction, causing death by dangerous driving, perjury and many of the offences under the Forgery Act 1913. It seems that offences are triable on indictment only, either because of their exceptional gravity or because, for other reasons such as anticipated complexity of issues, it is considered unsuitable that they be triable summarily.

2 Indictable Offences Triable on Indictment or Summarily

Numerous offences, now set out in the First Schedule to the Magistrates' Courts Act 1952, which formerly could only be tried on indictment are now triable summarily with the consent of the defendant. Among these are many of the offences under the Theft Act 1968 (including theft, obtaining by deception and handling stolen goods), and certain offences under the Malicious Damage Act 1861 and the Forgery Act 1913.

In cases falling under this head it is for the court to decide, having regard to the nature of the charge and the circumstances of the case, whether to deal with the case summarily, but the court cannot so proceed unless it first informs the defendant of his right to be tried by jury on indictment and the defendant elects to be tried summarily.

Where a person over fourteen but under seventeen is charged with *any* offence, other than homicide, the court may proceed summarily if, having been informed of his right to be tried by a jury, the defendant consents to summary trial.[12]

Where a person who is under fourteen is charged with *any* offence, other than homicide, he *must* be tried summarily, unless he is charged jointly with a person

---

[10] Note that the jurisdiction of quarter sessions to try indictable offences is limited. They may not, *e.g.*, try offences punishable by death or by imprisonment for life. See Criminal Law Act 1967, Sch. 1, List B.

[11] See Jackson, *Machinery of Justice*, 5th ed. (1967), pp. 100–106, 112–114.

[12] Magistrates' Courts Act 1952, s. 20.

over fourteen in which case the court may, if it considers it necessary in the interests of justice, commit both for trial.[13]

3   Offences which are both Indictable and Summary

It is now common for the Legislature to provide that an offence shall be triable either on indictment or summarily and further to provide different maximum punishments depending on the mode of trial. What happens in these cases is that the court proceeds as if the offence were not a summary offence unless it determines on the application of the prosecutor to proceed summarily. If no application is made by the prosecutor before evidence is called then the court begins to enquire into the information as examining justices, but if at any time during the enquiry the court feels, having regard to any representations made by the prosecution or the defendant and to the nature of the case, it is proper to do so, the court may:

(a) if the punishment prescribed for the offence *as a summary offence* is not more than imprisonment for three months, proceed to deal with the case summarily;

(b) if the punishment prescribed for the offence *as a summary offence* is more than imprisonment for three months, proceed to deal with the case summarily if, and only if, the defendant, having been informed of his right to be tried by a jury, elects to be tried summarily.[14]

4   Summary Offences Triable Summarily or on Indictment

Whenever a summary offence carries a maximum punishment in excess of imprisonment for three months, the defendant may, unless the offence is an assault or an offence under s. 1 of the Vagrancy Act 1898, claim to be tried by a jury. The court must again inform the defendant of his right and cannot proceed to determine the charge unless he elects to be tried summarily.[15]

5   Offences which are Summary only

Offences falling within this category, and there are very many of them, must be exclusively summary offences not carrying a punishment in excess of imprisonment for three months.

---

[13] Magistrates' Courts Act 1952, s. 21.
[14] Magistrates' Courts Act 1952, s. 18. The distinction between (a) and (b) above results from s. 18 (6) and s. 25 (1) of the Act.
[15] Magistrates' Courts Act 1952, s. 25 (1).

CHAPTER 4

The Elements of a Crime

Before a man can be convicted of a crime it is usually necessary for the prosecution to prove (a) that a certain event or a certain state of affairs, which is forbidden by the criminal law, has been caused by his conduct and (b) that this
conduct was accompanied by a prescribed state of mind. The event, or state of
affairs, is usually called the *actus reus* and the state of mind the *mens rea* of the
crime. Both these elements must be proved beyond reasonable doubt by the
prosecution. Though it is absolutely clear that D killed P—that is, he has
caused an *actus reus*—he must be acquitted of murder if the killing might
reasonably have been accidental; for, if that is the case, it has not been proved
beyond reasonable doubt that he has *mens rea*. It was so laid down by the House
of Lords in *Woolmington* v. *Director of Public Prosecutions*[1] where it was held,
overruling earlier authorities, that it is a misdirection to tell a jury that D must
satisfy them that the killing was an accident. The true rule is that the jury must
acquit even though they are not satisfied that D's story is true, if they think it
might reasonably be true. They should convict only if satisfied beyond reasonable doubt that it is *not* true. This rule is of general application[2] and there is
only one clearly established exception to it at common law—the defence of
insanity[3] Statute, however, has created many exceptions. Where an onus of
proof is put upon D, he satisfies it if he proves his case on a balance of probabilities—the same standard as that on the plaintiff in a civil action—and he need
not prove it beyond reasonable doubt.[4]

The principle that a man is not criminally liable for his conduct unless the
prescribed state of mind is also present is frequently stated in the form of a
Latin maxim: *actus non facit reum nisi mens sit rea*. The two elements of *actus
reus* and *mens rea* require separate consideration.

---

[1] [1935] A.C. 462.
[2] *Mancini* v. *Director of Public Prosecutions*, [1942] A.C. 1; [1941] 3 All E.R. 272 (provocation); *Chan Kau* v. *R.*, [1955] A.C. 206; [1955] 1 All E.R. 266; *Lobell*, [1957] 1 Q.B.
547; [1957] 1 All E.R. 734 (self-defence); *Bratty* v. *A.G. for Northern Ireland*, [1963]
A.C. 386; [1961] 3 All E.R. 523 (automatism); *Gill*, [1963] 2 All E.R. 688 (duress).
[3] Below, p. 122.
[4] *Carr-Briant*, [1943] K.B. 607; [1943] 2 All E.R. 156.

1 THE ACTUS REUS

1 The Nature of an Actus Reus

A crime may, for the purpose of analysis, be divided into two elements, *actus reus* and *mens rea*. *Mens rea* is to be found in the mind of the accused. It follows that the *actus reus* includes all the elements in the definition of the crime except those which relate to the accused's state of mind and is not merely an "act" in the ordinary, popular usage of that term. It is made up not only of the accused's conduct and its consequences but also of the surrounding circumstances, in so far as they are relevant.[5] Circumstances are relevant in so far as they are included in the definition of the crime. The definition of theft, for example, requires that it be proved that D dishonestly appropriated property *belonging to another*. If the property belonged to no one (because it had been abandoned) D's appropriation could not constitute the *actus reus* of theft. However dishonest he might be, he could not be convicted of theft because an essential constituent of the crime is missing.[6]

Sometimes a particular state of mind on the part of the *victim* is required by the definition of the crime. If so, that state of mind is part of the *actus reus* and, if the prosecution are unable to prove its existence, they must fail. If D is prosecuted for rape, it must be shown that P did not consent to the act of intercourse. The absence of consent by P is an essential constituent of the *actus reus*. But in many crimes the consent of the victim is entirely irrelevant. If D is charged with the murder of P, it is no defence for him to show that P asked to be killed.

It is apparent from these examples that it is only by looking at the definition of the particular crime that we can see what circumstances are material to the *actus reus*. We find this definition, in the case of common law crimes, in the decisions of the courts and, in the case of statutory crimes, in the words of the statute, as construed by the courts. Many factors may be relevant; for example, in bigamy, the fact that D is validly married; in treason committed abroad, that D is a British national (or under the protection of the Crown for some other reason); in handling stolen goods, that the goods have, in fact, been stolen; and so on. In general, it may be said that, if the absence of any fact (other than the accused's state of mind) will negative the commission of the crime, that fact is part of the *actus reus*.

2 An Actus Reus must be Proved

If there is no *actus reus* there can be no crime. Although D believes that he is appropriating P's property he cannot in any circumstances be guilty of theft if the property belongs to no one. D has the *mens rea* but the *actus reus*, the other fundamental element of the crime, is lacking. D may assault P with intent to ravish her against her will but, if in fact she consents, his act cannot amount to

---

[5] It should be said that this is not the only possible definition of an *actus reus*, and that a more limited view is taken of it by some writers. It is thought, however, that it is the most useful conception of the *actus reus* and is adopted throughout this book. *Cf.* Williams, C.L.G.P., 16 and [1958] Crim. L.R. at 830.

[6] Whether he could be convicted of an attempt to commit theft is another matter, considered below, p. 171.

rape. D may intend to marry during the lifetime of his wife but if, unknown to him, she is dead, he cannot commit bigamy. If D makes a statement, which he believes to be false, for the purpose of obtaining money, he cannot be convicted of obtaining by deception if the statement is, in fact, true.

In *Deller*,[7] D induced P to purchase his car by representing (*inter alia*) that it was free from encumbrances. D had previously executed a document which purported to mortgage the car to a finance company and, no doubt, he thought he was telling a lie. He was charged with obtaining by false pretences.[8] It then appeared that the document by which the transaction had been effected was probably void in law as an unregistered bill of sale. If it was void the car *was* free from encumbrances—". . . quite accidentally and, strange as it may sound, dishonestly, the appellant had told the truth".[9] D's conviction was, therefore, quashed by the Court of Criminal Appeal, for, though he had *mens rea*, no *actus reus* had been established.

A case which is sometimes said to be inconsistent with this fundamental principle, but which is worth discussing because it illustrates the difficulties which may arise in connection with its application, is *Dadson*.[10]

D was a constable, employed to watch a copse from which wood had been stolen. He carried a loaded gun. P emerged from the copse carrying wood which he had stolen, and, ignoring D's calls to stop, ran away. D, having no other means of bringing him to justice, fired and wounded him in the leg. He was convicted of shooting at P with intent to cause him grievous bodily harm. It was assumed in this case that it was perfectly lawful to wound an escaping felon if this was the only way of arresting him;[11] but stealing growing wood was not, under s. 39 of the Larceny Act 1827, a felony unless P had two previous convictions for the same offence. In fact P had been repeatedly convicted of stealing wood, but D did not know this. ERLE, J., told the jury that the alleged felony, *being unknown to the prisoner*, constituted no justification. On a case reserved the judges thought the conviction right: D was not justified in firing at P because the fact that P was committing a felony was not known to D at the time.[12]

The argument runs that this case is wrong because, if we ignore D's state of mind and look at the actual facts, what he did was perfectly lawful; that there was no *actus reus*. It is submitted that this is going too far. It is important to distinguish between two types of defence which may be raised. In the first type, D merely denies the existence of an element (other than the *mens rea*) in the definition of the crime. If D makes out the defence he certainly cannot be convicted whatever his state of mind. This is what happened in *Deller*.[13] In the second type, D admits that all the elements in the definition of the crime have been established and goes on to assert other facts which afford him a defence in law. The establishment of this type of defence may require D to assert the existence of a mental element as well as external facts. A successful defence of

---

[7] (1952), 36 Cr. App. Rep. 184.
[8] Under s. 32 of the Larceny Act 1916, now replaced by s. 15 of the Theft Act 1968, below, p. 383. The same principles are applicable.
[9] *Ibid.*, at 191.
[10] (1850), 2 Den. 35; see Williams, C.L.G.P., 23 *et seq.* His view that Dadson could properly have been convicted of an attempt renders academic the question whether Dadson was properly convicted of the complete crime. See below, pp. 171-174.
[11] On this point, see below, p. 229.
[12] For a discussion of this problem in the modern law, see below, p. 231.
[13] *Supra.*

duress cannot be made out by showing that D was threatened with dire consequences if he did not commit the crime charged, if he was unaware of the threat.
Acts, so provocative as to cause the most reasonable of men to lose his self-
control, will not afford a defence to a charge of murder if they were unknown to
D or had no effect on his mind.

In *Dadson*[14] D did not deny that he shot at P or that he intended to cause him
grievous bodily harm. He admitted the necessary constituents of the crime but
went on to assert other facts which, he alleged, made his act lawful. Whether
his act was lawful depended on what were the constituents of the defence which
he raised; and the case decides that the defence, like duress and provocation,
required the assertion not merely of external facts, but also of a state of mind.
A doctrine of *actus reus* which says that such a course *must* be wrong, as contravening a fundamental principle, is much too constricting. Whether the defence
should consist simply in the external facts, or in the facts plus the state of mind,
is a matter of policy; and it was a not unreasonable decision of policy to say that
a man who deliberately shot another should be guilty of an offence unless he
knew of circumstances justifying his conduct.

Dadson then, is perfectly reconcilable with *Deller*. It does not decide that a
man cannot be convicted where there is no *actus reus*: there was an *actus reus* for
D did unlawfully wound P. All that the case decided was that the defence to
wounding, "I was arresting an escaping felon," is a defence which requires a
mental as well as a physical element and, the mental element lacking, the
wounding was unlawful.

Of course, the law relating to felonies is now repealed but problems similar in
principle to *Dadson* may still arise. If the facts of that case occurred again, the
question would be whether D had used only such force as was "reasonable in
the circumstances." How this question should be decided is considered below.[15]

3 Analysis of an Actus Reus

Some writers have suggested that "an act" is nothing more than a willed
muscular movement— for example, the deliberate crooking of a finger. But if
D crooked his finger around the trigger of a loaded pistol which was pointing at
P, with the result that P was killed, to say "D crooked his finger" would be a
most misleading way of describing D's "act". It would be more natural and
realistic to say, "D shot P". This way of describing the act takes account of
the circumstances surrounding the willed muscular movement (in so far as they
are relevant) and its consequences (again, in so far as they are relevant), and, for
ordinary purposes, it is obviously the sensible way of describing it. But for the
purposes of the criminal law it is sometimes necessary to break down an "act",
so comprehensively described, into the constituents of (i) the conduct which is
the central feature of the crime, and (ii) the surrounding material circumstances.
One reason for so doing will soon appear. When we consider *mens rea* we will
see that the law's requirements as to the mental state which must be proved are
not necessarily the same for each of the different elements in the *actus reus*. To

---

[14] Above, p. 29.
[15] See p. 231. For a defence of *Dadson*, see Hall, *General Principles*, 228 and Perkins,
Criminal Law, 39. And *cf.* the crime of perjury, below, p. 509, where D may be convicted
if he makes a statement on oath which he believes to be false though it is in fact true.

take a crime where the cases show this to be so,[16] s. 20 of the Sexual Offences Act 1956, provides:

> "It is an offence for a person acting without lawful authority or excuse to take an unmarried girl under the age of sixteen out of the possession of her parent or guardian against his will."

Here the conduct which is the central feature of the crime is the physical act of taking away the girl. The material circumstances are:

(a) the absence of lawful authority or excuse;
(b) that the girl is unmarried and under sixteen;
(c) that she was in the possession of her parent or guardian.

If any one of these circumstances is not present the crime is not committed. Thus if D was acting under the order of a competent court; or if P was married,[17] or seventeen; or if she was not in the possession of any parent or guardian, in none of these cases would there be an *actus reus*.

This example illustrates the fact that the *actus reus* of a crime may include negative factors—that is, in this case, the absence of lawful authority or excuse. If there is a lawful excuse for the doing of the act (apart from the accused's state of mind), there is no *actus reus*. So when a hangman executes a condemned prisoner, or a soldier in battle shoots an enemy, the killing is not the *actus reus* of any crime for there is a lawful excuse for it. To drive a motor vehicle at 50 m.p.h. through a built-up area is generally the *actus reus* of a crime under s. 19 (1) of the Road Traffic Act 1960; but if the vehicle is a fire engine going to a fire, or an ambulance to an accident, there is a lawful excuse under s. 25 of the Act and, therefore, no *actus reus*.

4 The Conduct must be Willed

If the *actus reus* includes an act, that act must be willed by the accused. If a man is unable to control a movement of his limbs it seems obvious that he should not be held criminally liable for that movement or any of its consequences. Thus D was acquitted of murder where he killed a girl, according to his story (which the jury must have found might reasonably be true) in his sleep.[18] If the movement is an uncontrolled one it is often said, indeed, that it is not an "act" at all. The beating of the heart is a muscular movement, but it would be strange to describe it as an act.

> "An act is a muscular contraction and something more. A spasm is not an act. The contraction of the muscles must be willed".[19]

Whether an involuntary muscular movement is to be considered an involuntary act, or not an act at all, does not seem, however, to be of any great importance; for it is clear that it does not entail criminal liability.[20] It is a defence, now

---

[16] See below, pp. 43, 305.
[17] If under sixteen, she could be validly married if domiciled abroad at the time of the marriage. See *M.* v. *K.*, [1968] Crim. L.R. 341.
[18] *Boshears* (1961), *The Times*, February 18.
[19] Holmes, *The Common Law*, 54.
[20] Some writers regard the "voluntariness" of the accused's conduct as an element in his *mens rea:* see Turner in M.A.C.L. 195, 199 and Kenny, *Outlines*, 29. Others consider it to be part of the *actus reus:* see Williams, C.L.G.P. § 8. It is thought that to indulge in controversy on the matter would be fruitless. The only thing that exists in

commonly called "automatism", for D to show that his act may have been involuntary.

In *Charlson*,[1] D, a devoted and indulgent father, made a sudden and savage attack on his son, striking him on the head with a mallet and throwing him from a window. He was charged in three counts with various offences against the person and, at his trial, evidence was given to the effect that there was a possibility that he was suffering from a cerebral tumour. A person who was so afflicted, according to the medical evidence, would be liable to an outburst of impulsive violence over which he would have no control at all. BARRY, J., directed the jury that if D was acting as an automaton without any real knowledge of what he was doing, if his actions were purely automatic and his mind had no control over the movement of his limbs, he should be acquitted on all counts. If the jury were left in doubt upon the matter and thought he might well have been acting as an automaton then, too, they should acquit. In other words, once some evidence of automatism had been given, the burden of proving that the accused's act was voluntary was on the Crown.[2]

Again, in a prosecution for dangerous driving[3] when the defence of automatism was raised (unsuccessfully, for there was no evidence of it whatever) PEARSON, J., put the following cases:

> "(1) The man in the driving seat is having an epileptic fit, so that he is unconscious and there are merely spasmodic movements of his arms and legs. (2) By the onset of some disease he has been reduced to a state of coma and is completely unconscious. (3) He is stunned by a blow on the head from a stone which passing traffic has thrown up from the roadway. (4) He is attacked by a swarm of bees so that he is for the time being disabled and prevented from exercising any directional control over the vehicle, and any movements of his arms and legs are solely caused by the action of the bees."[4]

In none of these cases, in the learned judge's view, could it be said that the man in the driving seat was driving and, therefore, he would not be criminally

---

law is *a crime*; and it is only for purposes of analytical convenience that it is divided into *actus reus* and *mens rea*. Once it is agreed that voluntariness is essential, it does not matter how it is classified. Yet in *Harrison-Owen*, [1951] 2 All E.R. 726, the C.C.A. held inadmissible evidence tending to prove the voluntariness of an act, though they apparently thought the same evidence might be admissible to prove that a voluntary act was not accidental—*i.e.*, done with *mens rea*. The logical effect of the evidence would seem to be the same for both purposes and the decision is doubted by Lord DENNING in *Bratty* v. *A.G. for Northern Ireland*, [1963] A.C. 386 at p. 410; [1961] 3 All E.R. 523 at p. 533 and criticised by Williams, C.L.G.P. at 14. For another view as to importance of classifying voluntariness as part of the *actus*, see Patient, [1968] Crim. L.R. 23.

[1] [1955] 1 All E.R. 859; approved on the point under discussion by the House of Lords in *Bratty* v. *A.G. for Northern Ireland*, [1963] A.C. 386 at p. 407; [1961] 3 All E.R. 523 at p. 531. *Cf.* Lord DENNING, [1961] 3 All E.R. at p. 533, and below, p. 117.

[2] It is now clear that this is in accordance with principle, notwithstanding the *dictum* by Lord GODDARD, C.J., in *Hill* v. *Baxter*, [1958] 1 Q.B. 277; [1958] 1 All E.R. 193, that the burden of proof is on the accused; the matter seems to have been settled beyond doubt by *Spurge*, [1961] 2 Q.B. 205; [1961] 2 All E.R. 688; *Budd*, [1962] Crim. L.R. 49, and *Sell*, [1962] Crim. L.R. 463; see also *Bratty* v. *A.G. for Northern Ireland*, [1963] A.C. 386; [1961] 3 All E.R. 523. D must adduce evidence sufficient to lay a foundation for the offence: *Dervish*, [1968] Crim. L.R. 37; *Cook* v. *Atchison*, [1968] Crim. L.R. 266. Where the alleged automatism is due to a "defect of reason from disease of the mind", the plea is one of insanity and the onus of proof is on the accused: below, p. 122.

[3] *Hill* v. *Baxter*, above, footnote 2.

[4] [1958] 1 Q.B. 277 at p. 286; [1958] 1 All E.R. 193 at p. 197. It appears that automatism not amounting to insanity may result from sleepwalking: *Boshears* (above, p. 31); *Bratty's Case* (*supra*) (*dicta*); concussion: *Scott*, [1967] V.R. 276 (below, p. 46); *Bratty's Case* (*dicta*); or a hypoglycaemic episode: *Watmore* v. *Jenkins*, [1962] 2 Q.B. 572; [1962] 2 All E.R. 868.

liable for the consequence of the movements of his limbs. Of course, it may well be that the man who had the epileptic fit was guilty of dangerous driving by being on the road at all[5]; but then he would be held responsible for the act which he had done voluntarily—taking the car on the road in the first place.[6] The answer would probably depend, as PEARSON, J., suggested,

> "on the degree and frequency of the epilepsy and the degree of probability that an epileptic fit might come upon him."[7]

Lord DENNING has suggested that "it is not every involuntary act which leads to a complete acquittal"; and that a man, "so drunk that he does not know what he is doing", may be convicted of unlawful wounding or manslaughter.[8] Certainly, if D is so drunk that he puts the baby on the fire in mistake for a log of wood,[9] he is guilty of manslaughter; but this is not an involuntary act. If D's drunkenness prevents him from controlling his bodily movements at all, it is submitted that he can be guilty of no crime, except perhaps in the case where the drunkenness was self-induced with the intention of committing crime.[10]

5 Causation

When the definition of an *actus reus* requires the occurrence of certain consequences it is necessary to prove that it was the conduct of the accused which caused those consequences to occur. In murder or manslaughter, for example, it is necessary to prove that the act of the accused caused the death. If the death came about solely through some other cause then the crime is not committed, even though all the other elements of the *actus reus* and the *mens rea* are present.

In *White*[11] it appeared that D put potassium cyanide into a drink called "nectar" with intent to murder his mother. She was found dead shortly afterwards with the glass, three parts filled, beside her. The medical evidence showed that she had died, not of poison, but of heart failure. D was acquitted of murder and convicted of an attempt to murder. Although the consequence which D intended occurred, he did not cause it to occur and there was no *actus reus* of murder. A less obvious example is *Hensler*.[12] There D wrote a begging letter to P, declaring that he was "a poor shipwrecked widow" and telling other lies. P, because he remembered something which had been told him previously, was not deceived but, nevertheless, sent five shillings. D was convicted of an *attempt* to obtain five shillings by false pretences. Once again the consequence which D intended (and which was[13] part of the *actus reus* of obtaining by false pretences) occurred but it was not D's false pretence which caused it to occur. It was as if a rogue, having tried unsuccessfully to break into a safe with an inadequate implement, were to be presented by the owner with the contents. The rogue would have got what he wanted, yet failed to bring about the *actus reus* of the crime.

---

[5] Below, p. 336.
[6] *Cf. McBride*, [1962] 2 Q.B. 167; [1961] 3 All E.R. 6.
[7] [1958] 1 Q.B. at p. 287; [1958] 1 All E.R. at p. 198.
[8] *Bratty* v. *A.G. for Northern Ireland*, [1963] A.C. 386 at p. 460; [1961] 3 All E.R. 523 at p. 533.
[9] See below, p. 131.
[10] See below, p. 135.
[11] [1910] 2 K.B. 124.
[12] (1870), 11 Cox C. C. 570; below, p. 173.
[13] As it now is of obtaining by deception: below, p. 386.

Problems of causation have given rise to much difficulty and controversy in the law of tort and contract. These difficulties have been less commonly encountered in criminal cases. The reason probably is that a man will usually be held criminally liable only for such consequences of his conduct as he foresaw (or, in crimes of negligence, *ought* to have foreseen) to be likely to occur. The problem, in the criminal law, more usually takes the form of an investigation into what the accused foresaw (or ought to have foreseen) than an enquiry into problems of causation. If he foresaw (or ought to have foreseen) the harm as likely to occur, it is usually obvious that it is not too remote a consequence; if he did not foresee it (or, in crimes of negligence, there is no reason why he should have foreseen it), the problem of causation does not arise, for he has no *mens rea* (or is not negligent).

The problems of D's foresight, on the one hand, and of causation on the other are, however, distinct questions and both may have to be answered in a criminal case. The cases of *White* and *Hensler*, considered above, are both cases where D foresaw a consequence, and that consequence occurred, yet he did not cause it.

Since, however, the problem almost invariably arises in connection with cases of murder and manslaughter, detailed discussion of it is postponed to the chapters on homicide.[14] For the present it is sufficient to note the rule, which is almost invariable, that D should have caused the *actus reus*.[15]

6   A "State of Affairs" as an Actus Reus

A crime may be so defined that it can be committed although there is no "act" in the sense considered above. There may be no necessity for any "willed muscular movement". Instead it may be enough if a specified "state of affairs" is proved to exist. Under the Road Traffic Act 1960, s. 6 (2), for example, any person who, when in charge of a motor vehicle on a road or other public place is unfit to drive through drink or drugs, commits an offence. It is not *taking* charge of the vehicle, or *becoming* unfit which is the offence; but simply *being* in charge and *being* unfit. So long as this state of affairs continues, the *actus reus* of the crime is committed. The *actus reus* may even be in process of being committed while D is sleeping peacefully,[16] for he may still be "in charge". A person commits an offence if, when not at his place of abode, he *has with him* any article for use in the course of or in connection with burglary, etc. So long as he has the article with him, he is committing the offence. Of course, in both of these examples the accused will, almost invariably, have done the acts of taking charge, getting drunk, or taking up the article, but such acts seem, technically, to be no part of the crime. This seems to follow from *Larsonneur*,[17] where D was convicted under the Aliens Order 1920, in that she,

> "being an alien to whom leave to land in the United Kingdom has been refused was found in the United Kingdom".

---

[14] See below, pp. 184 *et seq.*

[15] The one reported exception seems to be *Larsonneur, infra.*

[16] *Duck* v. *Peacock*, [1949] 1 All E.R. 318; but see the defence provided by Road Traffic Act 1956, s. 9 (1) proviso, now re-enacted in Road Traffic Act 1960, s. 6 (1), below, pp. 339, 341.

[17] (1933), 24 Cr. App. Rep. 74. *Cf. Walters*, [1968] 3 All E.R. 863 (being an incorrigible rogue). See the criticism of *Larsonneur* by Howard, *Strict Responsibility*, 47.

In this case D had done no voluntary act at all, but was brought into the United Kingdom in the custody of the police. The circumstances of her entry into the country were, the Court of Criminal Appeal said, "perfectly immaterial". "Being in the United Kingdom", in these circumstances, was the *actus reus* of the crime.

Larsonneur's case is peculiar in that the statute was so drafted that, not only was it unnecessary to prove that D caused the *actus reus*, but also no *mens rea* was required on her part. Such an unjust result could hardly arise under any of the other statutes considered in this section since the state of affairs is required to be accompanied by some guilty knowledge or intention on the part of the accused.

It was held[18] at common law that "being in possession" was an insufficient act to constitute the *actus reus* of a crime, but there are many cases where, by statute, mere possession is enough. Thus possession of dangerous drugs, explosive substances, firearms and forged bank-notes all constitute the *actus reus* of various crimes. "Being in possession" does not involve an act in the sense of a muscular movement at all, for a man may possess goods merely by knowingly[19] keeping them in his house. "Being in possession" is simply a state of affairs, which, in certain circumstances, involves criminal liability.

7 Omissions[20]

An *actus reus* may also consist in a failure to take action where action is required by the criminal law. The common law very rarely punished omissions.[1] It seems to have been thought that the function of the criminal law was to prevent men from doing positive harm and it was left to public opinion, morality and religion to encourage the doing of good works. The usual illustration of the common law attitude is that of a group of people who watch a child, whom they could easily save, drown in a shallow pool.[2] If they are in no special relationship with the child, it is said that, however grossly immoral their conduct, they commit no crime. If, however, one of them were the parent or guardian of the child this relationship would impose a duty to act, violation of which would be a breach of the criminal law.

The question is to determine when the criminal law imposes a duty to act. It is thought that it is not possible to answer this with any general statement of principle, for none is to be found in the cases. It can be said, however, that the common law seems never to have imposed a duty to act in protection of another's property. The duty to protect another's person arose only where there was some special relationship—such as parent or guardian—with that other; or where the accused had undertaken a duty gratuitously[3] or by

---

[18] *Heath* (1810), Russ. & Ry. 184; *Dugdale* v. *R* (1853), 1 E. & B. 435.

[19] A man may possess a thing in the civil law although he does not know of its existence; but knowledge will usually be required in criminal law: *cf. Warner* v. *Metropolitan Police Commissioner*, below, p. 78; *Cugullere*, [1961] 2 All E.R. 343; below, p. 286.

[20] Glazebrook (1960), 76 L.Q.R. 386; Graham Hughes (1958), 67 Y.L.J. 590.

[1] An instance of a common law crime consisting purely of an omission was misprision of felony now abolished by the Criminal Law Act 1967. Misprision of treason, however, survives; below, p. 557.

[2] See J. B. Ames (1908), 22 Harv. L. Rev. at 112–113; Stephen, 3 H.C.L. 10.

[3] *Instan*, [1893] 1 Q.B. 450, D omitted to give food to P, her aunt and a helpless invalid. There probably was a contract for P paid both for her own and D's food; but the court found there was "a common law duty imposed upon D".

contract. In the latter case, the contractual duty would suffice to make him *criminally* liable for injuries to persons, not parties to the contract, incurred in consequence of his omission to act.

In *Pittwood*[4] a railway crossing gate-keeper opened the gate to let a cart pass and went off to his lunch, forgetting to shut it again. Ten minutes later a hay-cart while crossing the line was struck by a train. D was convicted of man-slaughter. It was argued on his behalf that he owed a duty of care only to his employers, the railway company, with whom he contracted. WRIGHT, J., held, however, that

> "there was gross and criminal negligence, as the man was paid to keep the gate shut and protect the public . . . A man might incur criminal liability from a duty arising out of contract".[5]

In *Gibbins and Proctor*[6] a man and the woman with whom he was living were held guilty of murder of the man's child where the woman, with the man's concurrence, withheld food from the child, intending it death or grievous bodily harm. By living with the man and receiving money from him for food, the woman assumed a duty towards the child.

A duty to act may also arise where D is responsible for the creation of a dan-gerous situation. According to an American case,[7] if D accidentally starts a fire, his wilful omission to do anything to put it out makes him liable for arson. If D, sitting alone in the passenger seat of a car, were accidentally to knock off the handbrake, so that the car ran away, it is submitted that he could be convicted of murder if he wilfully omitted to pull the brake on again, intending the car to run over and kill P. D locks the door of a room, not knowing that P is inside. Having learned that P is within, he omits to unlock the door. Should he not be liable for false imprisonment?[8]

Statute has made omissions criminal in many cases. If, for example, owing to the presence of a motor vehicle on a road, an accident occurs, causing damage or injury to any person, vehicle or animal, the driver of the vehicle is required to give his name and address to any person having reasonable grounds for requiring him to do so, or to report the accident to the police within twenty-four hours.[9] A person legally liable to maintain a child commits a crime if he fails to provide him with adequate food, clothing, medical aid or lodging.[10]

There are many provisions which make it illegal to do one thing unless some other thing is also done. Broadcasting a dramatic or musical performance with-out the consent of the performers,[11] driving a car without third-party insurance,[12] selling ice-cream in a public place without conspicuously displaying a notice of

---

[4] (1902), 19 T.L.R. 37.

[5] WRIGHT, J., said that this was not a mere case of non feasance, but of misfeasance. However D's breach of duty was not in opening the gate, but in omitting to close it again. *Cf.*, however, *Smith* (1869), 11 Cox C. C. 210, where on similar facts LUSH, J., ruled that there was no duty.

[6] (1918), 13 Cr. App. Rep. 134.

[7] *Commonwealth* v. *Cali* (1923), 247 Mass. 20; 141 N.E. 516. Note that this could not be arson in English law since the statute requires that D shall have "unlawfully and mal-iciously *set fire to* . . .": Malicious Damage Act 1861, ss. 1–6.

[8] Andenaes, *G.P.C.L. of Norway*, 135; and see *Fagan* v. *Metropolitan Police Com-missioner*, [1968] 3 All E.R. 442; below, p. 253.

[9] Road Traffic Act 1960, s. 77.

[10] Children and Young Persons Act 1933, s. 1 (2) (a).

[11] Copyright Act 1956, Sixth Schedule, Part I, IB.

[12] Road Traffic Act 1960, s. 201.

the vendor's name and address,[13] are examples. Such crimes are not purely offences of omission, for a positive act is part of the *actus reus*. The omission is an equally essential part, but the emphasis is obviously placed mainly on the positive element. The omission tends to be regarded as one of the surrounding circumstances: that is, not having obtained the performers' consent, it is criminal to broadcast the performance. Crimes with elements of both omission and commission do not then involve any special problem; it is those of mere omission which occasion difficulty.

2 MENS REA [14]

It is a widely held view of legal historians that until the twelfth century a man might be held liable for many harms, simply because his conduct caused them, without proof of any blameworthy state of mind whatsoever on his part. Under the influence of Canon law and the Roman law, a change gradually took place and the courts began to require proof of an element of moral blameworthiness— "a guilty mind" of some kind. In the developed common law of crime, some such mental element is always necessary, and is known as *mens rea*.

1 Definition of Terms

Mens rea is a technical term. It is often loosely translated as "a guilty mind", but this translation is frequently misleading. A man may have *mens rea*, as it is generally understood today, without any feeling of guilt on his part. He may, indeed, be acting with a perfectly clear conscience, believing his act to be morally, and even legally, right, and yet be held to have *mens rea*. In order properly to appreciate the meaning of the term it is necessary to distinguish between a number of different possible mental attitudes which a man may have with respect to the *actus reus* of the crime in question. These are: (a) intention, (b) recklessness, (c) negligence and (d) blameless inadvertence.

(a) *Intention*.—There exist numerous crimes which are so defined as to require proof of intention to bring about various consequences. It is therefore very important to know what is meant by "intention". It is clear that a man intends a consequence of his act when he foresees that it may result and desires that it should do so. If the consequence is desired it is immaterial that the chance of its resulting may be small. Thus if D, hoping to kill P, were to shoot at him from a mile's range, knowing that the chances of killing him were a thousand to one, it would be an intentional killing if the one chance came up.

Where the consequence is not desired for its own sake, difficulties arise. The problem occurs where D, in deciding whether to act, contemplates two

---

[13] Food and Drugs Act 1955, s. 22.
[14] Turner, "The Mental Element in Crimes at Common Law", M.A.C.L. 195; Williams, *The Mental Element in Crime* and C.L.G.P., Ch. 2; Hart, "Negligence, *Mens Rea* and Criminal Responsibility", in *Oxford Essays in Jurisprudence*, 29; Smith, "The Guilty Mind in the Criminal Law" (1960), 76 L.Q.R. 78.

consequences, (A) and (B).   (A), considered in isolation, is a consequence which
D does not desire, indeed its occurrence may be abhorrent to him.   (B), however,
he wants badly.   Now it may be that it is apparent to D that he cannot have (B)
without having (A) as well.   Suppose that P has made a will leaving the whole of
his large estate to D.   D does not desire P's death (consequence (A)), for he
loves P.   He does desire to enjoy his inheritance immediately (consequence (B)).
If he gives P what he knows to be a fatal dose of poison, he surely intends P's
death, though he says with truth that it causes him great pain.   Or again, D
wishes to injure O (consequence (B)) who is standing at the window of P's house.
He does not wish to break P's window (consequence (A)).   If knowing the window to be closed, he throws the stone through it at P, can it be doubted that he
intends to break the window?

In these examples, the occurrence of consequence (A) is a condition precedent
to the occurrence of consequence (B).   In the nature of things, (as D knows) (B)
cannot happen, unless (A) happens first.   It might be argued that D *does* desire
(A) as well as (B); in any other circumstances, he would rather that (A) did not
occur but, in the actual circumstances, he would rather it did.   But whether he
desires it or not, few would dispute that (A) is intended.

The matter might be thought to be more debateable where (A) is not a condition of (B); that is, it is *possible* for (B) to happen without (A) also occurring, but
as D knows, to cause (B) is virtually certain to cause (A) as well.   D, wishing to
collect the insurance on a cargo (consequence (B)), puts a time bomb in a plane
to blow it up in mid-Atlantic.   He knows that the explosion, short of a near-
miracle, will kill the crew (consequence (A)).   He does not desire their deaths
and, provided that the cargo was destroyed, he would be delighted if they should
escape.   Since escape can hardly have been regarded as a serious possibility,
however, it would seem that this type of case should not be treated as distinguishable from those discussed in the previous two paragraphs.   In principle then, it
might be concluded that a person intends those consequences of his act—

(i) which he desires to bring about;

(ii) which he knows to be conditions precedent to the occurrence of the
consequences which he desires; and

(iii) which he knows to be virtually certain to result from his act.

When one turns to the actual law on the point, however, the position is by no
means so clear.   Of course, it is perfectly clear that in the case where D gave P
the poison to accelerate the inheritance, the courts would say that he intended to
cause death.   His intention to inherit P's property would be regarded as a mere
motive, irrelevant except for the purposes of proof.   But in other circumstances,
difficult to distinguish in principle, different results have been reached. Thus
in *Ahlers*,[15] a German consul who assisted German nationals to return
home after the declaration of war in 1914 was held to intend to do his duty as
consul and not to intend to aid the King's enemies.   In *Steane*,[16] D, who during
the Second World War gave broadcasts which would assist the enemy was held to
intend to save himself and his family from the horrors of the concentration camp

---

[15] [1915] 1 K.B. 616.   *Cf. Kupfer*, [1915] 2 K.B. 321.
[16] [1947] K.B. 997; [1947] 1 All E.R. 813.

and not to assist the enemy. In *Thorne* v. *Motor Trade Association*[17] Lord ATKIN thought that to put a trader's name on a "stop list" so that his business would certainly be ruined might be "an act done in lawful furtherance of business interests, and . . . without any express intent to injure the person whose name is published." In *Sinnasamy Selvanayagam* v. *R.*,[18] the Privy Council thought (*obiter*) that if D remained in occupation of his home in defiance of a lawful order to quit, knowing that the owner of the property would be annoyed, his "dominant intention" was simply to retain his home and he was not guilty of an offence under the Ceylon Penal Code of remaining in occupation with intent to annoy the owner.

Yet in *Ahlers*, *Steane* and *Thorne* the consequence held not to have been intended seems to have been a condition of that which was intended. The consul's duty could be done *only* by assisting the enemy; Steane could save his family *only* by giving the enemy the assistance they desired; the Motor Trade Association could promote business interests by this act *only* if they injured the trader. Why were not the consul's desire to do his duty, Steane's desire to save his family, the Association's desire to promote business interests, mere motives for the more immediate result?

On the other hand, it has been held that a man has an intent to aid in the commission of crime if he knows that his act will have that result though its occurrence is a matter of indifference to him. "If one man deliberately sells a gun to another to be used for murdering a third, he may be indifferent about whether the third man lives or dies and interested only in the cash profit to be made out of the sale"—but he intends to aid the murderer: *National Coal Board* v. *Gamble*,[19] *per* DEVLIN, J.

This seems to be the better view in principle, but it is clear that, in examining the state of the law we must, whenever the concept of intention is in issue, inquire whether it bears the broad meaning attributed to it by DEVLIN, J., or the narrow meaning which was attributed to it in *Steane* and the other cases considered above. It will be convenient to refer to the narrow meaning as "direct" intention and the broad meaning as "oblique" intention.

An act may be intentional with respect to circumstances as well as consequences. Intention here means *either* knowledge *or* hope that the circumstances exist. D receives a car which he knows to be stolen. This is an intentional handling of stolen goods even though D, perhaps, would much prefer that the car was not stolen. Again,

"he who steals a letter containing a cheque, intentionally steals the cheque also if he hopes that the letter may contain one, even though he well knows that the odds against the existence of such a circumstance are very great."[1]

(b) *Recklessness*.[2]—A man is reckless with respect to a consequence of his act, when he foresees the probability that it will occur, but does not desire it nor

---

[17] [1937] A.C. 797.
[18] [1951] A.C. 83. The Board declined, *ibid.* at p. 87, to find that D contemplated that he would induce in the mind of the "owner" (a government superintendent) "an emotion so inappropriate to a government officer and so unprofitable, as annoyance".
[19] [1959] 1 Q.B. 11; [1958] 3 All E.R. 203; below, p. 85.
[20] *Cf.* Bentham, *Principles of Morals and Legislation* (Harrison ed.), 202.
[1] Salmond, *Jurisprudence* (11th ed. 1957), 411.
[2] For an interesting discussion of the meaning of recklessness, see (1961), 24 M.L.R. 592 and (1962), 25 M.L.R. 49, 55 and 437.

foresee it as substantially certain. Recklessness with respect to circumstances means realisation that the circumstances may exist, without either knowing or hoping that they do. D points a gun at P and pulls the trigger. If he does not know it is loaded, but realises the possibility that it may be, he is reckless with respect to that circumstance, whether he hopes it is unloaded or just does not care whether it is loaded or not. If he is reckless with respect to this circumstance, it follows that he is also at least reckless with respect to the consequence of the death of P; that is, he foresees that it may very well occur, but neither desires it, nor foresees it as certain. Again if D buys goods from a notorious fence, realising the likelihood that they have been stolen, he is reckless as to that circumstance.

A person who acts recklessly is, then, taking a deliberate risk; and the word connotes that the risk is an unjustifiable one.[3] The operator of aircraft, the surgeon performing an operation and the promoter of a tightrope act in a circus must all foresee that their acts might cause death; but we should not describe them as reckless, unless the risk taken was unjustifiable. Whether the risk is justifiable depends on the social value of the activity involved, as well as on the probability of the occurrence of the foreseen evil. It is an objective question—that is, it is a question to be answered by the jury and D's opinion is irrelevant. Recklessness is therefore sometimes described as "advertent negligence."

(c) *Negligence.*—A man acts negligently when he brings about a consequence which a reasonable and prudent man would have foreseen and avoided. A man acts negligently with respect to a circumstance when a reasonable man would have been aware of the existence of the circumstance and, because of its existence, would have avoided acting in that manner.   In this case, it is irrelevant that D does not foresee the consequence and is not aware of the circumstance. D points a gun at P and pulls the trigger either believing that the gun is unloaded or not even considering the possibility that it may be. If any reasonable man would have realised the possibility that the gun might be loaded and accordingly avoided acting in this way, then D is negligent with respect to that circumstance. If the gun goes off and kills P, it follows that D is negligent with respect to that consequence. Again, X, a notorious car thief, offers to sell to D, at an absurdly low price, a car which is concealed in a wood. The possibility that it is a stolen car does not occur to D. If a reasonable man would have appreciated that possibility and accordingly avoided buying the car, D is negligent with respect to the circumstance of the car's being stolen.

Since foresight and awareness need not be proved, this concept is sometimes designated "inadvertent negligence" to distinguish it from recklessness. It should be noted, however, that when negligence is sufficient to found liability, recklessness and intention are, *a fortiori*, sufficient. The prosecution do not have to prove foresight and awareness, but they do not have to prove the absence of foresight and awareness. It is sufficient to prove certain conduct in certain circumstances, and unnecessary to prove anything at all about the accused's state of mind. Evidence of knowledge may be relevant, however, where the case is that no reasonable man, with the knowledge possessed by the accused, would have acted as he did.[4]

---

[3] Williams, C.L.G.P., s. 25; Model Penal Code s. 2.02 (*c*).
[4] Below, p. 54.

(d) *Blameless inadvertence.*—Finally, a man may reasonably fail to foresee a consequence that follows from his act—as when a slight slap causes the death of an apparently healthy person—or reasonably fail to consider the possibility of the existence of a circumstance—as when goods, which are in fact stolen, are bought in the normal course of business from a trader of high repute.

2 The Meaning of Mens Rea

We are now in a position to consider the meaning of *mens rea*. If the *actus reus* of a crime consists of a number of defined consequences and circumstances which, in the view of the law, constitute an evil to be prevented by criminal sanctions, the most blameworthy state of mind with respect to those consequences and circumstances is clearly intention, followed by recklessness, negligence and blameless inadvertence in that order. A consideration of the examples of a killing and a receipt of stolen goods, which are discussed in connection with each state of mind will have shown that this is so. It seems obvious that the intentional man is fully responsible for the *actus reus* and should be held guilty; it seems equally obvious that the blamelessly inadvertent man is not at all responsible and *should* be acquitted. Somewhere between the two a line must be drawn; and the common law usually—but not invariably—drew it between recklessness and negligence. The reckless man was liable, the negligent man was not. This does not mean that it is not necessary to draw the distinction between intention and recklessness for, as will appear below, in some cases intention *only* will suffice. These cases may be regarded as exceptions, however, to a general principle which does not distinguish between intention and recklessness. A definition of *mens rea*, taking account of this general principle of the common law, would therefore include (as well, in some cases, as a further element considered next) the following: *Intention or recklessness with respect to all those circumstances and consequences of the accused's act (or the state of affairs) which constitute the* actus reus *of the crime in question.*

3 The Requirement of an Ulterior Intent

This principle, by itself, would amount to a definition of the *mens rea* of many crimes, but it does not meet all cases. A crime is frequently so defined that the *mens rea* includes an intention to produce some further consequence beyond the *actus reus* of the crime in question. Burglary will serve as an example. It is not enough that D intended to enter a building as a trespasser, that is to achieve the *actus reus* of burglary. It is necessary to go further and to show that D had the intention of committing one of a number of specified offences in the dwelling house. The actual commission of one of those offences is no part of the *actus reus* of burglary which is complete as soon as D enters. Causing grievous bodily harm with intent to resist the lawful apprehension of any person,[5] placing gunpowder near a building with intent to do bodily injury to any person,[6] are instances of similar crimes. Where such an ulterior intent must be proved, it is

---

[5] Offences against the Person Act 1861, s. 18.
[6] *Ibid.*, s. 30.

sometimes referred to as a "specific intent".[7] This term, however, is one which should be regarded with caution.[8] It is variously used to mean (i) whatever intention has to be proved to establish guilt of the particular crime before the court;[9] (ii) a "direct" as distinct from an "oblique" intention;[10] or (iii) an intention ulterior to the *actus reus*. The phrase "ulterior intent" is therefore preferred to describe the third concept. The nature of the ulterior intent required varies widely from crime to crime—an intent to commit one of a number of specified offences in burglary, an intent to defraud in forgery, an intent permanently to deprive the owner in theft and so on.

Before leaving this subject, attention should be drawn to the fact that, where an ulterior intent is required, recklessness is not enough. On a charge of wounding with intent to cause grievous bodily harm, proof that D was reckless whether he caused grievous bodily harm will not suffice. Yet, paradoxically, if death resulted from the wound, D's recklessness would probably be enough to found liability for murder.

It should again be emphasised that not all crimes require an ulterior intent. In rape, for example, it is enough that the accused intended the *actus reus*—intercourse with a woman without her consent—and no ulterior intention need be proved. The result is that the best we can do by way of a general definition of *mens rea* is as follows: "Intention or recklessness with respect to all the consequences and circumstances of the accused's act (or the state of affairs) which constitute the *actus reus, together with any ulterior intent which the definition of the crime requires.*"

4   The Extent to which Mens Rea is required varies from Crime to Crime

Mens rea, as so defined, is not required for all crimes, for (a) even at common law there were many exceptions to it and (b) statutory crimes are frequently interpreted so as to exclude the necessity for either intention or recklessness with respect to some one or more elements in the *actus reus*.

Sometimes it is enough to prove only negligence; sometimes even this is not necessary and D may be convicted although he was blamelessly inadvertent as to a circumstance of the *actus reus*. In the latter case we shall say that the crime imposes "strict liability" as to that circumstance.

The offence under s. 20 of the Sexual Offences Act 1956 discussed above[11] will serve as an illustration. It has been held that, as to the circumstance that the girl is under sixteen, the accused may be blamelessly inadvertent and yet may be convicted. In *Prince*,[12] D took a girl out of the possession and against the will of her father and mother. He knew he was doing this; but, as the jury found, he believed her statement that she was eighteen and his belief was reasonable, for she looked very much older than sixteen. In fact, she was under sixteen and D therefore brought about the *actus reus* of the crime. He was not even negligent, let alone reckless or intentional as to the girl's age. In spite of his blameless inadvertence as to this important circumstance in the *actus reus*, D was convicted.

---

[7] See Perkins, "A Rationale of *Mens Rea*" (1939), 52 Harv. L. Rev. 905, 924.
[8] See Cross, [1961] Crim. L.R. 510.
[9] *Director of Public Prosecutions* v. *Beard*, [1920] A.C. 479 at pp. 501–502; below, p. 134.
[10] Above, p. 39. *Steane*, [1947] K.B. 997 at p. 1004; [1947] 1 All E.R. 813 at p. 816.
[11] See p. 31; and below, pp. 305–307.
[12] (1875), L.R. 2 C.C.R. 154.

Yet in *Hibbert*[13] D took away and seduced a young girl but was acquitted because it was not proved that he knew, or had any reason to believe, that she was in the possession of her parents. BRAMWELL, B., though upholding the conviction in *Prince*, thought D would have a good defence if he believed he had the father's consent. That the girl is (a) under sixteen, (b) in the possession of her parents, and (c) that they do not consent, are circumstances which are equally essential to the existence of an *actus reus*, yet *mens rea* is, as the law stands,[14] required as to (b) and (c) but not as to (a).

It is not suggested that this sort of situation—which arises in connection with several crimes—is a very happy one. On the face of it, it is illogical and unjust. An ideal rule would seem to be that stated at the beginning of this section, requiring intention or recklessness as to *all* the elements in the *actus reus*. Presumably no element is included in the definition of an *actus reus* unless it contributes to the heinousness of the offence. If the accused is blamelessly inadvertent with respect to *any* one element in the offence, and does not, therefore, appreciate the full heinousness of his conduct, is it then proper to hold him responsible for it?

That the law should impose strict liability to one circumstance and yet require *mens rea* as to another in the same crime may be partly a result of historical development for the courts' attitude to the problem of *mens rea* and especially to how far a requirement of *mens rea* should be imported into statutory offences, has varied from time to time. One element may have fallen to be construed by a court devoted to strict liability, another by a court which adhered to the principles of *mens rea*. This may explain how the law came to be in the state it is, but it certainly does not justify it.

Yet at the same time it must be conceded that there is sometimes a real difficulty in requiring *mens rea* as to all the elements of the *actus reus*. Particularly it would seem that the "ideal rule" might lead to unsatisfactory results where the definition of the *actus reus* includes a circumstance of a morally indifferent nature. Whether the girl is fifteen years and eleven months or sixteen years and one month when the accused takes her out of her parents' possession does not affect the morality of the accused's conduct to any appreciable extent. The line drawn by the law is necessarily an arbitrary one. Where this is so, it may well happen that the accused acts without adverting to the question of age at all, being unaware of its legal significance. If the girl is in fact fifteen years and eleven months it would be hardly a satisfactory rule which required the acquittal of the accused who had not adverted to this question. The case, it will be noted, differs in a respect which might be thought material from that where D has a positive belief as in *Prince*, that the girl is eighteen. Williams, indeed, attempts[15] to resolve the difficulty by distinguishing between cases of "mistaken knowledge" (where there is a positive belief) which will negative recklessness, and "simple ignorance" (where the question is not adverted to at all) which, he maintains, will not. He put the following case.[16]

"Suppose that a statute is passed making it an offence intentionally or recklessly to destroy documents over a hundred years old without the consent of a

---

[13] (1869), L.R. 1 C.C.R. 184.
[14] It is arguable that *Hibbert* is inconsistent with *Prince* but it was not overruled in this latter case.
[15] C.L.G.P., 151.
[16] In the first edition of C.L.G.P. at 123.

Historical Documents Commission. D clears out his father's attic and burns all the papers. He does not know the law and does not consider the question whether the papers include some above a hundred years old."

This, of course, is a case of simple ignorance and, in Williams's submission, D's act is therefore reckless. If this view is to be accepted at all, it is clear that it cannot be applied to *all* circumstances. A failure to advert to a circumstance which, if it is observed, plainly renders the transaction illegal, cannot conceivably be classed as recklessness. Thus if D were to receive stolen goods in perfectly innocent circumstances and without adverting at all to the possibility that they might be stolen (a case of simple ignorance), it surely could not be contended that he received the goods recklessly. Perhaps the difference is that the document burner necessarily knows that the document has some age and, *ex hypothesi*, does not care what it is. Equally it might be said that the taker of the girl knows that she has some age, and does not care what the age is. It is obviously not possible to say that the receiver of the goods does not care whether they are stolen or not when he does not advert to that possibility. This suggests that Williams's principle should be limited to cases of age, time or any other cases where the law draws an arbitrary line as to a circumstance which everyone knows to exist in some degree.

What the judges have in fact done in cases like *Prince*, then, it is submitted, is to impose strict liability in respect of circumstances of a morally indifferent nature, or where an arbitrary line is drawn. Some such cases are, perhaps, justifiable to effectuate a particular policy but they are a departure from the "ideal rule" stated above and should be confined to the minimum.

5 Transferred Malice

If D, with the *mens rea* of a particular crime, does an act which causes the *actus reus* of the same crime, he is guilty, even though the result, in some respects, is an unintended one. D intends to murder O and, in the dusk, shoots at a man whom he believes to be O. He hits and kills the man at whom he aims, who is in fact P. In one sense this is obviously an unintended result; but D did intend to cause the *actus reus* which he has caused and he is guilty of murder. Again, D intends to enter a house, No. 6 King Street, and steal therein. In the dark he mistakenly enters No. 7. He is guilty of burglary.[17]

The law, however, carries this principle still farther. Suppose, now, that D, intending to murder O, shoots at a man who is in fact O, but 'misses and kills P who, unknown to D, was standing close by. This is an unintended result in a different—and more fundamental—respect than the example considered above. Yet, once again, D, with the *mens rea* of a particular crime, has caused the *actus reus* of the same crime; and, once again, he is guilty of murder. The application of the principle to cases of this second type is known as the doctrine of "transferred malice".

In *Latimer*,[18] D had a quarrel in a public house with O. He took off his belt and aimed a blow at O which struck him lightly, but the belt bounded off and struck P who was standing close by and wounded her severely. The jury found that the blow was unlawfully aimed at O, but that the striking of P "was purely accidental and not such a consequence of the blow as the prisoner ought to have

---

[17] See *Wrigley*, [1957] Crim. L.R. 57.
[18] (1886), 17 Q.B.D. 359.

expected"—that is, he was not even negligent with respect to this result. It was held, on a case reserved, that D was properly convicted of unlawfully and maliciously wounding P.

It is important to notice the limitations of this doctrine. It operates only when the *actus reus* and the *mens rea* of the *same* crime coincide. If D, with the *mens rea* of one crime, does an act which causes the *actus reus* of a different crime, he cannot, as a general rule, be convicted of either offence. D shoots at P's dog with intent to kill it but misses and kills P who, unknown to D, was standing close by. Obviously he cannot be convicted of maliciously killing the dog, for he has not done so; nor can he be convicted of murder,[19] for he has not the *mens rea* for that crime. A similar result follows where D shoots at P with intent to kill him and, quite accidentally, kills P's dog: D is guilty of neither crime. In *Pembliton*[20] D was involved in a fight outside a public house, and, as a result, was charged with maliciously breaking a window. The jury found

> "that the prisoner threw the stone which broke the window, but that he threw it at the people he had been fighting with, intending to strike one or more of them with it, but not intending to break the window."[1]

His conviction was quashed by the Court for Crown Cases Reserved, for there was no finding that he had the *mens rea* of the crime, the *actus reus* of which he has caused. Lord COLERIDGE pointed out that it would have been different if there had been a finding that he was reckless as to the consequence which had occurred—but there was no such finding. The intent which is transferred must be a *mens rea*, an intent to cause an *actus reus*. If D shoots at O with intent to kill, because O is making a murderous attack on him and this is the only way in which he can preserve his own life, he does not intend an *actus reus*, for to kill in these circumstances is justified. If, however, D misses O and inadvertently kills P, an innocent bystander he does cause an *actus reus* but he is not guilty of murder for there is no *mens rea* to transfer; the result which he intended was a perfectly lawful one.[2]

It has been suggested by Williams[3] that the doctrine of transferred malice should be applied only where the actual consequence was brought about negligently: that is, where D, when shooting at O, *ought* to have appreciated that there was a risk of killing P. There is, however, no suggestion in the cases that the rule is to be thus limited and it will be noted that the doctrine was applied in *Latimer* even though there was an express finding that D was not negligent with respect to the consequence which actually occurred. It would, moreover, be illogical to make the commission of a crime requiring *mens rea* depend on the presence or absence of negligence.

Williams regards the doctrine of transferred malice as a "rather arbitrary exception to normal principles". He rejects the argument that "the result is *not* unintended, for the intention was to kill, and the result is a killing." He writes:[4]

> "This argument . . . sounds plausible only because part of the real intention is omitted. Although the result in the sense of a killing was intended, the result in the sense of a killing of P was not intended. After all the accused

---

[19] As to whether it could be manslaughter, see below, pp. 216 *et seq.* and 222.
[20] (1874), L.R. 2 C.C.R. 119.
[1] *Ibid.*, at p. 120.
[2] Below, p. 230; and *cf. Gross* (1913), 23 Cox C.C. 455, below, p. 206.
[3] C.L.G.P. § 48.
[4] C.L.G.P. at 135; and see 9 J.S.P.T.L. at 170–171.

is not indicted for killing in the abstract; he is indicted for killing P; and it should therefore, on a strict view, be necessary to establish *mens rea* in relation to the killing of P."

The answer to this, it is submitted, is that D's act is unintentional only in a respect which is immaterial. The test of materiality in a difference of result is whether it affects the existence of the *actus reus* which D intended. Thus it would be immaterial that D intended to shoot P in the heart but, because of a quite unexpected movement by P, shot him (unintentionally) in the head. The *actus reus* of murder is the killing of a human being—*any* human being—under the Queen's Peace, and his identity is irrelevant.

6 Coincidence of Actus Reus and Mens Rea

The *mens rea* must coincide in point of time with the act which causes the *actus reus*. "If I happen to kill my neighbour accidentally, I do not become a murderer by thereafter expressing joy over his death. My happiness over the result is not the same as a willingness to commit the illegal act."[5] *Mens rea* implies an intention to do a present act, not a future act. Suppose that D is driving to P's house, bent on killing P. A person steps under the wheels of D's car, giving D no chance to avoid him, and is killed. It is P. Clearly, D is not guilty of murder. One who walks out of gaol while in a state of automatism does not commit the offence of escape[6] by deliberately remaining at large.[7] One apparent exception to this rule, which is discussed below,[8] is that where D takes drink with the object of giving himself courage to commit a particular crime. If he commits that very crime when too drunk to be able to form a *mens rea*, it seems that he is guilty.

Where the *actus reus* is a continuing act, it is sufficient that D has *mens rea* during its continuance.[9] Where the *actus reus* is part of a larger transaction, it may be sufficient that D has *mens rea* during the transaction, though not at the moment the *actus reus* is accomplished. D inflicts a wound upon P with intent to kill him. Then, believing that he has killed P he disposes, as he thinks, of the "corpse." In fact P was not killed by the wound but dies as a result of the act of disposal. D has undoubtedly caused the *actus reus* of murder by the act of disposal but he did not, at that time have *mens rea*. In an Indian and a South African[10] case it has been held, accordingly, that D must be acquitted of murder and convicted only of attempted murder. But in *Thabo Meli*[11] the Privy Council held that it was

> "impossible to divide up what was really one series of acts in this way. There is no doubt that the accused set out to do all these acts in order to achieve their plan, and as parts of their plan: and it is much too refined a ground of judgment to say that, because they were at a misapprehension at one stage and thought that their guilty purpose was achieved before it was achieved, therefore they are to escape the penalties of the law."

---

[5] Andanaes, *C.L.G.P. of Norway*, 194.
[6] Below, p. 515.
[7] *Scott*, [1967] V.R. 276; discussed by Howard in [1967] Crim. L.R. at 406.
[8] Page 35; and *cf.* cases considered above, p. 36, where the deliberate omission to prevent the consequences of an earlier act may ground liability.
[9] *Fagan* v. *Metropolitan Police Commissioner*, [1968] 3 All E.R. 442; below, p. 253.
[10] *Khandu* (1890) I.L.R. 15 Bomb. 194; *Shorty*, [1950] S.R. 280.
[11] [1954] 1 All E.R. 373.

This suggests that the answer might be different where there was no ante-cedent plan to dispose of the body and *Thabo Meli* has been distinguished on this ground in South Africa[12] and New Zealand[13] But in *Church*[14] the Court of Criminal Appeal applied *Thabo Meli* on a manslaughter charge where D, in a sudden fight, knocked P unconscious and, wrongly believing her to be dead, threw her into the river where she drowned. Here there was no antecedent plan. The point was not considered by the court, but it was apparently thought to be enough that the accused's conduct constituted "a series of acts which culminated in [P's] death." If *Church* is rightly decided perhaps the principle is that the transaction is continuing so long as D is covering up the homicide he believes he has committed. So that if he leaves the "body" in his attic and P dies of starvation a month later, he is guilty; but if he is carrying the "body" from the scene of the crime to hand it over to the police and accidentally drops it and kills P, he is not.

The problem is not confined to cases where D supposes P to be dead. D stuns P and gags him. P dies from suffocation, because of the gag. If the blow was struck with intent to do grievous bodily harm, D would have been guilty of murder if P had died from it. The gag was inserted with no intention to cause any harm whatever; but it was this act which killed. If this was all part of a pre-arranged plan, it would seem right that *Thabo Meli* should apply. Where there was no such plan, the New Zealand Court of Appeal held *Thabo Meli* inapplic-able.[15] The principle tentatively suggested in the previous paragraph would have led to a different result; but the Court held that, in any event, the terms of the relevant legislation excluded the application of the doctrine.

7 Motive usually does not affect Liability

If D causes an *actus reus* with *mens rea*, he is guilty of the crime and it is entirely irrelevant to his guilt that he had a good motive. The mother who kills her imbecile and suffering child out of motives of compassion is just as guilty of murder as is the man who kills for gain. On the other hand, if either the *actus reus* or the *mens rea* of any crime is lacking, no motive, however evil, will make a man guilty of a crime.

A contrary view, it is true, has been put by an American writer:[16]

> "Suppose a grave felony is about to be committed under such circumstances that the killing of the offender to prevent the crime would be justified by law, and at that very moment he is shot and killed. If the slayer was prompted by the social impulse to promote the social security by preventing the felony he is guilty of no offence; if he had no such impulse but merely acted upon the urge to satisfy an old grudge by killing a personal enemy, he is guilty of murder. The intent is the same in either case—to kill the person; the difference between innocence and guilt lies in the motive which prompted this intent."

It is submitted, however, that (assuming that D knew of the facts which justified the killing) this view is contrary to principle. If it were correct, it would seem to follow that D, the public executioner, would be guilty of murder in hanging X, who had been condemned to death by a competent court, if it were

---

[12] *Chiswibo*, 1961 (2) S.A. 714.
[13] *Ramsay*, [1967] N.Z.L.R. 1005.
[14] [1966] 1 Q.B. 59; [1965] 2 All E.R. 72.
[15] *Ramsay*, [1967] N.Z.L.R. 1005.
[16] Perkins, *Criminal Law*, 723.

shown that D had postponed his retirement to carry out this particular execution because he had a grudge against X and derived particular pleasure from hanging him. This can hardly be the law—and, indeed, the Australian Court of Criminal Appeal has held, in effect, that it is not.[17]

Sometimes, when we speak of motive, we mean an emotion such as jealousy or greed, and sometimes we mean a species of intention. For example, D intends (a) to put poison in his uncle's tea, (b) to cause his uncle's death and (c) to inherit his money. We would normally say that (c) is his motive. Applying our test of "desired consequence" (c) is certainly also intended. The reason why it is considered merely a motive is that it is a consequence ulterior to the *mens rea* and the *actus reus*; it is no part of the crime. If this criterion as to the nature of motive be adopted then it follows that motive, by definition, is irrelevant to criminal responsibility—that is, a man may be lawfully convicted of a crime whatever his motive may be, or even if he has no motive.

In some exceptional cases motive is relevant. In a prosecution for libel, if a defence of fair comment or qualified privilege is set up, it can be defeated by proof of motive in the sense of spite or ill-will. Similar evil motives may be relevant in conspiracy, while in blackmail contrary to the Theft Act 1968, s. 21,[18] the accused's motive may be relevant in ascertaining whether his demand was unwarranted. [19]

As *evidence*, motive is always relevant. This means simply that, if the prosecution can prove that D had a motive for committing the crime, they may do so since the existence of a motive makes it more likely that D in fact did commit it. Men do not usually act without a motive.

Motive is important again when the question of punishment is in issue. When the law allows the judge a discretion in sentencing, he will obviously be more leniently disposed towards the convicted person who acted with a good motive. When the judge has no discretion (as in murder) a good motive may similarly be a factor in inducing a favourable exercise of the Crown's prerogative of mercy.

8   Ignorance of the Law is No Defence

In our discussion of the general principles of *mens rea* nothing has been said about whether the accused knows his act is against the law, for, in the great majority of cases, it is irrelevant whether he knows it or not. It must usually be proved that D intended to cause, or was reckless whether he caused, the event or state of affairs which, as a matter of fact, is forbidden by law; but it is quite immaterial to his conviction (though it may affect his punishment) whether he *knew* that the event or state of affairs was forbidden by law. This is so even though it also appears that D's ignorance of the law was quite reasonable and even, apparently, if it was quite impossible[20] for him to know of the prohibition in question. A native of Baghdad was convicted of committing an unnatural offence on board a ship lying in an English port in spite of his plea that the act was lawful in his own country and that he did not know English law.[1] It was held

---

[17] *McKay*, [1957] A.L.R. 648; below, p. 233. See Morris, "The Slain Chicken Thief", 2 Sydney L.R. 414.
[18] See below, p. 405.
[19] *Cf. Adams*, below, p. 184; *Chandler* v. *D.P.P.*, below, p. 562.
[20] *Bailey*, below, p. 49.
[1] *Esop* (1836), 7 C. & P. 456.

that a Frenchman might be guilty of murder in the course of duelling in England, even if he did not know that duelling was against English law.[2] In *Bailey*,[3] D was convicted of an offence created by a statute which was passed while he was on the high seas although he committed the act before the end of the voyage when he could not possibly have known of the statute.[4] In each of these cases it might be argued that D at least intended something immoral; but that makes no difference. So, if a statute forbids the sale of a house for a price above a stated figure, D, who helps to negotiate a sale at a price of which he is aware, and which is in excess of the stated figure, has *mens rea* even though he affirmatively believes a sale at the particular price to be lawful.[5] He intends the occurrence of that event which the law forbids. If, on the other hand, D is misled as to the price and believes it to be a figure which is, in fact, below the statutory maximum, then he has no *mens rea*.[6] The event which he now intends is not forbidden by the law.

In the case of the most serious crimes the problem does not arise; everyone knows it is against the law to murder, rob or rape. In the case of many less serious crimes, however, a man may very easily, and without negligence, be ignorant that a particular act is a crime. In such cases there will usually be nothing immoral about the act; and the conviction of a morally innocent person requires justification. Various justifications for the rule have been advanced. Blackstone[7] thought that "every person of discretion" may know the law—a proposition which is manifestly untrue today. Austin[8] based the rule upon the difficulty of disproving ignorance of the law, while Holmes,[9] who considered this no more difficult a question than many which are investigated in the courts, thought that to admit the plea would be to encourage ignorance of the law. A modern writer[10] argues that to allow the defence would be to contradict one of the fundamental postulates of a legal order: that rules of law enforce objective meanings, to be ascertained by the courts:

> "If that plea [*sc.* ignorance of the law] were valid, the consequence would be: whenever a defendant in a criminal case thought the law was thus and so, he is to be treated as though the law were thus and so, that is, *the law actually is thus and so.*"[11]

As this writer points out, the criminal law represents an objective code of ethics which must prevail over individual convictions and he therefore argues:[12]

> "Thus, while a person who acts in accordance with his honest convictions is certainly not as culpable as one who commits a harm knowing it is wrong, it is also true that conscience sometimes leads one astray. *Mens rea* underlines the essential difference. Penal liability based on it implies the objective wrongness of the harm proscribed—regardless of motive or conviction. This may fall short of perfect justice but the ethics of a legal order must be objective."

Unfortunately, however, much modern legislation is devoid of moral content,

---

[2] *Barronet and Allain* (1852), Dears. C.C. 51.
[3] (1800), Russ. & Ry 1.
[4] But the judges recommended a pardon.
[5] *Johnson v. Youden*, [1950] 1 K.B. 544; [1950] 1 All E.R. 300.
[6] *Ibid.*
[7] *Commentaries*, iv, 27.
[8] *Lectures on Jurisprudence*, 497.
[9] *The Common Law*, 48.
[10] Jerome Hall, "Ignorance and Mistake in Criminal Law", (1957), 33 Ind. L.J.1. *Cf. General Principles*, 382–383.
[11] 33 Ind. L.J. at 19.
[12] *Ibid.*, at 22.

apart from the moral obligation to obey the law. One who, being ignorant of the law, sells goods at a price in excess of the maximum fixed by statute could hardly be said to have been led astray by his conscience while the "harm proscribed" lacks "objective wrongness".

The common law rule is not universally followed and the arguments by which it is supported have been found "not very convincing to those used to another system".[13] In Scandinavian criminal law, ignorance of the law is, in varying degrees, a defence. Thus, in Norway, a man will not be excused for ignorance of "the general rules of society which apply to everybody" or "the special rules governing the business or activity in which the individual is engaged". But "a fisherman need not study the legislation on industry"; a servant may be excused for *bona fide* and reasonable obedience to illegal orders of his master; or a stranger for breaking a rule which he could not be expected to know about; or liability may be negatived because the legislation is very new, or its interpretation doubtful. Such rules seem to have much to commend them, compared with the rigid and uncompromising attitude of English law. They seek to relate guilt to moral responsibility in a way in which our rule does not.[14]

9 Mistake of Law may Negative Mens Rea

If D, with *mens rea*, causes the *actus reus*, he is guilty and it will not avail him to say that he did not know the *actus reus* was forbidden by the criminal law. But the *actus reus* may be so defined that a mistake of law may result in D's not being intentional or reckless with respect to some element in it and so in his not having *mens rea*. In such a case, his mistake should, in principle, afford him a defence. Bigamy is the best illustration of this. The *actus reus* of that crime is going through a ceremony of marriage when married. If D, knowing that he was already married to X, were to marry P, it would certainly be no defence for him to say that he thought the law allowed him a plurality of wives. Here he would simply be saying he did not know the *actus reus* was forbidden by the criminal law. But if, owing to a misunderstanding of the law, he wrongly supposed that his first marriage had been dissolved, then he would have a good defence, at all events if the mistake were a reasonable one. In this case D did not intend, *being married*, to go through a ceremony of marriage, for he believed he was not married—that is, he had no *mens rea* as to an important circumstance in the *actus reus*. Therefore his mistake as *to the law of divorce* would,[15] indirectly, afford a defence. Likewise in *National Coal Board* v. *Gamble*[16] it was accepted that a mistake by the weighbridge operator about his right to withhold the ticket (a question of civil law) might be "a genuine belief in the existence of circumstances which, if true, would negative an intention to aid."

---

[13] Andenaes, "*Ignorantia Juris* in Scandinavian Law" in *Essays in Criminal Science* (ed. Mueller), 217 at 222.

[14] An exception to the general rule is created by the Statutory Instruments Act 1946, s. 3. On a charge brought under a statutory instrument it is a defence for D to prove that the instrument had not been issued at the time of the alleged offence; unless the Crown then proves that reasonable steps had been taken to bring it to the notice of the public, or persons likely to be affected by it, or D. See *Defiant Cycle Co., Ltd.* v. *Newell*, [1953] 2 All E.R. 38. The Privy Council has held that, in a jurisdiction where there is no similar provision, a person who is unaware that a ministerial order applying a prohibition to him has been made, may set up his ignorance as a lack of *mens rea*: *Lim Chin Aik* v. *R.*, [1963] A.C. 160, below, p. 69.

[15] The actual state of the law on the point is considered below, p. 483.

[16] [1959] 1 Q.B. 11, at p. 25, *per* DEVLIN, J. The facts are set out below, p. 85.

This principle will operate only when the definition of the *actus reus* contains some legal concept like "being married". It is probably also confined to the case where the legal concept belongs to the civil law—as the notion of marriage does—and not to the criminal law.[17] Suppose that X obtains goods from P by deception and gives them to D, who knows all the facts. We have already seen that it will not avail D to say he does not know handling stolen goods is a crime. Equally, it is thought it will not avail him to say that he did not know that it is against the criminal law to obtain goods by deception and that goods so obtained are "stolen" for this purpose. "Stolen" is a concept of the criminal, not the civil law, and ignorance of it is no defence.

10 Absence of a "Claim of Right" as an Element in Mens Rea

Sometimes the *mens rea* of an offence is so defined as to require the absence of a claim of right. In other words, if D believed he had a right to do the act in question, he had no *mens rea* and therefore was not guilty of the crime. This defence will prevail even if D's belief is mistaken and is based upon an entirely wrong view of the law. It is available in a number of important crimes, including theft,[18] malicious damage to property,[19] and a number of other offences requiring wilfulness or fraud. These crimes then are, in a sense, exceptional in that a mistake of law may, indirectly, operate as a defence by preventing the accused from having *mens rea* in acting as he did. It is important to notice the narrow limits within which this defence operates. The mistake must be one which leads the accused to believe he has a right to act as he does; it is not enough that he simply believes his act is not a crime. Here too, the distinction between mistake as to the criminal and as to the civil law seems to be important. Thus if D, having read in an out-of-date book on criminal law that it is not stealing to take another's title deeds to land,[20] were to take P's deeds, thinking that this was a way in which he could injure P without any risk of being punished, he could, no doubt, be convicted of theft under s. 1 of the Theft Act 1968. He had no claim of right. It would be otherwise if D, owing to a misunderstanding of the law of property, thought that the title deeds were his, and that P was wrongfully withholding them from him. Here, clearly, he had a claim of right. Thus, while a mistake as to the criminal law only will not give rise to a claim of right, an error as to the civil law may do so.

It certainly cannot be asserted with confidence that the absence of a claim of right is a *general* requirement of *mens rea*, as it is in the case of theft and the other crimes referred to above. The question will therefore be considered in relation to specific crimes discussed below.

11 Proof of Intention and Foresight

There was formerly high authority[1] for the view that there is an irrebuttable presumption of law that a person foresees and intends the natural consequences of

---

[17] It seems that a distinction between mistakes of civil and mistakes of criminal law was found to be untenable in German law: *Honig* (1963), 54 J. Cr. L. & Cr. at 285. But the distinction taken in the text seems to be a necessary consequence of the concept of *mens rea*.

[18] Below, p. 370.

[19] Below, p. 461.

[20] This was the rule at common law.

[1] *Director of Public Prosecutions* v. *Smith*, [1961] A.C. 290; [1960] 3 All E.R. 161, below, p. 197.

his acts. Proof that he did an act the natural consequence of which was death, was conclusive proof that he intended to kill, in the absence of evidence of insanity or incapacity to form an intent. To what extent, if at all, this actually represented the law was disputed: but it is now clear beyond all doubt that it is not the law. The question in every case is as to the actual intention of the person charged at the time when he did the act. Section 8 of the Criminal Justice Act 1967 provides:

> "A court or jury in determining whether a person has committed an offence,
>
> (a) shall not be bound in law to infer that he intended or foresaw a result of his actions by reason only of its being a natural and probable consequence of those actions; but
>
> (b) shall decide whether he did intend or foresee that result by reference to all the evidence drawing such inferences from the evidence as appear proper in the circumstances."

To what extent intention or foresight need be proved in any particular case depends on the law relating to the crime which is in issue. Section 8 is concerned with *how* intention or foresight must be proved, not *when* it must be proved. On a charge of manslaughter, for example, it remains unnecessary to prove that D intended or foresaw that death was likely to result from his act. It may be that the section has been so construed[2] as to affect the law of murder but, if so, this should be regarded as exceptional.

Section 8 is confined to the *result* of D's actions. As we have seen, D's knowledge of the circumstances surrounding his actions is frequently no less significant than his foresight of the results of them. The distinction between consequences and circumstances is likely to be material in the interpretation of the section. If a broad view were taken of "result", it could incorporate the relevant circumstances. The removal of a girl *under the age of sixteen* from the custody of her parents was a result which *Prince*[3] neither intended nor foresaw. It is certain, however, that s. 8 will not be construed so as to affect that case, or other cases of strict liability. *Prince* was not decided on the ground that he must be taken to have foreseen that his act would result in the removal of a girl under sixteen; but on the ground that it was quite irrelevant whether he foresaw it or not, or whether it was a natural consequence or not; it was enough that he did it. It is necessary, therefore, to consider in respect of each crime the extent to which foresight of consequences and knowledge of circumstances must be proved and, subject to the possibly anomalous case of murder, s. 8 has no effect on the law in this respect.

It might be thought, at first sight, that proof of intention and foresight presents almost insuperable difficulties. Direct evidence of a man's state of mind, except through his own confession, is not available. But the difficulties, in practice, are not so great. If D points a loaded gun at P's head, pulls the trigger and shoots him dead, it is reasonable to infer that D intended and foresaw P's death. A jury might well be convinced by such evidence that D intended to kill. If D offered an explanation of any kind—he thought the gun was unloaded, or he intended to fire above P's head—and the jury thought that it might reasonably be true, then they should acquit him of an intention to kill. If he offered no

---

[2] *Wallett*, [1968] 2 All E.R. 296, below, p. 198.
[3] (1875), L.R. 2 C.C.R. 154, above, p. 42.

explanation, as s. 8 makes clear, the jury would not be bound to convict him of having such an intention; they would have to ask themselves whether, in the light of all the evidence, they were satisfied beyond reasonable doubt. Sometimes D's acts may afford apparently overwhelming evidence of his intention to produce a particular result but evidence to the contrary is always admissible and the question must be left to the jury.[4]

---

[4] *Riley*, [1967] Crim. L.R. 656, is a striking instance of the rebuttal of apparently conclusive evidence of an intent.

CHAPTER 5

Crimes of Negligence*

1 NEGLIGENCE AS FAILURE TO COMPLY WITH AN OBJECTIVE STANDARD

It is clear that some crimes may be committed although D is neither intentional nor reckless with respect to some element in the *actus reus*, provided that he is negligent with respect to it. D does not advert at all to the particular element— but a reasonable man in his position would have done so and, consequently, would not have acted as D did. Writers differ as to whether negligence can properly be described as *mens rea*.[1] On the one hand, it is argued that the absence of foresight or knowledge is just as much a state of mind as its presence.[2] On the other hand, negligence may be proved simply by showing that D's conduct failed to measure up to an objective standard, and, therefore, without proving anything as to what was going on in his head. If it were necessary to prove that D did not foresee the relevant consequence, that would certainly require proof of a state of mind; but it is not—proof of D's conduct suffices. It could never be a defence to a charge of a crime of negligence to show that the negligent act was done recklessly or intentionally; and it will not avail D to show that he was most anxious to avoid causing the harm which has in fact resulted and (subject to one recent decision[3]) that was taking all the care of which he was capable. In this book, therefore, the term "*mens rea*" will be restricted to intention and reckless-ness. Crimes requiring *mens rea* will be contrasted with crimes of negligence. This is not to say that a person's state of mind is always irrelevant when negli-gence is in issue. He may, for example, have special knowledge which an ordi-nary person would not possess. The question then is, whether a reasonable man, with that knowledge, would have acted as he did. Behaviour with a revolver which is possibly not negligent in the case of an ordinary person with no special knowledge might be grossly negligent if committed by a firearms expert.[4] If D has less knowledge or foresight than the reasonable man this, it seems, will not

---

* See Hart, "Negligence, *Mens Rea* and Criminal Responsibility" in *Oxford Essays in Jurisprudence*, 29. The question of liability for negligence in manslaughter and under the Road Traffic Acts is considered in detail below, pp. 222–227 and 331–338.
  [1] Edwards, *Mens Rea*, 206.
  [2] *Cf.* Salmond on *Jurisprudence* (11th ed.), 429.
  [3] *Hudson*, [1965] 1 All E.R. 721, below, p. 299.
  [4] *Cf. Lamb*, [1967] 2 Q.B. 981; [1967] 2 All E.R. 1282; below, p. 221.

help him; but if he has more knowledge or foresight, a higher standard will be expected of him.

2 NEGLIGENCE AS THE BASIS OF LIABILITY

There are very few crimes in English law in which negligence is the gist of the offence. Manslaughter is the most conspicuous example and, indeed, the only serious crime in this category. Generally, in serious crimes, intention or reck-lessness is required as to the central features of the offence, but negligence with respect to some subsidiary element in the *actus reus* is sometimes enough.

So under s. 19 of the Sexual Offences Act 1956,[5] it is an offence to take an unmarried girl under the age of eighteen out of the possession of her parent or guardian against his will with the intent that she shall have unlawful sexual inter-course with men or with a particular man. It is expressly provided, however, that it is a defence "If he believes her to be of the age of eighteen or over and *has reasonable cause for the belief*". It follows that an honest but unreasonable belief that the girl is over eighteen is no defence. Negligence with respect to that element will suffice, though, of course, it must be shown that D intended[6] to take the girl out of the possession of her parent, and had the ulterior intent as to unlawful sexual intercourse.

If there had been a similar provision in the section in issue in *Prince*'s case,[7] he would, of course, have been acquitted. But such a provision, as well as catching the negligent person, disposes of another difficult case. It deals satis-factorily with the case of the man who does not advert to the girl's age at all (simple ignorance), for he cannot say that "he believed her to be of the age of eighteen or over". Such a person will have no defence even though he had reasonable ground for believing the girl to be over eighteen[8] and was therefore not negligent.

Apart from specific statutory instances of liability for negligence, there exists a general principle which might involve liability for negligence as to a relevant circumstance in almost any crime. This is the rule, upon which the courts have generally insisted, that mistake of fact is a valid defence to a criminal charge only if it is reasonable. According to this view, if D goes through a ceremony of marriage believing, wrongly and on unreasonable grounds, that his wife is dead, he is guilty of bigamy. This, in effect, is to turn bigamy into a crime of negli-gence so far as this element of the offence is concerned. D is to be held liable because he did not take sufficient care to ascertain that his wife was dead, before going through the second ceremony. As mistake of fact is a possible defence to any crime where the definition of the *actus reus* includes circumstances, it follows that this theory (which is criticised below[9]) is capable of turning almost any crime into one of negligence, so far as circumstances are concerned.[10]

In the examples just considered, the negligence is as to a subsidiary element only. Occasionally, negligence is the central feature of the crime. Under the Road Traffic Act 1960, s. 3 (1), for example, it is an offence to drive a motor

---

[5] Below, p. 305.
[6] *Cf. Hibbert*, above, p. 43 and *Hudson*, below, p. 299.
[7] Above, p. 42.
[8] *Cf. Harrison*, [1938] 3 All E.R. 134.
[9] See pp. 129–131.
[10] As to consequences, see s. 8 of the Criminal Justice Act 1967, above, p. 52.

vehicle on a road without due care and attention or without reasonable consideration for other persons using the road. On a charge of driving without due care,
it is clear that negligence is the gist of the offence. This section, it has been held,
establishes

> "an objective standard, impersonal and universal, fixed in relation to the safety
> of other users of the highway. It is in no way related to the degree of pro-
> ficiency or degree of experience to be attained by the individual driver".

So a learner driver, who was "exercising all the skill and attention to be expected
from a person with his short experience" but who failed to attain the required
standard, was held guilty.[11] The offence may be committed by making an error
of judgment of a kind which a reasonably prudent and skilful driver would not
make.[12] It will be noted that it is not necessary to prove that any harmful consequence ensued; it is enough to show that D drove in such a manner that a
reasonable man in his position would have foreseen the likelihood of some
harm occurring.

3 DEGREES OF NEGLIGENCE

It has been said that there can be no

> "degrees of inadvertence when that word is used to denote a state of mind,
> since it means that in the man's mind there has been a complete absence of a
> particular thought, a nullity; and of nullity there can be no degrees."[13]

However this may be, if negligence is considered as a failure to comply with a
standard of conduct, then it is clear that there are degrees of it. It may be negligent to drive a car at 40 m.p.h. on a particular piece of road. If so, it is more
negligent to do so with defective brakes, more still if there is a fog or ice on the
road and so on. English law does, in fact, recognise different degrees of negligence. It has been stated repeatedly by the courts that negligence which will
found civil liability is not necessarily enough on a charge of manslaughter,
though that crime may be committed negligently.[14] Within the criminal law,
the slight degree of negligence sufficient to amount to lack of due care and attention on a charge under s. 3 (1) of the Road Traffic Act 1960 is manifestly inadequate on a charge of manslaughter if death results.[15]

Of course these different degrees of negligence are incapable of precise definition and much must necessarily depend upon the judgment of the particular
jury (or bench of magistrates) and their own standard in the matter in question.
The fact that the line is difficult to draw is not a good reason for not attempting
to draw it, if there are practical reasons for making the distinction.[16]

4 SHOULD NEGLIGENCE BE A GROUND OF LIABILITY?

Distinguished academic writers have strongly contended that negligence
should have no place in criminal liability. Turner acknowledges that negligence
connotes that D was

---

[11] *McCrone* v. *Riding*, [1938] 1 All E.R. 157; below, p. 332.
[12] *Simpson* v. *Peat*, [1952] 2 Q.B. 24; [1952] 1 All E.R. 447.
[13] Kenny, *Outlines*, 39, criticised by Hart in *Oxford Essays in Jurisprudence* at 41.
[14] Below, p. 226.
[15] *Andrews* v. *Director of Public Prosecutions*, [1937] A.C. 576; [1937] 2 All E.R. 552.
[16] See Hart in *Oxford Essays in Jurisprudence*, at 42: "Negligence is gross if the precautions to be taken against harm are very simple, such as persons who are but poorly
endowed with physical and mental capacities can easily take."

"in some measure blameworthy, and that we should expect an ordinary reasonable man to foresee the possibility of the consequences and to regulate his conduct so as to avoid them;"[17]

but contends that the moral test, on which criminal liability should be (and, indeed, is) based, is that of foresight of the consequences of one's conduct. Hall goes further and finds it difficult to accept that negligently caused harm reflects a moral fault.[18] He rejects the view that punishment stimulates care, arguing that the deterrent theory postulates a man who weighs the possibility of punishment in the balance before acting; but the inadvertent harm-doer, by definition, does not do this. Hall appears to suggest[19] that the courts themselves do not really believe that punishment deters negligence, pointing out that sentences, even for negligent homicides, are relatively light. He rejects the thesis that negligent persons may be ethically blameworthy in so far as they are insensitive to the rights of others. In the case of negligently caused motor-car accidents, for example, he argues that

"it seems much more probable that a dull mind, slow reactions, awkwardness and other ethically irrelevant factors were the underlying cause."[19]

Williams[20] acknowledges that "it is possible for punishment to bring about greater foresight, by causing the subject to stop and think before committing himself to a course of conduct;" but thinks that this justification does not go very far and that the law is wise in penalising negligence only exceptionally.

Hart[1] has recently challenged the commonly accepted criterion of foresight. The reason why it is thought proper to punish (in most cases) the man who foresees the forbidden harm is that he can choose to cause it or not; but in some cases of negligence, at least, it may be said,

" 'he could have thought about what he was doing' with just as much rational confidence as one can say of any intentional wrong-doing, 'he could have done otherwise'."

Hart's approach to negligence, however, differs from that so far generally adopted by the courts. He would not enforce an objective, external and impersonal standard which took no account of the individual's lack of capacity. He would recognise that punishment might[2] be proper only if two questions are answered in the affirmative:[3]

"(i) Did the accused fail to take those precautions which any reasonable man with normal capacities would in the circumstances have taken ?

(ii) Could the accused, given his mental and physical capacities, have taken those precautions ?"

Such an approach would remove some objections; but, apart from one recent case,[4] it is not the present approach of the courts and it is thought that there would be difficulties in applying it. If there is a variable standard, how is the court to ascertain the capacities of the individual defendant ?

---

[17] M.A.C.L. 207.
[18] *General Principles*, 136.
[19] *Ibid.*, 138. And *cf.* Keedy in 22 Harv. L. Rev. at p. 84: ". . . a man should not be held criminal because of lack of intelligence."
[20] C.L.G.P. 123.
[1] *Oxford Essays in Jurisprudence*, 29.
[2] Hart is not concerned to *advocate* the punishment of negligence, but only to dispel the belief that liability for negligence is a form of strict or absolute liability.
[3] *Ibid.*, at p. 46.
[4] *Hudson*, [1965] 1 All E.R. 721.

Hall argues[5] that negligence should be controlled in other ways—by re-examining whether negligent persons should be able to escape completely from civil liability by insurance; by more vigorous control of licences to operate dangerous instrumentalities; and by more education and instruction.

The negligent handling of certain instruments—notably motor-vehicles —can have such drastic consequences that society is almost bound to adopt any measures which seem to have a reasonable prospect of inducing greater care; and it seems reasonable to suppose that the threat of punishment does have an effect on the care used in the handling of such instruments. It may well be that in those areas of the law where at present strict liability prevails, negligence will, in future, have a greater part to play.[6] Both Parliament and the courts have recently shown an inclination to move in this direction. The Trade Descriptions Act 1968 creates a number of offences, some of which replace earlier offences of strict liability, and provides by s. 24 that it is a defence to prove (i) that the commission of the offence was due (*inter alia*) to a mistake or accident and (ii) that D "took all reasonable precautions and exercised all due diligence to avoid the commission of such an offence by himself or any person under his control." Thus, though the prosecution do not have to prove negligence, it is a defence for D to show that he was not negligent.

Where there is no such express provision in a statute, there is now a distinct possibility that the court might hold one to be implied. In the very recent case of *Sweet* v. *Parsley*[7] the House of Lords looked with favour on a doctrine developed in Australia.[8]

> "When a statutory prohibition is cast in terms which at first sight appear to impose strict responsibility, they should be understood merely as imposing responsibility for negligence but emphasising that the burden of rebutting negligence by affirmative proof of reasonable mistake rests upon the defendant."[9]

---

[5] "Negligent Behaviour should be excluded from Penal Liability", 63 Col. L. R. 632.
[6] Below, p. 69.
[7] [1969] 1 All E.R. 347 at pp. 351 *per* Lord REID, 357 *per* Lord PEARCE and p. 362 *per* Lord DIPLOCK.
[8] *Maher* v. *Musson* (1934), 52 C.L.R. 100; *Proudman* v. *Dayman* (1941), 67 C.L.R. 536.
[9] Howard, "Strict Responsibility in the High Court of Australia" (1960), 76 L.Q.R. 547 at p. 566. And see below, pp. 68–70.

CHAPTER 6

Crimes of Strict Liability

1 THE POSITION AT COMMON LAW AND BY STATUTE

Crimes which do not require intention, recklessness or even negligence as to one or more elements in the *actus reus* are known as offences of strict liability or, sometimes, "of absolute prohibition".[1] The latter term is somewhat misleading in so far as it suggests that an accused whose conduct has caused[2] an *actus reus* will necessarily be held liable. It is common to say that "no *mens rea*" need be proved in the case of these offences. This is inaccurate. *Prince*[3] is acknowledged to be the leading case of strict liability; yet, as we have seen, to secure a conviction of the offence in question, it must be proved that D intended to take a girl out of her father's possession without his consent. The fact is that an offence is regarded—and properly regarded—as one of strict liability if no *mens rea* need be proved as to a single element in the *actus reus*. The single element will usually be one of great significance; but it by no means follows that *mens rea* should not be required as to the remaining constitutents of the offence. Thus, on a charge of selling meat unfit for human consumption, it is unnecessary to prove that D knew that the meat was unfit; but it probably must be proved that he at least intended *to sell meat*.[4] Liability is thus not "absolute" and the term "strict liability" will be preferred throughout this book.

Crimes of strict liability are almost invariably the creation of statute. It is usually said[5] that there were only two exceptions at common law to the rule

---

[1] For discussions of these offences, see Jackson "Absolute Prohibition in Statutory Offences", M.A.C.L. 262; Edwards, *Mens Rea*; Sayre, "Public Welfare Offences", (1933), 33 Col. L.R. 55; Howard, *Strict Responsibility*.

[2] In *Kilbride* v. *Lake*, [1962] N.Z.L.R. 590, D was acquitted of permitting a vehicle not displaying a current warrant of fitness to be on the highway, when the warrant was detached during his absence. The court took the view that there was an *actus reus* (*sed quaere?*) but that D had not caused it and he was not liable even if the offence was one of strict liability. *Cf. Parker* v. *Alder*, [1899] 1 Q.B. 20; below, p. 71.

[3] (1875), L.R. 2 C.C.R. 154; above, p. 42.

[4] *Gleeson* v. *Hobson*, [1907] V.L.R. 148 at 157, *per* CUSSEN, J.; Cross & Jones, *Introduction to Criminal Law* (5th ed.) 95.

[5] But the matter is by no means so clear as is sometimes thought. See below, pp. 545 and 549.

requiring *mens rea*. These were public nuisance and criminal libel. In the former any master might be held liable for the act of his servant even though he himself did not know it had taken place; while in the latter a newspaper proprietor was liable for libels published by his servants without his authority or consent. Public nuisance, however, is an anomalous crime and is treated in several respects rather as if it were a civil action than an indictable offence; while in criminal libel the rule has been modified by the Libel Act 1843 which makes it a defence for the defendant to prove that the publication was without actual malice or gross negligence on his part and that he has published an apology. It will be noted, moreover, that both cases are instances of vicarious liability.[6] To these two instances, a recent decision[7] shows that we must add a third—contempt of court. It is an offence to publish inaccurate reports of the evidence at a trial in such a manner that the jurors might be influenced in their decision, even though the publisher believes in good faith and on reasonable grounds that the reports are accurate.[8]

Apart from these instances, the common law always required *mens rea*, at least as to the more important elements in the *actus reus*, subject to the qualifications in respect of murder and manslaughter considered below.[9] It is very different with statutory offences. In a great many cases, the courts have held that Parliament intended to impose strict liability and have convicted defendants who lacked *mens rea*, not merely as to some subsidiary matter, but as to the central feature of the *actus reus*.

The validity of the imposition of strict liability has recently received the sanction of the House of Lords in *Warner* v. *Metropolitan Police Commissioner*,[10] the first case on this point to reach our highest tribunal; but the very different attitude adopted by the House in the subsequent case of *Sweet* v. *Parsley*[11] suggests that any further expansion of strict liability will be very closely scrutinized.

The case which has been said[12] to be the first to impose strict liability is *Woodrow*.[13] D was found guilty of having in his possession adulterated tobacco, although he did not know it was adulterated. The prosecution emphasised the purpose of the statute—it was for the protection of the revenue—and the absence of "knowingly" or any similar word. The court relied on a section of the Act which empowered the commissioners of excise to forbear to prosecute where there was no "intention of fraud or of offending against this Act"—the implication being that the crime was still committed even when there was no fraud or intention of offending against the Act. PARKE, B., thought that the prosecution would very rarely be able to prove knowledge; and that the public inconvenience which would follow if they were required to do so would be greater than the injustice to the individual if they were not. Even the exercise of reasonable care

---

[6] See below, p. 98.
[7] *Evening Standard*, [1954] 1 Q.B. 578; [1954] 1 All E.R. 1026; below, p. 529.
[8] This too is sometimes said to be an instance of vicarious liability; but see below, p. 529.
[9] See pp. 197–200, 216–222 and 227–228.
[10] [1968] 2 All E.R. 356, Lord REID (whose speech deserves careful study) dissenting on this issue. The case is more fully considered below, p. 78.
[11] [1969] 1 All E.R. 347. Recent cases before *Sweet* v. *Parsley* suggested an extension of strict liability; see *Patel* v. *Comptroller of Customs*, [1966] A.C. 356; [1965] 3 All E.R. 593 (P.C.); *Salter*, [1968] 2 All E.R. 951; *Cummerson*, [1968] 2 All E.R. 863.
[12] By Sayre, *op. cit.*
[13] (1846), 15 M. & W. 404.

would not have saved D; according to PARKE, B., he was liable even if the adulteration was discoverable only by a "nice chemical analysis".[14]

A number of other well-known cases may be taken as examples. In *Bishop*,[15] D advertised in the newspapers for patients suffering from "hysteria, nervousness and perverseness" and received into her house several young women so described, who were in fact lunatics. She was charged[16] with receiving two or more lunatics into her house, not being an asylum or hospital registered under the Act. STEPHEN, J., told the jury that an honest belief on D's part that the women were *not* lunatics would be immaterial. The jury found D guilty, adding that she honestly and on reasonable grounds, believed that her patients were not lunatics. The conviction was affirmed. Mellor, for the prosecution pointed out: "Nothing as to *knowingly* receiving lunatics occurs in the section"; and DENMAN, J., said that if knowledge were required, the object of the statute might be frustrated.

In *Hobbs* v. *Winchester Corporation*,[17] the plaintiff, a butcher, was suing for compensation for certain unsound meat which had been destroyed under the Public Health Act 1875. That Act provided that, where any person sustained damage in relation to any matter as to which he was not himself in default, full compensation should be paid. The question was: was the plaintiff in default? He was unaware, and he could not have discovered by any examination which he could reasonably be expected to make that the meat was unsound. It was held by the Court of Appeal, reversing CHANNELL, J., that the plaintiff was in default because he was guilty of the crime of selling unsound meat. KENNEDY, L.J., said:[18]

> "The clear object, the important object [of the statute] . . . is as far as possible to protect the buyer of that which, in the opinion at all events of most people, is a necessity of human life, from buying and consuming meat that is unwholesome and unfit for the food of man; and I should say that the natural inference from the statute and its object is that the peril to the butcher from innocently selling unsound meat is deemed by the legislature to be much less than the peril to the public which would follow from the necessity of proving in each case a *mens rea*.
>
> "I think that the policy of the Act is this: that if a man chooses for profit to engage in a business which involves the offering for sale of that which may be deadly or injurious to health he must take that risk, and that it is not a sufficient defence for anyone who chooses to embark on such a business to say 'I could not have discovered the disease unless I had an analyst on the premises.'"

In *Cundy* v. *Le Cocq*,[19] D was convicted of selling intoxicating liquor to a drunken person contrary to s. 13 of the Licensing Act 1872. It was proved that D did not know the person was drunk and nothing had occurred to show that he

---

[14] The judges suggested that D might have taken a warranty from the person from whom he bought the tobacco, indemnifying him against the consequences of a prosecution (fine and forfeiture). But there are difficulties about this. In *Askey* v. *Golden Wine Co.*, [1948] 2 All E.R. 35 at p. 38, DENNING, J., said: "It is . . . a principle of our law that the punishment inflicted by a criminal court is personal to the offender and that the civil courts will not entertain an action by the offender to recover an indemnity against consequences of that punishment."

[15] (1880), 5 Q.B.D. 259.

[16] Under 8 & 9 Vict. c. 100, s. 44.

[17] [1910] 2 K.B. 471 (C.A.).

[18] *Ibid.*, at p. 483.

[19] (1884), 13 Q.B.D. 207.

was drunk. While some sections of the Act contained the word "knowingly", s. 13 did not do so. The Divisional Court held that it was not necessary to consider whether D knew, or had means of knowing, or could with ordinary care have detected, that the person served was drunk. If he served a drink to a person who was in fact drunk, he was guilty.

It will be noted that it was established in each of these cases that D was not even negligent. The convictions were upheld notwithstanding D's blameless inadvertence as to the crucial factor in the *actus reus*. This is a very remarkable and, on the face of it, unjust result, and certainly requires explanation.

2 RECOGNITION OF OFFENCES OF STRICT LIABILITY

Since these offences are always the creation of statute, the courts, in enforcing them, profess merely to be implementing the expressed intention of Parliament. This is mere lip-service.

> "The fact is that Parliament has no intention whatever of troubling itself about *mens rea*. If it had, the thing could have been settled long ago. All that Parliament would have to do would be to use express words that left no room for implication. One is driven to the conclusion that the reason why Parliament has never done that is that it prefers to leave the point to the judges and does not want to legislate about it."[20]

This is not to say that the judges ignore the words of the statutes. On the contrary, they pay the closest regard to them. Certain words are considered as particularly apt to import *mens rea* into an offence, but no single word is conclusive. The court obviously has regard to the whole of the statute in which the offence is to be found. It may look at other statutes in the same or related fields, or at statutes which have been repealed and replaced by that in issue, seeking the intention of Parliament in significant changes of wording which may have been made. Usually, however, these sources will leave the court with a fairly free hand. Consequently the decision is often governed by what the court considers to be the social object of the statute. *Hobbs* v. *Winchester Corporation* is a clear example of this. Other examples are considered below.

1 The Offence in its Statutory Context

In the cases considered above, the absence of the word "knowingly" was considered important. If it could be said that wherever that (or a similar) word is to be found, *mens rea* is required; and where no such word appears, strict liability is intended, the position would be simple but, unfortunately, this is far from being the case. *Mens rea* has often been required where no such word is used, for, according to DEVLIN, J.,

> "All that the word 'knowingly' does is to say expressly what is normally implied";[1]

---

[20] Devlin, *Samples of Lawmaking*, at 71. But *cf.* Lord REID in *Sweet* v. *Parsley*, [1969] 1 All E.R. at p. 351.

[1] *Roper* v. *Taylor's Garage*, [1951] 2 T.L.R. 284 at p. 288. But Lord MORRIS thought this "too sweeping"; *Warner*, [1968] 2 All E.R. at 377. See *Sleep* (1861), 30 L.J.M.C. 170; *Core* v. *James* (1871), L.R. 7 Q.B. 135; *Nichols* v. *Hall* (1873), L.R. 8 C.P. 322.

and even where the word "knowingly" is used, *mens rea* will not necessarily be required as to all the elements in the *actus reus*. The presence or absence of such a word may, nevertheless, be a most important factor. If it is used in one section and not in another, the implication is strong that *mens rea* is required in the first case and not in the second. Even this is not conclusive; and *mens rea* has been required where the word was not used, even though it appeared in another part of the *same* section.

In *Sherras* v. *De Rutzen*,[2] D was charged with supplying liquor to a constable on duty, contrary to s. 16 (2) of the Licensing Act 1872. The policeman was not wearing his armlet which, it was admitted, is an indication that he is off duty. D, who was in the habit—quite lawfully—of serving constables in uniform but without their armlets, made no enquiry and took it for granted that the policeman was off duty. Section 16 (1) of the Act made it an offence for a licensee *knowingly* to harbour or suffer to remain on his premises any constable on duty. Section 16 (2) did not include the word "knowingly". Yet D's conviction was quashed. DAY, J., said that the only inference to be drawn was that under s. 16 (1) the prosecution had to prove knowledge, while under s. 16 (2) the defendant had to prove he had no knowledge.[3] WRIGHT, J., made no attempt to reconcile the two sub-sections, contenting himself with pointing out that[4]

> "if guilty knowledge is not necessary, no care on the part of the publican could save him from conviction . . . since it would be as easy for the constable to deny that he was on duty when asked, or to produce a forged permission from his superior officer as to remove his armlet before entering the public house."

If the word "knowingly" is used, *mens rea* as to all the elements of the *actus reus* is usually required. But, as mentioned above, even this rule is not without exceptions. It was an offence under the Intoxicating Liquors (Sale to Children) Act 1901, s. 24,[5] for a licensee knowingly to sell intoxicating liquor to children under fourteen

> "excepting such intoxicating liquors as are sold or delivered in corked and sealed vessels. . . ."

The requirement of knowledge extends to the child's age, so that D is not liable if he believes the child to be over fourteen;[6] but in *Brooks* v. *Mason*[7] it was held that a mistaken belief that the bottle was properly corked and sealed was no defence. This case turned on the fact that D's ignorance was as to an exception from the offence; but this was not true of *Dacey*,[8] where it was held that D could be convicted of "knowingly" possessing an explosive substance for an unlawful object, even if he did not know that the substance was explosive. Happily, this decision has been overruled by *Hallam*;[9] D is guilty[10] only if he knows the substance is an explosive.

---

[2] [1895] 1 Q.B. 918.
[3] This view was doubted by DEVLIN, J., in *Roper* v. *Taylor's Garage* (above). If DAY, J., intended to refer to the *evidential* burden only, the *dictum* is unobjectionable. See Edwards, *Mens Rea*, 90–97.
[4] [1895] 1 Q.B. 918 at p. 923.
[5] Re-enacted in the Licensing Act 1953, s. 128, which was subsequently repealed: *cf.* now the Licensing Act 1964, s. 169.
[6] *Groom* v. *Grimes* (1903), 89 L.T. 129.
[7] [1902] 2 K.B. 743. *Cf. Gaumont British Distributors, Ltd.* v. *Henry*, [1939] 2 K.B. 711; [1939] 2 All E.R. 808.
[8] [1939] 2 All E.R. 641.
[9] [1957] 1 Q.B. 569; [1957] 1 All E.R. 665.
[10] Under the Explosive Substances Act 1883.

2 The Offence in its Social Context

The courts are greatly influenced in their construction of the statute by the degree of social danger which they believe to be involved in the offence in question. The greater the degree of social danger, the more likely is the offence to be interpreted as one of strict liability. Thus, the economic dangers through which the country is passing were the basis of the decision in *St. Margaret's Trust Ltd.*[11] In this case D Limited, a finance company, was charged with disposing of a car on hire purchase without a deposit of at least 50 per cent of the purchase price having been paid as required by the Hire Purchase Order[12] then in force. A car dealer and his customers had fraudulently misled D Limited into advancing more than 50 per cent by stating a falsely inflated price for the cars which were the subjects of the transactions. It was admitted that D Limited had acted innocently throughout and supposed that a deposit of at least 50 per cent had been paid. The company was, nevertheless, convicted.

The reasons given by the court had very little to do with the words of the statute. It is true DONOVAN, J., said:[13]

> "The words of the order themselves are an express and unqualified prohibition of the acts done in this case by St. Margaret's Trust Ltd."

But this means no more than that no such word as "knowingly" was used. He went on:

> "The object of the order was to help to defend the currency against the peril of inflation which, if unchecked, would bring disaster on the country. There is no need to elaborate this. The present generation has witnessed the collapse of the currency in other countries and the consequent chaos, misery and widespread ruin. It would not be at all surprising if Parliament, determined to prevent similar calamities here, enacted measures which it intended to be absolute prohibitions of acts which might increase the risk in however small a degree. Indeed that would be the natural expectation. There would be little point in enacting that no one should breach the defences against a flood, and at the same time excusing anyone who did it innocently."[13]

A second example may be found in the offences concerning dangerous drugs. The dangers of drug addiction are constantly stressed on all hands at the present time. In *Yeandel* v. *Fisher*, PARKER, L.C.J., said:

> "I certainly take judicial notice of the fact that drugs are a great danger today and legislation has been tightening up the control of drugs in all its aspects."[14]

In that case and in *Sweet* v. *Parsley*[14] the Divisional Court held that D was guilty of being "concerned in the management of premises used for the purpose of smoking cannabis" though he did not know and had no means of knowing that such smoking was taking place. In *Lockyer* v. *Gibb*[15] the court held that D was guilty of being in unauthorised possession of a drug if he knew he had control of a thing which was in fact a dangerous drug though he did not know and had no reason to know this. The latter ruling was modified by the House of Lords in

---

[11] [1958] 2 All E.R. 289; [1958] 1 W.L.R. 522.
[12] S.I. 1956 No. 180. See now S.I. 1964 No. 942.
[13] [1958] 2 All E.R. 289 at p. 293. Would the floodgates really have been opened in this way, if the case had been decided differently?
[14] *Yeandel* v. *Fisher*, [1966] 1 Q.B. 440 at p. 446; [1965] 3 All E.R. 158; *Sweet* v. *Parsley*, [1968] 2 All E.R. 337 (D.C.), reversed, [1969] 1 All E.R. 347 (H.L.).
[15] [1966] 2 All E.R. 653 (D.C.).

Warner:[16] the word "possession" connotes that D knew or at least ought to have known what kind of thing he had; but no further mental element is required. In *Sweet* v. *Parsley*[14] the House reversed the former ruling: no offence is committed unless it is the manager's purpose that cannabis be smoked on the premises. *Mens rea* should not be dispensed with unless Parliament has given a clear indication that it so intends—the social danger involved was not a sufficient reason.

As a third example, we may take road traffic offences. Parliament has provided the twin offences of dangerous driving and driving without due care and attention.[17] Dangerous driving is obviously the more serious offence since it carries a maximum penalty of two years' (or, if death is caused, five years') imprisonment on indictment, whereas "careless driving" is punishable only by three months. Consequently it seemed reasonable to argue that, while some degree of negligence was obviously necessary to constitute "careless" driving, a higher degree must be proved to constitute "dangerous" driving. This distinction was invalidated by the decision in *Evans*[18] where it was held correct to direct a jury, on a charge of dangerous driving that the "slightest negligence" would be enough and that it was immaterial that the driver was doing "his incompetent best." In *Ball and Loughlin*[19] the court went still further and held that dangerous driving is an offence of strict liability. D, the driver of a scout car so constructed that he could see only to the front and not to the sides, halted at a major road. His colleague, standing in the turret of the vehicle, instructed him that the road was clear. D drove forward into the path of a motor-cyclist who was killed. It was held that the jury had been correctly directed as follows:

> ". . . once you are satisfied looking at it objectively that it was what you think it right to describe as dangerous driving, well, then, it does not matter whether the driver was being deliberately reckless, whether he was being what you would call momentarily inattentive, whether he was a most incompetent person doing his best, or whether he was a good driver doing his best in very difficult circumstances."

This interpretation produces the absurd result that a higher degree of culpability must be proved on a charge of careless than of dangerous driving—where indeed, no culpability whatever need be proved. Had Ball been charged with careless driving, it is evident that he would have been acquitted unless the court was satisfied that he was not doing all that could be expected of a reasonable driver in all the circumstances.[20] The decision may perhaps be explained, though not justified, by the current concern about death on the roads.

3 The Severity of the Punishment

It is often argued that the provision for a severe maximum punishment shows that strict liability could not have been intended by Parliament. To some extent, this is in conflict with the principle previously discussed, since the provision for only a slight punishment would suggest that Parliament thought the social danger involved to be slight. Certainly, the courts do not seem to have been deterred in recent years from imposing strict liability in the case of offences carrying heavy maximum sentences—an offence under section 9 (1) (b) of the

---

[16] [1968] 2 All E.R. 356.
[17] Below, p. 331.
[18] [1963] 1 Q.B. 412; [1962] 3 All E.R. 1086.
[19] (1966), 50 Cr. App. R. 266.
[20] *Cf. Liddon* v. *Stringer*, [1967] Crim. L.R. 371, and commentary thereon.

Dangerous Drugs Act 1964 is punishable with ten years' imprisonment and causing death by dangerous driving is punishable with five.

4   The Presumption in Favour of Mens Rea

According to a much-cited dictum of WRIGHT, J., in *Sherras* v. *de Rutzen*:[1]

> "There is a presumption that *mens rea*, or evil intention, or knowledge of the
> wrongfulness of the act, is an essential ingredient in every offence; but that
> presumption is liable to be displaced either by the words of the statute
> creating the offence or by the subject-matter with which it deals, and both
> must be considered."

This presumption seems to have been generally followed by the courts until
the latter part of the nineteenth century. After the case of *Prince*[2] (1875) the
courts showed a greater readiness to interpret statutory offences to impose strict
liability. It has been said[3] that the doctrine of *mens rea* reached its nadir in
Wheat (1921),[4] now happily overruled. Much depended on the view of the
Lord Chief Justice of the day because of his dominant position in criminal
appeals.[5] GODDARD, L.C.J., frequently asserted that there is a presumption in
favour of *mens rea*[6] but was far from consistent in his decisions.[7] The trend in
recent years, culminating in *Warner*[8] seems to have been in favour of strict
liability; but in *Sweet* v. *Parsley*[9] the House of Lords has re-affirmed principles
which were beginning to look old-fashioned: ". . . whenever a section is silent
as to *mens rea* there is a presumption that, in order to give effect to the will of
Parliament, we must read in words appropriate to require *mens rea*;" and ". . . it
is a universal principle that if a penal provision is reasonably capable of two
interpretations, that interpretation which is most favourable to the accused must
be adopted."[10] According to Lord DIPLOCK,[11] the implication of *mens rea*

> ". . . stems from the principle that it is contrary to a rational and civilised
> criminal code, such as Parliament must be presumed to have intended, to
> penalise one who has performed his duty as a citizen to ascertain what acts
> are prohibited by law (*ignorantia juris non excusat*) and has taken all proper
> care to inform himself of any facts which would make his conduct unlawful."

3   LIABILITY IS STRICT, NOT "ABSOLUTE"

It was observed at the beginning of this chapter that the need for a mental element
is not ruled out completely by the fact that an offence is one of strict liability. It

---

[1] [1895] 1 Q.B. 918 at p. 921, above, p. 63.
[2] See above, p. 42.
[3] Williams, C.L.G.P., 178.
[4] [1921] 2 K.B. 119, overruled by *Gould*, [1968] 2 Q.B. 65; [1968] 1 All E.R. 849,
considered below, p. 483.
[5] Though the Lord Chief Justice's influence is still very great, his dominance has
probably been diminished since provision was made for an appeal to the House of Lords
from decisions of the Divisional Court (by the Administration of Justice Act 1960) and
since the functions of the Court of Criminal Appeal were transferred to the Court of
Appeal (by the Criminal Appeal Act 1966). See now Criminal Appeal Act 1968.
[6] *E.g.*, *Evans* v. *Dell*, [1937] 1 All E.R. 349; *Brend* v. *Wood* (1946), 175 L.T. 306 at
p. 307; *Harding* v. *Price*, [1948] 1 K.B. 695 at pp. 700–702; [1948] 1 All E.R. 283 at
p. 285; *Younghusband* v. *Luftig*, [1949] 2 K.B. 354 at pp. 369–370; [1949] 2 All E.R. 72
at p. 80; *Reynolds* v. *Austin*, [1951] 2 K.B. 135 at p. 147; [1951] 1 All E.R. 606 at p. 610.
[7] See, *e.g.*, *Kat* v. *Diment*, [1951] 1 K.B. 34; [1950] 2 All E.R. 657.
[8] *Warner* v. *Met. Police Commr.*, [1968] 2 All E.R. 356.
[9] Above, p. 64.
[10] *Per* Lord REID at pp. 349–350.
[11] At p. 362.

may be necessary to prove that D was aware of all the circumstances of the offence save that in respect of which strict liability is imposed. When the court holds that it is an offence of strict liability to sell meat which is unfit for human consumption, it decides that a reasonable mistake as to that particular fact is not a defence. It does not decide that any other defence is unavailable to D; and indeed, we have seen that a mistake as to other circumstances of the *actus reus* may afford a defence.[12] There is no reason why all other defences should not be available as they are in the case of offences requiring full *mens rea*. Though dangerous driving is an offence of strict liability, it is clearly a defence if D was in a state of automatism when he "drove" the vehicle.[13] It is perfectly clear that a child under the age of ten could in no circumstances be convicted of an offence of strict liability[14] and it is submitted that a child between ten and fourteen could be convicted only if it were proved that he knew his act was "wrong.'[15] It is submitted, therefore that other general defences—insanity, necessity, duress and coercion—should be available equally on a charge of an offence of strict liability as in the case of any other offence.[16]

It may that *Larsonneur*[17] is an authority for the proposition that compulsion is not a defence to a charge of strict liability. The case was not really argued on this point, however, and it is submitted that, even in an offence such as that— requiring no act and no *mens rea* whatever—compulsion should be a defence. If D were to get drunk in the privacy of his home and be carried by malicious companions and left in the street while in a stupor, he should have a defence to a charge of being found drunk in a highway.[18]

4 ARGUMENTS FOR AND AGAINST STRICT LIABILITY

The proliferation of offences of strict liability while generally deplored by legal writers, has been welcomed by the distinguished social scientist, Lady Wootton, on the ground that "nothing has dealt so devastating a blow at the punitive concept of the criminal process . . ."[19]

> "If, however, the primary function of the courts is conceived as the prevention of forbidden acts, there is little cause to be disturbed by the multiplication of offences of strict liability. If the law says that certain things are not to be done, it is illogical to confine this prohibition to occasions on which they are done from malice aforethought; for at least the material consequences of an action, and the reasons for prohibiting it are the same whether it is the result of sinister malicious plotting, of negligence or of sheer accident."[20]

Accepting that the primary function of the courts is the prevention of forbidden acts, there remains the question, what acts should be regarded as forbidden? Surely only such acts as we can assert ought not to have been done. Suppose

---

[12] Above, p. 59.
[13] *Hill* v. *Baxter*, [1958] 1 Q.B. 277; [1958] 1 All E.R. 193; *Budd*, [1962] Crim. L.R. 49; *Watmore* v. *Jenkins*, [1962] 2 Q.B. 572; [1962] 2 All E.R. 868. See Patient, "Some Remarks about the Element of Voluntariness in Absolute Offences", [1968] Crim. L.R. 23.
[14] Below, p. 110.
[15] Below, p. 111. *Cf.* CAVE, J., in *Tolson* (1889), 23 Q.B.D. 168 at p. 182 and Lord DIPLOCK in *Sweet* v. *Parsley*, [1969] 1 All E.R. at p. 361.
[16] For discussion of this question see Sayre, "Public Welfare Offences" (1933), 33 Col. Law Rev. 55 at 75–78; Howard, *Strict Liability*, Chapter 9.
[17] (1933) 24 Cr. App. R. 74; above, p. 34.
[18] Licensing Act 1872, s. 12. *Cf. O'Sullivan* v. *Fisher*, [1954] S.A.S.R. 33, discussed by Howard, *op. cit.*, at 193.
[19] *Crime and the Criminal Law*, 48.
[20] *Ibid.*, 51.

that a butcher, who has taken all reasonable precautions has the misfortune to sell some meat which is unfit for human consumption. That it was so unfit is undiscoverable by any precaution which a butcher can be expected to take. Ought the butcher to have acted as he did? Unless we want butchers to stop selling meat, it would seem that the answer should be in the affirmative; we want butchers, who have taken all reasonable precautions to sell meat—the act of this butcher was not one which the law should seek to prevent. Some of the judges who upheld the conviction of *Prince* did so on the ground that men should be deterred from taking girls out of the possession of their parents, whatever the girl's age. This reasoning can hardly be applied to many modern offences of strict liability. We do not wish to deter people from driving cars, being concerned in the management of premises or financing hire purchase transactions. These acts, if done with all proper care, are not such acts as the law should seek to prevent. The fallacy in the argument lies in looking at the harm done in isolation from the circumstances in which it was brought about. Many acts, which have in fact caused harm, *ought* to have been done. The surgeon performing a justified operation with all proper skill may cause death.

Another argument that is frequently advanced in favour of strict liability is that, without it, many guilty people would escape—"that there is neither time nor personnel available to litigate the culpability of each particular infraction."[1] This argument assumes that it is possible to deal with these cases without deciding whether D had *mens rea* or not, whether he was negligent or not. Certainly D may be convicted without deciding these questions, but how can he be sentenced? Clearly the court will deal differently with (i) the butcher who knew that the meat was tainted; (ii) the butcher who did not know, but ought to have known; and (iii) the butcher who did not know and had no means of finding out. Sentence can hardly be imposed without deciding into which category the convicted person falls. Treating the offence as one of strict liability, in the case of jury trial, merely removes the decision of these vital questions of fact from the jury and puts them in the hands of the judge; in the case of summary trial, it removes the questions from the sphere of strict proof according to law and leaves them to be decided in the much more informal way in which questions of fact relating purely to sentence are decided. If the rules relating to proof at the trial have any value at all, it is extraordinary that they should not be applied to the most important facts in the case. That the sentence should be imposed by the judge on a basis of fact different from that on which the jury convicted is deplorable; but it is always possible in the case of strict liability unless the judge questions the jury as to the grounds of their decision—and there are difficulties about this.[2]

The argument which is probably most frequently advanced by the courts for imposing strict liability is that it is necessary to do so in the interests of the public. Now it may be conceded that in many of the instances where strict liability has been imposed, the public does need protection against negligence and,

---

[1] Wechsler, "The Model Penal Code", in *Modern Advances in Criminology* (ed., J. Ll. J. Edwards) (1965), 73. The argument was met by the authors of the Code by "the creation of a grade of offense which may be prosecuted in a criminal court but which is not denominated criminal and which entails upon conviction no severer sentence than a fine or civil penalty or forfeiture".

[2] *Cf.* comment on *Lockyer* v. *Gibb*, [1966] Crim. L.R. 504; *Dalas* (1966), *The Times*, September 28, *Warner*, [1967] 3 All E.R. 93; [1967] Crim. L.R. 528 and commentary thereon.

assuming that the threat of punishment can make the potential harmdoer more careful, there may be a valid ground for imposing liability for negligence as well as where there is *mens rea*. This is a plausible argument in favour of strict liability if there were no middle way between *mens rea* and strict liability—that is liability for negligence—and the judges have generally proceeded on the basis that there is no such middle way. Liability for negligence has rarely been spelled out of a statute except where, as in driving without due care, it is explicitly required. Lord DEVLIN has explained this:[3]

> "It is not easy to find a way of construing a statute apparently expressed in terms of absolute liability so as to produce the requirement of negligence. Take, for example, an offence like driving a car while it has defective brakes. It is easy enough to read into a statute a word like 'wilfully' but you cannot just read in 'carelessly'. You cannot show that no one should carelessly drive a car with defective brakes; you are not trying to get at careless driving. What you want to say is that no one may drive a car without taking care to see that the brakes are not defective. That is not so easy to frame as a matter of construction and it has never been done."

The case against strict liability, then, is, first, that it is unnecessary. It results in the conviction of persons who have behaved impeccably and who should not be required to alter their conduct in any way. Secondly, that it is unjust. Even if an absolute discharge be given (as in *Ball*)[4] D may feel rightly aggrieved at having been formally convicted of an offence for which he bore no responsibility. It is significant that Ball thought it worthwhile to appeal. Moreover, a conviction may have far-reaching consequences outside the courts,[5] so that it is no answer to say that only a nominal penalty is imposed.[6]

The imposition of liability for negligence would in fact meet the arguments of most of those who favour strict liability. Thus Roscoe Pound, in a passage which has been frequently and uncritically accepted as a justification for such offences, wrote:[7]

> "The good sense of the courts has introduced a doctrine of acting at one's peril with respect to statutory crimes which expresses the needs of society. Such statutes are not meant to punish the vicious will but to put pressure upon the thoughtless and inefficient to do their whole duty in the interest of public health or safety or morals."

The "thoughtless and inefficient" are, of course, the negligent. The objection to offences of strict liability is not that these persons are penalised, but that others who are completely innocent are also liable to conviction. Though Lord DEVLIN was sceptical about the possibility of introducing the criterion of negligence in the lecture from which the above quotation is taken he stated a principle from the bench which came very close to imposing such a requirement.[8] The point was taken up by the Privy Council in *Lim Chin Aik*:[9]

> ". . . it is not enough in their Lordship's opinion merely to label the statute as one dealing with a grave social evil and from that to infer that strict liability was intended. It is pertinent also to inquire whether putting the defendant under strict liability will assist in the enforcement of the regulations. That

---

[3] *Samples of Lawmaking*, 76.
[4] (1966), 50 Cr. App. R. 266, above, p. 65.
[5] As in the case of *Sweet* v. *Parsley*, [1968] 2 All E.R. 337.
[6] This was accepted by the Privy Council in *Lim Chin Aik*, [1963] A.C. 160 at 175 and by Lord REID in *Warner*, [1968] 2 All E.R. at 366.
[7] *The Spirit of the Common Law*, 52.
[8] In *Reynolds* v. *Austin*, [1951] 2 K.B. 135 at p. 150; [1951] 1 All E.R. 606 at p. 612.
[9] [1963] A.C. at p. 174; [1963] 1 All E.R. at p. 228.

means that there must be something he can do, directly or indirectly, by supervision or inspection, by improvement of his business methods or by exhorting those whom he may be expected to influence or control, which will promote the observance of the regulations. Unless this is so there is no reason in penalising him, and it cannot be inferred that the legislature imposed strict liability merely in order to find a luckless victim."

If there is something that D can do to prevent the commission of the crime this presumably means that he was not doing all he should, that he was in some way negligent. It is not clear, however, that these observations, notwithstanding their high authority have had much influence in subsequent cases, at least, until *Sweet* v. *Parsley*.[10] In *Warner* v. *Commissioner of Metropolitan Police*,[11] the first case on strict liability to reach the House of Lords, the majority (Lord GUEST dissenting on this issue) held that a mental element was required because the offence was one of being in possession. Only Lord REID thought that any mental element beyond that required to establish possession was necessary. The offence was punishable with two years' imprisonment and, as Lord REID said, "would be regarded as a truly criminal and disgraceful offence, so that a stigma would attach to a person convicted of it."[12] Yet, subject to the necessity for the mental element implicit in possession, the offence was an "absolute" one. The House rejected the possibility of a "half-way house" that was argued before them—that proof of physical possession should throw upon the accused the onus of proving his innocence on a balance of probabilities. In *Sweet* v. *Parsley*,[10] the House seemed to have undergone a remarkable change in its whole attitude to strict liability. The possibility of a defence to an apparently absolute offence by proving (*per* Lords REID and PEARCE) that all reasonable care had been taken or merely (*per* Lord DIPLOCK) raising a reasonable doubt whether all such care had been taken, was recognised. The former approach is difficult to reconcile with *Woolmington's Case*[13] and would still leave perfectly innocent persons liable to conviction. Lord DIPLOCK's approach is preferable; but it remains to be seen what influence these expressions of opinion will have. It may well be that a solution will still have to be sought in legislation.[14]

5 STATUTORY DEFENCES

Occasionally the drastic effect of a statute imposing strict liability is mitigated by the provision of a statutory defence. Where, for example, a person is accused of contravening the provisions of the Food and Drugs Act 1955 he is

"upon information duly laid by him and on giving to the prosecution not less than three clear days' notice of his intention . . . entitled to have any person, to whose act or default he alleges that the contravention of the provisions in question was due, brought before the court in the proceedings; and if, after the contravention has been proved, the original defendant proves that the contravention was due to the act or default of that other person, that other person may be convicted of the offence, and, if the original defendant proved that he has used all due diligence to secure that the provisions in question were complied with, he shall be acquitted of the offence."[15]

---

[10] [1969] 1 All E.R. 347.
[11] [1968] 2 All E.R. 356.
[12] At p. 365.
[13] [1935] A.C. 462, above, p. 27.
[14] See 118 New L.J. at p. 453 for proposals made by the Bar Council to the Law Commission.
[15] Section 113 (1).

In order to escape liability under this provision the defendant must prove two things: (a) that the contravention was due to the act or default of the third party and (b) that he himself used all due diligence to comply with the requirements of the Act. If he can establish only (a) and not (b) then both the original defendant and the third party are liable to conviction. If the court is left in doubt as to who caused the contravention then the original defendant must be convicted and the third party acquitted.[16] The third party might be, for example, a servant of the original defendant or a supplier of the goods in question. If he is a supplier, he, in his turn, might join the person from whom he received the goods, and so on, until the manufacturer is joined—and he might join his servant. There is also a provision[17] for short-circuiting this complicated procedure, and acting directly against the person ultimately responsible without joining the intermediate parties.

It is not necessary to prove any *mens rea* or negligence on the part of the third party. So if a shopkeeper is charged with selling a toffee with a nail in it,[18] he can escape liability by showing that there was no negligence on his own part and that the nail was in the toffee when he received it from the manufacturer. It is not necessary to show that the manufacturer knew, or ought to have known, that the nail was in the toffee when supplied. Indeed it is no defence for the manufacturer to satisfy the court that he has used every reasonable precaution to prevent any such occurrence. In other words, though a number of defendants may escape liability under this provision by showing that they got the offending article from someone else and were not themselves negligent, there must always be someone at the end of the line who will be subject to unmitigated strict liability.

Another limitation on the effectiveness of this particular defence is that it would seem that it will be of no avail if the third party who is in default is not identifiable so that no information can be laid (though, if he is identifiable and an information is laid it is immaterial that he cannot be brought before the court, because, for example, his whereabouts are not known).[19]

In *Parker* v. *Alder*,[20] D, a milk salesman, in pursuance of a contract of sale delivered some milk in a pure and unadulterated condition to a railway station for carriage to London. Under this contract, the property in the milk passed when it was delivered in London. When the milk was delivered it was found to be adulterated by 9 per cent of added water. The luckless D, without any fault on his part, had sold adulterated milk and the Divisional Court held that he was guilty of an offence under s. 6 of the Food and Drugs Act 1875.

The statutory defence we have been considering was not then in force; but it would seem that, in spite of it, D would be in no better position today.

Statutory defences do not always take this complicated form. More commonly they simply impose on the accused the burden of proving that he had no *mens rea* and was not negligent. Thus one who sells feeding stuffs containing deleterious ingredients is liable unless he proves "that he did not know and could not with

---

[16] *Moore* v. *Ray*, [1951] 1 K.B. 98; [1950] 2 All E.R. 561.
[17] Section 113 (3).
[18] *Lindley* v. *G. W. Horner & Co.*, [1950] 1 All E.R. 234.
[19] *Malcolm* v. *Cheek*, [1948] 1 K.B. 400; [1947] 2 All E.R. 881.
[20] [1899] 1 Q.B. 20.

reasonable care have known that the article contained" such an ingredient.[1] The effect of such a provision is that the prosecution need do no more than prove that the accused did the prohibited act and it is then for him to establish, if he can, that he did it innocently.   Such provisions are a distinct advance; but they are still a deviation from the fundamental principle that the prosecution must prove the whole of their case; and an extensive use of offences of strict liability, even when so qualified, is to be deplored.

---

[1] Fertilisers and Feeding Stuffs Act 1926, s. 7 (1).   See too, Weights and Measures Act 1963, ss. 26 and 27; Trade Descriptions Act 1968, s. 24; Post Office Act 1953, s. 63 (1). The provision of a statutory defence may be an indication to the court that an offence of strict liability is intended.   *Cf.* Sexual Offences Act 1956, s. 6, below, pp. 165 and 296, and Obscene Publications Act 1959, s. 2 (5), below, pp. 496–497.

CHAPTER 7

The Effect of
Particular Words*

Certain words, which have a bearing on whether *mens rea* need be proved, tend to be commonly used in criminal statutes and their interpretation in many cases has given them a more or less well-settled meaning which requires examination.

1 Knowingly

Thus, the word, "knowingly", as has already appeared repeatedly, is apt to introduce a requirement of *mens rea*[2] as to all the elements of the offence though it has not invariably been held to do so.[3] This seems to be the clearest word which can be used and it is probably safe to assume that the word will in future import a requirement of *mens rea* except, possibly, as to an exception clause in the definition of the crime.[4]

"Knowingly", for this purpose, includes the state of mind of the man who suspects the truth, but deliberately avoids finding out, "shutting his eyes to an obvious means of knowledge"[5] or deliberately refraining from "making enquiries the results of which he might not care to have".[6] "Connivance", as this attitude of mind is sometimes called, is closely akin to recklessness.[7]

If, as DEVLIN, J., says, "knowingly" only says expressly what is normally implied,[8] it is generally superfluous and its use in some but not all sections of a statute, puzzling. Three explanations have been offered: (1) that the sections where the word is not used create offences of strict liability—a view inconsistent with DEVLIN, J.'s *dictum* and rejected in *Sherras* v. *de Rutzen*[8] in favour of

---

* Edwards, *Mens Rea*; Williams, C.L.G.P., Ch. 5; Howard, *Strict Responsibility*, Ch. 6.

[1] See *Gaumont British Distributors* v. *Henry*, [1939] 2 K.B. 711; [1939] 2 All E.R. 808, and *A.-G.* v. *Cozens* (1934), 50 T.L.R. 320.

[2] *Brooks* v. *Mason*, [1902] 2 K.B. 743; *Dacey*, [1939] 2 All E.R. 641, overruled by *Hallam*, [1957] 1 Q.B. 569; [1957] 1 All E.R. 665. And see Sexual Offences Act 1956, ss. 25 and 26, below, p. 299.

[3] See *Brooks* v. *Mason*, above, p. 63.

[4] *Roper* v. *Taylor's Garages, Ltd.*, [1951] 2 T.L.R. 284 at p. 288, *per* DEVLIN, J.

[5] *Evans* v. *Dell*, [1937] 1 All E.R. 349 at p. 353, *per* HEWART, C.J. But *cf. Van Dusen* v. *Kritz*, [1936] 2 K.B. 176.

[6] See Edwards, *Mens Rea*, 202–205; Williams, C.L.G.P., 159.

[7] See *Roper*, above, p. 63.

[8] Above, p. 63.

(2) that the absence of the word shifts the onus of proof on to the defence;[9] (3) Williams argues that the requirements of *mens rea* are satisfied by "simple ignorance"[10] where "knowingly" is not used, but not where it is. For example, D makes a reproduction of a musical or dramatic performance without obtaining the consent of the performer. D does not know that this is an offence and consequently does not even consider whether the performers have consented or not. He is not guilty of "knowingly" committing the offence:[11] but, according to this view, he would be guilty (simple ignorance being equated with recklessness) if the statute had omitted the word "knowingly". In *Sherras* v. *de Rutzen*,[12] the publican had a positive belief that the constable was off duty. According to this view, he would have been guilty if (being ignorant that it was against the law to serve constables on duty) he had not directed his mind to the question whether the constable was on or off duty. This third solution involves giving an extended meaning to recklessness in statutory offences; but it may well be the most satisfactory explanation of Parliament's action. If so, of course, "knowingly" does say something more than is normally implied.

2 Maliciously

Another adverb commonly found in statutes is "maliciously". Many offences containing this word are examined below.[13] At one time this adverb was taken, in its natural and popular meaning, to require a generally wicked intention and improper motive.[14] Later, however, the word came simply to denote a requirement of recklessness or intention with respect to the *actus reus* of the crime in question: that is to import a requirement of *mens rea*. It probably also denotes the absence of a claim of right.[15] It is therefore no longer sufficient for the judge to tell the jury that D was malicious if he did the act "wickedly".[16] The question is whether he knew of the circumstances and foresaw the consequences which constitute the *actus reus* of the offence charged; or, in some cases, which constitute harm of the same kind, though not necessarily of the same degree as that specified in the definition of the *actus reus*.[17]

3 Wilfully

The term "wilfully" has been less consistently interpreted. Sometimes it is held to import a requirement of *mens rea*.[18] Thus in *Eaton* v. *Cobb*,[19] D, a motorist, was found not guilty of wilfully obstructing the free passage of the highway when, after looking in his mirror and seeing the road apparently clear, he opened his car door in the path of a cyclist. He wilfully opened the car door, but did not "wilfully obstruct". In other cases it has been held to do no more

---

[9] Followed in *Harding* v. *Price*, [1948] 1 K.B. 695; [1948] 1 All E.R. 283, but doubted by DEVLIN, J., in *Roper*, above, by the Privy Council in *Lim Chin Aik* v. *R.*, [1963] A.C. 160 at p. 173 and disapproved by Lord PEARCE in *Warner*, [1968] 2 All E.R. 356 at p. 386.
[10] C.L.G.P. §§ 54 and 59; above, pp. 43–44.
[11] *Gaumont British Distributors* v. *Henry*, above, pp. 63 and 73.
[12] Above, p. 63.
[13] See pp. 264–271 and 455–473.
[14] *Fordham* (1839), 4 J.P. 397; *Prestney* (1849), 3 Cox C.C. 505; *Mathews and Twig* (1876), 14 Cox C.C. 5.
[15] Edwards, *Mens Rea*, 21–27.
[16] *Cunningham*, [1957] 2 Q.B. 396; [1957] 2 All E.R. 412; below, p. 270, footnote 19.
[17] *Mowatt*, [1968] 1 Q.B. 421; [1967] 3 All E.R. 47; below, p. 267.
[18] *Roper* v. *Knott*, [1898] 1 Q.B. 868; *Morris* v. *Edmonds* (1897), 77 L.T. 56; *Younghusband* v. *Luftig*, [1949] 2 K.B. 354; [1949] 2 All E.R. 72; *Wilson* v. *Inyang*, [1951] 2 K.B. 799; [1951] 2 All E.R. 237; *Bullock* v. *Turnbull*, [1952] 2 Lloyd's Rep. 303; *Rice* v. *Connolly*, [1966] 2 Q.B. 414; [1966] 2 All E.R. 649, below, p. 263.
[19] [1950] 1 All E.R. 1016.

than impose a requirement that D's conduct be voluntary and not to extend to his knowledge of circumstances or foresight of consequences.

In *Hudson* v. *MacRae*[20] it was held that D was guilty of unlawful and wilful fishing in water where another person has a private right of fishing, under s. 24 of the Larceny Act 1861[1], though he believed the public had a right to fish there. And in *Cotterill* v. *Penn*[2] it was held that D was guilty of "unlawfully and wilfully" killing a house pigeon under s. 23 of the Larceny Act 1861 (repealed) where he shot a bird honestly thinking it was a wild pigeon. It was enough that he shot the bird he aimed at, though it would have been different, according to Lord BLACKBURN in the former case and Lord HEWART in the latter, if the section had used the word "maliciously". In the earlier case of *Horton* v. *Gwynne*[3] DARLING, J., suggested that it would be different if D shot at a crow, missed and killed a pigeon. "Wilful", according to this view, required an intention to kill the bird that was killed, but not an intention to kill a *house pigeon*.

It is submitted that the better view is that "wilful" should be held to apply to all the elements in the offence. It seems an abuse of language to say that one who shoots a bird he believes to be a wild pigeon, wilfully *shoots a house pigeon*. If he was reckless, and shot at the bird, not knowing whether it was wild or tame, that is another matter.[4]

4 "Permitting", "Suffering", or "Allowing"

The meaning of these three words appears to be the same. The most commonly used is "permitting" and this has been consistently held in recent cases to import a requirement of *mens rea*.[5] In some earlier cases, however, a different view was taken. Where an offence of permitting has once been interpreted to impose strict liability, that interpretation will be followed though, if the section had fallen to be construed for the first time today, a different result would probably be reached.

In *James & Son, Ltd.* v. *Smee*[6] the court had to consider the Motor Vehicles (Construction and Use) Regulations 1951 under which it was an offence, "If any person uses or causes or permits to be used" a vehicle in contravention of the regulations. "Using", "causing" and "permitting" are three separate offences; and the court held that *using* a vehicle in contravention of a regulation (in that it had a defective braking system) was an offence of strict liability;[7] but D was charged with *permitting* the use, "which, in our opinion, at once imports a state of mind". Knowledge of the defect, or wilful blindness had to be proved. Similarly, selling liquor to a drunken person is an offence of strict liability,[8] but *permitting* drunkenness requires *mens rea*.[9] In *Goldsmith* v. *Deakin*[10] LAWRENCE, J., said that "the word 'permit' means 'intentionally allow', in the sense that one has to consider the state of the defendant's mind." In that case it was held that wilful blindness or recklessness ("if . . . he . . . did not care whether or not it

---

[20] (1863), 4 B. & S. 585; *Wells* v. *Hardy*, [1964] 2 Q.B. 447; [1964] 1 All E.R. 953.
[1] See now Theft Act 1968, Sch. 2, para. 2.
[2] [1936] 1 K.B. 53. *Cf.* Stallybrass in M.A.C.L. at 460 *et seq.*
[3] [1921] 2 K.B. 661.
[4] *Cf. Holroyd* (1841), 2 Mood & R. 339 (wilful obstruction satisfied by recklessness).
[5] See cases referred to in comment on *Tapsell* v. *Maslen*, [1967] Crim. L.R. 53.
[6] [1955] 1 Q.B. 78; [1954] 3 All E.R. 273.
[7] *Green* v. *Burnett*, decided at the same time as *James* v. *Smee*.
[8] *Cundy* v. *Le Cocq*, above, p. 61.
[9] *Somerset* v. *Wade*, [1894] 1 Q.B. 574.
[10] (1933), 150 L.T. 157 at 158.

was used, in contravention of the statute, he did . . . permit the use") was enough.

On the other hand, it has been held that D may permit a false invoice to the prejudice of the purchaser, contrary to the Fertilisers and Feeding Stuffs Act 1893,[11] even though he does not know it to be false; it is enough that he permits to be sent out an invoice which is, in fact, false.[12] D may be convicted of permitting a vehicle to be used on the highway without a third-party policy of insurance being in force in respect of it although he believes, on reasonable grounds, that there is such a policy in force.[13]

Though attempts have been made[14] to distinguish between them, it is probable that "permitting" and "suffering" mean precisely the same thing.[15] If so, it would not be surprising to find that the courts have been little more consistent in the interpretation of the latter word than the former. It has been held in a number of cases that a licensee "suffers" gaming to be carried on, in the licensed premises, only if he knows of, or connives, at the gaming.[16]

Out of line with these authorities is the judgment of MANISTY, J., in *Bond* v. *Evans*[17] in which he held that *suffering* gaming is an offence of strict liability, pointing out (i) that in other sections the statute used the phrases *"knowingly suffers"* and *"knowingly permits"*, and (ii) that the earlier statute had used "knowingly" in relation to suffering gaming but the present statute did not. These are no light arguments, but nevertheless they have not, as *Sherras* v. *de Rutzen*[18] and *Harding* v. *Price*[19] show, always been found conclusive. STEPHEN, J., concurred but his judgment, though not absolutely clear, is evidently based on the fact that the gaming was suffered by D's servant who had *mens rea* and for whose acts D was, in the circumstances vicariously liable.[20] The case is distinguishable from earlier authorities on this ground.

If the observations in *James* v. *Smee* and *Goldsmith* v. *Deakin* are applied, the use of the adverbs "knowingly", or "wilfully" to qualify "permitting" or "suffering" is superfluous;[1] yet the very fact that they are used sometimes can give force to the argument that, where they are not used, strict liability is intended. The three possible solutions to the occasional use of the word "knowingly" which have already been considered, are however again applicable.[2]

---

[11] See now Fertilisers and Feeding Stuffs Act 1926.

[12] *Korten* v. *West Sussex County Council* (1903), 72 L.J.K.B. 514, followed in *Laird* v. *Dobell*, [1906] 1 K.B. 131.

[13] *Lyons* v. *May*, [1948] 2 All E.R. 1062. *Cf. Boss* v. *Kingston*, [1963] 1 All E.R. 177.

[14] *E.g.*, by DARLING, J., in *Rochford Rural Council* v. *Port of London Authority*, [1914] 2 K.B. 916 at p. 924.

[15] *Bond* v. *Evans* (1888), 21 Q.B.D. 249 at p. 257, *per* STEPHEN, J.; *Somerset* v. *Wade*, [1894] 1 Q.B. 574 at p. 576, *per* MATHEW, J.

[16] *Bosley* v. *Davies* (1875), 1 Q.B D. 84, followed in *Redgate* v. *Haynes* (1876), 1 Q.B.D. 89, and *Somerset* v. *Hart* (1884), 12 Q.B.D. 360.

[17] (1888), 21 Q.B.D. 249.

[18] Above, p. 63.

[19] Above, p. 74.

[20] See below, p. 101.

[1] And *cf.* DEVLIN, J., in *Roper* v. *Taylors Garages, Ltd.*, above p. 62.

[2] *Lomas* v. *Peek*, [1947] 2 All E.R. 574, suggests that the words, when they qualify "permitting", are generally superfluous. They were omitted from an information charging an offence under the Licensing (Consolidation) Act 1910 which uses the words. It was held that the omission of these "technical words" was irrelevant. "If a man permits a thing to be done, it means that he gives permission for it to be done, and if a man gives permission for a thing to be done, he knows what is to be done or what is being done, and, if he knows that, it follows that it is wilful"—*per* Lord GODDARD, C.J.

5 Causing

The interpretation of this word prolongs the sorry tale of inconsistency. On the one hand, D did not *cause* to be presented a play containing words disapproved by the Lord Chamberlain, so as to incur liability under the Theatres Act 1843 s. 15, if he did not know that the offending words were being included.[3] The owner of a steam engine did not cause it to be erected within twenty-five yards of the highway, contrary to the Highway Act 1835 if he had no knowledge that the machine was being so placed.[4] Nor, under the same Act, did a surveyor cause to be laid on the highway a heap of stone, if he did not know that the carter to whom he had given general directions as to the repairing of the road, was going to and did so lay the stones.[5] The manager of a colliery was not liable for causing horses belonging to the colliery to be ill-treated, when he had no knowledge of the cruelty.[6]

On the other hand, in *Korten* v. *West Sussex County Council* and *Laird* v. *Dobell*[7] the courts did not distinguish between "causing" and "permitting", holding both to impose strict liability. In *Moses* v. *Midland Rly*.[8] it was held that causing any substance to flow into any waters with the result that fish are poisoned or killed, contrary to the Salmon Fishery Act 1861, did not require *mens rea*. In *Wurzal* v. *Wilson*[9] it was held that D caused a vehicle to be used as an express carriage when he did not know but ought to have known that it was an express carriage within the meaning of the Act.

Edwards[10] argues that

"Whereas . . 'permits', 'suffers' and 'allows' all denote passive acquiescence in the commission of the prohibited act, 'causes' is a far more positive epithet and indicates an express authorisation of the forbidden event."

It is, moreover, a stronger term than some of the verbs used to denote the conduct of an accessory before the fact where *mens rea* is required.[11]

6 Fraudulently

It would seem that nothing could be more apt to introduce a requirement of *mens rea* than the word "fraudulently" or the term "with intent to defraud"; and generally it is clear that this is their effect; and that, moreover, dishonesty is required so that a claim of right is a defence.[12]

It should be noted, however, that not even the requirement of fraud has been invariably sufficient to preclude the courts from interpreting an offence as one of strict liability. Under the Merchandise Marks Act 1887, s. 2, it was an offence, *inter alia*, to apply any false trade description to goods. It was a defence if D "proves that he acted without intent to defraud". It was held that this

---

[3] *Lovelace* v. *Director of Public Prosecutions*, [1954] 3 All E.R. 481; see now Theatres Act 1968, s. 2, below, p. 500.

[4] *Harrison* v. *Leaper* (1862), 5 L.T. 640.

[5] *Hardcastle* v. *Bielby*, [1892] 1 Q.B. 709.

[6] *Small* v. *Warr* (1882), 47 J.P. 20.

[7] Above, p. 76, footnote 12.

[8] (1915), 84 L.J.K.B. 2181.

[9] [1965] 1 All E.R. 26, following *Browning* v. *J. W. H. Watson (Rochester), Ltd.*, [1953] 2 All E.R. 775.

[10] *Mens Rea*, 254.

[11] Below, p. 94.

[12] *Cf.* Theft, deception and forgery; below, Ch. 15.

was available only if D proved that he did the act by accident or mistake: *Kat v. Diment*.[13]   An honest belief that the description was true was irrelevant[14] if it was intentionally applied and, in fact, false.   The 1887 Act has now been repealed by the Trade Descriptions Act 1968 and the corresponding provision (s. 24) does not refer to intent to defraud.   It is hoped that the courts will never again interpret "defraud" to cover honest conduct.

7   Corruptly

Like "fraudulently" this word, in its natural sense, seems to imply dishonesty; but, like "fraudulently", it has been narrowly construed.   Under the Corrupt Practices Prevention Act 1854 it was an offence corruptly to offer money to a voter on account of his having voted in a particular way.   The view of the majority of judges seems to have been that nothing more than an intention to do the act specified was required.   There need be no dishonesty.[15]   Thus the word "corruptly" was held to add nothing to the meaning of the section in which it was used.

Recently it was held[16] that, if D offers a bribe to a public servant, it is no defence to a charge under the Public Bodies Corrupt Practices Act 1889 that he did so only with the intention of exposing the public servant.   D acted "corruptly" because he deliberately did an act which the law forbids as tending to corrupt others.

8   Possession

Just as one cannot "permit" without a certain state of mind, so one cannot "possess" without a mental element.   In all of the many crimes where this word is used, some mental element is therefore imported into the offence.   In *Lockyer* v. *Gibb*[17] PARKER, L.C.J., said that

> ". . . if something were slipped into your basket and you had not the vaguest notion it was there you could not be said to be in possession of it."

A man is not guilty of possessing a dangerous drug when it has been "planted" on him.[18]   If D were to borrow a car in which a drug was concealed, he would not be in possession of it if he did not know it was there.[19]   Lord PARKER's view was that if D knew he was in control of the thing, which was in fact a drug, he was in possession (and was guilty of the offence) even though he supposed that it was aspirin or even sweets.   In *Warner* v. *Metropolitan Police Commissioner*[20] the majority[1] of the House of Lords held that this was too restricted a view of the mental element in possession.   In that case, a parcel found in a van driven by D contained a prohibited drug.   D said that he believed that it contained

---

[13] [1951] 1 K.B. 34; [1950] 2 All E.R. 657, and see *Brinson* v. *Hunt Brothers*, [1963] Crim. L.R. 48.

[14] *Mercer* v. *Co-operative Retail Services, Ltd.*, [1964] Crim. L.R. 51.

[15] *Cooper* v. *Slade* (1858), 6 H.L.Cas. 746 at p. 773, *per* WILLES, J.   And see *Bewdley Election Petition* (1869), 19 L.T. 676, *per* BLACKBURN, J.   *Cf. Calland*, [1967] Crim. L.R. 236.

[16] *Smith*, [1960] 2 Q.B. 423; [1960] 1 All E.R. 256.

[17] [1967] 2 Q.B. 243 at p. 248.

[18] *Per* Lord PEARCE in *Warner, infra*, footnote, 20 at p. 388.

[19] *Carpenter*, [1960] Crim. L.R. 633, approved by Lord WILBERFORCE in *Warner*, below, footnote 20 at p. 394.

[20] [1968] 2 All E.R. 356.

[1] Lords MORRIS and GUEST agreeing with Lord PARKER.

scent. The Court of Appeal, following *Lockyer* v. *Gibb*, held that this could be no defence; but the majority of the House of Lords held that D, though undoubtedly in possession of the parcel, was not in possession of its contents if the following conditions were satisfied: (i) D believed the contents were scent and not drugs; (ii) scent and drugs are different in kind and not merely in quality; (iii) D did not have a reasonable opportunity to ascertain the contents of the parcel; and (iv) he did not suspect that there was anything wrong with the contents of the parcel. If the jury were satisfied that any one of these conditions was not fulfilled, then D would apparently be in possession. If D were proved to be in possession, then no other mental element need be proved.

It should be noted that for some purposes, the mental element sufficient to found possession is more restricted even than that which Lord PARKER thought to be enough. Thus an intention to exclude others from one's property is enough, for some purposes, to found possession of things in or on the property.[2] Though the drug may have been planted in D's basket or his car without his knowledge, it would seem that he could sue for trespass if it were wrongfully removed by another; his general intention to exclude others being enough. When we are concerned with criminal offences of possession, however, it would seem likely that the more elaborate mental element specified in *Warner* will be required. It is obvious that this may prove a source of considerable difficulty to juries and those who have to direct them.

---

[2] *Elwes* v. *Brigg Gas Co.* (1886), 23 Ch. D. 562; *South Staffs. Water Co.* v. *Sharman*, [1896] 2 Q.B. 44; *Hibbert* v. *McKiernan*, [1948] 2 K.B. 142.

CHAPTER 8

Modes of Participation in Crime

1 ACCOMPLICES

The person who directly and immediately causes the *actus reus* of a crime is not necessarily the only one who is criminally liable for it. By the Accessories and Abettors Act 1861, s. 8:

"Whosoever shall aid, abet, counsel or procure the commission of any misdemeanour at common law or by virtue of any act passed or to be passed, shall be liable to be tried, indicted and punished as a principal offender."

The effect of s. 1 of the Criminal Law Act 1967[1] is that this provision is now applicable to all offences whether they were formerly felonies or misdemeanours. The distinctions which existed in the law of felonies between principals in the first degree and in the second degree and accessories before the fact have now entirely disappeared. The change is one of form rather than of substance. No one becomes liable to conviction, as a result of this reform, who was not liable before it; and no one is exempt from liability who was not exempt before. The modes of participation in crime which the law recognises are unchanged.

It continues to be necessary, for some purposes,[2] to distinguish between the participant who was designated "principal in the first degree" in the law of felonies and other participants in the offence. He might, therefore, conveniently be designated "the principal" and the other participants in the offence, "secondary parties".[3] There are basically two types of activity which will found liability as a secondary party. The first, "aiding and abetting", was the activity of the principal in the second degree to felony. The second, "counselling or procuring," was the activity of the accessory before the fact.[4] The old cases on

---

[1] Above, p. 23.
[2] Below, pp. 94–95.
[3] It will be noted that the Accessories and Abettors Act does not provide that secondary parties are principal offenders but that they are liable to be proceeded against as if they were.
[4] "Aid" and "abet" seem to be synonyms as do "counsel" and "procure". The terms "abet", "abettor", "counsel" and "counsellor" will therefore be used henceforth to denote the respective activities and actors.

participation in felonies remain valid authorities on the limits of criminal liability. To be liable, a person who is not the principal offender must be proved to be either an abettor or a counsellor, though it is quite sufficient to show that he must have been one or the other.

1 The Principal Offender

Where there are several participants in a crime the principal offender is the one whose act is the most immediate cause of the *actus reus*. In murder, for example, he is the man who, with *mens rea*, fires the gun or administers the poison which causes death; in theft, the man, who, with *mens rea*, appropriates the thing which is stolen; in bigamy, the person who, knowing himself to be already married, goes through a second ceremony of marriage; and so on. The *actus reus* may be directly brought about by the act of someone who is not a participant in the crime at all (that is, who has no *mens rea*, or who has some defence, such as infancy or insanity). Such a person is usually described as an "innocent agent" and, in such a case, the principal offender is the participant in the crime whose act is the most immediate cause of the innocent agent's act. So if D, intending to kill P, gives to P's daughter a poison which, he says, will cure P's cold, and she innocently administers the poison, causing P's death, then D is guilty as the principal offender.[5] If the daughter had had *mens rea* then she would, of course, have been the principal. Where D, a collector of money, makes a false statement to his employer's book-keeper, knowing that the statement will be entered in the books, and it is so entered by the innocent book-keeper, D is guilty, as a principal, of falsifying his employer's accounts.[6] Where D induces a child, aged eleven, to take money from a till and give it to D, D is a principal only if the child is exempt from criminal liability which, in the case of a child of that age, depends on whether he knows the act is wrong.[7] If the child does know his act is wrong, then he is the principal and D is a counsellor.[8]

It is, of course, perfectly possible to have two principals in the same crime. If D1 and D2 make an attack on P intending to murder him and the combined effect of their blows is to kill him, plainly both are guilty of murder[9] as principals.

2 Abettors

An abettor is one who is present assisting or encouraging the principal at the time of the commission of the offence. A conspirator who was present at the commission of the crime was a principal in the second degree under the law of felonies, whether he gave assistance or encouragement at that time or not.[10] Since, however, a conspirator appears to be liable as a counsellor, whether he is present or not, unless he has previously retracted his agreement[11] to the commission of the crime, this variety of abetting seems no longer to be of any

---

[5] (1634), Kelyng 53; *Michael* (1840), 9 C. & P. 356; below, p. 192.

[6] *Butt* (1884), 15 Cox C.C. 564.

[7] See below, p. 111. And see *Tyler* (1838), 8 C. & P. 616 (liability for act of lunatic).

[8] *Manley* (1844), 1 Cox C.C. 104. The child was actually nine. A child under ten is now incapable of crime, so D would be the principal whether the nine-year-old knew the act was wrong or not. See also *Mazeau* (1840), 9 C. & P. 676.

[9] *Macklin and Murphy*'s case (1838), 2 Lewin C.C. 225.

[10] Williams, C.L.G.P., s. 120.

[11] Hawkins, 2 P.C. c. 29, s. 16; *Croft*, [1944] K.B. 295; below, p. 96. Williams, C.L.G.P. s. 123, argues that ". . . this proposition would be vexatious if pressed to its fullest extent; it would mean that a minor participant in a vast organisation could be charged as participant in every crime committed incidentally to the criminal purpose."

significance. If an unretracted conspiracy can be proved, D can be convicted of the crime, and it is irrelevant that he was not present when it was committed.

Assistance given before the offence is committed will ground liability as a counsellor, so it is only as regards the conclusion of the offence that time becomes important. Assistance given when the principal is no longer in the course of the commission of the offence—to enable him to escape or to reap the benefits of the crime—does not amount to abetting. Where D1 broke into a warehouse, stole butter and deposited it in the street thirty yards from the warehouse door, D2 who came to assist in carrying it off was held not guilty of abetting in larceny.[12] Larceny was to some extent a continuing offence and it was sometimes difficult to determine the point at which it concluded.[13] Under the new law of theft, this particular problem is unlikely to arise: D2 would be guilty of theft through his own appropriation of the property.[14] A similar problem could occur, however, under s. 11[15] (removal of articles from places open to the public) or s. 12[16] (taking motor vehicle or other conveyance without authority) of the Theft Act; and the general principle remains valid. Assistance given to a murderer, after his victim is dead, to a rapist after he has completed the act of intercourse, or to a bigamist after the second ceremony of marriage, cannot ground liability for the crime in question. If a person is near enough to give assistance to the principal, either by warning or otherwise, he may be held liable as an abettor even though he is some considerable distance from the actual scene of the crime[17] or is outside the house in which the crime is being committed.

What is the position when the principal himself is not present at the moment of the completion of the crime? If two or more persons conspire to employ an innocent agent both are liable as principals for the agent's acts and it is immaterial that the agent was instructed by the one in the absence of the other. The innocent agent's acts are considered the acts of both conspirators.[18] Where there is no innocent agent, the same considerations cannot apply. D1, in pursuance of an agreement with D2, leaves poison to be taken by P, or sets a trap into which P falls. It is thought that D2 will be liable as a secondary party.

A person is not guilty merely because he is present at the scene of a crime and does nothing to prevent it.[19] He must either (a) give active assistance or encouragement (in which case it is immaterial that there was no prior agreement to do so[20]) or (b) have agreed that the crime should be committed. In *Allan*[1] it was held that one who remains present at an affray, nursing a secret intention to help if the need arises but doing nothing to evince that intention, does not thereby

---

See examples given in Model Penal Code, T.D. No. 1, p. 19. But it seems scarcely satisfactory to say that D should be guilty of those offences within the scope of the conspiracy at which he happens to be present (though he does nothing) and not guilty of those offences within the scope of the conspiracy at which he is not present.

[12] *King* (1817), Russ. & Ry. 332; see also *Kelly* (1820), Russ. & Ry. 421.

[13] *Cf. Atwell and O'Donnell* (1801), 2 East P.C. 768.

[14] *Cf.* the similar problem which arises in distinguishing handling from theft; Smith, *Law of Theft*, §§ [601]–[604], below, p. 429.

[15] Below, p. 398.

[16] Below, p. 400.

[17] Hawkins, 2 P.C. c. 29, §§ 7 and 8; Foster, 350; *Betts and Ridley* (1930), 22 Cr. App. Rep. 148.

[18] *Bull and Schmidt* (1845), 1 Cox C.C. 281.

[19] *Atkinson* (1869), 11 Cox C.C. 330; but it is an offence to refuse to assist a constable to suppress a breach of the peace when called upon to do so: *Brown* (1841), C. & M. 314.

[20] *Mohan v. R.*, [1967] 2 All E.R. 58.

[1] [1963] 2 All E.R. 897; see also *Tansley v. Painter* (1968), 112 Sol. Jo. 1005.

become an abettor. Thus in the leading case of *Coney*[2] it was held that proof of mere voluntary presence at a prize-fight, without more, is, at the most only *prima facie* and not conclusive evidence of abetting the battery of which the contestants are guilty. Presence at such an event is certainly capable of amounting to an actual encouragement. If there were no spectators there would be no fight and, therefore, each spectator, by his presence, contributes to the incentive to the contestants. As MATHEW, J., (dissenting) said:[3]

> "The chief incentive to the wretched combatants to fight on until (as happens too often) dreadful injuries have been inflicted and life endangered or sacrificed, is the presence of spectators watching with keen interest every incident of the fight."

Voluntary presence at such an event, then, is some evidence on which a jury might find that the accused was there with the intention of encouraging the fight. Coney's conviction was quashed because the majority of the court thought that the chairman's direction was capable of being understood to mean that voluntary presence was *conclusive* evidence of an intention to encourage. If the direction had made it clear that presence was *prima facie* evidence only, no doubt the conviction would have been sustained. So in *Wilcox* v. *Jeffrey*[4] it was held that D's presence at a public performance by H, a celebrated alien performer on the saxophone, who had been given permission to land only on condition that he would take no employment, was a sufficient aiding and abetting of H in his contravention of the Aliens Order 1920. D's behaviour before and after the performance supplied further evidence of his intention to encourage; for he had met H at the airport and he afterwards reported the performance in laudatory terms in the periodical of which he was the proprietor.

It would seem that where the evidence establishes mere presence without any positive act, a prior agreement that the crime be committed must be proved. But if some positive act of assistance is voluntarily done, with knowledge of the circumstances constituting the offence, that is enough to sustain a conviction; and it is irrelevant, in the latter case, that the aid is not given with the motive or purpose of encouraging the crime.[5] So if D2 handed a gun to D1 knowing that D1 intended to shoot P, it would not avail D2 to say that he hoped that D1 would not use the gun.[6]

Where D has a right to control the actions of another and he deliberately refrains from exercising it, his inactivity may be a positive encouragement to the other to perform an illegal act, and, therefore, an aiding and abetting. So if a licensee of a public house stands by and watches his customers drinking after hours, he is guilty of aiding and abetting them in doing so.[7] Again in *Du Cros* v. *Lambourne*,[8] it was proved that D's car had been driven at a dangerous speed but it was not proved whether D or E was driving. It was held that, nevertheless, D could be convicted. If E was driving she was doing so in D's

---

[2] (1882), 8 Q.B.D. 534.
[3] *Ibid.*, at p. 544.
[4] [1951] 1 All E.R. 464.
[5] *National Coal Board* v. *Gamble*, [1959], 1 Q.B. 11; [1958] 3 All E.R. 203; below, p. 85.
[6] *Cf.*, however, *Fretwell* (1864), Le. & Ca. 443; below, p. 85.
[7] *Thomas* v. *Lindop*, [1950] 1 All E.R. 966 at p. 968, *per* Lord GODDARD, C.J.; *Ferguson* v. *Weaving*, [1951] 1 K.B. 814; [1951] 1 All E.R. 412.
[8] [1907] 1 K.B. 40; *cf.* also *Rubie* v. *Faulkner*, [1940] 1 K.B. 571; [1940] 1 All E.R. 285; *Harris*, [1964] Crim. L.R. 54.

presence, with his consent and approval; for he was in control and could and ought to have prevented her from driving in a dangerous manner. D was equally liable whether he was a principal or an abettor.[9] The result would presumably have been different if it had been E's own car, for D would then have had no right of control, and could only have been convicted if active instigation to drive at such speed had been proved. In *Baldessare*,[10] D1 and D2 unlawfully took X's car and D1 drove it recklessly and caused P's death. It was held that D2 was guilty of manslaughter as an abettor. In this case (as prosecuting counsel put it)

> "The common purpose to drive recklessly was . . . shown by the fact that both men were driving in a car which did not belong to them and the jury were entitled to infer that the driver was the agent of the passenger. It matters not whose hand was actually controlling the car at the time."

These cases should be contrasted with *Richardson*,[11] where D1 and D2 accosted P in the street with intent to rob him but, on discovering that he only had $2\frac{1}{2}d.$, either D1 or D2 (it was not proved which) said, "Do not take that" and abandoned the enterprise. The other, however, robbed P of his $2\frac{1}{2}d.$ Here both had to be acquitted; for, while one of them was certainly guilty as a principal in the first degree, the other was not an aider and abettor and was, therefore, not guilty of robbing at all.[12]

3   Counselling

A counsellor is one who, before the commission of the crime, conspires to commit it, advises its commission or knowingly gives assistance to one or more of the principals. One whose participation in the events prior to the crime does not involve conspiracy, advice or encouragement to commit it, and who does not assist the commission in any way, is not liable.

This rule received what has been regarded as a generous interpretation in *Taylor*.[13] A and B quarrelled and agreed to fight. They each agreed to put down £1 so that the £2 might be paid to the winner. D agreed to hold the stakes. A and B fought, A received injuries of which he died and B was convicted of manslaughter. D was not present at the fight. He paid over the £2 to B, not knowing at that time that A's life was in danger. It was held that D was not liable as an accessory. There was no evidence that he encouraged the two men to fight, and, as BRAMWELL, B., said, "Nothing that the accused did assisted or enabled the fight to take place."[14] The stake was, after all, a collateral transaction, and the fight could well have taken place without it.

In cases where D advises the commission of the crime, there is convincing evidence that he intends it to be committed. Where he merely gives assistance, this is not necessarily so. Whether a man is guilty who knowingly gives assistance, but hopes that the crime will not be committed, is a question on which the

---

[9] *Cf. Swindall and Osborne* (1846), 2 Car. & Kir. 230; *Salmon* (1880), 6 Q.B.D. 79; *Iremonger* v. *Wynne*, [1957] Crim. L.R. 624; Williams, C.L.G.P. § 137, n. 23.

[10] (1930), 22 Cr. App. Rep. 70.

[11] (1785), 1 Leach 387.

[12] No doubt he was guilty of a conspiracy to rob; below, p. 151; and possibly of attempted robbery; below, p. 166.

[13] (1875), L.R. 2 C.C.R. 147, criticised in Williams, C.L.G.P., 365; Kenny, *Outlines*, 110.

[14] (1875), L.R. 2 C.C.R. 147 at p. 149.

authorities are not easy to reconcile. In *Fretwell*,[15] a woman, who had become pregnant by D, asked D to procure for her an abortifacient and threatened to kill herself if he did not do so. He did supply her with corrosive sublimate which she took and, in consequence, died. Now at common law this was self-murder by her and D was charged with murder as an accessory. It was held that he was not guilty, ERLE, C.J., saying:[16]

> ". . . the prisoner was unwilling that the woman should take the poison. He procured it for her at her instigation and under a threat by her of self-destruction . . . the facts of the case are quite consistent with the supposition that he hoped and expected that she would change her mind and not resort to it."

In *National Coal Board* v. *Gamble*,[17] E, a lorry driver, had his employer's lorry filled with coal at a colliery belonging to the defendant Board. When the lorry was driven on to the weighbridge operated by the defendants' servant, F, it appeared, and F so informed E, that its load exceeded by nearly four tons that permitted by the Motor Vehicles (Construction and Use) Regulations. E said he would take the risk, F gave him a weighbridge ticket and E committed the offence by driving the overloaded lorry on the highway. The property in the coal did not pass until the ticket was handed over and, therefore, E could not properly have left the colliery without it. It was held that the Board, through F,[18] was guilty of the misdemeanour. The decision was based on the assumption that D knew he had the right to prevent the lorry leaving the colliery with the coal. Had he not known this, he should have been acquitted. SLADE, J., dissenting, accepted the argument of the defence that the Board was not liable because F's act was not done with the motive of assisting in the commission of the crime. Presumably F was indifferent whether E drove his overloaded lorry on the road or not—he probably thought that it was none of his business. The majority, (Lord GODDARD, C.J., and DEVLIN, J.) however, thought that motive was irrelevant and that it was enough that a positive act of assistance had been voluntarily done with knowledge of the circumstances constituting the offence. DEVLIN, J., said:[19]

> "If one man deliberately sells to another a gun to be used for murdering a third, he may be indifferent about whether the third man lives or dies and interested only in the cash profit to be made out of the sale, but he can still be an aider and abettor. To hold otherwise would be to negative the rule that *mens rea* is a matter of intent only and does not depend on desire or motive."

This result is in accord with two previous decisions. In *Cook* v. *Stockwell*,[20] D, a brewer, supplied large quantities of beer to some cottages, knowing very well that they were re-selling it, without being licensed to do so, to soldiers quartered near by. In *Cafferata* v. *Wilson*,[1] D, a wholesaler, sold a firearm to E, who kept a general shop, but was not registered as a firearms dealer. Presumably D knew that E was going to re-sell the firearm, which he in fact did. In both cases D was held liable as an accessory to the illegal sale.

The cases might be reconciled on the very narrow ground that Fretwell actually hoped that the crime would not be committed, whereas the accessories

---

[15] (1862) Le & Ca. 161.
[16] (1862), Le. & Ca. at p. 164.
[17] [1959] 1 Q.B. 11; [1958] 3 All E.R. 203.
[18] See, however, below, pp. 104 and 106.
[19] [1959] 1 Q.B. 11 at p. 23.
[20] (1915), 84 L.J.K.B. 2187.
[1] [1936] 3 All E.R. 149.

in the three later cases were merely indifferent whether it was committed or not.[2]
It is submitted, however, that this would involve too close an examination into
a man's motives to be a practical test in the criminal law. A man himself may
often be unable to say with certainty whether he hoped a thing would not
happen or was merely indifferent whether it occurred or not. It is submitted,
with respect, that the principles stated in *National Coal Board* v. *Gamble* are to
be preferred to the decision in *Fretwell*. The latter case is perhaps best regarded
as one in which the court strained the principles governing the liability of accessories in order to mitigate the severity of the rule which treated suicide as
murder,[3] and that it is a decision which should not be followed.

Williams's view is to the contrary. He argues:[4]

> "The seller of an ordinary marketable commodity is not his buyer's keeper
> in criminal law unless he is specifically made so by statute. Any other rule
> would be too wide an extension of criminal responsibility."

Williams would now accept that:

> ". . . the seller of a motor car would become a party to crime if he knew that
> the buyer proposed to drive the car himself and was subject to epileptic fits—
> because danger to life is involved; it is very like selling a revolver to a would-
> be murderer."[5]

The other example given to demonstrate the extravagance of the rule, is:

> ". . . the vendor of a hotel would become a party to crime if he knew at the
> time of sale that the purchaser intended to carry on illegal after-hour trading."

This certainly appears a startling conclusion, but only because the sale is a big
one and the crime a small one. If the purchaser intended to use the hotel as a
headquarters for espionage, or even for use as a brothel, the conclusion would
seem less startling; and there is no difference in principle. Most principles of
liability bring in some cases where no prosecution should be brought; and the
sale of the hotel for after-hour trading may be one of these.

Another difficult question which arises in this connection is the extent to which
D must know the details of the crime which he is alleged to have counselled. It
seems clear that if he knows the type of crime which is contemplated, that would
be enough, even if he did not know the person or thing which was to be the
subject of it or time, place or other circumstances in which the crime was to be
carried out. Thus, if X were to tell D that he wanted to borrow his revolver to
shoot someone, it would not be necessary to prove that D knew who was to be
shot or where and when the shooting was to take place. Or if D were to lend X
his jemmy, knowing that X intended to commit a burglary with it, it would be
immaterial that D did not know where or when the burglary was to take place.

The case of *Lomas*[6] has been relied on for the proposition that "there must be
some particular crime in view".[7] That was a case in which D had a jemmy
belonging to a burglar, K. He returned the jemmy to K, who committed a
burglary with it. It was held that D was not liable as an accessory. However, in
the later case of *Bullock*,[8] the Court of Criminal Appeal held that *Lomas* was no
authority for this proposition. That case turned on the fact that it was K's own

---

[2] Williams, C.L.G.P., § 124.
[3] As to which, see below, p. 237.
[4] C.L.G.P., § 124 at p. 373.
[5] 9 J.S.P.T.L. (N.S.) at p. 171.
[6] (1913), 9 Cr. App. Rep. 220.
[7] Headnote in (1913), 9 Cr. App. Rep. 220.
[8] [1955] 1 All E.R. 15 (C.C.A.).

jemmy; as D was not entitled to withhold it, his doing what he had no right not to do could not make him an accessory. As DEVLIN, J., put it in *National Coal Board* v. *Gamble*,[9] D, although physically performing a positive act, was, in law, only refraining from detinue.[10] *Bullock* does not assist very greatly in the solution of the problem. The facts were that D was charged with two offences of house-breaking. In each case a different car was used for the crime and in each case that car had been hired by D. His defence was an alibi. He said that the cars must have been taken away during the night without his knowledge. The prose-cution's case was that D was present at the breaking and entering. It appeared, however, from questions which the jury put to the judge, that they thought it possible that D's alibi was true but that, on each occasion, he lent the car for the purpose of committing the crime. The judge directed that, in such a case, D would be an accessory before the fact. On appeal it was argued that this was an insufficient direction and, particularly, that the jury ought to have been told that D could only be convicted if he knew that his car was being used for the specific crime. The court held the direction adequate, apparently on the grounds that, in the particular circumstances, if D had lent the car for an unlawful pur-pose, he must have known what that purpose was.

The point was directly raised in *Bainbridge*.[11] D purchased some oxygen-cutting equipment which was used six weeks later for breaking into a bank at Stoke Newington. D's story was that he had bought the equipment for one Shakeshaft, that he suspected Shakeshaft wanted it for something illegal—perhaps breaking up stolen goods—but that he did not know that it was going to be used for any such purpose as it was in fact used. Judge AARVOLD directed that it was essential to prove that D knew the type of crime that was going to be committed: it was not enough that he knew that some kind of illegality was con-templated; but that, if he knew breaking and entering and stealing was in-tended, it was not necessary to prove that he knew that the Midland Bank, Stoke Newington, was going to be broken into. The Court of Criminal Appeal held that this was a correct direction.

Again, where D has supplied E with the means of committing a crime of a particular type, is he to be held liable for all the crimes of that type which E may thereafter commit? What if the Midland at Stoke Newington was the second, third or fourth bank which E had feloniously broken and entered with Bain-bridge's apparatus? Williams questions whether D should be subject to such unforeseeable and perhaps far-reaching liability.[12] Yet, once it is conceded that D need not know the details of any specific crime, it is difficult to see why he should be liable for any one crime of the type contemplated and not for others.[13]

The case leaves some unsolved problems. Whether a crime is of the same type as another may not always be easy to discover. If D lends a jemmy to E, contemplating that E intends to enter a house in order to steal, is D guilty of any offence if E enters a house intending to rape?[14] Clearly, D cannot be convicted of rape, because that is an offence of a different type; but he is probably guilty of burglary, because burglary was the crime he had in view—though this particular

---

[9] [1959] 1 Q.B. 11 at p. 20; [1958] 3 All E.R. 203 at p. 207.
[10] Yet it is difficult to suppose that an action by a burglar for the wrongful detention of his jemmy would succeed!
[11] [1959] 3 All E.R. 200; (1959), 43 Cr. App. Rep. 194.
[12] C.L.G.P., § 124.
[13] On the question of the withdrawal of an accessory before the fact, see below, p. 95.
[14] See below, p. 408.

variety of burglary may be abhorrent to him. If D contemplates theft and E commits robbery, D is not guilty of robbery but might be convicted of the theft which is included in it.[15] Is theft an offence of the same type as removing an article from a place open to the public[16] or taking a motor vehicle without authority?[17] Is robbery an offence of the same type as blackmail?

4   Liability of Secondary Party for Unforeseen Consequences

Where two persons embark on a joint unlawful enterprise each is equally liable for the consequences of such acts of the other as are done in pursuance of the agreement. The abettor is, then, liable for unforeseen consequences to the same extent as the principal. So in *Baldessare*,[18] the driver was held liable for the unintended and unforeseen death which he caused and his passenger was equally liable. If, in a crime requiring *mens rea*, one of the parties goes beyond what was agreed upon, then the other is not liable for the unforeseen consequences of that unauthorised act. In an old case three soldiers went to rob an orchard. Two climbed a pear tree while the third stood at the gate with a drawn sword. When the owner's son intervened, the sentinel stabbed and killed him. HOLT, C.J., held that he was guilty of murder, but that the other two were innocent. It would have been otherwise if they had all set out with a common intention to oppose interference with deadly force.[19]

In a modern case,[20] two gangs of boys engaged in a fight on Clapham Common. One of them, E, carried a knife with which he inflicted a fatal stab wound. There being no evidence that D, another member of the same gang, knew that E carried a knife, it was held that D, though guilty of a common assault, was not an accomplice in the murder.[1] If E had killed with a blow of his fist, D would have been guilty of manslaughter, because the blow was delivered in pursuance of the agreement. But, because the use of a knife was not within his contemplation at all, he was not responsible for the death which resulted from it.[2]

It is quite different where D knows that E is carrying a knife and that he may use it. If E uses the knife to kill, D will be liable for murder or manslaughter, according to his own *mens rea*—that is, according to the sort of use of the knife that he contemplated. If D expected E to use the knife to cause grievous bodily harm (presumably including any stabbing), D would be liable for murder.[3] If he expected E merely to use it to threaten, he would be liable for manslaughter.[4] This is so even though E goes beyond D's expectations and stabs with intent to kill, because the use of a knife is within "the scope of the concerted action".[5] If E had used a revolver which D did not know he had, that would appear to be outside the scope of the concerted action.[6]

---

[15] Below, p. 380.
[16] Theft Act 1968, s. 11. Below, p. 398.
[17] Theft Act 1968, s. 12. Below, p. 400.
[18] Above, p. 84.
[19] (1697), Foster, 353.
[20] *Davies* v. *Director of Public Prosecutions*, [1954] A.C. 378; [1954] 1 All E.R. 507 (H.L.).
[1] *Cf.*, *Murtagh and Kennedy*, [1955] Crim. L.R. 315.
[2] *Caton* (1874), 12 Cox C.C. 624; *Anderson and Morris*, [1966] 2 Q.B. 110; [1966] 2 All E.R. 644.
[3] *Betts and Ridley* (1930), 22 Cr. App. Rep. 148 (C.C.A.).
[4] *Larkin*, [1943] 1 All E.R. 217 (C.C.A.); below, p. 220, footnote 6.
[5] *Smith*, [1964] Crim. L.R. 129 (C.C.A.); *Betty* (1963), 48 Cr. App. Rep. 6 (C.C.A.).
[6] 48 Cr. App. Rep. 6 at p. 10.

These examples concern possible liability by abetting. The same principles govern liability by counselling. Foster, in a passage which has been relied on by the Court of Criminal Appeal in a case concerning abetting,[7] stated the law as follows:

> "If the principal totally and substantially varieth, if being solicited to commit a felony of one kind he wilfully and knowingly committeth a felony of another, he shall stand single in that offence, and the person soliciting will not be involved in his guilt. . . . But if the principal in substance complieth with the temptation, varying only in circumstance of time or place, or in the manner of execution, in these cases the person soliciting to the offence will, if absent, be an accessory before the fact, if present a principal."

Similarly, the counsellor is not liable where the principal deliberately commits an offence of the same kind as that counselled upon a different subject: thus D is not liable if he advises E to kill X and E intentionally kills Y; or to burn X's house and he intentionally burns Y's; or to steal X's bicycle and he intentionally steals X's car. But D is liable if he advises E to poison X and he shoots him; or to rob X when he is returning home at night and he robs him when he is going to work in the morning.

What is the position where E commits the very same crime counselled by D, but does so in circumstances materially different from those foreseen by D? In a South African case,[8] D1, D2 and E agreed with P that E should kill P to procure the money for which P's life was insured and to avoid P's prosecution for fraud. At the last moment, P withdrew his consent to die but E nevertheless killed him. It was not proved that D1 and D2 foresaw the possibility that E might kill P even if he withdrew his consent and that they had been reckless whether he did so kill him. It was held that the common purpose was murder with the consent of the victim and that E had acted outside that common purpose. D1 and D2, accordingly, were not guilty of murder—though they were guilty of attempted murder, since E had reached the stage of an attempt before P withdrew his consent. HOLMES, J.A., dissenting, thought ". . . looking squarely at the whole train of events, the conspiracy was fulfilled in death, and there is no room for exquisite niceties of logic about the exact limits of the mandate in the conspiratorial common purpose." It is submitted that the better view is that of the majority. If E knows that a condition precedent of the agreement has not been performed, he is no longer engaged on the joint enterprise. If D conspires with E that E shall murder P if he finds out that P is committing adultery with D's wife and E, having discovered that P is not committing adultery, nevertheless kills him, D should not be liable for murder, though he remains liable for conspiracy to murder.

According to Foster,[9] the doctrine of transferred malice[10] applies to counsellors: that is, if D advises E to kill X and E shoots at X, misses and kills Y, D is guilty of the murder of Y; or if D advises E to burn X's house and the flames spread and burn Y's house, D is guilty of arson of Y's house. The difference between these cases and those considered in the preceding paragraph is that here D's departure from his instructions is an accidental result of his attempt to execute them; there, D is not attempting to execute his instructions but has

---

[7] *Crown Law*, 369, quoted in *Betts and Ridley* (1930), 22 Cr. App. Rep. 148 at p. 155.
[8] *S. v. Robinson and Others*, 1968 (1) S.A. 666.
[9] *Crown Law*, 370.
[10] Above, p. 44.

6*

embarked on a new and independent enterprise. The distinction is thought to be sound in principle.

The old and famous case of *Saunders and Archer*,[11] in its result at least, is reconcilable with it. D1, intending to murder his wife, on the advice of D2, gave her a poisoned apple to eat. She ate a little of it and gave the rest to their child. D1 loved the child, yet he stood by and watched it eat the poison, of which it soon died. It was held that D1 was guilty of murder, but the judges agreed that D2, who, of course, was not present when the child ate the apple, was not an accessory to this murder.

If D1 had been absent when the child ate the apple it is thought that this would have been a case of transferred malice and D2 would have been liable; but D1's presence and failure to act made the killing of the child, in effect, a deliberate, and not an accidental, departure from the agreed plan. It was—as it is well put in Kenny,[12]

> "as if Saunders had changed his mind and on a later occasion had used such poison as Archer had named in order to murder some quite different person of whom Archer had never heard."

Foster, however, stated the rule rather more widely than this:[13]

> "So whenever the principal goeth beyond the terms of the solicitation, *if in the event the felony committed was a probable consequence of what was ordered or advised*, the person giving such orders or advice will be an accessory to that felony."

This would make a counsellor liable for negligence in failing to foresee what he ought, as a reasonable man, to have foreseen, which, it is submitted, would be going too far. It is true that he may be held liable for negligently unforeseen consequences where the principal in the first degree may likewise be held liable,[14] but, where the crime is one requiring *mens rea*, it is submitted that actual foresight of the consequences in question must be proved equally for the counsellor as for the abettor. Take the following case: D advises E to steal money from P's house by breaking the gas-meter from the wall. E does so, with the result that the gas escapes and P is injured. It is established that E is guilty of maliciously administering a noxious thing[15] only if he actually foresaw that injury of the particular kind might be caused.[16]

Foster's rule would fix D with liability simply because the result was a probable consequence of his action. It is submitted that the true rule is that the counsellor must have such foresight of the consequence of his action as is necessary for the conviction of the principal in the first degree. In this example, D may be convicted, only if he foresaw the likelihood that the coal gas would be administered to someone.

5   Conviction of Secondary Party and Acquittal of Principal in the First Degree

Even if the alleged principal has been acquitted, a conviction of another as

---

[11] (1576), 2 Plowden 473.
[12] *Outlines*, 112.
[13] *Crown Law*, 370. See, to the same effect, Stephen, *Digest*, Art 20.
[14] *Baldessare* (1930), 22 Cr. App. Rep. 70.
[15] Offences against the Person Act 1861, s. 23; below, p. 269.
[16] *Cunningham*, [1957] 2 Q.B. 396; [1957] 2 All E.R. 412; below, p. 270, footnote 19.

abettor or counsellor may be logical. This is so even if it is assumed[17] that a secondary party may be convicted only when the principal himself is guilty. The acquittal of the alleged principal, so far from being conclusive that no crime was committed, would not even be admitted as evidence at a subsequent trial of the secondary parties.[18] A second jury may be satisfied beyond reasonable doubt that the crime was committed upon evidence which the first jury found unconvincing; evidence may be admissible against the secondary party which was not admissible against the principal, or fresh evidence may have come to light or the principal may have been acquitted because the prosecution offered no evidence against him. The position would seem to be the same where the secondary party is tried first and convicted and the principal is subsequently acquitted[19] and when the parties are jointly indicted. In *Hughes*,[20] after the prosecution had offered no evidence against E, he was acquitted and called as a witness for the Crown, with the result that D was convicted by the same jury as an accessory before the fact to E's alleged crime. But in *Anthony*[1] it was said, *obiter*, that a jury cannot acquit E and at the same time find D guilty of counselling him to commit the crime. If E and D are tried together and the evidence tending to show that E committed the crime is the same against both, then it would be inconsistent to acquit E and convict D.[2] Where, however, there is evidence admissible against D but not against E that E committed the crime (as, for example, a confession by D that he saw E committing the crime and went to assist him) it would be perfectly logical to acquit E and convict D of abetting him. In *Humphreys and Turner*,[3] which was just such a case, CHAPMAN, J., held that D might be convicted, distinguishing the dicta in *Anthony* as applicable only to felonies. It is submitted that, since the Criminal Law Act 1967 came into force, the rule stated in *Humphreys and Turner* is applicable to all offences.

6 Conviction of Secondary Party where there is no Principal

It is one thing for a court which is trying D2 alone to reject or ignore the holding of another court that D1 was not a principal in the first degree and to hold that he was; and that, therefore, D2 might be convicted as a secondary party to D1's crime. It is quite another thing for a court to hold at one and the same time, (i) that D1 was, in law, not guilty[4] and (ii) that D2 was guilty, as a

---

[17] Contrary to the view expressed below, p. 94.

[18] *Remillard* v. *R.* (1921), 62 S.C.R. 21 at p. 26: "As between Romeo Remillard and the Crown the verdict of the jury who tried him is no doubt conclusive as to the nature of his crime. As between Joseph Remillard and the Crown it determines nothing": *per* ANGLIN, J. The rule in *Hollington* v. *Hewthorn*, [1943] K.B. 587; [1943] 2 All E.R. 35, though repealed for civil cases by the Civil Evidence Act 1968, will continue to apply in criminal cases.

[19] In *Rowley*, [1948] 1 All E.R. 570, D's conviction was quashed when, after he had pleaded guilty as an accessory after the fact, the alleged principals were acquitted by the jury. While in the particular circumstances the quashing of the conviction was, with respect, justifiable, HUMPHREYS, J.'s *dictum*, "As a result, there is error on the record which cannot be erased by amendment", seems inconsistent with principle. See [1958] 3 All E.R. 300 at p. 303.

[20] (1860), Bell C.C. 242.

[1] [1965] 1 All E.R. 440. *Cf. Surujpaul* v. *R.*, [1958] 3 All E.R. 300 at pp. 302–303.

[2] *Surujpaul* v. *R.*, [1958] 3 All E.R. 300.

[3] [1965] 3 All E.R. 689.

[4] Not merely that there was not enough evidence to convict him, but that there was evidence which established his innocence.

secondary party, of D1's crime. These propositions seem to be inconsistent and irreconcilable with a passage in Russell[5] which has received judicial approval:[6]

> ". . . when the law relating to principals and accessories as such is under consideration there is only one crime, although there may be more than one person criminally liable in respect of it; . . . There is one crime, and that it has been committed must be established before there can be any question of criminal guilt of participation in it."

This seems, indeed, to be an obvious enough principle: a man cannot be guilty of having abetted a crime, or counselled it, unless the crime has actually been committed by the principal offender. But, with great respect, it is not entirely clear that it can be accepted without qualification. In the first place it is clear that, where two crimes have the same *actus reus* and the principal is convicted of the greater crime, an abettor may be convicted of the less. So if a passenger in a car urges the driver to drive close to P so as to frighten him, and the driver deliberately runs him over and kills him, the driver is guilty of murder and the passenger of manslaughter.[7] The *actus reus* is the same for both crimes, but the *mens rea* differs, and each party is held liable to the extent of his own *mens rea*. This case might be justified on the ground that the greater includes the less and, therefore, that the abettor's crime being included within murder, has been committed by the principal. But this reasoning cannot be applied to a case where the abettor is convicted of a greater crime. According to Hawkins[8]

> "if there were malice in the abettor, and none in the person who struck the party it will be murder as to the abettor, and manslaughter only as to the other".

Hawkins thus contemplates the possibility of a person being convicted as an abettor of a crime which the principal cannot be said to have committed in any sense, except that he has caused the *actus reus*. Illogical though this sounds, it is very sensible in result; for, if the person actually doing the killing had a complete defence, (for example, insanity) the "abettor" would be liable as the principal offender. Why should his guilt be less because the killer has only a partial defence? Take the following case: E, accompanied by his friend D, returns to his home and finds his wife in the act of adultery. D, who is perfectly self-possessed, at once cries out, "Kill her!" and E, deprived of his self-control, instantly does so.

As will appear below,[9] E, in these circumstances, has the defence of provocation, which reduces to manslaughter a killing which would otherwise be murder. If D had done the killing with his own hand, no such defence would be available to him. Why, then, should he be able to shelter behind E's defence?[10]

Though Hawkins thought that the abettor might be guilty of a greater crime than the principal in the first degree, he was emphatic that the rule was otherwise with respect to accessories before the fact:

> "I take it to be an uncontroverted rule [that the offence of the accessory can never rise higher than that of the principal]; it seeming incongruous and absurd

---

[5] 12th ed. by J. W. C. Turner, 128.
[6] *Surujpaul* v. *R.*, [1958] 3 All E.R. at p. 310 (P.C.).
[7] *Murtagh and Kennedy*, [1955] Crim. L.R. 315.
[8] 2 P.C., c. 29, § 7. To the same effect, see East, 1 P.C. 350.
[9] See p. 207.
[10] In the Canadian case of *Remillard* v. *R.* (1921), 62 S.C.R. 21, it was held that the defence was not available.

that he who is punished only as a partaker of the guilt of another, should be adjudged guilty of a higher crime than the other. And therefore it seems clear that if a wife or servant cause a stranger to murder the husband or master, and are absent when the murder is committed, they cannot be said to be accessories to petit treason, but to murder only, because the offence of the principal is but murder. But if such wife or servant had been present when the murder was committed, they would have been guilty of petit treason, and the stranger of murder."[11]

With respect, it would seem no less incongruous and absurd to distinguish between the principal in the second degree and accessory before in this way. D gives E a poison, telling him that it is an emetic, and suggests that he adminster it secretly to P in order to cause him discomfort. If E does so and P dies, E is probably guilty of manslaughter. It would seem absurd that D's liability for murder should depend on whether he was present or absent when the poison was administered. Equally it would seem absurd that D should be guilty of murder if he had told E that it was a medicine which would do P good, and of manslaughter if he told him that it was something which would cause P pain. Even if Hawkins stated the law correctly for felonies, however, it is submitted that no such distinction can be drawn between abettors and counsellors of misdemeanours, the law of which now applies to all offences. If D, in the above examples, knew that the medicine would kill, surely he should be liable for murder in both cases.

The true principle, it is suggested, is that where the principal has caused an *actus reus*, the liability of each of the secondary parties should be assessed according to his own *mens rea*. If there is no *actus reus*, then certainly no one can be convicted.

In *Morris* v. *Tolman*,[12] D was charged with abetting the owner of a vehicle in using that vehicle for a purpose for which the vehicle had not been licensed. The statute (the Roads Act 1920) was so phrased that the offence could be committed only by the licence-holder. It was held that, there being no evidence that the licence-holder had used the vehicle for a purpose other than that for which it was licensed, D must be acquitted. Though he, in fact, had used the vehicle, that was not an *actus reus*. Again, in *Thornton* v. *Mitchell*,[13] D, a bus conductor, negligently signalled to the driver of his bus to reverse, so that two pedestrians, whom it was not possible for the driver to see, were knocked down and one of them killed. The driver having been acquitted of careless driving, it was held that the conductor must be acquitted of abetting.[14] Again, there was no *actus reus*. The driver's acquittal shows that he committed no *actus reus*, for careless driving is a crime which requires no *mens rea* beyond an intention to drive and D could not be said to have driven the bus. There would have been no such obstacle in the way of convicting D for manslaughter. That would simply have raised the question whether D's negligence was sufficiently great.[15]

An alternative way of looking at these cases would be to say that in each of them D was not liable because he was incapable of being a principal offender,

---

[11] 2 P.C., c. 29, § 15.
[12] [1923] 1 K.B. 166.
[13] [1940] 1 All E.R. 339.
[14] Yet, if the conductor had been charged with abetting dangerous driving, he should have been convicted; for the driving, though not careless, was dangerous: *Ball and Loughlin* (1966), 50 Cr. App. Rep. 266, above, p. 65.
[15] See above, p. 54, and below, p. 222.

not being a licence-holder or a driver, respectively.[16] This rule, however, would produce unsatisfactory results in a number of situations. It is well settled that a person can be convicted as a secondary party to a crime which he is personally incapable of committing as a principal offender. Thus a woman[17] or a boy under fourteen[18] could be convicted of abetting a rape; a bachelor could be convicted of abetting a bigamous marriage. Should the boy, or the woman or the bachelor be acquitted because the person committing the rape, or the person going through the ceremony of marriage was insane, or lacked *mens rea*, or was exempt from criminal liability for some other reason? D's conduct would certainly be none the less heinous, and though incapable of committing an *actus reus* personally, D would have caused one to occur and have done so with *mens rea*. It does not seem feasible to extend the doctrine of the innocent agent to this situation. If D, through an innocent agent, has killed P, it is not unreasonable for the indictment to state, "D . . . murdered P". If D, a bachelor procures E to go through a ceremony of marriage, it would be quite plainly untrue for the indictment to state, "D . . . married . . ., during the life of his wife . . ." for he did not marry anyone, nor did he have a wife. Is there any reason why the indictment should not state, "E . . . married F, during the life of his wife . . . D . . . was present, aiding, abetting and assisting the said E to commit the said crime"? There is one case where the result at least supports this view, though the reasoning on which it is based is very far from clear. In *Bourne*,[19] D, by duress, compelled his wife to have connection with a dog. He was charged with abetting her to commit buggery. It was argued that, as the wife could not be convicted, since she acted under the coercion of her husband,[20] he must be acquitted. This argument was rejected. The Court of Criminal Appeal assumed that the wife was entitled to be acquitted, but held that, nevertheless, D's conviction as an abettor could stand.[1] Williams has suggested that Bourne

> "could well have been convicted of the substantive crime as principal in the first degree, acting through the innocent agency of his wife".[2]

It is, with respect, difficult to follow this, for there is the same difficulty over the indictment as with the bigamy example. An allegation that "Bourne . . . committed buggery with a dog" would not have been true. If, however, Williams is correct, it is submitted that there is no reason why, in the bigamy example, D should not also be convicted as a principal offender. It is thought, however, that to hold that abetting (with *mens rea*) of a mere *actus reus* is indictable, is a more elegant solution and is in accordance with the authorities.

7   Mens Rea of Secondary Parties

The question whether it must be proved that a secondary party *desires* the commission of the crime has already been considered. It has also been observed that a secondary party may be held liable for unforeseen *consequences* of the joint

---

[16] See Williams, C.L.G.P., §§ 120, 129 (4).
[17] *Ram and Ram* (1893), 17 Cox C.C. 609.
[18] *Eldershaw* (1828), 3 C. & P. 396, *per* VAUGHAN, B. See below, p. 112.
[19] (1952), 36 Cr. App. Rep. 125 (C.C.A.); *cf. Kemp and Else*, below, p. 486.
[20] See below, p. 145
[1] For further discussion of this case, see Edwards (1953), 69 L.Q.R. 226, and Cross (1953), 69 L.Q.R. 354.
[2] C.L.G.P., § 129 at p. 389.

enterprise to the same extent as the principal. As to the *circumstances*, the rule is different; it seems now to be quite clear it is necessary that the secondary party should always have full *mens rea* in the sense of knowledge of, or wilful blindness towards, the circumstances which must be proved in order to constitute the offence:

> "Before a person can be convicted of aiding and abetting the commission of an offence he must at least know the essential matters which constitute that offence. He need not actually know that an offence has been committed, because he may not know that the facts constitute an offence and ignorance of the law is not a defence."[3]

This principle applies even in the case of an offence of strict liability: in such a crime the principal offender may, but an abettor may not, be convicted without *mens rea*. The reason is that abetting is a common law notion. It was never necessary for a statute creating an offence to specify that it should also be an offence to abet or counsel it. The common law, now codified in the Accessories and Abettors Act 1861,[4] was that so to act created liability to conviction of the offence abetted or counselled. It is natural that the normal principles of liability at common law should apply. The result, however, is to emphasise the anomalous nature of offences of strict liability, for the alleged abettor who has no *mens rea* must be acquitted even if he was negligent[5] whereas the principal who has caused the *actus reus* must be convicted even if he took all proper care.

In *Callow* v. *Tillstone*,[6] D, a veterinary surgeon was charged with abetting the exposure for sale of unsound meat. At the request of a butcher, G, he examined the carcase of a heifer which had eaten yew leaves and been killed by the farmer just before it would have died of yew poisoning. He gave G a certificate that the meat was sound. The examination had been negligently conducted and the meat was tainted. G, relying on the certificate, exposed the meat for sale and was convicted. The justices, holding that D's negligence had caused the exposure, convicted him of abetting. It was held that his conviction must be quashed.[7]

Thus, if Prince[8] had been assisted by a friend, D, who had driven him away with the girl in a hansom cab, it would have been a defence for D (even though it was not for Prince) to show that he believed the girl to be over sixteen or even that he did not know what age she was.

8 Repentance by Secondary Party

If D, having counselled E to commit a crime, or being present, abetting E in the commission of it, withdraws from the project before the crime is constituted

---

[3] *Johnson* v. *Youden*, [1950] 1 K.B. 544 at p. 546; (*cf.* [1950] 1 All E.R. 300 at p. 302) *per* Lord GODDARD, C.J.; see above, pp. 48–49. See also *Ackroyds Air Travel, Ltd.* v. *Director of Public Prosecutions*, [1950] 1 All E.R. 933 at p. 936; *Thomas* v. *Lindop*, [1950] 1 All E.R. 966 at p. 968; *Ferguson* v. *Weaving*, [1951] 1 K.B. 814; [1951] 1 All E.R. 412; *Bateman* v. *Evans* (1964), 108 Sol. Jo. 522; *Smith* v. *Jenner*, [1968] Crim. L.R. 99. *Lenzi* v. *Miller* (1965), S.A.S.R. 1 is to the contrary, but seems to confuse aiding and abetting with vicarious liability.
[4] Above p. 80. *Cf. McCarthy*, [1964] Crim. L.R. 225.
[5] *Carter* v. *Mace*, [1949] 2 All E. R. 714 (D.C.) is to the contrary, but in *Davies, Turner & Co., Ltd.* v. *Brodie*, [1954] 3 All E.R. 283 (D.C.) that case was said to lay down no principle of law and to be decided on its own particular facts. See J. Montgomerie in (1950), 66 L.Q.R. 222.
[6] (1900), 83 L.T. 411 (D.C.).
[7] See also *Bowker* v. *Premier Drug Co., Ltd.*, [1928] 1 K.B. 217 at p. 227.
[8] Above, p. 42.

and communicates his withdrawal to E, he may escape liability for the contemplated crime—but not necessarily for incitement or conspiracy. Even a communicated withdrawal may leave D liable if he neglects to avert a danger which he has helped to create.[9] The *mens rea* must coincide[10] with the act of counselling, not necessarily with the commission of the counselled offence. If D repents but does not communicate his repentance, according to such authority as there is, he remains liable.[11] What, however, is the position where D has no means of communicating with E? If he has sold E safebreaking equipment, does he continue liable for E's breakings[12] after he has become a reformed character and repented of his criminality? It must surely be an effective withdrawal to advise the police of the proposed crime, but it is not clear in what other way, if any, D can escape liability.

If D's withdrawal is involuntary, as where he is arrested before E completes the crime, he will be liable as a counsellor or even an abettor if, though in custody, he is still assisting or encouraging E.[13]

9   Victims as Parties to Crime[14]

It has been noted[15] that when a statute creates a crime it does not generally provide that it shall be an offence to aid, abet, counsel or procure it. Such a provision is unnecessary, for it follows by implication of law. There is, however, one exception to this rule. Where the statute is designed expressly for the protection of a certain class of persons it may be construed as excluding by implication the liability of any member of that class of persons who is the victim of the offence, even though that member does in fact aid, abet, counsel or procure the offence.

In *Tyrrell*[16] D, a girl between the ages of thirteen and sixteen, abetted E to have unlawful sexual intercourse with her. This was an offence by E under the Criminal Law Amendment Act 1885, s. 5.[17] It was held, however, that D could not be convicted of abetting because the Act

> "was passed for the purpose of protecting women and girls against themselves."[18]

The decisions on sodomy with boys under the age of fourteen seem to be explicable only on the assumption that the courts have applied a similar principle.[19] On the other hand, it has been held that a woman who is not pregnant can be convicted of abetting the use upon herself by another of an instrument with intent to procure her miscarriage, although the clear implication of the

---

[9] Williams, C.L.G.P., § 127.
[10] Above, p. 46.
[11] Hale, 1 P.C. 618; Stephen, *Digest* (4th ed.) Art 42; Williams, C.L.G.P., § 127; *Croft*, [1944] 1 K.B. 295; [1944] 2 All E.R. 483.
[12] Above, p. 87.
[13] *Craig and Bentley*, below, p. 201.
[14] Hogan, [1962] Crim. L.R. 683.
[15] Above, pp. 94–95.
[16] [1894] 1 Q.B. 710.
[17] See now Sexual Offences Act 1956, s.6; below, p. 296.
[18] *Per* Lord COLERIDGE, C.J., at p. 712. Both the Chief Justice and MATHEW, J., pointed out that there was nothing in the Act to say that the girl should be guilty of aiding and abetting; but, it is submitted, no importance could be attached to that, for statutes hardly ever do.
[19] Below, p. 112.

statute[1] is that such a woman cannot be convicted of *using* an instrument on herself with that intent.[2] However, a pregnant woman can be convicted under the same section of using an instrument on herself so it cannot be argued that this section was passed for the protection of *women* and it would be curious that Parliament should have intended to protect non-pregnant women from themselves, but not pregnant women.

How far the rule in *Tyrrell* extends has not been settled. The court referred to "women" as well as girls; and it may well be that it extends to the offences of procuration of women to be prostitutes and of brothel keeping which were in the 1885 Act and are now in the Sexual Offences Act 1956.[3] It will obviously extend to intercourse with girls under thirteen and defectives;[4] to permitting premises to be used for intercourse with young girls and defectives;[5] and to at least some offences of abduction.[6] It is not settled whether it applies to the prostitute who abets a man who is living off her earnings; but it is thought that the better view is that she cannot be convicted.[7]

In all these cases, it seems clear that the protection of the law extends only to a person of the class who is a *victim*. Thus it is thought, a girl under sixteen could be convicted of abetting E in having intercourse with another girl, P; a boy of fourteen could be convicted of abetting E in sodomy with another boy under fourteen; a prostitute could abet E in keeping a brothel in which she was not a participant, or of living off the earnings of another prostitute.

Though it is obviously in the field of sexual offences that this rule will find its major sphere of operation, it should be noted that it is not confined to such cases and may, for example, be applied to a tenant in respect of criminal legislation passed to protect tenants.[8]

10 Instigation for the Purpose of Entrapment

A policeman or other law enforcement officer or his agent may have a defence when he knowingly does acts which amount to counselling or abetting an offence if his sole purpose is to entrap the principal offender. So in *Mullins*[9] when D, who was apparently acting with the authority of the police, attended a treasonable conspiracy, endeavoured to persuade strangers to join in and advocated the use of violence, MAULE, J., rejected an argument that D's evidence required corroboration as that of an accomplice. A person employed by the government as a spy does not deserve to be blamed

"if he instigates offences no further than by pretending to concur with the perpetrators."[10]

D's conduct, in fact, seems to have gone somewhat further than this. This was

---

[1] Offences against the Person Act 1861, s. 58; below, p. 243.
[2] *Sockett* (1908), 72 J.P. 428; below, p. 244.
[3] Below, p. 308 *et seq.*
[4] Below, p. 296 and 298.
[5] Below, p. 299.
[6] Below, p. 305. The rule was not applied in a Tasmanian case of abduction of a girl under eighteen: *Preston*, [1962] Tas. S.R. 141; but this turned on the construction of the Tasmanian Criminal Code.
[7] Hogan, [1962] Crim. L.R. at pp. 692–693.
[8] *Grace Rymer Investments, Ltd.* v. *Waite*, [1958] Ch. 831; [1958] 2 All E.R. 777.
[9] (1848), 3 Cox C.C. 526.
[10] *Ibid.* at p. 531.

certainly so in *Bickley*[11] where D, a woman acting on behalf of the police, asked E to give her something to procure an abortion and was held not to be an accomplice.

On the other hand, Lord GODDARD, C.J., expressed disapproval of such conduct in *Brannan* v. *Peek*:[12]

> "If . . . a bookmaker commits an offence by taking a bet in a public house, it is just as much an offence for a police constable to make a bet with him in a public house, and it is quite wrong that the police officer should be instructed to commit this offence."

Notwithstanding these remarks, it is probable that the police officer does have a defence in these circumstances, should he be charged. It would be wise, however, for police authorities to bear in mind the recommendation of the Royal Commission on Police Powers:[13]

> "As a general rule, the police should observe only, without participating in an offence, except in cases where an offence is habitually committed in circumstances in which observation by a third party is *ex hypothesi* impossible. Where participation is essential it should only be resorted to on the express and written authority of the Chief Constable."

With these cases may be compared that of *Smith*[14] where a private citizen took it upon himself to instigate crime with the object of procuring a conviction and was himself convicted. But even in the case of a private citizen it should be a defence to pretend to concur with the perpetrators[15] merely for the purpose of betraying them—as where a taxi-driver drives burglars to the scene of the crime, with the intention of fetching police when he has left them there.

2 VICARIOUS LIABILITY[16]

In the law of tort, a master is held liable for all acts of his servant performed in the course of the servant's employment. In the criminal law, a master is generally not so liable. In the leading civil case of *Lloyd* v. *Grace, Smith & Co.*[17] a solicitor's managing clerk, without the knowledge of his employer, induced a widow to give him instructions to sell certain property, to hand over the title deeds and to sign two documents which were neither read over nor explained to her, but which she believed were necessary for the sale. The documents were, in fact, a conveyance to the clerk of the property, of which he dishonestly disposed for his own benefit. It was held that, since the clerk was acting within the scope of his authority, his employer was liable. Now it is very likely that the clerk was guilty of certain criminal offences—perhaps larceny of the title deeds and fraudulent conversion of the money; but it is perfectly clear that his employer could never have been made criminally liable for those acts for which he bore civil liability. An employer is similarly liable in tort where the fraud in-

---

[11] (1909), 73 J.P. 239 (C.C.A.). See also *Browning* v. *J. W. H. Watson (Rochester), Ltd.,* [1953] 2 All E.R. 775 (D.C.); *Marsh* v. *Johnston,* [1959] Crim. L.R. 444.
[12] [1948] 1 K.B. 68 at p. 72 (*cf.* [1947] 2 All E.R. 572 at pp. 573, 574).
[13] Cmd. 3297 (1928), 116.
[14] [1960] 2 Q.B. 423; [1960] 1 All E.R. 256; above p. 78.
[15] See *Mullins*, footnote 9, above.
[16] Williams, C.L.G.P., Ch. 7, and "*Mens Rea* and Vicarious Responsibility" ((1956) 9 C.L.P. 57; F. B. Sayer "Criminal Responsibility for the Acts of Another" 1930), 43, Harv. L. R. 689; Baty, *Vicarious Liability* (1916), especially Ch. X.
[17] [1912] A.C. 716 (H.L.).

volves a forgery,[18] and for acts which amount to obtaining by deception, assault and battery, manslaughter and so on; but in none of these cases would he be criminally liable simply on the ground that his servant was acting in the course of his employment. The doctrine of vicarious liability in tort developed in the early part of the eighteenth century, but it was made clear by the leading case of *Huggins*[19] that there was to be no parallel development in the criminal law. Huggins, the warden of the Fleet, was charged with the murder of a prisoner whose death had been caused by the servant of Huggins's deputy. It was held that, though the servant was guilty, Huggins was not, since the acts were done without his knowledge. RAYMOND, C.J., said:[20]

> "It is a point not to be disputed, but that in criminal cases the principal is not answerable for the act of the deputy as he is in civil cases: they must each answer for their own acts, and stand or fall by their own behaviour. All the authors that treat of criminal proceedings proceed on the foundation of this distinction; that to affect the superior by the act of his deputy, there must be the command of the superior which is not found in this case."

A master can be held liable for his servants' crimes, as a general rule, only where he is a participant in them within the rules stated in the preceding section. Two exceptions to this have already been noted:[1] in public nuisance and criminal libel a master has been held liable for his servants' acts although he is, personally, perfectly innocent. These were the only exceptions at common law; but now, by statute, there are many such offences.

1 Strict Liability and Vicarious Liability Distinguished

Vicarious liability is by no means the same thing as strict liability. The point requires emphasis for there is an unhappy judicial tendency to confuse the two concepts. A statute may require *mens rea* and yet impose vicarious responsibility. It has already been noted that supplying liquor to a constable on duty is an offence requiring *mens rea*,[2] yet a licensee may be vicariously liable for his servants' act in so doing[3] and the same considerations apply to the offence of suffering gaming to be carried on in licensed premises.[4] Conversely, it is clearly possible for a statute to create strict liability without imposing vicarious responsibility. When the courts have once held that a statute imposes strict liability, then it is very probable that they will take the further step of holding it to impose vicarious liability also.[5] But there is no logical reason which compels such a holding; and in some offences which are now held to impose strict liability—like dangerous driving[6]—it is inconceivable that a master will be held vicariously liable.

---

[18] *Uxbridge Permanent Building Society* v. *Pickard*, [1939] 2 K.B. 248; [1939] 2 All E.R. 344.

[19] (1730), 2 Stra. 883.

[20] *Ibid.*, at p. 885.

[1] Above, p. 60 and see "Contempt of Court", below, p. 529.

[2] *Sherras* v. *De Rutzen*, above p. 63.

[3] *Mullins* v. *Collins* (1874), L.R. 9 Q.B. 292.

[4] *Bosley* v. *Davies* (1875), 1 Q.B.D. 84 (*mens rea* required); *Bond* v. *Evans* (1888), 21 Q.B.D. 249 (licensee liable for servants' acts); Licensing Act 1872, s. 16.

[5] *Dicta* to the effect that an offence of strict liability necessarily imposes vicarious responsibility are not difficult to find: see, *e.g.*, *Barker* v. *Levinson*, [1951] 1 K.B. 342 at p. 345; [1950] 2 All E.R. 825 at p. 827; *James & Son, Ltd.* v. *Smee*, [1955] 1 Q.B. 78 at p. 95; [1954] 3 All E.R. 273 at p. 280, *per* SLADE, J.

[6] See above, p. 65.

As in the case of strict liability, so with vicarious liability it may well be argued that the development is the work of the courts rather than of Parliament. A statute rarely, if ever, says in terms that a master is to be liable for his servants' crimes. It is not uncommon, however, for the courts to detect such an intention in statutes which create summary offences. The reason most commonly advanced by the judges for holding a master liable is that the statute would be "rendered nugatory"[7]—and the will of Parliament thereby defeated—if he were not. Two quite distinct principles, differing somewhat in their effect, underlie the various decisions. In the first place, a person may be held liable for the acts of another where he has delegated to that other the performance of certain duties cast on him by Act of Parliament. In the second place, a master may be held liable because acts which are done physically by the servant may, in law, be the master's acts. These two types of case require separate consideration.

2   The Delegation Principle

A good illustration of the application of this principle may be found in the case of *Allen* v. *Whitehead*.[8]   Under the Metropolitan Police Act 1839, s. 44, it is an offence to

> "knowingly permit or suffer prostitutes or persons of notoriously bad character to meet together and remain in a place where refreshments are sold and consumed".

D, the occupier of a café, while receiving the profits of the business, did not himself manage it, but employed a manager. Having had a warning from the police, D instructed his manager that no prostitutes were to be allowed to congregate on the premises and had a notice to that effect displayed on the walls. He visited the premises once or twice a week and there was no evidence that any misconduct took place in his presence. Then, on eight consecutive days, a number of women, known to the manager to be prostitutes, met together and remained there between the hours of 8 p.m. and 4 a.m. It was held by the Divisional Court, reversing the Metropolitan Magistrate, that D's ignorance of the facts was no defence. The acts of the servant and his *mens rea* were both to be imputed to his master, not simply because he was a servant, but because the management of the house had been delegated to him.

So in *Linnet* v. *Metropolitan Police Commissioner*[9] it was held, following *Allen* v. *Whitehead*,[8] that one of two co-licensees was liable for the acts of the other in knowingly permitting disorderly conduct in the licensed premises, contrary to s. 44 of the same Act, although the other was neither his servant nor his partner,[10] but simply his delegate in "keeping" the premises.

The argument that vicarious responsibility is necessary to make the statute operative applies with especial force to cases of this type. Where the statute is so phrased that the offence can be committed only by the master, there would indeed be a real difficulty in making the statute effective without vicarious liability. Under the Metropolitan Police Act 1839, s. 44, the offence may be

---

[7] *Mullins* v. *Collins* (1874), L.R. 9 Q.B. 292 at p. 295, *per* BLACKBURN and QUAIN, JJ.; *Coppen* v. *Moore* (*No. 2*), [1898] 2 Q.B. 306 at p. 314, *per* Lord RUSSELL C.J.; *Allen* v. *Whitehead, infra.*

[8] [1930] 1 K.B. 211.

[9] [1946] K.B. 290; [1946] 1 All E.R. 380.

[10] Both were, in fact, the employees of a limited company. The company was not charged, no doubt for the good reason that it was not the licensee.

committed only by a person "who shall *have or keep* any house . . .". Presumably the manager in *Allen* v. *Whitehead* was not such a person and if, therefore, the absentee "keeper" were not liable for his manager's acts, the statute could be ignored with impunity. The position is the same in many of the offences under the Licensing Acts; only the licensee can commit the offences. The difficulty has been well put by Lord RUSSELL, C.J.:[11]

> "We may take as an illustration the case of a sporting publican who attends race-meetings all over the country, and leaves a manager in charge of his public-house; is it to be said that there is no remedy under this section[12] if drink is sold by the manager in charge to any number of drunken persons? It is clear that there is no machinery by which the person actually selling can be convicted; a penalty can only be inflicted on the licensee."

In all these cases concerning licences the doctrine comes into play only when—as in *Allen* v. *Whitehead*—the licensee has delegated the management of the premises to another.[13] The authority for this proposition is *Somerset* v. *Hart*.[14] While D the licensee was serving in the bar, the potman permitted gaming to take place in another room. There was no evidence of knowledge or wilful blindness on D's part and the court held that he was rightly acquitted. Lord COLERIDGE, C.J., said:[15]

> "where no actual knowledge is shown there must, as it seems to me, be something to show either that the gaming took place with the knowledge of some person clothed with the landlord's authority, or that there was something like connivance on his part . . ."

If the licensee's delegate sub-delegates his responsibilities, the licensee is liable for the sub-delegate's acts,[16] but he is not liable for the acts of an inferior servant to whom control of the premises has not been delegated.[17]

It seems clear, however, that the delegation need by no means be so complete as that which took place in *Allen* v. *Whitehead*. It may be of part of the premises only (in *Bond* v. *Evans*[18] it was a skittle alley connected with the rest of the premises) and it may be of a most temporary nature (in *Redgate* v. *Haynes*[19] the licensee had merely gone to bed, leaving the hall porter in charge for the night); while in *Police Commissioner* v. *Cartman*[20] the question of delegation seems to have been entirely overlooked. The case seems to have been decided simply on the ground that the act done was within the scope of the servant's employment.[21] While it is necessary that the act should be so done, it is not sufficient unless there has also been a delegation.[1] A licensee whose duties are being performed by

---

[11] In *Police Commissioners* v. *Cartman*, [1896] 1 Q.B. 655 at p. 658.
[12] Licensing Act 1872, s. 13. *Cf. Cundy* v. *Le Cocq*, above, p. 61, which establishes that offence is also one of strict liability.
[13] *Cf.* Williams, C.L.G.P., § 95; Edwards, *Mens Rea*, 226–227.
[14] (1884), 12 Q.B.D. 360; and see *Emary* v. *Nolloth*, [1903] 2 K.B. 264; *McKenna* v. *Harding* (1905), 69 J.P. 354.
[15] (1884), 12 Q.B.D. 360 at p. 364.
[16] *Crabtree* v. *Hole* (1879), 43 J.P. 799.
[17] *Allchorn* v. *Hopkins* (1905), 69 J.P. 355.
[18] (1888), 21 Q.B.D. 249.
[19] (1876), 1 Q.B.D. 89; and see *Crabtree* v. *Hole*, above, footnote 16.
[20] [1896] 1 Q.B. 655.
[21] The evidence showed that the licensee was "a considerable distance away and out of sight of the bar", but *McKenna* v. *Harding* (1905), 69 J.P. 354, establishes that a licensee who is out of sight of the bar, but within call, has not necessarily delegated his responsibility.
[1] *Vane* v. *Yiannopoulos*, [1965] A.C. 486; [1964] 3 All E.R. 820.

another because he has been dismissed is not liable for the other's acts.[2] Some doubt was cast on the validity of the delegation principle by the House of Lords in *Vane* v. *Yiannopoulos*.[3] Since there was no delegation in that case their lord-ships' remarks were *obiter*. Lords MORRIS and DONOVAN could find no statutory authority for the doctrine and, though they did not find it necessary to pronounce on its validity, Lord DONOVAN thought that "If a decision that 'knowingly' means 'knowingly' will make the provision difficult to enforce, the remedy lies with the legislature." Lord REID found the delegation principle hard to justify; but while it may have been unwarranted in the first instance, it was now too late to upset such a long standing practice. Lord EVERSHED thought that a licensee may "fairly and sensibly" be held liable where he has delegated his powers and Lord HODSON expressed no opinion. The doctrine has subsequently been applied in the Divisional Court[4] and the Court of Appeal and it must be presumed that it will continue to apply unimpaired.

3 Where the Servant's Act is his Master's Act in Law

The most obvious application of the second principle occurs in the many cases where "selling" is the central feature of the *actus reus*, under statutes like the Trade Descriptions Act, the Food and Drugs Acts and the Fertilisers and Feed-ing Stuffs Act. Now a "sale" consists in the transfer of property in goods from A to B[5] and the seller, in law, is necessarily the person in whom the property is vested at the commencement of the transaction. It is not a great step, therefore, for the court to say that the employer has committed the *actus reus* of "selling" even though he was nowhere near when the incident took place. In *Coppen* v. *Moore (No. 2)*,[6] D owned six shops, in which he sold American hams. He gave strict instructions that these hams were to be described as "breakfast hams" and were not to be sold under any specific name of place of origin. In the absence of D, and without the knowledge of the manager of the branch, one of the assistants sold a ham as a "Scotch ham". D was convicted, under the Merchandise Marks Act 1887, s. 2 (2), of selling goods "to which any . . . false trade description is applied". Lord RUSSELL, C.J., said:[7]

> "It cannot be doubted that the appellant sold the ham in question, although the transaction was carried out by his servants. In other words he was the seller, although not the actual salesman. It is clear also, as already stated, that the ham was sold with a 'false trade description' which was material. If so, there is evidence establishing a prima facie case of an offence against the Act having been *committed by the appellant*".

The court was clearly influenced by the fact that D (like many other employers) carried on his business in a number of branches and could not possibly be in direct control of each one so that, if actual knowledge of the particular trans-action had to be proved, he could hardly be made liable. The court did not however, apply the principle of delegation which is to be found in the licensing cases. By construing the Act in accordance with the principles of the civil law and so holding that D had himself committed an *actus reus*, the court introduced

---

[2] *Duncan* v. *Hart*, [1968] Crim. L.R. 42.
[3] See footnote 1 on p. 101.
[4] *Ross* v. *Moss*, [1965] 2 Q.B. 396; [1965] 3 All E.R. 145; *Winson*, [1968] 1 All E.R. 197.
[5] This is so in the criminal as well as the civil law: *Watson* v. *Coupland*, [1945] 1 All E.R. 217.
[6] [1898] 2 Q.B. 306.
[7] *Ibid.*, at p. 313.

a more far-reaching principle.[8] Comparison with *Allchorn* v. *Hopkins*[9] will show that, under the delegation principle, D would not have been liable for the act of the assistant to whom control of the premises had not been delegated.[10]

There are many cases not involving a sale where a similar principle has been invoked. Just as it is the master who, in law, "sells" goods with which his servant is actually dealing, so too is he "in possession" of goods which are actually in his servants hands[11] and so can be made liable for offences of "being in possession" (of which there are many[12]) through his servants. A producer of plays "presents" a play even though he may be miles away when it is performed and was liable, under s. 15 of the Theatres Act 1843 (now repealed[13]), if words were introduced, even without his knowledge, which had not been allowed by the Lord Chamberlain.[14]

The owners of a van, supplied to the bailiff of their farm, "keep" a van which is not "used solely for the conveyance of goods or burden in the course of trade" without a licence[15] if the bailiff uses it, without their knowledge or authority, to take his wife for a day out at Clacton.[16] A master "uses" his vehicle in contravention of the Motor Vehicles (Constructions and Use) Regulations if his servant so uses it.[17] It is quite understandable that a court should hold that an employer "presents" a play or "keeps" a vehicle, for these verbs are apt to describe his function and inapt to describe that of his servants. It is less clear that this is so in the case of "uses". This could very well refer to the servant's use and Williams suggests that,[18] as a result of cases like *Green* v. *Burnett*,[19] perhaps,

> "we are now to witness the compiling of a new 'judicial dictionary' which will distinguish between those verbs in respect of which the servant's conduct can be regarded as the master's and those in which it cannot".

4 Mode of Participation of Master and Servant

In those cases where it is only the licensee, keeper of the refreshment house, or other designated person in whom it is an offence to do the act in question, it is apparent that the licensee, etc., who is held vicariously liable is a principal for he alone possesses the personal characteristic which is an essential part of

---

[8] If the same reasoning as that followed in *Coppen* v. *Moore* had been used in the licence cases, where the offence involved "selling", a licensee who owned his stock might have been convicted, notwithstanding the absence of delegation. But this reasoning has not been followed: *McKenna* v. *Harding* (1905), 69 J.P. 354; *Vane* v. *Yiannopoullos*, [1965] A.C. 486; [1964] 3 All E.R. 820. But see *Goodfellow* v. *Johnson*, [1965] 1 All E.R. 941; [1965] Crim. L.R. 304 and commentary thereon.

[9] Above, p. 101, footnote 17.

[10] It was within the scope of the servant's authority in *Coppen* v. *Moore*, above, to sell hams. A master is not liable where a servant boy, who has no authority to sell anything, supplies his master's whisky to a customer out of hours: *Adams* v. *Camfoni*, [1929] 1 K.B. 95. In this case there was no sale by the master.

[11] See below, p. 104.

[12] For examples, see above, p. 78.

[13] See Theatres Act 1968; below, p. 500.

[14] *Grade* v. *Director of Public Prosecutions*, [1942] 2 All E.R. 118. The defendant had, in fact been called up for service in the R.A.F. The result would have been different if D had been charged with "causing" the play to be presented: *Lovelace* v. *Director of Public Prosecutions*, [1954] 3 All E.R. 481, above, p. 77, footnote 3.

[15] Contrary to s. 27 of the Customs and Inland Revenue Duties Act 1869.

[16] *Strutt* v. *Clift*, [1911] 1 K.B. 1.

[17] *Green* v. *Burnett*, [1955] 1 Q.B. 78; [1954] 3 All E.R. 273; and see *Quality Dairies (York), Ltd.* v. *Pedley*, [1952] 1 K.B. 275; [1952] 1 All E.R. 380.

[18] (1956), 9 C.L.P.

[19] Above, footnote 17.

the *actus reus* and no one else is qualified to fill that role. The servant who actually performs the act is plainly incapable of being a principal, but it seems that he may be convicted as an abettor,[20]—strange though this appears when he is the only participant in the crime who is present.

Where the *actus reus* does not include a personal characteristic of the master and the servant is capable of being a principal, then it seems that he may be held to be a joint principal with his master. In crimes of "selling" and being "in possession" the court allows the prosecution the best of both worlds by having regard to the legal act when dealing with the master and the physical act when dealing with the servant. So it is held that the servant, as well as the master, "sells"[1] or is "in possession".[2] But the servant whose "use" of a vehicle has been held to be use by his master has been convicted in *Griffiths* v. *Studebaker* (above) of abetting and in *Green* v. *Burnett* (above) as a principal. It is submitted that when the servant is capable of being a principal it is more logical to hold him liable as such (for he is the real offender) and not as an abettor.

The precise nature of the servant's liability is of more than academic interest for two reasons. First, if the crime is one of strict liability, *mens rea* must nevertheless be proved if he is to be convicted as an abettor but not if he is a principal.[3] Secondly, where there is a statutory defence enabling one held vicariously liable to escape if he can bring the "actual offender" before the court, it is difficult to suppose that the production of an abettor (even though he is the real offender) will suffice, but a joint principal certainly will.[4]

5 No Vicarious Liability for Abetting, or Attempting Crimes

Abetting is a common law notion and therefore, as we have seen,[5] requires *mens rea* even where the offence abetted is one of strict liability. For the same reasons there can be no vicarious responsibility for abetting an offence, even though the offence itself may be one imposing vicarious liability. In *Ferguson* v. *Weaving*[6] D, a licensee, was charged with abetting several of her customers in consuming liquor on the licensed premises outside the permitted hours, contrary to the Licensing Act 1921, s. 4. It appeared that she had taken all proper means to ensure that drinking ceased when "Time" was called. But the waiters in the concert room, contrary to their instructions, made no attempt to collect the customers' drinks and, while D was visiting the several other rooms in the premises, the offence was committed. It was assumed that control of the concert room had been delegated. While accepting that the waiters might have been guilty of abetting the court was emphatic that D could not be. Lord GODDARD, C.J., said:[7]

---

[20] *Griffiths* v. *Studebakers, Ltd.*, [1924] 1 K.B. 102; *Ross* v. *Moss*, [1965] 2 Q.B. 396; [1965] 3 All E.R. 145.

[1] *Hotchin* v. *Hindmarsh*, [1891] 2 Q.B. 181. *Cf. Goodfellow* v. *Johnson*, [1965] 1 All E.R. 941.

[2] *Melias, Ltd.* v. *Preston*, [1957] 2 Q.B. 380; [1957] 2 All E.R. 449.

[3] Above, p. 103.

[4] *Melias, Ltd.* v. *Preston*, above.

[5] Above, p. 94.

[6] [1951] 1 K.B. 814; [1951] 1 All E.R. 412. See also *Thomas* v. *Lindop*, [1950] 1 All E.R. 966; *John Henshall (Quarries), Ltd* . v. *Harvey*, [1965] 1 All E.R. 725. *Provincial Motor Cab Co., Ltd.* v. *Dunning*, [1909] 2 K.B. 599 overlooks this principle and is a doubtful decision.

[7] [1951] 1 K.B. 814 at p. 821; [1951] 1 All E.R. 412 at p. 415.

"She can aid and abet the customers if she knows that the customers are committing an offence, but we are not prepared to hold that their knowledge can be imputed to her so as to make her, not a principal offender, but an aider and abettor. So to hold would be to establish a new principle in criminal law and one for which there is no authority."

Had there been a substantive offence of *permitting* drinking on licensed premises after hours, it is fairly clear that the court could have held D guilty; for in that case the acts, and the *mens rea*, of the servant would have been attributed to her.

An attempt is likewise a common law notion, and it has been said that there can be no vicarious liability for attempting to commit a crime, even though the crime attempted imposes vicarious liability.[8]

6 The Special Position of Corporations[9]

A corporation is a legal person but it has no physical existence and cannot, therefore, either act or form an intention of any kind except through its directors or servants. As each director and servant is also a legal person quite distinct from the corporation, it follows that a corporation's legal liabilities are all, in a sense, vicarious. If a corporation's criminal liability for the acts of its servants and agents were co-extensive with that of a natural person, it could be made liable only for those crimes which fall within the narrow limits which govern the vicarious liability of natural persons. A corporation's liability is in fact much wider than that, and therefore requires separate consideration.

It was formerly thought that a corporation could not be indicted for a crime at all.[10] Personal appearance was necessary at assizes and quarter-sessions and the corporation, having no physical person, could not appear. In the Court of King's Bench however, appearance by attorney was allowed and a way out of this difficulty was found by removing the indictment into that court by writ of *certiorari*;[11] but now this is unnecessary and, by statute,[12] a corporation may appear and plead through a representative. A second difficulty which has gone was that at one time all felonies were punished by death and, as the corporation was incapable of suffering the prescribed punishment, there was no point in trying it. Further objections which have been raised are that, since a corporation is a creature of the law, it can only do such acts as it is legally empowered to do, so that any crime is necessarily *ultra vires*; and that the corporation, having neither body nor mind, cannot perform the acts or form the intents which are a prerequisite of criminal liability. The *ultra vires* doctrine, however, seems to have been ignored in both the law of tort and crime and to apply only in the law of contract and property,[13] while the minds and bodies of the officers and servants of the corporation have been taken to supply its lack of mental and physical faculties. This has been done in two distinct ways:

(a) By holding that a corporation is vicariously liable for the acts of its servants and agents where a natural person would similarly be liable; for

---

[8] *Gardner* v. *Akeroyd*, [1952] 2 Q.B. 743; [1952] 2 All E.R. 306; below, pp. 165–166.
[9] See Williams, C.L.G.P., Ch. 22; R. S. Welsh, "The Criminal Liability of Corporations" (1946), 62 L.Q.R. 345; R. Burrows (1948), 1 *Journal of Criminal Science*, 1.
[10] *Anon* (1701), 12 Mod. Rep. 560, *per* HOLT, C.J.
[11] *Birmingham and Gloucester Rail. Co.* (1842), 3 Q.B. 223.
[12] Criminal Justice Act 1925, s. 33.
[13] *Cf.* Winfield, *Text Book of the Law of Tort* (4th ed.), 128.

example, in public nuisance at common law,[14] or when a statute imposes vicarious responsibility.[15]

(b) By holding that (i) in every corporation there are certain persons who control and direct its activities, and (ii) those persons, when acting in the company's business, are considered to be the company for this purpose. Their acts and states of mind are the company's acts and states of mind and it is held liable, not for the acts of its servants, but for what are deemed to be its own acts.

The type of case where it is most obviously proper that a corporation should be held liable arises where a statute imposes a duty upon a corporation to act and no action is taken. It was in such cases that the earliest developments took place. In 1842, in *Birmingham and Gloucester Rail. Co.*,[16] a corporation was convicted for failing to fulfil a statutory duty. Four years later, in *Great North of England Rail. Co.*,[17] counsel sought to confine the effect of that decision to cases of nonfeasance where there was no agent who could be indicted, arguing that, in the case of misfeasance, only the agents who had done the wrongful acts were liable. The court held that the distinction was unfounded. Even if it were discoverable, it was incongruous that the corporation should be liable for the one type of wrong and not the other. From holding that a corporation could be liable for breach of a statutory duty it was not a great step forward to impose liability in those cases where a natural person would similarly be liable for his servants' acts—for example in public nuisance at common law, or where statute imposes vicarious responsibility.[18]

There was a further important development in 1944. In that year it was held in three cases that a corporation may be held liable for acts of its employees which would certainly *not* render liable a natural person in the same situation. The principle has been well stated by DENNING, L.J.:[19]

> "A company may in many ways be likened to a human body. It has a brain and a nerve centre which controls what it does. It also has hands which hold the tools and act in accordance with directions from the centre. Some of the people in the company are mere servants and agents who are nothing more than hands to do the work and cannot be said to represent the mind or will. Others are directors and managers who represent the directing mind and will of the company and control what it does. The state of mind of these managers is the state of mind of the company and is treated by the law as such."[20]

In *Director of Public Prosecutions* v. *Kent and Sussex Contractors, Ltd.*:[1] D Ltd. was charged with offences under a Defence of the Realm regulation which required an intent to deceive. The justices found that the transport manager of the company had the requisite intention but dismissed the information on the ground that an act of will or state of mind could not be imputed to the company.

---

[14] *Great North of England Rail. Co.* (1846), 9 Q.B. 315.
[15] *Griffiths* v. *Studebakers, Ltd.*, [1924] 1 K.B. 102; *Mousell Brothers* v. *London and North Western Rail. Co.*, [1917] 2 K.B. 836.
[16] (1842), 3 Q.B. 223.
[17] (1846), 9 Q.B. 315.
[18] *Mousell Brothers* v. *London and North Western Rail Co.*, [1917] 2 K.B. 836; *Griffiths* v. *Studebakers, Ltd.*, [1924] 1 K.B. 102.
[19] *H. L. Bolton (Engineering) Co., Ltd.* v. *T. J. Graham & Sons, Ltd.*, [1957] 1 Q.B. at 172.
[20] Thus, it is thought that a company could be guilty of abetting an offence through its managing director—though there is no *vicarious* liability in abetting (above, p. 94).
[1] [1944] K.B. 146; [1944] 1 All E.R. 119.

The Divisional Court held that the conclusion was wrong and sent the case back with a direction that there was ample evidence that the *company* had done the act in question, with intent to deceive.

That decision was approved by the Court of Criminal Appeal in *I.C.R. Haulage Co., Ltd.*,[2] where the convictions of a company, its managing director and nine other persons of a common law conspiracy to defraud were upheld. STABLE, J., said:[3]

". . . the acts of the managing director were the acts of the company and the fraud of that person was the fraud of the company."

Now a natural person could never be held vicariously liable for a common law conspiracy, and the case is therefore an excellent illustration of the wider liability of corporations.

The third of the 1944 cases is more controversial. In *Moore v. I. Bresler, Ltd.*[4] the company was convicted of making certain returns in respect of purchase tax, which were false in material particulars, with intent to deceive, contrary to the Finance (No. 2) Act 1940, s. 35 The returns were actually made by the secretary of the company, and the sales manager of the branch concerned, and were made with the object of concealing the fraudulent sale which these two had made of the company's property. Welch criticises the case[5] on the ground (*inter alia*) that, in identifying these two agents with the company, the court went too far down the scale,

"blurring the distinction in law between the agents of a corporation and the legal *persona* itself."

Certainly the case goes beyond the other two, which both involved directors, and leaves an unanswered question as to how far "down the scale" the courts will go for this purpose. The distinction between the "brains" and the "hands" of the company is not clear-cut. Lord CALDECOTE, C.J., said they were "important officials".[6] This was, no doubt, true; but it can hardly be supposed that every "important official" of, say, the National Coal Board can affect the Board with criminal liability. The rule must surely be confined to those officials who are at the heart of the company's affairs, and *Moore v. Bresler, Ltd.* may perhaps be regarded as an illustration of its extreme limits. In *Magna Plant Ltd. v. Mitchell*[7] a company was held not liable for a crime committed by its depot engineer.

There are certain existing limitations on the liability of a corporation. (1) It can only be convicted of offences which are punishable with a fine. These include most offences;[8] but exclude murder. (2) There are other offences which it is quite inconceivable that an official of a corporation should commit within the scope of his employment; for example, bigamy, rape and incest and, possibly, perjury.[9]

---

[2] [1944] K.B. 551; [1944] 1 All E.R. 691. *Cf. McDonnell*, [1966] 1 Q.B. 233; [1966] 1 All E.R. 193, below, p. 155.

[3] [1944] K.B. at p. 559; [1944] 1 All E.R. at p. 695

[4] [1944] 2 All E.R. 515.

[5] (1946), 62 L.Q.R. at p. 358.

[6] [1944] 2 All E.R. 515 at p. 516.

[7] [1966] Crim. L.R. 394.

[8] See Summary Jurisdiction Act 1879, s. 4, and Criminal Justice Act 1948, s. 13.

[9] Even in some of these cases it is not inconceivable that a corporation might be held liable as a secondary party. *E.g.*, the managing director of an incorporated Marriage Advisory Bureau, negotiates a marriage which he knows to be bigamous. *Cf.* Cross and Jones, *Introduction to Criminal Law*, (6th ed.), 100.

In *Cory Brothers & Co.*,[10] it was held that a corporation could not be indicted for any felony or for a misdemeanour involving personal violence, but in *I.C.R. Haulage, Ltd.* STABLE, J., pointed out that this was a branch of law which had developed and, if the matter came before the court today, the result might well be different.[11] A corporation has in fact been recently tried for manslaughter but acquitted on the merits.[12] *Dicta* to the effect that a corporation cannot be convicted of fraudulent conversion[13] (now a variety of theft) are almost certainly out of date, and it is probable that the only limitations on the criminal liability of corporations are those stated above.

The social purpose underlying corporate criminal liability does not appear to have been considered by the English courts. The fine imposed is ultimately borne by the shareholders who, in most cases, are not responsible, in any sense, for the offence. If they really had control over the directors and so over the management of the company, this might afford some justification; but it is generally recognised that they have no such control over large, public companies.[14] Moreover fines may be inflicted on the Boards of nationalised industries, where there are no shareholders and the consumers of the product, who ultimately pay the fine, have no rights whatever to appoint or dismiss the officials concerned.[15]

Since the persons actually responsible for the offence may, in the great majority of cases, be convicted, is there any need to impose this additional penalty? Arguments in favour of corporate liability are that there may be difficulty in fixing individuals with liability where someone among the "brains" of the corporation has undoubtedly authorised the offence. Corporate liability ensures that the offence will not go unpunished and that a fine proportionate to the gravity of the offence may be imposed, when it might be out of proportion to the means of the individuals concerned. The imposition of liability on the organisation gives all of those directing it an interest in the prevention of illegalities—and they are in a position to prevent them, though the shareholders are not. Since, moreover, the names of the officers will mean nothing to the public, only the conviction of the corporation itself will serve to warn the public of the wrongful acts—operating buses with faulty brakes, or selling mouldy pies—which are committed in its name. None of these reasons seems to be very compelling and the necessity for corporate criminal liability awaits demonstration.

Statutory Liability of Officers.—It is now common form[16] to include the fol-

---

[10] [1927] 1 K.B. 810.

[11] [1944] K.B. 551 at p. 556; [1944] 1 All E.R. 691 at p. 694. *Cf.* the rejected argument of Artemus Jones, K.C., in *Cory Bros. Ltd.*: "The old difficulties as to procedure and punishment having disappeared, it follows that the *dicta* of the judges to the effect that a corporation cannot be indictable for a felony have ceased to have any application on the principle *cessante ratione legis cessat ipsa lex*."

[12] *Northern Star Mining Construction Co., Ltd.*, Glamorgan Assizes, February 1, 1965, unreported.

[13] *Grubb*, [1915] 2 K.B. 683.

[14] Pennington, (2nd ed.) *Company Law*, 481 *et seq.*

[15] In 1951 the Yorkshire Electricity Board was fined £20,000 for contravening a Defence Regulation. It has been suggested that the object of such a prosecution was to demonstrate that nationalised industries are not above the law.

[16] See for example Building Control Act 1966, s. 9 (5), Prices and Incomes Act 1966, s. 22, Industrial Development Act 1966, s. 10, Veterinary Surgeons Act 1966, s. 20 (5) and Sea Fisheries Regulations Act 1966, s. 11 (6).

lowing provision in statutes creating offences likely to be committed by corporations:

> "Where an offence . . . committed by a body corporate is proved to have been committed with the consent or connivance of, or to be attributable to any neglect on the part of, any director, manager, secretary or other similar officer of the body corporate or any person who was purporting to act in any such capacity, he as well as the body corporate shall be guilty of that offence and shall be liable to be proceeded against and punished accordingly."

So far as "consent" and "connivance" are concerned the provision probably effects only a slight extension of the law; for the officer who expressly consents or connives at the commission of the offence will be liable as a secondary party under the principles considered above. There may be a consent which does not amount to counselling or abetting, however; and the words "attributable to any neglect on the part of"[17] clearly impose a wider liability in making the officer liable for his negligence in failing to prevent the offence.

Unincorporated Bodies.—Occasionally statute makes provision for the criminal liability of an unincorporated body. Thus under the Prices and Incomes Act 1966 proceedings may be brought against "a trade union, trade union organisation, or employers' organisation, being an unincorporated body" in the name of that body and not in that of any of its members.

---

[17] These words are omitted from s. 18 of the Theft Act, below, p. 435.

CHAPTER 9

General Defences

Where D has caused an *actus reus* with the appropriate *mens rea*, he will generally be held liable. But this is not invariably so for there are certain defences which may still be available even in this situation. As well as special defences which apply in the case of particular crimes, there are certain defences which apply in the case of crimes generally and it is these with which we are concerned in this chapter.

1 INFANCY

Infants are persons under twenty-one years of age. As such, they are (with some exceptions) incapable of making contracts or wills but the law imposes no such limitations on their ability to commit crimes, for, as Kenny put it,

> "a child knows right from wrong long before he knows how to make a prudent speculation or a wise will".[1]

For the purpose of the criminal law, infants are divided into three categories.

1 Children under Ten Years

The first category is those who are entirely exempt from criminal responsibility in all circumstances. At common law a child was so exempt until the day before his seventh birthday.[2] Now, by statute,[3] the age is raised to ten. The rule is commonly stated as a conclusive presumption that the child is *doli incapax*. Even though there may be the clearest evidence that the child caused an *actus reus* with *mens rea*, he cannot be convicted once it appears that he had not, at the time he did the act, attained the age of ten. Nor is this a mere procedural bar; no crime at all is committed by the infant with the result that one who instigated him to do the act is a principal and not a secondary party.[4] And

---

[1] *Outlines*, 80.
[2] By a curious rule of common law a person attains a specified age in law on the day preceding the anniversary of his birthday: *Re Shurey, Savory* v. *Shurey*, [1918] 1 Ch. 263.
[3] Children and Young Persons Act 1933, s. 50, as amended by the Children and Young Persons Act 1963, s. 16, which raised the age from eight. The Ingleby Committee had recommended that the age be raised to twelve.
[4] Above, p. 81.

where a husband and wife were charged with receiving from their son (aged seven years) a child's tricycle, knowing it to have been stolen, it was held that they must be acquitted on the ground that, since the child could not steal, the tricycle was not stolen.[5] The only remedy which may be available in the case of a child under ten who commits a crime is to bring the child before the court as being in need of care and protection.[6] This is not a criminal proceeding, so there is no lower age limit nor is there a finding of guilt; yet the result may be that the child is sent to an approved school—which is generally regarded as a severe punishment. Ten is comparatively low age for the beginning of criminal responsibility; but, as the Ingleby Committee pointed out:[7]

> "In many countries the 'age of criminal responsibility' is used to signify the age at which a person becomes liable to the 'ordinary' or 'full' penalties of the law. In this sense, the age of criminal responsibility in England is difficult to state: it is certainly much higher than eight."[8]

The recent White Paper on "Children in Trouble" proposes that children between ten and fourteen should no longer be liable to criminal prosecution. A child who committed an offence would, instead, be subject to civil proceedings before a juvenile court if he was not receiving "such care, protection and guidance as a good parent may reasonably be expected to give".[9]

2 Children over Ten and under Fourteen Years

The second category of infants is a "twilight zone"[10] in which they are exempt from criminal responsibility unless it is proved, not only that they caused an *actus reus* with *mens rea*, but also that they did so with a "mischievous discretion".[11] In this category are children over ten and under fourteen years of age. Proof of mischievous discretion, according to Hale,[12] involved showing that the child could "discern between good and evil at the time of the offence committed". The fact that the child hid himself after committing the crime was regarded as sufficient evidence of this. In a case in 1748[13] a boy of ten was convicted of murder on evidence which showed that, after killing a five-year-old girl, he had concealed the body and told lies about what had happened. The younger a child is the stronger is the evidence required to establish mischievous discretion.[14]

In a modern case, *Gorrie*,[15] where a thirteen-year-old boy was charged with the manslaughter of a schoolmate, who had died from septic pyaemia resulting from a trifling stab wound with a pen-knife, SALTER, J., told the jury that they must be satisfied

---

[5] *Walters* v. *Lunt*, [1951] 2 All E.R. 645; and *cf. Marsh* v. *Loader* (1863), 14 C.B. N.S. 535.
[6] See Children and Young Persons Act 1963, ss. 2–7.
[7] Cmd. 1191, p. 30. For the special rules governing the treatment of children and young persons, see Children and Young Persons Acts 1933 and 1963.
[8] As the age then was. Above, footnote 3.
[9] See comments of Wootton and Napley in [1968] Crim. L.R. 465 and 474.
[10] Williams, [1954] Crim. L.R. at p. 494.
[11] Hale, 1 P.C. 630.
[12] 1 P.C. 26.
[13] *York*, see Foster, 70.
[14] *X.* v. *X.*, [1958] Crim. L.R. 805.
[15] (1919), 83 J.P. 136. See also *Owen* (1830), 4 C. & P. 236; *Manley* (1844), 1 Cox C.C. 104, and *Smith* (1845), 9 J.P. 682.

"that when the boy did this he knew he was doing what was wrong—not merely what was wrong, but what was gravely wrong, seriously wrong."

Proof that the child knew that the act was against the law—he would not have done it if a policeman had been watching—is undoubtedly sufficient; but it also seems clear that knowledge of legal wrongness is not necessary, if the child knew that the act was morally wrong.

Since it is now the duty of every court, in dealing with a child or young person, to "have regard to the welfare of the child or young person",[16] and merely retributive punishment is ruled out, it has been argued[17] that this test is now out of date:

"It saves the child not from prison, transportation or the gallows, but from the probation officer, the foster parent, or the approved school. The paradoxical result is that, the more warped the child's moral standards, the safer he is from the correctional treatment of the criminal law."

The Ingleby Committee were impressed by similar arguments and by evidence that, because courts find difficulty in applying the presumption and differ in the degree of proof they require, there is inconsistency in the administration of the law. They recommended that the *doli incapax* presumption be abolished; but this recommendation has not been acted on.

There is another special rule of exemption for a boy under fourteen in that he cannot be convicted of rape,[18] assault with intent to commit rape,[19] offences involving carnal knowledge,[20] or sodomy.[1] The rule is theoretically based on a presumption of incapacity[2] but, as no evidence is admissible in rebuttal, it is in effect a rule of law. When a boy has done acts which, but for his age, would amount to one of these offences he may be convicted of an indecent assault. He may also be convicted of abetting another to commit those offences of which he is himself incapable.[3]

3 Persons over Fourteen Years

Above the age of fourteen an infant is presumed to be "responsible for his actions entirely as if he were forty";[4] but there are, of course, very important differences in the treatment of young persons under the modern law.[5] In the case of these infants the prosecution need prove only the usual *mens rea* required in the case of a person of full age to obtain a conviction.

2 INSANITY[6]

1 Insanity before the Trial

An accused person's sanity may become relevant at two stages before the trial

---

[16] Children and Young Persons Act 1933, s. 44 (1).
[17] By Williams, [1954] Crim. L.R. 493 at p. 495.
[18] *Groombridge* (1836), 7 C. & P. 582.
[19] *Philips* (1839), 8 C. & P. 736.
[20] *Waite*, [1892] 2 Q.B. 600. Whether a conviction for attempted rape or carnal knowledge is possible is considered below, p. 294.
[1] *Tatam* (1921), 15 Cr. App. Rep. 132, holding that a boy under fourteen cannot be an accomplice to sodomy. But see below, p. 321.
[2] But see below, p. 321.
[3] Above, p. 94.
[4] *Smith* (1845), 1 Cox C.C. 260, *per* ERLE, J.
[5] See above, footnote 7.
[6] Walker, *Crime and Insanity in England*; Williams, C.L.G.P., Chapter 10.

It is inaccurate to speak of "a defence" in these preliminary proceedings, for the effect of a finding of insanity of the appropriate kind is to prevent the accused being tried at all. It is thought convenient to deal briefly with these matters here, however, because of their very close relationship with the defence of insanity at the trial.

Where D has been committed in custody for trial, and the Home Secretary is satisfied by reports from at least two medical practitioners that he is suffering from mental illness, psychopathic disorder, sub-normality or severe sub-normality, he may order that D be detained in a hospital, if he is of opinion having regard to the public interest that it is expedient to do so.[7] The Home Secretary exercised the corresponding power under the Criminal Lunatics Act 1884 only

"where the prisoner's condition is such that immediate removal to a mental hospital is necessary, that it would not be practicable to bring him before a court, or that the trial is likely to have an injurious effect on his mental state."[8]

The basis for this practice—

"that the issue of insanity should be determined by the jury whenever possible and the power should be exercised only when there is likely to be a scandal if the prisoner is brought up for trial . . ."[9]

—is presumably still applicable. The second stage is when the accused is brought up for trial. He may then be found unfit to plead on arraignment under s. 4 of the Criminal Procedure (Insanity) Act 1964.[8] The question at this stage is whether he is able to understand the charge and the difference between pleas of guilty and not guilty, to challenge jurors, to instruct counsel and to follow the evidence. If he is able to do these things, he has a right to be tried if he so wishes, even though he is not capable of acting in his best interests.[11] The same principle must, theoretically, be applicable where the prosecution contend that D is fit to plead and he denies it; but it might be more leniently applied in such a case.

It was held in *Podola*[12] that a man is fit to plead where an hysterical amnesia prevents him from remembering events during the whole of the period material to the question whether he committed the crime alleged, but whose mind is otherwise completely normal. The court was prepared to concede that a deaf mute is "insane"—the word used in the Criminal Lunatics Act 1800—but declined

"to extend the meaning of the word to include persons who are mentally normal at the time of the hearing of the proceedings against them and are perfectly capable of instructing their solicitors as to what submission their counsel is to put forward with regard to the commission of the crime."[13]

---

[7] Mental Health Act 1959, ss. 72–73.

[8] R.C.C.P., Cmd. 8932, p. 76.

[9] *Ibid.*

[10] Replacing s. 2 of the Criminal Lunatics Act 1800.

[11] *Robertson*, [1968] 3 All E.R. 557 (C.A.).

[12] [1960] 1 Q.B. 325; [1959] 3 All E.R. 418. The jury had found that Podola was not suffering from hysterical amnesia and the question before the Court of Criminal Appeal concerned the onus of proof of that issue; but the Court held that this question could only arise if the alleged amnesia could in law bring Podola within the scope of s. 2 of the Criminal Lunatics Act 1800. The Court's decision on this point thus appears to be part of the *ratio decidendi* of the case.

[13] [1960] 1 Q.B. at p. 356; [1959] 3 All E.R. at p. 433. The word "insane" is not used in s. 4 of the 1964 Act; but the law is unchanged. *Cf.* Cmd. 2149, p. 7.

But is a person suffering from hysterical amnesia so capable? If the actual facts justify a defence of accident or alibi but D is unable to remember them, the defence, in the absence of volunteer witnesses, cannot be raised. On the other hand it would be unsatisfactory if, for example, there could be no trial of a motorist who had suffered concussion in an accident, alleged to have been caused by his dangerous driving, and who could not remember what he did. It would be still less satisfactory in the case of one whose failure to recall the relevant events arose from drunkenness.[14]

The issue may be raised by the judge on his own initiative or at the request of the prosecution or the defence. Where neither party raises the issue, the judge should do so if he has doubts about the accused's fitness.[15] He may resolve his doubts by reading the medical reports, but it is undesirable for him to hear medical evidence.[15]

If the question is raised by either party, or if the judge has doubts, the issue must be tried by a jury specially empanelled for the purpose.[16] If the accused is found unfit to plead, the court makes an order that he be admitted to the hospital specified by the Home Secretary,[17] where he may be detained without limitation of time, the power to discharge him being exercisable only with the Home Secretary's consent.[18]

The general view expressed by witnesses before the Royal Commission on Capital Punishment was that:

> "someone who is certifiably insane may often nevertheless be fit to plead to the indictment and follow the proceedings at the trial and that, if he is, he should ordinarily be allowed to do so, because it is in principle desirable that a person charged with a criminal offence should, whenever possible, be tried, so that the question whether he committed the crime may be determined by a jury. Moreover, we were told that, as is not unnatural, persons who have been found insane on arraignment and ordered to be detained during H.M. pleasure sometimes exhibit a strong sense of grievance on the ground that they have not been proved to have committed any crime and ought not therefore to be detained in an institution for 'criminal lunatics'."[19]

Podola's case also decides, overruling earlier authorities, that, where D raises the issue of fitness to plead, the onus of proving that he is unfit is on him. By analogy to the rule prevailing when a defence of insanity is raised at the trial,[20] D is required to prove his case, not beyond reasonable doubt, but on a balance of probabilities. If the issue is raised by the prosecution and disputed by the defence then the burden is on the prosecution and the matter must be proved beyond reasonable doubt.[1] If the issue is raised by the judge and disputed by D, presumably the onus is again on the prosecution.[2]

---

[14] *Broadhurst* v. *R.*, [1964] A.C. 441 at p. 451; [1964] 1 All E.R. 111 at p. 116 (P.C.).
[15] *MacCarthy*, [1966] 1 All E.R. 447, discussed by A. R. Poole, "Standing Mute and Fitness to Plead", [1966] Crim. L.R. 6.
[16] Criminal Procedure (Insanity) Act 1964. s. 4 (4).
[17] Criminal Procedure (Insanity) Act 1964, s. 5 (1) (c) and Sched. I.
[18] Mental Health Act 1959, ss. 47 and 65.
[19] Report, Cmd. 8932, p. 78. The terms, "Her Majesty's Pleasure" and "criminal lunatic" are no longer used. In fact about half the prisoners found unfit to plead are detained in Broadmoor or other special hospitals, the remainder being detained in local hospitals: Cmd. 2149, para. 21 (4).
[20] See below, p. 122.
[1] *Per* Edmund Davies, J., at first instance, [1960] 1 Q.B. 325 at p. 329; [1959] 3 All E.R. 418 at p. 442; *Robertson*, [1968] 3 All E.R. 557 (C.A.).
[2] According to Podola's counsel, Mr. Lawton, it has been the normal practice in recent years for the prosecution to call the evidence.

The effect of *Podola*'s case is that a man may be convicted although a jury was not satisfied that he was capable of making out a proper defence at his trial. Moreover the reasoning of the court has been criticised[3] on the ground, *inter alia*, that the prosecution, in bringing the charge at all, is implicitly alleging that D is fit to stand his trial; and that he, in denying that he is so fit, is merely denying that the prosecution have established all the elements in their case.

Time of trial of fitness to plead.—A difficult problem may arise where there is evidence both of a substantive defence to the charge and of unfitness to plead. Until recently the predominant view[4] appeared to be that, where the court was aware of the issue as to unfitness, it was its duty to see that that issue was tried, even though no application was made by either prosecution or defence, before allowing the trial of the general issue to proceed. If it should then be found that D was unfit he was deprived of his right to raise the substantive defence. He might then be ordered to be detained indefinitely although there was a defence witness in court who could prove that D was ten miles away at the time of the alleged crime.[5] There were however two cases in which DEVLIN[6] and FINNE-MORE,[7] JJ., respectively held that the general issue should be tried first, and the question whether D was fit to plead should be tried and determined by the jury only if the general issue was determined against him.[8]

The conflict is now resolved by s. 4 of the Criminal Procedure (Insanity) Act 1964. The general rule remains that the question of fitness to plead is to be determined as soon as it arises[9] but the judge is now given a discretion to postpone it until any time up to the opening of the case for the defence, where, having regard to the nature of D's supposed disability, he considers it is expedient and in D's interests to do so.[10] If, at the end of the case for the prosecution, there is insufficient evidence to justify a conviction, then the jury should be directed to acquit. If, on the other hand, there is a substantial case against the accused, the issue of fitness to plead will be determined there and then by another jury specially empanelled for the purpose or by the trial jury as the judge shall direct. Where the defence on the substantive issue depends on some positive evidence (for example, of alibi) rather than on the weakness of the prosecution's case, it would be possible to request the judge to call the witness before the end of the prosecution's case.[11]

2 Insanity at the Trial[12]

If the accused is found fit to plead or, if that issue is not raised, he may raise the defence of insanity at his trial. It is important to notice that, whereas at the two preliminary stages we were concerned with the accused's sanity *at the time of the inquiry*, at the trial the question concerns the accused's sanity *at the time when he did the act*. The fact that he was insane in the medical sense is not in

---

[3] By Dean, [1960] Crim. L.R. 79 at p. 82.

[4] *Beynon*, [1957] 2 Q.B. 111; [1957] 2 All E.R. 513 (BYRNE, J.); *Podola*, [1960] 1 Q.B. 325, at pp. 349–350; [1959] 3 All E.R. 418 at p. 429 (C.C.A.).

[5] *Per* DEVLIN, J. in *Roberts*, [1954] 2 Q.B. at pp. 335–336; [1953] 2 All E.R. at p. 344.

[6] *Roberts*, [1954] 2 Q.B. 329; [1953] 2 All E.R. 340.

[7] *Pickstone*, [1954] Crim. L.R. 565.

[8] In both cases the jury returned a verdict of not guilty, so it was unnecessary to determine whether he was fit to plead.

[9] Criminal Procedure (Insanity) Act 1964, s. 4 (3).

[10] *Ibid.*, s. 4 (2).   [11] See Cmd. 2149, para. 24.

[12] See generally, Williams, C.L.G.P., Chapter 9; Ellenbogen, "The Principles of Criminal Law relating to Insanity", 1 *Journal of Criminal Science*, 178.

itself sufficient to afford a defence. There is a legal criterion of responsibility defined by the common law and set out in authoritative form in the "M'Naghten Rules", formulated by the judges in 1843. Daniel M'Naghten, intending to murder Sir Robert Peel, killed the statesman's secretary by mistake. His acquittal of murder[13] on the ground of insanity provoked controversy and was debated in the House of Lords, which sought the advice of the judges and submitted to them a number of questions. The answers to those questions became the famous Rules.[14] Answers to hypothetical questions, even by all the judges, are not, strictly speaking, a source of law; but the Rules have now been accepted and acted on by the courts for so long and so consistently, that there is no doubt that they represent the law. In a sense, the Rules are now obsolete since they are invoked by way of defence on only one or two occasions each year. It is necessary to consider them, however, (a) because they still remain the legal test of responsibility and (b) because of their relationship with other defences, especially automatism and diminished responsibility. The basic propositions of the law are to be found in the answer to Questions 2 and 3:[15]

> ". . . the jurors ought to be told in all cases that every man is presumed to be sane, and to possess a sufficient degree of reason to be responsible for his crimes, until the contrary be proved to their satisfaction; and that to establish a defence on the ground of insanity, it must be clearly proved that, at the time of the committing of the act, the party accused was labouring under such a defect of reason, from disease of the mind, as not to know the nature and quality of the act he was doing, or, if he did know it, that he did not know he was doing what was wrong."

It will be seen that there are two lines of defence open to an accused person: (i) He must be acquitted if, because of a disease of the mind, he did not know the nature and quality of his act; (ii) even if he did know the nature and quality of his act, he must be acquitted if, because of a disease of the mind, he did not know it was "wrong". The two limbs of the rule require separate consideration.

(i) *The nature and quality of his act.*—The phrase "nature and quality of his act" refers to the physical nature and quality of the act and not to its moral or legal quality.[16] Illustrations given by leading writers are:

> "A kills B under an insane delusion that he is breaking a jar"[17]

and

> "the madman who cut a woman's throat under the idea that he was cutting a loaf of bread."[18]

Of course, a man who was under such a delusion as these, apart altogether from insanity, could never be convicted of murder,[19] simply because he has no *mens rea*. The important practical difference, however, is that, if the delusion arose from a disease of the mind, he will be liable to be indefinitely detained in a special hospital whereas if it arose from some other cause, he will go entirely free. What is a "disease of the mind" is, then, an important as well as a difficult question which has given rise to some decisions that are not easy to reconcile.

---

[13] 4 St. Tr. N.S. 847.
[14] 10 Cl. & F. 200.   [15] 10 Cl. & F. at p. 210.
[16] *Codère* (1916), 12 Cr. App. Rep. 21.
[17] Stephen, *Digest* (8th ed.), 6.
[18] Kenny, *Outlines*, 76.
[19] Manslaughter, however, might be another matter.

In *Charlson*[20] the facts of which are given above,[1] D was entirely acquitted on the direction of BARRY, J., that he was not guilty if he was

"acting as an automaton without any real knowledge of what he was doing."[2]

This condition, if it existed at all, was caused by a cerebral tumour. The defence of insanity was not raised and the prison medical officer gave evidence that D was sane and was not suffering from a disease of the mind.

BARRY, J., did not go into the question of the distinction between mental and physical diseases, but that problem had to be faced by DEVLIN, J., in *Kemp*,[3] when he sought to distinguish *Charlson*.[20]

D made an entirely motiveless and irrational attack on his wife with a hammer. He was charged with causing grievous bodily harm to her with intent to murder her. It appeared that he suffered from arteriosclerosis which caused a congestion of blood in his brain. As a result he suffered a temporary lapse of consciousness during which he made the attack. It was conceded that D did not know the nature and quality of his act and that he suffered from a defect of reason but it was argued on his behalf that this arose, not from any mental disease, but from a purely physical one. It was argued that, if a physical disease caused the brain cells to degenerate (as in time, it might), then it would be a disease of the mind; but until it did so, it was said, this temporary interference with the working of the brain was like a concussion or something of that sort and not a disease of the mind. DEVLIN, J., rejected this argument and held that D was suffering from a disease of the mind. He said:[4]

"The law is not concerned with the brain but with the mind, in the sense that 'mind' is ordinarily used, the mental faculties of reason, memory and understanding. If one reads for 'disease of the mind' 'disease of the brain,' it would follow that in many cases pleas of insanity would not be established because it could not be proved that the brain had been affected in any way, either by degeneration of the cells or in any other way. In my judgment the condition of the brain is irrelevant and so is the question of whether the condition of the mind is curable or incurable, transitory or permanent."

The object of the inclusion in the Rules of the words "disease of the mind" was to exclude "defects of reason caused simply by brutish stupidity without rational power."[5]

DEVLIN, J., purported to distinguish *Charlson* on the ground that there the doctors were agreed that D was not suffering from a mental disease; in *Kemp* they disagreed. But, as DEVLIN, J., himself said,[6] the question whether a particular condition amounts to a "disease of the mind" within the Rules is not a medical but a legal question to be decided in accordance with the ordinary rules of interpretation, and it is submitted with respect that the facts of the cases are indistinguishable. If Kemp was suffering from a disease of the mind, so was Charlson. It is further submitted that *Kemp* is the preferable decision, for it is obviously desirable that persons who are subject to uncontrollable outbursts of this nature should be subject to restraint.[7]

---

[20] [1955] 1 All E.R. 859.
[1] See p. 32.
[2] [1955] 1 All E.R. at p. 862.
[3] [1957] 1 Q.B. 399; [1956] 3 All E.R. 249.
[4] [1957] 1 Q.B. at p. 407; [1956] 3 All E.R. at p. 253.
[5] *Ibid.*, at pp. 407 and 254.
[6] *Ibid.*, at pp. 406 and 253.
[7] In *Bratty* v. *A.-G. for Northern Ireland*, [1963] A.C. 386 at pp. 410–412; [1961] 3 All E.R. 523 at pp. 533–534 (H.L.) Lord DENNING approved of *Kemp* and disapproved of *Charlson, obiter.*

(ii) *Knowledge that the act is wrong.*—The question is not whether the accused is able to distinguish between right and wrong in general, but whether he was able to appreciate the wrongness of the particular act he was doing at the particular time. It has always been clear that if D knew his act was contrary to law, he knew it was "wrong" for this purpose. Thus in their first answer the judges in *M'Naghten*'s case said:[8]

> ". . . notwithstanding the party accused did the act complained of with a view, under the influence of insane delusion, of redressing or revenging some supposed grievance or injury, or of producing some public benefit, he is nevertheless punishable, according to the nature of the crime committed, if he knew at the time of committing such crime that he was acting contrary to law; by which expression we understand your lordships to mean the law of the land."

Even if D did not know his act was contrary to law, he was still liable if he knew that it was wrong "according to the ordinary standard adopted by reasonable men".[9] The fact that the accused thought his act was right was irrelevant if he knew that people generally considered it wrong. This again seems to be supported by the Rules:[10]

> "If the question were to be put as to the knowledge of the accused solely and exclusively with reference to the law of the land, it might tend to confound the jury, by inducing them to believe that an actual knowledge of the law of the land was essential to lead to a conviction: whereas the law is administered upon the principle that everyone must be taken conclusively to know it, without proof that he does know it. If the accused was conscious that the act was one which he ought not to do, and if that act was at the same time contrary to the law of the land, he is punishable."

A recent case, however suggests that the courts are concerned only with the accused's knowledge of legal wrongness.

In *Windle*,[11] D, unhappily married to a woman, P, who was always speaking of committing suicide and who, according to medical evidence at the trial, was certifiably insane, killed P by the administration of 100 aspirins. He then gave himself up to the police, saying, "I suppose they will hang me for this." A medical witness for the defence said that D was suffering from a form of communicated insanity known as *folie à deux*. Rebutting medical evidence was called, but the doctors on both sides agreed that he knew he was doing an act which the law forbade. DEVLIN, J., thereupon withdrew the issue from the jury. So far the decision accords perfectly with the law as stated above but, in the Court of Criminal Appeal, Lord GODDARD, C.J., in upholding the conviction, said:[12]

> "Courts of law can only distinguish between that which is in accordance with the law and that which is contrary to law. . . . The law cannot embark on the question and it would be an unfortunate thing if it were left to juries to consider whether some particular act was morally right or wrong. The test must be whether it is contrary to law. . . .
>
> In the opinion of the court there is no doubt that in the M'Naghten Rules 'wrong' means contrary to law and not 'wrong' according to the opinion of one man or of a number of people on the question whether a particular act might or might not be justified."

---

[8] 10 Cl. & F. at p. 209.
[9] *Codère* (1916), 12 Cr. App. Rep. 21 at p. 27.
[10] 10 Cl. & F. at p. 210.
[11] [1952] 2 Q.B. 826; [1952] 2 All E.R. 1.
[12] [1952] 2 Q.B. 826 at pp. 833, 834; [1952] 2 All E.R. 1 at pp. 1, 2.

It is thought that *Windle*[11] is in accordance with authority in rejecting the arguments of the defence that D should be acquitted if, knowing his act to be against the law, he also believed it to be morally right. But the effect of the *obiter dictum*—it was no more than that—that "wrong" means simply "legally wrong", would seem to be to widen the defence by making it available to a man who knows that his act is morally wrong but, owing to disease of the mind, fails to appreciate that it is also legally wrong. Such a case was not before the court and seems unlikely to arise.

The High Court of Australia has refused to follow *Windle*. In *Stapleton*[13] they made a detailed examination of the English law, before and after M'Naghten and came to the conclusion that *Windle* was wrongly decided. Their view was that if D believed his act to be right according to the ordinary standard of reasonable men he was entitled to be acquitted even if he knew it to be legally wrong. This would extend the scope of the defence, not only beyond what was laid down in *Windle*, but beyond what the law was believed to be before that case. While such an extension of the law may be desirable, it is difficult to reconcile with the M'Naghten Rules and to justify on the authorities.[14] It is unlikely to be followed by the courts in England.

(iii) *Insane delusions.*—The judges were asked in *M'Naghten*'s case:

"If a person under an insane delusion as to existing facts commits an offence in consequence thereof, is he thereby excused?"

They replied:[15]

> ... the answer must, of course, depend on the nature of the delusion: but making the same assumption as we did before, namely, that he labours under such partial delusion only, and is not in other respects insane, we think he must be considered in the same situation as to responsibility as if the facts with respect to which the delusion exists were real. For example, if under the influence of his delusion he supposes another man to be in the act of attempting to take away his life, and he kills that man, as he supposes, in self-defence, he would be exempt from punishment. If his delusion was that the deceased had inflicted a serious injury to his character and fortune, and he killed him in revenge for such supposed injury, he would be liable to punishment."

This seems to add nothing to the earlier answers. The insane delusions that the judges had in mind seem to have been factual errors of the kind which prevent a man from knowing the nature and quality of his act or knowing it is wrong. The example given seems to fall within those rules.

The proposition that the insane person "must be considered in the same situation as to responsibility as if the facts with respect to which the delusion exists were real"[16] must be treated with caution. It must always be remembered that there must be an actual *actus reus*, accompanied by the appropriate *mens rea*, for a conviction. Suppose that D strangles his wife's poodle under the insane delusion that it is her illegitimate child. If the supposed facts were real he would be guilty of murder—but that is plainly impossible as there is no *actus reus*.

---

[13] (1952), 86 C.L.R. 358.
[14] *Stapleton* is discussed in a note by N. Morris (1953), 16 M.L.R. 435, which is criticised by Montrose (1954), 17 M.L.R. 383.
[15] 10 Cl. & F. at p. 211.
[16] *Supra.*

Nor is there any crime in respect of the dog, for there is no *mens rea*. The rule seems merely to emphasise that delusions which do not prevent D from having *mens rea* will afford no defence. As Lord HEWART, C.J., rather crudely put it, "the mere fact that a man thinks he is John the Baptist does not entitle him to shoot his mother".[17] A case often discussed is that of a man who is under the insane delusion that he is obeying a divine command. Some American courts have held that such a belief affords a defence. Yet if the accused knows that his act is forbidden by law, it seems clear he is liable. Stephen certainly thought that this was so:[18]

> "My own opinion is that if a special divine order were given to a man to commit murder, I should certainly hang him for it, unless I got a special divine order not to hang him."

(iv) *Irresistible impulse.*—It is recognised by psychiatrists that a man may know the nature and quality of an act, may even know that it is wrong, and yet perform it under an impulse that is almost or quite uncontrollable. Such a man has no defence under the Rules. The matter was considered in *Kopsch*:[19] D, according to his own admission, killed his uncle's wife. He said that he strangled her with his necktie at her own request. (If this was an insane delusion, it would not, of course, afford a defence under the rules stated above.) There was evidence that he had acted under the direction of his sub-conscious mind. Counsel argued that the judge should have directed the jury that a person under an impulse which he cannot control is not criminally responsible. This was described by Lord HEWART, C.J., as a

> "fantastic theory . . . which if it were to become part of our criminal law, would be merely subversive."[20]

The judges have steadily opposed the admissibility of such a defence on the ground of the difficulty—or impossibility—of distinguishing between an impulse which proves irresistible because of insanity and one which is irresistible because of ordinary motives of greed, jealousy or revenge. The view has also been expressed that the harder an impulse is to resist, the greater is the need for a deterrent.[21]

The law does not recognise irresistible impulse even as a symptom from which a jury might deduce insanity within the meaning of the Rules.[1] If, however, medical evidence were tendered in a particular case that the uncontrollable impulse, to which the accused in that case had allegedly been subject, was a symptom that he did not know his act was wrong, it would be open to the jury to act on that evidence.[2] But it is not permissible for a judge to make use in one case of medical knowledge which he may have acquired from the evidence in another, in his direction to the jury.[3]

---

[17] Hewart, *Essays*, 224.

[18] 2 H.C.L. 160, n. 1.

[19] (1925), 19 Cr. App. Rep. 50 (C.C.A.). See also *True* (1922), 16 Cr. App. Rep 164; *Sodeman*, [1936] 2 All E.R. 1138 (P.C.).

[20] (1925), 19 Cr. App. Rep. 50 at p. 51.

[21] As a Canadian judge, RIDDELL, J., put it: "If you cannot resist an impulse in any other way, we will hang a rope in front of your eyes, and perhaps that will help": *Creighton* (1909), 14 Can. Crim. Cas. 349.

[1] *A.-G. for South Australia* v. *Brown*, [1960] A.C. 432; [1960] 1 All E.R. 734 (P.C.).

[2] *Ibid.* See also *Sodeman* (1936), 55 C.L.R. 192 at p. 203.

[3] [1960] A.C. 432 at p. 449.

Although the M'Naghten Rules remain unaltered a partial defence of irresistible impulse has, as will appear below[4] now been admitted into the law through the new defence of diminished responsibility.

(v) *Proposals for Reform.*—Almost from the moment of their formulation the Rules have been subjected to vigorous criticism, primarily by doctors, but also by lawyers. The Rules, being based on outdated psychological views, are too narrow, it is said, and exclude many persons who ought not to be held responsible. They are concerned only with defects of reason and take no account of emotional or volitional factors whereas modern medical science is unwilling to divide the mind into separate compartments and to consider the intellect apart from the emotions and the will. In 1923 a committee under the chairmanship of Lord ATKIN recommended that a prisoner should not be held responsible

"when the act is committed under an impulse which the prisoner was by mental disease in substance deprived of any power to resist."[5]

The recommendation was not implemented. In 1953 the Royal Commission on Capital Punishment[6] made much more far-reaching proposals. They thought that the question of responsibility is not primarily a matter of law or of medicine, but of morals and, therefore, most appropriately decided by a jury of ordinary men and women. They thought that the best course would be to abrogate the rules altogether and

"leave the jury to determine whether at the time of the act the accused was suffering from disease of the mind (or mental deficiency) to such a degree that he ought not to be held responsible."[7]

This meant abandoning the assumption that it is necessary to have a rule of law defining the relation of insanity to criminal responsibility; but the Commission thought this assumption had broken down in practice anyway.[8] As an alternative, which they thought less satisfactory but better than leaving the Rules unchanged, the Commission recommended that a third limb be added to the Rules: that the accused "was incapable of preventing himself from committing it"[9]... Neither of their recommendations has been implemented and the M'Naghten Rules remain intact.

The Rules still have their defenders and the case for them has been most cogently put by Lord DEVLIN:

"As it is a matter of theory, I think there is something logical—it may be astringently logical, but it is logical—in selecting as the test of responsibility to the law, reason and reason alone. It is reason which makes a man responsible to the law. It is reason which gives him sovereignty over animate and inanimate things. It is what distinguishes him from the animals, which emotional disorder does not; it is what makes him man; it is what makes him subject to the law. So it is fitting that nothing other than a defect of reason should give complete absolution."[10]

---

[4] See p. 124.
[5] Cmd. 2005.
[6] Cmd. 8932.
[7] *Ibid.*, para. 333. *Cf.* Walker's criticism, *op. cit.* at 110–111: "By what criterion could one tell whether this or that case 'ought' to have been included? Could the criterion be expressed in words, or was it ineffable?"
[8] The Commission was impressed by Lord COOPER's view that "However much you charge a jury as to the M'Naghten Rules or any other test, the question they would put to themselves when they retire is—'Is this man mad or is he not?'": Report, para. 322.
[9] *Ibid.*, paras. 317 and 313.
[10] "Mental Abnormality and the Criminal Law" in *Changing Legal Objectives* (Ed. R. St. J. MacDonald, Toronto, 1963) 71 at 85. *Cf.* A. F. Goldstein, *The Insanity Defence* (1967).

(vi) *Burden of Proof.*—The M'Naghten Rules laid it down that

> "every man is presumed to be sane, and to possess a sufficient degree of reason to be responsible for his crimes, until the contrary be proved to [the jury's] satisfaction; and that to establish a defence on the ground of insanity, it must be clearly proved, etc."[11]

It seems from these words that the judges were intending to put the burden of proof squarely on the accused, and so it has always been subsequently assumed.[12] Insanity is stated to be the one exception at common law to the rule that it is the duty of the prosecution to prove the prisoner's guilt in all particulars.[13] He does not have to satisfy that heavy onus of proof beyond reasonable doubt which rests on the prosecution but is entitled to a verdict in his favour if he proves his case on a balance of probabilities, the standard which rests on the plaintiff in a civil action. If the jury think it is more likely than not that he is insane within the meaning of the Rules, then he is entitled to their verdict.

When, however, consideration is given to what has to be proved to establish insanity under the first limb of the Rules, there is an apparent conflict with the general rule requiring the prosecution to prove *mens rea.* This requires proof that the accused was either intentional or reckless with respect to all those consequences and circumstances of his act which constitute the *actus reus* of the crime with which he is charged. But this, in effect, is to prove that the accused *did* know the nature and quality of his act. The general rule, therefore, says that the prosecution must prove these facts; the special rule relating to insanity says that the defence must disprove them. Williams argues[14] that the only burden on the accused is the "evidential" one of introducing sufficient evidence to raise a reasonable doubt in the jury's minds; and that the burden of *proof* is on the prosecution. This solution appears to be the only way of resolving the inconsistency; but, as yet, not even the difficulty, let alone the suggested solution, has been judicially recognised in England.[15]

This problem does not arise when the accused's defence takes the form that he did not know that his act was wrong. Here he is setting up the existence of facts which are quite outside the prosecution's case and there is no inconsistency in putting the onus on the prisoner. It is very strange that the onus of proof should be on the Crown if the defence is based on the first limb of the Rules and on the prisoner if it should be on the second. Yet the authorities[16] seem clearly to establish that the onus in the case of the second limb is on the prisoner. It is not possible to argue that the courts really meant the evidential burden, for they have said very clearly that the burden is one of proof "on a balance of probabilities", the same standard that the plaintiff in a civil action must satisfy. Whatever may be the position regarding the first limb of the defence then, it seems clear that, under the second, the onus is on the prisoner.

The anomaly is emphasised by the decision of the House of Lords in *Bratty* v. *A.-G. for Northern Ireland*[17] that, where the defence is automatism arising

---

[11] 10 Cl. & F at 210.
[12] *Stokes* (1848), 3 Car & Kir. 185; *Layton* (1849), 4 Cox C.C. 149; *Smith* (1910), 6 Cr. App. Rep. 19; *Coelho* (1914), 30 T.L. R. 535; *Bratty* v. *A.-G. for Northern Ireland,* [1963] A.C. 836; [1961] 3 All E.R. 523.
[13] *Woolmington* v. *Director of Public Prosecutions,* [1935] A.C. 462.
[14] C.L.G.P., § 165.
[15] *Cf.,* however, *Cottle,* [1958] N.Z.L.R. 999 at p. 1019 *per* NORTH, J.
[16] *Sodeman* v. *R.,* [1936] 2 All E.R. 1138; *Carr-Briant,* [1943] K.B. 607; [1943] 2 All E.R. 156.
[17] [1963] A.C. 386; [1961] 3 All E.R. 523.

otherwise than through a disease of the mind, the burden of proof is on the prosecution. Assuming for the moment that both *Charlson* and *Kemp*[18] were rightly decided, the effect of this is that Charlson was not guilty unless the prosecution proved beyond reasonable doubt that he was not in a state of automatism, whereas Kemp was guilty unless he proved on a balance of probabilities, that he was in a state of automatism. In his speech in *Bratty* Lord DENNING agreed with DEVLIN, J.,[19] that what is a disease of the mind is a question for the judge and did not agree with BARRY, J.'s assumption that a cerebral tumour was not a disease of the mind; but he thought that automatism arising from concussion or sleepwalking does not arise from a disease of the mind and that, in such a case, the onus of proof is on the Crown.

It is difficult to see why a man whose alleged disability arises from a disease of the mind should be convicted whereas one whose alleged disability arises from some other cause, would, in exactly the same circumstances, be acquitted.

(vii) *The special verdict of insanity and the right of appeal.*—Where a defence under the M'Naghten Rules was established, the correct verdict until recently was

> "guilty of the act or omission charged but insane, so as not to be responsible, according to law, for his actions at the time when the act was done or the omission made."

Despite the form of the verdict it was well settled that it was one of acquittal and no appeal lay from the finding either of guilty of doing the act charged, or of insanity.[20]

The anomalous form of the "guilty but insane" verdict had been repeatedly criticised and, by s. 1 of the Criminal Procedure (Insanity) Act 1964, it is provided that it shall be replaced by a special verdict that "the accused is not guilty by reason of insanity". Although it may seem, at first sight, highly illogical to give the accused a right of appeal from an acquittal, this too was a highly desirable reform which was effected by the 1964 Act. If it were the case that a special verdict of insanity could be found only where D himself had so pleaded, it would be reasonable that there should be no appeal; but this was not the case. Thus it will be recalled that in *Kemp*[1] D's contention was that he should be entirely acquitted, but it was held that the medical evidence established insanity within the M'Naghten Rules. The issue was decided against D, yet he had no right of appeal. A similar position arose where, after the Homicide Act 1957, D raised the defence of diminished responsibility and the prosecution were thereupon allowed to introduce evidence of insanity with the M'Naghten Rules.[2] For these reasons, a right of appeal to the Court of Appeal and the House of Lords is provided by s. 12 of the Criminal Appeal Act 1968, subject to the same conditions as apply in criminal appeals generally. The right of appeal is not limited to the case where the issue is decided against D's contention in the court below. It is now possible for D to appeal against the finding (no longer express

---

[18] Above, p. 117.
[19] [1961] 3 All E.R. at p. 534. If D puts his state of mind in issue, it is immaterial whether he describes his defence as "insanity" or not. Whether he has raised the defence is a question of law. If the judge rules that his evidence tends to disclose a defect of reason from disease of the mind, then D is raising insanity; otherwise he is not. *Cf. Stanecki*, [1966] V.R. 141; *Meddings*, [1966] V.R. 306; *Jeffrey*, [1967] V.R. 467.
[20] *Felstead* v. *R.*, [1914] A.C. 534; *Duke*, [1963] 1 Q.B. 210; [1961] 3 All E.R. 737.
[1] Above, p. 117.
[2] Below, p. 124.

but now implicit in the verdict) that he did the act or against the finding that he was insane when he did so.

(viii) *Function of the Jury.*—It has been laid down for defences of both insanity and diminished responsibility that:[3]

". . . it is for the jury and not for medical men of whatever eminence to determine the issue. Unless and until Parliament ordains that this question is to be determined by a panel of medical men, it is to a jury, after a proper direction by a judge, that by the law of this country the decision is to be entrusted."

The jury must, however, act on the evidence; so that, if the medical evidence is all one way (and in favour of the accused) and there is nothing in the facts or surrounding circumstances which could lead to a contrary conclusion, then a verdict against the medical evidence will be upset.[4] If there are facts which, in the opinion of the court, justify the jury in coming to a different conclusion from the experts then their verdict will be upheld. The jury hardly seems an appropriate body to decide between conflicting experts, still less to reject their united opinion on a matter of this sort.

3 DIMINISHED RESPONSIBILITY[5]

The Homicide Act 1957, s. 2, introduced into the law a new defence to murder, known as "diminished responsibility", which entitles the accused not to be acquitted altogether, but to be found guilty only of manslaughter.[6] By s. 2 (2) the Act expressly puts the burden of proof on the prisoner and it has been held that, as in the case of insanity, the standard of proof required is not beyond reasonable doubt but on a balance of probabilities.[7] Consideration of this defence is, strictly speaking, out of place here, for it is not a general defence, but applies only to murder. In practice, however, the scope of the new defence is almost the same as insanity, for the Rules themselves are rarely relied on outside murder cases. Except in murder, the prospect of indefinite and possibly lifelong confinement in Broadmoor is far worse than the ordinary punishment for the crime. Similarly it is reasonable to suppose that prisoners generally will prefer a conviction for manslaughter to an "acquittal" on the ground of insanity. Since the new defence includes all cases which also fall within the M'Naghten Rules (as well as other cases where there was formerly no defence) it is clear that the importance of the Rules in practice is much diminished. Contrary to some predictions at the time of the Act, however, the Rules have not become obsolete.[8]

One reason for this is that where D, being charged with murder, raises the defence of diminished responsibility and the Crown have evidence that he is insane within the Rules, they may adduce or elicit evidence tending to show that this is so. This is now settled by the 1964 Act, s. 6, resolving a conflict in the

---

[3] *Rivett* (1950), 34 Cr. App. Rep. 87, at 94; *Latham*, [1965] Crim. L.R. 434.
[4] *Matheson* (1958), 42 Cr. App. Rep. 145; *Bailey*, [1961] Crim. L.R. 828.
[5] Williams (1960), 1 Med. Sci. & L., 41; Wootton (1960), 76 L.Q.R. 224; Sparks (1964), 27 M.L.R. 9; Walker, *Crime and Insanity in England*, 138–164.
[6] The defence is borrowed from the law of Scotland, where it was a judicial creation, originating in the decision of Lord DEAS in *H.M. Advocate* v. *Dingwall* (1867), 5 Irv. 466. See T. B. Smith, [1957] Crim. L.R. 354 and Lord KEITH, [1959] Jur. Rev. 109. For English developments, see Williams (1960), 1 Med. Sci. & L. 41; Edwards in *Essays in Criminal Science*, 301.
[7] *Dunbar*, [1958] 1 Q.B. 1; [1957] 2 All E.R. 737. Where the medical evidence of diminished responsibility is based on certain facts, it is for the defence to prove those facts: *Din* (1962), 46 Cr. App. Rep. 269.
[8] Though the number of cases in which they are relied on is small.

cases. In *Bastian*[9] Donovan, J., had held that it was the *duty* of the prosecution to set up insanity in these circumstances. This was remarkable in that the Crown was now contending for what was, technically, a verdict of acquittal, while D was asserting that he should be convicted of manslaughter! It was, nevertheless realistic. Obviously, a verdict of guilty of manslaughter will often be preferable from D's point of view to a verdict of not guilty on the ground of insanity; but the latter verdict may well be in the public interest and it seems right that the Crown should be allowed to seek to achieve it. The other view was put by Lawton, J., in *Price*:[10]

> "Prosecutors prosecute. They do not ask juries to return a verdict of acquittal."

But Lawton, J.'s more formidable objection to the *Bastian* procedure was that it deprived D of his right of appeal if the jury accepted the Crown's and rejected his submissions. That objection being removed, by the 1964 Act there was no other obstacle of substance to the ratification by that Act of the *Bastian* rule.[11] The Act also provides for the converse situation. Where D sets up insanity, the prosecution may contend that he was suffering only from diminished responsibility.[12]

Thus, strangely, the roles of the prosecution and defence may be reversed, according to which of them is contending that the prisoner is insane. It seems clear in principle that the Crown must establish whichever contention it puts forward beyond reasonable doubt.[13] It must follow that D rebuts the Crown's case if he can raise a doubt.

The Act does not deal with the situation where D's state of mind is put in issue otherwise than by pleading insanity or diminished responsibility—for example, by raising the defence of automatism. However, the Criminal Law Revision Committee[14] did not think that the limited provision in the Act should throw any doubt on the right of the prosecution to call evidence in cases such as *Kemp*.[15] The prosecution may not, however, lead evidence of D's insanity, when the defence have not put the state of D's mind in issue,[16] even though this course is desired by the defence. The prosecution should supply the defence with a copy of any statement or report which a prison medical officer may have made on that crime and should make him available as a defence witness.[17]

1 The Nature of the Defence

The Homicide Act 1957, s. 2, enacts:

> "(1) Where a person kills or is a party to the killing of another, he shall not be convicted of murder if he was suffering from such abnormality of mind (whether arising from a condition of arrested or retarded development of mind or any inherent causes or induced by disease or injury) as substantially

---

[9] [1958] 1 All E.R. 568 n.

[10] [1963] 2 Q.B. 1 at p. 7.

[11] The Act does not, however, say that it is the *duty* of the Crown to seek to establish insanity.

[12] It had been so held at common law by Elwes, J., in *Nott* (1958), 43 Cr. App. Rep. 8.

[13] *Grant*, [1960] Crim. L.R. 424, *per* Paull, J.

[14] Cmd. 2149, para. 41.

[15] Above, p. 117.

[16] *Dixon*, [1961] 3 All E.R. 460 n., *per* Jones, J.

[17] *Casey* (1947), 32 Cr. App. Rep. 91 (C.C.A.). See Samuels, "Can the Prosecution allege that the Accused is Insane?" [1960] Crim. L.R. 453; [1961] Crim. L.R. 308.

impaired his mental responsibility for his acts and omissions in doing or being a party to the killing.

(2) . . .

(3) A person who but for this section would be liable, whether as principal or as accessory, to be convicted of murder shall be liable instead to be convicted of manslaughter."

In early cases where the defence was raised, it was held that it was the duty of the judge, in summing up, simply to read the section to the jury and invite them to apply the tests stated therein without further explanation; it was not for the judge to re-define the definition which had been laid down by Parliament. In *Spriggs*[18] prosecuting counsel argued that D had a high intelligence quotient and could not, therefore, be suffering from abnormality of mind. There was evidence that D lacked ability to control his emotions and his counsel submitted that such a condition came within the ambit of s. 2. In summing up the judge gave no ruling as to these conflicting submissions but simply left it to the jury to say whether they were satisfied that the accused came within the statutory definition. It was held by the Court of Criminal Appeal that this was a proper course. Yet it is a well established rule that the interpretation of statutes is exclusively a matter for the court, and this course left the jury free to choose between the alternative interpretations of the section. It now seems clear, however, that the decision in *Spriggs* is wrong and the true rule is that it was the duty of the judge to direct the jury as to the meaning to be attached to s. 2.

In *Byrne*[19] the trial judge directed the jury as to the meaning of s. 2 and did so in substantially the same terms as those urged by counsel for the prosecution in *Spriggs*; that is, that difficulty or even inability of an accused person to exercise will-power to control his physical acts could not amount to such abnormality of mind as substantially impaired his mental responsibilities. The Court of Criminal Appeal held that this was a wrong direction and that Byrne's conviction must be quashed. Obviously the jury in *Spriggs* may have elected to follow just such a view of the law and it seems to follow that Spriggs's conviction should have been quashed. Subsequently in *Terry*[20] the court expressly stated that

". . . in the light of [the interpretation that this court put on the section in *Byrne*] it seems to this court that it would no longer be proper merely to put the section before the jury but that a proper explanation of the terms of the section as interpreted in *Byrne* ought to be put before the jury."[1]

The facts of *Byrne*[2] were that D strangled a young woman in a Y.W.C.A. hostel and, after her death, committed horrifying mutilations on her body. Evidence was tendered to the effect that D, from an early age, had been subject to perverted violent desires; that the impulse or urge of those desires was stronger than the normal impulse or urge of sex, so that D found it very difficult or, perhaps, impossible in some cases to resist putting the desire into practice and that the act of killing the girl was done under such an impulse or urge. The court held that it was wrong to say that these facts did not constitute evidence which would bring a case within the section. Lord PARKER, C.J., said:[3]

---

[18] [1958] 1 Q.B. 270; [1958] 1 All E.R. 300. *Cf. Rolph*, [1962] Qd. R. 262.
[19] [1960] 2 Q.B. 396; [1960] 3 All E.R. 1.
[20] [1961] 2 Q.B. 314; [1961] 2 All E.R. 569.
[1] [1961] 2 All E.R. at p. 574.
[2] [1960] 2 Q.B. 396; [1960] 3 All E.R. 1.
[3] [1960] 2 Q.B. 396 at p. 403; [1960] 3 All E.R. 1 at p. 4.

" 'Abnormality of mind', which has to be contrasted with the time-honoured expression in the M'Naghten Rules, 'defect of reason', means a state of mind so different from that of ordinary human beings that the reasonable man would term it abnormal. It appears to us to be wide enough to cover the mind's activities in all its aspects, not only the perception of physical acts and matters and the ability to form a rational judgment whether an act is right or wrong, but also the ability to exercise will-power to control physical acts in accordance with that rational judgment."

Thus, the defence of irresistible impulse is at last admitted into the law (but only of murder) by way of diminished responsibility. The difficulties of proof, which deterred the judges from allowing the defence under the M'Naghten Rules, remain:

". . . the step between 'he did not resist his impulse' and 'he could not resist his impulse' is, as the evidence in this case shows, one which is incapable of scientific proof. *A fortiori*, there is no scientific measurement of the degree of difficulty which an abnormal person finds in controlling his impulses."

The only way to deal with the problem is for the jury to approach it "in a broad common-sense way".[4] They are entitled to take into account not only the medical evidence but also the acts or statements of the accused and his demeanour and other relevant material. Even when they are satisfied that D was suffering from abnormality of mind there remains the question whether the abnormality was such as substantially to impair his mental responsibility—a question of degree and essentially one for the jury.

It is not necessary that the impulse on which D acted should be found by the jury to be *irresistible*; it is sufficient that the difficulty which D experienced in controlling it (or, rather, *failing* to control it) was *substantially* greater than would be experienced in like circumstances by an ordinary man, not suffering from mental abnormality.[5] The test appears to be one of moral responsibility. A man whose impulse is irresistible bears *no* moral responsibility for his act, for he has no choice; a man whose impulse is much more difficult to resist than that of an ordinary man bears a diminished degree of moral responsibility for his act.

The court has from time to time approved directions following those given in Scottish cases and which, in effect, tell the jury that what must be proved is a mental state "bordering on, though not amounting to insanity"[6] or "not quite mad but a border-line case".[7] Care must be taken in giving such a direction to avoid any suggestion that "insanity" in this context bears the very narrow meaning of that form of insanity which is a defence under the M'Naghten Rules. If the word is used at all it must be used in "its broad popular sense".[8] A man may know the nature and quality of his act perfectly well and be aware that it is wrong in law and yet unable to prevent himself from doing it. Such a person in no way borders on insanity within the M'Naghten Rules; yet he should be able to rely on the defence of diminished responsibility. The Privy Council has pointed out that there may be cases in which the type of abnormality relied on cannot be related to any of the generally recognised types of insanity.[9]

---

[4] [1960] 2 Q.B. 396 at p. 404; [1960] 2 All E.R. 1 at p. 5, *per* Lord PARKER, C.J.
[5] *Byrne, supra*; *Simcox*, [1964] Crim. L.R. 402; *Lloyd*, [1966] 1 All E.R. 107. But *cf.* Sparks, *op. cit.*, at 16–19.
[6] *H.M. Advocate* v. *Braithwaite*, 1945 S.C. (J) 55, *per* Lord COOPER.
[7] *Spriggs*, [1958] 1 Q.B. 270 at p. 276; [1958] 1 All E.R. 300 at p. 304, *per* Lord GODDARD, C.J.
[8] *Rose* v. *R.*, [1961] A.C. 496; [1961] 1 All E.R. 859.
[9] *Ibid.*

It is thought, moreover, that this direction is generally unsatisfactory. It follows Scottish directions but the Scottish law of irresponsibility on the ground of insanity appears to be wider than the M'Naghten Rules[10] and diminished responsibility is now interpreted more favourably to the accused in England than in Scotland.[11] Under English law, persons who are actually insane in the "broad popular sense" may well be outside the scope of the M'Naghten Rules and have to rely on diminished responsibility.

2   The Effect of the Introduction of Diminished Responsibility

Diminished responsibility has been pleaded with success in cases where one would have thought there was no chance of a defence of insanity succeeding—mercy killers, deserted spouses or disappointed lovers who killed while in a state of depression, persons with chronic anxiety states, and so on.[12]   It is surprising that there has been no spectacular increase in the number of persons escaping conviction for murder on the ground of their mental abnormality.   In fact, the proportion of persons committed for trial for murder who escape conviction on the ground of their mental abnormality has remained much the same since the Homicide Act as it was before.   The proportion found insane on arraignment and the proportion acquitted on the ground of insanity have sharply declined.   This suggests that persons who were formerly found insane on arraignment or acquitted on the ground of insanity now plead diminished responsibility instead; and that only a very few persons escape conviction who would not have done so before 1957.[13]   The difference is that instead of being compelled to send the mentally abnormal person to a mental hospital, the court may sentence him to imprisonment, put him on probation or make a hospital order as it thinks appropriate in its discretion.   In view of the wide range of types of person who shelter under the umbrella of diminished responsibility, it seems desirable that there should be this flexibility in the means of dealing with them.

3   Hospital Orders

It remains to notice that, of much wider practical importance than either insanity or diminished responsibility, is the courts' power to make hospital orders.   Under s. 60 of the Mental Health Act 1959, a person who is proved to have committed an offence may be committed to a mental hospital or to the guardianship of a local health authority.   The offence must be one punishable with imprisonment and offences where the sentence is fixed by law (in effect, murder) are excluded.   The order can be made only on the evidence of two medical practitioners (one on the list approved by the local health authority as having special experience in the diagnosis or treatment of mental disorder) who agree that detention for treatment or reception into guardianship is warranted.

A court of assize or quarter sessions may, if it thinks it necessary for the protection of the public, make a "restriction order" for an indefinite or a specified

---

[10] *Cf.* T. B. Smith, *The United Kingdom; The Development of Its Laws and Constitution*, 719.
[11] Walker, *op. cit.*, 155–156.
[12] Wootton, *Crime and the Criminal Law*, 86.
[13] Walker, *op. cit.* 158–160.

period. The offender then may not be discharged, given leave of absence or transferred to another hospital without the consent of the Home Secretary.

The relative importance of hospital orders in practice is seen by the fact that in 1967, nine persons were found unfit to plead, only one was acquitted on the ground of insanity, fifty-six charges of murder were reduced to manslaughter on the ground of diminished responsibility, but 1,244 hospital and guardianship orders were made.[14]

4 MISTAKE[15]

Mistake is a defence where it prevents D from having the *mens rea* which the law requires for the crime with which he is charged. Where the law requires intention or recklessness with respect to some element in the *actus reus*, a mistake which precludes both states of mind will excuse.[16] Where negligence is enough, then only a *reasonable* mistake can afford a defence; for an unreasonable mistake, by definition, is one which a reasonable man would not make and is, therefore, negligent.[17] Where strict liability is imposed, then even a reasonable mistake will not excuse.[18] A mistake which does not preclude *mens rea* is irrelevant and no defence.[19] Mistake of law is generally no defence, for usually knowledge that the act is forbidden by law is no part of *mens rea*; but where the *mens rea* involves some legal concept,[20] or the absence of a claim of right,[1] then it may do so.

All this appears in the general discussion of *mens rea*, above. Since the "defence" of mistake is simply a claim of "no *mens rea*," a denial that the prosecution has proved its case, it may well be asked why it is thought necessary to re-consider the matter here. The answer must be that mistake has not always been treated either by courts or text-writers as if it were simply a denial of the prosecution's case, but has been regarded as a special defence requiring the prisoner to introduce evidence, not only as to the fact of the mistake, but also as to its reasonableness. In the leading case of *Tolson*,[2] D was deserted by her husband and was informed by reliable persons who might reasonably be expected to know the fact, that he had been lost in a ship bound for America. More than five years later, believing herself to be a widow, she married again. Her husband then re-appeared. The Court for Crown Cases Reserved, by a majority of nine to five, held that she was not guilty of bigamy. The majority all relied on the maxim, *actus non facit reum nisi mens sit rea*, yet all emphasised that the defence was allowed because of D's belief in good faith and *on reasonable grounds* that her husband was dead.[3] The implication is that an unreasonable belief would not have afforded a defence and, therefore, that bigamy, in

---

[14] Criminal Statistics, England and Wales, 1967, Cmd. 3689.
[15] Keedy, "Ignorance and Mistake in the Criminal Law" (1908), 22 Harv. L.R. 75; Williams, C.L.G.P., Ch. 5; Hall, *General Principles*, Ch. XI; Williams, "Homicide and the Supernatural" (1949), 65 L.Q.R. 491; Howard, "The Reasonableness of Mistake in the Criminal Law" (1961), 4 Univ. Q.L.J. 45.
[16] See above, p. 41.
[17] Above, p. 54.
[18] Above, p. 59.
[19] Above, p. 44.
[20] Above, p. 50.
[1] Above, p. 51.
[2] (1889), 23 Q.B.D. 168.
[3] *Cf. Bank of New South Wales* v. *Piper*, [1897] A.C. 383 at pp. 389–390 (P.C.).

one respect at least, is a crime of negligence. This, indeed, has now been confirmed by the decision of the Court of Criminal Appeal in *King*[4] that an unreasonable belief that the first marriage is void is no defence. Suppose that D, a woman with implicit faith in fortune-tellers, is informed by a crystalgazer that her husband, whom she has not seen for three weeks, is dead and that she thereupon marries again. However sincerely she may believe in her husband's death, she has no defence if he is alive. Yet her fault is not a disregard for the sanctity of marriage or a wish to "prostitute a solemn ceremony";[5] it is simply undue credulousness. A conviction for bigamy hardly seems an appropriate way of dealing with this condition.

In one modern case the Divisional Court departed from the view that only a reasonable mistake could excuse. In *Wilson* v. *Inyang*[6] Lord GODDARD recognised that

> "A man may believe that which no other man of common sense would believe, but yet he may honestly believe it"

and the court held such a belief to be a defence. D was an African who had lived in England for two years. He published an advertisement, offering to visit patients and describing himself as a "Naturopath physician, N.D., M.R.D.P." He was not a registered medical practitioner and was charged with "wilfully and falsely" using the title of physician, contrary to s. 40 of the Medical Act 1858. The magistrate held that he genuinely believed that he was entitled so to describe himself although in similar circumstances, no person brought up and educated in England could reasonably have held such a belief. It was held that he was rightly acquitted.

The decision was the more remarkable in that only two years before, in a prosecution[7] under the same section, Lord GODDARD, C.J., in holding that a man did not act wilfully and falsely if he honestly believed he was within his rights in describing himself as he did, remarked, *obiter*: "He must, of course, have a reasonable ground for his belief." In *Wilson* v. *Inyang*[8] Lord GODDARD modified his view. Unreasonableness was only evidence that the belief was not honestly held.

The case was hailed[9] at the time as

> "the most important contribution ever made to criminal jurisprudence by an English Divisional Court"

and as one repudiating

> "in general terms the hoary error that a mistake to afford a defence to a criminal charge must be reasonable."

But the "hoary error" is probably too firmly established to be got rid of so easily; and the decision in *King*[10] is evidence of its continuing vitality.

The mistake which Inyang made seems to have been a mistake of law for he knew all the facts and the question whether he was "entitled" to describe himself as he did was one of law. Similarly, where a claim of right has been held to be a

---

[4] [1963] 3 All E.R. 561 and see, to the same effect, *Gould*, [1968] 1 All E.R. 849, below, p. 483; and *Sweet* v. *Parsley*, [1969] 1 All E.R. at p. 363, *per* Lord DIPLOCK.
[5] See below, p. 485.
[6] [1951] 2 All E.R. 237 at p. 240 (*cf.* [1951] 2 K.B. 799 at p. 803).
[7] *Younghusband* v. *Luftig*, [1949] 2 K.B. 354; [1949] 2 All E.R. 72.
[8] [1951] 2 K.B. 799; [1951] 2 All E.R. 237.
[9] By Williams (1951), 14 M L.R. 485.
[10] *Supra*, footnote 4.

defence, the courts seem to have regarded reasonableness as irrelevant.[11] It is possible that a distinction is to be drawn between mistakes of fact and mistakes of law, reasonableness being necessary in the former but not in the latter; but it is thought that the better view is that reasonableness should only be evidence in both types of case.

5 DRUNKENNESS

1 Drunkenness as Evidence of the Absence of Mens Rea

Drunkenness is like mistake in that it operates as a defence only if it negatives the *mens rea* of the crime charged. In both cases D is simply denying that the prosecution has proved its case—by introducing evidence which tends to disprove that he had the *mens rea* alleged.

> ". . . if there is material suggesting intoxication, the jury should be directed to take it into account and to determine whether it is weighty enough to leave them with a reasonable doubt about the accused's guilty intent."[12]

Indeed, in many of the cases where drunkenness is relevant, the defence, in substance, is one of mistake, and the evidence of drunkenness is circumstantial evidence that the mistake was made. Two examples recently quoted by Lord DENNING[13] are: (i) where a nurse got so drunk at a christening that she put the baby on the fire in mistake for a log of wood;[14] and where a drunken man thought his friend, lying in bed, was a theatrical dummy and stabbed him to death.[15] Lord DENNING said there would be a defence to murder in each of these cases. These mistakes were highly unreasonable and, in the case of a sober man, it would be extremely difficult to persuade a jury that they were made. The relevance of the evidence of drunkenness is simply that it makes these mistakes much more credible.[16]

The limitations of the defence which follow from this principle should be carefully noted. In the first place, if the crime is one of strict liability and the mistake relates to a fact as to which no *mens rea* need be proved, drunkenness cannot be a defence. If the crime is one of negligence, then the unreasonable nature of the accused's conduct will itself ground liability. So Lord DENNING stated that the killings in the two examples quoted above would be manslaughter —a crime which may be committed negligently.[17] *A fortiori*, if the crime were one of strict liability. Even in crimes of strict liability, however, some mental

---

[11] *Bernhard*, [1938] 2 K.B. 264; [1938] 2 All E.R. 140; *Boden* (1844), 1 Car. & Kir. 395; *Hall* (1828), 3 C. & P. 409; and *Knight* (1908), 1 Cr. App. Rep. 186. And *cf.* Malicious Damage, below, pp. 461–467.

[12] *Broadhurst* v. *R.*, [1964] A.C. 441 at p. 463; [1964] 1 All E.R. 111 at p. 123 (P.C.), *per* Lord DEVLIN.

[13] In *A.-G. for Northern Ireland* v. *Gallagher*, [1963] A.C. 349 at p. 381; [1961] 3 All E.R. 299 at p. 313.

[14] (1748), 18 *Gentleman's Magazine*, 570; quoted in Kenny, *Outlines*, 29.

[15] (1951), *The Times*, January 13.

[16] In *Director of Public Prosecutions* v. *Beard*, [1920] A.C. 479 at pp. 501–502. The House of Lords speak of taking into account *incapacity* to form an intent with the other circumstances. As Lord DEVLIN points out in *Broadhurst*, [1964] A.C. 441 at p. 461; [1964] 1 All E.R. 111 at p. 122, if D were *incapable* of forming the intent, he could not have formed it, and it is pointless to take into account other circumstances. It is submitted that the question is not whether D *could* have formed the necessary intent but whether he *did*.

[17] Below, p. 222.

element must be proved[18] and, if drunkenness negatives that, it is a defence. So, if D is in a state of automatism as a result of drink, he should have a defence (subject to *Gallagher's Case*[19]) to a charge of any crime.[20] Secondly, if the accused's drunkenness was not such as to negative *mens rea*, it is no answer for him on any charge to say that he would not have behaved as he did, but for the drink. The effect of alcohol is to weaken the restraints and inhibitions which normally govern men's conduct. So a man may well commit an assault or a theft, for example, when he is drunk which he would never dream of committing when sober. If he had the *mens rea* required for the crime, he is guilty, even though the drink impaired or negatived his ability to judge between right and wrong,[1] and even though, in his drunken state, he found the impulse to act as he did irresistible.[2]

2   Drunkenness causing Insanity or Abnormality of Mind

If excessive drinking causes actual insanity, such as *delirium tremens*, then the M'Naghten Rules will be applied in exactly the same way as where insanity arises from any other causes:

> "... drunkenness is one thing and the diseases to which drunkenness leads are different things; and if a man by drunkenness brings on a state of disease which causes such a degree of madness, even for a time, which would have relieved him from responsibility if it had been caused in any other way, then he would not be criminally responsible."[3]

It has already been seen[4] that there are serious difficulties in defining a "disease of the mind" and the distinction between temporary insanity induced by drink and simple drunkenness is far from clear-cut. The distinction becomes important in the case of a man who does not know that his act is wrong because of excessive drinking. If he is suffering from temporary insanity he is entitled to a verdict of not guilty on the ground of insanity; but if he is merely drunk he should be convicted.[5]

The effect of drunkenness upon diminished responsibility has not yet been settled.[6] It has been argued[7] that drink can produce a toxic effect on the brain which would be an "injury" within s. 2 of the Homicide Act 1957;[8] but the court thought it very doubtful whether the *transient* effect of drink could amount to an injury. Presumably a permanent injury to the brain produced by drink would

---

[18] Above, p. 66.

[19] Below, p. 135.

[20] *Keogh*, [1964] V.R. 400.

[1] *Director of Public Prosecutions* v. *Beard*, [1920] A.C. 479 at pp. 502–504.

[2] A *dictum* by COLERIDGE, J., in *Monkhouse* (1849), 4 Cox C.C. 55, that drunkenness which prevented the accused restraining himself from committing the act would be a defence, was disapproved in *Director of Public Prosecutions* v. *Beard*, [1920] A.C. at p. 498.

[3] *Davis* (1881), 14 Cox C.C. 563 at p. 564, *per* STEPHEN, J., approved by the House of Lords in *Director of Public Prosecutions* v. *Beard*, [1920] A.C. at p. 501.

[4] Above, pp. 116–117.

[5] In case of simple drunkenness the judge should not introduce the question whether the prisoner knew he was doing wrong— for "it is a dangerous and confusing question"— *per* Lord BIRKENHEAD in *Director of Public Prosecutions* v. *Beard*, [1920] A.C. at p. 506.

[6] The Scottish rule is that a person who is not suffering from diminished responsibility when sober cannot avail himself of that defence when drunk: *Carraher* v. *H.M. Adv.* 1946 S.G.(J.) 108; *H.M. Adv.* v. *MacLeod* 1956 J.C. 20.

[7] In *Di Duca* (1959), 43 Cr. App. Rep. 167. See also *Dowdall* (1960), *The Times*, January 22.

[8] Above, p. 125.

be held to be an injury within the section. Difficult questions may arise where a substantial impairment arises as a result of a combination of inherent abnormality and drink.[9]

3 Drunkenness and Recklessness

The principles set out above are often obscured in the judgments by emphatic statements that drunkenness can be a defence only where a "specific intention" is an essential ingredient of the crime.[10] This term is, as has been seen,[11] ambiguous; but if the meaning intended is one which would exclude from the scope of the defence cases where recklessness is a sufficient *mens rea*, then it is submitted the *dicta* are contrary to principle. Suppose D, being drunk, stabs and inflicts grievous bodily harm on his friend whom he believes to be a theatrical dummy. He has a defence to a charge of wounding with intent to cause grievous bodily harm[12] because the "specific intent" is negatived. But in malicious wounding,[13] recklessness will do. May D be convicted of this crime although he is not reckless? Surely not. As Lord BIRKENHEAD said, after dealing with examples of crimes requiring specific intents:[14]

> "It is true that in such cases the specific intent must be proved to constitute the particular crime, but this is, on ultimate analysis, only in accordance with the ordinary law applicable to crime, for, speaking generally (and apart from certain special offences), a person cannot be convicted of a crime unless the *mens* was *rea*."

It would indeed be a strange and irrational departure from this fundamental principle to allow convictions in crimes which may be committed recklessly where there was no recklessness; and it is thought that, whenever the law requires any variety of *mens rea*, there can be no conviction if that *mens rea* is not proved, whether the accused was drunk or sober at the time. Even if this were incorrect before October 1, 1967, it is submitted that s. 8 of the Criminal Justice Act 1967[15] requires the jury to decide "whether he [the accused] did . . . foresee that result by reference to all the evidence"; and that the section cannot be read as if it contained the words, "except evidence of drunkenness".

4 Involuntary Drunkenness

It has been said that .

> "Involuntary drunkenness is a defence, as when the accused's companions put alcohol into his ginger beer."[16]

This evidently means that such a man would have a defence if he committed an *actus reus* with *mens rea* and it is difficult to understand precisely in what the defence consists. If a man intends to kill and does kill, it can hardly be a defence

---

[9] *Clarke and King*, [1962] Crim. L.R. 836.
[10] *Director of Public Prosecutions* v. *Beard*, [1920] A.C. at pp. 499, 501, 504; *A.-G. for Northern Ireland* v. *Gallagher*, [1963] A.C. 349 at p. 381; [1961] 3 All E.R. 299 at p. 313; *Bratty* v. *A.-G. for Northern Ireland*, [1963] A.C. 386 at p. 410; [1961] 3 All E.R. 523 at p. 533, *per* Lord DENNING.
[11] Above, p. 41.
[12] Offences against the Person Act 1861, s. 18; below, p. 264.
[13] *Ibid.*, s. 20; below, p. 264.
[14] [1920] A.C. at p. 504.
[15] Above, p. 52.
[16] Williams, C.L.G.P., 562.

simply to prove that he has some alcohol in his blood which he did not intend to have. Presumably he has at least to show that he would not have committed the crime but for the alcohol; but this is such a highly speculative matter as to be incapable of satisfactory proof. There is no English authority on the matter. It is true that Hale[17] distinguishes between voluntary and involuntary drunkenness; but this was because he did not allow voluntary drunkenness as a defence at all, even where it negatived *mens rea* and it by no means follows that he regarded involuntary drunkenness, not negativing *mens rea*, as a defence.[18]

5 The Leading Cases

The leading cases, *Meade*[19] and *Director of Public Prosecutions* v. *Beard*,[20] are complicated by their involvement with the law of murder and require some elucidation.

In *Meade*,[19] D, who had been drinking, brutally ill-treated a woman during the greater part of a night and eventually struck her a violent blow with his fist which ruptured an intestine and caused her death. He was convicted of murder and appealed to the Court of Criminal Appeal on the ground that the direction might have led the jury to believe that they should acquit of murder and convict of manslaughter only if they found that he was insane. The Court of Criminal Appeal held that this was not the effect of the direction. The true rule, which the direction had, in substance, put before the jury, was formulated by the Court as follows:

> "A man is taken to intend the natural consequences of his acts. This presumption may be rebutted—(i) in the case of a sober man, in many ways; (ii) it may also be rebutted in the case of a man who is drunk by showing his mind to have been so affected by the drink he had taken that he was incapable of knowing that what he was doing was dangerous—that is likely to inflict serious injury. If this be proved, the presumption that he intended to do grievous bodily harm is rebutted."[1]

In *Beard*,[2] D who had been drinking, ravished a thirteen-year-old girl and, "in aid of the act of rape" he placed his hand upon her mouth to stop her from screaming, at the same time pressing his thumb upon her throat, with the result that she died of suffocation. His conviction for murder was quashed by the Court of Criminal Appeal on the ground that the law had not been stated to the jury as laid down in *Meade*:[3] they had not been told to acquit unless satisfied that he was capable of knowing that what he was doing was dangerous. The Crown appealed to the House of Lords which restored the conviction. As the law then was,[4] a man was guilty of murder if he caused death by an act of violence done in the course or furtherance of a felony involving violence. If he intended to do such an act, that was a sufficient malice aforethought and it was irrelevant that he neither intended nor foresaw that his act was likely to cause death or grievous bodily harm. The only intent which had to be proved in this case was,

---

[17] 1 P.C. 32.
[18] PARK, J.'s *dictum* in *Pearson's* Case (1835), 2 Lew. C.C. 144, must be read subject to the same qualification.
[19] [1909] 1 K.B. 895.
[20] [1920] A.C. 479.
[1] [1909] 1 K.B. at pp. 899–900.
[2] Above, footnote 20.
[3] [1909] 1 K.B. 895.
[4] See below, p. 200.

then, an intent to commit rape. Beard's drunkenness could excuse him only if it rendered him incapable of forming the intention to have sexual intercourse with the girl without her consent—which was manifestly not the case. The distinction between the two cases is that the only felony involved in Meade's conduct (apart from murder or manslaughter) was one which in itself required an intent to cause grievous bodily harm;[5] whereas rape requires no such intention.

6 Drunkenness induced with the Intention of Committing Crime

Has D a defence if, intending to commit a crime, he drinks in order to give himself Dutch courage and then commits the crime, having, at the time of the act, induced insanity within the M'Naghten Rules or such a state of drunkenness as to negative *mens rea*? The problem was raised by *A.-G. for Northern Ireland* v. *Gallagher*.[6] D, having decided to kill his wife, bought a knife and a bottle of whisky. He drank much of the whisky and then killed his wife with the knife. The defence was that he was either insane or so drunk as to be incapable of forming the necessary intent at the time he did the act. The Court of Criminal. Appeal in Northern Ireland reversed his conviction for murder on the ground that the judge had misdirected the jury in telling them to apply the M'Naghten Rules to D's state of mind at the time before he took the alcohol and not at the time of committing the act. The majority of the House of Lords apparently did not dissent from the view of the Court of Criminal Appeal that such a direction would be

> "at variance with the specific terms of the M'Naghten Rules which definitely fix the crucial time as the time of committing the act."[7]

They differed, however, in their interpretation of the summing up and held that it did direct the jury's attention to the time of committing the act. In that case, of course, it was not necessary to decide the problem because the jury, by their verdict, had found that D had *mens rea* and was not insane.

Lord DENNING, however, seems to have taken the view that the Court of Criminal Appeal's interpretation of the summing up was correct and that the direction, so interpreted, was right in law. He said:[8]

> "My Lords, I think the law on this point should take a clear stand. If a man, whilst sane and sober, forms an intention to kill and makes preparation for it knowing it is a wrong thing to do, and then gets himself drunk so as to give himself Dutch courage to do the killing, and whilst drunk carries out his intention, he cannot rely on this self-induced drunkenness as a defence to a charge of murder, nor even as reducing it to manslaughter. He cannot say he got himself into such a stupid state that he was incapable of an intent to kill. So also, when he is a psychopath, he cannot by drinking rely on his self-induced defect of reason as a defence of insanity. The wickedness of his mind before he got drunk is enough to condemn him, coupled with the act which he intended to do and did do."

The difficulty about this is that an intention to do an act at some time in the future is not *mens rea*.[9] The *mens rea* must generally coincide with the conduct which causes the *actus reus*. If D, having resolved to murder his wife at midnight, drops off to sleep and, while still asleep, strangles her at midnight, it is thought that he is not guilty of murder (though he may be liable for manslaughter

---

[5] Offences against the Person Act 1861, s. 18.
[6] [1963] A.C. 349; [1961] 3 All E.R. 299.
[7] See [1963] A.C. 349 at p. 376; [1961] 3 All E.R. 299 at p. 310.
[8] [1963] A.C. 349 at p. 382; [1961] 3 All E.R. 299 at p. 314.
[9] Above, p. 46.

on the ground of his negligence). The case of deliberately induced drunkenness, however, is probably different. The true analogy, it is thought, is the case where a man uses an innocent agent as an instrument with which to commit crime. It has been seen[10] that if D induces an irresponsible person to kill, D is guilty of murder. Is not the position substantially the same where D induces in himself a state of irresponsibility with the intention that he shall kill while in that state? Should not the responsible D be liable for the foreseen and intended acts of the irresponsible D? So regarded, a conviction would not be incompatible with the wording of the M'Naghten Rules. The result, certainly, seems to be one required by policy and it is thought the courts will achieve it if the problem should be squarely raised before them.

Everything that has been said above in relation to alcohol would seem, in principle, to be equally applicable to mistake, insanity or abnormality induced by taking drugs.

6 NECESSITY[11]

We are not concerned here with cases where a man is compelled by physical force to go through the motions of an *actus reus* without any choice on his part. In such cases he will almost[12] invariably have a defence on the more fundamental ground that he did no act.

> "If there be an actual forcing of a man, as if A by force takes the arm of B and the weapon in his hand and therewith stabs C whereof he dies, this is murder in A but B is not guilty."[13]

The problem now to be discussed is the more difficult one that arises where D is able to choose between two courses, one of which involves breaking the criminal law and the other some evil to himself or others of such magnitude that it may be thought to justify the infraction of the criminal law. In an American case the master of a ship was held not guilty of violating an embargo act by illegal entry into a port when, as the result of storms, this course was "necessary" for the preservation of the vessel and the cargo and lives of those on board.[14] This was not a case where the ship was driven, willy-nilly, by the storm, but one where the captain made a deliberate choice to break the law in order to avert a greater evil; and was held justified in doing so.

To what extent a defence of necessity prevails in English law has not been settled with any degree of certainty. Stephen thought it

> "a subject on which the law of England is so vague that, if cases raising the question should ever occur the judges would practically be able to lay down any rule which they considered expedient."[15]

---

[10] Above, p. 81.

[11] See Hall, *General Principles*, Ch. XII; Williams, C.L.G.P., Ch. 17. and (1953), 6 C.L.P., 216; Stephen, *Digest*, Art. 11 and 2 H.C.L. 108–110; Fuller "The Speluncean Explorers" (1949), 62 Harv. L.R. 616; Wechsler and Michael (1937), 37 Col. L.R. 701 at 737–739.

[12] *Cf. Larsonneur* (above, p. 34) and *Kensington Borough Council* v. *Walters*, [1960] 1 Q.B. 361; [1959] 3 All E.R. 652, where D was held liable to pay the local authority the cost of repairing a street refuge into which his car had been propelled by another car, which collided with him without fault on D's part. This case (which was a civil proceeding) is criticised in [1960] Crim. L.R. 62 and by Turner, [1960] Crim. L.R. 89 and 168.

[13] Hale, 1 P.C. 434.

[14] *The William Gray*, 29 Fed. Cas. 1300, No. 17, 694.

[15] 2 H.C.L. 108.

His own opinion on the matter was that

> "it is just possible to imagine cases in which the expediency of breaking the law is so overwhelmingly great that people may be justified in breaking it, but these cases cannot be defined beforehand, and must be adjudicated upon by a jury afterwards, the jury not being under the pressure of the motives which influenced the alleged offenders."[16]

In spite of these doubts, Williams has submitted "with some assurance" that the defence of necessity is recognised by English law[17] and, particularly, by the criminal law,[18] arguing that the

> "peculiarity of necessity as a doctrine of law is the difficulty or impossibility of formulating it with any approach to precision."

Certainly the earlier writers generally quoted maxims supporting necessity as a defence[19] and, in 1550, Serjeant Pollard, in an argument which apparently found favour with the judges of the Exchequer Chamber said:[20]

> ". . . in every law there are some things which when they happen a man may break the words of the law, and yet not break the law itself; and such things are exempted out of the penalty of the law, and the law privileges them although they are done against the letter of it, for breaking the words of the law is not breaking the law, so as the intent of the law is not broken. And therefore the words of the law of nature, of the law of this realm, and of other realms and of the law of God will also yield and give way to some acts and things done against the words of the same laws, and that is, where the words of them are broken to avoid greater inconveniences, or through necessity, or by compulsion. . . ."

Moreover, it always seems to have been recognised that it was justifiable (in the conditions of those days) to pull down a house to prevent a fire from spreading, for a prisoner to leave a burning gaol contrary to the express words of a statute and for the crew of a ship to jettison the cargo in order to save the ship. The judges have accepted *obiter* that it would be a defence to the common law misdemeanour of exposing an infected person in the streets to show that the defendant was taking her infected child to obtain medical advice.[1] It has long been recognised that it is lawful to kill one who makes an illegal attack if that is necessary in self-defence.[2] Prison officials may—indeed, must—forcibly feed prisoners if that is necessary to preserve their health and, *a fortiori*, their lives.[3] It was a defence to the statutory felony of procuring an abortion to show that the act was done in good faith for the purpose only of preserving the life of the mother,[4] although at that time there was no provision for such a defence in any statute.[5] But, on the other hand, writers from Hale onwards have denied that necessity can be a defence to the larceny of food and clothing.[6] It might be argued that this case depends on the proposition that English law did not admit the possibility of a genuine necessity in such circumstances; for

---

[16] *Ibid.*, 109.
[17] 6 C.L.P., 216.
[18] C.L.G.P., 724 *et seq.*
[19] See 6 C.L.P., at 218.
[20] *Reniger* v. *Fogossa* (1552), 1 Plowden 1 at p. 18.
[1] *Vantandillo* (1815), 4 M. & S. 73; below, p. 543.
[2] Below, p. 230.
[3] *Leigh* v. *Gladstone* (1909), 26 T.L.R. 139.
[4] *Bourne*, [1939] 1 K.B. 687; [1938] 3 All E.R. 615; below, p. 242.
[5] See now Abortion Act 1967, below, p. 246.
[6] See 1 P.C. 54; Blackstone, *Commentaries*, iv, 31.

"by the laws of this kingdom, sufficient provision is made for the supply of such necessities by collections for the poor and by the power of the civil magistrate."[7]

More difficult to dispose of, however, is the case of *Dudley and Stephens*,[8] where the defence of necessity was expressly raised before the Queen's Bench Division and emphatically rejected. Three men and a boy of the crew of a yacht were shipwrecked and had to take to an open boat. After eighteen days in the boat, having been without food and water for several days, the two accused suggested to the third man that they should kill and eat the boy. He declined to fall in with this plan but, two days later, the accused killed the boy who was now in a very weak condition. The three men then fed on the boy's body and, four days later, they were rescued. The accused were indicted for murder. The jury, by a special verdict, found that the men would probably have died within the four days had they not fed on the boy's body, that the boy would probably have died before them and that, at the time of the killing, there was no appreciable chance of saving life, except by killing one for the others to eat.

The accused were convicted of murder, but the sentence was commuted to six months' imprisonment. The *ratio decidendi* is not obvious. Stephen said that he could discover no principle in the judgment.[9]

Lord COLERIDGE, C.J., however, began by casting doubt on whether necessity really existed:

"The verdict finds in terms that 'if the men had not fed upon the body of the boy they would *probably* not have survived,' and that 'The boy being in a much weaker condition was *likely* to have died before them.' They might possibly have been picked up next day by a passing ship; they might possibly not have been picked up at all; and in either case it is obvious that the killing of this boy would have been an unnecessary and profitless act."[10]

It is arguable that the case decided nothing about necessity, in that it was based on the premise that no necessity existed. But there is no certainty in human affairs; in any emergency, however hopeless the situation may seem, there is always the possibility of some unforeseen intervention. The most that can ever be postulated is a high degree of probability. If necessity is not admitted where there is a high degree of probability of disastrous consequences if action is not taken, then it can never be admitted. It has been well said that "modern legal systems . . . . do not require omniscience of human beings".[11] It is, therefore, difficult to avoid the conclusion that *Dudley* decided that it was no defence that the killing of one was necessary to preserve the lives of three.

Lord COLERIDGE, C.J., examined the pronouncements of writers of authority and found nothing in them to justify the extension of a defence to such a case as this. Killing by the use of force necessary to preserve one's own life in self-defence was a well-recognised, but an entirely different case from the killing of an innocent person. Moreover,

---

[7] Hale, *loc. cit.*
[8] (1884), 14 Q.B.D. 273. On the instructions of HUDDLESTON, B., the jury found the facts in a special verdict and the judge then adjourned the assizes to the Royal Courts of Justice where the case was argued before a court of five judges (Lord COLERIDGE, C.J., GROVE and DENMAN, JJ., POLLOCK and HUDDLESTON, BB.)
[9] *Digest* (8th ed.), 10, n. 2.
[10] 14 Q.B.D. at p. 279. *Cf.* CARDOZO, J.: "Who shall know when masts and sails of rescue may emerge out of the fog?" *Selected Writings*, 390.
[11] Hall, *General Principles*, 434.

"If ... Lord Hale is clear—as he is—that extreme necessity of hunger does not justify larceny, what would he have said to the doctrine that it justified murder ?[12]

Apart from authority, the court clearly thought that the law ought not to afford a defence in such a case. They thought, first, that it would be too great a departure from morality; and, secondly, that the principle would be dangerous because of the difficulty of measuring necessity and of selecting the victim.

"Though law and morality are not the same, and many things may be immoral which are not necessarily illegal, yet the absolute divorce of law from morality would be of fatal consequence; and such divorce would follow if the temptation to murder in this case were to be held by law an absolute defence to it."[13]

It is not easy to see how this far-reaching consequence would follow from the admission of a defence in the particular circumstances so rare that there was, and is, no comparable reported case in English law. But the second reason is more convincing:

"Who is to be the judge of this sort of necessity? By what measure is the comparative value of lives to be measured? Is it to be strength or intellect, or what? It is plain that the principle leaves to him who is to profit by it to determine the necessity which will justify him in deliberately taking another's life to save his own."[14]

The answer to the first question must surely be that it would be for a jury, under the direction of the judge, to say whether, on the facts known to D, a true necessity existed; and that it would be no defence merely to show that D believed the act was necessary. But the difficulty of choice is a very real one. If the boy had been able to resist, surely the law would not deny him the right to do so and to kill if that was the only way in which he could preserve his own life ?[15] But if the boy was not forbidden by the law from killing in self-defence this could only be either because the act of the aggressors was illegal or because the law had abdicated and gave no answer to the problem. If it is unlawful neither for A to kill B nor for B to kill A, might, indeed, is right, and anarchy, not law, prevails.[16] The law, surely, must provide an answer; and, if the choice must be made, surely it is better to say that the boy may kill his aggressors than that they may kill him?

Williams finds as the "one satisfying reason" in the judgment that it was no more necessary to kill the boy than one of the grown men and adds: "To hinge guilt on this would indicate that lots should have been cast ..."[17] If the boy had agreed to be bound by the casting of lots, he would have been consenting to

---

[12] 14 Q.B.D. at p. 283.

[13] *Ibid.*, at p. 287.

[14] *Ibid.*

[15] *Cf.* Stephen, discussing *U.S.* v. *Holmes*, 26 Fed. Cas. 360 (1842) (below, p. 140). "Suppose one of the party in the boat had a revolver and was able to use it, and refused either to draw lots or to allow himself or his wife or daughter to be made to do so or thrown overboard, could anyone deny that he was acting in self-defence and the defence of his nearest relations, and would he violate any legal duty in so doing?" 2 H.C.L. 109. Professor Hall replies: ". . . a correct statement of the legal import of such conduct is that not only was he not acting in self-defence (any more than does one who resists a legal arrest or self-defence, itself) but, also, that he was guilty of inflicting a proscribed harm": *General Principles*, 435.

[16] *Cf.* the mythical TATTING, J., in the "Speluncean Explorers", who withdraws from a similar case, finding it legally insoluble: (1949), 62 Harv. L.R. 616 at pp. 626–631.

[17] C.L.G.P., 744.

die; and consent in such a situation may be a defence. Captain Oates took his life when he left Scott and his companions; yet he was regarded, not as a felon, but as a hero. If the boy had not consented, the drawing of lots would be hardly more rational than trial by ordeal—yet more civilized than a free-for-all. In fact, the court disapproved, *obiter*, of a ruling in an American case, *U.S.* v. *Holmes*,[18] that the drawing of lots in similar circumstances would legalise a killing. Holmes, a member of the crew of a wrecked ship, was cast adrift in an overcrowded boat. In order to prevent the boat sinking, the mate gave orders to throw the male passengers overboard and Holmes assisted in throwing over sixteen men. No doubt, if his act was criminal at all, it was murder; but a grand jury refused to indict him for murder and so he was charged with manslaughter. The judge directed that the law was that passengers must be preferred to seamen; only enough seamen to navigate the boat ought to have been saved; and the passengers whom necessity requires to be cast over must be chosen by lot. As this had not been done (none of the officers or crew went down with the ship) the jury found him guilty.

Stephen thought the method of selection "over refined"[19] and Lord COLERIDGE thought this

> "somewhat strange ground . . . can hardly . . . be an authority satisfactory to a court in this country."[20]

The English judges offered no alternative solution and, presumably, their view was that, in the absence of a self-sacrificing volunteer, it was the duty of all to die. This was also the view of the distinguished American judge, CARDOZO, J.:

> "Where two or more are overtaken by a common disaster, there is no right on the part of one to save the lives of some, by the killing of another. There is no rule of human jettison."[1]

One argument is that in circumstances like these the threat of punishment cannot deter. But even faced with imminent death a man may be influenced by the fact that one of the courses open to him is murder. *Something* deterred the third man from joining in Dudley's and Stephens's plan though he was in equally dire straits and it is noteworthy that, immediately before killing,

> "the prisoner Dudley offered a prayer asking for forgiveness for them all if either of them should be tempted to commit a rash act, and that their souls might be saved."[2]

This does not sound like the conduct of a man who had ceased to take account of how his conduct was to be judged.

In the light of *Dudley* it is not easy to say how far a defence of necessity is available beyond the specific cases noted above. Some things seem to be clear.

(a) Where A kills B whom he knows to be innocent it is no defence that this was necessary in order to save his own life. A much discussed problem in this context is the following:

> ". . . two persons being shipwrecked and getting on the same plank; it is found not able to save them both, and one thrusts the other from it whereby he is drowned."[3]

---

[18] 26 Fed. Cas. 360 (1842).
[19] 2 H.C.L. 108.
[20] 14 Q.B.D. at p. 285.
[1] *Selected Writings*, 390.
[2] 14 Q.B.D. at p. 274.
[3] East, 1 P.C. 294.

East simply said of this case that "necessity may be urged"; Hawkins said, "It is said to be justifiable";[4] and Holmes regarded the case as a doubtful one.[5] Bacon thought A's conduct was justified and went so far as to extend justification to the case where B had hold of the plank first and A came and thrust him off.[6] It seems clear now that English law would not excuse either of these acts.[7] What if, in the last-mentioned case B had repelled A? This seems properly analogous to self-defence[8] and certainly *Dudley* is distinguishable. B would be justified.

(b) Similarly, it could not be a defence that A had killed B as the only means of saving C. For example, X has threatened A's wife, C, with instant death unless A kills B.[9] Nor does it appear to make any difference that A's object was to save a number of persons; Dudley killed to save himself and two others. Yet there are difficulties about a logical application of this rule to all cases: would it not be lawful to open a dike with the effect of drowning the half-dozen inhabitants of a farm, if this was the only way of saving a dam from bursting and inundating a whole town?[10]

Perhaps the difference here is that the choice is clear; it is *either* the half-dozen *or* the hundreds who must perish; but in *Dudley* there was no clear choice between the boy on the one hand and the men on the other. It must be conceded that it was not "more necessary to kill him than one of the grown men";[11] it is arguable that it is "more necessary to save the hundred than the half-dozen." But this case is not absolutely clear. Suppose that the farmer, knowing all the facts, has a rifle with which he can kill the man opening the dam. Does the law deny him the right to shoot to kill in order to preserve his own life and the lives of his family? Is he not essentially in the same position as the first man on the plank? He is the one at present in possession of safety. If it is lawful to drown him in order to preserve the hundred lives, then it must follow that he is deprived of his right of self-defence and is under a duty to die a heroic and unresisting death. The law rarely, if ever, imposes such high standards.[12]

It has been contended that there is or should be a doctrine of necessity generally applicable throughout the criminal law. The tentative draft of the American model penal code runs:

> "Conduct which the actor believes to be necessary to avoid an evil to himself or to another is justifiable, provided that:
>
> (a) the evil sought to be avoided by such conduct is greater than that sought to be prevented by the law defining the offence charged . . ."[13]

---

[4] Hawkins, 1 P.C. 326.
[5] *The Common Law*, 47.
[6] *Maxims*, reg. 25.
[7] Stephen's contention (*Digest*, 10, n. 2) that this case is distinguishable from *Dudley* is unconvincing: "Here the successful man does no direct bodily harm to the other. He leaves him the chance of getting another plank." But the problem pre-supposes that the men believe there are no other planks about.
[8] Below p. 230.
[9] Wechsler and Michael (1937), 37 Col. L.R. 739. And see below, p. 142.
[10] American Model Penal Code, Tentative Draft No. 8, S3. O2 Comments, p. 8: ". . . he can rightly point out that the object of the law of homicide is to save life, and that by his conduct he has effected a net saving of innocent lives . . . the numerical preponderance in the lives saved surely establishes an ethical and legal justification for the act."
[11] (1884), 14 Q.B.D. at pp. 287–288.
[12] But *cf.* Professor Hall's view in footnote 15, p. 139, above.
[13] Tentative draft No. 8, Art 3. (for which Glanville Williams was special consultant). It is subject to qualifications not necessary to be noted here.

It is clear that it cannot be stated with confidence that the present English law goes so far; and it is thought that there is much wisdom in the advice of STEPHEN, J., against seeking to anticipate such cases. The defence of necessity at present, then, does not go beyond the few well-recognised instances; and, no doubt, any development of the law will be similarly piecemeal.

7 DURESS (OR COMPULSION) AND COERCION[14]

The defences here to be considered are closely related to that of necessity. Once again, D is faced with a choice of evils: shall he break the criminal law or submit to the infliction of some evil on himself or on another? These might be regarded as special cases of necessity, the only peculiarity being that need arises out of the wrongful threats of another to inflict some harm if the criminal action is not taken. The terms "duress", "compulsion" and "coercion" are often used as if they were synonymous; but some writers reserve "coercion" for a special defence available to wives under pressure from their husbands, and this convenient practice will be followed here.

1 Duress

Though it is rarely raised, there is no doubt that a defence of duress does exist but there are difficulties in defining its limits. It has most commonly been raised in treason cases and it is clear that duress can be a defence to a charge of treason.

As long ago as 1419 in *Oldcastle's* case[15] the accused who were charged with treason in supplying victuals to Sir John Oldcastle and his fellow rebels were acquitted on the ground that they acted *pro timore mortis, et quod recesserunt quam cito potuerunt.* The existence of the defence was admitted, *obiter*, by LEE, C.J., in *M'Growther*,[16] a trial for treason committed in the 1745 rebellion and by Lord MANSFIELD in *Stratton*:[17]

> "... if a man is forced to commit acts of high treason, if it appears really force, and such as human nature could not be expected to resist and the jury are of that opinion, the man is not guilty of high treason."

Much more recently, in *Purdy*[18] OLIVER, J., directed a jury that fear of death would be a defence to a British prisoner of war who was charged with treason in having assisted with German propaganda in the second world war. Against this, Lord GODDARD, C.J., said in *Steane*[19] that the defence did not apply to treason, but this remark appears to have been made *per incuriam*.

Hale distinguished cases occurring in time of peace from those occurring (as did all the cases considered above) "in times of war, or public insurrection or rebellion"; when compulsion or fear of death might excuse "some acts in themselves capital which admit no excuse in time of peace."[20] In time of peace,

---

[14] See Edwards (1951), 14 M.L.R. 297; Williams, C.L.G.P., Ch. 18; Hall, *General Principles*, 436 *et seq.*
[15] Hale (1419), 1 P.C. 50; East, 1 P.C. 70.
[16] Foster, 13; 18 St. Tr. 391.
[17] (1779), 1 Doug. K.B. 239.
[18] (1946), 10 J. Cr. L. 182.
[19] [1947] K.B. 997 at p. 1005; [1947] 1 All E.R. 813 at p. 817.
[20] 1 P.C. 49.

"if a man be menaced with death unless he will commit an act of treason or murder or robbery, the fear of death will not excuse him, if he commit the fact."[1]

This rule might appear illogical and it might be said that, if a distinction is to be made between peace and war, it is in wartime that the defence should be excluded, for then anyone might be expected to give up his life in the defence of the realm.[2] Hale's reason, however, would appear to be that in wartime the ordinary legal remedies may not be available to a man who has fallen into enemy (or rebel) hands whereas in peacetime,

"the law hath provided a sufficient remedy against such fears by applying himself to the courts and officers of justice for a writ or precept *de securitate pacis*".[3]

Hale's reasoning is cogently criticised by Stephen[4] on the ground that in most cases there would be no time to resort to the protection of the law; but it is arguable that Hale's rule excluding the defence was not intended to be applicable, even in peacetime, to cases where there is no time to invoke legal remedies. Conversely, it is clear that, in wartime, the defence is not available to one who has the opportunity to put himself under the protection of the lawfully established authorities. Unless duress is to be a defence, as Stephen believed, only when the compulsion is applied by a body of rebels or rioters,[5] the logic of the reason underlying Hale's rule would go no farther than to exclude from the defence cases where D is in a position to seek legal protection from threats and fails to do so. This is in accordance with the principle of all the authorities. Thus in *M'Growther*'s case LEE, C.J., said:[6]

"The only force that doth excuse, is a force upon *the person*, and present fear of death; and this force and fear must continue all the time the party remains with the rebels. It is incumbent on every man, who makes force his defence, to show an actual force, and that he quitted the service as soon as he could."

It is submitted that this is the better way of interpreting the law as stated by Hale. It makes no difference to D, who is acting under a threat supported by a gun in his back whether it is held by an enemy, a rebel, a rioter or a criminal on a frolic of his own.

It must not be supposed that threats, even of death, will necessarily be a defence to every act of treason. In *Oldcastle*'s case[7] Hale emphasises that the accused's act was *only* furnishing of victuals and he appears to question whether, if they had taken a more active part in the rebellion, they would have been excused. Stephen thought the defence only applied where the offender took a subordinate part. If, as appears to be generally accepted, duress is not a defence to a charge of murder, it would be surprising if it were allowed where the expected consequence of the treasonable act was the death of one or more innocent persons.

---

[1] *Ibid.*, 51.
[2] *Cf.* Edwards (1951), 14 M.L.R. at p. 301.
[3] 1 P.C. 51.
[4] 2 H.C.L. 107.
[5] 2 H.C.L. 106.
[6] Foster at p. 14.
[7] Hale, 1 P.C. 50.

The authorities[8] generally except murder from the scope of the defence and in *Tyler*,[9] an indictment for murder, DENMAN, J., directed the jury that

> "no man from a fear of consequences to himself, has a right to make himself a party to committing a mischief on mankind".

In the case of lesser crimes it is reasonable to assume that it is of general application. The authorities are few; but in *Crutchley*[10] it appears to have been allowed on an indictment for maliciously damaging a threshing machine. PATTESON, J., admitted evidence to the effect that the prisoner and others had been compelled by a mob to join them and to give one blow to each machine that the mob broke; and, apparently on this evidence, D was acquitted. In modern cases the defence has been accepted as available on charges of larceny,[11] receiving stolen goods[12] and arson.[13] In *Bourne*,[14] the Court of Criminal Appeal appears to have accepted that the defence would apply to a charge of buggery. In *Verrier and Anderson*[15] it was assumed that duress was a defence to a charge of conspiracy to defraud.

What is a sufficiently serious threat to amount to duress? Hale speaks of threats of death and so do the judges in *M'Growther*[16] and *Purdy*;[17] Blackstone refers to "death or other bodily harm", Stephen to death or grievous bodily harm and Lord GODDARD, C.J., in *Steane*[18] to violence or imprisonment. It is clear that the threat must be one of immediate action and not of unpleasantness at some time in the future. There is no case in which a threat of injury to property, as distinct from the person, has been admitted. In *M'Growther*[19] D, who was a tenant of the Duke of Perth, called witnesses who proved that the Duke had threatened to burn the houses and drive off the cattle of any of his tenants who refused to follow him. LEE, C.J., directed that this could be no defence. But that was a case of treason and it does not necessarily follow that such a threat would not be enough on some lesser charge. It has been noted above that there is some authority for saying that the seriousness of the accused's conduct is a proper factor to be taken into consideration in these cases; and it would seem to follow that the law makes some effort to weigh in the balance the evils between which the accused had to choose. If the evil he caused by submitting to the threat was clearly less than that which would have been inflicted had he defied it, there are cogent reasons for allowing a defence; even if the threat was not of death or even grievous bodily harm. Williams has argued strongly in favour of such a principle, which is, of course, closely analogous to that adopted in the American model penal code in relation to necessity.[20] But, again, this is in advance of judicial thought on the matter. The only rule that

---

[8] Blackstone, *Commentaries*, iv, 30: ". . . he ought rather to die himself than escape by the murder of an innocent." East, 1 P.C. 225 (but see also p. 294).

[9] (1838), 8 C. & P. 616 at p. 620.

[10] (1831), 5 C. & P. 133.

[11] *Gill*, [1963] 2 All E.R. 688 (C.C.A.).

[12] *A.-G.* v. *Whelan*, [1934] I. R. 518 (Irish C.C.A.).

[13] *Shiartos* (LAWTON, J.) 1961, Sept. 19 unreported but referred to in *Gill*, above, footnote 11.

[14] (1952), 36 Cr. App. Rep. 125; above, p. 94.

[15] [1965] Crim. L.R. 732.

[16] Above, p. 143.   [17] Above, p. 142.

[18] [1947] K.B. at p. 1005; [1947] 1 All E.R. at p. 816.

[19] Above, p. 143.

[20] Above, p. 141.

can be stated with confidence at the present time is that threats of death (and probably grievous bodily harm) will excuse crimes other than murder.

In principle, it is clear that, while the prisoner should have the evidential burden, the onus of disproving duress should be on the Crown,[1] but until recently there were doubts about this because of Lord GODDARD's remark in *Steane*,[2] that "Duress is a matter of defence and the onus of proving it is on the accused". This, however, was *obiter* and it has now been held in *Gill*[3] that it must be construed as referring only to the evidential burden, since Lord GODDARD was contrasting proof of duress with that of a specific intent, where both the evidential burden and the burden of proof are on the Crown.[4]

2 Coercion

Though the terminology used by judges and writers is by no means uniform, the term "coercion" is generally reserved for a special defence that was available at common law only to a wife who committed certain crimes in the presence of her husband. It was then presumed that she acted under such coercion as to entitle her to be excused, unless the prosecution were able to prove that she took the initiative in committing the offence. The exact extent of the defence is uncertain. It did not apply to treason or murder; Hale[5] excluded manslaughter as well and Hawkins ruled out robbery.[6]

Earlier authorities allowed the defence only in the case of felonies but later it seems to have been extended to misdemeanours—but excluding brothel-keeping;

> "for this is an offence touching the domestic economy or government of the home in which the wife has a principal share."[7]

Various theoretical justifications were advanced for the rule—the identity of husband and wife, the wife's subjection to her husband and her duty to obey him—but the practical reason for its application to felonies was that it saved a woman from the death penalty when her husband was able, but she was not, to plead benefit of clergy.[8] This reason disappeared in 1692 when benefit of clergy was extended to women, yet the rule continued and its scope increased.

In 1925, however, the presumption was abolished by the Criminal Justice Act, s. 47:

> "Any presumption of law that an offence committed by a wife in the presence of her husband is committed under the coercion of the husband is hereby abolished, but on a charge against a wife for any offence other than treason or murder, it shall be a good defence to prove that the offence was committed in the presence of, and under the coercion of, the husband."

At first sight, it would seem that all Parliament has done is to shift the burden of proof. But there are difficulties about this, for the question at once arises,

---

[1] *Woolmington* v. *Director of Public Prosecutions*, [1935] A.C. 462.
[2] [1947] 1 K.B. at pp. 1005–1006; [1947] 1 All E.R. at p. 817.
[3] [1963] 2 All E.R. 688. (C.C.A.). *Bone*, [1968] 2 All. E.R. 644.
[4] *Cf*. Williams, C.L.G.P., 762, n. 13 whose argument was accepted in *Gill*. Hall, however, accepts American authorities which put the onus on the prisoner: *General Principles*, 443.
[5] 1 P.C. 45.
[6] 1 P.C. 4; but the editor of the 8th ed. (J. Curwood) doubted this.
[7] Blackstone, *Commentaries*, iv, 29.
[8] Hale, 1 P.C. 45; 2 Lew C.C. 232n.

proof of what? and it is not very easy to answer. "Coercion" at common law was really a fiction applied when the wife committed a crime in the presence of the husband and there was no evidence of initiative by the wife. The common law gives little guidance as to what is required now coercion is a matter of affirmative proof. One solution is to hold that it simply means the same as duress and puts the wife in the same situation as anyone else. The difficulty about that is that it would appear to put the wife in a *worse* position; for (i) the onus of disproving duress is on the Crown[9] and (ii) duress applies to treason.[10] The first difficulty might be got over by holding that the statute puts on the wife only the evidential burden (which defendants relying on duress have, but wives relying on coercion at common law did not) of introducing so much evidence as might raise a reasonable doubt whether she was under duress. The second difficulty is less easy to get over. Of course, it may be that, owing to the uncertainties of this branch of the criminal law, Parliament thought that duress did not apply to treason and that, if it does, wives have been put in a worse position by accident.[11]

The alternative is to hold that coercion is a wider defence than duress and is available to wives in addition to the general defence. This would seem to have been the real intention and the better view. In the debate on the Bill the Solicitor-General told the House that the section gives the married woman

> "a rather wider and more extended line of defence than pure compulsion, because coercion imports coercion in the moral, possibly even in the spiritual realm, whereas compulsion imports something only in the physical realm."[12]

The recommendation of the Avory Committee[13] that wives should be put in the same position as persons generally was not adopted. Far from there being the "endless litigation" which one member feared, there is only one reported case[14] in which the defence has been relied on.[15] It is by no means clear what a wife has to prove to succeed—moral and spiritual, as distinct from physical, coercion are somewhat intangible. Edwards suggests—as possibilities—the wife who has been

> "tamed into believing that failure to obey her husband's every command would inevitably result in her being doomed to suffer the fires of hell;"

or who has

> "been inculcated with her husband's teaching that to steal from the rich to help the poor was right and just;"

and,

> "what about threats not to provide any money to purchase food for the wife and children, or to desert the wife or to bring a concubine home to live under the same roof"[16]

---

[9] Above, p. 145.
[10] Above, p. 142.
[11] *Cf.*, however, Williams, C.L.G.P., 765· "The Act can be regarded as merely an incomplete statement of the common law, and the common law still exists to supplement its deficiency."
[12] Parl. Deb., H. of C. (1925), 188, col. 875.
[13] Cmd. 1677.
[14] *Pierce* (1941), 5 J. Cr. L. 124. *Cf. Bourne* (above p. 94) where duress rather than coercion seems to have been relied on.
[15] Perhaps the view of Mr. Greaves-Lord, M.P., has proved correct: ". . . how many women are there who have been coerced like that, who dare go into the witness box in order to convict the very persons under whose coercion the woman had committed the crime?" Parl. Deb., H. of C., 188, col. 870.
[16] (1951) 14 M.L.R. at p. 311.

Williams suggests that

> "Perhaps it is enough to show that the wife is meek and tractable, under the domination of her husband, and unable to influence him."[17]

The answer to these questions must await the decisions of the court when such cases arise.

The defence will no doubt be confined, as it was at common law, strictly to the case of husband and wife and will not be extended to an unmarried couple living as man and wife.[18] Yet a woman in such a situation may be as much under coercion as any married woman; while children, to whom no such defence is available, may be even more under the influence of their parents. Edwards argues for the retention of the defence, urging that

> "there still remains a considerable proportion of married women who regard their husbands as their lord and master to disobey whose commands would be unthinkable;"[19]

but it is thought that the very absence of cases in which it has been relied goes a long way towards showing that it is an unnecessary anomaly at the present day.

8 SUPERIOR ORDERS

Though there is little authority on this question, it is safe to assert that it is not a defence for D merely to show that the act was done by him in obedience to the orders of a superior, whether military or civil. The fact that D was acting under orders may, nevertheless, be very relevant. It may negative *mens rea* by, for example, showing that D was acting under a mistake of fact or that he had a claim of right[20] to do as he did, where that is a defence; or, where the charge is one of negligence,[1] it may show that he was acting reasonably.

The only question (which has been discussed mainly in connection with military orders) is whether orders are a defence where they do not negative *mens rea* or negligence, but give rise to a reasonable mistake of law. *The Manual of Military Law*[2] now asserts as "the better view" that they do not. *Dicta* in some of the cases suggest that they might. In a South African case[3] which has been much cited, SOLOMON, J., said:

> "I think it is a safe rule to lay down that if a soldier honestly believes he is doing his duty in obeying the commands of his superior, and if the orders are not so manifestly illegal that he must or ought to have known they are unlawful, the private soldier would be protected by the orders of his superior officer. . ."

The only English authority[4] directly on the point holds that it is not a defence to a charge of murder for D to show that he fired under the mistaken impression that it was his duty to do so. D was, no doubt, making a mistake of law, but there is no finding as to its reasonableness. If mistake of law does not afford a defence where it is reasonable on other grounds, it should not, in principle, afford a defence because it is reasonable as arising from the orders of a superior. If the result is harsh, it is because the rule (if it be the rule[5]) that reasonable mistake of law is not a defence is a harsh general rule.[6]

---

[17] C.L.G.P., 766.
[18] *Court* (1912), 7 Cr. App. Rep. 127.
[19] (1951), 14 M.L.R. at 312–313.
[20] *James* (1837), 8 C. & P. 131.
[1] *Trainer* (1864), 4 F. & F. 105.
[2] (1956), Part I, 117.
[3] *Smith* (1900), 17 S.C.R. 561; 17 C.G.H. 561.
[4] *Thomas* (1816), Ms. of BAILEY, J., Turner and Armitage, *Cases on Criminal Law*, 67.
[5] See above, p. 131.
[6] For further discussion, see Stephen, 1 H.C.L., 204–206; Dicey, *Law of the Constitution* (10th ed.), 302–306; Williams, C.L.G.P., 105.

CHAPTER 10

Incitement, Conspiracy and Attempt

1 INCITEMENT

The mere incitement of another to commit an indictable offence is a common law misdemeanour, whether the incitement is successful in persuading the other to commit, or to attempt to commit the offence or not.   It was so held in the leading case of *Higgins*[1] where Lord KENYON said:[2]

> "But it is argued, that a mere intent to commit evil is not indictable, without an act done; but is there not an act done, when it is charged that the defendant solicited another to commit a felony?   The solicitation is an act: and the answer given at the Bar is decisive, that it would be sufficient to constitute an overt act of high treason."

In principle, it would seem necessary that the incitement should have been communicated,[3] but the matter is of small practical importance since in the case of a failure of communication, there would at least be an attempt to incite.[4]

Where under the rule in *Tyrrell*[5] a victim is incapable of being an abettor, he is equally incapable of incitement; but the procedural requirements of the ulterior offence—such as the consent of the Director of Public Prosecutions[6]—do not necessarily apply to a charge of incitement.

If the offence incited is actually committed, then, as seen above, D becomes a participant in the offence and may be dealt with as a principal offender.

---

[1] (1801), 2 East 5.
[2] *Ibid.*, at p. 170.
[3] *Banks* (1873), 12 Cox C.C. 393 (letter, suggesting the murder of a child not yet born, intercepted.   Held an attempt to incite under Offences against the Person Act 1861, s. 4; below, p. 234).   Statutory offences of "soliciting" may be different; *cf.* *Horton* v. *Mead*, [1913] 1 K.B. 154; below, p. 316.
[4] It is of *some* importance, because a magistrates' court has no power to convict of an attempt on a charge of the full offence. Below, p. 176.
[5] Above, p. 96.   Tyrrell was acquitted of incitement as well as abetting.
[6] *Assistant Recorder of Hull, ex p. Morgan*, [1969] 1 All E.R. 416.

1 The Crime Incited

(i) *A summary offence.*—Incitement to commit even a summary offence is indictable. This was implicit in the Magistrates' Courts Act 1952[7] which provides that an incitement to commit a summary offence may be dealt with summarily with the consent of the accused; and in *Curr*[8] the Court of Appeal took the view that this settled the matter. It seems extraordinary that the mere incitement to commit an offence should be regarded as more serious than the actual commission of that offence. This is the result, for the incitement, being a common law misdemeanour, may be punished with fine and imprisonment at the discretion of the court—that is, much more heavily than any summary offence. Moreover, other safeguards, such as periods of limitation which attach to summary offences, are inapplicable when the charge is incitement.

Conspiracy to commit a summary offence is similarly indictable.[9] This might be justified on the ground that the combination to do an unlawful act is more dangerous than the actual doing of the act by one person. It would be difficult to contend, however, that mere incitement to a crime is more dangerous than the crime itself. It is true that some incitements are attempts to conspire but these could be indicted as such.[10] The rule that incitement to commit summary offences is indictable is quite irrational.

(ii) *Another inchoate offence.*—An indictment will lie for inciting to conspire;[11] and an incitement to conspire would seem necessarily to amount to an attempt to conspire.[12] Presumably the same act could properly be charged in either way.

Whereas, generally, an indictment for inciting to attempt would be inept, it may be an appropriate charge in the special circumstances considered below.

2 Mens Rea

As in the case of counselling and abetting, it must be proved that D knew of (or deliberately closed his eyes to) all the circumstances which render the act incited the crime in question. To constitute an incitement there must, however, be, in addition, an element of persuasion,[13] which is not necessary in the case of counselling or abetting. If D sells a gun to E, knowing that E intends to murder P, it is probable that D is guilty of murder if E does kill P;[14] but, if E does not kill P, it would seem impossible, on those facts alone, to convict D of incitement.

Among the circumstances is the *mens rea* of the person incited. If D believes that the person does not have *mens rea* for the crime in question, then he intends to commit that crime through an innocent agent, but he is not guilty of incite-

---

[7] See s. 19 (8), and First Schedule, para. 20. Williams, C.L.G.P. § 193, suggested that the Schedule may be concerned only with "offences of incitement created by special statutes". This possibility was not referred to by the court in *Curr*, below.

[8] [1967] 1 All E.R. 478.

[9] *Blamires Transport Services, Ltd.*, [1964] 1 Q.B. 278; [1963] 3 All E.R. 170; below, p. 157.

[10] If the incitement were charged as an attempt to conspire, it would seem to follow from *Blamires* case that an indictment would lie.

[11] *De Kromme* (1892), 17 Cox C.C. 492.

[12] In *De Kromme*, at p. 494, Lord COLERIDGE, C.J., said, "There was an attempt to bring another mind into combination to do this."

[13] *Christian* (1913), 78 J.P. 112; below, p. 295. And see below, p. 234.

[14] Above, p. 85.

ment. In *Curr*[15] D was acquitted of inciting women to commit offences under the Family Allowances Act 1945 because it was not proved that the women had the guilty knowledge necessary to constitute that offence. The real question, it is submitted, should have been, not whether the women actually had the knowledge, but whether D believed they had. In that event he should have been guilty. But if he believed that they did not have the guilty knowledge, he was not guilty of incitement, whether they had it or not.[16] If D urges E to accept the gift of a necklace, which is in fact stolen, he is not guilty of inciting E to handle stolen goods if he believes E to be unaware that the necklace is stolen; even though in fact she is so aware.

3   Impossibility

It is irrelevant that the crime incited is impossible of commission. So in *McDonough*[17] D was convicted of inciting E to receive certain lamb carcases, knowing them to be stolen, although in fact no lamb carcases were in existence at the time. It does not appear whether D knew that there were no carcases. If he believed the carcases were in existence, the decision seems clearly correct and is supported by the analogy of the cases on attempts.[18] If he knew there were no carcases it is arguable that he should have been acquitted as lacking *mens rea*.[19] Thus in *Brown*[20] D was charged with inciting women to take a noxious thing with intent to procure abortion. DARLING, J., directed that, if D knew that the thing was not noxious but that the women would take it thinking it was, *they* would be guilty of an attempt,[21] but *he* would not be guilty of incitement. It is thought, however that, in such circumstances, an indictment for inciting *to attempt* should lie and that *Brown* should be re-considered. It is established that E may be convicted of attempting to pick a pocket which is in fact empty.[22] If D incites E to attempt to steal from a pocket which D knows to be empty, he is asking E to do an act, which, in the circumstances known to D, will amount to the misdemeanour of attempt. As a matter of fact, he *is* inciting E to commit that misdemeanour; and there seems to be no reason why he should not be held liable in law.[1]

It should be noted that the result might have been different if, in *McDonough*,[2] D had incited E to receive *certain existing* carcases which both wrongly believed to be stolen. Here, if the whole transaction which they contemplated were performed, the *actus reus* of no crime would result; and the *dicta* in *Percy Dalton, Ltd.*[3] which were said in *McDonough*[4] to be "obviously right" suggest that an indictment for incitement, no less than attempt, would fail in such a case.

---

[15] Above, footnote 8.
[16] *Cf. Bourne* (1952), 36 Cr. App. Rep. 125, above, p. 94.
[17] (1962), 47 Cr. App. Rep. 37. D may be convicted of inciting the murder of a person yet unborn: *Shephard*, [1919] 2 K.B. 125; but that is not a case of impossibility.
[18] Below, p. 171.
[19] Williams, C.L.G.P., § 194.
[20] (1899), 63 J.P. 790.
[21] On this question, see below, p. 174.
[22] Below, pp. 170-171.
[1] It is true, as Williams points out (§ 193), that an indictment for inciting to a common law attempt would generally be inept; but the ineptitude does not seem to exist in the special circumstances of the problems discussed here.
[2] Above, footnote 15.
[3] (1949), 33 Cr. App. Rep. 102; below, p. 172; but see now *Millar and Page*, below, p. 173.
[4] (1962), 47 Cr. App. Rep. 37 at p. 41.

2 CONSPIRACY[5]

Conspiracy consists in the agreement between two or more persons to effect some "unlawful" purpose. The word "unlawful" is used in a special sense which is examined in detail below.[6] The crime is complete so soon as the parties agree, and it is quite immaterial that they never begin to put their agreement into effect.[7] The *actus reus*, then, is the agreement, which, of course, is not a mere mental operation but must involve spoken or written words or other overt acts. Conspiracy thus occupies an intermediate stage between incitement and attempt. Most conspiracies probably begin with the incitement by one of another to commit a crime. When the other agrees, there is a conspiracy; but obviously further action is required before there can be an attempt. Conspiracy is another common law misdemeanour, punishable with fine or imprisonment at the discretion of the court, except in the case of murder where, by statute,[8] there is a maximum punishment of ten years.

1 The Actus Reus—an Agreement

It may be that an agreement in the strict sense required by the law of contract is not necessary[9] but the parties must at least have reached a decision to perpetrate the unlawful object. In *Walker*[10] a conviction was quashed although it was "perfectly clear" that D had discussed with others the proposition of stealing a payroll, because it was not proved that they had got beyond the stage of negotiation when D withdrew.

If an agreement is reached, it is immaterial that it is subject to express or implied reservations.[11] If it were otherwise, no one could ever be convicted of conspiracy for every agreement like every contract, is subject to implied reservations.

If A agrees to sell B certain goods, known to both to be stolen, at "a price to be agreed between us", they have not (apart from the question of illegality) reached the stage of a concluded contract.[12] Is there an indictable conspiracy? It is thought that there probably is; though it is arguable that the situation is no different from that where the parties are bargaining as to the price of stolen goods and are clearly, therefore, still at the stage of negotiation. If the parties are trying to reach agreement, the question is of no practical importance since it would seem that there is an attempt to conspire which, as a common law misdemeanour, is punishable in the same way as the conspiracy itself.

---

[5] Williams, C.L.G.P., Ch. 15; Wright, *Law of Criminal Conspiracies and Agreements* (1873); Stephen, 2 H.C.L. 227; Winfield, *History of Conspiracy and Abuse of Legal Procedure*; Sayre (1922), 35 Harv. L.R. 393.

[6] See p. 157.

[7] In the *Bridgewater* case (unreported) referred to by Lord COLERIDGE, C.J., in the *Mogul Steamship* case (1888), 21 Q.B.D. 544 at p. 549, D was convicted although he withdrew from the combination immediately.

[8] Offences against the Person Act 1861, s. 4.

[9] *Cf.* Williams, C.L.G.P., § 212.

[10] [1962] Crim. L.R. 458. *Cf. Mulcahy* v. *R.* (1868), L.R. 3 H.L. 306 at p. 317.

[11] *Mills*, [1963] 1 Q.B. 522; [1963] 1 All E.R. 202.

[12] *May and Butcher* v. *R.*, [1934] 2 K.B. 17n. (H.L.)

2 The Mens Rea

Conspiracy is a common law offence and, accordingly, *mens rea* must be proved. D must intend to carry out the unlawful purpose.[13] He must know of the facts which make the purpose unlawful. In *Churchill* v. *Walton*[14] the House of Lords held that this is so even when the offence which the parties have agreed to commit is one of strict liability:

> "If what they agreed to do was, on the facts known to them, an unlawful act,[15] they are guilty of conspiracy and cannot excuse themselves by saying that, owing to their ignorance of the law, they did not realise that such an act was a crime. If, on the facts known to them, what they agreed to do was lawful, they are not rendered artificially guilty by the existence of other facts, not known to them, giving a different and criminal quality to the act agreed on."

So if D1 and D2, wrongly believing a girl to be over sixteen, agree to take her out of the possession of her parents, they do not commit conspiracy. But if they know her to be under sixteen, and believe that it is lawful so to take her, then they are guilty of conspiracy. This is in accordance with the general principle that ignorance of the criminal law is no defence,[16] but, in the case of offences with no moral content, it may operate very harshly.

In *Jacobs*[17] D1 and D2 agreed to buy from E 300 gross razor blades at 42s. per gross. The controlled price, under the Prices of Goods Act 1939 was 15s. On a charge of conspiring to contravene the Act, WROTTESLEY, J., directed that it was not necessary that the accused should have known that the price in question was an excessive one. The Court of Criminal Appeal held that this was correct; the accused knew all the facts and were ignorant (if at all) only of the law.

Since the accused in that case were dealers in the goods in question, the court's view that they were "ignorant of the matters which it was their bounden duty to know" was valid; but the principle is equally applicable to persons who could not reasonably be expected to know of the rule of law in question.

The case of *Clayton*[18] is probably similarly explicable. It concerned an agreement to sell goods in excess of a statutory quota. The defence was that D believed, on erroneous legal advice, that he was entitled to a quota of unspecified dimensions until the Board of Trade chose to impose conditions. This seems to be simply a mistake as to interpretation of a criminal statute.[19]

3 Proof of the Agreement

The question of what is a sufficient agreement to found a charge of conspiracy is one of several questions in the criminal law which are aggravated by a confusion between the substantive law and the law of evidence. The actual agreement in most cases will probably take place in private and direct evidence of it will rarely be available. A very frequent way of proving it is by showing that the parties concerted in the pursuit of a common object in such a manner as to show that their actions must have been co-ordinated by arrangement beforehand.[20] The danger is that the importance attached to the acts done may obscure the

---

[13] *Thomson* (1965), 50 Cr. App. Rep. 1 (LAWTON, J.)
[14] Reversing the Court of Criminal Appeal: [1967] 2 A.C. 224; [1967] 1 All E.R. 497.
[15] The act may be "unlawful" for this purpose without being a crime; below, p. 157.
[16] Above, p. 48.
[17] [1944] K.B. 417.
[18] (1943), reported in 33 Cr. App. Rep. 113.
[19] *Cf. Johnson* v. *Youden* (above, p. 49).
[20] *Cooper and Compton*, [1947] 2 All E.R. 701; *Hammersley* (1958), 42 Cr. App. Rep. 207.

fact that these acts do not in themselves constitute a conspiracy, but are only evidence of it. If the jury are left in reasonable doubt, when all the evidence is in, whether the two accused persons were acting in pursuance of an agreement, they should acquit, even though the evidence shows that they were simultaneously pursuing the same object.[21]

It may not be necessary to show that the persons accused of conspiring together were in direct communication with one another. Thus, it may be that the conspiracy revolves around some third party, X, who is in touch with each of D1, D2, D3, though they are not in touch with one another (a "wheel conspiracy"); or D1 may communicate with X, X with D2, D2 with Y, Y with D3 (a "chain conspiracy"). Provided that the result is that they have a common design—for example, to rob a particular bank—D1, D2 and D3 may properly be indicted for conspiring together though they have never been in touch with one another until they meet in the dock.

> "What has to be ascertained is always the same matter: is it true to say . . . that the acts of the accused were done in pursuance of a criminal purpose held in common between them ?"[1]

These propositions, for which there is ample authority,[2] are stated in the case of *Meyrick*,[1] though that case itself seems a questionable application of them. D1 and D2, night-club proprietors, each offered bribes to a police sergeant, E, to induce him to connive at breaches of the licensing laws. They were convicted of conspiring to contravene the licensing laws and

> "to effect a public mischief by obstructing the police . . . in the execution of their public duty and by corrupting officers of that force."

The jury were directed that there must be a "common design" and, by their verdict of guilty, they so found but it is difficult to see how the evidence justified this finding. The design of each night club proprietor was simply to evade the licensing laws in respect of his own premises.

Meyrick was distinguished in *Griffiths*[3] on the rather unconvincing ground that

> ". . . the conspiracy alleged [in *Meyrick*] was . . . in relation to a comparatively small geographical area, namely Soho. In view of the size and nature of the locality, there were clearly facts upon which a jury could come to the conclusion that the night club proprietors in that district well knew what was happening generally in relation to the police."[4]

Even if D1 and D2 each knew that the other had made a similar agreement with E, it would seem that there were two conspiracies not one. PAULL, J., has put the following example:

---

[21] Where there are counts for both conspiracy and the ulterior crime and the only evidence of conspiracy is the collaboration of the parties in the completion of the ulterior crime, the only logical verdicts are guilty of both conspiracy and the ulterior crime or not guilty of both. Thus in *Cooper and Compton*, [1947] 2 All E.R. 701, the court quashed a verdict of guilty of conspiracy as inconsistent with a verdict of not guilty of larceny. Conversely, in *Beach and Owens*, [1957] Crim. L.R. 687, a verdict of guilty of attempt to pervert the course of justice was quashed as inconsistent with a verdict of not guilty of conspiracy.
[1] *Meyrick* (1929), 21 Cr. App. Rep. 94 at p. 102. *Cf. Griffiths and Others*, [1965] 2 All E.R. 448.
[2] See *e.g.*, *Cooper and Compton* (above, p. 152); *Sweetland and Another* (1957), 42 Cr. App. Rep. 62.
[3] (1965) 49 Cr. App. Rep. 279.
[4] *Ibid.*, at p. 291.

"I employ an accountant to make out my tax return. He and his clerk are both present when I am about to sign the return. I notice an item in my expenses of £100 and say: 'I don't remember incurring this expense.' The clerk says: 'Well, actually I put it in. You didn't incur it, but I didn't think you would object to a few pounds being saved. The accountant indicates his agreement to this attitude. After some hesitation I agree to let it stand. On those bare facts I cannot be charged with fifty others in a conspiracy to defraud the Exchequer of £100,000 on the basis that this accountant and his clerk have persuaded 500 other clients to make false returns, some being false in one way, some in another, or even all in the same way. I have not knowingly attached myself to a general agreement to defraud."[5]

It is submitted that the position would be no different if the accountant had said: "We do this for all our clients"; there would still have been a series of conspiracies, not one general conspiracy. The convictions in *Griffiths* were indeed quashed on the ground that the evidence, while perhaps sufficient to establish a series of separate conspiracies, did not establish the single "wheel conspiracy" alleged.

4 Conspiracy where the Contemplated Offence is Committed

The courts discourage the charging of conspiracy where there is evidence of the complete crime:

". . . when the proof intended to be submitted to a jury is proof of the actual commission of crime, it is not the proper course to charge the parties with conspiracy to commit it, for the course operates, it is manifest, unfairly and unjustly against the parties accused; the prosecutors are thus enabled to combine in one indictment a variety of offences, which, if treated individually, as they ought to be, would exclude the possibility of giving evidence against one defendant to the prejudice of others, and which deprive defendants of the advantage of calling their co-defendants as witnesses."[6]

Though these sentiments have been approved recently by the Court of Criminal Appeal,[7] it is not at all clear that evidence is admissible on a conspiracy charge which would not be admissible on a joint trial for the complete crime. In both cases D1 may be prejudiced by evidence admissible only against D2. The real objection to conspiracy, as it has been commonly used in recent years, has been pointed out by Williams.[8] It is—

". . . to the use of a conspiracy count to give a semblance of unity to a prosecution which, by combining a number of charges and several defendants, results in a complicated and protracted trial. The jury system is unworkable unless the prosecution is confined to a relatively simple issue which can be disposed of in a relatively short time."

No better illustration could be imagined than *Griffiths*[9] where a supplier of lime, his accountant and seven farmers were charged with conspiracy to defraud the government of the subsidy payable to farmers for spreading lime on their land. In addition to the conspiracy count, there were 24 other counts alleging substantive offences of false pretences. There were 60 prosecution and 35 defence witnesses and 263 exhibits including accounts and schedules. The jury had to return no less than 78 verdicts and the trial lasted 10 weeks—at the end of which, not surprisingly, all the convictions had to be quashed.

---

[5] *Ibid. Cf.* the argument of MADDOCKS in *Meyrick*, 45 T.L.R. at p. 422.
[6] COCKBURN, C.J., in *Boulton* (1871), 12 Cox C.C. 87 at p. 93.
[7] *West*, [1948] 1 K.B. 709 at p. 720; [1948] 1 All E.R. 718 at p. 723.
[8] C.L.G.P., 684; and see *The Proof of Guilt* (3rd ed.), Ch. 9.
[9] Above, footnote 1.

5 Two or More Parties

The requirement of two or more parties for a conspiracy is self-evident. If the managing director of a company resolves to perpetrate an illegality in the company's name, but communicates this to no one, there is no conspiracy between him and the company. To allow an indictment would be to

> "offend against the basic concept of a conspiracy, namely an agreement of two or more to do an unlawful act . . . it would be artificial to take the view that the company, although it is clearly a separate legal entity can be regarded here as a separate entity or a separate mind. . ."[10]

It appears that husband and wife are one person for this purpose and cannot, therefore, conspire together. The law is so stated in leading text-books[11] though there appears to be no English case in which it has been so decided;[12] but in *Mawji* v. *R.*,[13] an appeal from Tanganyika, the Privy Council assumed that the rule was part of English law; and, since the Penal Code of Tanganyika provided that it was to be interpreted in accordance with English principles, it was part of the law of Tanganyika also and, moreover, applied to a potentially polygamous marriage. The reason for the rule seems to be the common law fiction that husband and wife are one person with one will. The continuance of the rule might be rationalised on the basis of a policy against making marital confidence the subject of legal proceedings; but it is not obvious why this policy should extend protection to agreements to commit crime.

The rule applies only when the parties are married at the time of the agreement. Marriage after conspiracy is no defence.[14] Where husband and wife agree with a third party, for example, a daughter, all are guilty of conspiracy.[15]

6 Acquittal of the only other Alleged Conspirators

One person may properly be indicted and tried alone for conspiracy with others who are dead, or unknown, or simply not charged. But where two or more persons are indicted and tried together and all but one are acquitted, the conviction of the one cannot stand, unless he is alleged to have conspired with others in addition to those charged with him, or with persons unknown. The reason given is that a person cannot conspire by himself. It is not, however, a satisfactory rule;[16] for it may be that there is evidence admissible against D1 that he conspired with D2 which is not admissible against D2. The rule is, however, well established. Thus in *Thompson*[17] D1 was charged with conspiring with D2, D3 and persons unknown. He was convicted and D2 and D3 acquitted. It was held, ERLE, J., dissenting, that D1's conviction could not stand, there being no evidence that he had conspired with anyone other than

---

[10] *McDonnell*, [1966] 1 Q.B. 233; [1966] 1 All E.R. 193 (NIELD, J.). *Cf. I.C.R. Haulage Co.*, above, p. 107.

[11] *E.g.*, Hawkins, 1 P.C., c. 27, § 8; Archbold, § 46.

[12] See Williams, C.L.G.P., § 215 and (1947), 10 M.L.R. 20.

[13] [1957] A.C. 526; [1957] 1 All E.R. 385. The rule has also been followed in Canada: *Kowbel*, [1954] S.C.R. 498; New Zealand: *McKechie*, [1926] N.Z.L.R. 1, and U.S.A.: Perkins, *Criminal Law*, 537.

[14] *Robinson's* case (1746), 1 Leach 37.

[15] *Whitehouse* (1852), 6 Cox C.C. 38. *Quaere* whether two wives of a polygamous marriage could be convicted of conspiring together.

[16] See the cogent criticism by C. S. Greaves, a former editor of Russell (10th ed., 674, n. 9); Williams, C.L.G.P. (2nd ed.), § 213.

[17] (1851), 16 Q.B. 832; *cf. Kannangara Aratchige Dharmasena* v. *R.*, [1950] A.C. 1; *Doyle*, [1963] Crim. L.R. 37; *Anthony*, [1965] 1 All E.R. 440. See above, p. 91.

D2 or D3. ERLE, J.'s view was that the jury may have been satisfied that D1 conspired with either D2 or D3 but not satisfied which; and in such a case he thought a conviction proper. This view is logical and has much to commend it; but it was not accepted by the remainder of the court. The rule applies equally where one party has pleaded guilty and the other is acquitted[18] or even where the jury disagree as to the other.[19] It has not been settled whether the rule applies to separate trials so as to avoid the conviction of D1 for conspiring with D2 where D2 is subsequently acquitted.

7 Immunity of the only other Alleged Conspirators

Where D is alleged to have conspired with E, the fact that E would most certainly have to be acquitted of conspiracy if he were charged may not be a bar to the conviction of D if E is not charged. If so this makes the rule appear rather absurd. D will be acquitted if E is charged but convicted if he is not! In *Duguid*,[20] D agreed with E to remove E's child from the possession of her lawful guardian. This would have been a crime by D under the Offences against the Person Act 1861 s. 56;[1] but that section provides that no person who is, *inter alios*, the mother of the child can be convicted of the offence. D's conviction for conspiracy was upheld. The court declined to decide whether E could have been convicted of the substantive crime or of the conspiracy, ALVERSTONE, C.J., saying[2]—

> "I am clearly of the opinion that no immunity of one of the persons, which would prevent her being proceeded against in respect of acts done by herself, has any bearing upon the question whether a conspiracy between her and another person to do an unlawful act was a conspiracy against the criminal law."

While it seems fairly clear that E could not have been convicted of the substantive offence, there is some authority that she could, in fact, have been convicted of the conspiracy. In *Whitchurch*,[3] D was convicted of conspiring to procure her own abortion, although she could not have been convicted of the substantive offence as she was not in fact pregnant.[4] The result may be technically justified on the ground that D would have been guilty as an aider and abettor if the offence had been completed;[5] but it has been criticised as "gravely wrong for it sets at naught the limitation upon responsibility imposed by Parliament."[6]

If *Whitchurch* is right, the problem posed did not arise on the facts of *Duguid*; but since the court was unwilling to express any view as to whether E could have been convicted of conspiracy, it was presumably willing to uphold D's conviction even if he could not; and the case affords some authority for the absurd result stated above.

---

[18] *Plummer*, [1902] 2 K.B. 339 (C.C.R.). D1 had not been sentenced. It is not certain whether, if he had been sentenced, the sentence ought not to have been vacated.
[19] *Manning* (1883), 12 Q.B.D. 241.
[20] (1906), 70 J.P. 294.
[1] Below, p. 277.
[2] 70 J.P. 294 at p. 295.
[3] (1890), 24 Q.B.D. 420.
[4] See below, pp. 243–245.
[5] *Sockett* (1908), 72 J.P. 428.
[6] Williams, C.L.G.P., 673, criticised by Hogan in "Victims as Parties to Crime", [1962] Crim. L.R. 683; and see below, p. 244.

A similar problem arises where E purports to conspire with D but has no intention of going through with the illegal plan, as where he is a police spy. Looking at the facts objectively, there is such an agreement as (apart from the illegality) would be enforceable in the law of contract. It would seem then that there is an *actus reus*; and, as a matter of general principle, it would seem very proper that one who has brought about an *actus reus* with *mens rea* should be liable to conviction.[7] In some jurisdictions the contrary has been decided,[8] but the point has not arisen in England. The question is of no great practical importance where D is the instigator of the agreement for then he is surely guilty of an attempt to conspire, which is a common law misdemeanour.[9] Where E is the instigator of the agreement, it is less clear that D's concurrence is an attempt. It is submitted, however, that the better view is that D is guilty of conspiracy in both cases.

8 The "Unlawful" Object

(i) *A crime.*—The most obvious unlawful object is the commission of a crime, even a non-indictable crime.[10] This is anomalous in that the mere agreement to commit the crime is triable in a higher court and liable to be more severely punished than the commission of the crime itself. There is an exception where the offence punishable summarily is defined as an agreement, for then a conspiracy charge alleges "the very offence which is created by the Act . . . and which the Act makes triable only as a summary offence"; and, therefore, no indictment will lie.[11] The law to be contravened must be in force at the time of the agreement. An agreement to break a law which might be made in the future is not indictable.[12]

If the agreement contemplates an act to be committed abroad, in a country where it is criminal so to act, but the act committed abroad would not be *indictable* in England, the agreement, though made in England, is not indictable in England:[13]

> "The gist of the offence being the agreement, whether or not the object is attained, it may be asked why it should not be indictable if the object is situate abroad. I think the answer to this is that it is necessary to recognize the offence to aid in the preservation of the Queen's Peace and the maintenance of law and order within the realm with which, generally speaking, the criminal law is alone concerned."[14]

Thus an agreement in Dover to commit an assault in Calais is not indictable here, for the assault would not be indictable here. An agreement by a British

---

[7] Above, p. 94. But could E's *mens rea* be part of D's *actus reus*? Above p. 28.

[8] *Harris*, [1927] N.P.D. at p. 347 (South Africa); *O'Brien*, [1954] S.C.R. 666 (Canada); *Delaney* v. *State* (1932), 164 Tenn. 432 (Tennessee); *State* v. *Otu*, [1964] N.N.L.R. 113 (Nigeria). *Cf. Thomson* (1965), 50 Cr. App. Rep. 1. See Fridman in (1956), 19 M.L.R. 276.

[9] See *Harris*, above, footnote 8.

[10] *Blamires Transport Services, Ltd.*, [1964] 1 Q.B. 278; [1963] 3 All E.R. 170. See also *Costello and Bishop*, [1910] 1 K.B. 28; *Bunn* (1872), 12 Cox C.C. 316.

[11] *Barnett*, [1951] 2 K.B. 425; [1951] 1 All E.R. 917 (C.C.A.), holding that there could be no indictment for a conspiracy amounting to a bidding agreement under the Auctions (Bidding Agreements) Act 1927.

[12] *West*, [1948] 1 K.B. 709; [1948] 1 All E.R. 718.

[13] *Board of Trade* v. *Owen*, [1957] A.C. 602; [1957] 1 All E.R. 411. This rule was strongly criticised by WINN, L. J., in *Cox (Peter)*, [1968] 1 All E.R. 410 at p. 413–414; [1968] Crim. L.R. 163, and commentary thereon. For a full discussion, see Williams (1965), 81 L.Q.R. 276, 395 and 518, especially at p. 534.

[14] [1957] A.C. 602 at p. 625; [1957] 1 All E.R. 411 at p. 415, *per* Lord TUCKER.

citizen in Dover to commit murder or bigamy in Calais is indictable here; for murder and bigamy by a citizen of the United Kingdom and Colonies are indictable in England wherever in the world they are committed.[15]

In *Board of Trade* v. *Owen* the House reserved for future consideration the question—

> "whether a conspiracy in this country which is to be wholly carried out abroad may not be indictable here on proof that its performance would produce a public mischief in this country or injure a person here by causing him damage abroad."[16]

Where the agreement is that the act is to be committed *either* abroad *or* within the jurisdiction, then it is a conspiracy indictable here.[17]

(ii) *Fraud.*—According to Wright:[18]

> ". . . it has long been established law that a combination to defraud may be criminal, although the proposed deceit is not such as would be criminal apart from this combination."

Most agreements to defraud will now amount to obtaining by deception, either property contrary to s. 15, or a pecuniary advantage contrary to s. 16, of the Theft Act 1968.[19] Before the Theft Act it was held that an indictment for conspiracy would lie where the proposed fraud did not amount to any criminal offence,[20] but the wide terms of ss. 15 and 16 would now seem to cover all of the cases in which this device was used—they would now amount to conspiracies to commit a crime. Situations may still be envisaged, however, in which the proposed fraud is not itself an offence but in which conspiracy might be held to be a proper charge. For example, D1 and D2 agree to shift D1's boundary fence so as to appropriate some of P's land;[1] or they agree to deprive P temporarily of his property;[2] or dishonestly to use P's profit-earning chattel without his consent to make a profit for themselves.[3] It might be argued, however, that since Parliament has so recently decided that acts such as these are not offences when done by an individual, it would be wrong to hold that an agreement to commit them is a crime.

The object in view in most of the conspiracy to defraud cases was the commission of a tort and it has been suggested that it is open to the courts to confine the crime to such cases. Recently, in *Sinclair*,[4] it was held that to defraud is "to act with deliberate dishonesty to the prejudice of another person's right." The directors of a company were thus guilty of conspiracy where they agreed to take a risk with assets of the company by using them in a manner which was known not to be in the best interests of the company and to be prejudicial to the minority shareholders. Such conduct is not necessarily tortious and clearly the court did not look for a tort as an element of the crime.

---

[15] Below, pp. 181 and 479.

[16] [1957] A.C. 602 at p. 634; [1957] 1 All E.R. 411 at p. 422, *per* Lord TUCKER.

[17] *Kohn* (1864), 4 F. & F. 68; *Board of Trade* v. *Owen*, [1957] A.C. at p. 631; [1957] 1 All E.R. at p. 419.

[18] *Law of Criminal Conspiracies and Agreements* (1873), 11.

[19] Below, p. 382.

[20] See, *e.g.*, *Carlisle* (1854), Dears C.C. 337; *Hall* (1858), F. & F. 33; *Warburton* (1870), L.R. 1 C.C.R. 274; *Orman and Barber* (1880), 14 Cox C.C. 381; *Clucas*, [1949] 2 K.B. 226; [1949] 2 All E.R. 40.

[1] Below, p. 358.

[2] Below, p. 375.

[3] Smith, *Theft*, para. 89.

[4] [1968] 3 All E.R. 241, below, p. 375.

(iii) *Torts involving "malice".*[5]— Hawkins asserted that

"There can be no doubt, but that all confederacies whatsoever, wrongfully to prejudice a third person, are highly criminal at common law."

This broad proposition was unsupported by adequate authority,[6] but, as has so often happened in the history of English criminal law, the proposition was uncritically adopted in subsequent works.[7] Lord DENMAN let fall a similarly broad and even more influential dictum in 1832:[8] that the indictment must

"charge a conspiracy to do an unlawful act, or a lawful act by unlawful means."

Though Lord DENMAN himself seems to have doubted the wisdom of his remark a few years later,[9] it has been constantly cited ever since and is judicially regarded as authoritative at the present day. The difficulty is the vagueness of the words "unlawful" and "wrongful". If by these words Hawkins and DENMAN meant "criminal", their propositions are clearly correct and entirely unobjectionable; but if the word includes "tortious" then it extends the criminal law very widely indeed. But even the word "unlawful" may have a wider meaning still, for many contracts are "unlawful" which involve neither crime nor tort.[10] It appears that some, but not all of these agreements are at present held to amount to conspiracies.[11] And the borderline is not easily discoverable.

It is thought that it is certainly too wide to assert that a combination to commit any tort is a conspiracy. An agreement to commit a civil trespass is not indictable, even, Lord ELLENBOROUGH held,[12] where the object was to poach for hares with "divers bludgeons and other offensive weapons".[13]

Agreements to commit certain torts involving "malice", in the sense of spite or ill will,[14] on the other hand, are certainly indictable. Indeed, the law of conspiracy had its origin in cases of combinations to bring false indictments or false appeals of felony;[15] and an agreement to commit malicious prosecution is certainly a conspiracy.[16] So, it is said, is an agreement maliciously to defame; but it it not easy to find direct authority for this. Most of the cases involve some further element, such as fraud, as in *Timberley and Childe*[17] where it was held to be conspiracy to agree falsely to accuse P of being the father of a bastard child, *whereby he would have become liable for the maintenance of the child.* If the defamation were in writing, it would be libel[18] and criminal and thus within an

---

[5] 1 P.C., c. 27, § 2.
[6] See Sayre (1922), 35 Harv. L.R. at p. 402.
[7] *E.g., Burn's Justice* (4th ed.), 276.
[8] *Jones* (1832), 4 B. & Ad. 345 at p. 349.
[9] *Peck* (1839), 9 Ad. & El. 686 at p. 690: "I do not think the antithesis very correct."
[10] See *e.g.* Cheshire and Fifoot, *Law of Contract* (6th ed.), 283–319.
[11] *Porter*, [1910] 1 K.B. 369 at p. 372; *Boston* (1923), 33 C.L.R. 386 at p. 394. Contracts in restraint of trade are unlawful but not indictable.
[12] *Turner* (1811), 13 East 228.
[13] Lord CAMPBELL thought the decision wrong, on the ground that the trespass with intent to oppose interference with offensive weapons was itself indictable, no doubt as an unlawful assembly (below, p. 533): *Rowlands* (1851), 17 Q.B. 671; but Lord COLERIDGE, C.J., in the *Mogul S.S.* case (1888), 21 Q.B.D. at p. 551, approved of Lord ELLENBOROUGH's observations.
[14] See above, p. 48.
[15] Stephen, 2 H.C.L. 228; Sayre (1922), 35 Harv. L.R. 394 *et seq.*
[16] *Poulterers* case (1610), 9 Co. Rep. 55b; where the Court of Star Chamber held that, while the civil action would not lie, unless the prosecution and acquittal had taken place, the conspiracy was indictable as soon as it was made.
[17] (1663), 1 Sid. 68.
[18] See below, p. 548.

earlier paragraph; so it is only a false oral defamation which would need to be brought under this head.

It cannot be taken as settled that even the presence of malice will render an agreement to commit any tort whatever indictable. Would it, for example, be criminal to agree to trespass on other's land for the purpose of annoying him? It may be that maliciously to commit a private nuisance is indictable for in *Levy*[19] it was held that it was a conspiracy to make loud noises and violent knocking against the wall of a room in which a pregnant woman lay "to injure and terrify her". And if a nuisance why not a trespass? It has been suggested[20] that *Levy* should be supported on the ground that it was an agreement to insult and annoy;[1] but this will surely be a wider rather than a narrower ground, for "malice" will usually involve an intent to annoy.

(iv) *To commit a public mischief.*—A law imposing criminal liability for an agreement to commit any crime or tort would be very wide indeed, but at least it would be reasonably precise and definite. It is now, however, established by the authority of the highest court in the land in *Shaw* v. *Director of Public Prosecutions*[2]—that the scope of conspiracy is wider even than this. It is indictable to agree to commit a "public mischief". Public mischief is a concept which no doubt includes, but may also extend far beyond, the bounds of the criminal law. How far it extends is undetermined for the courts have as yet laid down no guiding principles beyond the fact that the object of the parties must be mischievous to the public. Whether it is thus mischievous is a question to be settled by the direction of a judge,[3] on the facts of each particular case. In *De Berenger*[4] it was an agreement to raise the price of government stocks by circulating false rumours of the death of Napoleon, whereby any member of the public dealing with the stocks on a particular day might have been defrauded. In *Brailsford*[5] it was an agreement to obtain a passport for A by falsely representing that it was intended for B. In *Porter*[6] it was an agreement by an accused person to indemnify his bail. In *Bassey*,[7] it was an agreement to present forged certificates in order to gain admission to an Inn of Court. In *Newland*[8] it was an agreement to divert decorated pottery from the export to the home market in defiance of the government's declared policy.[9]

Finally in *Shaw* it was an agreement "to corrupt public morals" by publishing the *Ladies Directory* which advertised the names and addresses of prostitutes with, in some cases, photographs, and, in others, particulars of sexual perversions which they were willing to practise. Corruption of public morals is clearly a narrower concept than public mischief and the decision could have been put solely on that narrower ground but both Viscount SIMONDS and Lord TUCKER (with whom Lord MORRIS and HODSON expressed their agreement)

---

[19] (1819), 2 Stark 458.
[20] Williams, C.L.G.P., 697.
[1] *Cf.* Lord HALSBURY in the *Mogul S.S.* case, [1892] A.C. at p. 38.
[2] [1962] A.C. 220; [1961] 2 All E.R. 446.
[3] Below, p. 163.
[4] (1814), 3 M. & S. 67.
[5] [1905] 2 K.B. 730; *cf.* cheating, below, p. 394.
[6] [1910] 1 K.B. 369.
[7] (1931), 22 Cr. App. Rep. 160.
[8] [1954] 1 Q.B. 158; [1953] 2 All E.R. 1067.
[9] Of which judicial notice was taken. *Cf. St. Margaret's Trust*, above, p. 64.

treated the case as an instance of a public mischief.[10] The concept thus comprehends widely divergent factual situations; and the House of Lords has asserted the right of the courts to continue to expand the scope of the criminal law. Viscount SIMONDS, with whom Lords MORRIS and HODSON concurred, said:[11]

"In the sphere of criminal law I entertain no doubt that there remains in the courts of law a residual power to enforce the supreme and fundamental purpose of the law, to conserve not only the safety and order but also the moral welfare of the State, and that it is their duty to guard it against attacks which may be the more insidious because they are novel and unprepared for. That is the broad head (call it public policy if you wish) within which the present indictment falls. It matters little what label is given to the offending act. To one of your Lordships it may appear an affront to public decency, to another considering that it may succeed in its obvious intention of provoking libidinous desires it will seem a corruption of public morals. Yet others may deem it aptly described as the creation of a public mischief or the undermining of moral conduct. The same act will not in all ages be regarded in the same way. The law must be related to the changing standards of life, not yielding to every shifting impulse of the popular will but having regard to fundamental assessments of human values and the purposes of society."[12]

It is interesting to note that all these cases could have been decided on a much narrower and less controversial ground. *De Berenger*[13] was, no doubt, a conspiracy to commit the tort of deceit and to defraud; and the other cases were agreements to commit crimes—in *Brailsford*,[14] obtaining by false pretences, in *Porter*,[15] a contempt of court,[16] in *Bassey*,[17] forgery, in *Newland*,[17] obtaining by false pretences and, probably, the procurement of a breach by the pottery manufacturers of the statutory regulations, and in *Shaw*, publication of an obscene article contrary to s. 2 (4) of the Obscene Publications Act 1959.[18] This perhaps indicates that the wide power has not been abused; but the proposition for which they stand is no less objectionable for that. More important is the fact that it would be open to a future court to limit the *rationes* of these cases to agreements to commit crimes or to defraud; but, until some such step is taken, it must be accepted that a conspiracy to effect a public mischief is indictable.

(v) *To commit or induce a breach of contract.*—An agreement to commit a breach of contract is probably not indictable at the present day. Kenny[19] said that it was where the breach was

---

[10] The Court of Criminal Appeal had held that conduct calculated or intended to corrupt public morals is a substantive common law misdemeanour. The House of Lords did not reject this view, but simply found it unnecessary to decide on it; the conspiracy to corrupt is indictable whether or not the actual corruption is.

[11] [1962] A.C. 220 at p. 267; [1961] 2 All E.R. 446 at p. 452.

[12] For a judicial view to the contrary, see Stephen, 3 H.C.L. 359. See Seaborne Davies, *Annual Survey of English Law* (1932), 276–277. For critcism of *Shaw*, see Seaborne Davies (1962), 6 J.S.P.T.L. (N.S.) 104; Goodhart (1961), 77 L.Q.R. 560; Hall Williams (1961), 24 M.L.R. 626; and [1961] Crim. L.R. 470.

[13] (1814), 3 M. & S. 67; above, p. 160.

[14] [1905] 2 K.B. 730; above, p. 160.

[15] [1910] 1 K.B. 369; above, p. 160.

[16] According to Williams, C.L.G.P., § 225, n. 25.

[17] Above, p. 160.

[18] Shaw was in fact convicted of this offence on another count at the same trial and his conviction was upheld and leave to appeal to the House of Lords on that count refused by the Court of Criminal Appeal. Below, p. 496. See the puzzling remarks by Lord REID, [1962] A.C. 220 at p. 280; [1961] 2 All E.R. 446 at p. 460; and see [1961] Crim. L.R. 473, n. 2a.

[19] *Outlines*, 429.

"under circumstances that are peculiarly injurious to the public."

But the authority cited[20] hardly supports this proposition and the only modern authority for it appears to be Lord BRAMWELL's dictum that an indictment may lie where "the public has a sufficient interest"[1] in the fulfilment of the contract. In view of the attitude of the majority of the House of Lords in *Shaw*, the matter cannot be taken to be settled; but it is thought that the better view is that an agreement should never be indictable on the ground only that it involves a breach of contract. If the breach of contract happens also to be "unlawful" in the sense discussed above then, of course, it will be no less indictable because it is a breach of contract.

An agreement to induce others to break their contracts is an agreement to commit a tort and was indictable at common law. In the most important class of case, however, such an agreement now has statutory protection for the Conspiracy and Protection of Property Act 1875, s. 3, provides:

> "An agreement or combination by two or more persons to do or procure to be done any act in contemplation or furtherance of a trade dispute shall not be indictable as a conspiracy if such act committed by one person would not be indictable as a crime".

A malicious agreement to induce a breach of contract, not falling within the protection of this section, presumably remains indictable.

9 Rationale of Conspiracy

So far as conspiracies to commit crimes are concerned, the rationale of conspiracy is not far to seek. Like attempt, to which it is closely related, it is an inchoate crime which enables legal intervention at an early stage to prevent the crime from reaching fruition. But, as appears above, it has long been accepted that a combination to do acts not in themselves criminal may be indictable. This is much less easily explicable. The traditional explanation is as follows:

> "The general principle on which the crime of conspiracy is founded is this, that the confederacy of several persons to effect any injurious object creates such a new and additional power to cause injury as requires criminal restraint; although none would be necessary were the same thing proposed, or even attempted to be done, by any person singly."[2]

This theory has been criticised[3] on the grounds (i) that it should be for the legislature, not the courts, to say what combinations should be illegal[4] and (ii) that a great corporation planning an act may be more dangerous than a group of individuals doing so. It may be answered to the second point that, under modern English law, the corporation would be guilty of conspiring with the officer or officers who actually made the plan.[5] The other objection is a formidable one. The House of Lords in *Shaw* urged[6] that the citizen is protected against arbitrariness by the presence of juries—

> ". . . who can be trusted to maintain the corporate good sense of the community and to discern attacks upon values that must be preserved. If there

---

[20] *Vertue* v. *Lord Clive* (1769), 4 Burr. 2472.
[1] *The Mogul Steamship* case, [1892] A.C. at p. 48.
[2] Criminal Law Commission, 7th Report (1843), 90. Goodhart suggests (77 L.Q.R. at 564) that the *Shaw* case perhaps illustrates the validity of this principle "because if Shaw had not acted in concert with the prostitutes by receiving payment for their advertisements, it is clear that the *Ladies Directory* would never have been published."
[3] By Sayre, *op. cit.*, at 420.
[4] Obviously numerous combinations—social and athletic clubs, and societies, etc., are perfectly lawful.
[5] Above, p. 107.
[6] [1962] A.C. 220 at p. 297; [1961] 2 All E.R. 446 at p. 467, *per* Lord MORRIS.

were prosecutions which were not genuinely and fairly warranted juries would be quick to perceive this."

It appears, however, that whether particular facts amount to a public mischief is a conclusion of law;[7] so that a jury could only afford protection by declining to follow a judicial direction. Moreover, as Seaborne Davies objects:[8]

"First, the jury system was never meant to be an alternative to a properly enunciated law. Second, it is no more the function of the jury than it is of the judiciary to act as legislators in penal matters."

3 ATTEMPT

It is an indictable misdemeanour at common law to attempt to commit an indictable offence, whether common law or statutory. It follows that if a new indictable offence is created by statute, it automatically becomes a common law misdemeanour to attempt to commit that offence. By s. 7 (2) of the Criminal Law Act 1967, the attempt is now punishable to the same extent as the completed offence.

There is some slight[9] authority for the view that an attempt to commit even a summary offence is indictable; and the fact that incitement[10] and conspiracy to commit a summary offence are indictable suggests that this is correct. The absurdity here is even greater than in the case of incitement,[11] for so many completed crimes necessarily comprehend an attempt, which may be charged notwithstanding the completion of the crime. The whole is a mere summary; offence; the part is indictable. It may be that the courts will not be prepared to press logic quite so far.

1 Mens Rea in Attempt[12]

It is implicit in the concept of an attempt that the person acting intends to do the act attempted; so that the *mens rea* of an attempt is essentially that of the complete crime. This proposition, however, requires qualification. It has been seen[13] that generally, though not invariably, recklessness as well as intention is a sufficient *mens rea* to ground liability for crimes at common law. Paradoxically, but inevitably, the law's requirements on a charge of attempting to commit a crime are stricter than on a charge of actually committing it; for the concept of attempt necessarily involves the notion of an intended consequence. Whenever the definition of the crime requires that some consequence be brought about by D's conduct, it must be proved, on a charge of attempting to commit that crime, that D intended that consequence; and this is so even if, on a charge of committing the complete crime, recklessness as to that consequence—or even some lesser degree of *mens rea*—would suffice. Thus, on a charge of maliciously causing injury to person or property, it would suffice to show that D foresaw that harm of the kind actually caused was likely to occur as a result of his act, even though he may have hoped that such harm would not occur.[14] This would obviously not do if the charge were one of attempting the same crime; there, it would be necessary to show that the accused actually intended the particular

---

[7] *Porter*, [1910] 1 K.B. at p. 372; *Boston* (1923), 33 C.L.R. at p. 392.
[8] (1961), 6 J.S.P.T.L. at p. 110.
[9] See "Attempts to Commit Summary Offences" (1922), 86 J.P.N. 550.
[10] *Curr*, [1967] 1 All E.R. 478, above, p. 149.
[11] *Blamires Transport Services, Ltd*, [1963] 3 All E.R. 170; above, p. 157.
[12] See Stuart, "Mens Rea, Negligence and Attempts", [1968] Crim. L.R. 647.
[13] Above, p. 157.
[14] *Welch* (1875), 1 Q.B.D. 23; below, p. 461.

type of harm which the definition of the crime he is charged with attempting requires.[15]

The anomaly is even greater where the substantive crime is one which does not require the full *mens rea* of intention or recklessness as to the consequence which is an essential ingredient of the *actus reus*.   Thus a man may be convicted of murder even though he did not foresee the possibility of the death of his victim if he intended to inflict grievous bodily harm upon him;[16] but it is established that, on a charge of attempted murder, nothing less than intention to kill will do. In *Whybrow*[17] D, by a device which he had constructed, administered an electric shock to his wife while she was in a bath.   PARKER, J., directed the jury that, if he did so with intent to kill his wife *or to do her grievous bodily harm*, he would be guilty of attempted murder.   The Court of Criminal Appeal held that this was a wrong direction.   It correctly described the *mens rea* on a charge of murder:[18]

> "But if the charge is one of attempted murder, the intent becomes the principal ingredient of the crime."

2   Recklessness in Attempt

It does not follow from this that intention is required as to all the elements of the *actus reus*.   The distinction between consequences and circumstances is important here.[19] Where the consequences are intended, recklessness with regard to the circumstances will suffice on a charge of attempt, provided that this would be so on a charge of committing the complete crime.   Intention is required as to the consequences because we cannot conceive of an attempt without it.   But there seems to be no obstacle to saying that there is an attempt in the following cases:

D posts a begging letter to P making a representation which he hopes will induce P to send him money.   He neither knows nor cares whether the representation is true or false.   It is false.

D, not knowing or caring whether his wife (whom he left a year ago) is alive or dead, is about to go through a form of marriage with P, but is prevented by the intervention of his wife at the altar.

D owns an umbrella of a common pattern.   He has mislaid it but, on leaving his club, he sees an umbrella of that pattern.   Being quite uncertain whether it is his, he puts out his hand to take it, intending to keep it as his own.   The umbrella is not his and, at that moment, its true owner appears.

In these cases D intends the consequences which are required for the crimes of obtaining by deception, bigamy and theft, respectively; but he is only

---

[15] Whether "intention" here includes consequences foreseen as certain but not desired (see above, p. 37) has not been decided. D attempts to explode a bomb with the object of demolishing a building. He knows there are people in the building who, inevitably, will be killed by the explosion. It is not D's object to kill these people—he would rather that they were not there. Is he guilty of attempted murder? The Model Penal Code gives an affirmative answer: s. 5101 (1) (b). So does Williams, *The Mental Element in Crime* at 24-25.

[16] Or even, it seems, foreseeing that grievous bodily harm is a likely consequence of his act, at least if it be an unlawful one; below, p. 196.

[17] (1951), 35 Cr. App. R. 141. See also *Loughlin*, [1959] Crim. L.R. 518. *Cf.* the similar anomaly which arises where the definition of a crime requires a "specific intent", as in wounding with intent to murder: *Foley*, [1959] Crim. L.R. 286; and see *Bourdon*, the offence (now repealed) of wounding with intent to murder: *Foley*, [1959] Crim. L.R. 286; and see *Bourdon* (1847), 2 C. & K. 366.

[18] 35 Cr. App. Rep. 141 at p. 147.

[19] Above, pp. 30 and 39.

reckless as to circumstances which are equally essential ingredients of the crime: that the representation be false, that the wife be alive and that the umbrella be that of another. Yet there seems to be no reason why he should not be guilty of an attempt in all three cases.

3 Negligence and Strict Liability in Attempt

It would be logical to go on to say that, similarly, where negligence as to a circumstance will suffice for the complete crime so it will on a charge of attempt; and, further, that where there is strict liability as to a circumstance on a charge of committing the complete crime,[20] no *mens rea* whatever need be proved with respect to that circumstance on a charge of attempt. At least there is nothing in the concept of an attempt which bars this holding.[1] But a strong argument from principle can be made against this view. Attempt, like abetting, is a common law notion. As has already appeared,[2] *mens rea* must be proved on a charge of abetting even an offence of strict liability; and, by analogy to that rule, it may well be that, while recklessness as to a circumstance will suffice on a charge of attempt where it will do so on a charge of the complete crime, the same is not true of negligence or strict liability; for *mens rea* at common law generally includes recklessness but does not include negligence or blameless inadvertence.

If, however, there is a common law offence which allows a conviction where there is negligence or blameless inadvertence as to a circumstance, there seems to be no reason why this should not be equally true of an attempt. Suppose, for instance, that there was strict liability as to the circumstance of time in burglary[3] as a common law offence, and as codified in the Larceny Act 1916. Was there any valid reason for requiring *mens rea* on a charge of attempted burglary? Most absolute prohibitions arise, however, from statute; and here the analogy of abetting is persuasive that *mens rea* should be required, even as to the absolutely prohibited circumstance, on a charge of attempt. The only case directly in point, however, goes the other way.

In *Collier*[4] D, a man under twenty-four who had not previously been charged with a like offence, was charged with attempting to have sexual intercourse with a girl under sixteen and over thirteen. Under s. 6 (3)[5] of the Sexual Offences Act 1956 it is a defence for such a man, charged with the substantive offence to prove that he believed on reasonable grounds that the girl was over sixteen. STREATFEILD, J., after hearing argument, held that the statutory defence was available on a charge of attempt as well as on a charge of committing the substantive offence. If *mens rea* had been required, this ruling would have been unnecessary, as the accused could have relied on the much broader defence of lack of *mens rea*. It is therefore implicit in the decision that *mens rea* is not required on a charge of attempting to commit this statutory offence—except to the limited extent that it is required on a charge of committing the substantive offence.

---

[20] For examples, see above, pp. 59 *et seq.*

[1] This is the rule adopted in the American Model Penal Code s. 5101: "A person is guilty of an attempt to commit a crime if, acting *with the kind of culpability otherwise required for the commission of the crime* he: (a) purposely engages in conduct which would constitute the crime if the attendant circumstances were as he believes them to be . . .".

[2] Above, pp. 94–95.

[3] See now Theft Act 1968, s. 9, below, p. 408.

[4] [1960] Crim. L.R. 204.

[5] Below, p. 296.

The judge presumably told the jury to convict, even if D believed the girl to be over sixteen, if they were not satisfied his belief was reasonable.

The only other case which is relevant to the problem is *Gardner* v. *Akeroyd*[6] where, however, a different point was in issue.

Under the Defence Regulations 1939 it was an offence to do acts preparatory to further offences under the regulations, including that of selling meat at a price exceeding the maximum fixed by statutory order. D was a butcher in whose shop were found parcels of meat bearing the names of purchasers and prices exceeding the maximum. The parcels had been prepared and the tickets affixed by an assistant during D's absence from the shop and without his knowledge. The Divisional Court held that if the parcels had actually been delivered D would have been vicariously liable for breach of the absolute prohibition of selling meat at a price in excess of the maximum; but that the offence of doing acts preparatory to the sale required *mens rea* and did not import vicarious liability. D was therefore rightly acquitted. Lord GODDARD, C.J., said:

> "That [vicarious liability] is a necessary doctrine for the proper enforcement of much modern legislation none would deny,[7] but it is not one to be extended. Just as in former days the term 'odious' was applied to some forms of estoppel, so it might be to vicarious liability. It makes a person guilty of an offence actually committed by another when he may have no knowledge that it was being committed or have done his best to prevent it. There is no case in the books where it has been applied to an attempt, and, for my part, I refuse so to extend and apply it. Were it to be applied, the consequences might be startling and unjust in the highest degree. For, once a servant had done an act amounting to an attempt, his master would be vicariously liable though he had intervened and frustrated the commission of the substantive offence."

This, of course, was *obiter*, the court being concerned with a statutory offence, not a common law attempt; and the *dicta* relate to a problem of vicarious liability rather than of *mens rea*—for the servant probably had *mens rea*. But it is certainly arguable that the same principle which excludes vicarious liability in attempt should also exclude strict liability, except, perhaps, in cases where those doctrines apply to common law offences.[8]

The question is, therefore, an open one. If there is a valid policy underlying the imposition of liability for negligence and strict liability in the substantive offence, it is difficult to see why it does not apply equally to the attempt. The only difference between the man who attempts and fails and another who attempts and succeeds may be chance. There is, *ex hypothesi*, no difference in moral blameworthiness between them and the one may be as dangerous as the other.

4   Actus Reus in Attempt

The courts seem at one time to have inclined to the view that any act done with intent to commit a felony or misdemeanour was an offence. It was held to be an offence at common law to procure counterfeit coin with intent to utter it in payment[9] and to procure indecent prints with intent to publish them.[10] It was

---

[6] [1952] 2 Q.B. 743 at p. 751; [1952] 2 All E.R. 306 at p. 311.
[7] *Sed quaere.* See C.L.G.P., § 99.
[8] See above, pp. 43 and 99.
[9] *Fuller and Robinson* (1816), R. & R. 308.
[10] *Dugdale* (1853), 1 E. & R. 435.

enough that the procuring was an act done in the commencement of a misdemeanour to render it indictable as a misdemeanour in itself. Being in possession of counterfeit coin, etc., was not regarded as an act;[11] but it might be
evidence of procuring. Had this development continued, there would have been
no need for the concept of the attempt as such; but it was interrupted by the
influential *dictum* of PARKE, B., in *Eagleton*: (1855)[12]

> "The mere intention to commit a misdemeanour is not criminal. Some act
> is required, and we do not think that all acts towards committing a mis-
> demeanour are indictable. Acts remotely leading towards the commission of
> the offence are not to be considered as attempts to commit it, but acts immedi-
> ately connected with it are . . ."

Even after this case, a conviction was upheld in *Roberts* (1855)[13] for procuring
a part of the necessary apparatus for making counterfeit coin; JERVIS, C.J., said
this was not an indictment for an attempt so it was irrelevant that the evidence
did not disclose an attempt. Three of the other four judges (including PARKE, B.),
however, thought that the act done was sufficiently proximate to amount to an
attempt. Since then the doctrine of proximity seems to have been strictly
applied; and in *Taylor* (1859)[14] POLLOCK, C.B., thought that buying matches
with intent to commit arson would not be a sufficiently proximate act to amount
to an attempt to commit arson.

Recently, in *Gurmit Singh*,[15] McNAIR, J., followed the old authorities in
upholding an indictment alleging that D unlawfully procured a rubber stamp
bearing the words, "Magistrate First Class Jullundur" with intent to use it to
forge a document in order to defraud. McNAIR, J., held that D's conduct did
not amount to an attempt to forge, but was an indictable act of preparation. If
the decision is correct and the old authorities are still good law, the importance of
the distinction between acts of preparation and attempts, on which so much
attention has been lavished, is of no significance; both are equally offences at
common law. Procuring a knife with intent to commit murder, an axe with
intent to commit malicious damage, a screwdriver with intent to commit
burglary, pen and paper with intent to obtain by deception, a wedding ring
with intent to commit bigamy, will all be crimes.[16] This might be a very
desirable development; but it is certainly unsafe to assume that it has yet come
to pass; and, in the meantime, it is necessary to consider the distinction between
acts of preparation and attempts. It is obvious that there may be many steps
towards the commission of a crime which cannot properly be described as an
attempt to commit it. D, intending to commit a murder, buys a gun and ammunition, does target practice, studies the habits of his victim, reconnoitres a
suitable place to lie in ambush, puts on a disguise and sets out to take up his
position. These are all acts of preparation but they could not properly be
described as attempted murder. D takes up his position, loads the gun, sees his
victim approaching, raises the gun, takes aim, puts his finger on the trigger and
squeezes it. Certainly he has now committed attempted murder. But he might
have been interrupted at any one of the stages described. At which stage had he

---

[11] *Heath* (1810), R. & R. 184; *Stewart* (1814), Russ & Ry. 288.
[12] Dears. 515.
[13] Dears. 539.
[14] 1 F. & F. 511.
[15] [1966] 2 Q.B. 53; [1965] 3 All E.R. 384.
[16] And, presumably, an *attempt* so to procure will also be an offence.

gone far enough for his conduct to be described as an attempt? This is a matter about which opinions may well differ; but it is an important question for it determines the borderline of criminal liability. Two cases may be compared to illustrate the difficulties of drawing the line. In *Button*[17] entries for two handicaps at a public athletic meeting were made in the name of Sims. Sims's recent performances were very moderate and, in consequence, he was given long starts. At the meeting D personated Sims, who was absent, and, being a good runner, won both races. On being questioned, he said he was Sims. The recorder directed the jury that if the prisoner made the false pretences wilfully, intentionally and fraudulently, with intent to obtain the prizes, he was guilty of attempting to obtain by false pretences. The court dismissed as "exceedingly subtle, but unsound", the argument that some other act had to be done in order to make the offence complete and that it must be shown that he had applied for the prizes. His conviction was affirmed.

In *Robinson*[18] D, a jeweller, having insured his stock against theft, concealed some of it in his premises, tied himself up with string and called for help. He told a policeman who broke in that he had been knocked down and his safe robbed. He valued the jewellery at £1,500. The policeman was not satisfied with the story and discovered the property concealed on the premises. D then confessed that he had hoped to get money from the insurers. His conviction of attempting to obtain £1,200 by false pretences was quashed. He could have been convicted if a claim had been made or if any step had been taken towards communicating the news of the burglary to the insurers. *Button*[19] was distinguished on the grounds that there D had made the false pretence, whereas here he was merely preparing the evidence to support a false pretence which he never made.

The most interesting effort to lay down a test is what has been called "the equivocality theory". This was propounded by Salmond[20] as follows:

> "An attempt is an act of such a nature that it is itself evidence of the criminal intent with which it is done. A criminal attempt bears criminal intent upon its face. *Res ipsa loquitur*. An act, on the other hand, which is in itself and on the face of it innocent, is not a criminal attempt, and cannot be made punishable by evidence *aliunde* as to the purpose with which it is done."

Salmond, as a New Zealand judge, applied this test[1] and it became established as the law in that Dominion. In England the theory was enunciated by Turner,[2] in an article published in 1934. A key passage was reproduced, verbatim, in *Archbold*[3] and recently received the approval of the Court of Appeal in *Davey* v. *Lee*[4]:

---

[17] [1900] 2 Q.B. 597 (C.C.R.).
[18] [1915] 2 K.B. 342 (C.C.A.).
[19] *Supra.*
[20] *Jurisprudence* (6th ed.), 346.
[1] *Barker*, [1924] N.Z.L.R. 856, followed in *Yelds*, [1928] N.Z.L.R. 18.
[2] " Attempts to Commit Crimes " (1934), 5 C.L.J. 230, reproduced in M.A.C.L., 273; Russell, 184–195; Kenny, 197. In applying this test we are directed to ignore "any evidence which *merely* goes to establish his intention, and which does not go to establish a step taken by him in order to achieve the results which he intended"; for this "is solely evidence of *mens rea* and is no evidence at all of *actus reus*". Thus D's account of his intention, either before or after the act, though evidence of his *mens rea*, would be ignored when deciding whether there was an *actus reus*. The New Zealand court held that it was permissible to take account of conversations which formed part of the *res gesta* in interpreting the acts which followed (*Mackie*, [1957] N.Z.L.R. 669 at p. 676) so that conversations making arrangements for the commission of the crime would be steps towards its commission. And see *Jones* v. *Brooks* (1968), 52 Cr. App. Rep. 614, below, p. 170.
[3] (36th ed.) § 4104.
[4] [1967] 2 All E.R. 423; [1967] Crim. L.R. 357 and commentary thereon.

". . . the *actus reus* necessary to constitute an attempt is complete if the prisoner does an act which is a step towards the commission of the specific crime, which is immediately and not merely remotely connected with the commission of it, and the doing of which cannot reasonably be regarded as having any other purpose than the commission of the specific crime."

In the meantime, Turner had himself come to the conclusion that the definition needed modification; to require that the act could not reasonably be regarded as having any other purpose than the commission of the specific crime went too far. It should be enough that the steps taken be sufficient

"to show, *prima facie*, the offender's intention to commit the crime which he is charged with attempting."[5]

Moreover, the test had been found to work so badly in New Zealand that it had been repealed by legislation.[6] Of all this, however, the editors of *Archbold* and the Court of Appeal seem to have been unaware. The test seems to be deficient in two respects. On the one hand

"There may be cases where one overt act demonstrates beyond all question the criminal intent, but yet of itself is not sufficiently proximate to constitute an attempt. . . ."[7]

Thus on a charge of attempting unlawfully to use an instrument with intent to procure miscarriage, there may be evidence of telephone conversations making arrangements for the illegal operation which establish beyond doubt D's intent to carry it out; yet he may be a hundred miles from the patient and, on a common-sense view, it may be impossible to say that there is an attempt. On the other hand, the facts may be such that on any common-sense view, D's conduct amounts to an attempt and yet it may not be unequivocal. In *Campbell and Bradley* v. *Ward*,[8] P, returning to his parked car, saw D emerging from the front seat. D ran away to another car in which were two accomplices. P jumped on the running board and pulled D out. D and his accomplices were apprehended; the accomplices confessed that D was trying to steal a car battery and had got into several cars for this purpose. All three were convicted of attempting to steal a battery. The accomplices appealed and their convictions were quashed. The court held that D's act, to be an attempt, must be both sufficiently proximate *and* unequivocal. It was sufficiently proximate (that is, the court thought it really was an attempt), but not unequivocal.

". . . The overt act done by [D] . . . is ambiguous as to the crime intended, and resort may not be had to the confessions in order to resolve the ambiguity. The act of getting into [P's] car or of interfering with it . . . if it can be regarded as evidencing any criminal intent at all, the most natural inference might be that there was an intention to take or convert the car. . . . If it were permissible to regard the act as sufficient evidence of an intent to steal, it is, in so far as the matter may be relevant, completely uninformative as to the object or objects to be stolen."[9]

It is indeed difficult to see how the test was passed in *Davey* v. *Lee*.[10] D was

---

[5] Russell (11th ed., 1958), 195, n. 52; (12th ed., 1964), 184, n. 53.
[6] Crimes Act 1961, s. 72 (3). "An act done or omitted with intent to commit an offence may constitute an attempt if it is immediately or proximately connected with the intended offence, whether or not there was any act unequivocally showing the intent to commit that offence."
[7] *Mackie*, [1957] N.Z.L.R. 669 at p. 675, *per* NORTH J. *Cf. Robinson*, above, p. 168.
[8] [1955] N.Z.L.R. 471.
[9] *Ibid.*, at p. 476.
[10] Above, p. 168.

convicted of attempting to steal copper on evidence that he had cut the wire of a compound in which were a copper store, an office building, dwelling houses and other stores. Though the copper store was situated at the end of the compound where the cutting took place, it is difficult to see that this act might not reasonably be regarded as having been done in order to steal money from the office or goods from one of the dwelling houses or the other stores. Already the inadequacies of the test are appearing; and in *Jones* v. *Brooks*[11] the divisional court upheld a conviction although the act was equivocal; the intention of the accused expressed at the time of the offence *and later* was not to be disregarded as part of the evidence of the *actus reus*.

It is one thing to point out the difficulties inherent in the equivocality test; it is quite another to propose a substitute for it. In fact, it is difficult to escape from Kenny's conclusion that

> "no abstract test can be given for determining whether an act is sufficiently proximate to be an attempt".[12]

This assumes that the question must be decided as one of common sense in each particular case. The law is necessarily vague; but perhaps it is better that it should be vague than capricious. Nevertheless, it is unfortunate that it causes difficulty to the police who must strike before an offence is consummated if they are not to appear to connive at the offence and yet, if they are to get a conviction, must not strike before it amounts to an attempt.[13]

Only one, not very helpful, rule can be asserted with confidence. If D has done the last act which he expects to do and which it is necessary for him to do in order to achieve the consequence alleged to be attempted, he is guilty.[14] But a man may be guilty of an attempt even though he has not gone so far and has other acts to do.[15]

It is logical that, once the steps taken towards the commission of an offence are sufficiently far advanced to amount to an attempt, it can make no difference whether the failure to complete the crime is due to a voluntary withdrawal by the prisoner, the intervention of the police, or any other reason. In *Taylor*[16] it was held that an attempt was committed where D approached a stack of corn with the intention of setting fire to it and lighted a match for that purpose but abandoned his plan on finding that he was being watched.

5   Where the Accused's Objective is Impossible of Achievement

It was thought at one time that there could be no conviction for an attempt to do an act which was impossible. The origin of this error—as it has subsequently been shown to be—was *McPherson*[17] where the decision was simply that, where

---

[11] (1968), 52 Cr. App. Rep. 614.
[12] *Cf.* Stephen *Digest* (8th ed.), Art. 29: "An act done with intent to commit that crime and forming part of a series of acts which would constitute its actual commission if it were not interrupted. The point at which such a series of acts begins cannot be defined; but depends on the circumstances of each particular case."
[13] See *Lawson*, [1959] Crim. L.R. 134; *Mills*, [1963] 1 Q.B. 522; [1963] 1 All E.R. 202.
[14] *Eagleton* (1855), Dears C.C. 515 at p. 538, *per* PARKE, B. *Cf. White*, above, p. 33; *Vreones*, [1891] 1 Q.B. 360; below, p. 512.
[15] In *White* (last footnote) D may have contemplated the administration of further doses. See also *Linneker*, [1906] 2 K.B. 99.
[16] (1859), 1 F. & F. 511; See also *Lankford*, [1959] Crim. L.R. 209.
[17] (1857), Dears & B. 197.

an indictment charged D with stealing certain specific goods, he could not be found guilty of attempting to steal other goods: "If you indict a man for stealing your watch, you cannot convict him of attempting to steal your umbrella." This point is clear enough; but certain *dicta* in the case misled the Court for Crown Cases Reserved to hold in *Collins*[18] that an attempt was established only where, if no interruption had taken place, the attempt could have been carried out successfully; and that, therefore, D could not be convicted of attempted larceny where he had put his hand into another's pocket with intent to steal but it was not proved that there was anything in the pocket. Doubt was cast on this decision in *Brown*[19] but, as the full offence was capable of commission in that case, the issue was not directly raised. But in *Ring, Atkins and Jackson*[20] where the facts were the same as in *Collins*, a conviction was upheld and it was stated that *McPherson* had been overruled by *Brown*. Though this may be technically inaccurate—as the point was not really in issue in *Brown*—it is clear that *Ring* itself settled the matter beyond doubt. So if D attempts to break open the front door of a bank, using an implement which is utterly inadequate for the purpose; if he attempts to poison P, using a dose which is far too weak to kill anyone;[1] if he tries to deceive P into giving him money by a false representation about a matter as to which P happens to know the truth;[2] in each of these cases the thing attempted is impossible, yet a conviction for an attempt to commit it would be proper.[3]

6   Where the Accused's Objective is not Criminal[4]

The prototype of the problem here to be discussed is the oft-cited hypothetical case put by BRAMWELL, B.,[5] of the man who sees an umbrella and resolves to steal it. He takes it and carries it away and finds out that it is his own. Plainly he is not guilty of theft—he has committed no *actus reus*. Can he be convicted of an attempt? Many similar cases may be put. For example:

D, who believes his wife A to be alive, goes through a ceremony of marriage with B. In fact, A was run over by a 'bus and killed five minutes before the ceremony. Is D guilty of attempted bigamy?

D receives a roll of oilcloth which he believes to be stolen property. In fact, unknown to D, after being stolen, the oilcloth came back into the possession of its owner and so ceased in law[6] to be stolen goods. Is D guilty of attempting to receive stolen goods?[7]

---

[18] (1864), 9 Cox C.C. 497.
[19] (1889), 24 Q.B.D. 357.
[20] (1892), 61 L.J.M.C. 116.
[1] *Cf. White*, above, p. 33.
[2] *Cf. Hensler*, above, p. 33.
[3] Holmes's view that "the act must come pretty near to accomplishing that result before the law will notice it" (*Commonwealth* v. *Kennedy* (1897), 170 Mass. 18) is difficult to reconcile with this rule. It is true that "proximate" means "pretty near"; but "proximate" must be treated as a term of art.
[4] See Smith, "Two Problems in Criminal Attempts" (1957), 70 Harv. L.R. 422; and "Two Problems in Criminal Attempts Re-examined", [1962] Crim. L.R. 135 and 212; Ryu (1957) 32 N.Y.U.L. Rev. 1170; Williams, "Criminal Attempt, A Reply", [1962] Crim. L.R. 300.
[5] In *Collins* (1864), 9 Cox C.C. 497 at p. 498.
[6] See below, p. 423.
[7] These are the facts of the American case of *Jaffé* (1906), 185 N.Y. 497; 78 N.E. 169, where a conviction for attempted receiving was quashed.

D, who believes that his car is subject to a mortgage, states that it is free from encumbrances in order to induce P to buy it and does induce him to do so. In fact, the document creating the supposed mortgage is void as an unregistered bill of sale and the car *is* in law free from encumbrances. Is D guilty of attempting to obtain by deception ?[8]

D has sexual intercourse with a woman whom he believes to be a mental defective. She is not a mental defective. Is he guilty of an attempt to have intercourse with a mental defective?[9]

In each of these cases D has *mens rea*. If the facts had been as he supposed them to be, there would have been an *actus reus* and D would have been guilty of the complete crime; but in each case, from the beginning of the transaction, an essential ingredient of the complete crime is missing. In fact, the commission of the crime in all these cases is impossible. These cases differ, however, from the group of cases of impossibility first considered in that in the cases in the first group D necessarily fails to achieve his objective—he fails to get anything out of the pocket, to break and enter, or to kill, respectively; and if he had succeeded, he would have been guilty of a crime. In the cases in the second group D, if he succeeds in his *objective*—going through the ceremony of marriage; receiving the goods he intends to receive; inducing the belief he intends to induce and getting money in consequence; and having sexual intercourse—commits no crime. Until very recently, the English courts showed no inclination to treat this type of case as an attempt. There are numerous cases of this type where the court has quashed a conviction for the complete crime—sometimes with expressions of regret—and has not used its power[10] to substitute a conviction for an attempt. One would certainly have expected the power to be used if the court thought that an attempt was made out; but the possibility does not appear to have been canvassed. The cases referred to therefore suggest, but by no means decide, that there is no attempt in such circumstances. The one case in which the matter was discussed also suggested that there was no attempt. In *Percy Dalton Ltd.*[11] where D Ltd. was charged with selling pears in excess of the permitted price. The transactions in question were sales of boxes of pears described as being of "46 lbs. or better". If the boxes had weighed only 46 lbs. the price at which they were sold was excessive; but if they weighed 46 lbs. 15 ozs., the price was lawful. There was evidence that the boxes were usually some 2 or 3 lbs. more than 46 lbs. net weight and the prosecution was unable to prove that the boxes in question weighed less than 46 lbs. 15 ozs. The jury, however, found D guilty of attempting to sell pears in excess of the permitted price. In

---

[8] These are the facts of *Deller* (1952), 36 Cr. App. Rep. 184, above, p. 29, where no reference was made to the possibility of conviction for an attempt.

[9] These are the facts of *Director of Public Prosecutions* v. *Head*, [1959] A.C. 83; [1958] 1 All E.R. 679, where, again, no reference was made to the possibility of conviction for an attempt. Williams concedes that it "would certainly look odd" if Head were convicted of an attempt. It would—but no odder than in the other cases discussed. See C.L.G.P., 653.

[10] Under s. 9 of the Criminal Procedure Act 1851. See *Schmidt* (1866), L.R. 1 C.C.R. 15 (receiving); *Villensky*, [1892] 2 Q.B. 597 (receiving); *Turvey* (1946), 31 Cr. App. Rep. 154 (larceny or receiving); *Deller* (1952), 36 Cr. App. Rep. 184 (obtaining by false pretences); *Director of Public Prosecutions* v. *Nieser*, [1959] 1 Q.B. 254; [1958] 3 All E.R. 662 (receiving); *Director of Public Prosecutions* v. *Head*, [1959] A.C. 83; [1958] 1 All E.R. 679; [1958] Crim. L.R. 330 (carnal knowledge of a mental defective); *Clayton and Halsey*, [1963] 1 Q.B. 163; [1962] 3 All E.R. 500 (publishing an obscene article). See also *Walters* v. *Lunt*, [1951] 2 All E.R. 645 (receiving); (1957), 70 Harv. L.R. 442–448.

[11] (1949), 33 Cr. App. Rep. 102.

quashing that conviction, BIRKETT, J., delivering the judgment of the Court of Criminal Appeal said:[12]

"Steps on the way to the commission of what would be a crime, if the acts were completed, may amount to attempts to commit that crime, to which, unless interrupted, they would have led; but steps on the way to the doing of something, which is thereafter done and which is no crime, cannot be regarded as attempts to commit a crime."

There does not appear to have been any evidence that D believed that the pears were under 46 lbs. 15 ozs. in weight. According to the *dictum* quoted above it would have made no difference if there had been such evidence, since the acquittal was required on the ground of the absence of an *actus reus*. The recent and only actual decision on the point, however, goes the other way. In *Millar and Page*[13] D1 and D2 approached a lorry driver and suggested that he should assist them in stealing the contents of his lorry. The driver reported the matter to his employer who told him to co-operate. He took the lorry to the place appointed by the accused and assisted them in unloading the bales. It was held that the accused must be acquitted of larceny because the taking was with the consent of the owner, but that they were guilty of an attempt. It would certainly have been outrageous if the accused had been guilty of no offence; but it is worth observing that they were certainly guilty of conspiracy; and that the absurdity arose from the law of larceny, now repealed, which required that the taking be without consent.

Millar and Page cannot be taken conclusively to have settled the question since no authorities were cited by the court and, in particular, no reference was made to the *dicta* in *Percy Dalton, Ltd.* which the court thought to be "obviously right" only three years previously.[14] The weight of academic authority would support the decision in *Millar and Page*. Thus Williams's view of *Percy Dalton, Ltd.* is that the jury's verdict would have been perfectly logical, if there had been evidence of *mens rea*.

"Supposing that the company thought the boxes to be underweight, they took steps that, on the facts as they thought them to be, were steps towards the commission of a crime; but they did not thereafter commit the full crime, being saved from this by their mistake. Thus the case was not one of taking 'steps on the way to the doing of something, which is thereafter done, and which is no crime' ".[15]

Hall takes a similar view:[16]

"In criminal attempts (excluding strict liability), one must take account of the defendant's *mens rea*, and if it is said that the defendant 'did everything he intended to do', that must therefore be understood to mean the actualisation (realisation or fulfilment) of his *mens rea*."

Williams relies on *Hensler*.[17] D wrote a begging letter, making false pretences to P who, knowing the pretence was false, sent the money requested. It was held that D was guilty of an attempt to obtain money by false pretences. It is submitted, however, that *Hensler* is not an authority on this point. When D completed the attempt by posting the letter, all the circumstances necessary for the complete crime *did* exist. It is true that he received the money which he

---

[12] *Ibid.*, at p. 110.
[13] (1965), 49 Cr. App. Rep. 241.
[14] *McDonough* (1962), 47 Cr. App. Rep. 37 at p. 41; above, p. 150.
[15] C.L.G.P., 649.
[16] *General Principles*, 598.
[17] (1870), 11 Cox C.C. 570.

hoped to get. But his case is exactly like that of a thief who tries to break into a safe with an entirely inadequate implement, where the owner, having observed his failure, opens the safe and presents him with the contents; it is unlike the case of *Millar and Page* where, long before the stage of an attempt could be reached, the circumstances necessary to constitute the offence no longer existed —the owner had given his consent.

The case for upholding convictions for attempt in these circumstances is that D is socially just as dangerous and morally just as bad as the person who completes the crime. It is merely by chance that he did not commit it; and criminal liability should not depend on chance. This is a formidable case. The argument against is that D, even if he completes the transaction and achieves his objective has not done anything contrary to law. Unlike an ordinary attempt, which would have resulted in a crime if carried through, this can never do so. Moreover, it looks absurd to say that a man who has actually had sexual intercourse with a woman, is not guilty thereby of having sexual intercourse with a defective, but of attempting to do so; that a man who has shot another in the leg and wounded him is not guilty of unlawful wounding, but of attempted unlawful wounding. The significance of the *actus reus* is greatly reduced. This may be no bad thing; but it would be a departure from the general insistence of the criminal law upon harm, either caused or in the process of being caused.

7　Importance of Defining the Act Attempted

If the *dicta* in *Percy Dalton, Ltd.*[18] be correct, it is of the first importance to determine precisely what is the act which D is alleged to have attempted. Exactly the same conduct may be an attempt to commit one act and not an attempt to commit another. This seems very obvious, but it can cause difficulty. This is seen in two cases (generally agreed to be in conflict) concerning attempts to administer a noxious thing with intent to procure miscarriage contrary to s. 58 of the Offences against the Person Act 1861.[19] It will be noted that, in both parts of this section, it is the administration of the noxious thing with intent to procure abortion which is the forbidden act. The crime is complete as soon as the noxious thing is administered.

In *Brown*[20] D was charged with inciting women

> "unlawfully to attempt to feloniously and unlawfully to [*sic*] administer to themselves divers noxious things with intent to procure their own miscarriage. . . ."

It was contended that the drugs which had been sold to the women as being capable of procuring abortion were in fact harmless and would not do so. The question, therefore, was whether the women were guilty of the attempt alleged in the indictment—that is, to administer to themselves noxious things—if they administered to themselves things which they believed to be noxious but which were in fact harmless. Brown's counsel got off on the wrong foot by mis-stating the thing alleged to have been attempted:

> "If a woman takes a noxious thing, though with intent to procure her abortion, she does not attempt *to procure her abortion*."[1]

---

[18] Above, p. 173.
[19] Below, p. 241.
[20] (1899), 63 J.P. 790.
[1] *Ibid.*, at p. 791.

It was perhaps because of this unfortunate start that DARLING, J., throughout his judgment, mis-stated the act which the women were alleged to have attempted. For example:[2]

> ". . . if the woman, believing she is taking a noxious thing within the statute, does, with intent to procure abortion, take a thing that is in fact harmless, she is guilty of an *attempt to procure abortion* within the meaning of the statute".

This proposition is perfectly accurate. The women were attempting to procure abortion. This was their object and they failed to accomplish it. The inadequacy of the drug used ought no more to afford a defence on a charge of attempted abortion than the inadequacy of the poison in *White's* case.[3] But DARLING, J., was directing his mind to the wrong question. The charge was not one of attempting to procure abortion but of attempting to administer a noxious thing. Now the women did intend to administer a noxious thing and there was a failure of intention, in one sense, for they administered only a harmless thing. But it is also true to say that the women intended to administer the very things they had been given and no other, and in that they succeeded—and this administration was no crime.

This seems to have been the point in the mind of ROWLATT, J., in the next case, *Osborn*,[4] which reached a different result. D was charged with attempting to administer noxious things to a woman with intent to procure her miscarriage. There was no evidence to show that that stuff which D had given to the girl and which she had taken was noxious. *Brown*[5] was not cited, but ROWLATT, J., spoke almost as if he had DARLING, J.'s remarks in mind:[6]

> "He is charged . . . with attempting to administer noxious things with intent to procure miscarriage; he is not charged with attempting to procure miscarriage, but with attempting to administer a noxious thing. . . ."

ROWLATT, J.'s judgment has been criticised and much of it is indeed confused; but his conclusion is defensible:[7]

> "If the thing was not noxious though he thought it was, he did not attempt to administer a noxious thing by administering the innoxious thing."

He succeeded in administering the very thing he intended to administer, the transaction was complete—and it was no crime. The fact that this was an attempt to do something else—to procure abortion—was irrelevant.

8 Successful Attempts

The view has been advanced that failure is essential to the very nature of an attempt, so that success rules out the possibility of a conviction for an attempt. In an American case it was said:

> "A failure to consummate the crime is as much an essential element of an attempt as the intent and performance of an overt act towards its commission."[8]

---

[2] *Ibid.*
[3] Above, pp. 170–171.
[4] (1919), 84 J.P. 63.
[5] Above, footnote 20.
[6] 84 J.P. at p. 63.
[7] *Ibid.*, at p. 64.
[8] *Commonwealth v. Crow* (1931), 303 Pa. 91 at p. 98, quoted in Michael and Wechsler, *Criminal Law and Its Administration*, 620–621. See also at 626.

Hall writes:[9] ". . . attempt implies failure . . ." It is thought, however, that there is no logical impossibility in holding a man to have attempted what he has succeeded in. If D writes a letter to P in which he deliberately makes false statements with intent to induce P to pay money to him, there is no doubt that an attempt to obtain by deception is committed as soon as D posts the letter. The attempt may fail for many reasons, or it may succeed; and there is no obvious reason why, if it succeeds, it should cease to be the attempt which, until that moment, it was. Moreover, such a rule would lead to the logical absurdity that a man would have to be acquitted entirely if it was uncertain whether he had succeeded or not; for, since it could not be proved beyond reasonable doubt that he had succeeded, he must be acquitted of the substantive crime; and, since it could not be proved that he had failed, he must be acquitted of the attempt. This can hardly be the law.

9 Merger

The result just noted, absurd as it is, would seem to have been the logical result of the common law doctrine or doctrines of merger as applied to attempts. There was a rule[10] that where D was charged with a misdemeanour and the facts proved, while establishing the misdemeanour, also showed that a felony had been committed, the misdemeanour merged in the felony and the accused had to be acquitted of the misdemeanour. Since an attempt is a common law misdemeanour, an attempt to commit a felony would merge in the complete offence.

This doctrine was almost certainly abolished so far as trial on indictment is concerned as long ago as 1851,[11] though the matter was disputed; but, with the abolition of felonies, there is plainly no scope for it any more. Moreover, s. 6 (4) of the Criminal Law Act 1967 now provides

> ". . . where a person is charged on indictment with attempting to commit an offence or with any assault or other act preliminary to an offence, but not with the completed offence, then (subject to the discretion of the court to discharge the jury with a view to the preferment of an indictment for the completed offence) he may be convicted of the offence charged notwithstanding that he is shown to be guilty of the completed offence."

Thus, in a trial on indictment, there can never be any question of an attempt merging in the completed offence. Unfortunately, however, this provision does not extend to summary trial. This is immaterial if the merger of attempts was an instance of the wider doctrine of merger of misdemeanours in felonies. However, in *Males*[12] the Court of Criminal Appeal left open the question whether an attempt to commit a misdemeanour would merge in the complete crime. It is submitted that there is no such doctrine of merger at common law; but if there were, then it survives so far as summary trial is concerned.

In *Rogers* v. *Arnott*[13] D was a bailee of a tape recorder which was the subject of a hire-purchase agreement made between two persons. P, a police officer, as a result of information received, made an appointment to meet him. D produced

---

[9] *General Principles*, 577.

[10] It is cogently argued by P. R. Glazebrook, "The Merging of Misdemeanours" (1962), 78 L.Q.R. 560, that merger "is no ancient principle of the common law, but an unhappy aberration with a short and fitful history which ought to have ended in 1844 and certainly did end in 1848 . . .".

[11] By the Criminal Procedure Act 1851, s. 12, now repealed by the Criminal Law Act.

[12] [1962] 2 Q.B. 500; [1961] 3 All E.R. 705.

[13] [1960] 2 Q.B. 244; [1960] 2 All E.R. 417.

the tape recorder, demonstrated it and offered to sell it to P, who thereupon disclosed his identity and arrested him. The defence, which was successful both before the magistrate and in Divisional Court, was that the offence amounted to the complete crime of larceny (a felony) and, *therefore* could not be an attempt to commit it. In both courts the argument was directed to the question whether D's conduct was the complete crime of larceny or not; and it seems to have been assumed that, if the answer to this question was in the affirmative, it followed that he could not be convicted of an attempt. The grounds for the decision are obscure. If, as is probable, it depended on the doctrine of merger of misdemeanours in felonies (which continued to apply to summary trial) it should be decided differently today, unless the submission above, that attempts to commit misdemeanours do not merge, is wrong.

10   Crimes which it is Impossible to Attempt

Stephen wrote that

> "there are a large number of crimes which it is impossible to attempt to commit"

and he instanced compassing the King's death, perjury, riot, libel, the offering of bad money and assault.[14] The first example may be accepted for, though an overt act as well as a mental operation is required to amount to compassing,[15] it would seem that any act directed towards accomplishing the end contemplated would suffice. But it is not at all clear that attempts are inconceivable in other cases. If D writes a letter defamatory of P to Q who never receives it or burns it unread, this looks like attempted libel; and equally, a little ingenuity could devise possible (if unlikely) attempts in the remaining cases.[16]

In *Moran*,[17] the Court of Criminal Appeal held that there could not be a verdict of attempting to demand money with menaces; "there is a demand or there is not". It may be accepted that, on the evidence before the jury in that particular case, either there was a demand (if the evidence was believed) or there was not (if the evidence was disbelieved) but, if this was intended to be a proposition of general application, it has been rightly criticised:

> "If D posts a letter to P demanding money with menaces, and the letter never reaches P, there is surely an attempt to demand."[18]

The alternative explanation of *Rogers* v. *Arnott*[19] is that larceny by a bailee was a crime which cannot be attempted. There is some slight evidence for this in that D's counsel said:

> "One has not heard of attempted fraudulent conversion because, if one attempts a fraudulent conversion, one commits the full offence. . . ."[20]

It is arguable that a man cannot attempt to assume the rights of an owner, which was the essence of the crime, without actually doing so. Since larceny by a bailee has provided the pattern for the new offence of theft,[1] this principle, if it be one, now has a much wider application.

---

[14] 2 H.C.L. 227.
[15] Below, p. 551.
[16] [1961] Crim. L.R. at p. 444.
[17] (1952), 36 Cr. App. R. 10.
[18] Williams, C.L.G.P., 615, n. 9; and see Edwards (1952), 15 M.L.R. 346; Russell, 995.
[19] Above, footnote 13.
[20] [1960] 2 Q.B. at p. 246.
[1] Below, p. 350.

There are three other types of case where an attempt is not possible. (i) Crimes purely of omission where the *actus reus* does not include any consequence of the omission, for example, misprision of treason or the statutory offences of omission discussed above.[2] (ii) Crimes which, by definition may be committed recklessly or negligently, but not intentionally. The only example which comes readily to mind is involuntary manslaughter. It is of the essence of this crime that the killing is done unintentionally, for an intentional killing (in the absence of diminished responsibility, provocation or a suicide pact) is necessarily murder.[3] It has been seen that it is of the essence of an attempt that the consequence required by the definition of a crime (that is, in the case of both murder and manslaughter, a killing) should have been intended. If there is an intention to produce this consequence the crime is necessarily attempted murder; if there is no intention to produce it, there cannot be an attempt at all. (iii) It is difficult to conceive of an attempt when the *actus reus* is a state of affairs, such as "being found".[4]

An attempt to commit voluntary manslaughter, on the other hand, is theoretically a possibility. This variety of manslaughter may be committed when death is intended.[5] If D, having received such provocation as would reduce murder to manslaughter, shoots at P with intent to kill him and misses, this would appear to be attempted manslaughter, assuming that the defence of provocation applies to a charge of attempted murder. It is reasonable to suppose that provocation, being a defence at common law, will be applied to such a charge.[6] It is not so clear that diminished responsibility and suicide pact, being statutory defences[7] available on a charge of murder, could properly be extended to charges of an attempt, though there is slight persuasive authority in favour of such an extension.[8]

---

[2] Page 36. But in the view of writers such as Williams and Hall, even attempted misprision is possible: D, who believes, wrongly, that X has committed treason, refrains from reporting him. See above, p. 173.

[3] Below, p. 196.

[4] Above, p. 34.

[5] *A.-.G. of Ceylon* v. *Kum Perera*, [1953] A.C. 200 at pp. 205–206; below, p. 205; and see *Lee Chun Chuen* v. *R.*, [1963] A.C. 220; [1963] 1 All E.R. 73.

[6] It was held that it does so apply in *Smith*, [1964] N.Z.L.R. 834 (WILSON, J.) and *Anderson*, [1965] Tas. S.R. 21 (CRAWFORD, J.). *Cf. Patience* (1837), 7 C. & P. 775. When attempted murder was, by statute, a felony, a conviction for attempted manslaughter on a charge of attempted murder was ruled out by the doctrine that, apart from statute, there could be no conviction for a misdemeanour on an indictment for felony. Since the Criminal Law Act 1967, this objection no longer applies. In Australia it has been held that provocation is a defence to a charge of wounding with intent to murder: *Newman*, [1948] V.L.R. 61; *Spartels*, [1953] V.L.R. 194; *contra Falla*, [1964] V.R. 78.

[7] Homicide Act 1957, ss. 2 and 4; see above, p. 124 and below, p. 239.

[8] *Collier*, [1960] Crim. L.R. 204; above, p. 165.

PART II

Particular Crimes

CHAPTER 11

Homicide

1 MURDER

The classic definition of murder is that of Coke:

> "Murder is when a man of sound memory, and of the age of discretion, unlawfully killeth within any county of the realm any reasonable creature *in rerum natura* under the king's peace, with malice aforethought, either expressed by the party or implied by law, so as the party wounded, or hurt, etc. die of the wound or hurt, etc. within a year and a day after the same."[1]

(1) WHO CAN COMMIT MURDER

"A man of sound memory, and of the age of discretion" means simply a man who is responsible according to the general principles which have been discussed above. Such a man is not insane within the M'Naghten Rules; he is over ten and, if under fourteen, he has a "mischievous discretion"; and, since 1957[2] he does not suffer from diminished responsibility.

(2) WHERE MURDER CAN BE COMMITTED

If the killing is by a citizen of the United Kingdom and Colonies, it need no longer take place within "any county of the realm". Murder and manslaughter are among the exceptional cases where the English courts have jurisdiction over offences committed abroad. By s. 9 of the Offences against the Person Act 1861 and s. 3 of the British Nationality Act 1948 a murder or manslaughter committed by a citizen of the United Kingdom and Colonies on land anywhere out of the United Kingdom may be tried in any county or place in England as if it had been committed there. Homicides on a British ship[3] or aircraft[4] are also triable here, whether committed by a British subject or not; but not those on a foreign ship, outside territorial waters.[5]

---

[1] 3 Inst. 47.

[2] See s. 2 of the Homicide Act 1957, above, p. 124.

[3] Not only when sailing on the high seas, but also when in the rivers of a foreign territory at a place below bridges, where the tide ebbs and flows and where great ships go: *Anderson* (1868), 1 C.C.R. 161.

[4] Civil Aviation Act 1949, s. 62.

[5] Jurisdiction over offences within territorial waters is given by the Territorial Waters Jurisdiction Act 1878, s. 2. And see Continental Shelf Act 1964, s. 3.

(3) WHO CAN BE THE VICTIM[6]

"A reasonable creature *in rerum natura*" includes any human being. The only problem that gives any difficulty concerns the unborn child. It is not murder to kill a child in the womb or while in the process of being born. At common law it was a "great misprision" (misdemeanour)[7] and it is now an offence under s. 58 of the Offences against the Person Act 1861,[8] or, where the child is capable of being born alive, under the Infant Life Preservation Act 1929.[9] To be the victim of a murder the child must be wholly expelled from the mother's body and it must be alive.[10] The cord and the after-birth need not have been expelled from the mother nor severed from the child.[11] The child, it is commonly said, must have an existence "independent of the mother".[12] The tests of independent existence which the courts have accepted are that the child should have an independent circulation, and that it should have breathed after birth. But there are difficulties about both these tests.

In *Brain* PARK, J., said:[13]

> ". . . it is not essential that it should have breathed at the time it was killed; as many children are born alive and yet do not breathe for some time after their birth."

And, according to Atkinson, there is no known means of determining at what instant the foetal and parental circulations are so dissociated as to allow the child to live without the help of the parental circulation; and this dissociation may precede birth.[14] There is thus a good deal of uncertainty about the precise moment at which the child comes under the protection of the law of murder, though the question does not seem to have troubled the courts in recent years.

If the child is poisoned or injured in the womb, is born alive and then dies of the poison or injury, this may be murder or manslaughter.[15] In *West*[16] MAULE, J., directed the jury:

> ". . . if a person intending to procure abortion does an act which causes a child to be born so much earlier than the natural time that it is born in a state much less capable of living and afterwards dies as a consequence of its exposure to the external world, the person who by her misconduct so brings a child into the world and puts it merely into a situation in which it cannot live is guilty of murder."

---

[6] Seaborne Davies, "Child-killing in English Law", M.A.C.L. 301; Williams, *Sanctity of Life and the Criminal Law*, 19–23; S. B. Atkinson, "Life, Birth and Live Birth" (1904), 20 L.Q.R. 134.

[7] 3 Co. Inst. 50. According to Hale, 1 P.C. 433, "a great crime". WILLES, J., said in 1866 (B.P.P. 21, p. 274) that the crime was obsolete. (See M.A.C.L. at 310). But *cf.* the revival of misprision of felony.

[8] Below, pp. 243–245.

[9] Below, p. 241.

[10] *Poulton* (1832), 5 C. & P. 329, *per* LITTLEDALE, J.; *Brain* (1834), 6 C. & P. 349 (PARK, J.); *Sellis* (1837), 7 C. & P. 850 (COLTMAN, J.).

[11] *Reeves* (1839), 9 C. & P. 25 (VAUGHAN, J.); *Trilloe* (1842), 2 Moo. C.C. 260 (ERSKINE, J., and C.C.R.).

[12] See the cases cited by Atkinson, 20 L.Q.R. at 143.

[13] (1834), 6 C. & P. at p. 350.

[14] 20 L.Q.R. at 145.

[15] 3 Co. Inst. 50; Hawkins, 1 P.C., c. 31, § 16; East, 1 P.C. 228; *contra* Hale, 1 P.C. 433.

[16] (1848), 2 Cox C.C. 500. See also *Kwok Chak Ming* (Hong Kong, 1963) discussed in [1963] Crim. L.R. 748.

In such a case, D would have the *mens rea* sufficient, at that time, for murder, since she intended to commit a felony.[17]   It was held in *Senior*[18] that where the pre-natal injury was caused by gross negligence or with a *mens rea* sufficient only for manslaughter, and death after birth resulted from it, then, similarly, a conviction for manslaughter was appropriate.   In that case a midwife,

> "being grossly ignorant of the art which he professed, and unable to deliver the woman with safety to herself and the child, as might have been done by a person of ordinary skill, broke and compressed the skull of the infant, and thereby occasioned its death immediately after it was born."

The judges held that a conviction for manslaughter was proper.   It would be logical to go on to hold that gross pre-natal neglect of the child by the mother, resulting in death after birth, should also be manslaughter; but this step has not been taken, and the rule appears to apply only to acts and not omissions.[19] Similar problems could arise as to the moment at which life ends, though these do not seem, in practice, to have troubled the courts.   Is P dead, and therefore incapable of being murdered, if his heart has stopped beating but a surgeon confidently expects to start it again, by an injection or mechanical means?[20]   Is P dead if he is in a "hopeless" condition and "kept alive" only by an apparatus of some kind?[21]   There is, at present, no certain answer to these questions which are being raised in an acute form by heart transplant operations.

All persons appear to be "under the Queen's peace", for this purpose even an alien enemy, "unless it be in the heat of war, and in the actual exercise thereof."[22] So also it is murder at common law if a man condemned to death be executed by someone other than the officer lawfully appointed, or if the officer lawfully appointed carries out the execution by an unauthorised method, as where he beheads a man condemned to be hanged.[1]   In *Page*[2] an argument that an Egyptian national who had been murdered in an Egyptian village by a British soldier was not within the Queen's peace, was rejected.[3]

(4) DEATH WITHIN A YEAR AND A DAY

The reason for this arbitrary rule lies in the difficulty of tracing the causation when there is a long interval between the act and the death:

> ". . . for if he die after that time, it cannot be discerned, as the law presumes, whether he died of the stroke or poison, etc. or a natural death."[4]

Whether a rule that may well have been justified in Coke's time should still be the law in the present state of medical science is, to say the least, doubtful.   But the rule undoubtedly remains valid both for murder and manslaughter.[5]   Thus

---

[17] Under 9 Geo. IV, c. 31, s. 13.
[18] (1832), 1 Mood. C.C. 346.
[19] *Knights* (1860), 2 F. & F. 46; *Izod* (1904), 20 Cox C.C. 690; and see the discussion by Davies, M.A.C.L. at 308–309.
[20] Williams, *Sanctity of Life and the Criminal Law*, 18.
[21] Elliott (1964), 4 Med. Sci. & L. 77; and see *ibid.*, at 550.
[22] Hale, 1 P.C. 433.
[1] *Ibid.*
[2] [1954] 1 Q.B. 170; [1953] 2 All E.R. 1355 (C.-M.A.C.).
[3] The real issue in that case was whether the court-martial assembled in the Canal Zone had jurisdiction to try the case.   It was admitted that, if D had been brought to this country and tried here, no question could have arisen as to the nationality of the victim. The court-martial was held to have jurisdiction under the Army Act.
[4] 3 Co. Inst. 52.
[5] *Quaere*, for other statutory forms of homicide, for example, causing death by dangerous driving.

in *Dyson*[6] D, who had inflicted injuries on a child in November, 1906, and again in November, 1907, was indicted for the manslaughter of the child which died on March 5, 1908. The judge directed the jury that they could find D guilty if they considered death to have been caused by the injuries inflicted in November, 1906. The Court of Criminal Appeal set aside the conviction:

> "It is still undoubtedly the law of the land that no person can be convicted of manslaughter where the death does not occur within a year and a day after the injury was inflicted, for in that event it must be attributed to some other cause."[7]

The law takes no note of a part of a day. If the blow is struck at any time on January 1, 1963, death must occur before midnight on January 1, 1964, to be within the rule.

(5) THE PROBLEM OF CAUSATION[8]

The year and a day rule is a convenient starting point for the whole question of causation. What must be caused is some acceleration of death. Since everyone must die sooner or later, it follows that every killing is merely an acceleration of death; and it makes no difference for this purpose that the victim is already suffering from a fatal disease or injury or is under sentence of death. Thus, in *Dyson*, the facts of which are given above, Lord ALVERSTONE, C.J., said:[9]

> "The proper question to have been submitted to the jury was whether the prisoner accelerated the child's death by the injuries which he inflicted in December, 1907. For if he did the fact that the child was already suffering from meningitis from which it would in any event have died before long, would afford no answer to the charge of causing its death."

In *Commonwealth* v. *Bowen*[10] PARKER, C.J., of the Supreme Court of Massachusetts directed that D was guilty of murder if he incited a condemned man to commit suicide on the eve of his execution in order to disappoint the sheriff and people who might assemble to see the execution; it was none the less murder because

> "justice was thirsting for a sacrifice, and that but a small portion of Jewett's earthly existence could in any event remain to him."

The administration of pain-saving drugs presents difficult problems. In the case of *Adams*[11] DEVLIN, J., directed the jury that there is no special defence justifying a doctor in giving drugs which would shorten life in the case of severe pain: "If life were cut short by weeks or months it was just as much murder as if it were cut short by years." He went on:

> "But that does not mean that a doctor aiding the sick or dying has to calculate in minutes or hours, or perhaps in days or weeks, the effect on a patient's life of the medicines which he administers. If the first purpose of medicine—the restoration of health—can no longer be achieved, there is still much for the doctor to do, and he is entitled to do all that is proper and necessary to relieve pain and suffering even if measures he takes may incidentally shorten life."

---

[6] [1908] 2 K.B. 454.

[7] *Ibid.*, at p. 456.

[8] Hart and Honoré, *Causation in the Law*, especially Chs. XII–XIV; Williams, "Causation in Homicide", [1957] Crim. L.R. 429 and 510; Camps and Havard, "Causation in Homicide—A Medical View", [1957] Crim. L.R. at 576.

[9] [1908] 2 K.B. at p. 457. And see Hale, 1 P.C. 428; *Fletcher* (1841), Russell, 417; *Martin* (1832), 5 C. &. P. 128 at p. 130.

[10] (1816), 13 Mass. 356.

[11] [1957] Crim. L.R. 365; (1957), *The Times*, April 9; Sybille Bedford, *The Best We Can Do*, at 192. The case is discussed by Hart and Honoré, *op. cit.*, at p. 308.

These passages are not easy to reconcile. If a doctor gives drugs with the object of relieving the pain and suffering of a dying man knowing that the drugs will certainly shorten life, then he intends to shorten life. If, as DEVLIN, J., held, and as must surely be the case, the doctor has a defence, it cannot be because his act has not caused death nor because he did not intend so to do. Perhaps this is a case in which motive affords an excuse. Would not a legatee, who administered the same drugs with the object of hastening his inheritance, be guilty of murder if his action accelerated the death to any appreciable extent?[12]

Alternatively, it may be that there is a defence in these cases only where the drugs are not a "substantial" cause of death; for, if the doctor is entitled to shorten life at all to save pain, presumably he may do this only where death is inevitable within a short time; hence the contrast made by the learned judge between "weeks or months" and "minutes or hours".

1   A Question of Fact and Law

Causation is a question of both fact and law. D's act cannot be held to be the cause of an event if the event would have occurred without it.[13] The act, that is, must be a *sine qua non* of the event and whether it is so is a question of fact. But there are many acts which are *sine qua non* of a homicide and yet are not either in law, or in ordinary parlance, the cause of it. If I invite P to dinner and he is run over and killed on the way, my invitation may be a *sine qua non* of his death, but no one would say I killed him and I have not caused his death in law. Whether a particular act which is a *sine qua non* of an alleged *actus reus* is also a cause of it is a question of law. In the cases considered below the judges have regularly ruled that, given a certain state of fact, D's act was, or was not, the cause of the *actus reus*. Thus, the case of *Jordan*[14] has been criticised[15] because medical experts were permitted to say that certain medical treatment, and not a wound inflicted by D, was the cause of P's death. The wound was certainly a *sine qua non* of the death for it led directly to the medical treatment; and whether it was "a cause", for the purpose of the decision, was a question of law, not of medicine. Certainly it was relevant and proper for the court to know if the medical treatment was effective to cause death, either in conjunction with, or independently of the wound; and perhaps all that the witnesses intended to say was that the treatment alone was the medical cause of death. The court was in error in holding that a jury would have felt bound to follow this evidence. It was not a matter for the jury but for the court itself.

2   Contributory Causes

It is clear that the act of the accused need not be the sole cause of death. In *Dyson* it would have been immaterial that the blows would not have caused the death but for the meningitis; it was enough that the death would not have been

---

[12] But the doctor who, following accepted medical practice, administered drugs which shortened life, would not be guilty because he knew that P had left him a legacy and was pleased at the prospect of receiving it sooner. See above, p. 47.

[13] With, possibly, one rather unlikely exception. Where D and E simultaneously and not acting in concert, each inflict a fatal injury on P, each must be held to have caused the death, though if either one of them had not acted, the death would still have occurred at the same time. See Hall, *General Principles*, 267.

[14] Discussed in detail, below, p. 190.

[15] By Williams at [1957] Crim. L.R. 431 and by Camps and Havard at [1957] Crim. L.R. 582.

caused by the meningitis at the time when it occurred but for the blows.[16] Contributory causes may be the acts of others including the acts of the deceased himself. The contributory negligence of the plaintiff in civil actions of negligence was an absolute defence at common law, but no such principle applied in murder or manslaughter. In *Swindall and Osborne*[17] where one or other of the two accused ran over and killed an old man, POLLOCK, C.B., directed the jury:

> "The prisoners are charged with contributing to the death of the deceased, by their negligence and improper conduct, and, if they did so, it matters not whether he was deaf or drunk or negligent, or in part contributed to his own death; for in this consists a great distinction between civil and criminal proceedings ... each party is responsible for any blame that may ensue, however large the share may be. ... Generally, it may be laid down, that, where one by his negligence, has contributed to the death of another, he is responsible. ..."

A case in which the negligence of third parties contributed to P's death is *Benge*.[18] D, a foreman platelayer, employed to take up a certain section of railway line, misread the time-table so that the line was up at a time when a train arrived. He placed a flagman at a distance of only 540 yards, instead of 1,000 yards as required by the company's regulations and entirely omitted to place fog signals, although the regulations specified that these should be put at 250-yard intervals for a distance of 1,000 yards. At D's trial for manslaughter it was urged that, in spite of his mistakes, the accident could not have happened if the other servants of the company had done their duty—if the flagman had gone the proper distance or if the engine driver had been keeping a proper look-out, which he was not. PIGOTT, B., ruled that this was no defence; if D's negligence mainly or substantially caused the accident, it was irrelevant that it might have been avoided if other persons had not been negligent.

Evidence of P's negligence may, however, be relevant in showing that D was not negligent at all or that his negligence was not gross.

The death is not attributable to the accused if the culpability of his act in no way contributed to it. In *Dalloway*[19] D was driving a cart on a highway with reins not in his hands but loose on the horse's back. A three-year-old child ran into the road a few yards in front of the horse and was struck by one of the wheels and killed. ERLE, J., directed the jury that, if the prisoner had reins and by using the reins could have saved the child, he was guilty of manslaughter; but that if they thought he could not have saved the child by the use of the reins, then they should acquit him. If D had not been driving the cart at all the incident could not have occurred; and in that sense, he "caused" it; but it was necessary to go further and show that the death was due to the culpable element in his act—the negligence in not using the reins.

---

[16] *Johnson* (1827), 1 Lew. C.C. 164, is difficult to reconcile with this principle. D struck P who died. The evidence was that P would not have died if he had been sober. HULLOCK, B., directed an acquittal. The case is inconsistent with *Murton* (1862), 3 F. & F. 492, and other cases and its correctness has frequently been questioned. See Roscoe, *Criminal Evidence* (16th ed.), 769 and Russell, 416, n. 79.

[17] (1846), 2 Car. & Kir. 230 above, p. 84. See also *Walker* (1824), 1 C. & P. 320 (GARROW, B.).

[18] (1865), 4 F. & F. 504. *Cf. Ledger* (1862), 2 F. & F. 857.

[19] (1847), 3 Cox C.C. 273.

3   A Substantial Cause

It is commonly said by judges and writers[20] that, while the accused's act need not be the sole cause of the death, it must be a substantial cause. What is a substantial cause is, of course, incapable of exact definition; but it seems clear that the notion of it is a necessary qualification in the doctrine of causation. This is particularly so because killing is merely an acceleration of death. Factors which produce a very trivial acceleration will be ignored. For example:

D and P are roped mountaineers. P has fallen over a thousand-foot precipice and is dragging D slowly after him. D cuts the rope and P falls to his death five seconds before both P and D would have fallen. Or where two persons independently inflict wounds on P:

> "... suppose one wound severed the jugular vein whereas the other barely broke the skin of the hand, and as the life blood gushed from the victim's neck, one drop oozed from the bruise on his finger ... metaphysicians will conclude that the extra drop of lost blood hastened the end by the infinitesimal fraction of a second. But the law will apply the *substantial factor* test and for juridical purposes the death will be imputed only to the severe injury in such an extreme case as this."[21]

These are, perhaps, rather unlikely examples but the principle would apply, for example, to the person visiting the dying man and contributing to his exhaustion by talking with him; and probably to the administration of pain-killing drugs which accelerate death.[1]

The problem of an intervening cause, which is discussed below[2] is sometimes put on the basis of substantial cause. Thus Hall writes:

> "For example, a slight wound may have necessitated going to a doctor or drugstore, and *en route* the slightly injured person was struck by an automobile or shot by his mortal enemy. The slight wound, though a necessary condition of the death, did not contribute substantially to it."[3]

4   Intervening Acts or Events

Difficult problems may arise where, after D has inflicted an injury on P, some other act or event intervenes before death. A number of cases must be distinguished.

1. P dies of the combined effect of the injury inflicted by D and the subsequent act or event; for example E also injures P, neither injury in itself being mortal. Or E, by his negligent treatment of P's wound, aggravates it and accelerates P's death from the wound. Here, according to the rule already enunciated, both D and E are guilty of homicide.

2. P dies as the result of some subsequent act or event which would have caused death in just the same way even if D had not inflicted the injury on P: for example, D administers poison to P but, before it takes any effect on P's body, P dies of a heart attack[4] or is shot dead by E. Here it is clear D is not guilty of

---

[20] See for example, *Benge* above, p. 186: *Smith*, [1959] 2 Q.B. 35 at pp. 42–43; [1959] 2 All E.R. 193 at p. 198 (below, p. 190); Hall, *General Principles*, 283; Perkins (1946), 36 J. Cr. L. & Cr. at p. 393, and *Criminal Law*, 606–607.

[21] Perkins, *Criminal Law*, 607. But *cf. Garforth*, [1954] Crim. L.R. 936; below, p. 220.

[1] Above, p. 184.

[2] *Infra.*

[3] Hall, *General Principles*, at 283, 393.

[4] *Cf. White*, above, p. 33; *Pankotai*, [1961] Crim. L.R. 546.

homicide, even though the dose of poison was a fatal one. He must be judged by what actually happened, not by what would have happened but for subsequent events.

3. P dies as the result of some act or event which would not have occurred but for the infliction of the injury by D. This is more difficult and two situations must be distinguished.

(a) Cases where death from the subsequent act or event was the natural consequence of D's act—that is, it was foreseeable as likely to occur in the normal course of events. Here D may be held to have caused the death.

(b) Cases where death from the act or event was not the natural consequence of D's act. Here D is not liable for homicide.

These propositions (a) and (b) seem to be the explanation of the examples given by Perkins[5]:

> ". . . if one man knocks down another and goes away leaving his victim not seriously hurt[6] but unconscious, on the floor of a building in which the assault occurred, and before the victim recovers consciousness he is killed in the fall of the building which is shaken down by a sudden earthquake, this is not homicide. The law attributes such a death to the 'Act of God' and not to the assault, even if it may be certain that the deceased would not have been in the building at the time of the earthquake, had he not been rendered unconscious. The blow was the occasion of the man's being there, but the blow was not the cause of the earthquake, nor was the deceased left in a position of obvious danger. On the other hand if the blow had been struck on the seashore, and the assailant had left his victim in imminent peril of an incoming tide which drowned him before consciousness returned, it would be homicide."

P's being drowned in the latter example was a "natural" consequence of D's action—that is, a consequence which might be expected to occur in the normal course of events. P's being killed by the falling building in the former was an abnormal and unforeseeable consequence.

The position seems to be the same where human intervention is involved, whether that intervention be intentional, negligent or merely accidental. The surgeon to whom the injured P is taken for an operation, deliberately kills him; or the ambulance driver, taking P to the hospital, negligently drives into a canal and drowns him; or a careless nurse gives him a deadly poison in mistake for a sleeping pill; or, as in a Kentucky case, *Bush* v. *Commonwealth*[7] the medical officer attending P inadvertently infects him with scarlet fever and he dies of that. None of these is an act which might be expected to occur in the ordinary course of events and they free D from liability. But if the injured P is receiving proper and skilful medical attention and he dies from the anaesthetic or the operation D will be liable. The receipt of such medical attention may be regarded as the natural consequence of the infliction of the wound. At one time the cases concerning medical treatment seemed to lay down a stricter rule, and this must be considered in more detail.

An intervening act by the original actor will not break the chain of causation so as to excuse him, where the intervening act is part of the same transaction;[8] but it is otherwise if the act which causes the *actus reus* is part of completely

---

[5] (1946), 36 J. Cr. L. & Cr. at 393.

[6] The result would appear to be the same if he were seriously hurt.

[7] (1880), 78 Ky. 268 (Kentucky Court of Appeals).

[8] See above, p. 46; Russell, 53–60, where the cases are set out; Williams, C.L.G.P., 65; Hart and Honoré, *Causation in the Law*, 298.

different transaction. For example, D, having wounded P, visits him in hospital and accidentally infects him with smallpox of which he dies.

5 Death caused by Medical Treatment of an Injury

The nineteenth-century cases seem to lay it down that, where the immediate cause of death is the medical treatment received by P consequent upon his injury by D, D is guilty of homicide, whether the treatment was proper or improper, negligent or not. If the treatment was given *bona fide* by competent medical officers, evidence was not admissible to show that it was improper or unskilful. In the earlier cases, this rule was applied only where the wound was dangerous to life. Later, and logically, it was extended to less serious injuries.

In *Pym*[9] ERLE, J., refused to admit evidence that it was the operation and not the wound which caused the death, and that the operation was unnecessary. In *McIntyre*[10] COLERIDGE, J., directed that it was murder if D, intending to kill, inflicted mortal injuries upon P, even though the immediate cause of P's death was the entry into her lungs of brandy given by a surgeon to restore her; if, however, the injury was not a mortal one, then D was guilty of an assault.[11] In *Clark and Bagg*[12] where the injuries were not of a dangerous character, WIGHT-MAN, J., directed the jury that, if they found that death occurred from bad medical treatment, they should find a verdict of assault. But in *Davis and Wagstaffe*,[13] MATHEW, J., after consultation with FIELD, J., went further. The injury which D inflicted upon P in that case was admittedly not mortal, and P died as the result of the administration of chloroform in the course of an operation to mend a broken jaw. MATHEW, J., directed the jury that:

". . . if although there might be no intent to do more than assault, still an injury was inflicted by one man on another which compelled the injured man to take medical advice, and death ensued from an operation advised by the medical man, for that death the assailant was in the eye of the law responsible."

This was logical. If D inflicts upon P an injury which renders advisable an operation, and P is killed by the anaesthetic, it is difficult to see why D has "caused" death any more where the injury is grievous than where it is slight. D's contribution to P's death consists, in both cases, in putting him in the situation in which an anaesthetic must be administered. If he intended the grievous or the slight injury, he had the *mens rea*, in the one case of murder, in the other of manslaughter; and he should be guilty of homicide in both cases or neither. MATHEW, J.'s ruling would not allow the question to be gone into at all in either case:

"For it would never do to have a serious injury by one man on another, and have the issue raised that death was due to want of skill on the part of the medical men."

These cases must now be regarded in the light of the recent decisions of the Court of Criminal Appeal in *Jordan*[14] and *Smith*.[15]

---

[9] (1846), 1 Cox C.C. 339 at p. 341; he said that ROLFE, B., was of the same opinion.
[10] (1847), 2 Cox C.C. 379.
[11] The jury in fact convicted of manslaughter.
[12] (1842), 6 J.P. 508.
[13] (1883), 15 Cox C.C. 174.
[14] (1956), 40 Cr. App. Rep. 152.
[15] [1959] 2 Q.B. 35; [1959] 2 All E.R. 193.

In *Jordan* D stabbed P who was admitted to hospital and died eight days later. At the trial,

> "it did not occur to the prosecution, the defence, the judge or the jury that there could be any doubt but that the stab caused death".[16]

In the Court of Criminal Appeal, the fresh evidence of two doctors was allowed to the effect that in their opinion death had not been caused by the stab wound, which was mainly healed at the time of death, but by the introduction (with a view to preventing infection) of terramycin after the deceased man had shown he was intolerant to it and by the intravenous introduction of large quantities of liquid. This treatment, according to the evidence, was "palpably wrong." The court held that if the jury had heard this evidence they would have felt precluded from saying that they were satisfied that the death was caused by the stab wound and they quashed the conviction. The case has been interpreted by Williams[17] as one where the medical treatment was grossly negligent, but he argues[18] that any degree of negligence which would be recognised by the civil courts should be enough. The court did not say in express terms that there was evidence of negligence, gross or otherwise, though it may reasonably be inferred that "palpably wrong" treatment is negligent.

While anxiously disclaiming any intention of setting a precedent[19] they stated the basis of their decision in even broader terms. They were "disposed to accept it as law that death resulting from any normal treatment employed to deal with a felonious injury may be regarded as caused by the felonious injury;" but it was "sufficient to point out here that this was not normal treatment." Surely treatment which is "not normal" is not necessarily negligent, even in the civil law.

The case gave rise to some concern in the medical profession and it was predicted[20] that the result of it would be that if, in future, the victim of a homicidal assault died as a result of the medical treatment instituted to save his life, it would not be considered homicide by the assailant if the treatment could be shown to be "not normal".

How far it is safe to rely on *Jordan* is doubtful, in view of the fact that it was distinguished by the Court of Criminal Appeal in *Smith*[1] as "a very particular case depending upon its exact facts." This is a formula which may be interpreted as a pronouncement that the case should never be followed.[2] *Smith* is distinguishable on the facts. In the course of a fight between soldiers of different regiments, D stabbed P twice with a bayonet. One of P's comrades, trying to carry P to the medical reception station, twice tripped and dropped him. At the reception station the medical officer, who was trying to cope with a number of other cases, did not realise that one of the wounds had pierced a lung and caused haemorrhage. He gave P treatment which, in the light of the information regarding P's condition available at the time of the trial, was "thoroughly bad and might well have affected his chances of recovery." D's conviction of

---

[16] See (1956), 40 Cr. App. Rep. 152 at p. 155.

[17] [1957] Crim. L.R. at p. 430.

[18] *Ibid.*, at p. 513.

[19] But no court has the right to preclude future courts from considering the effects of its decisions.

[20] By Camps and Havard, "Causation in Homicide—A Medical View", [1957] Crim. L.R. 576 at pp. 582–583.

[1] [1959] 2 Q.B. 35 at p. 43; [1959] 2 All E.R. 193 at p. 198.

[2] *Cf.* Williams, *Learning the Law* (7th ed.), 82.

murder was upheld and counsel's argument, that the court must be satisfied that the treatment was normal, and that this was abnormal, was brushed aside.

"... if at the time of death the original wound is still an operating cause and a substantial cause, then the death can properly be said to be the result of the wound, albeit that some other cause of death is also operating. Only if it can be said that the original wounding is merely the setting in which another cause operates can it be said that the death does not result from the wound. Putting it in another way, only if the second cause is so overwhelming as to make the original wound merely part of the history can it be said that death does not flow from the wound."[3]

Jordan's case was evidently one in which the wound was merely the setting in which (according to the new evidence) the medical treatment operated to cause death.

It is submitted that the following propositions at present represent the law:

1. Medical evidence is admissible to show that the medical treatment of a wound was the cause of death and that the wound itself was not.[4] This is so whether or not the wound is mortal.

2. If the medical treatment killed P, quite independently of the wound, and was grossly negligent, the wound is merely the setting for and not the cause of death. *Jordan* must be equated with the case where a nurse inadvertently administers a deadly poison to the patient.[5]

3. If the medical treatment killed P quite independently of the wound, but was not grossly negligent,[6] it is submitted that D remains guilty of homicide—murder, if he had malice aforethought, manslaughter if he had not.[7]

6 The Effect of Neglect by the Injured Person

As might be expected, the nineteenth-century rule was that neglect or maltreatment by the injured person of himself did not exempt D from liability for his ultimate death. In *Wall's* case[8] where the former governor of Goree was convicted[9] of the murder of a man by the illegal infliction on him of a flogging of 800 lashes, there was evidence that P had aggravated his condition by drinking spirits. MacDonald, L.C.B., told[10] the jury:

"... there is no apology for a man if he puts another in so dangerous and hazardous a situation by his treatment of him, that some degree of unskilfulness and mistaken treatment of himself may possibly accelerate the fatal catastrophe. One man is not at liberty to put another into such perilous circumstances as these, and to make it depend upon his own prudence, knowledge, skill or experience what may hurry on or complete that catastrophe, or on the other hand may render him service."

---

[3] *Per* Lord Parker, C.J., [1959] 2 Q.B. 35 at pp. 42–43; [1959] 2 All E.R. 193 at p. 198.

[4] *Jordan* must be authority for this at least. Moreover at the trial in *Smith* Dr. Camps gave evidence that, with proper treatment, P's chances of recovery were as high as 75 per cent.

[5] It is thought that this confines *Jordan* to its narrowest terms. It is not impossible for a subsequent court to hold that it extends to merely negligent, or even abnormal non-negligent treatment.

[6] Or, if Jordan be given the wider interpretation, not negligent or not abnormal.

[7] The proposition from *Smith* quoted above, is capable of a wider construction, exempting D *whenever* the treatment is the immediate cause of death, the original wound in such a case becoming merely part of the history. It is thought that such a radical departure from the authorities can hardly have been intended.

[8] (1802), 28 State Tr. 51.

[9] Twenty years after the event.

[10] *Ibid.*, at p. 145.

In *Holland*[11] D waylaid and assaulted P, cutting him severely across one of his fingers with an iron instrument. P refused to follow the surgeon's advice to have the finger amputated, although he was told that if he did not his life would be in great danger. The wound caused lockjaw, the finger was then amputated, but it was too late and P died of lockjaw. The surgeon's evidence was that if the finger had been amputated at first, P's life could probably have been saved. MAULE, J., told the jury that it made no difference whether the wound was in its own nature instantly mortal, or whether it became the cause of death by reason of the deceased not having adopted the best mode of treatment. The question was whether, in the end, the wound inflicted by the prisoner was the real cause of death. There is no modern English[12] authority on the point and it may be that an unreasonable refusal to follow medical advice might now be held, by analogy to *Jordan*, to exempt D from liability for the consequent death. It has been pointed out[13] that medical science has advanced greatly since 1841 and that a refusal to undergo an operation which, at that time, might not have been unreasonable, might be viewed in a different light today.

7 Intended Consequences

It is sometimes said that intended consequences cannot be too remote. This, however, is not always true, for the *sine qua non* rule remains applicable. Thus, in *White*[14] the consequence intended by D—the death of his mother—occurred; but its occurrence had nothing to do with D's act in administering the poison and would have happened just the same if D had done nothing. Even where the *sine qua non* rule is satisfied, the consequence, though intended, may be too remote where it occurs as a result of the intervention of some new cause. So in the cases of *Bush*[15] and *Jordan*[16] it may be that D intended P's death, and P's death occurred; moreover, in neither case would death have occurred without D's act; but in the one case it was caused by scarlet fever and not by D's bullet; and in the other it was caused by medical treatment and not by D's knife. Where the death occurs in the manner intended by D he will be guilty even if the course of events was not what he expected, for example, he shoots at P's head, but the bullet misses, ricochets and kills P by striking him in the back. The case of *Michael*[17] is perhaps a rather extreme example of this:

D's child, P, was in the care of a nurse, X. D, intending to murder the child, delivered to X a large quantity of laudanum, telling her it was a medicine to be administered to P. X did not think the child needed any medicine and left it untouched on the mantelpiece of her room. In X's absence, one of her children, Y, aged five, took the laudanum and administered a large dose to P who died. All the judges held that the jury were rightly directed that this administration by "an unconscious agent" was murder.

Hart and Honoré[18] criticise the case on the ground that the child was

---

[11] (1841), 2 Mood. & R. 351.
[12] And the South African case of *Mubila*, 1956 (1) S.A. 31, appears to be one where P would have died even if he had followed medical advice.
[13] By Hart and Honoré, *Causation in the Law*, at 231.
[14] Above, p. 33.
[15] (1880), 78 Ky. 268; above, p. 188.
[16] (1956), 40 Cr. App. Rep. 152.
[17] (1840), 9 C. & P. 356.
[18] *Op. cit.*, at p 301.

"not in any sense an agent, conscious or unconscious, of the mother, who intended [X] alone to give the poison to the child; but the decision may be justified on the ground that, in our terminology, the act of the child of five did not negative causal connexion between the prisoner's act and the death."

According to this view, the result would have been different if Y had been, not five, but fifteen.

It does not appear that Y knew, from the labelling of the bottle or otherwise, that this was "medicine" for P. If she did know this, and acted on that knowledge, then there seems no difficulty in imputing the death to D, whatever Y's age. No such fact being reported, however, the case must be treated as one where Y's intervention was in no way prompted by D's instructions. Thus, if Y had taken the poison herself, her death would have been just as much caused by D's act as was P's in the actual case; but it would require an extension of the decision to hold D guilty in such a case, for Y's death was not an intended consequence.[19] If such an extension be not made, the result is quite arbitrary, for it was pure chance whether Y administered the poison to P, or to herself or another child.

8 Special Instances of Causation

There are a few instances of causation which require special mention, by reason of the state of the authorities.

(i) *Killing by mental suffering or shock.*—The view of the earlier writers was that the law could take no cognisance of a killing caused merely by mental suffering or shock, because "no external act of violence was offered, whereof the common law can take notice and secret things belong to God."[20] Stephen thought[1] that the fear of encouraging prosecutions for witchcraft was the reason for the rule and that it was "a bad rule founded on ignorance now dispelled."

> "Suppose a man were intentionally killed by being kept awake till the nervous irritation of sleeplessness killed him, might not this be murder? Suppose a man kills a sick person intentionally by making a loud noise when sleep gives him a chance of life; or suppose knowing that a man has aneurism of the heart, his heir rushes into his room and roars in his ear, 'Your wife is dead!' intending to kill and killing him, why are not these acts murder? They are no more 'secret things belonging to God' than the operation of arsenic."

This view now represents the law. Hale's proposition was first modified in *Towers*[2] where D violently assaulted a young girl who was holding a four-and-a-half months'-old child in her arms. The girl screamed loudly, so frightening the baby that it cried till it was black in the face. From that day it had convulsions and died a month later. DENMAN, J., held that there was evidence to go to the jury of manslaughter. In the case of an adult person, he said that murder could not be committed by using language so strong or violent as to cause that person to die:

> "mere intimidation, causing a person to die from fright by working upon his fancy, was not murder";

---

[19] But the doctrine of transferred malice (above p. 44) would support such an extension.
[20] Hale, 1 P.C. 429; and see East, 1 P.C. 225.
[1] *Digest*, 217, n. 9.
[2] (1874), 12 Cox C.C. 530.

but that rule did not apply to a child of such tender years as this;

> ". . . if the man's act brought on the convulsions or brought them to a more
> dangerous extent, so that death would not have resulted otherwise, then it
> would be manslaughter."[3]

This was extended to the case of an adult person by RIDLEY, J., in *Hayward*.[4]
D, who was in a condition of violent excitement and had expressed his determination to "give his wife something", chased her from the house into the road
using violent threats against her. She fell dead. She was suffering from an
abnormal heart condition, such that any combination of physical exertion and
fright or strong emotion might cause death. RIDLEY, J., directed the jury that
no proof of actual physical violence was necessary, but that death from fright
alone, caused by an illegal act, such as a threat of violence, was enough.

(ii) *Killing by frightening P into taking his own life.*—This was recognised to be
homicide at an earlier stage than the previous category. In *Pitts*[5] ERSKINE, J.,
held that D was guilty of murder if P had thrown himself into a river and been
drowned from the apprehension of immediate violence by D; but the apprehension must have been well grounded, there being no other way of escape, and
the action must have been such as a reasonable man might take. These qualifications were not made by the Court for Crown Cases Reserved in *Halliday*[6]
where D was convicted of wilfully and maliciously inflicting grievous bodily
harm[7] on his wife who had jumped from a window and broken a leg in escaping
from him. Lord COLERIDGE, C.J., said:

> "If a man creates in another's mind an immediate sense of danger which
> causes such person to try to escape, and in so doing he injures himself, the
> person who creates such a state of mind is responsible for the injuries which
> result."

D should be guilty, *a fortiori*, where P, seeking to escape, not intentionally but
accidentally takes some step which causes his death. In *Curley*,[8] PHILLIMORE,
J., directed the jury:

> ". . . if from a well grounded fear of violence from the prisoner the deceased
> woman went to the window to call for assistance and by accident overbalanced
> herself, it would be a case of manslaughter."[9]

(iii) *Killing by perjury.*—It is sometimes said[10] that it is not homicide if D, by
giving false evidence, procures the conviction and execution of P. There is no
conclusive authority on the point. In *McDaniel*[11] D and others were in fact
convicted of the murder of P by falsely swearing to his guilt of robbery (in order
to obtain the reward) for which P was hanged; but judgment was respited "upon

---

[3] *Ibid.*, at p. 533.
[4] (1908), 21 Cox C.C. 692.
[5] (1842), Car. & M. 284.
[6] (1889), 61 L.T. 701.
[7] Clearly, it would have been at least manslaughter if she had died.
[8] (1909), 2 Cr. App. Rep. 96.
[9] The Court of Criminal Appeal was "inclined to think that the direction was right if
it was made clear to the jury that the accident was caused by the violence of the prisoner."
See also, DENMAN, J., in *Towers* (1874), 12 Cox C.C. 530; above, p. 193.
[10] The earlier authorities said that it was murder; but Coke (3 Inst. 48) said that it was
"not holden for murder at this day." Foster, *Crown Law* at 131, supported this, citing the
case of *Titus Oates* (1685), 10 State Tr. 1227, who, he thinks, would certainly have been
charged with murder by perjury if that had been a crime. East, 1 P.C. 333, is non-com-
mittal. Hawkins accepted the older view: 1 P.C., c. 13, § 5, 7.
[11] (1756), 1 Leach 44.

a doubt whether an indictment for murder would lie in this case:" and the Attorney-General declined to argue that it would, so the prisoners were discharged. Blackstone wrote[12] that he had

> "grounds to believe it was not from any apprehension that the point was not maintainable, but from other prudential reasons."

The "prudential reasons" appear to be

> "to avoid the danger of deterring witnesses from giving evidence upon capital prosecutions, if it must be at the peril of their own lives."

East[13] says that Lord MANSFIELD, C.J., took the same view of the law and that he and other judges supported the indictment.

The balance of authority is then, perhaps, against the rule; but if it exists, it is thought that it has nothing to do with causation[14] but it is a rule of policy, closely analogous to that which protects a witness from an action for defamation[15] or for damages for the injury suffered by conviction upon perjured evidence.[16]

(6) THE MENS REA OF MURDER

The *mens rea* of murder is traditionally called "malice aforethought". This is a technical term and it has a technical meaning quite different from the ordinary popular meaning of the two words. The phrase, it has been truly said,

> "is a mere arbitrary symbol . . ., for the 'malice' may have in it nothing really malicious; and need never be really 'aforethought' ".[17]

Thus a parent who kills a suffering child out of motives of compassion is "malicious" for this purpose; and there is sufficient forethought if an intention to kill is formed only a second before the fatal blow is struck. Neither ill-will nor premeditation is necessary.

The meaning of the term is of the utmost importance, for it is the presence or absence of malice aforethought which determines whether an unlawful killing is murder or manslaughter.

> "Murder is unlawful homicide with malice aforethought. Manslaughter is an unlawful homicide without malice aforethought."[18]

Its meaning (subject to s. 8 of the Criminal Justice Act 1967[19]) is a matter of common law; it can be ascertained only by reference to the cases. If the general definition of *mens rea* which has been considered above were applied to murder, we would simply be able to say that it was an intention to kill a reasonable creature in being and under the Queen's Peace, or recklessness whether or not that result occurred. But, as already noted, this general principle is not of universal application and curiously it is in murder, perhaps the most serious of all crimes, that we find remarkable divergences from it.

An examination of the authorities reveals, as the Royal Commission on Capital Punishment has said,[20] that malice aforethought

---

[12] *Commentaries*, iv, 196.
[13] 1 P.C. 333, n. (a).
[14] *Cf*. Hart and Honoré, *Causation in the Law*, at 363.
[15] *Watson* v. *M'Ewen*, [1905] A.C. 480.
[16] *Hargreaves* v. *Bretherton*, [1959] 1 Q.B. 45; [1958] 3 All E.R. 122; *Marrinan* v. *Vibart*, [1963] 1 Q.B. 528; [1962] 3 All E.R. 380.
[17] Kenny, *Outlines* (15th ed.), 153.
[18] *Per* STEPHEN, J., in *Doherty* (1887), 16 Cox C.C. 306 at p. 307.
[19] See above, p. 52 and below, p. 197.
[20] R.C.C.P., Cmd. 8932, p. 27.

"is simply a comprehensive name for a number of different mental attitudes, which have been variously defined at different stages in the development of the law, the presence of any one of which in the accused has been held by the courts to render a homicide particularly heinous and therefore to make it murder."

There is still a good deal of uncertainty as to the precise way in which these different mental attitudes should be defined.

The authorities suggest that they include the following:

(1) An intention to kill any person.

(2) An intention to cause grievous bodily harm to any person.

(3) An intention to do something unlawful to any person, foreseeing that death or grievous bodily harm is the natural and probable result; *or*

an intention to do any act, foreseeing that death or grievous bodily harm is the natural and probable result.

1   An Intention to Kill any Person

This is in accordance with the general principle of *mens rea* and presents no difficulty. D shoots at P with intent to kill him and does so; or misses and kills Q. In the latter case, D's malice is transferred[21] and he is no less guilty of murder. This is equally true of the other forms of malice aforethought.

2   An Intention to Cause Grievous Bodily Harm to any Person

"Grievous bodily harm" was formerly interpreted as including

"some harm which is sufficiently serious to interfere with the victim's health or comfort."[1]

This prompted DEVLIN, J., to remark:[2] "Murder by pin-prick is not a legal impossibility." Subsequently, however, the House of Lords held in *Director of Public Prosecutions* v. *Smith*[3] that there is

"no warrant for giving the words 'grievous bodily harm' a meaning other than that which the words convey in their ordinary and natural meaning. 'Bodily harm' needs no explanation, and 'grievous' means no more and no less than 'really serious'."

Thus, in *Errington and Others*[4] P who was drunk went to sleep on a chest. D and others covered and surrounded him with straw and threw a shovel of hot cinders on him. The straw ignited and P was burnt to death. PATTESON, J., told the jury that if D intended to do *any serious injury* to the deceased, although not to kill him, it was murder; but if his intention was only to frighten P in sport, then it was manslaughter. Another case, commonly cited as an illustration of this principle, is *Grey*.[5] A blacksmith whose servant was cheeky to him, struck the servant on the head with a bar of iron which he happened to have in his hand. The servant's skull was broken and he died. At the time it was lawful for a master to administer corporal punishment to his servant; but, said the court,[6]

---

[21] Above, p. 44; *Salisbury* (1553), 1 Plowd. 100.

[1] *Ashman* (1858), 1 F. & F. 88, *per* WILLES, J.; *Cox* (1818), Russ. & Ry. 362 (C.C.R.), *per* GRAHAM, B.; *Vickers*, [1957] 2 Q.B. 664; [1957] 2 All E.R. 741 (C.C.A.).

[2] [1954] Crim. L.R. at 669.

[3] [1961] A.C. 290 at p. 334; [1960] 3 All E.R. 161 at p. 171; and see *Miller*, [1951] V.L.R. 346 at p. 357.

[4] (1838), 2 Lew. C.C. 148, 217.

[5] (1666), Kel 64.

[6] *Ibid*.

"they must do it with such things as are fit for correction. . . . And a bar of iron is no instrument for correction. It is all one as if he had run him through with a sword."

This is a very old case and the principle is not very clearly to be collected from it; the court may well have been satisfied that Grey intended to kill. Indeed there are few cases in which the principle is clearly expressed until after 1877 when Stephen formulated the various heads of malice with some degree of precision.[7] But there can be no doubt that it is the law today. It was clearly accepted as such before the Homicide Act 1957 and, as appears below,[8] the Court of Criminal Appeal and the House of Lords have held that the Act makes no change in this respect.

3 Intention to do Something Unlawful to Someone with Foresight of Death or Grievous Bodily Harm

This heading of *mens rea* is derived from the notorious case of *Director of Public Prosecutions* v. *Smith*[9] as it appears to have been modified in effect by the Criminal Justice Act 1967, s. 8. In *Smith*, the House of Lords held[10] that, on a charge of murder, it must be proved that D was "unlawfully and voluntarily doing something to someone" and that a reasonable man, with D's actual knowledge of the "circumstances and nature of his acts" would have contemplated death or grievous bodily harm as the natural and probable result. This formula embodied two subjective elements—(i) the intention to do something unlawful to someone; and (ii) the knowledge of such circumstances as rendered the act so done likely to cause death or grievous bodily harm. There need be no proof of actual foresight on the accused's part of either death or grievous bodily harm, however. D might intend only a small degree of harm and fail to foresee, as a reasonable man would have foreseen, that the act was likely to cause grievous bodily harm. In that case he was guilty. The case was subjected to an immense amount of criticism,[11] and the question was considered by the Law Commission. The Commission formed the view that a subjective and not an objective test should be applied in ascertaining the intent required in murder. They proposed two clauses, the first of which became s. 8 of the Criminal Justice Act 1967 and is set out above.[12] The second, which defined the *mens rea* of murder, and is set out below,[13] has not been enacted into law. Had the whole of the Law Commission's recommendations been enacted, as they obviously intended, it would have been perfectly clear that the intent to kill, as defined in the second draft clause,

---

[7] *Digest,* Art. 264.
[8] See pp. 202–203.
[9] [1961] A.C. 290; [1960] 3 All E.R. 161.
[10] [1961] A.C. at p. 327; [1960] 3 All E.R. at p. 167.
[11] See, especially, Williams, "Constructive Malice Revived" (1962), 23 M.L.R. 605; SALMON, J., "The Criminal Law Relating to Intent" (1961), 14 C.L.P. 1; Cross, "The Need for a Re-Definition of Murder", [1960] Crim. L.R. 728; Lord MACDERMOTT, "Murder in 1963", *Presidential Address to the Holdsworth Club,* University of Birmingham, 1963; and the first edition of this work.
See also, DENNING, "Responsibility before the Law" (1961), Hebrew University Press; Prevezer, "Recent Developments in the Law of Murder" (1961), 14 C.L.P. 16; Smith, [1960] Crim. L.R. 765; Travers and Morris, "Imputed Intent to Murder or *Smith* v. *Smyth*" (1961), 35 A.L.J. 154.
[12] p. 52.
[13] p. 204.

would have to be proved on every charge of murder. The enactment of only the first draft clause left the law of murder in a somewhat doubtful position. There is no doubt the House of Lords when debating, in its legislative capacity, the clause which became s. 8, intended to reverse the effect of *Smith* and thought that they were doing so.[14] As has been seen, however, s. 8 relates to *how* intention and foresight must be proved, not *when* they must be proved. It is still necessary to look at the substantive law to ascertain the *mens rea* of the particular offence. That means that we must look at *Smith*, the leading case on the *mens rea* of murder, which has never been overruled. On this question, Viscount KILMUIR's speech was quite unequivocal.

> "The jury must, of course, in such a case as the present make up their minds on the evidence whether the accused was unlawfully and voluntarily doing something to someone. The unlawful and voluntary act must clearly be aimed at someone in order to eliminate cases of negligence or of careless or dangerous driving. Once, however, the jury are satisfied as to that, it matters not what the accused in fact contemplated as the probable result or whether he ever contemplated at all, provided he was in law responsible and accountable for his actions, that is, was a man capable of forming an intent, not insane within the M'Naghten Rules and not suffering from diminished responsibility. On the assumption that he is so accountable for his actions, the sole question is whether the unlawful and voluntary act was of such a kind that grievous bodily harm was the natural and probable result. The only test available for this is what the ordinary responsible man would, in all the circumstances of the case, have contemplated as the natural and probable result. That, indeed, has always been the law . . ."[15]

The view that *Smith* laid down a rule of the substantive law of murder and not a rule of evidence gained further force from subsequent decisions[16] which confined the case to the law of murder. If it had laid down a principle of proof, then it might have been expected to apply on charges on attempted murder, malicious wounding and other offences; but the courts held that this was not so. According to ordinary principles of interpretation, then, it would appear that s. 8 did no more than affirm that the "intention to do something unlawful to someone" must be subjectively proved—a matter which was never in doubt, anyway. It is clear, however, that *Smith* was disliked by the judges and was being largely ignored even before the Criminal Justice Act.[17] It is hardly surprising, therefore, to find the section being given the effect which it was undoubtedly intended to have, even though, on a proper construction, it is difficult to see how it can bear that meaning. At all events, in *Wallett*[18] the Court of Appeal assumed, apparently as self-evident, that *Smith* was reversed by the Criminal Justice Act. The judge had directed the jury that D was guilty if he did the act

> "knowing quite well at the time that he was doing something [which] any ordinary person like himself would know was doing her really serious bodily harm."

The reference to "any ordinary person" was held to be fatal to the resulting conviction. This is a very strict application of the rule which the section is taken

---

[14] 283 H. of L. Official Report 248–253.

[15] [1961] A.C. at p. 327; [1960] 3 All E.R. at p. 167.

[16] *Grimwood*, [1962] 2 Q.B. 621; [1962] 3 All E.R. 285 (C.C.A.); *Wilkins* v. *An Infant* (1965), 109 Sol. Jo. 850; [1965] Crim. L.R. 730.

[17] Buxton, "The Retreat from Smith", [1966] Crim. L.R. 195.

[18] [1968] 2 All E.R. 296.

to lay down and suggests that judges would be wise to eschew reference to the reasonable man or ordinary men, altogether.

What then, is the effect on the rule in *Smith*? That case required:

(1) an intention to do something unlawful to someone.

(2) knowledge of such circumstances as rendered the act likely to cause death or grievous bodily harm.

The objectivity of the test lay in the fact that it need not be proved that the accused intended or foresaw death or grievous bodily harm, and it must be taken that it is this element of objectivity which s. 8 is held to have removed. Thus the conclusion is that the *mens rea* of murder, defined in *Smith* and modified by the Criminal Justice Act, is: an intention to do something unlawful to someone, foreseeing that death or grievous bodily harm is the natural and probable result.

It would have been most unfortunate if *Smith* had been held still to be law after all; and the result is a desirable one; but it is not sound in principle to attribute to statutes an effect which they cannot properly bear, even to achieve so desirable an end. It poses difficult questions, for, if s. 8 is held to have modified the *mens rea* of murder, what about the *mens rea* of other offences? If the matter came before the House of Lords, it is respectfully submitted that the right course would be to hold that s. 8 did not affect the decision in *Smith* and then to over-rule that case by virtue of the House's newly assumed power to reverse its previous decisions.[19]

The alternative and wider formulation of this third head of malice aforethought does not require any intention to do any injury or legal wrong whatever to anyone. The classic example is that of the man who throws a heavy beam off the roof of a house in a town without looking to see whether anyone is passing below. In the light of the Criminal Justice Act, it must be taken that he realises the risk he is taking—he knows that someone might be hit by the beam and be killed or at least seriously injured; but he certainly does not wish to kill or injure anyone. The authority in favour of this rule is slight. The Royal Commission[20] relied on two cases.

In *Walters*[1] an unmarried woman gave birth to a child by the roadside. She carried it about a mile and then abandoned it, naked and without protection, and omitting to tie the umbilical cord. The child died. The Crown argued that this was murder, relying on Russell:[2]

> "If a man, however, does an act, the probable consequence of which may be, and eventually is, death, such killing may be murder; although no stroke be struck by himself, and no killing may have been primarily intended; as where a person carried his sick father against his will, in a severe season, from one town to another, by reason whereof he died; or where a harlot being delivered of a child, left it in an orchard covered only with leaves, in which condition it was killed by a kite;[3] or where a child was placed in a hogstye where it was devoured[4] . . ."

COLTMAN, J., directed the jury in much less severe terms than this:

> "If a party do any act with regard to a human being helpless and unable to provide for itself, which must necessarily lead to its death, the crime amounts

---

[19] [1966] 3 All E.R. 77, note
[20] Cmd. 8932 at p. 28.
[1] (1841), Car. & M. 164.
[2] Book 3, c.l. of the 2nd ed.
[3] These two cases are quoted from Hale, 1 P.C. 431, 432; Hawkins, 1 P.C., c. 31, §§5, 6.
[4] East, 1 P.C., c. 5, § 13.

to murder. But if the circumstances are not such that the party must have been aware that the result would be death, that would reduce the crime to manslaughter, provided the death was occasioned by an unlawful act, but not such as to imply a malicious mind."

The question for the jury, it seems, was whether she knew that the child *must* die or whether she thought it might be found and its life preserved. This seems to require an intention to kill. A case on these facts might, however be brought within the rule in *Smith* since the abandonment of the child would be an unlawful act and might well be sufficient evidence of foresight of death or grievous bodily harm.

The second case is the unreported one of *Desmond, Barrett*[5] where the accused exploded a barrel of gunpowder against the wall of a prison, with the intention of enabling a prisoner to escape, and killed a number of persons in the street. COCKBURN, C.J., told the jury that it was murder—

"If a man did an act, more especially if that were an illegal act, although its immediate purpose might not be to take life, yet if it were such that life was necessarily endangered by it—if a man did such an act, not with the purpose of taking life, but with the knowledge or belief that life was likely to be sacrificed by it."

STEPHEN, J., thought that the law was rightly stated in *Desmond* and that this ought to be the law. He followed that case in *Serné and another*[6] where D was alleged to have set fire to a house in which six people were sleeping in order to collect the insurance money. D's son was killed and STEPHEN, J., directed the jury that the accused were guilty of murder if they had caused death "by conduct which, to their knowledge, was likely to cause death and was therefore eminently dangerous in itself . . ." If they knew that they were placing people in deadly risk, ". . . it matters very little indeed whether the prisoners hoped the people would escape or whether they did not."

Kenny,[7] as long ago as 1901, thought:

"To treat this class of intentions as amounting to a murderous malice is perhaps impolitic; as being a more severe treatment than modern public opinion cordially approves."

It is supported by the general principle that no distinction is drawn at common law generally between intention and recklessness; but murder is so grave an offence and attended with such drastic consequences that it is arguable that a stricter rule should be applied and that foresight of the death or grievous bodily harm should be sufficient only where it is foreseen as so very highly probable as to be inevitable or almost inevitable.

4 Constructive Malice

There were, at common law, two additional forms of malice aforethought which have been abolished by the Homicide Act 1957.

1. Where a man caused death in the course or furtherance of committing a felony, that was murder; and the only intention that need be proved was the

---

[5] (1868), *The Times*, April 28; and Stephen's *Digest*, Art. 222.
[6] (1887), 16 Cox C.C. 311.
[7] Kenny described this form of malice aforethought as, "Intention to do an act intrinsically likely to kill though without any purpose of thereby inflicting any hurt whatever." His principal illustration (one much discussed in the older writers), based on *Hull* (1664), Kel. 40, is "the intention of any workman who recklessly throws things off the roof of a house in a town without looking over the edge to see if anyone is likely to be struck, or giving any warning": *Outlines* (15th ed.), 156.

mens rea of the felony. Thus accidentally to kill while attempting to steal, or while procuring an abortion, or while committing rape was automatically murder. It was necessary to prove only an intention to steal, to procure an abortion, or to rape as the case may be. There was no need to prove foresight of death or grievous bodily harm or even that a reasonable man would have foreseen death or grievous bodily harm. In this respect, the rule was stricter than the doctrine of *Smith*'s case.

Though the rule in this strict and rigorous form remained the law until 1957,[8] the judges in the present century had applied it leniently in the sense that they had restricted its operation to violent felonies. In cases such as abortion[9] they had confined it to instances where the operation was so conducted that the reasonable man would have foreseen the risk of death or grievous bodily harm—a development, which as has appeared,[10] bedevilled the cases concerning non-constructive malice. In the case of violent felonies, the rule was strictly applied up to the time of its abolition. The leading case was that of *Beard*[11] where, it will be recalled, the House of Lords held that D was guilty of murder because he had an intention to rape and it was quite immaterial whether he foresaw that his act was likely to cause death or grievous bodily harm.[12]

A secondary party was guilty of murder if he consented to the use of some degree of violence in the course of committing the contemplated felony. In *Betts and Ridley*[13] D2 agreed with D1 that P should be "pushed down" and robbed. D1 struck P a violent blow which killed him and it was held that D2 was equally guilty of the murder.[14]

2. Where death was caused in the course of resisting lawful arrest by an officer of justice, this was murder if only an intention to resist arrest by force was proved. The leading case is *Porter*.[15] D was arrested by a constable in a public house on suspicion of larceny. He resisted and the constable called on a private citizen, P, for assistance. P came to the policeman's aid. D kicked him in the abdomen and he died. BRETT, J., directed the jury that if the prisoner inflicted the kick in resistance to his lawful arrest, even although he did not intend to cause grievous bodily harm, he was guilty of murder. All that was necessary was an intention to kick in resistance to lawful arrest.[16]

These two forms of malice aforethought are abolished by s. 1 of the Homicide Act 1957 which provides:

"(1) Where a person kills another in the course or furtherance of some other offence, the killing shall not amount to murder unless done with the same malice aforethought (express or implied) as is required for a killing to amount to murder when not done in the course or furtherance of another offence.

---

[8] See R.C.C.P., Cmd. 8932, para. 85.
[9] *Whitmarsh* (1898), 62 J.P. 711; *Bottomley* (1903), 115 L.T. Jo. 88; *Lumley* (1911), 22 Cox C.C. 635. See Turner, M.A.C.L. at pp. 252–254.
[10] Above, pp. 197–200.
[11] Above, p. 134.
[12] The rule was applied where the attempted rape was never completed: *Stone*, [1937] 3 All E.R. 920.
[13] (1930), 22 Cr. App. Rep. 148.
[14] *Cf. Davies v. Director of Public Prosecutions*, [1954] A.C. 378; [1954] 1 All E.R. 507; above, p. 88, where no felony was in contemplation.
[15] (1873), 12 Cox C.C. 444. See also *Appleby* (1940), 28 Cr. App. Rep. 1.
[16] A direction followed by Lord GODDARD, C.J., in the case of *Craig and Bentley* (1952), *The Times*, December 10–13.

(2) For the purposes of the foregoing subsection, a killing done in the course or for the purpose of resisting an officer of justice, or of resisting or avoiding or preventing a lawful arrest, or of effecting or assisting an escape or rescue from legal custody, shall be treated as a killing in the course or furtherance of an offence."

This does not necessarily mean, of course, that men like Beard, Betts, Ridley and Porter would necessarily be acquitted of murder today. The direction to the jury would be different and they would have an additional chance of acquittal. The juries in each of these cases must have found that D intended to do "something unlawful to someone". The remaining question for the jury today would be whether Beard, Betts, Ridley and Porter, respectively, foresaw that his act was likely to cause death or grievous bodily harm.

5   Constructive Malice and Intent to cause Grievous Bodily Harm

The marginal note[17] to s. 1 of the Act[18] reads: "Abolition of 'constructive malice'." On the other hand, it is clear from the body of the section that something called "implied malice" is retained. Unfortunately, these terms have no precise meaning.[19] The Royal Commission on Capital Punishment thought that constructive malice comprehended only the two types of *mens rea* discussed in the previous paragraph.[20] No doubt, according to this view, "intent to cause grievous bodily harm" was implied malice. DEVLIN, J., however, thought this third form of malice was also "constructive".[1] There can be little doubt, however, that the draftsman of the bill intended the narrower meaning to attach to constructive malice; and no doubt at all that the sponsors so intended.[2]

An argument to give the section a wide effect can, however, be based on its wording. Suppose D strikes P with intent to cause him grievous bodily harm and does cause him such harm. This is an offence under s. 18 of the Offences against the Person Act 1861. P then dies. D, it is said, has killed P in the course or furtherance of another offence, that is, that under s. 18; and the Act says that this shall not amount to murder unless done with malice aforethought, express or implied. Therefore it is argued, "malice aforethought", must mean something more than an intent to cause grievous bodily harm. This argument is, however, untenable. If D wounded P with intent to kill him, this, when the Homicide Act was passed and until repealed by the Criminal Law Act 1967, was a substantive offence under s. 11 of the Offences against the Person Act 1861.[3] If P died, he was killed in the course or furtherance of another offence; but it was impossible to argue that on that account, some further intent, beyond intention to kill, was required. It is submitted, therefore, that arguments on these lines were rightly rejected by the Court of Criminal Appeal in *Vickers*.[4] D broke into

---

[17] It is not part of the Act and must be ignored on a point of construction: *Chandler* v. *Director of Public Prosecutions*, [1962] 1 All E.R. 142 at pp. 145, 146; but the court in *Vickers* did look at is as "some indication of the purpose" of the section.

[18] *Supra.*

[19] Stephen concluded that the distinction between express and implied malice was a distinction without a difference: *Digest*, 497.

[20] Report, paras. 77–90.

[1] "I take an intent to be 'constructive' when there is imputed to a man a state of mind other than his actual state of mind": [1954] Crim. L.R. at p. 668.

[2] See 560 H.C. Deb. 1163.

[3] It would now be attempted murder at common law.

[4] [1957] 2 Q.B. 664; [1957] 2 All E.R. 741.

a shop belonging to an old lady, P. He did not expect to be disturbed, as he knew she was deaf; but she discovered him, attacked him and scratched his face. In return, he struck many blows at her and killed her. HINCHCLIFFE, J., directed the jury that D was guilty of murder if, when he struck the blows, "he intended to do her serious bodily harm". After a first hearing before three judges (Lord GODDARD, C.J., BYRNE and DEVLIN, JJ.), at which "there was not complete unanimity", a full court of five (HILBERY and SLADE, JJ., joined the original court) unanimously held that this was a correct direction:[5]

> "The 'furtherance of some other offence' must refer to the offence he was committing or endeavouring to commit other than the killing, otherwise there would be no sense in it. . . . The killing was in the course or furtherance of . . . burglary."

This result was affirmed by the House of Lords in *Smith* where the contention ("but faintly adumbrated") that *Vickers* was wrongly decided was rejected.[6] It is thus finally settled that an intention to cause grievous bodily harm remains a variety of malice aforethought.[7]

(7) DEGREES OF MURDER

Until the Homicide Act 1957 all persons convicted of murder were automatically sentenced to death. By s. 5 of that Act certain types of murder were singled out and designated "capital murder". These continued to be punishable by death, while the remaining types of murder were punishable by imprisonment for life. In effect we had two degrees of murder.

The distinction between the two degrees of murder proved to be most unsatisfactory, and the death penalty for murder was suspended by the Murder (Abolition of Death Penalty) Act 1965. The distinction between capital and non-capital murder has thus disappeared, at least temporarily, and all persons convicted of murder must now be sentenced to imprisonment for life. The 1965 Act will however expire and capital murder revive on July 31, 1970, unless Parliament by affirmative resolution of both Houses otherwise determines. If the Act is allowed to expire, then the law existing immediately prior to the Act, except so far as it is repealed or amended by the Act, shall again operate as though the Act had not been passed. The law relating to capital murder, which was stated in the first edition of this work,[8] is omitted from this edition in the confident expectation that Parliament will not allow the revival of a distinction between two categories or murder which proved so discreditable to English law.

On sentencing a murderer, the judge may recommend to the Home Secretary the minimum period which should elapse before the prisoner is released on licence under the Prison Act 1952, s. 27.[9] Whether or not a recommendation has been made, the Home Secretary is required by s. 2 of the Act to consult the Lord Chief Justice and trial judge, if he is available, before releasing a murderer on licence.

---

[5] [1957] 2 Q.B. at p. 671; [1957] 2 All E.R. at p. 743.
[6] [1961] A.C. at p. 335; [1960] 3 All E.R. at p. 172.
[7] *Vickers* was vigorously attacked by Turner in [1958] Crim. L.R. 15 but his arguments are severely criticised in [1958] Crim. L.R. 714. See also [1957] Crim. L.R. 615.
[8] See pp. 197 *et seq.*
[9] Counsel must be allowed to plead in mitigation before a recommendation is made: *Todd*, [1966] Crim. L.R. 557; but no appeal lies from any such recommendation: *Aitken*, [1966] 2 All E.R. 453 n.

(8) PROPOSALS FOR REFORM

The second clause proposed by the Law Commission[10] and referred to above, would provide as follows:

(1) Where a person kills another, the killing shall not amount to murder unless done with an intent to kill.

(2) A person has an "intent to kill" if he means his actions to kill, or if he is willing for his actions, though meant for another purpose, to kill in accomplishing that purpose.

(3) It is immaterial whether the intent to kill is an intent to kill the person in fact killed or any particular person, so long as it is an intent to kill someone other than himself; and references to killing in subsection (2) above shall be construed accordingly.

This proposal would obviously eliminate intention to cause grievous bodily harm as a head of *mens rea*. How much farther it would go is less clear. It seems very arguable that, under this formula, recklessness as to death would be sufficient, so that the second rather than the first of the alternative formulations of head (3) of malice aforethought, above, would represent the law. That is, Desmond,[11] when he blew the hole in the prison wall, probably knew that it was not unlikely that someone would get killed. He was prepared to take that risk to get his friend out of gaol. Was he not then "willing for his actions, though meant for another purpose, to kill in accomplishing that purpose"? The Law Commission did not intend their proposal to go so far. They gave[12] the following examples:

> "A man who drives a car at an excessive speed down a crowded street, thereby killing a pedestrian, may know that by his reckless folly he runs the risk of killing that pedestrian, but, although he is aware of the risk, he may not be willing to kill him. He may be guilty of manslaughter because he has run an extreme risk; he is not guilty of murder if he was not willing to kill. On the other hand, it is desirable to bring within the definition of a murderer a man who . . . plants a powerful time-bomb in an aeroplane in order to blow it up in flight with the aim of recovering the proceeds of insurance on the cargo. Although he has a purpose other than killing (namely, the recovery of the insurance money) it is clear from the circumstances that at the time when he planted the bomb, he was willing to kill those in the aeroplane in accomplishing his purpose of recovering the insurance money . . ."

There is certainly a distinction between these two cases, but it does not seem to turn on the issue of "willingness to kill". The distinction is that in the second case D knows that his act is certain to cause death—only a miracle can save the passengers—whereas in the first case the driver knows that he has at least a chance of getting away with injuring no one. If, however, as the example says, he knows he runs the risk of killing by driving in this way, it is difficult to see that he is not willing to kill when he proceeds so to drive.[13]

If it is desirable to distinguish between these two cases on the basis of intention —and it is submitted that it is—the correct test of intention then is that considered above:[14] that a consequence is intended if it is desired or foreseen as

---

[10] "*Imputed Criminal Intent: Director of Public Prosecutions v. Smith*".
[11] *Desmond* (1868), *The Times*, April 28.
[12] At pp. 14–15.
[13] See criticism of the proposals by Cross (1967), 83 L.Q.R. 191–193.
[14] See p. 38.

certain to result from the act being done. If the distinction between murder and manslaughter is to be retained—and while manslaughter is defined so widely, this seems desirable—it is on these lines, it is submitted, that the distinction should most satisfactorily be drawn.

2 MANSLAUGHTER

(1) VOLUNTARY AND INVOLUNTARY

Manslaughter is a diverse crime, covering all unlawful homicides which are not murder. A wide variety of types of homicide fall within this category, but it is customary and useful to divide manslaughter into two main groups which are designated "voluntary" and "involuntary" manslaughter, respectively. The distinction is that in voluntary manslaughter D may have the malice aforethought of murder, but the presence of some defined mitigating circumstance reduces his crime to the less serious grade of criminal homicide. Where these circumstances are present, then, D may actually intend to kill and do so in pursuance of that intention and yet not be guilty of murder.[15] At common law, voluntary manslaughter occurred in one case only, where the killing was done under provocation. But now, by statute, two further categories must be added. Under the Homicide Act 1957, it is now manslaughter and not murder, notwithstanding the presence of malice aforethought, where (i) D is suffering from diminished responsibility; and[16] (ii) where D kills in pursuance of a suicide pact.[17] Diminished responsibility has already been considered, and the problem of the suicide pact is looked at in connection with the new statutory crime of abetting suicide.[18] This section, then, will be devoted to killing under provocation.

(2) PROVOCATION

Provocation is a defence to a charge of murder at[19] common law, entitling D to be convicted of manslaughter. The common law rule was stated by DEVLIN, J., in what the Court of Criminal Appeal described as a "classic direction", as follows:

> "Provocation is some act, or series of acts, done by the dead man to the accused, which would cause in any reasonable person, and actually causes in the accused, a sudden and temporary loss of self-control, rendering the accused so subject to passion as to make him or her for the moment not master of his mind."[20]

The common law rule has been modified by the Homicide Act 1957, s. 3, which provides:

> "Where on a charge of murder there is evidence on which the jury can find that the person charged was provoked (whether by things done or by things said or by both together) to lose his self-control, the question whether the provocation was enough to make a reasonable man do as he did shall be left to

---

[15] *A.-G. of Ceylon* v. *Perera*, [1953] A.C. 200 (P.C.); *Lee Chun Chuen* v. *R.*, [1963] A.C. 220; [1963] 3 All E.R. 73; *Parker* v. *R.*, [1964] 2 All E.R. 641; *contra, per* Lord SIMON in *Holmes* v. *Director of Public Prosecutions*, [1946] A.C. 588 at p. 598 (H.L.).
[16] Section 2.
[17] Section 4.
[18] Below, p. 237.
[19] Provocation is not a defence to a charge of wounding or any charge other than murder according to *Cunningham*, [1959] 1 Q.B. 288; [1958] 3 All E.R. 711. It may, however, be a defence to a charge of attempted murder now that that is a common law offence once more. Above, p. 178, footnote 7.
[20] *Duffy*, [1949] 1 All E.R. at p. 932.

be determined by the jury; and in determining that question the jury shall take into account everything both done and said according to the effect which, in their opinion, it would have on a reasonable man."

1   Provocation and Third Parties[1]

(i) *By whom the provocation may be given.*—Provocation, with the one exception discussed below, was, at common law, something done *by the dead man to the accused.* It was no defence for D, who had killed P, to say that he was provoked into doing so by the action of X.[2] Under the Homicide Act, however, the judge is bound to leave the defence to the jury if there is evidence that "the person charged was provoked . . . to lose his self-control." Provocation given by a third party is clearly capable of amounting to such evidence and, accordingly, in *Twine*[3], LAWTON, J., left the defence to the jury where D's girl friend's conduct caused him to lose his self-control and strike and kill the man she was with.

The defence was available, even at common law, if the blow was *aimed* at the provoker. If, by accident, it missed him and killed an innocent person, P, then the doctrine of transferred malice[4] operated and D was guilty of manslaughter only. In *Gross*[5] D, provoked by blows from her husband, fired at him, intending to kill him but missed and killed P. It was held that

"... if the firing at the person intended to be hit would be manslaughter, then, if the bullet strikes a third person not intended to be hit, the killing of that person equally would be manslaughter and not murder."[6]

If D were reckless whether he hit P, he would have an independent *mens rea* with respect to P, probably sufficient to fix him with liability for murder[7] at common law; but now the provocation given by the third party would be a defence.

(ii) *Acts directed against third parties.*—It is said that at common law provocation must consist in something done to D. Most commonly, provocation has consisted in some kind of physical attack on D. The case of the adulterous spouse might also be considered as one where something is "done to" D by the guilty pair. At least they are committing a matrimonial offence against him. Suppose, however, that D came upon P committing rape on his wife and instantly killed him. It is conceived that this would have been sufficient provocation at common law; it could hardly have been less provoking because the wife was not consenting. In *Fisher*,[8] PARK, J., said, *obiter*,[9] that if a father came upon a man in the act of committing an unnatural act with his young son and instantly killed him, this, by analogy to the adultery rule, would probably have been a sufficient provocation. In *Harrington*[10] COCKBURN, C.J., contemplated the possibility that a violent assault upon his daughter by her husband might be sufficient to reduce D's killing of the husband to manslaughter, but did not

---

[1] See O'Regan, "Indirect Provocation and Misdirected Retaliation", [1968] Crim. L.R. 319.
[2] *Simpson* (1915), 84 L.J.K.B. 1893 (C.C.A.). But see *Ho Chun Yuen*, [1961] H.K.L.R. 433, discussed in [1963] Crim. L.R. 756.
[3] [1967] Crim. L.R. 710.
[4] Above, p. 44.
[5] (1913), 23 Cox C.C. 455 (DARLING, J.); and see *Porritt*, [1961] 3 All E.R. 463.
[6] 23 Cox C.C. at p. 456.
[7] Above, p. 199.
[8] (1837), 8 C. & P. 182.
[9] The judge ruled as a matter of law that there had been a sufficient cooling time.
[10] (1866), 10 Cox C.C. 370. And see *Terry*, [1964] V.R. 248.

decide the point. Whatever the position at common law, however, it would seem, again, that if there is evidence that D was in fact provoked to lose his self-control, the defence must be left to the jury even though the provocative act was directed against another.

2 The Subjective Condition

Attention in the cases has tended to be concentrated on the objective condition because, if the facts are such as to satisfy a jury that a reasonable man would have lost his self-control, there will usually be no doubt that D did so. Under the Act, however, the first hurdle for D is to satisfy the judge that there is evidence—fit for the consideration of the jury—that *he* lost his self-control; and so this subjective element will be considered first.

Whether a person lost his self-control on a certain occasion is a question of fact and, as in the determination of facts generally, it is for the judge to decide whether any evidence has been produced, by the party having the onus of introducing it, on which a jury could decide in his favour; and for the jury to decide whether the onus is satisfied. In the situation now being considered, this means that the judge must say whether a reasonable jury, having heard the evidence, might not at least have a reasonable doubt whether the first condition of provocation was fulfilled. If he concludes that they might have a reasonable doubt, the jury must say, either that they have no doubt, or no reasonable doubt, that at least one of the conditions was not fulfilled (guilty of murder) or that they think it reasonably possible (or probable, or certain) that both conditions were fulfilled (guilty of manslaughter.)

In deciding this question of fact the jury is, naturally, entitled to take into account all the relevant circumstances; the nature of the provocative act and all the relevant conditions in which it took place, the sensitivity or otherwise of D and the time, if any, which elapsed between the provocation and the act which caused death. D's failure to testify to his loss of self-control is not necessarily fatal to his case. Provocation is commonly set up as an alternative to the complete defence of self-defence. The admission of loss of self-control would weaken or destroy the alternative defence; and the courts recognise that D has a tactical reason for not expressly asserting what may be the truth.[11] If the facts of the case speak for themselves and suggest a possible loss of self-control, then the judge must leave the defence to the jury even though it has not been raised in express terms either by the accused or his counsel.[12]

If D is of an unusually phlegmatic temperament and it appears that he did not lose his self-control, the fact that a reasonable man in like circumstances would have done so will not avail D in the least. A traditional example of extreme provocation is the finding of a spouse in the act of adultery;[13] but if D, on so finding his wife, were to read her a lecture on the enormity of her sin and then methodically to load a gun and shoot her, it is probable (for it remains a question of fact) either that the judge would rule that there was no evidence that D lost

---

[11] *Bullard* v. *R.*, [1957] A.C. 635; [1961] 3 All E.R. 470 n. *Rolle* v. *R.*, [1965] 3 All E.R. 582. *Lee Chun Chuen* v. *R.*, [1963] A.C. 220; [1963] 1 All E.R. 73.
[12] *Mancini* v. *D.P.P.*, [1942] A.C. 1.
[13] Killing, in such a case "is of the lowest degree of [manslaughter]; and therefore . . . the court directed the burning in the hand to be gently inflicted, because there could not be a greater provocation": Blackstone, *Commentaries*, iv, 192. And see the leading case of *Maddy* (1672), T. Raym. 212.

his self-control or that the jury would find that he did not. In that case, D would be guilty of murder and it would be irrelevant that the jury may think that a reasonable man in like circumstances would lose his self-control.

Great importance is attached in many of the cases to the presence of "cooling time" between the act of provocation and the killing. In *Hayward*[14] TINDAL, C.J., told the jury that the question for their consideration was—

> ". . . whether the mortal wound was given by the prisoner while smarting under a provocation so recent and so strong that the prisoner might not be considered at the moment the master of his own understanding; in which case, the law, in compassion to human infirmity, would hold the offence to amount to manslaughter only: or whether there had been time for the blood to cool, and for reason to resume its seat, before the mortal wound was given, in which case the crime would amount to wilful murder."[15]

Shortness of time in that case was in D's favour, but against him was the fact that he fetched the weapon from two or three hundred yards away. If this showed "contrivance and design", that was inconsistent with the "violent and ungovernable passion" which was necessary for the defence to succeed.

Cooling time is obviously a fact of very great importance in deciding this particular question; but it should always be remembered that it is not a matter of law, but one item of evidence in answering the question: was D deprived of his self-control when he did the fatal act?

3   The Objective Condition[16]

The older cases tended to lay down as a matter of law what was, and what was not, capable of amounting to provocation. It was only in the latter half of the nineteenth century that the rider was introduced that the provocation must be such as to affect a reasonable man. It will be noted that in his direction in *Hayward*[17] TINDAL, C.J., told the jury that, if the accused were deprived of his self-control,

> "*the law*, in compassion to human infirmity, would hold the offence to amount to be manslaughter only."

The jury were not invited to consider the question whether the reasonable man would have lost his self-control. Thus Hawkins[18] catalogues a number of instances of provocative acts of which he says

> "it is certain that it can amount to no more than manslaughter."

To what extent the categories of provocative acts were fixed by law before the Homicide Act is not certain,[19] but it seems probable that, even where the act was one recognised as capable of being provocation, it still had to pass the reasonable man test at the hands of the jury. If, for example, D had connived at his wife's adultery with P, it may be that his sudden finding of them in the act would not be regarded as a sufficient provocation.

---

[14] (1833), 6 C. & P. 157.
[15] *Ibid.*, at p. 159. This direction was approved by the Court of Criminal Appeal in *Hall* (1928), 21 Cr. App. Rep. 48. See also *Lynch* (1832), 5 C. & P. 324; *Eagle* (1862), 2 F. & F. 827; and *cf. Fisher*, above, p. 206.
[16] See Williams "Provocation and the Reasonable Man", [1954] Crim. L.R. 740; Edwards "Another View", [1954] Crim. L.R. 898.
[17] *Supra.*
[18] 1 P.C., c. 13, § 36; and see East, 1 P.C. 233.
[19] See the discussion between Williams and Edwards at [1954] Crim. L.R. 740 and 898.

The reasonable man seems to have made his first appearance in this branch of the law in *Welsh*[20] where KEATING, J., told the jury that, if there was evidence of provocation,

> "then it is for the jury whether it was such that they can attribute the act to the violence of passion naturally arising therefrom, and likely to be aroused thereby in the breast of a reasonable man."[1]

After several further references to the reasonable man, he said that the provocation must be

> "something which might naturally cause an ordinary and reasonably minded man to lose his self-control and commit such an act."[2]

This view was accepted by the Court of Criminal Appeal in *Lesbini*.[3] D went into a hall called "Fairyland" in which there was a rifle and revolver range. The girl in charge of the range made some impertinent remarks in D's hearing, referring to him as "Ikey". He said he wanted to shoot at the range and selected a revolver which the girl gave to him. He pointed it at her, saying, "Now I have got you", and shot her. At his trial for murder the defences of accident and insanity were rejected by the jury. In the Court of Criminal Appeal the defence of provocation was urged and it was argued that *Welsh*'s case did not apply where, as in the present case, D suffered from defective control and want of mental balance. AVORY, J., interjected that it would seem to follow from this that a bad-tempered man would be entitled to a verdict of manslaughter where a good-tempered one would be liable to be convicted of murder[4] and the court held that, to afford a defence, the provocation must be such as would affect the mind of a reasonable man, which was manifestly not so in the present case.

Before the Homicide Act, it was possible for the judge to withdraw the defence from the jury on the ground that no reasonable jury could find, on the evidence given, the reasonable man would have been provoked.[5] Thus the behaviour of the reasonable man and his characteristics were laid down as a matter of law. In *Alexander*[6] it was held that the judge rightly refused to allow counsel to submit to the jury that there was provocation where the acts would not have caused a normal person to lose his self-control but might have done so to the accused who was mentally deficient. In *Smith*,[7] where D had killed a two-and-a-half-year-old child by hitting her over the head with a broom, it was held that the fact that D was seven months pregnant was irrelevant. In *Holmes* v. *Director of Public Prosecutions*[8] the House of Lords held that, as a matter of law, a confession of adultery is insufficient provocation[9] where a husband kills his wife, and that the trial judge was right in so directing the jury. Their Lordships added[10] that "in no case could words alone, save in circumstances of a most extreme and exceptional character", reduce the crime to manslaughter. The Court of Criminal

---

[20] (1869), 11 Cox C.C. 336.
[1] *Ibid.*, at p. 338.
[2] *Ibid.*, at p. 339.
[3] [1914] 3 K.B. 1116.
[4] For a discussion of this argument, see below, p. 211.
[5] *Holmes* v. *Director of Public Prosecutions*, [1946] A.C. 588 at p. 597; [1946] 2 All E.R. 124 at p. 126.
[6] (1913), 9 Cr. App. Rep. 139.
[7] (1914), 11 Cr. App. Rep. 36.
[8] [1946] A.C. 588; [1946] 2 All E.R. 124.
[9] Likewise a declaration of intention to commit adultery: *Ellor* (1920), 15 Cr. App. Rep. 41.
[10] [1946] A.C. at p. 600; [1946] 2 All E.R. at p. 128.

Appeal held that the doctrine of finding in adultery did not extend to unmarried persons living as man and wife,[11] or to a fiancée.[12]

The reasonable man was held to be normal in body as well as in mind. In *Bedder v. Director of Public Prosecutions*[13] D, a youth of eighteen who was sexually impotent, attempted in vain to have sexual intercourse with P, a prostitute. P jeered at him and attempted to get away. He tried to hold her and she slapped him in the face, punched him in the stomach and kicked him in the genitals. D knew of his impotence and had allowed it to prey on his mind. SELLERS, J., directed the jury that they must consider the effect which P's acts would have had on an ordinary person, not on a man who is sexually impotent and the House of Lords held that this was a correct direction.

In *McCarthy*,[14] where D, who was drunk, "went raging" after (he alleged), an indecent assault and an invitation by P to commit sodomy, it was held that the jury were not entitled to consider the fact that D was worse for drink and consequently more excitable and likely to lose self-control if provoked.

The courts thus built up a quite detailed picture of the reasonable man and his reactions in various circumstances. Not only was he not unusually excitable or pugnacious; he was not mentally deficient, or under the influence of drink, he was physically normal—not impotent and presumably not blind, or a dwarf, or scarred as a result of war injuries;[15] if a woman, she was not pregnant. He lost his self-control on finding his wife in the act of adultery, but not on hearing her confession of it; nor on finding his mistress or his fiancée in the act. He retained his self-control in the face of words, however abusive, except perhaps in some undefined extreme and exceptional case; and probably remained unmoved even if his nose was pulled into the bargain.[16]

4 The Homicide Act 1957 and the Reasonable Man

To what extent does all this represent the law? The text is still objective;[17] but it is clear that it is no longer possible for the judge to withdraw the defence from the jury on the ground that no evidence has been adduced that the reasonable man would have been provoked. Once the judge has found that there is evidence on which the jury might find that the man in the dock was provoked to lose his self-control, he has made the only decision which the law now requires of him; the remaining decisions are for the jury. Section 3 of the Homicide Act 1957 is phrased in imperative terms:[18]

"... the question whether the provocation was enough to make a reasonable man do as he did *shall be left* to be determined by the jury ..."

Thus, if in *Alexander*[19] there was evidence that D was provoked, it would not be possible, today, for the judge to preclude counsel from submitting that, or the jury from considering whether, a reasonable man would have been provoked.

[11] *Greening*, [1913] 3 K.B. 846 (C.C.A.). This, strictly, was *obiter*, as there was no actual finding in adultery.

[12] *Palmer*, [1913] 2 K.B. 29 (C.C.A.). This was a case of confession of adultery but it was regarded as equivalent to a finding in adultery.

[13] [1954] 2 All E.R. 801; (1954), 38 Cr. App. Rep. 133.

[14] [1954] 2 Q.B. 105; [1954] 2 All E.R. 262.

[15] *Cf.* A. P. Marshall's argument in *Bedder v. Director of Public Prosecutions* at (1954), 38 Cr. App. Rep. at p. 136.

[16] *Holmes*, [1946] A.C. at p. 600.

[17] The "reasonable man" test is unaffected by s. 8 of the Criminal Justice Act 1967 (above, p. 52): *Williams*, [1968] Crim. L.R. 678.

[18] See *Phillips v. R.* (1968), 113 Sol. Jo. 14 (P.C.). The proposition in Archbold, 2508, is wrong.

[19] Above, p. 209.

To what extent may the judge now seek to control the jury in applying the reasonable man test? Clearly he may no longer advise them that the reasonable man is not provoked by words alone since the section refers to provocation by "things done or by things said or by both together." Nor, it seems reasonably clear, may he now instruct or advise them that the reasonable man does not lose his self-control on finding his fiancée or his mistress in adultery for, by s. 3 of the Act, the jury

> "shall take into account *everything* both done and said according to the effect which, *in their opinion*, it would have on a reasonable man."

The italicised words seem to make it reasonably clear that the jury are now to decide untrammelled by instructions or advice from the judge on these matters. May he, however, advise the jury as to the characteristics of the reasonable man— that he is not impotent, under the influence of alcohol, etc.? This is less clear. It can hardly be objectionable for the judge to remark, as EDMUND DAVIES, J., did in *Wardrope*[20] that the reasonable man is not a violent-tempered man, because this adds nothing to what is necessarily implicit in "reasonable"; and perhaps this is equally true of the judge's direction that he is not a drunken man. Unfortunately, this would seem to open the door to the continuance in the law of the whole of the pre-Homicide Act concept of the reasonable man.

It is said that this would be "unfortunate" particularly in view of the decision in *Bedder* v. *Director of Public Prosecutions*.[21] This was justified by Lord SIMONDS as follows:[22]

> "It would be plainly illogical not to recognise an unusually excitable or pugnacious temperament in the accused as a matter to be taken into account but yet to recognise for that purpose some unusual physical characteristic, be it impotence or another. Moreover, the proposed distinction appears to me to ignore the fundamental fact that the temper of a man which leads him to react in such and such a way to provocation is, or may be, itself conditioned by some physical defect. It is too subtle a refinement for my mind or, I think, for that of a jury to grasp that the temper may be ignored but the physical defect taken into account."

It is submitted, however, that the result of the case is utterly absurd. Does it make sense to ask a jury to consider the effect of taunts of impotence on a man who is not impotent? or of taunts of being a hunchback and a dwarf on a man of six feet with a fine, military bearing? or of being a "black . . .!" on a man with a fair skin?[1] Surely there is only one characteristic of the reasonable man which is important for the present purpose and that is that he should show a reasonable degree of restraint in the actual circumstances, including his physical characteristics, whatever they be.[2] In applying the test of the reasonable man at all we ask the jury, in effect, to put themselves into the situation in which D found himself, and to consider whether they, being, presumably, a reasonable cross-section of the community, would have lost control of themselves. As the situation will probably be one which the jury have never before experienced anyway, this will

---

[20] [1960] Crim. L.R. 770.
[21] [1954] 2 All E.R. 801 (H.L.).
[22] *Ibid.*, at pp. 803, 804.
[1] See C. C. Marsack, "Provocation in Trials for Murder", [1959] Crim. L.R. 697; C. Howard, "What Colour is the Reasonable Man?" [1961] Crim. L.R. 41.
[2] *Cf.* New Zealand Crimes Act 1961, s. 169 (2) (*a*): "In the circumstances of the case it was sufficient to deprive *a person having the power of self-control of an ordinary person, but otherwise having the characteristics of the offender*, of the power of self-control."

be a most difficult task; will it be rendered so much more difficult by their attempting to visualise themselves as having also the physical characteristics of the accused?

It is thought that there is much to be said in favour of simply leaving the question of the effect of the provocation on a reasonable man to the jury, without any attempt to describe the reasonable man. *Pace* Lord SIMONDS, the jury, as a matter of common sense,[3] would take account, for example, of D's impotence, and ask themselves, what would be the effect of the provocation on a man with these physicial characteristics, but having a reasonable degree of self-restraint?

The wording of the Act, and its obvious policy of removing the objective condition from the sphere of the judge to that of the jury, would seem to leave it open to the courts to regard *Bedder* v. *Director of Public Prosecutions*[4] as over-ruled and it is submitted that it is very desirable that they should do so.

> "No court has ever given,[5] nor do we think ever can give, a definition of what constitutes a reasonable or an average man. That must be left to the collective good sense of the jury."[6]

5 The Relationship between the Provocation and the Mode of Resentment

In *Mancini* v. *Director of Public Prosecutions*[7] D was charged with the murder of P who had been stabbed to death by an instrument with a two-edged blade, a sharp point and sharp sides, at least five inches long. D's story was that P was attacking him with an open pen-knife and MACNAGHTEN, J., told the jury that, if they believed this story, they should return a verdict of not guilty (on the ground of self-defence.) He did not direct them that, if they rejected the defence of self-defence, they still might find D guilty of manslaughter on the ground of provocation; and D appealed on the ground that he ought to have done so. His conviction was affirmed. By their verdict, the jury had rejected his story of the attack with the pen-knife; and the case had, therefore, to be treated as one in which, at the most, P made an unarmed attack on D. If there had been evidence of provocation, it would have been the judge's duty to direct the jury on it, even though the defence had not been set up;[8] but here there was no evidence. An attack by hand or fist

> "would not constitute provocation of a kind which could extenuate the sudden introduction and use of a lethal weapon like this dagger, and there was, therefore, . . . no adequate material to raise the issue of provocation."[9]

The House stated the law in general terms as follows:[10]

> ". . . it is of particular importance . . . to take into account the instrument with which the homicide was effected, for to retort, in the heat of passion induced

---

[3] This opinion is based on the invariable reaction of the many law students with whom we have discussed the case.
[4] And *Alexander* (1913), 9 Cr. App. Rep. 139; above, p. 209.
[5] But *cf.* above, p. 210.
[6] *Per* Lord GODDARD, C.J., in *McCarthy*, [1954] 2 Q.B. 105 at p. 112; [1954] 2 All E.R. 262 at p. 265.
[7] [1942] A.C.1; [1941] 3 All E.R. 272 (H.L.).
[8] Above, p. 207.   [9] [1942] A.C. at p. 10: [1941] 3 All E.R. at p. 278.
[10] [1942] A.C. at p. 9; [1941] 3 All E.R. at p. 277, *per* Lord SIMON.

by provocation, by a simple blow, is a very different thing from making use of a deadly instrument like a concealed dagger. In short, the mode of resentment must bear a reasonable relationship to the provocation if the offence is to be reduced to manslaughter."

This seems to pre-suppose that the reasonable man, even after he has lost his self-control, will continue to behave reasonably!—and that D, therefore, must do likewise. "Fists might be answered with fists, but not with a deadly weapon."[11] The Supreme Court of Hong Kong, in distinguishing *Mancini*, has recently condemned the rule as "illogical and contrary to common sense."[12] In New Zealand, the relationship between the mode of resentment and the provocation is merely a factor, though a weighty factor to be considered by the jury in deciding whether there was provocation.[13]

Is the "reasonable relationship" rule still the law after the Homicide Act? Some justification for its continuance might perhaps be found in the words of s. 3[14] which require the provocation to be such as "to make a reasonable man *do as he [the accused] did*," whereas in the case of the person charged the requirement is that he should "lose his self-control." But since it is now for the jury to say what, "in their opinion", would have been the effects of the provocation on a reasonable man, it would seem to be inconsistent with the words of the Act for the judge to tell them that they *must* hold that he does not do acts out of proportion to the provocation received. In *Church*[15] the Court seemed clearly to have re-affirmed the "reasonable relationship" rule; but in the very recent case of *Walker*[16] the Court has said that "it may well be" that s. 3 has abolished any rule *of law* requiring a reasonable relationship, though this remains a vital element for the jury's consideration. The Privy Council, on the other hand, has stated[17] that *Mancini* is not reversed by s. 3, while apparently inconsistently, regarding the reasonable relationship rule as merely a factor for the consideration of the jury.

6 Criticism of the Objective Test

The Royal Commission on Capital Punishment considered the criticisms which have been made of the objective test. These they summed up as follows:

"The test, it is said, is inequitable. If the accused is mentally abnormal or is of subnormal intelligence or is a foreigner of more excitable temperament or is for some other reason peculiarly susceptible to provocation, it is neither fair nor logical to judge him by the standard of the ordinary Englishman."[18]

The abolition of the test was, however, strongly opposed by the judges who gave evidence and the Lord Justice General, Lord COOPER, used the "bad-

---

[11] *Per* DEVLIN, J., in *Duffy*, [1949] 1 All E.R. 932. See also *McCarthy*, [1954] 2 Q.B. at pp. 109–110.

[12] *Ng Yiu-nam* v. *R.*, [1963] Crim. L.R. 850. But in *Lee Chun Chuen* v. *R.*, [1963] A.C. 220 at pp. 231–232; [1963] 1 All E.R. 73 at p. 79, an appeal from Hong Kong, Lord DEVLIN insisted on the need for the retaliation to be proportionate to the provocation.

[13] *Dougherty*, [1966] N.Z.L.R. 890.

[14] Above, p. 205.

[15] [1966] 1 Q.B. 59; [1965] 2 All E.R. 72; below, pp. 217–218.

[16] (1968), *The Times*, December 20.

[17] In *Phillips* (1968), 113 Sol. Jo. 14. See also *Wardrope*, [1960] Crim. L.R. 770; *Southgate*, [1963] Crim. L.R. 570 and commentaries on *Walker* and *Phillips* in [1969] Crim L.R. (March).

[18] R.C.C.P., Cmd. 8932, para. 141.

tempered man" argument relied on by AVORY, J., in *Lesbini*.[19] The Commission
were impressed by this and did not feel justified in recommending any change
in the law:[20]

> "It is a fundamental principle of the criminal law that it should be based on a
> generally accepted standard of conduct applicable to all citizens and it is
> important that this principle should not be infringed. Any departure might
> introduce a dangerous latitude into the law. Those idiosyncrasies of indi-
> vidual temperament or mentality that may make a man more easily provoked
> or more violent in his response to provocation, ought not, therefore, to affect
> his liability to conviction, although they may justify mitigation of sentence."

It was not surprising, then, that the legislature retained the objective test in the
1957 Act. Yet the arguments which have been advanced for its retention have
been subjected to convincing criticism.[1]

There is really nothing in the "bad-tempered man" argument as appears
from the following propositions:

(1) If the provocation was enough to cause the good tempered man to lose his
self-control and kill, *a fortiori* it was enough to cause the bad-tempered
man to do likewise; and both will be convicted of manslaughter.

(2) If the provocation was not enough to cause the good-tempered man to lose
his self-control, but was enough to cause the bad tempered man to do so—

   (a) if the good tempered man *does* kill, he is rightly convicted of murder;
   and no injustice is done to him if the bad-tempered man is acquitted,
   for he lost his self-control and their cases are thus quite different.

   (b) if the good-tempered man does not kill, no question arises as to any
   equity between him and the bad-tempered man who does: the one
   commits no crime and can hardly feel unjustly treated if the other who
   kills is found guilty only of manslaughter! This may happen under the
   existing law if the provocation is enough to provoke the reasonable, as
   well as the bad-tempered, man.

The only case where both men kill and are treated differently is 2 (a) and this
difference arises from the existing subjective test, which everyone agrees should
be retained.

It is an extraordinary thing that the objective test assumes that the reasonable
man may commit homicide! If the act were really one which a reasonable man
might be expected to do, it ought not to be a crime at all; but, in fact, the "man
in the Clapham omnibus" in modern English society does not give way to the
temptation to inflict death or grievous bodily harm, even under extreme provocation. If the test were strictly applied, surely the defence would never succeed.
It is tolerable because it is leniently applied by judges and juries.[2] Lenient
application of the rule is excusable and, indeed, inevitable; for it presents the

---

[19] Above, p. 209.
[20] R.C.C.P., para 143. Somewhat inconsistently, the Commissioners said that they
thought that the test would be too harsh if it were strictly carried out; but they consoled
themselves with the consideration that "In practice . . . the courts not infrequently give
weight to factors personal to the prisoner in considering a plea of provocation and where
there is a conviction of murder such factors are taken into account by the Home Secretary
and may often lead to commutation of sentence": para. 145.
[1] See Williams, [1954] Crim. L.R. 751; Kenny, *Outlines*, 178.
[2] *Simpson*, [1957] Crim. L.R. 815; *Fantle*, [1959] Crim. L.R. 584.

jury with insoluble problems—for example, how does the reasonable man react to taunts from a prostitute with whom he has failed to have intercourse. A strange "reasonable man", indeed!

It is submitted that the objective test should be abolished, and a purely subjective criterion applied.

7 Provocation arising from a Mistake of Fact

The authorities suggest that, where D is provoked partly as the result of a mistake of fact he is entitled to be treated as if the facts were as he mistakenly supposed them to be. Thus in *Brown*[3] D, a soldier, wrongly, but apparently reasonably, supposed that P was a member of a gang who were attacking him and his comrade. He struck P with a sword and killed him. The judges were clearly of the opinion that this was only manslaughter. In the other cases the mistake arose from drunkenness. In *Letenock*[4] the Court of Criminal Appeal substituted a verdict of manslaughter in the case of a soldier who had stabbed a corporal, where

> "The only element of doubt in the case is whether or not there was anything which might have caused the applicant, *in his drunken condition*, to believe that he was going to be struck."[5]

This decision is unaffected by *McCarthy*[6] which was not concerned with a mistake of fact but with the effect of the alcohol on D's self-restraint. So in *Wardrope*,[7] EDMUND DAVIES, J., told the jury both that the provocation "must be such as to deprive a reasonable man, not a drunken man . . . of self-control" and that

> "A person whose mind was so impaired by drink as to imagine himself attacked was entitled[8] to take such steps in defending himself as were necessary to meet the imagined attack as if it were real or not exaggerated. . . ."

Must the mistake be a reasonable one? The cases do not offer any clear guidance on the problem. It is submitted that, as in mistake generally, reasonableness *ought* to be irrelevant, except as evidence whether a genuine mistake was made or not; but, in view of the tendency of the courts to insist on reasonableness[9] in mistake, it cannot be asserted that they will not do so here. Certainly a drunken mistake is not a reasonable one and drunken mistakes appear to be allowed; but here again, the general attitude of the courts seems to have been more generous[10] in the case of drunken than in the case of other unreasonable mistakes.

(3) INVOLUNTARY MANSLAUGHTER

This category includes all varieties of unlawful homicide which are committed without malice aforethought. It is not surprising, therefore, that the *mens rea* (or lack of it) with which it may be committed, takes several forms. And, as the limits of malice aforethought are uncertain, it follows inevitably that there is a

---

[3] (1776), Leach 148.
[4] (1917), 12 Cr. App. Rep. 221 (C.C.A.).
[5] *Ibid.*, at p. 224.
[6] [1954] 2 Q.B. 105; [1954] 2 All E.R. 262; above, p. 210.
[7] [1960] Crim. L.R. 770.
[8] Wardrope also raised the defence of self-defence and the use of the word "entitled" (*cf. Southgate*, [1963] 2 All E.R. 833) suggests that it was to this defence that the judge was here referring; but he could hardly have intended the jury to consider D's mistake of fact for the purpose of the one defence and not for the other.
[9] See above, p. 130.
[10] Above, p. 131.

corresponding uncertainty as to the boundary of manslaughter. The difficulties do not end there, for there is another vague borderline between manslaughter and accidental death. Indeed, Lord ATKIN said[11] that

> ". . . of all crimes manslaughter appears to afford most difficulties of defini-
> tion, for it concerns homicide in so many and so varying conditions . . . the
> law . . . recognises murder on the one hand based mainly, though not ex-
> clusively,[12] on an intention to kill, and manslaughter on the other hand, based
> mainly, though not exclusively,[13] on the absence of intent to kill, but with the
> presence of an element of 'unlawfulness' which is the elusive factor."

This "elusive factor" is obviously difficult to define; but it would seem to comprise the following varieties and combinations of *mens rea* and negligence:

(1) An intention to do an unlawful act, or unlawfully to omit to act, being grossly negligent whether any personal injury, however slight, be caused.

(2) An intention to do any act, or to omit to act where there is a duty to do so, being grossly negligent whether death (or at least grievous bodily harm) be caused.

(3) An intention to do any act, being reckless whether any personal injury be caused.

(4) An intention to escape from lawful arrest.

Categories (1) and (2) are firmly established; categories (3) and (4) are, as will appear, based on rather slender authority.

1   Intention to do an unlawful act, being grossly negligent as to personal injury

(1) *Constructive Manslaughter.*—Coke laid it down that an intention to commit any unlawful act was a sufficient *mens rea* for murder[14] so that if D shot at P's hen with intent to kill it and accidentally killed P, this was murder, "for the act was unlawful". This savage doctrine was criticised by HOLT, C.J.,[15] and by the time Foster wrote his *Crown Law*,[16] it appears to have been modified by the proviso that the unlawful act must be a felony. Thus, if D shot at the hen intending to steal it, the killing of P was murder;

> "but if it was done wantonly and without that intention it will be barely
> manslaughter."

This was the doctrine of constructive murder which survived until the Homicide Act 1957. From Foster's time there existed a twin doctrine of constructive man-slaughter; that any death caused while in the course of committing an unlawful act, other than a felony, was manslaughter. An act was unlawful for this purpose even if it was only a tort, so that the only *mens rea* which needed to be proved was an intention to commit the tort.

---

[11] In *Andrews* v. *Director of Public Prosecutions*, [1937] A.C. 576 at p. 581; [1937] 2 All E.R. 552 at pp. 554–555.
[12] See above, p. 195.
[13] See above, p. 205.
[14] 3 Inst. 56. See Turner, M.A.C.L., 195 at 212 *et seq.* for a discussion of the historical development.
[15] *Keat* (1697), Comb, 406 at p. 409.
[16] (1762)—see p. 258.

Thus, in *Fenton*[17] D threw stones down a mine and broke some scaffolding with the result that a corf being lowered into the mine overturned and P was killed. TINDAL, C.J., told the jury:[18]

"If death ensues as the consequence of a wrongful act, an act which the party who commits it can neither justify nor excuse, it is not accidental death but manslaughter. . . . In the present instance the act was one of mere wantonness and sport, but still the act was wrongful, it was a trespass. The only question therefore is whether the death of the party is to be fairly and reasonably considered as a consequence of such wrongful act; if it followed from such wrongful act as an effect from a cause, the offence is manslaughter."

Even in the nineteenth century, this doctrine was not accepted without reservation by the judges. A notable refusal to follow it is the direction of FIELD, J., in *Franklin*.[19] D, while walking on Brighton pier

"took up a good sized box from the refreshment stall on the pier and threw it into the sea."

The box struck P and killed him. The prosecution urged that, quite apart from the question of negligence, it was sufficient to show that the death was caused by an unlawful act—the tort against the refreshment stallkeeper; and relied on *Fenton*. FIELD, J. (with whom MATHEW, J., agreed) held that the case must go to the jury "on the broad ground of negligence". Expressing his abhorrence of constructive crime, the judge asserted that

"the mere fact of a civil wrong committed by one person against another ought not to be used as an incident which is a necessary step in a criminal case."[20]

One *nisi prius* ruling of this sort, however, could not undermine so well-established a doctrine; and it was applied by the Court for Crown Cases Reserved in 1899 in *Senior*,[1] which is also a leading case on manslaughter by omission. D belonged to a sect called the "Peculiar People" who believed that making use of medical aid showed a want of faith in God. For this reason he omitted to procure medical aid for his child, aged eight months, who was suffering from pneumonia. The child died and the evidence was that its life would have been prolonged or saved by medical treatment. WILLS, J., directed the jury that if D was guilty of the misdemeanour under the Prevention of Cruelty to Children Act 1894,[2] of wilfully neglecting the child in a manner likely to cause injury to its health, and the child died because of the wilful neglect, that was manslaughter. It was held that this was a correct direction; it was no answer that the father was an affectionate parent and acted as he did from religious motives.[3]

Until the recent case of *Church*[4] there was no clear judicial repudiation of the doctrine but it has long been certain that it is at least modified and subject to certain limitations. It follows from the well-established rule[5] that negligence sufficient to found civil liability is not necessarily enough for criminal guilt,

---

[17] (1830), 1 Lew 179.
[18] *Ibid.*
[19] (1883), 15 Cox C.C. 163.
[20] *Ibid.*, at p. 165.
[1] [1899] 1 Q.B. 823.
[2] See now Children and Young Persons Act 1933, s. 1 (1).
[3] The court added *obiter* that they thought this a case in which "an indictment for gross and culpable neglect could be supported at common law."
[4] [1966] 1 Q.B. 59; [1965] 2 All E.R. 72; below, p. 218.
[5] Below, pp. 222–226.

10*

that death caused in the course of committing the tort of negligence is not necessarily manslaughter. But the limitation goes further than this: there are degrees of negligence which are *criminally* punishable which are yet not sufficient to found a charge of manslaughter. If, then, the unlawfulness, whether civil or criminal, of the act arises solely from the negligent manner in which it is performed, death caused by the act will not necessarily be manslaughter. This follows from the decision of the House of Lords in *Andrews* v. *Director of Public Prosecutions*.[6]

In that case DU PARCQ, J., told the jury that if D killed P in the course of committing an offence against s. 11 of the Road Traffic Act 1930 he was guilty of manslaughter. Lord ATKIN (who clearly regarded dangerous driving as a crime of negligence)[7] said that, if the summing up had rested there, there would have been misdirection:

> "There can be no doubt that this section covers driving with such a high degree of negligence as that, if death were caused, the offender would have committed manslaughter. But the converse is not true, and it is perfectly possible that a man may drive at a speed or in a manner dangerous to the public, and cause death, and yet not be guilty of manslaughter."[8]

This case has been accepted in some quarters[9] as destroying the doctrine of constructive manslaughter. It is, unfortunately, by no means certain that it goes so far. Lord ATKIN expressly distinguished[10] between acts which are unlawful because of the negligent manner in which they are performed and acts which are unlawful for some other reason:

> "There is an obvious difference in the law of manslaughter between doing an unlawful act and doing a lawful act with a degree of carelessness which the legislature makes criminal."

His Lordship's next sentence implies that killing in the course of unlawful acts generally *is* manslaughter:

> "If it were otherwise a man who killed another while driving without due care and attention would *ex necessitate* commit manslaughter."

This passage has been severely criticised[11] and it is certainly unhappily phrased. ". . . doing a lawful act with a degree of carelessness which the legislature makes criminal" is a contradiction in terms, for the act so done is plainly not a lawful act. But the distinction evidently intended, *viz.*, between acts which are unlawful because of negligent performance and acts which are unlawful for some other reason, is at least intelligible and, in view of the established distinction between civil and criminal negligence, a necessary limitation.

The doctrine has been further qualified by *Church*[12] where the Court of Criminal Appeal held that it is wrong to direct a jury that to cause death by any unlawful act in relation to a human being is necessarily manslaughter.

---

[6] [1937] A.C. 576; [1937] 2 All E.R. 552.
[7] See above, p. 65; below, p. 333.
[8] [1937] A.C. at p. 584; [1937] 2 All E.R. at pp. 556, 557.
[9] Stephen's *Digest* at 222; Russell at 591 *et seq.*; Archbold, § 2516.
[10] [1937] A.C. at p. 585; [1937] 2 All E.R. at p. 557.
[11] Turner, M.A.C.L. at 238.
[12] [1966] 1 Q.B. 59; [1965] 3 All E.R. 72. See also *Creamer*, [1966] 1 Q.B. 72 at p. 82; [1965] 3 All E.R. 257 at p. 262: "A man is guilty of involuntary manslaughter when he intends an unlawful act and one likely to do harm to the person and death results which was neither foreseen nor intended."

"For such a verdict inexorably to follow, the unlawful act must be such as all sober and reasonable people would inevitably recognise must subject the other person to, at least, the risk of some harm resulting therefrom, albeit not serious harm."[13]

There must then be evidence of (i) an intention to do an unlawful act and (ii) gross negligence as to some personal injury. The negligence must be gross ("all reasonable people would inevitably recognise" the risk) but the injury risked may be slight.

It follows that the intentional infliction of any degree of bodily injury by an unlawful act will amount to manslaughter if death results.

(2) *The need for and significance of the "unlawful act"*.—It must be proved that the act was an unlawful one for frequently it is lawful for one person to inflict some slight degree of bodily harm on another. If the infliction of such slight harm should happen to cause death, this will be an accidental death and not a crime. A shoulder charge in the course of a game of football is, no doubt, a law-ful act[14] and, if it chance to cause death, this will not be unlawful. It would be otherwise if precisely the same charge were inflicted on a person who had not consented to receive such treatment and who was not participating in the game. And, if excessive violence were used, even in the course of a lawful game, a resultant death would be manslaughter.[15]

Again, it is lawful in some circumstances for one person to inflict a degree of physical chastisement on another. A father may so chastise his children and may delegate this power to a schoolteacher.[16] If this should unhappily cause death, it will not be criminal, provided that D neither knew nor, as a reasonable man, ought to have known that death or grievous bodily harm was likely to result. If the chastisement is unlawful and it causes death, this is manslaughter.[17]

In *Woods*[18] D, a man aged twenty-one, had assumed control of the younger children at his father's request while the father was away. After the father's return, P, a younger brother, was cheeky to D, whereupon D hit him on the side of the face with the open hand. P died because he suffered from a peculiar con-dition of the gland in which the most trifling injury was likely to prove fatal. AVORY, J., told the jury that the elder brother, no longer being *in loco parentis*, had no right in law to strike a younger brother because he was cheeky and that, if the blow was unlawful, D was guilty of manslaughter, the younger brother's con-dition being no answer.

". . . if it was an unlawful blow, the person who strikes the blow must take the risk of the condition in which the person is."[19]

Alabaster[20] is a similar case and, according to DEVLIN, J.,

---

[13] At p. 70
[14] Below, p. 254.
[15] *Moore* (1898), 14 T.L.R. 229. What is excessive force is a difficult question. One answer would be: force greater than that to which P consented; and he consented to such force as the rules of the game allow. But in *Moore*, HAWKINS, J., refused to allow the rules to be put in evidence by the Crown "for it is not criminal and not necessarily either dan-gerous or malicious to break them." On the other hand, in *Bradshaw* (1878), 14 Cox C.C. 83, BRAMWELL, L.J., admitted evidence of the rules of the game for the defence as tending to show that D was not actuated by any malicious motive or intention and was not acting in a manner which he knew to be likely to be productive of death or injury. See below, p. 255.
[16] *Cleary* v. *Booth*, [1893] 1 Q.B. 465; but see below, p. 257.
[17] *Hopley* (1860), 2 F. & F. 202
[18] (1921), 85 J.P. 272.
[19] *Ibid.*
[20] (1912), 47 L.J.N. 397; and see *Pennington*, [1958] Crim. L.R. 690.

"it is not uncommon to find a prisoner charged with manslaughter because he struck his opponent a blow which he could not strictly justify and which, in a quite unforeseeable way, caused his death."[1]

In *Garforth*[2] D unlawfully assaulted P, not intending to occasion grievous bodily harm, and inflicted minor injuries which contributed to P's death although major injuries were inflicted at the same time by E who was convicted of murder. The Court of Criminal Appeal had no doubt that D was guilty of manslaughter. Most recently in *Sharmpal Singh*[3] the Privy Council held that D was guilty where he had used excessive force and killed his wife by squeezing her throat in the course of sexual intercourse; her injuries were such as to show that he had gone "well beyond the limits" permitted by the wife's submission to intercourse.

A battery which kills is necessarily manslaughter if it is intended (as most batteries are) to cause any degree of physical harm. If the battery is not intended to cause harm—as in the case of a mere touching without consent—the question must be asked whether any reasonable man would necessarily have foreseen the risk of some harm resulting—a question which in most such cases must surely be answered in the negative. Where D intends to commit, not a battery but an assault in the narrow sense of that term,[4] then the further question must always be asked, would any reasonable man necessarily have foreseen the risk of some harm resulting. In *Conner*[5] D was guilty of manslaughter where she threw a piece of iron at her child intending to frighten it and accidentally killed another of her own children as it came in through the door. The leading case, however, is now undoubtedly *Larkin*.[6] O had been committing "adultery" with D's mistress, P. D took a razor and, according to his story, pulled it out of his pocket with the intention only of terrifying O by the show of the razor. P, being groggy with drink, swayed against him and her throat was cut by the razor as he held it out for the purpose of frightening O. OLIVER, J., told the jury that, if this story were true, D was guilty of manslaughter and the Court of Criminal Appeal held that this was a correct direction. The distinction was again between acts which are unlawful only because negligently performed and acts which are otherwise unlawful:

> "If a person is engaged in doing a lawful act, and in the course of doing that lawful act behaves so negligently as to cause the death of some other person, then it is for the jury to say, upon a consideration of the whole of the facts of the case, whether the negligence proved against the accused person amounts to manslaughter, and it is the duty of the presiding judge to tell them that it will not amount to manslaughter unless the negligence is of a very high degree; the expression most commonly used is unless it shows the accused to have been reckless as to the consequences of the act. That is where the act is lawful. Where the act which a person is engaged in performing is unlawful, then, if at the same time it is a dangerous act, that is an act which is likely to injure another person, and quite inadvertently he causes the death of that other person by that act, then he is guilty of manslaughter."[7]

The doctrine thus requires that the act must be unlawful for some other reason than that it is negligent. If the act would have been lawful had it not been

---

[1] [1954] Crim. L.R. at p. 671.
[2] [1954] Crim. L.R. 936.
[3] [1962] A.C. 188 (P.C.).
[4] Below, p. 249.
[5] (1835), 7 C. & P. 438.
[6] [1943] 1 All E.R. 217. The case is reported only on another point in [1943] 1 K.B. 174.
[7] *Ibid.*, at p. 219, *per* HUMPHREYS, J.

performed negligently, it is not an unlawful act for this purpose, though it will still ground liability under the principle considered below[8] if the negligence was gross. In *Lamb*[9] D pointed a loaded gun at his friend, P, in jest. He did not intend to alarm P and P was not alarmed. Because they did not understand the way in which a revolver works, both thought that there was no danger; but, when P pulled the trigger, he shot and killed his friend. The pointing of the gun was not an assault because P did not apprehend any injury; nor was it an attempt to assault, since D did not intend to cause him apprehension. It was therefore a misdirection to tell the jury that this was an unlawful and dangerous act. It was not unlawful apart from the danger involved—no legal wrong would have been done if the gun had not gone off.

This variety of manslaughter is still properly described as "constructive", since it appears that the unlawfulness of the act may have no bearing whatever on responsibility for the death. If D casts down a banana skin on a public footpath and P slips on it and suffers fatal injuries, it would seem that there is *prima facie* case of manslaughter against D. He committed an offence against the Litter Act 1958 and everyone knows that this act is likely to cause some harm. If, however, the skin is cast down in a place to which the public do not have access, but where injury is no less likely to ensue, the present doctrine has no application for the act is not an unlawful one. D's responsibility for the death is the same in the two cases; but he would be liable in the second case only if he were grossly negligent within the next section.

(3) *Former felonies are now "unlawful acts".*—Before the Criminal Law Act, it was necessary to distinguish, for the purposes of the present rule, between an intention to commit a felony, and an intention to commit other unlawful acts. It will be recalled that death caused in the course of furtherance of a felony was murder at common law but that this doctrine of constructive malice was abolished by the Homicide Act 1957.[10] That Act simply prescribed (in effect) that such killings should not amount to murder and it seemed reasonable to assume that thereafter they amounted to manslaughter. Now that felonies have been abolished, it would seem that an intention to commit a former felony should be regarded in no way differently, for the purposes of manslaughter, from an intention to commit any other unlawful act.

The most common case was that where D caused death in the course of an attempt to procure an abortion.[11] Since such an attempt is punishable with life imprisonment, it seems unimportant as a practical matter whether it amounts to the further offence of manslaughter. Perhaps, however, some significance is attached to fixing D with criminal responsibility for the death. At all events, prosecutions for manslaughter in such cases have been brought in the past and may continue in the future. There is no doubt that D intends to do an unlawful act where the facts show that he is guilty of an offence under s. 58 of the Offences against the Person Act. The question now is whether any reasonable man would have foreseen the risk of some harm resulting. Clearly there is if the operation

---

[8] See p. 222.
[9] [1967] 2 Q.B. 981; [1967] 2 All E.R. 1282.
[10] Above, p. 201.
[11] *Newton and Stungo*, [1958] Crim. L.R. 469 (ASHWORTH, J.), discussed by Havard in [1958] Crim. L.R. 600; *Buck and Buck* (1960), 44 Cr. App. Rep. 213 (EDMUND DAVIES, J.); *creamer*, [1966] 1 Q.B. 72; [1965] 3 All E.R. 257 (C.C.A.).

was conducted negligently; but suppose that D took all proper care and performed the operation with skill. Could he argue that he reasonably expected benefit and not harm to result to the woman from the operation? Probably not. The physical act done to the woman, being forbidden by law and being an act to which she cannot lawfully consent, seems necessarily to amount to "harm" for legal purposes. Thus it seems probable that death caused in the course of attempting to procure an illegal abortion will continue necessarily to amount to manslaughter.

2 Killing by Gross Negligence

The question here is whether an act causing death which is not otherwise unlawful can amount to manslaughter because of the grossly negligent manner in which it was committed. Whether gross negligence is, and whether it ought to be, a ground of liability for manslaughter, are both matters on which opinions differ. Whether negligence *should* be a ground of liability has been discussed above.[12] Whether it *does* ground liability for manslaughter requires consideration here. It is well settled that the ordinary negligence which will suffice for civil liability is not enough and the argument of some writers that degrees of negligence do not exist, if accepted, would render further discussion pointless. This argument, however, as has been seen,[13] depends on the notion that negligence is a state of mind; whereas, in law, it would seem that negligence is *conduct* which fails to measure up to a required standard; and it is quite clear that there are degrees of such failure.

(i) *Is negligence a ground of liability?*—To answer this question the cases relied upon[14] as authority for the proposition that negligence does not ground liability for manslaughter must be examined.

A much-cited case is that of *Finney*.[15] D, an attendant at a lunatic asylum, told P, a lunatic whom he had bathed, to get out of the bath. P was able to understand what was said to him, but he did not, on this occasion, do as he was told. D's attention was distracted by a question from the attendant at the next bath; he put his hand on the hot tap in mistake for the cold one and projected a stream of scalding water over P and killed him. Lush, J., told the jury:[16]

> "If you think that indicates gross carelessness, then you should find the prisoner guilty of manslaughter; but if you think it inadvertence not amounting to culpability or what is properly termed an accident, then the prisoner is not liable."

It has been suggested that Lush, J., was telling the jury that inadvertence

---

[12] p. 56.

[13] Above, p. 56.

[14] By Turner in M.A.C.L. 216; and see Russell, Vol. 1, 43 *et seq.*, 592 *et seq.*, Kenny, *Outlines*, 183; Hall, *General Principles*, 122 *et seq.* The first case cited by Turner in M.A.C.L. 216 is *Townley* (1863), 3 F. & F. 839 at p. 846, which was a case where the defence to a charge of murder was insanity and Martin, B.'s direction was concerned solely with the question whether D knew the nature and quality of his act within the meaning of the M'Naghten Rules and had nothing to do with manslaughter by negligence or otherwise.

[15] (1874), 12 Cox C.C. 625.

[16] *Ibid.*, at p. 626.

cannot amount to culpability; but it will be noted that that is not what LUSH, J., said. Rather, he used the language of degrees of negligence:[17]

> "To render a person liable for neglect of duty there must be such a degree of culpability as to amount to gross negligence on his part. If you accept the prisoner's own statement, you find no such amount of negligence as would come within this definition."

The case may, moreover, fairly be looked at in the light of the same judge's direction in the case of *Jones*[18] the following day. D, in playing with P, a boy aged eight, pointed a gun at him and it went off. LUSH, J., told the jury:[19]

> "If a person points a gun without examining whether it is loaded or not, and it happens to be loaded and death results, he is guilty of negligence and manslaughter... If he held the gun pointed at the boy... and it went off what can that be but improperly and carelessly handling the gun as to be negligence and therefore manslaughter."

The jury were directed to convict here if they thought that D had behaved in a certain manner. They were given no instruction as to any requisite state of mind on D's part; and would have been justified in convicting even if they thought that the possibility of danger to the boy never entered into D's head.

In *Spencer*[20] where D, a doctor, caused the death of his patient, P, by administering to her a dose of strychnine in mistake for bismuth, WILLES, J., told the jury that, for conviction, the negligence must be such "as would amount to a culpable wrong and show an evil mind"; but the direction on the actual facts seems simply to distinguish between gross and ordinary negligence. WILLES, J., contrasted two ways in which the strychnine might have been administered:[1]

> "First, through gross negligence on the part of the prisoner. He might have kept his ordinary drugs and his poisons in such a way that he could not tell which he was using.... Secondly, the poison might have been administered by mistake, but a blunder alone would not render the prisoner criminally responsible."

Elliott[2] was an Irish case of a railway accident in which many persons were killed. D was the conductor of a train which failed to ascend a gradient. He chocked the wheels of the last six carriages and uncoupled them. They ran away and collided with another train. O'BRIEN, J., told the jury: "For intellectual defect, for mere mistake of judgment, he cannot be found guilty." But he also told them:[3]

> "But I cannot agree in the proposition which has been approached in the argument of counsel, that if by a wilful and forward confidence in his own opinion which was contrary to all reason and experience, that would not make the prisoner guilty."

---

[17] Hall (*General Principles*, 123) thinks there was an explicit exclusion of negligence and that LUSH, J., had recklessness clearly in mind, relying on the judge's statement: "Now, if the prisoner seeing that the man was in the bath, had knowingly turned on the tap and turned on the hot instead of the cold water, I should have said there was gross negligence." But it is clear that, in the case put, D did not know it was the *hot* tap he was turning—if he had, his act would have been intentional, not negligent, and he ought to have been charged with murder. Thus, in such a case D would still have been inadvertent as to the essential matter—the likelihood of injury to F.

[18] (1874), 12 Cox C.C. 628.
[19] *Ibid.*, at p. 629.
[20] (1867), 10 Cox C.C. 525.
[1] *Ibid.*, at p. 526.
[2] (1889), 16 Cox C.C. 710.
[3] *Ibid.*, at p. 714.

This seems again to be simply the familiar distinction between ordinary and gross negligence. The judge went on specifically to rule out the necessity for recklessness:

> "We cannot enter into the prisoner's mind—we must judge his conduct by certain external measures of reason. Nor is it necessary that there should be a conscious indifference in his mind—if such an expression may be used—as to the safety of passengers."[4]

In *Markuss*[5] D, a herbalist, prescribed for P a cure for a cold which killed her. WILLES, J., directed:[6]

> "Every person who dealt with the health of others was dealing with their lives, and every person who so dealt was bound to use reasonable care, and not to be grossly negligent . . . gross negligence consisted in rashness, where a person was not sufficiently skilled in dealing with dangerous medicines which should be carefully used, of the properties of which he was ignorant or how to administer a proper dose."

In *Doherty*,[7] a case of killing by shooting, STEPHEN, J., said:[8]

> "Manslaughter by negligence occurs when a person is doing anything dangerous in itself, or has charge of anything dangerous in itself, and conducts himself in regard to it in such a careless manner that the jury feel that he is guilty of culpable negligence and ought to be punished."

One case in which a reasonably unequivocal statement that recklessness is necessary is to be found is *Nicholls*,[9] where BRETT, J., told the jury that the negligence must be so great

> "that you must be of opinion that the prisoner had a wicked mind, in the sense that she was reckless and careless whether the creature had died or not."[10]

This was a case of killing by omission and one in which the judge clearly invited the jury to acquit. It would be dangerous to found any general proposition on it.

It is thought that these cases[11] cannot, with respect, be said to establish that "inadvertence does not ground liability at common law".[12] On the contrary, they seem generally to assume that gross negligence will suffice. Other authorities likewise support this view. Reference may be made to cases discussed above—*Pittwood*,[13] *Dalloway*,[14] *Benge*[15]—as well as to *Knight*[16] and *Kew and Jackson*[17] (negligent driving), *Rigmaidon*[18] (negligent slinging of a cask), *Dant*[19] (negligent pasturing of a horse near a public right of way) and the more modern cases

---

[4] *Cf.* EVE, J.'s definition (considered by Turner the "best judicial definition"(M.A.C.L. at p. 207)) of recklessness as "an attitude of mental indifference to obvious risks". *Hudston* v. *Viney*, [1921] 1 Ch. 98 at p. 104.
[5] (1864), 4 F. & F. 356.
[6] *Ibid.*, at p. 358; *cf. Noakes* (1866), 4 F. & F. 920.
[7] (1887), 16 Cox C.C. 306.
[8] *Ibid.*, at p. 309.
[9] (1874) 13 Cox C.C. 75.
[10] *Ibid.*, at p. 76.
[11] Other cases cited—*Cashill* v. *Wright* (1856), 6 E. & B. 891; *Chainey* (1914), 1 K.B. 137—seem to have little bearing on the problem. *Dabholkar*, [1948] A.C. 221, simply says that the negligence to be proved on a charge of negligent medical treatment under s. 222 of the Tanganyika Penal Code is less than that required for manslaughter, though of a higher degree than civil negligence.
[12] M.A.C.L. at 216.
[13] (1902), 19 T.L.R. 37; above, p. 36.
[14] (1847), 3 Cox C.C. 273; above, p. 186.
[15] (1865), 4 F. & F. 504; above, p. 186.
[16] (1828), 1 Lew. 168.
[17] (1872), 12 Cox C.C. 355.
[18] (1833), 1 Lew C.C. 180.
[19] (1865), Le. & Ca. 567.

of *Burdee*[20] (negligent medical treatment by an unqualified man, confident of his powers) and *Bateman*[1] (negligent medical treatment by a doctor).

The problem eventually came before the House of Lords in *Andrews* v. *Director of Public Prosecutions*;[2] but, unfortunately, the distinction between recklessness and negligence, now drawn by jurists, was not present to the minds of counsel or the court and the result is far from clear. On the one hand, there are passages which suggest that recklessness must be proved.

> "After all, manslaughter is a felony, and was capital, and men shrank from attaching the serious consequences of a conviction for felony to results produced *by mere inadvertence.*"[3]

and—

> "Probably of all the epithets that can be applied 'reckless' most nearly covers the case."[4]

But against this, Lord ATKIN began by saying that it was only necessary to consider manslaughter

> "from the point of view of an unintentional killing caused by negligence, that is, the omission of a duty to take care."[5]

He stated that he did not "find connotations of *mens rea* helpful in distinguishing between degrees of negligence;"[6] whereas if the true distinction is between recklessness and negligence, such connotations are most helpful. And the term "reckless" is used as an epithet to distinguish the criminal degree of negligence and not to describe a separate category of *mens rea*. Finally,

> " 'reckless' suggests an indifference to risk whereas the accused may have appreciated the risk and intended to avoid it and yet have shown such a high degree of negligence in the means adopted to avoid the risk as would justify a conviction."[7]

Moreover, the background to the case is a long history of liability for negligence and it is quite apparent that the House had no intention of overruling earlier authority but was simply applying what it conceived to be the existing law. It is thought, then, that the present law is that gross negligence may found liability for manslaughter.

Subsequent cases have certainly approved an objective test of negligence. In *Dunleavy*[8] the Irish Court of Criminal Appeal, dealing with a motor manslaughter charge, rejected the test of "reckless disregard for life" as more appropriate to murder:

> ". . . a more satisfactory way of indicating to a jury the high degree of negligence necessary . . . is to relate it to the risk or likelihood of substantial personal injury resulting from it . . .
> If . . . any reasonable driver, endowed with ordinary road sense and in full possession of his faculties, would realise, if he thought at all, that by driving in the manner which occasioned the fatality he was, without lawful excuse, incurring in a high degree, the risk of causing substantial personal injury to others, the crime of manslaughter appears to be clearly established."

---

[20] (1916), 12 Cr. App. Rep. 153.
[1] (1925), 19 Cr. App. Rep. 8.
[2] [1937] A.C. 576; [1937] 2 All E.R. 552.
[3] [1937] A.C. at pp. 581–582; [1937] 2 All E.R. at p. 555.
[4] [1937] A.C. at p. 583; [1937] 2 All E.R. at p. 556.
[5] [1937] A.C. at p. 581; [1937] 2 All E.R. at p. 555.
[6] [1937] A.C. at p. 583; [1937] 2 All E.R. at p. 556.
[7] *Ibid.*
[8] [1948] Irish Reports 95.

In *Lamb*,[9] which is discussed above, the Court of Appeal said, obiter,

> ". . . it would, of course, have been fully open to a jury, if properly directed, to find the accused guilty, because they considered his view as to there being no danger was formed in a criminally negligent way."

Thus, D might have been guilty although he had no foresight of any injury whatsoever and though he had no intention of doing anything unlawful.

(ii) *The definition of "gross negligence".*—Matters of degree always present difficulties of definition, and "gross negligence" is no exception. The best-known attempt is that of Lord HEWART in *Bateman*:[10]

> "In explaining to juries the test which they should apply to determine whether the negligence, in the particular case, amounted or did not amount to a crime, judges have used many epithets such as 'culpable', 'criminal', 'gross', 'wicked', 'clear', 'complete'. But whatever epithet be used and whether an epithet be used or not, in order to establish criminal liability the facts must be such that, in the opinion of the jury, the negligence of the accused went beyond a mere matter of compensation between subjects and showed such disregard for the life and safety of others as to amount to a crime against the State and conduct deserving of punishment."

This passage has been criticised[11] on the grounds that (i) it is circular in that it tells the jury to convict if they think that D is guilty of a crime and (ii) it leaves a question of law to the jury. These criticisms are well founded; yet, if we are to have a crime based on a certain degree of negligence, no other test is possible— the jury must say whether the negligence is bad enough to attract criminal liability. The "*Bateman* test" has the virtue that it draws attention to the fact that there exists civil liability for less degrees of negligence and that criminal liability should be reserved for gross aberrations.

Bateman received general approval from Lord ATKIN in *Andrews*, though he noted its circular nature[12] and it seems to be accepted as an authoritative statement.

(iii) *What consequence must be foreseeable?*—Negligence does not exist in the abstract. It must be negligence as to some particular consequence; that is, it must appear that a reasonable man in the position of D would have foreseen a particular kind of consequence as likely to occur from the conduct in question. Williams suggests that the negligence required for manslaughter is negligence as to death and not as an injury short of death. If negligence as to any degree of injury would suffice, then this head of manslaughter would swallow the head first considered, and it would be irrelevant whether the act was unlawful (apart from negligence) or not. The very fact that the "unlawful act" doctrine exists suggests that negligence as to some greater degree of harm is necessary to establish liability for manslaughter by gross negligence. Williams's example is:

> "D by gross negligence bumps into P; P falls against Q who is secretly carrying explosives, and P is blown up. This is not manslaughter in D for his negligence was only as to the bumping."[13]

---

[9] [1967] 2 Q.B. 981 at p. 980; [1967] 2 All E.R. 1282 at p. 1285, above, p. 221.
[10] (1925), 19 Cr. App. Rep. 8 at p. 11.
[11] By Turner, M.A.C.L. 211; Russell, 592–594; Turner, M.A.C.L. 210, 211.
[12] [1937] A.C. at p. 583; [1937] 2 All E.R. at p. 556; and see the Court of Criminal Appeal, [1937] W.N. 69.
[13] C.L.G.P. at p. 111. Williams points out that it is no longer held in the law of tort that negligence as to one consequence makes the defendant liable as to a completely different consequence: *The Wagon Mound*, [1961] A.C. 388; [1961] 1 All E.R. 404. But it is now

D has done an unlawful act to P—a negligent battery is a tort—but he did not *intend* to do an unlawful act so as to attract the operation of the unlawful act doctrine. While it seems to be clear that an intentional slight injury to the person entails liability for manslaughter[14] if death results, and a reckless injury *may* do so,[15] it would surely be going too far to extend this principle to negligent injuries. A negligent injury should be enough only where death (or, at the very least, grievous bodily harm) was foreseeable.[16]

3 Intention to do any Act, being Reckless whether any Personal Injury be Caused

Authority for this variety of *mens rea* is not very extensive. It is, of course, supported by the general principle that the criminal law equates intention and recklessness and by the recent case of *Pike*.[17] There D administered carbon tetrachloride (C.T.C.) to his mistress for the purpose of increasing sexual satisfaction. He had done this to women over a number of years with no apparent ill-effects except temporary loss of consciousness but, on this occasion, it caused P's death. HILBERY, J., directed that he was guilty if he knew that inhaling C.T.C. would expose P to the danger of physical harm and yet recklessly caused or allowed her to inhale it and the Court of Criminal Appeal held that this was a correct direction. It is arguable that this very briefly reported direction means that the jury must be satisfied that there was recklessness *as to death*. The jury were told that they were entitled to take into account the fact that D knew that C.T.C. made people unconscious, "for any anaesthesia is a step on the way to death."[18] But this interpretation is difficult to reconcile with the requirement by the judge of foresight of the danger merely of physical harm and not of death; and, on the whole, it seems likely that the case is authority for the rule that recklessness as to physical harm less than death or grievous bodily harm is enough.

Moreover, the cases in the preceding paragraph are of deaths caused in the course of a battery or an assault; and assault and battery can probably be commited recklessly as well as intentionally.[19]

4 An Intention to Escape from Lawful Arrest

An intention violently to resist lawful arrest was a sufficient *mens rea* for murder at common law if death resulted. This form of constructive murder was abolished by the Homicide Act 1957, s. 1. That Act does not, however, say such a killing, in the absence of malice aforethought, is a lawful homicide; and it is reasonable to infer that the effect is to transform it into manslaughter. Since, however, it is implicit in this situation that there is an intention to do an unlawful

---

clear that it is still the law that the negligent tortfeasor takes the victim of personal injuries as he finds him and negligence as to some slight injury may entail liability for death if that is caused: *Smith* v. *Leech Brain & Co. Ltd.*, [1962] 2 Q.B. 405; [1961] 3 All E.R. 1159; *Warren* v. *Scruttons, Ltd.*, [1962] 1 Lloyd's Rep. 497. Yet it does not follow that, because this may be the right rule in tort, it should also be followed in crime.

[14] Above, p. 219.
[15] *infra.*
[16] It is not a crime to cause *non-fatal* injuries by gross negligence. It seems illogical to make liability depend on the fact of death and not on the nature of the negligence. But this lack of logic runs through the whole of manslaughter.
[17] [1961] Crim. L.R. 114; affirmed, [1961] Crim. L.R. 547.
[18] *Ibid.*, at p. 116.
[19] *Chapin* (1909), 74 J.P. 71. *Ackroyd* v. *Barett* (1894), 11 T.L.R. 115; below, p. 254.

act which is likely to inflict some harm, such cases no longer seem to call for any special mention but can be brought within the general rule discussed above. The question remains, however, whether it is enough that D intends to escape from unlawful arrest, but does not intend any violence to the person of another.

In the leading case of *Porter*,[20] BRETT, J., told the jury that if D kicked P in resistance of his lawful arrest, he was guilty of murder even though he did not intend to cause grievous bodily harm (this was the doctrine of constructive murder). He added:[1]

> "But if, in the course of the struggle, he kicked the man not intending to kick him, then he was only guilty of manslaughter."

He further directed that the questions for the jury

> "were whether the prisoner inflicted the kick wilfully, and intending to inflict grievous injury, or intending to resist arrest, or whether it was only accidental in the course of the struggle;"

and that if they thought

> "that the kick was accidental, in the course of a wild struggle, then he would only be guilty of manslaughter."

This makes it clear that, for manslaughter, nothing more was required than an intention to escape—for example, to pull oneself free from the restraining arm of the arresting officer or to run away.

Nothing has happened in the meantime to overrule BRETT, J.'s direction on manslaughter, and it would appear to be still the law. The very strict rule which it lays down, however, was perhaps a corollary of the equally draconian rule concerning murder. Now that the murder rule has gone, might it not be that its corollary should be regarded as repealed by implication? Since killing by a *deliberate* kick, not intended to cause grievous bodily harm, in the course of resisting arrest is now manslaughter and not murder, ought it not now to be the law that killing by an *accidental* kick in the course of resisting arrest is an accidental death—in law as well as in fact?

3 DEFENCES TO MURDER AND MANSLAUGHTER

It has been traditional in English criminal law books to devote a section to "Lawful Homicides". Historically, there were good reasons for this, since the common law distinguished two categories of such homicides—"justifiable" and "excusable". A merely excusable homicide resulted in the forfeiture of the killer's movable property to the Crown, whereas the justifiable homicide imposed no legal burden whatever upon him. The distinction has been of no importance since forfeiture of goods was abolished in 1828.[2] Any homicide which is not murder or manslaughter under the principles considered above—for example, a death caused by an accident not involving gross negligence—is simply a lawful homicide and there is no point in adding illustrations of such cases.

There are, however, cases in which the conditions of liability for murder or manslaughter, described above, are fulfilled, but in which the existence of further facts affords a defence. These cases, which clearly do require consideration, are those in which death is caused:

---

[20] (1873), 12 Cox C.C. 444.
[1] *Ibid.* at p. 446.
[2] 8 & 9 Geo. IV c. 31.

(a) in carrying out the sentence of a competent court;

(b) in preventing crime or arresting offenders;

(c) in defence of one's own person or that of another;

(d) in defence of property.

(1) ONUS OF PROOF

Though it is convenient to speak of the conditions which must be established to make out these defences, it must always be borne in mind that there is no onus of proof on the accused who raises them. He has the evidential burden of "laying a foundation" for the defence; but, when he has so done, he must not be convicted unless the jury are satisfied beyond reasonable doubt that the conditions of the defence, or one of them, are not made out.[3]

(2) THE DEFENCES

1 Killing in Carrying out the Sentence of the Court

Clearly, the executioner who carries out the sentence of death imposed by a lawful court commits no *actus reus*. It has always been said,[4] however, that if the sentence were carried out in an unauthorised manner—for example, by beheading or poisoning a man who has been sentenced to be hanged—this would be murder. Likewise if the sentence be carried out by anyone other than the authorised executioner. Such problems are unlikely to arise at the present day.

2 Killing in the Course of Preventing Crime or Arresting Offenders

The common law on this subject was both complex and uncertain;[5] but now, by the Criminal Law Act 1967, s. 3:

> (1) A person may use such force as is reasonable in the circumstances in the prevention of crime, or in effecting or assisting in the lawful arrest of offenders or suspected offenders or of persons unlawfully at large.
>
> (2) Subsection (1) above shall replace the rules of the common law on the question when force used for a purpose mentioned in the subsection is justified by that purpose.

Since the common law rules are no longer in point, the question now seems to be simply one of what is reasonable in the particular circumstances of the case. The view of the Criminal Law Revision Committee[6] was;

> "No doubt if a question arose on clause [now 'section'] 3, the court, in considering what was reasonable force, would take into account all the circumstances, including in particular the nature and degree of force used, the seriousness of the evil to be prevented and the possibility of preventing it by other means; but there is no need to specify in the clause the criteria for deciding the question. Since the clause is framed in general terms, it is not limited to arrestable or any other class of offences, though in the case of very trivial offences it would very likely be held that it would not be reasonable to use even the slightest force to prevent them."

It cannot be reasonable to cause death unless (*a*) it was *necessary* to do so in order to prevent the crime or effect the arrest and (*b*) the evil which would follow

---

[3] *Chan Kau* v. *R.*, [1955] A.C. 206; [1955] 1 All E.R. 266; *Lobell*, [1957] 1 Q.B. 547; [1957] 1 All E.R. 734.

[4] For example, Hale, 1 P.C. 501; Co. 3 Inst. 52.

[5] See the first edition of this book at pp. 230–238.

[6] Cmd. 2659, para. 23.

from failure to prevent the crime or effect the arrest is so great that a reasonable man might think himself justified in taking another's life to avert that evil. It is likely, therefore, that killing will be justifiable to prevent unlawful killing or grievous bodily harm, or to arrest a man who is likely to cause death or grievous bodily harm if left at liberty. The whole question is somewhat speculative. Is it reasonable to kill in order to prevent rape? Or robbery, when the property involved is very valuable, and when it is of small value?[7] How much force may be used to prevent the destruction of a great work of art? In the last resort, these questions would presumably have to be answered by a jury though only if the judge ruled that there was evidence on which a reasonable jury could find that the defence was made out.

The standard of reasonableness to be applied in the situations under consideration should not be a strict one. The celebrated *dictum* of HOLMES, J., that "Detached reflection cannot be demanded in the presence of an uplifted knife"[8] should be borne in mind. The situations envisaged relate to crises when reasonable men might well make mistakes which they would not make in other circumstances. Even in the law of tort, D is not considered to be contributorily negligent when, being endangered by P's negligence, in "the agony of the moment" he chooses the wrong course in trying to save himself.[9] *A fortiori*, he should not lightly be held at fault for the purposes of the criminal law, and when he is endangered, not by mere negligence, but by wilful wrongdoing.

3 Self Defence

Self defence and defence of others almost invariably arise out of an attempt to commit a crime by the assailant and thus consist in the use of force to prevent the commission of the crime. The purpose of the person attacked, when he acts in self-defence, is not the enforcement of the law but his own self-preservation; but the degree of force which is permissible is presumably the same. An inquiry into D's motives is not practicable.[10] Technical questions were formerly raised whether action in defence of another could be justified outside the relationships of master and servant, parent and child and husband and wife; but in *Duffy*[11] the Court of Criminal Appeal held that a woman would be justified in using reasonable force when it was necessary to do so in defence of her sister, not because they were sisters, but because "there is a general liberty as between strangers to prevent a felony". That general liberty now extends to all offences. It is submitted that the principles applicable are the same whether the defence be put on grounds of self defence or on grounds of prevention of crime. The degree of force permissible should not differ, for example, in the case of a master defending his servant from the case of a brother defending his sister—or, indeed, that of a complete stranger coming to the defence of another under unlawful attack.

There were formerly technical rules about the duty to retreat before using

---

[7] Where a butcher used a butcher's knife to frustrate the robbery of his takings, his action met with the approval of the coroner, though the robber died; (1967), *The Times*, September 16.

[8] *Brown* v. *United States*, 256 U.S. 335; 41 S. Ct. 501; 65 Law Ed. 961 (1921).

[9] *Jones* v. *Boyce* (1816), 1 Stark. 493; *Admiralty Commissioners* v. *S.S. Volute*, [1922] 1 A.C. 129, at p. 136. *Cf. Swadling* v. *Cooper*, [1931] A.C. at p. 9.

[10] Above, p. 47.

[11] [1967] 1 Q.B. 63; [1966] 1 All E.R. 62 (C.C.A.).

force, or at least fatal force. It is submitted that this is now simply a factor to be taken into account in deciding whether it was necessary to use force, and whether the force used was reasonable.

In a very few cases the attacker may not be committing a crime because, for example, he is a child under ten, insane, in a state of automatism or under a material mistake of fact. If D is unaware of the circumstances which exempt the attacker, then s. 3 of the Criminal Law Act will still, indirectly, afford him a defence to any criminal charge which may be brought, provided he is acting reasonaby in the light of the circumstances as they reasonably appear to him; for he intends to use force in the prevention of crime, as that section allows, and therefore has no *mens rea*. Where D does know of the circumstances in question, then s. 3 is entirely inapplicable, but it is submitted that the question should be decided on similar principles. A person should be allowed to use reasonable force in defending himself or another against an unjustifiable attack, even if the attacker is not criminally responsible.

4 Defence of Property

The defender of property, like the defender of the person, is generally engaged in the prevention of crime and, accordingly, s. 3 of the Criminal Law Act is likely to provide the criterion in future. It can rarely, if ever, be reasonable to use deadly force merely for the protection of property. Would it have been reasonable to kill even one of the Great Train Robbers to prevent them from getting away with their millions of pounds of loot, or to kill a man about to destroy a priceless old master?—even assuming that no means short of killing could prevent the commission of the crime.

In the modern case of *Hussey*[12] it was stated that it would be lawful for a man to kill one who would dispossess him of his home. Even if this were the law at the time, it would seem impossible now to contend that such conduct would be reasonable; for legal redress would be available if the householder were wrongly evicted.

(3) REASONABLE FORCE USED BY ONE WHO DOES NOT KNOW IT TO BE REASONABLE

Suppose that D uses force against P which is unreasonable in the light of the circumstances known to D, but reasonable in the light of all the actual circumstances. This is the problem of *Dadson*,[13] which has been discussed above. It is arguable that the rule in that case is reversed by s. 3 of the Criminal Law Act 1967;[14] D has used only such force as was "reasonable in the circumstances". But this really begs the question, what are the circumstances? Why should not the state of D's mind be a relevant circumstance? Suppose that P, a notorious practical joker, points a gun at D and says, "You have got to die". D believes the gun to be a toy but, being irritated by P's practical jokes, strikes him a fatal blow with a hatchet. It transpires that P's gun was real and loaded and P undoubtedly intended to kill D. All the external circumstances for a defence of self-defence existed—but would it not be remarkable (these facts being proved) if D were guilty of no offence? It would certainly seem to be open

---

[12] (1924), 18 Cr. App. Rep. 160 (C.C.A.).
[13] (1850), 3 Car. & Kir. 148; above, p. 29.
[14] Above, p. 229.

to the court to hold that D's awareness of the facts is one of the relevant circumstances and, as suggested above,[15] considerations of policy might dictate that this
is the right course.

(4) USE OF EXCESSIVE FORCE

If D uses more force than is reasonable in preventing crime or arresting an
offender, then the use of force is plainly unlawful. D will probably be liable to
P in damages; but it does not follow that he is criminally liable. He should be
liable in a criminal court only if he has *mens rea*. It is necessary to distinguish
between the cases (a) where the force used is excessive only because D has made
a mistake of fact, as by supposing that P is armed with a knife when he is not;
and (b) where the force used is excessive because D over-estimates the amount of
force which it is reasonable to use in the known circumstances as (it is submitted)
by supposing that it is reasonable to kill to prevent himself being evicted from
his home.

It is clear that D should not be guilty of an offence where he has made a
reasonable mistake of fact and if, had the facts been as he believed them to be, the
force used would have been reasonable. This would be in accordance with the
principle which governed this question before the Criminal Law Act. But,
where the mistake was unreasonable, the authorities were to the effect that it
could not afford a defence even though, had the supposed facts been true,
the force used would have been reasonable; so in *Rose*[16] LOPES, J., told the jury
explicitly that if D had no reasonable grounds for his belief that his mother's life
was in danger, they should convict him of murder. This accords with the common attitude of the courts to mistakes of fact;[17] but it is again submitted that it
is not in accord with the fundamental principles of *mens rea*. It would be
particularly inappropriate to allow an unreasonable mistake no effect on a charge
of murder, since we have two grades of homicide, and the lower of these, manslaughter, may be committed negligently. An unreasonable mistake is negligence. It is therefore submitted that if D has killed, in the belief, arising from
an unreasonable mistake of fact, that it was necessary to do so to prevent crime
or in self-defence, he should be convicted of manslaughter, if his mistake was a
grossly unreasonable one. Unless his mistake could be said to amount to gross
negligence, he should have a complete defence.

The more difficult question is that which arises where D makes no mistake of
fact, but, having correctly appraised the factual situation, takes the view that it is
reasonable to kill, in circumstances in which no reasonable man could so decide.
He must be guilty at least of manslaughter and it is very arguable that he would
be rightly convicted of murder. His mistake is now one, in effect, of law. He
supposes, for example, that it is reasonable to kill someone trespassing on his
land. This does not seem to differ in principle from the case of the man who
kills a deformed child because he thinks it a reasonable, even a lawful, thing to do.
Such a person is plainly guilty of murder. As a matter of practice and subject to
the Australian developments considered in the next section, it certainly seems
highly likely that the English courts will take the view that an objective standard
of reasonableness must be applied to the situation envisaged in this paragraph.[18]

---

[15] See p. 30.

[16] (1884), 15 Cox C.C. 540   *cf. Weston* (1879), 14 Cox C.C. 346.

[17] Above, p. 129.

[18] *Cf.* Annotations to Criminal Law Act 1967, s. 3, in *Current Law Statutes*, 1967,
where a contrary view was canvassed.

(5) THE EFFECT OF THE DEFENCES[19]

It is clear that if one of the defences now being considered is made out, D is entitled to be acquitted. It is generally assumed in modern English text-books that, if the defence is not made out, D will be convicted of murder. That is, if the use of some force in self-defence or the prevention of crime is justifiable, but D uses excessive force, he is guilty of murder. There is a complete defence or no defence. It has already been suggested that this is an oversimplified view, in that action taken upon an unreasonable mistake of fact should amount at most to manslaughter if the killing would have been reasonable, had the facts been as they were unreasonably supposed to be. Recent authorities in Australia seem to go further and to suggest that killing by excessive force, even where there is no mistake of fact, should be manslaughter and not murder, if some force was justified.

"... if the occasion warrants action in self defence or for the prevention of felony or the apprehension of the felon but the person taking action acts beyond the necessity of the occasion and kills the offender the crime is manslaughter—not murder."[20]

The qualified defence seems to be applicable in Australia in the case of self-defence where (1) D honestly and reasonably thought he was defending himself; and (2) homicide would have been justified if excessive force had not been used; but (3) D used more force than was reasonably necessary. This principle has been mainly applied in self-defence cases,[1] but it originated in *McKay*,[2] which concerned the use of excessive force in the arrest of a felon and the defence of property and it is logical that, if it applies at all, it should apply to any of the defences now being considered.[3]

It is not certain that the Australian rule is also the law of England. In *Hassin*[4] the Court of Criminal Appeal described as "a novelty in present times" a submission that if D exceeded the bounds of self-defence, the proper verdict was manslaughter. It was not necessary to decide the point in that case. However, Hale[5] said that one who exceeded the right of self-defence by standing his ground when he should have retreated, was guilty only of manslaughter; and it was expressly so held in *Odgers*.[6] Moreover, the Australian courts and writers have relied largely on English authorities.[7] Some of these are far from clear and, in particular, several of them probably turned on provocation rather than self-defence.[8] But, allowing for this, it is thought that there is respectable authority

---

[19] See N. Morris "The Slain Chicken Thief" (1958), 2 Sydney L. Rev. 414; and "A New Qualified Defence to Murder" (1960), 1 Adelaide L. Rev. 23; Morris and Howard, *Studies in Criminal Law* (1964), Ch. IV; Howard, [1964] Crim. L.R. 448.
[20] *McKay* (1957), A.L.R. 648 at p. 649, *per* LOWE, J.
[1] *Howe*, [1958] S.A.S.R. 95; (1958), C.L.R. 448; *Bufalo*, [1958] V.R. 363; *Haley* (1959), 76 W.N. (N.S.W.) 550; *Tikos (No. 1)*, [1963] V.R. 285; *Tikos (No. 2)*, [1963] V.R. 306.
[2] [1957] V.R. 560.
[3] It has been argued the principle is of general application and should govern duress, coercion and necessity. Thus, even if duress, coercion and necessity do not afford a complete defence to murder, they might reduce the offence to manslaughter: Morris and Howard, *op. cit.*, 142. The idea is undeniably attractive but it is as yet unsupported by authority.
[4] [1963] Crim. L.R. 852.
[5] 1 P.C. 479.
[6] (1843), 2 Mood. & R. 479.
[7] *Cook* (1639), Cro. Car. 537; *Scully* (1824), 1 C. & P. 319; *Patience* (1837), 7 C. & P. 775; *Whalley* (1835), 7 C. & P. 245; *Allen* (1867), 17 L.T. 222; *Weston* (1879), 14 Cox C.C. 346; *Symondson* (1896), 60 J.P. 645; *Biggin*, [1920] 1 K.B. 213.
[8] For example, *Patience; Weston*.

in favour of the qualified defence in English law and the Australian cases now provide a body of strong persuasive authority.

Against such a rule, however, is the direction in *Rose*[9] that if D's belief that he was defending his mother was unreasonable, he was guilty of murder;[10] and more formidably, *Mancini*.[11] It will be recalled that, in the latter case the judge told the jury that if they believed D's story that he was being attacked with a pen-knife, they should acquit: but he did not tell them that, though they disbelieved this story, the killing might be manslaughter and not murder if D was, in truth defending himself, but by excessive force. The Australian courts have not found *Mancini* to be an obstacle to their doctrine, either because the point was not argued there[12] or because the case was treated as one of a common brawl where there was no room for self defence.[13] It need be no obstacle in the way of the approval of a qualified defence in English law.

4 OFFENCES ANCILLARY TO MURDER

Parliament was not content to leave to the common law the punishment of acts preliminary to murder. The Offences against the Person Act 1861 created offences of conspiracy, solicitation, attempt and threats to murder. The offences of attempt were particularly complicated[14] and, fortunately, have now been repealed by the Criminal Law Act 1967. Attempts to commit murder are now governed by the common law principles discussed above.

(1) CONSPIRACY AND SOLICITATION

By s. 4 of the Offences against the Person Act 1861, it is a misdemeanour punishable with ten years' imprisonment to

> "conspire, confederate and agree to murder any person",

or to

> "solicit, encourage, persuade or endeavour to persuade or . . . propose to any person, to murder any other person."

The first part of this provision adds nothing to the common law of conspiracy except perhaps on a jurisdictional point. It is expressly provided that the person to be murdered need not be a British subject or within the jurisdiction; but this would generally not be necessary at common law either, since murder by a citizen of the United Kingdom and Colonies is indictable here though committed abroad.[15] The section, however, would catch aliens who conspired within the jurisdiction to commit murder abroad and who might otherwise be immune under the rule in *Board of Trade* v. *Owen*.[16]

The second part, subject to the same point concerning jurisdiction, seems to add nothing to the common law of incitement. The offence may be committed

---

[9] (1884), 15 Cox C.C. 540.
[10] Williams submits that that was a misdirection and that it would have been at the most manslaughter: C.L.G.P. 208, n. 6.
[11] Above, p. 212.
[12] (1958), 100 C.L.R. at p. 476.
[13] [1958] S.A.S.R. at pp. 120–121.
[14] See the first edition of this book, pp. 250–253.
[15] Above, p. 181. *Cf.* Greaves's note on the subject in Russell, 612, n. 2.
[16] [1957] A.C. 602; [1957] 1 All E.R. 411; above, p. 158.

by the publication of an article in a newspaper and it is immaterial that the readers of the newspapers are not identified.[17] It seems, however, that the offence is not committed unless the mind of the person solicited, etc., is reached. Lord ALVERSTONE, C.J., so held in *Krause*,[18] applying this limitation even to "endeavour to persuade" which might be thought to cover an unsuccessful attempt to communicate. He held, however, that there was a common law attempt to commit the statutory offence where it was not proved that the offending letters, though sent, had ever reached the addressee.[19] If it is proved that the letter or other publication did reach the addressee, it is not necessary to prove that his mind was in any way affected by it.[20]

In deciding whether the words amount to a solicitation, etc., the jury will take account of (a) the language used; (b) the occasion on which it was used; (c) the persons to whom the words were used, and (d) the circumstances surrounding their use. In *Diamond*,[20] where COLERIDGE, J., so directed in leaving to the jury an article extolling the virtues of the assassins of tyrants, the occasion was just after an attempt on the life of the Viceroy of India, and the persons addressed were not "a debating society of philosophers or divines" but "anybody whom the paper would reach in this country or in Ireland."

The proposed victims need not be named, provided that they are a sufficiently well-defined class. Where the indictment used the words "sovereigns and rulers of Europe" PHILLIMORE, J., thought "rulers" a somewhat vague word, but there were some eighteen or twenty sovereigns in Europe and that was a sufficiently well-defined class.[1]

(2) WRITTEN THREATS TO MURDER

By s. 16 of the Offences against the Person Act 1861 it is an offence punishable with ten years' imprisonment maliciously to,

> "send, deliver or utter[2] or directly or indirectly cause to be received, knowing the contents thereof, any letter or writing threatening to kill or murder any person. . . ."

The term "maliciously" would here seem to rule out any accidental or merely negligent sending, etc., of a letter. It seems probable that actual knowledge of the contents of the letter must be proved[3] but presumably a reckless as well as an intentional sending, etc., would be enough. It was held under an earlier statute that a letter was sent or uttered when it was left by D under a tablecloth where he knew it would be found by the addressee.[4]

The threat may be to murder a person other than the one to whom the letter is sent;[5] and it is immaterial that there is no real intention to carry out the threat.[6] It was said that the word "malicious" implies the

---

[17] *Most* (1881), 7 Q.B.D. 244.
[18] (1902), 66 J.P. 121. Contrast *Horton v. Mead*, below, p. 317.
[19] See also *Banks* (1873), 12 Cox C.C. 393 at p. 399, *per* QUAIN, J.
[20] (1920), 84 J.P. 211; *Most, supra*; *Krause, supra*.
[1] *Antonelli and Barberi* (1905), 70 J.P. 4.
[2] See below, p. 452.
[3] *Cf. Director of Public Prosecutions v. Nieser*, [1959] 1 Q.B. 254; [1958] 3 All E.R. 622.
[4] *Jones* (1851), 5 Cox C.C. 226.
[5] *Syme* (1911), 6 Cr. App. Rep. 257.
[6] *Ibid.*

"doing of that which a person has no legal right to do and his doing it in order to secure some object by means which are improper."[7]

This seems, however, to require an improper motive and it must be doubtful whether the word "maliciously" requires this, in view of *Cunningham*.[8] It is submitted that the offence would be committed whatever the object of sender and even if he had no object in view. Since murder, by definition, is never justifiable it seems unnecessary to seek some ulterior evil motive.

It is somewhat curious that written threats to murder should be made thus severely punishable where there is no penalty for oral threats to murder unless they amount to a common assault.[9] The latter are likely to be the more terrifying since the necessary proximity of the threatener means that there will usually be an immediate possibility of the threat being fulfilled.

(3) CONCEALMENT OF BIRTH

This offence when first created by statute in 1623[10] was limited to (i) an illegiti-mate child who (ii) was born alive and whose body was disposed of so as to conceal its death (iii) by its mother. The current statute, the Offences against the Person Act 1861, s. 60, is subject to none of these limitations; it applies to any child, legitimate or not and whether born alive or not, whose body is disposed of so as to conceal its birth, by anyone. The section provides:

"If any woman shall be delivered of a child, every person who shall, by any secret disposition of the dead body of the said child, whether such child died before, at, or after its birth, endeavour to conceal the birth thereof, shall be guilty of a misdemeanour, and being convicted thereof shall be liable, at the discretion of the court, to be imprisoned for any term not exceeding two years. . . ."

The expressed object of the original statute was to catch those women who would otherwise escape on a murder charge through the difficulty of proving live-birth and it was provided, indeed, that the woman should suffer death as in the case of murder. Under a later Act,[11] which repealed the 1623 provision, con-viction of the new offence thereby created was possible only after an acquittal on an indictment for murder; but the current offence is an independent substantive crime for which an indictment will lie in the first instance. It was formerly the law that a person acquitted of murder, infanticide or child destruction might be convicted, on the same indictment, of concealment of birth; but this rule was abolished by the Criminal Law Act 1967, Sch. 2.

The test of a "secret disposition" seems to be whether there was a likelihood that the body would be found. So, said BOVILL, C.J., it would be a secret dis-position

"if the body were placed in the middle of a moor in the winter, or on the top of a mountain, or in any other secluded place, where the body would not be likely to be found."[12]

---

[7] DARLING, J., approved by the C.C.A. (1911), 6 Cr. App. Rep. at p. 260.
[8] Above, p. 74.
[9] Below, p. 249.
[10] 21 Jac. 1. c. 27.
[11] 43 Geo. 3 c. 58.
[12] *Brown* (1870), L.R. 1 C.C.R. 244.

If a body were thrown from a cliff top to the sea-shore, it might be a secret disposition if the place were secluded, not if it were much frequented.[13] So where the body was left in a closed but unlocked box in D's bedroom in such a way as to attract the attention of those who daily entered the room, it was held that there was no secret disposition.[14]

The accused must be proved to have done some act of disposition after the child has died. If the living body of the child is concealed and thereafter dies in the place of concealment, this offence is not committed,[15] though it is probable that murder or manslaughter is. Where it is uncertain whether the child died before or after the concealment the safe course would be to indict for murder, since a conviction for either manslaughter (if malice aforethought were not proved) or concealment (if death before concealment were not proved) would be appropriate on that indictment.

According to ERLE, J., in *Berriman*[16] the child must have

> "arrived at that stage of maturity at the time of birth that it might have been a living child";

so that the concealment of a foetus but a few months old would be no offence.[17]

(4) OTHER OFFENCES

It is a common law misdemeanour to dispose of or destroy a dead body with intent to prevent an inquest from being held.[18] It is an offence under the Perjury Act 1911 wilfully to make a false statement relating to births or deaths, or the live birth of a child.[19] And it is a summary offence under the Births and Deaths Registration Act 1953, s. 36, to fail to give information concerning births and deaths when under a duty, as defined in that Act, to do so.

5 COMPLICITY IN SUICIDE AND SUICIDE PACTS[20]

It was felony at common law for a sane person of the age of responsibility to kill himself either intentionally or in the course of trying to kill another.[1] Such a suicide was regarded as self-murder. Though the offender was, in the nature of things, personally beyond the reach of the law, his guilt was not without important consequences at common law, since it resulted in the forfeiture of his property. The results were more important, however, where the attempt failed, for then:

---

[13] *Ibid.*

[14] *George* (1868), 11 Cox C.C. 41. *Cf. Sleep* (1864), 9 Cox C.C. 559; *Rosenburg* (1906), 70 J.P. 264.

[15] *Coxhead* (1845), 1 Car. & Kir. 623 (decided under Geo. 4, c. 31, but the principle is the same); *May* (1867), 10 Cox C.C. 448.

[16] (1854), 6 Cox C.C. 388 at p. 390.

[17] *Colmer* (1864), 9 Cox C.C. 506 is to the contrary but is doubted by Russell, 611, n. 69 and Archbold, § 2607.

[18] Below, p. 514.

[19] Below, p. 511.

[20] For general discussions, see Williams, *The Sanctity of Life*, Ch. 7; St. John Stevas, *Life, Death and the Law*, Ch. 6; Second Report of the Criminal Law Revision Committee, Cmd. 1187 (1960).

[1] Hawkins, 1 P.C. 77.

(i) Since D had attempted to commit a felony he was guilty, under ordinary common law principles, of the misdemeanour of attempted suicide.[2]

(ii) If D, in the course of trying to kill himself, killed another, he was guilty of murder under the doctrine of transferred malice.[3]

Though suicide was regarded as "not a very serious crime",[4] an intention to commit it was thus the *mens rea* of murder. Moreover, one who was an accessory or principal in the second degree to the suicide of another was likewise guilty of murder as a secondary party. It followed that the survivor of a suicide pact was also guilty of murder, for, even if he did not actually kill, he was an aider and abettor, or at least an accessory before the fact to the other party's self-murder.

Suicide has now ceased to be a crime by virtue of the Suicide Act 1961 which simply provides that

> "The rule of law whereby it is a crime for a person to commit suicide is hereby abrogated."

It inevitably follows that (i) attempted suicide has also now ceased to be criminal; and (ii) that there is no room for the doctrine of transferred malice where D kills P in the course of trying to kill himself, for there is no malice to transfer.

In the latter case, D's liability will now depend on the general principles of murder and manslaughter. Thus, if the death of P were utterly unforeseeable, it would be accidental death; if a reasonable man would certainly have foreseen the likelihood of killing (or, perhaps, seriously injuring) another, it will probably be manslaughter; and if D himself foresaw this, it may be murder.[5]

(1) COMPLICITY IN ANOTHER'S SUICIDE

Section 2 of the Suicide Act creates a new offence:

> "A person who aids, abets, counsels or procures the suicide of another or an attempt by another to commit suicide, shall be liable on conviction on indictment to imprisonment for a term not exceeding fourteen years."

This establishes, in effect, that one can be a secondary party to a suicide, though there cannot any longer be a principal offender[6]. The discussion, above,[7] of counselling and abetting as modes of participating in crime would seem to be applicable to this section.

There were very sound reasons for the abolition of the felony of suicide. The felon was beyond the reach of punishment; the legal sanction was not an effective deterrent—there were some 5,000 suicides a year; and the effect was merely to add to the distress and pain of the bereaved relatives. The most important practical effect of the Act, however, was its repeal by implication of the crime of attempted suicide. This also recognised the realities of the situation for it had been the practice for many years to institute proceedings only where it was

---

[2] Not the felony of attempted murder under Offences against the Person Act 1861, s. 15: *Burgess* (1862), 9 Cox C.C. 247; *Mann*, [1914] 2 K.B. 107. Section 15 has been repealed by the Criminal Law Act 1967.
[3] *Hopwood* (1913), 8 Cr. App. Rep. 143; *Spence* (1957), 41 Cr. App. Rep. 80. Above, p. 44.
[4] *French* (1955), 39 Cr. App. Rep. 192, *per* Lord GODDARD, C.J.
[5] See above, p. 199.
[6] *Cf.* the words of the Accessories and Abettors Act 1861, ss. 2, 8, and the Magistrates' Courts Act 1952, s. 35.
[7] See pp. 81 *et seq.*

necessary for the accused's protection, for example, because no relatives and friends were willing to give help. Thus, in 1959, of a total of 4,980 suicide attempts known to the police (and an estimated total of 25,000 actual attempts concealed from the police) only 518 prosecutions were brought. The protection of the attempter may now be secured under Part IV of the Mental Health Act 1959.

The new crime of complicity in suicide is one which covers a variety of situations varying almost infinitely in moral culpability; from D who encourages P to suicide for the purpose of inheriting his property, to that of D who merely supplies a deadly drug to a suffering and dying P who is anxious to accelerate the end. In order to achieve consistency in the bringing of prosecutions, this is made one of those crimes in which the consent of the Director of Public Prosecutions is required.[8]

(2) SUICIDE PACTS

A party to a suicide pact who aids, abets, counsels or procures the other party to commit suicide is of course guilty of the offence under s. 2 of the Suicide Act.[9]

The survivor of such a pact may, however, have either himself killed the deceased or have procured a third party to do it. Such cases do not fall within the Suicide Act, but within the Homicide Act 1957, s. 4 (1), which, as amended by the Suicide Act provides:

> "It shall be manslaughter and shall not be murder for a person acting in pursuance of a suicide pact between him and another to kill the other or be party to the other being killed by a third person."

"Suicide pact" is defined by s. 4 (3) of the Homicide Act as

> "a common agreement between two or more persons having for its object the death of all of them, whether or not each is to take his own life, but nothing done by a person who enters into a suicide pact shall be treated as done by him in pursuance of the pact unless it is done while he has the settled intention of dying in pursuance of the pact."

The onus on a charge of murder of establishing the defence of suicide pact is put by s. 4 (2) on the accused and the standard of proof required is, no doubt, a balance of probabilities.

The distinction between complicity in suicide and manslaughter by suicide pact is not entirely satisfactory. The latter, being punishable with life imprisonment, is evidently the more serious crime; yet, since the person guilty of it always intends to die himself, it is difficult to see how it can compare in moral heinousness with the case of D who incites P to die in order that he may live and enjoy P's property.

The distinction between the two crimes will frequently be very fine. If D and P agree to gas themselves and D alone survives, it appears that he will be liable under the Homicide Act if he turned on the tap[10] and under the Suicide Act if P did. It may frequently be difficult to establish who did such an act and this is recognised by the provision in s. 2 (2) of the Suicide Act that, on the trial of an indictment for murder or manslaughter, the jury may find the accused

---

[8] Williams argues in favour of the legalisation of the abetting of a suicide for unselfish reasons: *The Sanctity of Life*, 271–276.

[9] Until the enactment of the Suicide Act, this was manslaughter under the Homicide Act 1957, s. 4.

[10] But if D pours out a glass of poison and P takes it, he will be liable under the Suicide Act.

guilty of complicity in suicide if that is proved. If D is charged with murder and he establishes on a balance of probabilities that P committed suicide in pursuance of a suicide pact he is entitled to be acquitted of murder and may presumably be convicted of complicity in suicide since he has, in effect, admitted his guilt. If, however, D were charged with complicity and it appeared that he had killed P, he would have to be acquitted.

6 INFANTICIDE[11]

The Infanticide Act 1938, s. 1 (1), provides:

> "Where a woman by any wilful act or omission causes the death of her child being a child under the age of twelve months, but at the time of the act or omission the balance of her mind was disturbed by reason of her not having fully recovered from the effect of giving birth to the child or by reason of the effect of lactation consequent upon the birth of the child, then, notwithstanding that the circumstances were such that but for this Act the offence would have amounted to murder, she shall be guilty of [an offence], to wit of infanticide, and may for such offence be dealt with and punished as if she had been guilty of the offence of manslaughter of the child."

This enactment replaces a statute of 1922 which confined the defence to a "newly-born" child, a term which the Court of Criminal Appeal had held to be inapplicable to a child of thirty-five days, so that the mother was convicted of murder.[12] The 1922 Act was itself the result of an agitation over very many years during which it was practically impossible to get convictions of murder by mothers of their young children because of the disapproval of public and professional opinion of a law which regarded such killings as ordinary murders. Where a conviction was obtained, the judge had to pronounce a sentence of death which everyone, except perhaps the prisoner, knew would not be carried out. A number of reasons were advanced why infanticide should be considered less reprehensible than other killings: (i) The injury done to the child was less, for it was incapable of the kind of suffering which might be undergone by the adult victim of a murder; (ii) the loss of its family was less great; (iii) the crime did not create the sense of insecurity in society which other murders caused; (iv) generally, the heinousness of the crime was less, the motive very frequently being the concealment of the shame of the birth of an illegitimate child; and (v), where the killing is done by the mother, her responsibility may be reduced by the disturbance of her mind caused by the stress of the birth. It is, of course, the last of these considerations which is the governing one in the present legislation. The killing of an infant by persons other than the mother, or by the mother if the balance of her mind is not disturbed, remains murder.

The Act provides by s. 1 (2) that a woman indicted for the murder of her child under the age of twelve months may be acquitted of murder and convicted of manslaughter if the conditions of s. 1 (1) are satisfied.

Where the charge is murder, an evidential burden on the issue of disturbance will fall on D; but the onus of *proof* remains with the Crown. Where the charge is infanticide, the onus of proving disturbance appears to be on the Crown; but this, of course, is unlikely to be contested.

---

[11] Seaborne Davies, "Child-Killing in English Law" (1937), 1 M.L.R. 203; M.A.C.L. 301; Williams, *The Sanctity of Life*, 25–45.
[12] *O'Donoghue* (1927), 20 Cr. App. Rep. 132.

The Act has been criticised by Williams[13] on the ground that:

"it may be said to be an illogical compromise between the law of murder and humane feeling. It recognises the inadequacy of the present law of insanity for the case of infanticide, and has the advantage of sparing the woman the agnony of a murder trial where there are strong circumstances of mitigation. Yet it allows the conviction of a woman who may in fact have been afflicted by puerperal mania, a real temporary insanity. If the woman was insane, the verdict should be one of insanity and conviction should be out of the question."

This may be thought to be a criticism of the general law relating to insanity rather than of this particular rule. Williams also expresses regret that "the Act was not extended to cover the mother who, deranged by the birth of a child, thereupon kills an older child.[14] The mother's responsibility is presumably diminished in a similar way in this situation as in that contemplated by the Act, but it may be that the other considerations referred to above justify a distinction between the killing of the new-born child and that of other children. But the general defence to murder of diminished responsibility is, in any case, available where the circumstances warrant.

7 CHILD DESTRUCTION AND ABORTION[15]

(1) CHILD DESTRUCTION

It has already been observed that it is not murder to kill a child in the womb or while in the process of being born.[16] Though the killing of the child in these circumstances appears to have been a misdemeanour at common law, the present law on the subject is statutory. Section 58 of the Offences against the Person Act 1861 (subject to the Abortion Act 1967[17]) prohibits attempts to procure miscarriage from any time after the conception of the child until its birth; and s. 1 of the Infant Life (Preservation) Act 1929 prohibits the killing of any child which is capable of being born alive. The two offences thus overlap. The latter provision reads:

"(1) Subject as hereinafter in this subsection provided, any person who, with intent to destroy the life of a child capable of being born alive, by any wilful act causes a child to die before it has an existence independent of its mother, shall be guilty of an offence, to wit, of child destruction, and shall be liable on conviction thereof on indictment to imprisonment for life: Provided that no person shall be found guilty of an offence under this section unless it is proved that the act which caused the death of the child was not done in good faith for the purpose only of preserving the life of the mother.

(2) For the purposes of this Act, evidence that a woman had at any material time been pregnant for a period of twenty-eight weeks or more shall be *prima facie* proof that she was at that time pregnant of a child capable of being born alive."

The jury may convict of this offence on an indictment for murder, manslaughter, infanticide or an offence under s. 58 of the Offences against the Person Act 1861; and on an indictment for child destruction, they may convict of an offence under s. 58 of the Offences against the Person Act 1861.

---

[13] *The Sanctity of Life* at 37.
[14] *Op. cit.*, 39.
[15] See Williams, *The Sanctity of Life and the Criminal Law*, 139–223 (1958), and "The Legalization of Medical Abortion" *The Eugenics Review*, April, 1964; B. M. Dickens, *Abortion and the Law* (1966).
[16] See above, p. 182.
[17] See below, p. 246.

The Abortion Act 1967 now legalises abortion in certain circumstances and subject to certain formalities, but it is provided that this shall not affect the offence of child destruction. Where a viable foetus is destroyed, it is no defence to show that the conditions prescribed in the 1967 Act were satisfied. Conversely, if the formalities prescribed by the 1967 Act are not complied with, it may be no defence to a charge under s. 58 of the Offences against the Person Act to show that the act was done in good faith for the purpose only of preserving the life of the mother. Where the foetus is viable, it is safe to procure an abortion only if both (a) the conditions of the 1967 Act are satisfied and (b) it is done in good faith for the purpose only of preserving the life of the mother.

A wider meaning was given to the words "for the purpose only of preserving the life of the mother", by MACNAGHTEN, J., in *Bourne*.[18] This was *obiter*, so far as the Infant Life Preservation Act was concerned, since the charge was brought under the Offences against the Person Act 1861; but MACNAGHTEN, J., took the view that those words represented the common law and were implicit in the 1861 Act by virtue of the word "unlawfully". He said:

> "As I have said, I think those words ['for the purpose of preserving the life of the mother'] ought to be construed in a reasonable sense, and if the doctor is of opinion, on reasonable grounds and with adequate knowledge, that the probable consequence of the continuance of the pregnancy will be to make the woman a physical or mental wreck, the jury are quite entitled to take the view that the doctor who under these circumstances and in that honest belief, operates, is operating for the purpose of preserving the life of the mother."[19]

Both before and after this, however, the judge stressed that the test was whether the operation was performed in good faith for the purpose of preserving the *life* of the girl and the passage may be intended to refer only to such injuries to health as will shorten life for the judge had said:[20]

> ". . . life depends upon health and health may be so gravely impaired that death results."

Informed medical opinion construed the judgment in the wider sense[1] and this appears to have been vindicated. In *Bergmann and Ferguson*[2] MORRIS, J., is reported to have said that the court will not look too narrowly into the question of danger to life where danger to health is anticipated. Then in *Newton and Stungo*[3] ASHWORTH, J., stated in his direction to the jury:

> "Such use of an instrument is unlawful unless the use is made in good faith for the purposes of preserving the life *or health* of the woman",

adding that this included mental as well as physical health. Newton was acquitted of manslaughter by criminal negligence, but convicted of manslaughter by unlawfully using an instrument[4] and of the offence under s. 58. He did not appeal (obviously the direction was favourable to him) and we thus have no appellate ruling on the question; but it is thought likely that ASHWORTH, J.'s view would be accepted by the appellate courts.

---

[18] [1939] 1 K.B. 687; [1938] 3 All E.R. 615.
[19] [1939] 1 K.B. at pp. 693, 694; [1938] 3 All E.R. at p. 619.
[20] [1939] 1 K.B. at p. 692; [1938] 3 All E.R. at p. 617.
[1] Havard, [1958] Crim. L.R. at p. 605.
[2] 1948 (unreported); *The Sanctity of Life*, 154; 1 B.M.J. 1008.
[3] [1958] Crim. L.R. 469, fully considered by Havard in "Therapeutic Abortion", [1958] Crim. L.R. 600.
[4] That is, constructive manslaughter; see above, p. 221.

The criterion of the defence as it has been applied by the courts is a subjective one; that is, the question is not whether the operation is in fact necessary to preserve the life of the mother but whether D believes it to be necessary.[5] In answering this question the court will take account of the size of the fee, a large fee being evidence of bad faith;[6] and whether D followed accepted medical practice.[7] What is the position if the operation was in fact necessary, but was performed by D in bad faith, to oblige, as he thought, the mere convenience of the woman and for a high fee? One view might be that there is no *actus reus* here,[8] but it is thought more likely that the defence will be limited to the case of a *bona fide* belief.[9] Thus, in *Newton* it does not seem to have been decided that an operation was unnecessary; only that Newton did not *bona fide* believe it to be necessary.[10]

These cases all relate to s. 58 of the 1861 Act, where they are probably no longer in point.[11] Since they purport to be an interpretation of the proviso in the 1929 Act, however, they cannot be ignored in considering child destruction. On the other hand it is quite possible that the court, when actually confronted with the interpretation of the proviso, might take a stricter and narrower view of what constitutes the preservation of the life of the mother.

(2) ATTEMPTING TO PROCURE MISCARRIAGE

The common law misdemeanour of abortion applied only after the child had quickened in the womb. To procure an abortion before this occurred was no crime. A statute of 1803[12] enacted that it should be a felony punishable by death to administer a poison with intent to procure the miscarriage of a woman quick with child and a felony punishable with imprisonment or transportation for fourteen years to administer poison with a like intent to a woman who was not proved to be quick with child. The distinction between quick and non-quick women gave rise to complications and it disappeared in the re-enactment of the law by the Offences against the Person Act 1839[13] which established the law in substantially in its modern form. The current statute is the Offences against the Person Act 1861, which provides by s. 58:

"Every woman being with child who, with intent to procure her own miscarriage, shall unlawfully administer to herself any poison or other noxious thing, or shall unlawfully use any instrument or other means whatsoever with the like intent, and whosoever, with intent to procure the miscarriage of any woman, whether she be or be not with child, shall unlawfully administer to her

---

[5] *Bergmann and Ferguson* cited in *The Sanctity of Life*, 165.
[6] A significant difference between the case of Newton and that of Stungo (who was acquitted) seems to have been that Stungo took a very small fee, Newton a high one.
[7] See Havard, [1958] Crim. L.R. at pp. 607, 608.
[8] *Cf.* The discussion of *Dadson*, above, p. 29 and p. 231.
[9] *Cf.* Williams, *The Sanctity of Life*, 166, who would agree with this conclusion on the ground that the crime is in the nature of an attempt. But it is just as much a substantive crime as burglary.
[10] But even if it was necessary to carry out the operation, it was probably not necessary to carry it out in the way it was done—in a consulting room, the patient being sent back to a hotel in a taxi afterwards.
[11] *Infra.*
[12] 43 Geo. III. c. 58.
[13] 1 Vic. c. 85.

or cause to be taken by her any poison or other noxious thing, or shall unlawfully use any instrument or other means whatsoever with the like intent, shall
be guilty of an offence, and being convicted thereof shall be liable . . . to
imprisonment for life. . . ."

The extension of the law was of great practical importance, since most self-
induced abortions occur before quickening.

The statute makes it clear beyond all doubt that the offence may be committed by the woman herself as well as by others, the only distinction being that
if the woman herself is charged, it must be proved that she is in fact pregnant,
whereas this is not necessary if the accused is someone other than the mother
herself.

The Act is not confined to the use of a "poison or other noxious thing" or
"any instrument"; the "other means" include manual interference, even though
no instrument is employed and the medical evidence is that the act could not, in
the circumstances, cause a miscarriage.[14]   The *actus reus* consists simply in the
administration of the poison or other noxious thing or the *use* of the instrument or
other means.

The Act distinguishes between "poison" and "noxious thing" and it has been
held that in the case of something other than a "recognised poison" the thing
must be administered in such quantity as to be in fact harmful though not
necessarily abortifacient.[15]   A sleeping pill has been held not to be noxious;[16]
and the administration in harmless quantities of oil of juniper was no *actus reus*;[17]
but DENMAN, J., said that it would be otherwise if a thing, innocuous when
administered in small quantities, were to be administered in such quantities as
to be noxious.   FIELD and STEPHEN, JJ., thought that if the thing were a "recognised poison" the offence might be committed even though the quantity given
was so small as to be incapable of doing harm.   The distinction is hardly a logical
one for "recognised poisons" may be beneficial when taken in small quantities
and in such a case the thing taken is no more poisonous than the oil of juniper
was noxious.   According to one view,[18] the accused in these cases might have
been convicted of an attempt to administer a noxious thing; but this view does
not seem, at least until recently, to have commended itself to the courts.

It has been observed that the section makes a distinction between the case
where the woman administers, etc., the thing to herself and that where it is
administered to her by another.   In the former case the woman must be proved
to be with child, in the latter case, she need not.   The importance of this distinction has been diminished by the decision in *Whitchurch*[19] that a woman who
is not pregnant may be convicted of conspiring with another to procure her own
abortion and in the decision in *Sockett* that such a woman[20] may be convicted of
aiding and abetting in the offence of the other, if it is complete.   Thus, in effect,
the woman will be excused on the ground that she is not with child only in cases
where she is not acting in concert with another.   While one view is that this interpretation has "set at naught" the intention of Parliament,[1] it has been argued

---

[14] *Spicer*, [1955] Crim. L.R. 772.
[15] *Marlow* (1964), 49 Cr. App. Rep. 49 (BRABIN, J.); *Douglas*, [1966] N.Z.L.R. 45.
[16] *Weatherall*, [1968] Crim. L.R. 115 (Judge BRODRICK).
[17] *Cramp* (1880), 5 Q.B.D. 307.
[18] Above, p. 173. *Cf. Perry* (1847), 2 Cox C.C. 223; *Isaacs* (1862), 32 L.J.M.C. 52;
Hennah (1877), 13 Cox C.C. 547.
[19] (1890), 24 Q.B.D. 420; above, p. 156.
[20] (1908), 72 J.P. 428; above, p. 97.
[1] Williams, C.L.G.P., 673.

elsewhere[2] that it would have been perfectly reasonable for Parliament to discriminate between the non-pregnant woman who calls in the back-street or professional abortionist and the non-pregnant woman who administers to herself an abortifacient in the solitude of her own bedroom. The point is perhaps not of great practical importance as it appears that it is not the practice to prosecute the mother today.[3]

(3) KNOWINGLY SUPPLYING OR PROCURING POISON, ETC.

Section 59 of the Offences against the Person Act makes a substantive crime of certain preparatory acts, some of which might amount to counselling or abetting the offence under s. 58. It provides:

> "Whosoever shall unlawfully supply or procure any poison or other noxious thing, or any instrument or thing whatsoever, knowing that the same is intended to be unlawfully used or employed with intent to procure the miscarriage of any woman, whether she be or be not with child, shall be guilty of a misdemeanour, and being convicted thereof shall be liable . . . to imprisonment . . . for any term not exceeding five years . . ."

It has recently been held[4] that the word "procure", on the first occasion on which it is used in the section, means "get possession of something of which you have not got possession already"; so D's conviction was quashed when there was no evidence as to how or when he had come into the possession of the instruments and the judge had directed the jury that the word was

> "wide enough to include getting instruments or getting them together or preparing them for use".[5]

This leaves a gap in the legislation. As Crown counsel said:[6]

> ". . . if a defendant went to a chemist and bought an instrument to abort A, he would have committed an offence, but if he then put the instrument away in a cupboard and later, for the purpose of aborting B went to the cupboard and took the instrument he would not have committed an offence."

The words, "knowing that the same is intended to be unlawfully used" have been construed in an extraordinarily wide sense and one highly unfavourable to the accused. Their natural meaning is surely that some person other than the accused must intend the unlawful user and that the accused must know of that intention. But it has been held that it is enough if the accused *believes* that the poison, etc., is to be so used, so that it is no defence for him to show that the person supplied did not intend to use it[7] or that the person supplied was a policeman who had obtained the thing by false representations about a purely fictitious woman.[8] This construction was defended by ERLE, C.J., the rest of the Court concurring, on the extraordinary ground that

---

[2] Hogan, [1962] Crim. L.R. at p. 690.
[3] *Cf. The Sanctity of Life* at p. 146; *Peake* (1932), 97 J.P.N. 353.
[4] *Mills,* [1963] 1 Q.B. 522; [1963] 1 All E.R. 202, following *Scully* (1903), 23 N.Z.L.R. 380.
[5] [1963] 1 Q.B. at p. 524.
[6] [1963] 1 Q.B. at p. 526.
[7] *Hillman* (1863), 9 Cox C.C. 386 (C.C.R.).
[8] *Titley* (1880), 14 Cox C.C. 502 (STEPHEN, J.).

"The defendant knew what his own intention was, and that was that the substance procured by him should be employed with intent to procure miscarriage."[9]

This attitude contrasts strikingly with the strict construction of the word "procure"; and these two cases, which have been dissented from in Victoria,[10] though followed elsewhere in the Commonwealth,[11] deserve re-consideration.

(4) THE ABORTION ACT 1967[12]

The law relating to abortion is modified in important respects by the Abortion Act 1967. In the Act:

"'the law relating to abortion' means ss. 58 and 59 of the Offences against the Person Act 1861, and any rule of law relating to the procurement of abortion."

Section 1 of the Act provides:

1 Medical termination of pregnancy.—(1) Subject to the provisions of this section, a person shall not be guilty of an offence under the law relating to abortion when a pregnancy is terminated by a registered medical practitioner if two registered medical practioners are of the opinion, formed in good faith—

(a) that the continuance of the pregnancy would involve risk to the life of the pregnant woman, or of injury to the physical or mental health of the pregnant woman or any existing children of her family, greater than if the pregnancy were terminated; or

(b) that there is a substantial risk that if the child were born it would suffer from such physical or mental abnormalities as to be seriously handicapped.

(2) In determining whether the continuance of a pregnancy would involve such risk of injury to health as is mentioned in paragraph (a) of subsection (1) of this section, account may be taken of the pregnant woman's actual or reasonably foreseeable environment.

(3) Except as provided by subsection (4) of this section, any treatment for the termination of pregnancy must be carried out in a hospital vested in the Minister of Health or the Secretary of State under the National Health Service Acts, or in a place for the time being approved for the purposes of this section by the said Minister or the Secretary of State.

(4) Subsection (3) of this section, and so much of subsection (1) as relates to the opinion of two registered medical practitioners, shall not apply to the termination of a pregnancy by a registered medical practitioner in a case where he is of the opinion, formed in good faith, that the termination is immediately necessary to save the life or to prevent grave permanent injury to the physical or mental health of the pregnant woman.

Section 2 of the Act gives the Minister of Health powers to require the opinion of medical practitioners to be certified in a particular form and notice of the termination of pregnancy and other information to be given.

The defences provided by the Act are available "when a pregnancy is terminated". It has been argued[13] that it follows that an offence will be committed if an abortion operation is left unfinished or if the woman is not pregnant. This can

---

[9] (1863), 9 Cox C.C. at p. 387.
[10] *Hyland* (1898), 24 V. L.R. 101.
[11] *Scully* (1903), 23 N.Z.L.R. 380; *Nosworthy* (1907), 26 N.Z.L.R. 536; *Neil*, [1909] St. R. Qd. 225; *Freestone*, [1913] T.P.D. 758; *Irwin* v. *R.* (1968), 68 D.L.R. (2d) 485.
[12] See Hoggett, "The Abortion Act 1967", [1968] Crim. L.R. 247: *A Guide to the Abortion Act* 1967 (Abortion Law Reform Association).
[13] By Hoggett, [1968] Crim. L.R. at p. 256.

hardly be so, since, if the conditions of the Act are otherwise fulfilled, the steps taken to procure abortion are taken without *mens rea*—there is no intent *unlawfully* to adminster anything or *unlawfully* to use any instrument. But apart from the question of *mens rea*, it is submitted that there can be no offence; the legalisation of an abortion must include the steps which are taken towards it. Are we really to say that these are criminal until the operation is complete, when they are retrospectively authorised or alternatively that they are lawful until the operation is discontinued or the woman is discovered not to be pregnant when, retrospectively, they become unlawful? When the conditions of the Act are otherwise satisfied, it is submitted that D is not unlawfully administering, etc., and that this is so whether the pregnancy be actually terminated or not.

Section 1 (1) (*a*) clearly affords a greater protection than did *Bourne*. Indeed, on a literal reading, it could justify the termination of most pregnancies in their early stages, since some risk is necessarily involved in child bearing whereas the risks involved in an abortion operation at this stage are very slight.[14] The Act also allows the interests of the children of the woman's family to be taken into account for the first time. These expressions are not defined in the Act, but it has been argued[15] that "family" means the sociological and not the legal unit, so as to include illegitimate children and perhaps children who have been accepted as members of the family. The view has been expressed[16] that a person over twenty-one could be a child of the family for this purpose if, for example, he were severely subnormal. The eugenic justification for abortion provided by s. 1 (1) (*b*) is also an innovation in the law. It presents difficulties of interpretation as to what is a "substantial risk" and when physical and mental abnormalities amount to serious handicaps. While these questions must be of great concern to the medical profession, it is perhaps unlikely that they will require consideration by the courts.

By s. 5 (2) of the Abortion Act:

> "For the purposes of the law relating to abortion, anything done with intent to procure the miscarriage of a woman is unlawfully done unless authorised by section 1 of this Act."

It seems clear that this is intended entirely to supersede the law as laid down in *Bourne*.[17] Abortions, and the steps to procure them which are proscribed, are unlawful unless they can be justified by the 1967 Act. It is submitted, however, that this provision cannot have been intended entirely to eliminate the operation of general defences to crime. To take extreme examples, a child under the age of ten or a person within the M'Naghten rules could surely not be convicted of committing or, (slightly more likely) abetting an abortion. If this be conceded, then duress ought equally to operate as a defence; and if duress, why not necessity? And so we are back to admitting *Bourne's* case into the law. A possible interpretation of the Act would be to allow general defences, other than necessity. Construing s. 5 (2) in the light of the previous law, a court might conclude that its obvious purpose was to overrule *Bourne*; and that it would be unreasonable to extend its operation beyond that.

A limited defence of necessity would seem desirable in principle. The defence

---

[14] ". . . it follows that a pregnancy may lawfully be terminated in order to secure a relatively small improvement in the woman's medical condition": *A Guide to the Abortion Act 1967*, p. 11.

[15] Hoggett, *op. cit.* at 249; *A Guide to the Abortion Act 1967*, p. 6.

[16] *Ibid.*

[17] Above, p. 242.

would necessarily be limited in scope by the fact that, in the great majority of cases where it is necessary to procure an abortion, this is lawful by statute so that there is no room for the operation of any broader defence. But suppose that a qualified doctor who is not a registered medical practitioner and so does not come within the terms of s. 1 (4) above, forms the opinion in good faith that immediate termination of a pregnancy is necessary in order to save the life of the mother who is in a remote place and beyond the help of any registered medical practitioner. Is it the law that he must let the woman die when he could save her by terminating the pregnancy?

In *Bourne* MACNAGHTEN, J., took the view that there was not only a right but a duty to perform the operation where a woman's life could be saved only by the doctor procuring an abortion:

". . . if a case arose where the life of a woman could be saved by performing the operation and the doctor refused to perform it because of his religious opinions and the woman died, he would be in grave peril of being brought before this court on a charge of manslaughter by negligence. He would have no better defence than a person who, again from some religious reason, refused to call in a doctor to attend his sick child, where a doctor could have been called in and the life of the child could have been saved."[18]

Section 4 of the Abortion Act now provides:

"(1) Subject to subsection (2) of this section, no person shall be under any duty, whether by contract or by any statutory or other legal requirement, to participate in any treatment authorised by this Act to which he has a conscientious objection:

Provided that in any legal proceedings the burden of proof of conscientious objection shall rest on the person claiming to rely on it."

(2) Nothing in subsection (1) of this section shall affect any duty to participate in treatment which is necessary to save the life or to prevent grave permanent injury to the physical or mental health of a pregnant woman."

Section 4 (2) does not create any duty, but it does appear to recognise at least the possibility of a duty at common law. The only authority for this appears to be *Bourne*. It will be noted that MACNAGHTEN, J., dealt only with the case where the woman died, whereas the Act refers to grave permanent injury to physical or mental health. MACNAGHTEN, J., appeared to regard the doctor's liability as one arising from gross negligence; and this is indeed confined to cases where death is caused.[19] There is no general criminal liability for causing grievous bodily harm by gross negligence as distinct from recklessness. If, however, the doctor is under a duty to act, and he knows all the circumstances giving rise to that duty and foresees the consequences of not fulfilling it, it would seem that he has the *mens rea* necessary to found a conviction for causing grievous bodily harm contrary to s. 18 of the Offences against the Person Act.[20] The only doubtful link in this argument appears to be the existence of the duty; but the Act strengthens the case for its existence. Clearly, a doctor with conscientious objections could fulfil his duty by referring the patient to another doctor who does not have such objections; and it is submitted that the doctor has a duty to do this, where an abortion is necessary to save the woman from death or grave permanent injury. The question of a duty to participate in the operation can arise only where there is no effective substitute for the doctor concerned. Where the patient has conscientious objections there can be no duty to perform the operation since, clearly, it can only be lawfully performed with consent.

---

[18] [1939] 1 K.B. at p. 693; [1939] 3 All E.R. at p. 618.
[19] Above, p. 227, footnote 16.
[20] Below, p. 264.

CHAPTER 12

Non-Fatal Offences against the Person

1 ASSAULT AND BATTERY[1]

Assault and Battery are two distinct crimes at common law;[2] but it is common in ordinary usage, and even in statutes, to use the term "assault" to cover both. By s. 47 of the Offences against the Person Act 1861 a "common assault", which includes battery, is punishable on indictment with one year's imprisonment; and by s. 42, it is punishable on summary conviction with two months' imprisonment or a fine not exceeding five pounds.

By s. 43, a common assault on a male child under fourteen[3] or any female[4] is punishable on summary conviction with six months' imprisonment or a fine not exceeding twenty pounds, if the justices think the offence is of so aggravated a nature that it cannot be sufficiently punished under s. 42. "Aggravated" here means aggravated in some way which does not amount to a distinct offence recognised by the law, and does not include rape, an assault with intent to rape or an indecent assault.[5]

An assault is any act by which D, intentionally or (possibly) recklessly, causes P to apprehend immediate and unlawful personal violence.[6] A battery is any act by which D, intentionally or (possibly) recklessly, inflicts unlawful personal violence upon P.[7] An assault is often described as an attempt to commit a

---

[1] Turner, "Assault at Common Law", M.A.C.L. 344; Williams "Assault and Words", [1957] Crim. L.R. 219.

[2] So a conviction for "assault or battery" must be quashed: *Jones* v. *Sherwood*, [1942] 1 K.B. 127.

[3] The section does not create a separate offence: the proper course is to lay an information for a common assault and for the justices to deal with it under s. 42 or s. 43 as appropriate.

[4] *Holden* v. *King* (1876), 46 L.J.Q.B. 75.

[5] *Re Thompson* (1860), 6 H. & N. 193 (rape); *Baker* (1883), 47 J.P. 666 (indecent assault).

[6] A definition in almost identical terms was approved in *Fagan* v. *Met. Police Comr.*, [1968] 3 All E.R. at p. 445, below, p. 253.

[7] *Rolfe* (1952), 36 Cr. App. Rep. 4.

battery or other crime of personal violence;[8] but this is too narrow, for an assault may be committed where D has no intention to carry out a battery. Assault is an independent crime and should be treated as such.

It should be noted that assault and battery are also torts; and many, though not all, of the principles appear to be equally applicable in both branches of the law. Consequently, some of the cases cited below are civil actions.

(1) ELEMENTS OF ASSAULT

1 Actus Reus

Typical instances of an assault would be where D rides or drives at P, points a loaded gun or sword or knife at him, shakes a fist under his nose and so on. If these acts were unobserved by P there would be no assault—as where D approaches P from behind, or P is asleep or insensible or too young to appreciate what D appears likely to do. Similarly there can be no assault if it is obvious to P that D is unable to carry out his threat, as where D shakes his fist at P who is safely locked inside his car. In *Stephens* v. *Myers*,[9] D advanced with clenched fist towards P, the chairman of a parish meeting, but was stopped before he reached him. TINDAL, C.J., directed that it was an assault if

> "his blow would almost immediately have reached the chairman if he had not been stopped";[10]

or if

> "within a second or two of time he would have reached the plaintiff."

The chief justice also said that

> "there must, in all cases, be the means of carrying the threat into effect."[11]

But this goes too far. Such propositions have caused difficulty in the situation where D points an unloaded gun at P but the position, in principle, appears to be clear. If P knows the gun is unloaded, there is no assault, for then he could not be put in fear. If P believes the gun is, or may be loaded, there is an *actus reus*, for now he suffers the apprehension which is an essential element of the crime. Though there are *dicta* to the contrary this is the effect of the one clear ruling on the point.[12]

It has been generally accepted that mere words cannot constitute an assault.

---

[8] For example, by Archbold, § 2631.
[9] (1830), 4 C. & P. 349.
[10] *Ibid.*, at p. 350.
[11] *Ibid.*
[12] *St. George* (1840), 9 C. & P. 483 (PARKE, B.). The case was wrongly decided in that PARKE, B., should not have let common assault go to the jury when the indictment was for felony. See above, p. 178, footnote 7 and *Wilson*, [1955] 1 All E.R. 744 at p. 745. But this does not affect the authority of the ruling on the assault point. As the case was left to the jury on this ruling, it appears to be *ratio decidendi* and not *dictum* as is commonly stated. On the other hand, in *Baker* (1843), 1 Car. & Kir. 254, ROLFE, B., and in *James* (1844), 1 Car. & Kir. 530, TINDAL, C.J., holding that no indictment would lie under s. 3 of 1 Vic. c. 85 (later s. 14 of the Offences against the Person Act 1861, now repealed) for pointing an unloaded pistol, said *obiter* that it was not a common assault either. And in a civil case, *Blake* v. *Barnard* (1840), 9 C. & P. 626, Lord ABINGER said: "If the pistol was not loaded there would be no assault". But the better view is that that case turned on the fact that the plaintiff had pleaded that the gun was loaded: Russell 564; Street, *Torts*, 22. *Contra*, Winfield on *Tort*, 254.

It has been recently held in Canada[13] that there was no assault where a man with a jacket over his arm went up to the box-office of a theatre and said to the cashier, "I've got a gun, give me all your money or I'll shoot." It would probably have been different if it had been proved that D simulated the pointing of a gun. In England, there seems to be no more authority for the proposition than a *dictum* of HOLROYD, J., in *Meade and Belt*[14] that "no words or singing are equivalent to an assault." The proposition has been rightly questioned by recent writers.

> "If the plaintiff turns a corner to be confronted by a motionless robber who, with gun in hand, commands 'Hands up', why should not this be an assault ?"[15]

Moreover,

> "The opinion would deny the possibility of an assault (as opposed to a battery) in pitch darkness, when a gesture cannot be seen but menacing words can be heard."[16]

In *Wilson*[17] Lord GODDARD said of the accused:

> "He called out 'Get out the knives', *which itself would be an assault*, in addition to kicking the gamekeeper."

This was a mere *dictum*—but it surely counterbalances that in *Meade*?

It is clear that a threat to inflict harm at some time in the future cannot amount to an assault[18]—an apprehension of immediate personal violence is essential. As already noted, an oral threat even to murder P, and even if made in his presence, is not an offence unless it amounts to an assault.

Whether or not words may amount to an assault, it is clear that they may negative one. In the famous case of *Tuberville* v. *Savage*[19] D laid his hand upon his sword, saying, "If it were not assize time I would not take such language." If D had said nothing, it is clear that the court would have held this to be evidence of an assault; but

> "the declaration of [D][20] was, that he would not assault him, the judges being in town."[1]

If the words had not accompanied the act, but followed it, again there would presumably have been an assault, for the words could not undo a crime already constituted by the apprehension aroused in P.

In *Blake* v *Barnard*,[2] Lord ABINGER applied the same principle to the situation where D presented a pistol at P's head and said that if P was not quiet he would blow his brains out. This differs from *Tuberville* v. *Savage* in that D's declared intention not to shoot was conditional on P's doing as he was told. It has been forcefully argued[3] that this is a vital distinction and that D should not have been acquitted of an assault on that ground—

---

[13] *Byrne*, [1968] 3 C.C.C. 179 (Br. Col. C. of A.).
[14] (1823), 1 Lew C.C. 184.
[15] Street, *Torts*, 22.
[16] Williams, [1957] Crim. L.R. at 224.
[17] [1955] 1 All E.R. 744 at p. 745.
[18] *Stephens* v. *Myers*, above, p. 250; and see *Police* v. *Greaves*, [1964] N.Z.L.R. 295; *Fagan*, [1968] 3 All E.R. 442; below p. 253, footnote 14.
[19] (1669), 1 Mod. Rep. 3. But *cf. Light* (1857), D. & B. 332.
[20] D was in fact the plaintiff in an action for assault arising out of a fight which followed the incident described.
[1] *Ibid.*
[2] (1840), 9 C. & P. 626.
[3] By Williams, [1957] Crim. L.R. at p. 220.

"Otherwise, indeed, the highwayman who says 'Your money or your life,' at the same time presenting a weapon, would not be guilty of assault at common law—a proposition which it is impossible to believe."

Thus in *Read* v. *Coker*,[4] where D and his servants had surrounded P, tucking up their sleeves and aprons and had threatened to break his neck *if he did not leave the premises*, the Court of Common Pleas had no doubt that this was an assault. Yet P was already a trespasser in that case, having been told to go. The threat amounted to an assault presumably only because it was of excessive force.[5]

It has generally been assumed that an act of some kind is an essential ingredient of assault; but a recent case[6] suggests the possibility of an assault by omission. Where D inadvertently causes P to apprehend immediate violence and subsequently wilfully declines to withdraw the threat, his omission might constitute an assault.

2 Mens Rea

The cases generally refer to the necessity for an intention[7] in assault. In the earlier authorities, where assault was described as an *attempt* to inflict violence it was consistent to hold that nothing less than an intention to inflict it would do. According to the modern view, however, it would be an assault if D struck in the direction of P, intending only to alarm him and not to touch him; but it could not be an attempted battery. It is submitted that it would be in accordance with principle[8] to hold D guilty if he were merely reckless whether P might not be alarmed by his gesture. It may be, though there is no authority on the point, that a civil action will lie for a negligent assault;[9] but, in principle, it should not be a crime.

It is often said that D must have had a *hostile* intention in assault and battery.[10] So far as assault is concerned, this adds nothing to intentionally or recklessly causing apprehension. It would be no defence that D was friendly with P and did it for a joke—unless P's consent could be implied.

3 Attempt to Assault

It has been questioned whether there can be an attempt to assault, since assault itself was regarded as an attempt to commit a battery. It is submitted that, since assault itself is now wider than attempted battery, there is no reason why there should not be attempt to commit it; as where D points an unloaded gun at P, intending to frighten him, but P, knowing the gun is unloaded, is unperturbed.[11]

---

[4] (1853), 13 C.B. 850.
[5] *Cf. Osborn* v. *Veitch* (1858), 1 F. & F. 317 (Pointing a gun at half-cock ("cocking it is an instantaneous act") to resist an unlawful arrest held an assault, because "To shoot a man is not a lawful way of repelling an unlawful assault": *per* WILLES, J.).
[6] *Fagan* v. *Met. Police Comr.*, [1968] 3 All E.R. 442, below, p. 253.
[7] *Tuberville* v. *Savage* (1669), 1 Mod. Rep. 3; *Coward* v. *Baddeley* (1859), 28 L.J. Ex 260.
[8] *Cf. Cunningham*, [1957] 2 Q.B. 396; [1957] 2 All E.R. 412. Above, p. 74.
[9] Street, *Torts*, 21.
[10] *Coward* v. *Baddeley* (1859), 28 L.J. Ex. 260; *Fairclough* v. *Whipp*, [1951] 2 All E.R. 834; *Director of Public Prosecutions* v. *Rogers*, [1953] 2 All E.R. 644.
[11] "Is Criminal Assault a Separate Substantive Crime or is it an Attempted Battery?" (1945), 33 Ky. L.J. 189; *State* v. *Wilson* (1955), 218 Ore. 575; 346 P. 2d. 115.

(2) BATTERY

1 Actus Reus

This consists in the infliction of unlawful personal violence by D upon P. It used to be said that every battery involves an assault; but this is plainly not so, for in battery there need be no apprehension of the impending violence. A blow from behind is not any less a battery because P was unaware that it was coming. It is generally said that D must have done some act and that it is not enough that he stood still and obstructed P's passage[12] like an inanimate object. But suppose D is sitting at the corner of a corridor with his legs stretched across it. He hears P running down the corridor and deliberately remains still with the intention that P, on turning the corner, shall fall over his legs. Why should not this be a battery? It would be if D had put out his legs with the intention of tripping up P. There is certainly no battery where D has no control over the incident, as where his horse unexpectedly runs away with him;[13] but this might be put on the ground of lack of *mens rea*. It might be otherwise if D foresaw, when he mounted, that this might happen. There may be a battery where D inadvertently applies force to P and then wrongfully refuses to withdraw it. In *Fagan*,[14] where D accidentally drove his mini-car on to a constable's foot and then intentionally left it there, the court held that there was a continuing act, not a mere omission.

"Violence" here includes the smallest degree of personal contact—a mere touching without consent is enough. But there is an implied consent to that degree of contact which is necessary or customary in everyday usage. In *Tuberville* v. *Savage*[15] it was said that it is no assault to strike another on the hand, arm or breast in ordinary discourse. Touching another to attract his attention is not a battery,[16] even if, as in *Coward* v. *Baddeley*,[17] P has already told D to go away and mind his own business. In *Coward* v. *Baddeley*, the court put its decision on the ground of lack of hostility, but there are difficulties in requiring the act to be hostile, and not only in indecent assaults.[18] If D, out of concern for P's morals, were to drag P away to prevent him watching an indecent exhibition, this would surely be a battery; but would it be "hostile"?

For this purpose the person of the victim includes the clothes he is wearing; PARKE, B., ruled that there was a common assault where D slashed P's clothes with a knife:

"surely it is an assault on a man's person to inflict injury to the clothes on his back. In the ordinary case of a blow on the back, there is clearly an assault, though the blow is received by the coat on the person."[19]

Presumably in this example, however, it is necessary that the blow be felt by P, for there is no injury to his clothes.

Most batteries are directly inflicted, as by D's striking P with his fist or an instrument, or by a missile thrown by him, or by spitting upon P. But it is not

---

[12] *Innes* v. *Wylie* (1844), 1 Car. & Kir. 257.
[13] *Gibbon* v. *Pepper* (1695), 2 Salk. 637.
[14] [1968] 3 All E.R. 442; above, pp. 36, 46 and 249.
[15] (1669), 1 Mod. Rep. 3; above, p. 251.
[16] *Rawlings* v. *Till* (1837), 3 M. & W. 28, *per* PARKE, B.
[17] (1859), 28 L.J. Ex. 260.
[18] Below, p. 302.
[19] *Day* (1845), 1 Cox C.C. 207.

essential that the violence should have been so directly inflicted. Thus STEPHEN and WILLS, JJ., thought there would be a battery where D digs a pit for P to fall into, or, as in *Martin*[20] he causes P to rush into an obstruction. It would undoubtedly be a battery to set a dog on another.[1] If D beat O's horse causing it to run down P, this would be battery by D.[2] No doubt the famous civil case of *Scott* v. *Shepherd*[3] is equally good for the criminal law. D throws a squib into a market house. First E and then F flings the squib away in order to save himself from injury. It explodes and injures P. This is a battery by D.

2 Mens Rea

The tort of battery may be committed intentionally, recklessly or negligently; and in America it is apparently well established[4] that "criminal negligence" will found a prosecution for battery. But there is no authority in England for such an extension of criminal liability and it is submitted that it must be proved that D intentionally, or at least recklessly, applied force to the person of another.[5] It is not certain that even recklessness is enough. In *Bradshaw*[6] BRAMWELL, L.J., ruled that if a footballer, in charging,

> "was indifferent and reckless as to whether he would produce serious injury[7] or not, then the act would be unlawful."

But "unlawful" here could have meant merely tortious; and in *Ackroyd* v. *Barett*[8] a conviction for battery by reckless cycling[9] was quashed after a submission that there must be an intention to assault. It may look odd to convict reckless road users of battery; but, if they are reckless whether they cause personal injury, why not?

(3) DEFENCES TO ASSAULT AND BATTERY

1 Consent

(i) *Effect of consent.*—It is of the essence of both offences that they are done against the will of the victim.[10] Consent therefore negatives either crime and the onus of proving the absence of consent is on the Crown.[11] Fraud does not necessarily negative consent. It does so only if it deceives P as to the identity of the person or the nature of the act.[12] In *Clarence*[13] P consented to intercourse with D and, although she would not have consented had she been aware of the disease which D knew he was suffering, this was no assault. If D told P that he was going to inject him with a vaccine and then injected a poison instead, it is thought that this would be a battery, but if he injected the vaccine with a dirty

---

[20] Below, p. 265.

[1] *Plunkett* v. *Matchell*, [1958] Crim. L.R. 252.

[2] *Gibbon* v. *Pepper* (1695), 2 Salk 637 (*obiter*).

[3] (1773), 2 Wm. Bl. 892.

[4] Perkins, *Criminal Law*, 85.

[5] There seems to be a suggestion in *Plunkett* v. *Matchell* (*supra*) that negligence would be enough. *Sed quaere.*

[6] (1878), 14 Cox C.C. 83.

[7] There being consent to the force ordinarily incident to football.

[8] (1894), 11 T.L.R. 115. The case is a weak authority in that no one appeared to support the conviction.

[9] This is an offence under the Road Traffic Act 1960; see below, p. 331, footnote 14.

[10] *Christopherson* v. *Bare* (1848), 11 Q.B. 473.

[11] *Donovan*, [1934] 2 K.B. 498, following *May*, [1912] 3 K.B. 572.

[12] But *cf.* the rule in trespass to land and, therefore, in burglary, below p. 411.

[13] (1888), 22 Q.B.D. 23, below, p. 265.

needle, there would, as in *Clarence*, be no battery even though D knew that P would not have consented to injection with a dirty needle. Where D1, a doctor, by falsely pretending that D2 was a medical student, obtained P's consent to D2's presence at a vaginal examination of P, it was held that both D1 and D2 were guilty of indecent assault.[14] The medical examination to which P consented was different in nature from the indecent exhibition of her body to prurient eyes to which she was subjected. In *Burrell* v. *Harmer*[15] consent was held to be no defence to a charge of assault occasioning actual bodily harm, where D tattooed boys aged 12 and 13, causing their arms to become inflamed and painful. The court took the view that the boys were unable to understand the nature of the act. But in what sense did they not understand it? Consent may also be negatived by duress which may be implied from the relationship between the parties— for example where D is acting as a schoolmaster, and P a thirteen year-old pupil.[16] As in rape and indecent assault,[17] submission is not consent. But an unfounded belief in P's consent ought to afford a defence, at least if it is reasonable, and, in principle, even if it is not.[18]

(ii) *Limitations on consent.*[19]—It is clear that there are limits to the degree of physical harm to which a person can effectively consent but where the line is to be drawn is by no means clear. To take the most obvious example, it is no defence on a charge of murder for D to say that P asked to be killed. "Prize fights" have long been held to be batteries. It seems that "prize fight" in this context signifies a fight without gloves, or otherwise likely to cause more serious injury than boxing under the Queensberry rules. Thus, in *Coney*,[20] CAVE, J., said:

> "The true view is, I think, that a blow struck in anger, or which is likely or is intended to do corporal hurt, is an assault, but that a blow struck in sport, and not likely, nor intended to cause bodily harm, is not an assault, and that, an assault being a breach of the peace and unlawful the consent of the person struck is immaterial. If this view is correct a blow struck in a prize-fight is clearly an assault; but playing with single-sticks or wrestling do not involve an assault; nor does boxing with gloves in the ordinary way, and not with the ferocity and severe punishment to the boxers deposed to in *R* v. *Orton*."[1]

If blows struck in boxing are lawful, it is clear that it is permissible to submit to the infliction of some degree of bodily harm. If it were not so, not only boxing but many other sports would be unlawful. The shoulder charge delivered in a game of football would clearly be a battery if it were inflicted on an unwilling passer-by. It is only lawful in the game because P has obviously consented to D's doing what the rules permit. He has consented to nothing more and, for this reason, it is submitted that *Moore*,[2] holding the rules inadmissible

---

[14] *Bolduc and Bird* (1967), 61 D.L.R. (2d) 494 (British Columbia C. of A.). *Cf. Rosinski* (1824), 1 Mood. C.C. 19.
[15] [1967] Crim. L.R. 169 and commentary thereon.
[16] *Nichol* (1807), Russ. & Ry. 130.
[17] Below, pp. 291 and 301.
[18] The point was raised by the jury, but not clearly answered in *Donovan*, [1934] 2 K.B. at p. 506.
[19] Williams, "Consent and Public Policy", [1962] Crim. L.R. 74 and 154.
[20] (1882), 8 Q.B.D. at p. 539; above, p. 83.
[1] (1878), 39 L.T. 293. The contestants wore gloves but it was held that the jury were rightly directed that it was a prize fight if they intended to fight on until one gave in from exhaustion or injury.
[2] (1898), 14 T.L.R. 229.

in evidence in favour of the prosecution, is a bad decision.[3] But P cannot consent to acts which are likely to cause him death or serious injury, so that rules of the game permitting such acts would be irrelevant.[4]

The seriousness of the bodily harm likely to be incurred is, then, a very important factor in determining whether consent is legally operative; but it is clearly not the only factor involved. Account must also be taken of the purpose of D and P. Surgical operations for medical purposes are obviously lawful[5] although they involve the infliction of wounds upon the patient. But it may be otherwise if the purpose of the operation is against public policy. So Coke tells us that in 1604,

> "a young strong and lustie rogue, to make himself impotent, thereby to have the more colour to begge or to be relieved without putting himself to any labour, caused his companion to strike off his left hand":

and that both of them were convicted of mayhem.[6] Maiming, even with consent, was unlawful because it deprived the king of a fighting man. In early Victorian times when soldiers, as part of their drill, had to bite cartridges, a soldier got a dentist to pull out his front teeth to avoid the drill. STEPHEN, J., thought that both were guilty of a crime.[7] DENNING, L.J., followed these instances in discussing, *obiter*, the legality of a sterilisation operation:

> "When it is done with the man's consent for a just cause, it is quite lawful, as, for instance, when it is done to prevent the transmission of an hereditary disease; but when it is done without just cause or excuse, it is unlawful, even though the man consents to it. Take a case where a sterilisation operation is done so as to enable a man to have the pleasure of sexual intercourse without shouldering the responsibilities attaching to it. The operation is then plainly injurious to the public interest."[8]

This was unnecessary to the decision and the other judges were careful to express no opinion on the point. The legality of a sterilisation operation is thus not settled. A similar doubt applies to the case of a man with uncontrollable sexual impulses who is willing to undergo a castration operation. The Court of Criminal Appeal in *Cowburn*[9] was asked to give its blessing to such an operation and declined to do so, as the issue was not before it. Public policy might well be served by such an operation.[10] but it is impossible to be certain of the attitude the courts would take, for "public policy" is a notoriously elusive and slippery doctrine. It was invoked to justify conviction for a relatively slight degree of harm in *Donovan*.[11] D, for his sexual gratification, beat a seventeen-year-old girl with a cane in circumstances of indecency. He was convicted of both indecent assault and common assault. The judge failed to direct the jury

---

[3] Williams justifies the case on the ground that "the players are deemed to consent even to an application of force that is in breach of the rules of the game, if it is the sort of thing that may be expected to happen during the game." But proof of breach of the rules ought to establish at least a prima facie case. The rules are admissible in favour of the defence as tending to negative malice: *Bradshaw* (1878), 14 Cox C.C. 83.

[4] *Bradshaw, supra;* and see above, p. 219, footnote 15.

[5] Stephen, *Digest*, Art. 310.

[6] 1 Co. Inst. 127a and b.

[7] *Digest* (3rd ed.), 142.

[8] *Bravery* v. *Bravery*, [1954] 3 All E.R. 59, at pp. 67, 68.

[9] [1959] Crim. L.R. 590.

[10] See Havard, [1959] Crim. L.R. 554 at p. 555: "The Scandinavian experience has shown that voluntary castration is particularly efficacious in these cases and may permit an early rehabilitation in the community."

[11] [1934] 2 K.B. 498.

that the onus of negativing consent was on the Crown, but the Court of Criminal Appeal held that, if the blows were likely or intended to cause bodily harm, this omission was immaterial because D was guilty whether P consented or not. The conviction was quashed because the question whether the blows were likely or intended to cause bodily harm was not put to the jury, and

> "There are many gradations between a slight tap and a severe blow . . .".[12]

Thus, P's consent to "a slight tap" would have been operative notwithstanding D's evil motives. But it was clearly these motives which rendered unlawful a degree of force which, in other circumstances, might have been permissible. The decision suggests[13] that the infliction of any degree of bodily harm, however slight,[14] is a battery unless P consents *and* the action can be positively justified by some rule of policy, such as that validating "manly sports". This leaves the law in an uncertain state and one depending very much on the views of the judges as to what is desirable, and what is undesirable, conduct.

2 Lawful Correction

Parents are entitled to inflict moderate and reasonable physical chastisement on their children; but—

> "If it be administered for the gratification of passion or rage or if it be immoderate or excessive in its nature or degree, or if it be protracted beyond the child's powers of endurance or with an instrument unfitted for the purpose and calculated to produce danger to life and limb . . .".[15]

—then it is unlawful. If the chastisement is moderate, it would be impracticable for the courts to inquire very closely into the validity of the parents' motives. Where the force is immoderate, his motives are irrelevant. School teachers are in the same position as parents with regard to the conduct of the child at, or on its way to or from school.[16] It has always been said that the teacher is a delegate of the parent in this matter but it has been questioned whether this basis for the rule can be accepted any longer,[17] since a parent has a statutory duty to secure the education of his child.[18] Yet the Act preserves the general principle that pupils are to be educated in accordance with the wishes of their parents,

> "so far as is compatible with the provision of efficient instruction and training. . . ."

While corporal punishment is recognised in schools it is so clearly desirable that all pupils should be in the same position that the right of parents to forbid such punishment might fall foul of this proviso.

The ancient right to chastise a wife, a servant or an apprentice may now be regarded as obsolete.

3 Self-Defence

Since self-defence may afford a defence to murder, obviously it may do so to lesser offences against the person and subject to similar conditions. The matter

---

[12] *Ibid.*, at p. 510.
[13] See *ibid.* at p. 509.
[14] There were seven or eight red marks on P's body. This was sufficient evidence of bodily harm to go to the jury.
[15] *Hopley* (1860), 2 F. & F. 202 at p. 206, *per* COCKBURN, C.J
[16] *Cleary* v. *Booth*, [1893] 1 Q.B. 465; *Newport (Salop.)* JJ., [1929] 2 K.B. 416; *Mansell* v. *Griffin*, [1908] 1 K.B. 160.
[17] Street, *Torts*, 87.
[18] Education Act 1944, s. 36.

is now regulated by s. 3 of the Criminal Law Act 1967.[19] An attack which would not justify D in killing might justify him in the use of some less degree of force, and so afford a defence to a charge of wounding, or, *a fortiori*, common assault. But the use of greater force than is reasonable to repel the attack will result in liability to conviction for common assault,[20] or whatever offence the degree of harm caused and intended warrants. Reasonable force may be used in defence of property so that D was not guilty of an assault when he struck a bailiff who was unlawfully using force to enter D's home.[21]

2 AGGRAVATED ASSAULTS

The Offences against the Person Act 1861 singles out certain varieties of assault as being especially heinous and provides a more severe punishment for them. Some of these were, no doubt, intended to deal with matters causing public concern at the time, and appear rather curious today.

Thus, obstructing or assaulting a clergyman in the discharge of his duties in a place of worship or burial place, or who is on his way to or from such duties is a misdemeanour punishable with two years' imprisonment under s. 36. Assaulting a magistrate or other person in the exercise of his duty concerning the preservation of a vessel in distress or a wreck is a misdemeanour punishable with seven years' imprisonment.

Such provisions are rarely invoked at the present day and need not be considered further. But s. 38, now in part replaced by s. 51 of the Police Act 1964, is still important.

(1) ASSAULT ON, RESISTANCE TO, OR OBSTRUCTION OF CONSTABLES

By s. 51 of the Police Act 1964:

"(1) Any person who assaults a constable in the execution of his duty, or a person assisting a constable in the execution of his duty, shall be guilty of an offence and liable:

(a) on summary conviction to imprisonment for a term not exceeding six months, or to a fine not exceeding £100, or to both;

(b) on conviction on indictment to imprisonment for a term not exceeding two years or to a fine or to both.

(2) Subsection (2) of section 23 of the Firearms Act 1937, shall apply to offences under subsection (1) of this section.

(3) Any person who resists or wilfully obstructs a constable in the execution of his duty, or a person assisting a constable in the execution of his duty, shall be guilty of an offence and liable on summary conviction to imprisonment for a term not exceeding one month or to a fine not exceeding £20, or to both."

Though the section is headed "Assaults on Constables", there are three crimes here, only one of which necessarily amounts to an assault. Resistance to a constable may occur without an assault, as where D has been arrested by P and tears himself from P's grasp and escapes. Obstruction, as appears below, embraces many situations which do not amount to an assault. On the other hand, both resistance and obstruction clearly may include assaults. The nature of assault and resistance require no further consideration but obstruction presents

---

[19] Above, p. 229.
[20] *Driscoll* (1841), Car. & M. 214; *Morse* (1910), 4 Cr. App. Rep. 50.
[21] *Vaughan* v. *McKenzie*, [1968] 1 All E.R. 1154; [1968] Crim. L.R. 265 and commentary thereon.

problems and is examined in some detail below. The first question—when is a constable[1] acting in the course of his duty?—is common to all three crimes. But the *mens rea* of assault and resistance, on the one hand, and obstruction on the other require separate consideration.

1 A Constable Acting in the Execution of his Duty

When a policeman is acting in the course of his duty is a question which can give rise to difficult problems. In *Prebble*[2] P, a constable, at the request of the landlord, turned some persons out of a public house, and was assaulted by one of them, D. The court held that, while his action may have been very laudable and proper, P was not acting in the execution of his duty, since there was no nuisance or danger of a breach of the peace. Obviously, the constable was acting lawfully, since D was convicted of a common assault. This suggests that it is not enough that P is doing something which he may lawfully do while on duty. Must his act then be something which he *must* do? Such an argument was advanced in *Betts* v. *Stevens*[3] where police officers were obstructed when operating a speed trap. It was pointed out that there was no statutory duty to operate such a trap. The answer accepted by the court in that case was that the policeman obstructed was in the execution of his duty because he was obeying the orders of a superior officer. It is difficult to suppose, however, that the result would have been different if it had been the senior officer himself who was obstructed. It can hardly be necessary to prove that the act the officer was doing was one which it would have been a tort or a crime for him not to do. So to hold would be to give much too narrow an interpretation to the section. In the recent case of *Waterfield*[4] the Court of Criminal Appeal said:

> "In the judgment of this court it would be difficult, and in the present case it is unnecessary, to reduce within specific limits the general terms in which the duties of police constables have been expressed. In most cases it is probably more convenient to consider what the police constable was actually doing and in particular whether such conduct was *prima facie* an unlawful interference with a person's liberty or property. If so, it is then relevant to consider whether (a) such conduct falls within the general scope of any duty imposed by statute or recognised at common law and (b) whether such conduct, albeit within the general scope of such a duty, involved an unjustifiable use of powers associated with the duty."

If the police officer's conduct falls within the scope of the general "duty" to prevent crime and to bring offenders to justice, then it would seem to be within the protection of the statute, if it was lawful. Thus in *McArdle* v. *Wallace*,[5] P was held to be acting in the execution of his duty as a constable when he entered a café to make inquiries regarding some property which he thought might have been stolen. He was told to leave but did not do so and was then assaulted. At the time of the assault he was no longer acting in the execution of his duty since he became a trespasser when he refused to leave: for a constable can hardly have a duty to break the law. Since a constable has no power to detain for questioning, the use of reasonable force to escape from such detention is not an assault[6]; and

---

[1] *I.e.* a person holding the *office*, not the rank of constable.
[2] (1858), 1 F. & F. 325. [3] [1910] 1 K.B. 1.
[4] [1964] 1 Q.B. 164 at p. 170; [1963] 3 All E.R. 659 at p. 661.
[5] [1964] Crim. L.R. 467; *Davis* v. *Lisle*, [1936] 2 K.B. 434; [1936] 2 All E.R. 213; *Robson* v. *Hallett*, [1967] 2 All E.R. 407; *McGowan* v. *Chief Constable of Hull*, [1968] Crim. L.R. 34.
[6] *Kenlin* v. *Gardner*, [1967] 2 Q.B. 510; [1966] 3 All E.R. 931.

the use of excessive force, while a common assault (or wounding etc.) would not be an offence under s. 51. *Waterfield*[7] is a more difficult case. P had been informed that a car had been involved in a serious offence. Evidently acting on the instructions of a superior officer, he attempted to prevent D, the owner of the car, from removing it from the place on the road where it was parked. D drove the car at P, thus assaulting him, in order to remove it. The court held that P was not "entitled" to prevent removal of the car and therefore was not acting in the execution of his duty. The difficulty is that the judgment nowhere specifies in what respect P's act was unlawful. He simply stood in front of the car. It has been pertinently asked, why, if it was not an unlawful act, was it not one that P might properly do in fulfilment of the general duty to bring offenders to justice?[8] It may be, however, that the answer is that P was guilty of obstructing the highway under the Highways Act 1959;[9] but there was no finding that the road was a highway.

Prebble[10] is reconcilable, on the view advanced above, only on the basis that there is no "general duty" on a police officer to assist citizens in the enforcement of their private rights. The nature of the "general duty" is therefore somewhat vague, and there must be doubt whether the police officer is protected by the section when he is doing many acts which he may lawfully do—from rescuing a stranded cat to acting as a midwife.

Probably the most important application of the provision is in the context of the constable's duty to prevent breaches of the peace which he reasonably apprehends.[11] If it appears (i) that facts existed from which a constable could reasonably have anticipated a breach, as a real and not merely as a remote possibility; and (ii) that he did so anticipate, then he is under a duty to take such steps as he reasonably thinks are necessary.[12] In *Piddington* v. *Bates*, it was held that P was acting in the course of his duty in forbidding D to join two persons picketing the entrance to certain premises. Notwithstanding the provision of the Trade Disputes Act 1906 that it is lawful for "one or more" persons to picket, the police have a duty to limit the number of pickets if it is necessary to maintain the peace.

Even where no breach of the peace is anticipated, a constable may be under a duty to give instructions to members of the public—for example, to remove an obstruction from the highway—and a deliberate refusal to obey such an instruction may amount to an obstruction of the police.

2 Mens Rea in Cases of Assault and Resistance

It has been held in *Forbes and Webb*[13] that the only *mens rea* required is an intention to assault (or, presumably, to resist) and that ignorance that P is a constable is no defence.[14] Williams has said that

> "The only useful comment that can be made upon *Forbes* is that it is a mere direction to the jury by a recorder and is unsound."[15]

But in *Prince*[16] six of the judges seem to have accepted it as correct; in *Maxwell*

---

[7] [1964] 1 Q.B. 164; [1963] 3 All E.R. 659.
[8] See "The Arrest of a Motor-Car", by P. J. Fitzgerald, [1965] Crim. L.R. 23.
[9] Below, p. 547.
[10] (1858), 1 F. & F. 325.
[11] *Duncan* v. *Jones*, [1936] K.B. 218.
[12] *Piddington* v. *Bates*, [1960] 3 All E.R. 660.
[13] (1865), 10 Cox C.C. 362.
[14] For a full examination of the law on this matter, see Howard (1963), 79 L.Q.R. 247.
[15] C.L.G.P. 194.
[16] Above, p. 42.

and Clanchy[17] a Divisional Court, holding that there was evidence to support a jury's finding that D knew P was a policeman, said, *obiter*, that they wished to cast no doubt on *Forbes*; it was followed by MAXWELL TURNER, J., in *Mark*;[18] and in *Reynhoudt*[19] a majority of the High Court of Australia (TAYLOR, MENZIES and OWEN, JJ., DIXON, C.J., and KITTO, J., dissenting) arrived at a similar result on the construction of the equivalent provision in Victorian legislation. It is submitted that the better view is that of the dissenting judges in *Reynhoudt*— that at least the chance of P's being a peace officer in the execution of his duty must be foreseen by D when he makes the assault.[20] Such a view avoids any difficulty arising from the fact that s. 36[1] of the 1861 Act uses the words "to the knowledge of the offender", whereas no such words were used in s. 38 or its successor.

Nevertheless, the present English law is that laid down in *Forbes*. This is implicit in *McBride* v. *Turnock*,[2] where D struck at O, who was not a constable, and hit P, who was. Although he had no intention of assaulting P, the Divisional Court held he was guilty of assaulting a constable in the execution of his duty. The *mens rea* for this crime being only that of a common assault, D's "malice" was transferable.[3] No better illustration could be given of the unsatisfactory nature of the rule in *Forbes*.

It is essential that it be proved that D intended an *assault* (or resistance); so that if he reasonably believed in the existence of such facts as would have justified his act in law, he must be acquitted. So in *Mark*,[4] the jury were told that if D acted under honest and reasonable belief that P was not a constable acting in the execution of his duty but a person engaged in committing a felony or breach of the peace, they should acquit. The requirement of reasonableness is unsatisfactory. Why should D be convicted if he assaults a policeman in the execution of his duty in the honest but unreasonable belief that he is going to the aid of a victim of a crime? D may be foolish, impetuous or merely short-sighted, but his intention, far from being criminal, is laudable.[5]

3 Wilful Obstruction[6]

(i) *The meaning of obstruction.*—A wide interpretation of "obstruction" has been accepted in England. It is not necessary that there should be any interference with the officer himself by physical force or threats. To give a warning to a person who has committed a crime so as to enable him to escape detection by police is enough. Thus in *Betts* v. *Stevens*,[7] D warned the drivers who were exceeding the speed limit that there was a police trap ahead. But it is not an offence to warn a driver who is not exceeding the speed limit of such a trap.[8]

---

[17] (1909), 73 J.P. 176.
[18] [1961] Crim. L.R. 173.
[19] (1962), 36 A.L.J. 26.
[20] This was the view of the majority of the court in *Galvin* (*No. 2*), [1961] V.R. 740, overruling *Galvin* (*No. 1*), [1961] V.R. 733. BARRY, J., thought actual knowledge necessary. SHOLL, J., adhered to his view in *Galvin* (*No. 1*) that the offence was one of strict liability. See also *McLeod* (1955), 111 C.C.C. 106.
[1] Above, p. 258.
[2] [1964] Crim. L R. 456.
[3] Above, p. 44.
[4] *Supra.*
[5] But the case accords with the general attitude of the courts to "mistake". Above, p. 129.
[6] See Coutts (1956), 19 M.L.R. 411.
[7] [1910] 1 K.B. 1.
[8] *Bastable* v. *Little*, [1907] 1 K.B. 59.

It is very strange that it should be a crime to tell a man who is committing a continuing offence to stop doing so even though the motive is to frustrate the police; but the court was influenced by the practical difficulties then facing the police of getting direct evidence of violation of speed limits. It is obviously different where the police tell an offender to desist from an offence. Here deliberate refusal may amount to an obstruction, as where D is obstructing the highway and refuses to obey the instructions of a constable to move.[9] It is not necessary that the constable should anticipate a breach of the peace. It is probable, however, that a constable has no power to arrest D for obstructing him, unless a breach of the peace has occurred or is anticipated.[10]

Presumably it must be proved that some named officer was obstructed; it would hardly be enough that D warned E in general terms that if he did not stop committing an offence he would be found out; or if he advised E to get a television licence because the detector van was visiting his street next week—apart from the fact that the operators of the van would not be constables.

Hinchliffe v. *Sheldon*[11] might be thought to go further than *Betts* v. *Stevens*[12] in that it was only suspected, and not proved, that an offence was being committed; but there the warning was tantamount to a physical obstruction.[13] D, a publican's son, shouted a warning to his parents that the police were outside the public house. It was 11.17 p.m. and the lights were on in the bar, so presumably the police suspected that liquor was being consumed after hours. There was a delay of eight minutes before the police were admitted and no offence was detected. *Bastable* v. *Little*[14] was distinguished on the ground that the police had a right to enter the licensed premises under the Licensing Act 1953. Whether an offence was being committed or not, an entry under this statutory right was in execution of their duty; and their *entry* was obstructed.

Lord GODDARD, C.J., defined "obstructing" as

"making it more difficult for the police to carry out their duties."[15]

This is far wider than was necessary for the decision. But the *dictum* has been applied in New Zealand in a case where D, a bystander, merely advised E not to answer any questions put to him by P, a police officer, investigating a suspected offence.[16] E was perfectly entitled to remain silent but his doing so undoubtedly made it more difficult for P to carry out his duty of investigating crime. An earlier decision in[17] the Supreme Court of Victoria is to the contrary and is to be preferred. Surely a solicitor who advises his client to say nothing cannot be guilty of an offence, though he undoubtedly makes things more difficult for the police; and why should a solicitor be in a different situation from anyone else?

In England, it has been held that refusal to answer a constable's question, though it undoubtedly makes it more difficult for the police to carry out their duties, does not amount to wilful obstruction: *Rice* v. *Connolly*.[18] It would,

---

[9] *Tynan* v. *Balmer*, [1967] 1 Q.B. 91; [1966] 2 All E.R. 133; *Donaldson* v. *Police*, [1968] N.Z.L.R. 32.
[10] *Gelberg* v. *Miller*, [1961] 1 All E.R. 291.
[11] [1955] 3 All E.R. 406.
[12] Above, p. 259.
[13] See Coutts, *op. cit.*
[14] *Supra.*
[15] [1955] 3 All E.R. at p. 408.
[16] *Steele* v. *Kingsbeer*, [1957] N.Z.L.R. 552.
[17] *Hogben* v. *Chandler*, [1940] V.L.R. 285.
[18] [1966] 2 Q.B. 414; [1966] 2 All E.R. 649 (D.C.).

apparently be different if D were to tell the police a false story.[19] These difficulties would not arise if the Act had been held to be limited to physical interference; and it has been held[20] to be so limited in Scotland where "obstruct"
has been construed *ejusdem generis* with "assault" and "resist".[1] D was held not
guilty when he told lies to the police to conceal an offence of which he was guilty.
There is much to be said in favour of the Scottish view.[2]

(ii) *Mens rea.*—The obstruction of the officer must be "wilful". "Assault"
and "resist" are not so qualified and this would seem to afford a good reason why
Forbes[3] should not be applied to this part of the section. Though a narrow interpretation has sometimes been put on "wilful",[4] it is submitted that, in this context, it must require that D knew that there was at least a chance that P was a
constable in the execution of his duty. In *Rice* v. *Connolly*[5] it was said that
"wilfully" means not only "intentionally" but also "without lawful excuse."
This is difficult to follow. "Wilfully" must surely refer to the state of mind of
the defendant. But whether he has a lawful excuse for what he does generally
depends on D's conduct and the circumstances in which he acts.[6] In that case,
D would have been no more "wilful" if he had told a false story. The difference
seems to lie in the conduct which the court considers to be permissible. "Wilfully" may of course import the absence of any *belief* on D's part of circumstances
of lawful excuse.[7] If the story told by D were in fact false, but D believed it to be
true, the constable might be obstructed, but he would not be "wilfully" obstructed.

(3) ASSAULT OCCASIONING ACTUAL BODILY HARM

By s. 47 of the Offences against the Person Act 1861, an assault occasioning actual
bodily harm is punishable on indictment with five years' imprisonment. " 'Bodily
harm' ", according to the House of Lords in *Director of Public Prosecutions* v.
Smith[8]

> "needs no explanation. 'Grievous' means no more and no less than 'really
> serious' ".

It seems to follow that, under s. 47, the harm need not be really serious.

In *Miller*,[9] LYNSKEY, J., quoted the statement formerly contained in Archbold:[10]

> "Actual bodily harm includes any hurt or injury calculated to interfere
> with the health or comfort of the prosecutor . . ."

---

[19] *Ibid.*; *Matthews* v. *Dwan*, [1949] N.Z.L.R. 1037.
[20] *Curlett* v. *M'Kechnie*, 1938 S.C.J. 176.
[1] The re-arrangement of these offences by the Police Act precludes the application of the
ejusdem generis rule; but it could have been applied when they were contained in the
Offences against the Person Act 1861.
[2] See Coutts, *op. cit.*
[3] Above, p. 260.
[4] Above, p. 74.
[5] Above, p. 262.
[6] See comment at [1966] Crim. L.R. 390.
[7] *Cf.* below, p. 457–458.
[8] [1961] A.C. 290 at p. 334; [1960] 3 All E.R. 161 at p. 71; Above, p. 197.
[9] [1954] 2 Q.B. 282, at p. 292; [1954] 2 All E.R. 529 at p. 534; below, p. 289. *Cf.*
Burrell v. *Harmer*, [1967] Crim. L.R. 169 and commentary thereon; above, p. 255.
[10] 32nd ed., p. 959.

LYNSKEY, J., held that this included a hysterical and nervous condition resulting from an assault, taking the view that an injury to the state of a man's mind is actual bodily harm.

Since—absurdly—the maximum punishment for this offence is the same as that for maliciously inflicting grievous bodily harm contrary to s. 20 of the same Act—which also requires proof of an assault[11]—it would seem that the prosecutor could, with advantage, always indict for an offence under s. 47, whatever the degree of harm caused, thus incurring the burden of proving a less degree of harm.

The *mens rea* would appear to be merely that of an assault—at the most of an assault being reckless whether some bodily harm might be caused.

3 WOUNDING AND GRIEVOUS BODILY HARM

Sections 18 and 20 of the Offences against the Person Act 1861 create offences of wounding and causing or inflicting grievous bodily harm. By s. 18, as amended by the Criminal Law Act 1967:

> "Whosoever shall unlawfully and maliciously by any means whatsoever wound or cause any grievous bodily harm to any person with intent to do some grievous bodily harm to any person or with intent to resist or prevent the lawful apprehension or detainer of any person, shall be guilty of an offence, and being convicted thereof shall be liable to imprisonment for life."

By s. 20:

> "Whosoever shall unlawfully and maliciously wound or inflict any grievous bodily harm upon any other person, either with or without any weapon or instrument shall be guilty of a misdemeanour, and being convicted thereof shall be liable to imprisonment for five years."

The two sections are closely associated with one another and it is convenient to consider them together. Each creates two offences, one of wounding and the other of causing (s. 18) or inflicting (s. 20) grievous bodily harm.

(1) THE ACTUS REUS

1 To Wound

In order to constitute a wound, the continuity of the whole skin must be broken.[12] It is not enough that the cuticle or outer skin be broken if the inner skin remains intact.[13] Where P was treated with such violence that his collar-bone was broken, it was held that there was no wound if his skin was intact.[14] It was held to be a wound, however, where the lining membrane of the urethra was ruptured and bled, evidence being given that the membrane is precisely the same in character as that which lines the cheek and the external and internal skin of the lip.[15]

It was held that there was no wounding under the 1837 Act[16] where P, in warding off D's attempt to cut his throat, struck his hands against a knife held by

---

[11] Below, p. 265.
[12] *Moriarty* v. *Brooks* (1834), 6 C. & P. 684.
[13] *M'Loughlin* (1838), 8 C. & P. 635.
[14] *Wood* (1830), 1 Mood. C.C. 278.
[15] *Waltham* (1849), 3 Cox C.C. 442. Contrast *Jones* (1849), 3 Cox C.C. 441, where there was internal bleeding but no evidence of where it came from.
[16] 1 Vic. c. 85, s. 4.

D and cut them;[17] and where P was knocked down by D and wounded by falling on iron trams.[18] That Act did not contain the words "by any means whatsoever", and it is probable that these cases would now be decided differently. Even under the earlier law, D was guilty where he struck P on the hat with a gun and the hard rim of the hat caused a wound.[19]

2 To Cause or Inflict Grievous Bodily Harm

As already noted,[20] this was formerly interpreted to include any harm which seriously interferes with health or comfort;[1] but in *Smith*[2] the House of Lords said that there was no warrant for giving the words a meaning other than that which they convey in their ordinary and natural meaning. This was *obiter*, so far as the statutory offences are concerned, but it has since been followed in *Metharam*[3] where it was held to be misdirection to use the old formula. Grievous bodily harm may cover cases where there is no wounding as, for instance, the broken collar-bone in *Wood*.[4] Conversely, there might be a technical "wounding" which could not be said to amount to grievous bodily harm.

Where s. 18 uses the word "cause", s. 20[5] uses "inflict". The effect may be that s. 18 is wider than s. 20. Bodily harm is not "inflicted" under s. 20 unless it is caused by an assault of some kind.[6] In *Clarence*,[6] the Court for Crown Cases Reserved held by a majority of nine to four that D who, knowing that he was suffering from gonorrhoea, had intercourse with his wife and infected her, was not guilty of inflicting grievous bodily harm. He had acted "unlawfully", for his conduct constituted cruelty under the divorce laws and was grounds for a judicial separation; but the word "inflict", in this context, implied an assault and here there was no assault. STEPHEN, J., said:[7]

> "The words appear to me to mean the direct causing of some grievous injury to the body itself with a weapon as by a cut with a knife, or without a weapon, as by a blow with the fist, or by pushing a person down. Indeed though the word 'assault' is not used in the section, I think the words imply an assault and battery of which a wound or grievous bodily harm is the manifest, immediate and obvious result."

To constitute an assault, and so an offence under s. 20, it is not necessary that the injury should be directly inflicted. Thus WILLS, J., while holding an assault to be necessary, nevertheless expressed in *Clarence* his approval of *Martin*.[8] Shortly before the end of a performance in a theatre D put out the lights on the landing of the gallery staircase and over the pay office and placed an iron bar across the doorway. The audience was seized by panic and rushed down the stairs, forcing those in front against the iron bar and causing them serious

---

[17] *Becket* (1836), 1 Mood. & R. 526, (PARKE, B.); *Day* (1845), 1 Cox C.C. 207; above, p. 253. *Cf. Coleman*, (1920), 84 J.P. 112.
[18] *Spooner* (1853), 6 Cox C.C. 392.
[19] *Sheard* (1837), 2 Mood. C.C. 13.
[20] Above, p. 181.
[1] *Ashman* (1858), 1 F. & F. 88.
[2] [1961] A.C. 290; [1960] 3 All E.R. 161; above, p. 197.
[3] [1961] 3 All E.R. 200.
[4] Above, p. 264, footnote 14.
[5] Above, p. 264.
[6] *Taylor* (1869), L.R. 1 C.C.R. 194; *Clarence* (1888), 22 Q.B.D. 23.
[7] (1889), 22 Q.B.D. at p. 41.
[8] (1881), 8 Q.B.D. 54. WILLS, J., agreed with STEPHEN, J., that "a man who digs a pit for another to fall into, whereby that other is injured" would be within the section.

injuries. He was convicted of inflicting grievous bodily harm. The judges seem to have directed their attention solely to the question of *mens rea* and to have assumed that there was an *actus reus*.

Martin was followed in *Halliday*,[9] where D so terrified his wife, P, that she attempted to get out of a window. Her daughter caught and held her. D, uttering threats, *approached within reach of P* and told the daughter to let her go. The daughter did so and P fell into the street and was injured. Lord COLERIDGE, C.J., stated the principle broadly:[10]

> "If a man creates in another man's mind an immediate sense of danger which causes such a person to try to escape, and in so doing he injures himself, the person who creates such a state of mind is responsible for the injuries which result."

This proposition does not necessarily involve an assault in the technical sense and it is submitted that, notwithstanding the observations in *Clarence*,[11] so to require would be too restrictive of s. 20. *Clarence* can well be confined to narrower grounds; for example, (i) that this section was not intended to apply to the administration of poison[12] and (ii) that P did in fact consent. If *Clarence* is correct, there still remains the question whether it governs s. 18. HAWKINS, J., thought that if the charge in *Clarence* had been under s. 18 no one could have doubted that

> "he would have fallen within not only the spirit but the precise language of the section, according to the strictest interpretation which could be applied to it";[13]

HAWKINS, J., was dissenting but his view on this point seems to be correct. Clearly, the ordinary meaning of "cause" is wider than that attributed by the majority to "inflict". This is not a strong point, however, for the meaning given to "inflict" was also an unnaturally narrow one. Indeed—as HAWKINS, J., pointed out—under s. 23 of the Act, there is an offence of inflicting grievous bodily harm by administering poison[14] which, plainly, does not involve an assault. On the other hand, one of the reasons given by STEPHEN, J.,[15] for confining "inflict" to assaults was that s. 20 was a re-enactment of an earlier section[16] which began by reciting the expediency of making further provision for "aggravated assaults". Section 18 replaced a section in a different statute[17] which contained no similar preamble. The main point is that the words, "by any means whatsoever", which occur in s. 18 and not in s. 20 are very strong indeed. They seem to cover a case of poisoning or of causing grievous bodily harm by deliberate omission to act where there is a duty to do so.[18]

(2) THE MENS REA

1 **Malice**

Both sections contain the word "maliciously". According to the general

---

[9] (1889), 61 L.T. 701.
[10] *Ibid.* at p. 702.
[11] Above, footnote 7.
[12] STEPHEN, J., 22 Q.B.D. at pp. 41–42.
[13] (1888), 22 Q.B.D. at p. 48.
[14] Below, p. 269.
[15] At p. 41.
[16] Section 4 of 14 & 15 Vic. c. 19.
[17] Section 4 of 7 Will, 4 & 1 Vic. c. 85.
[18] *Cf.* above, p. 248.

principles discussed above,[19] this might be expected to mean that it must be proved that D intended or was reckless whether he wounded or caused grievous bodily harm. This requires qualification.[20]

Where, under s. 18, the charge is of causing grievous bodily harm with intent to do grievous bodily harm, the word "maliciously" obviously has no part to play. Any *mens rea* which it might import is comprehended within the ulterior intent. Where the charge is wounding with intent to do grievous bodily harm, the word can be given meaning, though the occasion to invoke it is unlikely to arise. It is possible for D to intend to do grievous bodily harm, without intending to wound. If he in fact wounds and is charged accordingly, then it is arguable that it must be proved, not only that he intended to cause grievous bodily harm, but also that he foresaw that he might wound, otherwise the wounding is not malicious.

Where the charge is of wounding or causing grievous bodily harm with intent to resist lawful apprehension, then there is no difficulty in giving meaning to "maliciously" and it is submitted that meaning should be given to that word. A mere intent to resist lawful apprehension should not found liability for a charge of wounding or causing grievous bodily harm. It is submitted that the Court of Appeal went too far in *Mowatt*[1] in saying that "In section 18 the word 'maliciously' adds nothing."

The observation was *obiter*, the court in that case being concerned with an appeal from conviction under s. 20. The court held that, under this section,—

> ". . . the word 'maliciously' does import upon the part of the person who unlawfully inflicts the wound or other grievous bodily harm an awareness that his act may have the consequence of causing some physical harm to some other person. That is what is meant by 'the particular kind of harm' in the citation from Professor Kenny.[2] It is quite unnecessary that the accused should have foreseen that his unlawful act might cause physical harm of the gravity described in the section, *i.e.*, a wound or serious physical injury. It is enough that he should have foreseen that some physical harm to some person, albeit of a minor character, might result."

If this be correct for s. 20, then it is submitted that it is also correct for s. 18, where the charge does not specify an ulterior intent which necessarily comprehends injury to the person. It is submitted, however, that the statement in *Mowatt* is unsound in principle. A person who intends some injury less than wounding or grievous bodily harm intends to commit another offence under the Offences against the Person Act, that of assault occasioning actual bodily harm, contrary to s. 47.[3] This appears to be a less serious offence than that under s. 20 and it is wrong that the *mens rea* of the less offence should suffice for liability for the greater. In fact, offences under both s. 20 and s. 47 are punishable with five years' imprisonment.[4] This is quite irrational, and no doubt happens because the

---

[19] See p. 74.

[20] See MacKenna, J., in [1966] Crim. L.R. 548 at p. 533.

[1] [1968] 1 Q.B. 421; [1967] 3 All E.R. 47. See Buxton, "Negligence and Constructive Crime", [1969] Crim. L.R. (March). See also *Ward* (1872), L.R. 1 C.C.R. 356.

[2] *Outlines of Criminal Law* (19th ed.), 211. The citation is the passage approved by the Court of Criminal Appeal in *Cunningham*, [1957] 2 Q.B. 396; [1957] 2 All E.R. 412; above, p. 74; below, p. 270.

[3] Above, p. 263.

[4] Thus the prosecution might always use s. 47 where the onus on the Crown is much less, so that s. 20 would become redundant except where the jury acquit on a charge under s. 18 and convict instead of an offence under s. 20, which they may do though that offence be not expressly charged: Criminal Law Act 1967, s. 6 (3).

Act, like most of the 1861 legislation is a rag-bag of offences brought together from a variety of statutes with little or no attempt to introduce uniformity or consistency. Thus the accused who intends harm of a minor character and is convicted of an offence under s. 20 cannot be more severely punished than for the offence which he intended; but this should not be allowed to obscure the violation of principle involved. A rational system, if it distinguished at all between causing actual and causing grievous bodily harm, would provide for different penalties and the *mens rea* of the less should not be sufficient to found liability for the greater offence.

Whatever consequence it is that must be foreseen, it is clear that there must be proof that the accused person actually foresaw that consequence. Any doubt there may have been about this has been dispelled by the Criminal Justice Act 1968, s. 8.[5] *Mowatt* was decided before the Act came into force, and certain observations in the case are therefore suspect. It was said[6] that where the act:

"... was a direct assault which any ordinary person would be bound to realise was likely to cause some physical harm to the other person .. and the defence put forward on behalf of the accused is not that the assault was accidental or that he did not realise that it might cause some physical harm to the victim, but is some other defence such as that he did not do the alleged act or that he did it in self-defence, it is unnecessary to deal specifically in the summing up with what is meant by the word 'maliciously' in the section."

This suggests that the jury need not be directed on the issue because they are bound to infer that D foresaw the result by reason of its being a natural and probable consequence of his actions. This is directly contrary to the words of s. 8. Under s. 10 of the Criminal Justice Act 1967, formal admissions may be made; but, if D has not admitted his malice, then it is submitted that it must be proved like every other element in the crime. The fact that the evidence appears to the judge to be overwhelming is not a good reason for not leaving it to the jury.

Similar considerations apply to the case of *Wilkins* v. *An Infant*[7] where the justices had dismissed an information under s. 20 against a fifteen year old boy on the ground that, while an older person might have foreseen the consequences (of firing an air gun at a hut in which children were playing) the defendant was too young to do s. The decision of the divisional court that this was the wrong approach and that the conclusion could not stand is obviously correct; but the court went on to direct the justices to convict. This again seems to be a decision that D must have foreseen because an ordinary person would have done so. The court, so far as appears, had not seen or heard the evidence of the boy. How then could they be certain that *this* boy foresaw the consequences of his act? It would seem that the right course, especially since the Criminal Justice Act 1967, would be to send such a case back to the justices with a direction to apply their minds to the right question and decide accordingly.

2   The ulterior intent

Section 18 alone requires an ulterior intent which may be either an intent to do grievous bodily harm or an intent to resist or prevent the lawful apprehension or detainer of any person. A count is not bad for duplicity because it specifies the

---

[5] Above, p. 52.
[6] At p. 426–427.
[7] (1965), 109 Sol. Jo. 850; [1965] Crim. L.R. 730.

ulterior intent in the alternative; the intents specified "are variations of method rather than creations of separate offences in themselves", according to *Naismith*[8]—though it is difficult to see how an ulterior intent can be equated with a "method".

The intent specified in the indictment must be proved. It is not enough to prove another variety of intent described in the section. So D had to be acquitted where the various counts of the indictment charged intent to murder, to disable, or to do some grievous bodily harm and the jury found that the acts were done to resist and prevent D's apprehension *and for no other purpose*.[9] But if D intends to prevent his apprehension and, in order to do so, intends to cause grievous bodily harm, he may be convicted under an indictment charging only the latter intent. It is immaterial which is the principal and which the subordinate intent.[10]

If D intends to cause grievous bodily harm to O and, striking at O, he by accident wounds another person P, he may be convicted of wounding P with intent to cause grievous bodily harm to O.[11] If D intends to cause grievous bodily harm to O, and strikes the person he aims at who is in fact P, he may be convicted of wounding P with intent to cause grievous bodily harm to P.[12]

The intent to cause grievous bodily harm requires no further consideration. The intent to resist lawful apprehension is obviously negatived if the attempted apprehension is believed to be, and is, unlawful.[13] But if the apprehension is lawful, it has been held[14] that it is no defence that D believed it unlawful. This was put on the ground that ignorance of the law was not a defence. It does not follow that D should be convicted if he wrongly believed in a state of *facts* such that, if it had existed, the arrest would have been unlawful. In such a case, it is submitted that he should be acquitted, at all events if his belief was reasonable. It is, moreover, arguable that even a mistake of law should afford a defence, being a mistake of civil law which negatives *mens rea*.[15]

4 ADMINISTERING POISON

(1) THE ACTUS REUS

Sections 23 and 24 of the Offences against the Person Act 1861 create offences, punishable with ten and five years' imprisonment, respectively, with a similar *actus reus*. In each case, the definition includes the words—

> ". . . unlawfully . . . administer to or cause to be administered to or taken by any other person any poison or other destructive or noxious thing. . . ."[16]

---

[8] [1961] 2 All E.R. 735 (C.–M.A.C.).

[9] *Duffin and Marshall* (1818), Russ. & Ry. 365; *cf. Boyce* (1824), 1 Moo. C.C. 29.

[10] *Gillow* (1825), 1 Mood. C.C. 85. *Cf. Cox* (1818), Russ. & Ry. 362. In *Woodburne and Coke* (1722), 16 State Tr. 53, the defence to an indictment charging intent to maim and disfigure was that D intended to kill. Lord KING, C.J., directed (at p. 81) that the latter intent did not exclude the former. WILLES, J., and EYRE, B., expressed some dissatisfaction with this case: East, 1 P.C. 400; and *cf. Sullivan* (1841), C. & M. 209.

[11] *Cf.*, the doctrine of "transferred malice", above, p. 44. In *Jarvis* (1837), 2 Mood & R. 40, GURNEY, B., directed that D could be convicted of shooting at P with intent to injure P although D had in fact aimed at O, but missed. This seems hardly satisfactory as D in fact neither shot at P nor intended to injure him. But *Hunt* (1825), 1 Mood, C.C. 93, seems to be to the same effect. *Cf. Ryan* (1839), 2 M. & R. 213, and *Hewlett* (1858), 1 F. & F. 91, which are to the contrary.

[12] *Smith* (1855), Dears. 559, 560; *Stopford* (1870), 11 Cox C.C. 643.

[13] *Walker* (1854), Dears. C.C. 358; *Sanders* (1867), L.R. 1 C.C.R. 75.

[14] *Bentley* (1850), 4 Cox C.C. 406.

[15] Above, p. 50.

[16] The meaning of poison, etc., is considered above, p. 244.

But under s. 23, the *actus* includes a further element—

". . . so as thereby to endanger the life of such person, or so as thereby to inflict upon such person any grievous bodily harm . . .".

A poison is "administered" by D if it is left by him for P who takes it up and consumes it.[17]   In the case of a poison intended to be swallowed, it seems that it is not administered until it is taken into the stomach.[18]   But clearly to leave the poison, intending it to be taken, would be an áttempt.

(2) THE MENS REA

Under s. 23 the only *mens rea* required is intention or recklessness as to the administration of a noxious thing. This, at least, is plainly required by the use in the section of the word "maliciously"; and, of course, it has been so held in the leading case of *Cunningham*.[19]   It may be, however, on present authority, that the requirement of malice does not extend to the second part of the *actus*— so as to endanger life or inflict grievous bodily harm.

Section 24 requires an ulterior intent:

"with intent to injure aggrieve or annoy such person".

Where D put a sleeping tablet in P's tea to enable him to search her handbag and find letters to prove she was committing adultery, it was held that there was insufficient evidence of intent to injure aggrieve or annoy.[20]   This suggests that the inquiry as to intent should be limited to the direct physical effect of the thing administered. But surely D would have an intent to injure aggrieve or annoy if he administered a sleeping pill to P with intent to rape her. It is submitted that regard should be had to the whole object which D had in mind.

The contrast between "so as thereby to" in s. 23 and "with intent to" in s. 24, does perhaps suggest that no *mens rea* is required as to the second part of the *actus* in s. 23; and it seems to have been so held in a civil case. *Tully* v. *Corrie*[1] was an action for false imprisonment in which the defence was that the plaintiff had committed a felony which an offence under s. 23 then was. The jury found that a noxious thing had been administered, but not with intent to inflict grievous bodily harm; and that grievous bodily harm had resulted. The Court of Queen's Bench upheld COCKBURN, C.J.'s direction of a verdict for the defendant. MELLOR, J., said:[2]

"The mere administration of poison with intent only to injure or annoy is of itself only a misdemeanour [s. 24]; but its administration if it actually causes grievous bodily harm, *or with intent to cause such injury* is a felony."

In the first place, it may be pointed out that the italicised proposition is unsupportable. Clearly the grievous bodily harm must actually be caused (or life

---

[17] *Harley* (1830), 4 C. & P. 369; *Dale* (1852), 6 Cox C.C. 14. D would more appropriately be charged with "causing . . . to be taken".
[18] *Cadman* (1825), *Carrington's Supplement*, 237. The report to the contrary in Ryan and Moody 114 is said to be inaccurate: *Harley* (above), *per* PARK, J.: and 6 Cox C.C. 16, n. (c). But see *Walford* (1899), 34 L. Jo. 116, *per* WILLS, J.
[19] [1957] 2 Q.B. 396; [1957] 2 All E.R. 412; D tore the gas meter from the wall of an unoccupied house to steal money from it. The gas seeped into the neighbouring houses and was taken by P, whose life was endangered. D's conviction under s. 23 was quashed because the judge directed the jury only that "malicious" meant "wicked".
[20] *Weatherall*, [1968] Crim. L.R. 115 (Judge BRODRICK); above, p. 244.
[1] (1867), 10 Cox C.C. 640.
[2] *Ibid.*, at p. 641.

actually endangered). Secondly, it is implicit in the case that D intended to administer a noxious thing and to injure, aggrieve or annoy; but there is no finding as to any state of mind with reference to endangering life or grievous bodily harm, and the case must decide that none is necessary.

This is an extraordinary result, in that a less culpable state of mind is required for the more serious offence than the less. It is submitted that *Tully* v. *Corrie* should be re-considered and that the requirement of malice should be extended to endangering life or inflicting grievous bodily harm. *Cunningham*, unfortunately, does not necessarily go so far. The court thought the jury should have been told that D must have foreseen that the coal gas might cause injury to someone. They did not say he must have foreseen that life would be endangered.

By s. 25, a person charged under s. 23 may be convicted of an offence under s. 24. But a person charged under s. 24 may not be convicted of an offence under s. 23.[3]

5 FALSE IMPRISONMENT

False imprisonment, like assault and battery, is both a misdemeanour at common law and a tort. The civil remedy is much more commonly invoked and most of the cases on this subject are civil actions. But, as will appear, it is probable that there are some important distinctions between the crime and the tort.

False imprisonment is committed where D unlawfully and intentionally or recklessly restrains P's freedom of movement from a particular place.

(1) THE ACTUS REUS

1 Imprisonment

The "imprisonment" may consist in confining P in a prison,[4] a house,[5] even P's own house,[6] a mine[7] or a vehicle;[8] or simply in detaining P in a public street[9] or any other place. It is enough that D orders P to accompany him to another place and P goes because he feels constrained to do so. P is not imprisoned if, on hearing D use words of arrest, he runs away or makes his escape by a trick.[10] If P goes voluntarily, and not in consequence of the command, he is not imprisoned.[11] An invitation by D to P to accompany him cannot be an imprisonment if it is made clear to P that he is entitled to refuse to go. Thus Lord LYNDHURST, C.B., thought there was no imprisonment where D asked a policeman to take P into custody, and the policeman objected, but said that if D and P "would be so good as to go with him", he would take the advice of his

---

[3] *Cf. Stokes* (1925), 19 Cr. App. Rep. 71.
[4] *Cobbett* v. *Grey* (1850), 4 Exch. 729.
[5] *Warner* v. *Riddiford* (1858), 4 C.B. N.S. 180.
[6] *Termes de la Ley*, approved by WARRINGTON and ATKIN, L.JJ. (1920), 122 L.T. at 51 and 53.
[7] *Herd* v. *Weardale Steel, Coal and Coke Co., Ltd.*, [1915] A.C. 67.
[8] By driving at such a speed that P dare not alight: *McDaniel* v. *State* (1942), 15 Tex. Cr. R. 115; *Burton* v. *Davies*, [1953] Q.S.R. 26.
[9] Blackstone, *Commentaries*, iii, 127.
[10] *Russen* v. *Lucas* (1824), 1 C. & P. 153.
[11] *Wood* v. *Lane* (1834), 6 C. & P. 774; *Arrowsmith* v. *Le Mesurier* (1806), 2 Bos. & P. (N.R.) 211.

superior.[12] The distinction between a command, amounting to an imprisonment, and a request not doing so, is a difficult one.[13] Probably ALDERSON, B. went too far in *Peters* v. *Stanway*[14] in holding that P was imprisoned if she went to the police station with a constable voluntarily but nevertheless in consequence of a charge against her.

Though some of the older authorities[15] speak of false imprisonment as a species of assault it is quite clear that no assault need be proved.[16] In *Linsberg*,[17] the Common Sergeant held that P, a doctor, was falsely imprisoned where D locked the door to prevent him leaving a confinement. The restraint need be only momentary, so that the offence would be complete if D tapped P on the shoulder and said, "You are my prisoner."[18] But a battery is not necessarily an imprisonment. In *Bird* v. *Jones*[19] P was involved in

> "a struggle during which no momentary detention of his person took place."

It is not an imprisonment wrongfully to prevent P from going in a particular direction, if he is free to go in other directions. This was decided in *Bird* v. *Jones*,[20] where COLERIDGE, J., said:

> "A prison may have its boundary large or narrow, visible and tangible, or, though real, still in the conception only;[1] it may itself be moveable or fixed: but a boundary it must have. . . .",

It would be otherwise if P could move off in other directions only by taking an unreasonable risk;[2] it could hardly be said that a man locked in a second-floor room was not imprisoned because he could have climbed down the drainpipe.

There is little authority on the question how large the area of confinement may be. It has been suggested that it would be tortious to confine a P to a large country estate or the Isle of Man;[3] but it could hardly be false imprisonment to prevent P from leaving Great Britain, still less to prevent him from entering. But a person who has actually landed and is not allowed to leave an airport building is imprisoned.[4] Is P also imprisoned, then, if he is not allowed to leave the ship which has docked in a British port?

It has been held by the Court of Appeal, DUKE, L.J., dissenting, in *Meering* v. *Graham-White Aviation Co., Ltd.*[5] that it is irrelevant that P does not know he is imprisoned. ATKIN, L.J., said:

> "It appears to me that a person could be imprisoned without his knowing it. I think a person can be imprisoned while he is asleep, while he is in a state of

---

[12] *Cant* v. *Parsons* (1834), 6 C. & P. 504.

[13] Williams in *Police Power and Individual Freedom* at p. 43.

[14] (1835), 6 C. & P. 737, followed in *Conn* v. *David Spencer, Ltd.*, [1930] 1 D.L.R. 805.

[15] For example, Hawkins, 1. P.C., c. 60, § 7; *Pocock* v. *Moore* (1825), Ry. & M. 321.

[16] *Grainger* v. *Hill* (1838), 4 Bing. N.C. 212; *Warner* v. *Riddiford* (1858), 4 C.B. N.S. 180.

[17] (1905), 69 J.P. 107.

[18] *Simpson* v. *Hill* (1795), 1 Esp. 431, *per* EYRE, C.J.; *Sandon* v. *Jervis* (1859), E.B. & E. 942, ". . . a mere touch constitutes an arrest, though the party be not actually taken;" *per* CROWDER, J.

[19] *Infra.*

[20] (1845), 7 Q.B. 742 (DENMAN, C.J., dissenting).

[1] For example, P is forbidden to move more than ten yards from the village pump.

[2] Street, *Torts*, 24.

[3] Street, *ibid.* In *Re Mwenya*, [1960] 1 Q.B. 241; [1959] 3 All E.R. 525, a writ of *habeas corpus* was sought for P who was confined to an area of some 1,500 square miles but he was released before it became necessary to decide whether he was imprisoned for the purpose of *habeas corpus*.

[4] *Kuchenmeister* v. *Home Office*, [1958] 1 Q.B. 496; [1958] 1 All E.R. 485.

[5] (1919), 122 L.T. 44.

drunkenness, while he is unconscious, and while he is a lunatic . . . though the imprisonment began and ceased while he was in that state."

A contrary decision of the Court of Exchequer[6] was not cited and the case has been heavily criticised;[7] but the arguments advanced against awarding damages in this situation are not applicable to the crime. D's conduct may not be damaging to P if P knows nothing about it, but it is not necessarily any less blameworthy for, in most cases, the fact that P remains in ignorance must be a matter of mere chance.[8]

Like other crimes, false imprisonment can be committed through an innocent agent. So D is responsible for the *actus reus* if, at his direction or request, a policeman takes P into custody,[9] or he signs the charge-sheet when the police have said they will not take the responsibility of detaining P unless he does;[10] but merely to give information to a constable, in consequence of which he decides to make an arrest has been held not to be actionable, at all events if D is *bona fide*.[11] *A fortiori*, it should not be *criminal*, for lack of *mens rea*; but why should D not be guilty if he deliberately supplies false information to a constable who, acting on his own authority but relying exclusively on D's information, arrests P? D has surely caused the *actus reus* with *mens rea* and may be liable for the ministerial act of the constable as distinct from the judicial act of the magistrate.[12] Where D is initially liable for false imprisonment his liability ceases on the intervention of some judicial act[13] authorising the detention or on any other event, breaking the chain of causation.[14]

Whatever may be the position in the law of tort,[15] it is thought that it would be immaterial in the criminal law that the imprisonment was not "directly" caused by D; and that it would be sufficient that he caused it with *mens rea*—as by digging a pit into which P falls and is trapped.[16]

Another question in the law of tort is whether it is possible falsely to imprison by mere omission in view of the requirement of a trespass. In *Herd v. Weardale Steel Coal and Coke Co., Ltd.*[17] P voluntarily descended into D's mine and, in breach of contract, stopped work and asked to be brought to the surface before the end of the shift. D's refusal to accede to this request was not a false imprisonment: he was under no duty to provide facilities for P to leave in breach of contract. Clearly, the result would be different if D were to take positive steps

---

[6] *Herring* v. *Boyle* (1834), 1 Cr. M. & R. 377.
[7] Williams in *Police Power and Individual Freedom* at 45–46; Street, *Torts*, 26.
[8] It might, however, be an attempt to imprison, under one theory of attempt; above, p. 173, footnotes 15 and 16.
[9] *Gosden* v. *Elphick and Bennett* (1849), 4 Exch. 445.
[10] *Austin* v. *Dowling* (1870), L.R. 5 C.P. 534. It is otherwise if D signs the charge sheet as a matter of form, when the police are detaining P on their own responsibility: *Grinham* v. *Willey* (1859), 4 H. & N. 496.
[11] *Gosden* v. *Elphick and Bennett*, above; *Grinham* v. *Willey, supra*: "We ought to take care that people are not put in peril for making complaint when a crime has been committed," *per* POLLOCK, C.B.
[12] See *Austin* v. *Dowling* (1870), L.R. 5 C. & P. at p. 540.
[13] *Lock* v. *Ashton* (1848), 12 Q.B. 871. *Cf. Marrinan* v. *Vibart*, [1963] 1 Q.B. 528; [1962] 3 All E.R. 380.
[14] *Harnett* v. *Bond*, [1925] A.C. 669. D's report caused P to be taken to an asylum; D was not liable for the imprisonment after the doctor at the asylum had examined P and decided to detain him. *Cf. Pike* v. *Waldrum*, [1952] 1 Lloyds Rep. 431.
[15] Street, *Torts*, 25.
[16] *Cf. Clarence* (1888), 22 Q.B.D. 23 at p. 36, *per* WILLS, J.
[17] [1915] A.C. 67 (H.L.).

to prevent P from leaving in breach of contract,[18] as by locking him in a factory. Buckley and Hamilton, L.JJ.,[19] thought that mere omission could not have been false imprisonment, even if it occurred when the shift was over: P's only civil remedy would have been in contract; but the House of Lords expressed no opinion on this point.

In *Mee* v. *Cruikshank*,[20] Wills J., held that a prison governor was under a duty to take steps to ensure that his officers did not detain a prisoner who had been acquitted. In that case there were acts of imprisonment by the prison officers but they were not the servants of D, the governor, and it seems to have been D's omission which rendered him liable in tort. Surely it ought to be false imprisonment if D, a gaoler, is under a duty to release P at midnight and deliberately omits to unlock his cell until noon the following day?[1] And it ought to make no difference that D's duty to release P arises out of a contract:

> "If a man gets into an express train and the doors are locked pending its arrival at its destination, he is not entitled, merely because the train has been stopped by signal, to call for the doors to be opened to let him out."[2]

But if he is kept locked in for a day at his destination this surely ought to be false imprisonment. And if the technicalities of the forms of action preclude a remedy in tort this is no reason why the omission should not be held to be criminal.

2   Unlawful Restraint

The imprisonment must be "false", that is, unlawful. Thus there is no false imprisonment in the following cases:

(i) *Where a constable arrests under a valid warrant.*—Where the justice lacks jurisdiction to issue the warrant, the constable is statutorily protected[3] from any action if he acts in obedience to it. As the term "action" is inappropriate to a criminal proceeding, a constable could not rely on the Act as a defence to a criminal prosecution; but he would probably have a good defence on the ground of lack of *mens rea*.[4]

(ii) *Where a constable or other person arrests without warrant under a power provided by s. 2 (2)–(7) of the Criminal Law Act 1967:*[5]

> (2) Any person may arrest without warrant anyone who is, or whom he, with reasonable cause, suspects to be, in the act of committing an arrestable offence.[6]

---

[18] Unless, perhaps, the contract was that P should be entitled to leave only on the fulfilment of some reasonable condition: *Robinson* v. *Balmain New Ferry Co., Ltd.*, [1910] A.C. 295 (P.C.). *Sed quaere* whether one is entitled to restrain another from leaving even if it is a breach of contract for him to do so? The contract can hardly be specifically enforceable.

[19] [1913] 3 K.B. at pp. 787 and 793.

[20] (1902), 20 Cox C.C. 210.

[1] See *Moone* v. *Rose* (1869), L.R. 4 Q.B. 486; *Lesley* (1860), Bell, C.C. 220; and *cf. Peacock* v. *Musgrave*, [1956] Crim. L.R. 414 (where damages were awarded for detention by the police, originally justified, but unreasonably prolonged) and *Lambert* v. *Hodgson* (1823), 1 Bing. 317.

[2] *Herd* v. *Weardale Steel Coal and Coke Co., Ltd.*, [1915] A.C. 67 at p. 71, *per* Lord Haldane.

[3] The Constables Protection Act 1750.

[4] Below, p. 276.

[5] See annotations in *Current Law Statutes Annotated*, 1967.

[6] For the definition of an "arrestable offence", see above, p. 24.

(3) Where an arrestable offence has been committed, any person may arrest without warrant anyone who is, or whom he, with reasonable cause, suspects to be, guilty of the offence.

(4) Where a constable, with reasonable cause, suspects that an arrestable offence has been committed, he may arrest without warrant anyone whom he, with reasonable cause, suspects to be guilty of the offence.

(5) A constable may arrest without warrant any person who is, or whom he, with reasonable cause, suspects to be, about to commit an arrestable offence.

(6) For the purpose of arresting a person under any power conferred by this section a constable may enter (if need be, by force) and search any place where that person is or where the constable, with reasonable cause, suspects him to be.

(7) This section shall not affect the operation of any enactment restricting the institution of proceedings for an offence, nor prejudice any power of arrest conferred by law apart from this section."

It will be noted that arrest is always lawful where D reasonably suspects P to be in the act of committing the arrestable offence, even though in fact P is not doing so: but that where D reasonably suspects that P *has committed* an arrestable offence, the arrest is unlawful if P is innocent, unless D happens to be a constable. This, in effect, re-enacts the rule laid down for arrest for felony in *Walters* v. *W. H. Smith & Sons, Ltd.*:[7] D suspected on reasonable grounds that P had stolen a number of books from his book stall. He arrested him on a charge of stealing a particular book. Though other books had certainly been stolen, this one had not been stolen by P or anyone else. Because the offence for which the arrest was made had not been committed, D was held liable in damages. The Criminal Law Revision Committee thought it right to preserve the rule, although they pointed out that it may be

"a trap to a private person who is careful instead of precipitate about deciding whether to arrest a person. If, for example, a store detective saw a person apparently shoplifting, he could arrest him under clause [now 'section'] 2 (2) on the ground that he had reasonable cause to suspect him of being in the act of committing an arrestable offence, and he would not be liable for unlawful arrest even if it turned out that he was wrong; but if he preferred out of caution to invite the other to the office to give him an opportunity of clearing himself, and then arrested him on being satisfied that he was guilty, the detective would be liable if this turned out to be wrong."[8]

The justification for the rule is that an increase in the powers of arrest of private persons would not be acceptable to public opinion and that it is desirable, where it is at all doubtful whether an offence has been committed, for a private person to put the matter in the hands of the police.[9] This hardly allows, however, for the case where the citizen has no opportunity to inform the police and must either let the suspected person escape or make an arrest himself.

The powers of arrest of a constable are thus wider under s. 2 than those of other persons in two respects. An arrest by a constable of a person reasonably suspected of having committed an arrestable offence is not unlawful even though the offence in question has never been committed.

---

[7] [1914] 1 K.B. 595.
[8] Cmnd. 2659, para. 14.
[9] *Ibid.*, para. 15.

Secondly a constable may arrest a person reasonably suspected to be *about to commit* an arrestable offence, whereas other persons must wait until he is *in the act* of committing the offence.

(iii) *Where a constable or other person arrests for a breach of peace which has occurred in his presence, or where there are reasonable grounds for believing that it may occur.*[10]—A breach of the peace includes a riot, an affray, or an assault or battery committed by P upon D[11] or another.[12] Members of an unlawful assembly may be arrested where it is reasonably suspected that there will be a breach of the peace.

(iv) *Where a constable or other person arrests under one of numerous statutory powers.*[13]

(2) MENS REA

Since the great majority of the cases are civil actions, there is little authority on the nature of the *mens rea* required for false imprisonment. It is submitted that the question should be governed by general principles and that D should be liable only if he intentionally or recklessly caused an *actus reus*. Thus it has been suggested that D would not have been criminally liable in *Walters* v. *W. H. Smith & Son, Ltd*,[14] since he believed, on reasonable grounds, that the felony for which he arrested P had been committed in which case there would have been no *actus reus*. This seems to be right in principle. Similarly, a belief that an arrestable offence had been committed should be defence on a criminal charge, though not to an action for damages. Even if the belief were unreasonable, it ought, according the submissions above,[15] to be a defence; but, because of the court's insistence that a mistake must be reasonable, it might not do so.

(3) KIDNAPPING

According to East[16]

"The most aggravated species of false imprisonment is the stealing and carrying away, or secreting of some person, sometimes called kidnapping, which is an offence at common law."

Blackstone[17] confines this offence to the case where the victim is sent into another country and East[18] appears to agree that this is strictly a constituent of kidnapping properly so-called.

According to Russell,[19] the offence is committed if a minor is taken away against the will of his friends or lawful guardians. If this is so, the offence may be slightly wider than false imprisonment. Consent, by a minor who understood the nature of the transaction, would afford a defence to false imprisonment, but

---

[10] *Light* (1857), D. & B. 332.
[11] *Coward* v. *Baddeley* (1859), 4 H. & N. 478.
[12] *Lewis* v. *Arnold* (1830), 4 C. & P. 354.
[13] Devlin (J.D.). *Police Procedure, Administration and Organisation* (1966), 308–327, Archbold, § 2811, and Williams, "The Interpretation of Statutory Powers of Arrest without Warrant", [1958] Crim. L.R. 73 and 154.
[14] Above, p. 275.
[15] See pp. 129–131.
[16] 1 P.C., 429.
[17] *Commentaries*, iv, 429.
[18] 1 P.C. 430.
[19] *Crime*, 692.

apparently not to kidnapping, if his parents or guardian did not consent. If the child is under fourteen and force or fraud is practised on the parent an offence is committed under the section next considered, even if the child goes willingly. If the child is a *girl* under sixteen, taking without the consent of the parents is an offence under s. 20 of the Sexual Offences Act 1956[20] even though she goes willingly. But if the child is a girl over sixteen or a boy of any age who goes willingly and no force or fraud is practised on anyone, kidnapping is the only charge. Kidnapping may therefore be of some small importance at the present day.

(4) CHILD-STEALING

Child-stealing is an offence, punishable with seven years' imprisonment.[1] The *actus reus* is—

> "unlawfully, either by force or fraud, [to] lead or take away, or decoy or entice away or detain, any child under the age of fourteen years."

The force or fraud may be directed either at the child or the parent.[2]
The *mens rea* is—

> "with intent to deprive any parent, guardian, or other person having the lawful care or charge of such child, of the possession of such child,"

or

> "with intent to steal any article upon or about the person of such child."

Where it is alleged that D intended to deprive the parent, etc., it is not necessary to show that this was intended to be a permanent deprivation as in larceny.[3]

The following persons are exempted from prosecution for "getting possession of such a child or taking such child . . .":

1. A person "who shall have claimed any right to possession of such child."
2. The mother of the child.
3. A person "who shall have claimed to be the father of the child where it is illegitimate."

It is curious that this exception is limited to cases of getting possession of, or taking, the child. The implication seems to be that there would be no defence to a prosecution on a charge of *detaining* the child. There seems to be no obvious reason for this.

Moreover, as observed above,[4] it may be possible to indict one of the exempted persons for a conspiracy with a non-exempted person to commit an offence under the section.

6 FIREARMS AND OFFENSIVE WEAPONS

One way of discouraging serious offences against the person is by regulating the use of firearms and offensive weapons and there is a good deal of criminal legislation on this subject.

---

[20] Below, p. 305.
[1] Offences against the Person Act 1861, s. 56.
[2] *Bellis* (1893), 17 Cox C.C. 660.
[3] *Powell* (1914), 79 J.P. 272.
[4] See p. 156.

(1) THE FIREARMS ACT 1968

The Firearms Act 1968 contains detailed regulations about firearms. It is an offence to purchase, acquire or possess any firearm or ammunition without a firearms certificate.[5] The Act provides for the grant, renewal, variation, revocation and production of certificates[6] and exempts various classes of persons from the necessity of holding a certificate.[7] It is a summary offence to manufacture, sell, transfer, repair, test or prove any firearm, or have it in one's possession for any of these purposes, or to expose it for sale or transfer, unless registered as a firearms dealer[8] and the Act makes detailed provision for registration.[9] It imposes restrictions on the purchase or possession of firearms and air weapons by young persons[10] and prohibits the sale of them to drunk or insane persons.[11] A person who has been sentenced to preventive detention or corrective training or imprisonment for three years or more, is prohibited from possessing a firearm or ammunition at any time. A person who has been sentenced for less than three years but not less than three months is prohibited from possessing a firearm or ammunition for five years from the date of his release. It is an offence to sell, etc., a firearm or ammunition to a person so prohibited.[12]

The Act creates a number of more serious offences which deserve more detailed consideration.

1 Prohibited Weapons

The Act distinguishes a separate category of prohibited weapons. These are weapons considered suitable for use only by the armed services and which have no proper function in civilian life.

A "prohibited weapon" is defined as, in effect, an automatic firearm (one which continues to discharge missiles while pressure is maintained on the trigger); any weapon

> "designed or adapted for the discharge of any noxious liquid gas or other thing"

and

> "any ammunition containing or designed or adapted to contain, any such noxious thing."[13]

It is an offence, punishable with two years' imprisonment, to manufacture, sell, transfer, purchase, acquire or have in one's possession any prohibited weapon without the consent of the Defence Council.

2 Use of Firearms or Imitation Firearms to Resist Arrest; and Possession of them, in relation to Certain Offences

By s. 17 (1) of the Act it is an offence, punishable with fourteen years' imprisonment,

---

[5] Firearms Act 1968, s. 1.
[6] *Ibid.*, ss. 26–32.
[7] *Ibid.*, ss. 7–12.
[8] *Ibid.*, s. 3.
[9] *Ibid.*, ss. 33–39.
[10] *Ibid.*, s. 22–24.
[11] *Ibid.*, s. 25.
[12] *Ibid.*, s. 21.
[13] *Ibid.*, s. 5 (1).

"To make or attempt to make any use whatsoever of a firearm or imitation firearm with intent to resist or prevent the lawful arrest or detention of himself or any other person."

By s. 17 (2), it is a misdemeanour punishable with seven years' imprisonment,

"If a person, at the time of his committing, or being arrested for an offence specified in Schedule 1 to this Act, has in his possession a firearm or imitation firearm . . . unless he shows that he had it in his possession for a lawful object."

The schedule specifies a wide range of offences under the Malicious Damage Act 1861, the Offences against the Person Act 1861, the Vagrancy Act 1824, the Prevention of Crimes Act 1871, the Theft Act 1968, the Police Act 1964, s. 217 of the Road Traffic Act 1960 and the Sexual Offences Act 1956.

The sentence under s. 17 (1) may be in addition to any imposed for any offence for which he is lawfully arrested or detained and that under s. 17 (2) may be in addition to any imposed for an offence in the Schedule.

"Firearm" is particularly defined for the purposes of this section as

"a lethal barrelled weapon of any description from which any shot, bullet or other missile can be discharged, and includes
(a) any prohibited weapon, whether it is such a lethal weapon as aforesaid or not"

and an "imitation firearm" means

"any thing which has the appearance of being a firearm"—except a weapon which has the appearance of a weapon "designed or adapted for the discharge of any noxious liquid, gas or other thing"[14]—"whether or not it is capable of discharging any shot, bullet or other missile.

This definition has been widely interpreted. In *Read* v. *Donovan*[15] Lord GODDARD went so far as to say that "lethal weapon" means "a weapon capable of causing injury . . ." This *dictum* was wider than was necessary for the decision, for there was evidence that the weapon was capable of killing at up to twenty feet. Lord PARKER has since said in *Moore* v. *Gooderham*,[16] that he does not feel that "too much attention" can be attached to that definition. In that case the court accepted, surely rightly, that the injury must be of a kind which may cause death. The court nevertheless held that an airgun was a lethal weapon because it might cause death if fired point-blank at some particularly vulnerable part. The question is not whether the weapon was designed or intended to cause death but whether it might do so if misused.

A real weapon which is incapable of firing is an imitation firearm within the definition. This was held in *Debreli*,[17] where D was in possession of an automatic pistol with the firing pin removed. Having regard to the mischief aimed at by the Act, the court held that it was sufficient that the weapon looked like a firearm and it was immaterial that it was not fabricated as an imitation. The court thus avoided the absurdity that a rubber model of an automatic pistol would have been within the Act but not the real pistol used in that case.

---

[14] It is not obvious why an imitation gas pistol, for example, should be excluded from the Act.
[15] [1947] 1 K.B. 326 at p. 327; [1947] 1 All E.R. at p. 37.
[16] [1960] 3 All E.R. 575 at p. 577.
[17] [1964] Crim. L.R. 53.

Rather remarkably, in view of the seriousness of the offence involved, it has been held that s. 17 (1) imposes strict liability in one respect. In *Pierre*,[18] the court held that it was unnecessary that D should know that the thing used is a firearm as defined in the section. No doubt it is necessary to prove that D intended to use the thing which he did use[19] and which is a firearm within the meaning of the section; but if D supposes it is something other than a firearm he will have no defence. Presumably the same construction must be applicable to s. 17 (2): it must be proved that D knows he has the thing,[20] but he need not know its nature. However, here it would be open to D to establish, on a balance of probabilities, that he had the thing for a lawful object. Thus if D has in his possession, for purposes of amateur dramatics, an object which he believes to be an imitation gas-pistol but which in fact is a real one and he happens to commit an offence within Schedule 1, he may be able to establish a defence; but if he encounters and strikes[1] with the pistol a police officer who is attempting to arrest him he will have no defence. Yet if the thing had been an imitation his offence would only have been the misdemeanour under s. 51 of the Police Act 1964,[2] punishable with two years' imprisonment.

In another respect, however, a benevolent construction has been put on s. 17 (2). On a literal reading of the sub-section the offence is committed when D is lawfully arrested for one of the specified offences, whether he has actually committed it or not. But in *Baker*[3] the court held that it must be proved not only that D was lawfully arrested for such an offence but also that he actually committed it.

> "The other construction results in the absurdity that a man who has committed no offence at all of the nature specified in Sched. 3 [now Sched. 1] might be liable to seven years' imprisonment as opposed to two years merely because a policeman had reasonable grounds for suspecting that he had committed one of those offences."[4]

Section 17 (2) is nevertheless a wide-ranging provision. D would appear to be liable under it even if at the time of his arrest many years had elapsed since he committed the specified offence and his possession of the firearm was in no way connected with it.

3   Possessing Firearms with Intent

By s. 16 of the Firearms Act 1968 it is an offence punishable with fourteen years' imprisonment,

> ". . . for a person to have in his possession any firearm or ammunition with intent by means thereof to endanger life or cause serious injury to property, or to enable another person by means thereof to endanger life or cause serious injury to property, whether any injury to person or property has been caused or not."

---

[18] [1963] Crim. L.R. 513.
[19] *Cf. Cugullere*, [1961] 2 All E.R. 343; below, p. 286.
[20] *McGuire and Page*, [1963] Crim. L.R. 572, where D1 is in possession, D2 must be shown to have knowledge and joint control.
[1] It is evidently not necessary that use should be made of the firearm as such—the Act says "any use whatsoever".
[2] Above, p. 258.
[3] [1961] 2 Q.B. 530; [1961] 3 All E.R. 703.
[4] [1962] 2 Q.B. at pp. 532, 533; [1961] 3 All E.R. at p. 704.

The definition of "firearm" for the purpose of this section includes, as well as those things which are firearms for the purposes of s. 17,[5]

"(b) any component part of such a lethal or prohibited weapon; and (c) any accessory to any such weapon designed or adapted to diminish the noise or flash caused by firing the weapon."[6]

On the other hand, imitation firearms are not within the section since one would hardly possess these with the necessary intent.

It is not necessary that the weapon should be presently capable of causing any injury whatsoever. A dummy revolver with the barrel and cartridge chambers only partially bored[7] and a revolver with holes pierced in the sides of the barrel so as to make it ineffective for the purpose of firing live ammunition[8] have both been held to be within the Act either because the whole thing, or the whole thing less the defective parts, was a "component part" of a lethal weapon.

It is likely that *Pierre*[9] would again be applicable but this is perhaps less serious as, even though D is unaware that the thing is a firearm as defined in the Act, he must be proved to believe that it is capable of endangering life or causing serious injury to property. A mistaken belief that the thing was an imitation would thus afford a defence, by negativing the intent.

The offence is clearly useful in penalising preparations for murder, etc., which would not amount to attempts—though there is obviously difficulty in establishing intent where no action has been taken. It may also be a useful alternative charge to shooting with intent to murder.[10]

4 Carrying and Trespassing with Firearms

By s. 20 of the Firearms Act 1968:

"(1) A person commits an offence if, while he has a firearm with him, he enters or is in any building or part of a building as a trespasser and without reasonable excuse (the proof whereof lies on him).

(2) A person commits an offence if, while he has a firearm with him, he enters or is on any land as a trespasser and without reasonable excuse (the proof whereof lies on him)."

An offence under s. 20 (1) is punishable on indictment with five years' imprisonment and an offence under s. 20 (2) is punishable on summary conviction with three months. The constituents of the offence under s. 20 (1) bear an obvious kinship with the new definition of burglary, to which reference may be made."[11]

By s. 18:

"(1) It is an offence for a person to have with him a firearm or imitation firearm with intent to commit an indictable offence, or to resist arrest or prevent the arrest of another, in either case while he has the firearm or imitation firearm with him."

This offence, which is punishable with ten years' imprisonment, differs from that under s. 16 in that the range of the ulterior intent is much wider and the

---

[5] Above, p. 279.
[6] Firearms Act 1968, s. 57 (1). This is the general definition of "firearm" in the Act, except where otherwise expressly provided.
[7] *Cafferata* v. *Wilson*, [1936] 3 All E.R. 149.
[8] *Muir* v. *Cassidy*, 1953 S.L.T. (Sh. Ct.) 4.
[9] Above, p. 280.
[10] *Edgecombe*, [1963] Crim. L.R. 574.
[11] Below, p. 408. Smith, *Law of Theft*, para. 454 *et seq.*

actus reus is probably narrower[12] in that to "have with" one is less extensive than to have in one's possession. If D has gone out, leaving the firearm at home, he may be guilty of an offence under s. 16, but not under s. 18. As the side-note indicates, s. 18 is concerned with "carrying".

By s. 19:

"A person commits an offence if, without lawful authority or reasonable excuse (the proof whereof lies on him) he has with him in a public place a loaded shot gun or loaded air weapon, or any other firearm (whether loaded or not) together with ammunition suitable for use in that firearm."

This offence, which is punishable with five years' imprisonment, is closely related to that in the Prevention of Crime Act 1953 and the discussion of the constituents of the offence under that statute[13] is probably applicable to s. 19 in so far as the same expressions are used. To carry a loaded shot gun or air weapon is not an offence under the Prevention of Crime Act unless it is intended for causing injury to the person. No such intent need be proved under s. 19. The defence of "reasonable excuse" seems to vest a wide discretion in the court. The definition of "public place"[14] is wider for the purposes of s. 19 than for the purposes of the Prevention of Crime Act, in that it apparently includes a place to which the public have access, whether they are permitted to or not.

(2) THE PREVENTION OF CRIME ACT 1953[15]

The Prevention of Crime Act 1953 is, according to its long title:

"An Act to prohibit the carrying of offensive weapons in public places, without lawful authority or reasonable excuse."

It goes much further than the Firearms Act 1968 in that, (i) in general, the mere carrying of the offensive weapon in a public place is an offence without proof of any ulterior intent or the commission of any other offence and (if it is a firearm) without proof that it was loaded or that ammunition was carried; and (ii) it extends to a much wider range of weapons. The Act provides:

"1.—(1) Any person who without lawful authority or reasonable excuse, the proof whereof shall lie on him, has with him in any public place any offensive weapon shall be guilty of an offence, and shall be liable—

(a) on summary conviction, to imprisonment for a term not exceeding three months or a fine not exceeding fifty pounds, or both;

(b) on conviction on indictment, to imprisonment for a term not exceeding two years or a fine not exceeding one hundred pounds, or both.

(2) Where any person is convicted of an offence under subsection (1) of this section the court may make an order for the forfeiture or disposal of any weapon in respect of which the offence was committed."

1 Offensive Weapons

"Offensive weapon" is defined by s. 1 (4) to mean

"any article made or adapted for use for causing injury to the person, or intended by the person having it with him for such use by him."

---

[12] But s. 18 extends to imitation firearms and not to ammunition, while s. 16 extends to ammunition but not to imitation firearms.
[13] *Infra.*
[14] Section 57 (1).
[15] Brownlie, [1961] Crim. L.R. 19.

It will be noted that this definition is narrower than that of "weapon of offence" in s. 10 (1) (*b*) of the Theft Act 1968. It does not include, as the Theft Act does, articles made, adapted or intended for *incapacitating* a person.[16]

There are three categories of offensive weapon: (i) Articles *made for causing injury* would include a service rifle or bayonet, a revolver, a cosh, knuckle-duster or dagger.[17] (ii) Articles *adapted for causing injury* would include razor blades inserted in a potato or cap-peak, a bottle broken for the purpose, a chair-leg studded with nails and so on. "Adapted" probably means altered to as to become suitable,[18] and it may be irrelevant that the alteration was not made with that intention.[19] (iii) It is very important to distinguish the third category of articles which are neither made nor adapted for causing injury, but are carried for that purpose. This includes a sheath-knife,[20] a shot-gun,[1] a razor,[2] a sandbag,[3] a pick-axe handle,[4] a bicycle chain, a stone[5] and, indeed almost anything that is solid and heavy or is otherwise injurious if brought into contact with the person, like acid or a drum of pepper.[6]

The importance of the distinction is that, in the case of articles "made or adapted", the prosecution have to prove no more than possession in a public place. D will then be convicted unless he can prove, on a balance of probability, that he had lawful authority or reasonable excuse. But if the article falls into the third category the onus is on the prosecution to show that it was carried with intent to injure.[7] The question in *Woodward* v. *Koessler*[8] was whether D intended to "cause injury to the person" if he intended merely to frighten or intimidate by displaying a knife. The court held that he did and that, therefore, the knife was an offensive weapon. This was a broad view to take of the meaning of a phrase in a penal statute; and more recently[9] the Court of Criminal Appeal has held that frightening is not enough unless it is "intimidation" and

> "of a sort which is capable of producing injury through the operation of shock."

Where D has used the article in a manner likely to cause injury, this will be at least evidence that he had it with him for that purpose; and more recent authorities suggest that it will be conclusive.

If D assumes or retains control of the article for the purpose of causing injury, he clearly has the thing with him for that purpose even though his control be

---

[16] Below, p. 417; Smith, *Law of Theft*, paras. 512–516.

[17] ". . . bludgeons, properly so-called, clubs and anything that is not in common use for any other purpose but a weapon are clearly offensive weapons within the meaning of the legislature" (the Smuggling Acts): (1784) 1 Leach 342 n. (a).

[18] Cf. *Davison* v. *Birmingham Industrial Co-operative Society* (1920), 90 L.J.K.B. 206; *Flower Freight Co., Ltd.* v. *Hammond*, [1963] 1 Q.B. 275; [1962] 3 All E.R. 950; and *Herrmann* v. *Metropolitan Leather Co., Ltd.*, [1942] Ch. 248; [1942] 1 All E.R. 294.

[19] *Ibid.* Cf. *Maddox* v. *Storer*, [1963] 1 Q.B. 451; [1962] 1 All E.R. 831.

[20] *Woodward* v. *Koessler*, [1958] 3 All E.R. 557.

[1] *Gipson*, [1963] Crim. L.R. 281; *Hodgson*, [1954] Crim. L.R. 379.

[2] *Petrie*, [1961] 1 All E.R. 466.

[3] *Ibid.*

[4] *Cugullere*, [1961] 2 All E.R. 343.

[5] *Harrison* v. *Thornton* (1966), 110 Sol. Jo. 444; [1966] Crim. L.R. 388 (D.C.).

[6] 120 J.P. 250. Also, no doubt, a stiletto heel which can be a very dangerous weapon: *The Times*, September 25, 1964.

[7] *Petrie*, [1961] 1 All E.R. 466.

[8] [1958] 3 All E.R. 557.

[9] *Edmonds*, [1963] 2 Q.B. 142; [1963] 1 All E.R. 828.

only momentary. So D was guilty of an offence under the Act where he picked up a stone and threw it at P who was fighting with D's friend.[10] The same must be true where D retains a control, which he would otherwise discard, for the purpose of causing injury. What of the case where D is, throughout, in possession for a lawful purpose yet uses the article to cause injury? Using his umbrella to keep off the rain, he pokes P in the eye as he passes by—and continues, using his umbrella to keep off the rain. Soon after the Act was passed, it was laid down in *Jura*[11] that, if possession is originally lawful, it does not become unlawful because the weapon is used in an illegal manner:

> "the Act . . . is meant to deal with a person who, with no excuse whatever, *goes out with* an offensive weapon . . ."[12]

But in *Woodward* v. *Koessler* DONOVAN, J., said *obiter*,[13]

> "All that one has to do for the purpose of ascertaining what the intention is is to look and see what use is in fact made of it. If it is found that the accused did in fact make use of it for the purpose of causing injury, he had it with him for that purpose."

This seems directly to contradict the decision in *Jura*,[14] where D shot and wounded a woman at a shooting gallery with an air rifle and yet was held not guilty on the ground that he had a reasonable excuse for carrying the rifle. This could hardly be so if he had it with him for the purpose of shooting a woman. Moreover, in so far as DONOVAN, J.'s *dictum* purports to be a statement of fact, it is not necessarily true. If, as was suggested in *Jura*, a gamekeeper at a shooting party were suddenly to lose his temper and fire his gun at someone, it would follow, according to DONOVAN, J., that he had the gun with him for that purpose. But in fact this is not true; he had it with him for the purpose of shooting grouse and that purpose only. What DONOVAN, J., seems to have done is to lay down a conclusive presumption of law; and that seems to have been accepted as the right approach by the Court of Criminal Appeal in *Powell*[15] where it was held that a toy pistol[16] was an offensive weapon because D had used it with intent to injure. Apparently it was irrelevant that he really had it with him because he was looking after it for someone. *Jura* "depends on the special facts of the case." It is submitted that the Court of Criminal Appeal's first thoughts were best. In the first place, the effect of *Powell* is to prohibit the *use* of offensive weapons in a public place. As the long title shows, it is at least very doubtful if this was intended to be the purpose of the Act; and the use of the weapon is indictable under other statutes. Secondly, it means that ordinary accessories carried for their ordinary and lawful purpose become offensive weapons when they are unlawfully used—a furled umbrella,[17] a handbag and a shoe worn by D are presumably all offensive weapons if used offensively in a public place. Thirdly, the decision seems to impose a severe limitation on the defence of lawful authority or reasonable excuse.

---

[10] *Harrison* v. *Thornton* (1966), 110 Sol. Jo. 444; [1966] Crim. L.R. 388.
[11] [1954] 1 Q.B. 503; [1954] 1 All E.R. 696.
[12] [1954] 1 Q.B. at p. 506; [1954] 1 All E.R. at p. 697 (italics supplied).
[13] [1958] 3 All E.R. 557 at p. 558.
[14] *Supra.*
[15] [1963] Crim. L.R. 511.
[16] Not made or adapted for causing injury.
[17] According to *The Times*, May 23, 1967, a metropolitan magistrate refused to hold that a furled umbrella was an offensive weapon, though it was used to make an assault. *Sed Quaere?*

2   Lawful Authority or Reasonable Excuse

It is not certain what, if anything, is the difference between "lawful authority" and "reasonable excuse": and the meaning of neither term has been precisely elucidated.[18] "Lawful authority" particularly presents difficulties. Before the Act, it was presumably generally lawful to be in possession of an offensive weapon in a public place—otherwise there would have been no necessity for the Act. Now it is generally unlawful. "Lawful authority" postulates some legal exception to the general rule of the Act; yet none is provided for and the words themselves are certainly not self-explanatory. Probably the exception means no more than that there must be a motive for the possession which the court considers reasonable. If the motive is the commission of some crime, then there is obviously no defence. But it is not necessarily enough to exempt D that his motives were entirely lawful.[19] In *Evans* v. *Wright*[20] D's defence was that he carried a knuckle-duster and a truncheon to guard against possible attempts to rob him of the wages he collected for his employees. The court held that the justices had rightly found that his explanation was an unreasonable one, because he had last collected wages a few days before and had left the truncheon in his car and the knuckle-duster in his pocket. It might have been otherwise if he had been in the course of, or just returned from, collecting wages. If the question is then simply one of reasonableness, this leaves a large measure of discretion in the courts. If the court approves of the motive there is a defence; if it disapproves, there is none.

Evans v. *Wright*[1] suggests that it may be reasonable in some circumstances to carry offensive weapons for the protection of property and *a fortiori*, therefore, the person.[2] But it is not reasonable for an Edinburgh taxi driver to carry two feet of rubber hose with a piece of metal inserted at one end, though he does so for defence against violent passengers whom taxi-drivers soemtimes encounter late at night.[2] Apparently exceptional circumstances are required to justify the carrying of offensive weapons, even for defence. The court will look at the particular time to which the charge relates and it is irrelevant that D had reasonable excuse at some earlier time—according to *Powell*[3], even a second or two earlier.

Where D has done nothing with the weapon, except to possess it, the "reasonable excuse" provision is workable; but where he has taken some offensive action, it is difficult to see how it can have any effect. To take the example of the gamekeeper, discussed above: he can show that his possession of the gun was perfectly lawful up to the moment when he turned it on the person who annoyed him—but that is irrelevant. What he has to justify is the possession of a gun which he has with him (so it is conclusively presumed) for the purpose of firing at an innocent person. It must follow that anyone who has taken offensive action is bound to fail in establishing the statutory defence.

---

[18] But see below, p. 287.

[19] *Cf.* s. 23 (2) of the Firearms Act 1937, above, p. 282, where possession "for a lawful object" is a defence.

[20] [1964] Crim. L.R. 466.

[1] Is it a reasonable excuse that a girl carries a drum of pepper to defend herself against the attentions of lorry-drivers who might give her lifts ? (1956), 120 J.P.N. 250.

[2] *Grieve* v. *Macleod*, 1967 S.L.T. 70.

[3] Above, p. 284.

3 A Public Place

Section 1 (4) of the Prevention of Crime Act 1953 provides:

> " 'public place' includes any highway and any other premises or place to which at the material time the public are permitted to have access whether on payment or otherwise."

This is very similar to the interpretation which has been placed upon s. 257 of the Road Traffic Act 1960 and reference may be made to the discussion of that provision.[4] It should always be borne in mind that the same term may bear different meanings according to the context in which it is found and that whether a place is public is a question of fact.[5] The jury are, of course entitled to draw reasonable inferences; so that where D produced an air pistol in a private dwelling-house which he was visiting, it was open to them to infer that he brought it to or took it away from the house through the public street.[6]

4 Mens Rea

The Court of Criminal Appeal has held that the words "has with him in any public place" mean "*knowingly* has with him in any public place."[7]

> "If some innocent person has a cosh slipped into his pocket by an escaping rogue, he would not be guilty of having it with him within the meaning of the section, because he would be quite innocent of any knowledge that it had been put into his pocket."[8]

Whether D must know of the facts which make the thing an offensive weapon within the Act has not been decided. Is D guilty if he has with him in a public place a revolver which he believes to be an imitation but which is real? Analogy with the Firearms Act 1937[9] would suggest that he is, but principle, it is submitted, requires acquittal.

(3) THE PUBLIC ORDER ACT 1936

By s. 4 of the Public Order Act 1936—

> "(1) Any person who, while present at any public meeting or on the occasion of any public procession, has with him any offensive weapon, otherwise than in pursuance of lawful authority, shall be guilty of an offence.
>
> (2) For the purposes of this section, a person shall not be deemed to be acting in pursuance of lawful authority unless he is acting in his capacity as a servant of the Crown or of either House of Parliament or of any local authority or as a constable or as a member of a recognised corps or as a member of a fire brigade."

---

[4] Below, p. 340; and see the discussion of the meaning of public place for other purposes at pp. 316, 318, 326–327 and 340.

[5] *Theodolou*, [1963] Crim. L.R. 573.

[6] *Mehmed*, [1963] Crim. L.R. 780.

[7] *Cugullere*, [1961] 2 All E.R. 343 at p. 344. *Cf. Warner* v. *Metropolitan Police Commissioner*, [1968] 2 All E.R. 356, above, p. 78.

[8] *Ibid. Cf. Roper* v. *Taylor's Garages, Ltd.*, [1951] 2 T.L.R. 284 at p. 288, *per* DEVLIN, J.; above, p. 54; and contrast the cautious approach of the court to a similar problem arising under the Dangerous Drugs Regulations 1953 where the question whether possession must be accompanied by *mens rea* was left open: *Carpenter*, [1960] Crim. L.R. 633.

[9] *Pierre*, above, p. 280.

A "public meeting" is defined[10] to include—

> "any meeting in a public place and any meeting which the public or any section thereof are permitted to attend, whether on payment or otherwise;"

and a "public place" is

> "any highway, public park or garden, any sea beach, and any public bridge, road, lane, footway, square, court, alley or passage, whether a thoroughfare or not; and includes any open space to which, for the time being, the public have or are permitted to have access, whether on payment or otherwise; . . ."

The offence is punishable only on summary conviction with three months imprisonment or a fine of £50 or both.

Almost all cases within the terms of this section will now also amount to the more serious offence under the Prevention of Crime Act 1953. The 1953 Act is in most respects wider. It is not confined to public meetings and its definition of "public place" is probably wider, for the 1936 Act appears to be confined to places out-of-doors. "Offensive weapon" has not been defined for the purposes of the 1936 Act, but any construction adopted is unlikely to be wider than the definition in the 1953 Act. Moreover, proof of the offence under the 1953 Act may be easier since, under the 1936 Act, the onus of disproving any "lawful authority" which may be set up is presumably[11] on the prosecution. In one respect only does the 1936 Act appear to be wider: "lawful authority or reasonable excuse" under the 1953 Act may well be wider than "lawful authority" as narrowly defined in s. 4 (2) of the 1936 Act. If D had with him a rifle, wrongly supposing that the rifle club to which he belonged had been approved by a Secretary of State, he would not have lawful authority under the 1936 Act, but he might have "reasonable excuse" under the 1953 Act.

(4) THE CUSTOMS AND EXCISE ACT 1952

By s. 72 of the Customs and Excise Act 1952 any person who is "armed with an offensive weapon or disguised in any way" when committing "smuggling" offences against the Act is liable on conviction on indictment to three years' imprisonment.

(5) THE NIGHT POACHING ACT 1828

Where three or more persons "unlawfully enter or be in" any land by night, for the purpose of taking or destroying game, and any of them is

> "armed with any gun, crossbow, fire arms, bludgeon, or any other offensive weapon",

all are guilty of an offence punishable with fourteen years' imprisonment under the Night Poaching Act 1828.

---

[10] By s. 9.
[11] But *cf.* s. 81 of Magistrates Courts Act 1952.

CHAPTER 13

Sexual Offences[*]

1 RAPE

Section 1 (1) of the Sexual Offences Act 1956 provides:

"It is an offence for a man to rape a woman."

By s. 37 and Schedule 2 the maximum punishment is life imprisonment. The statute tells us nothing more about the crime and its definition is therefore a matter of common law.

1 The Actus Reus

(i) *Unlawful sexual intercourse.*—The *actus reus* consists in having unlawful sexual intercourse with a woman without her consent.[1] The term "unlawful" in this context probably means simply intercourse outside the bonds of marriage.

"Sexual intercourse between husband and wife is sanctioned by law; all other sexual intercourse is unlawful."[2]

It was stated by Hale[3] that

"the husband cannot be guilty of a rape committed by himself upon his lawful wife, for by their mutual matrimonial consent and contract the wife hath given up herself in this kind unto her husband which she cannot retract."

This view of the law seems to have been so generally accepted that there was no recorded prosecution of a husband for himself committing rape upon his wife until 1949[4] when Byrne, J., in *Clarke*[5] accepted Hale's statement of the law as

---

* *Sexual Offences* (ed. Radzinowicz), A Report of the Cambridge Department of Criminal Science; Hughes, "Consent in Sexual Offences" (1962), 25 M.L.R. 319; Koh, "Consent in Sexual Offences", [1968] Crim. L.R. 81.
[1] Hale, 1 P.C. 627; Hawkins, 1 P.C., c. 16, § 2; East. 1 P.C. 434; Halsbury, Vol. 10, p. 746; Russell, 706.
[2] Perkins, *Criminal Law*, 115. *Cf. Chapman*, [1959] 1 Q.B. 100; [1958] 3 All E.R. 143; [1958] Crim. L.R. 623 and commentary. But sexual intercourse within marriage may be "unlawful" in criminal law if it is such as affords grounds for divorce or separation: *Clarence* (1888), 22 Q.B.D. 23; above, p. 254.
[3] 1 P.C. 629.
[4] Morris and Turner, (1952–55), 2 Univ. Q.L.J. at 256.
[5] [1949] 2 All E.R. 448.

generally correct but held that an indictment would lie in that case, because the justices had made an order providing that the wife should no longer be bound to co-habit with the accused.

> "The position, therefore, was that the wife, by process of law, namely, by marriage, had given consent to the husband to exercise the marital right during such time as the ordinary relations created by the marriage contract subsisted between them, but by a further process of law, namely the justices' order, her consent to marital intercourse was revoked."[6]

In *Miller*,[7] the only direct authority, LYNSKEY, J., after a careful examination of the authorities, concluded that Hale's proposition was correct and that the husband, who was charged with rape, had no case to answer. In that case, the wife had presented a petition for divorce before the act of intercourse but LYNSKEY, J., held, distinguishing *Clarke*, that this was immaterial. He said, *obiter*, that if there had been an agreement to separate, particularly if it had contained a non-molestation clause, the wife's consent would have been revoked. Presumably consent would also be revoked by a decree nisi of divorce or nullity.

It seems therefore that, with the above qualifications, Hale's statement probably represents the law but it cannot be taken to be settled beyond all doubt. In *Clarence*[8] the matter was considered, *obiter*, by the Court for Crown Cases Reserved and WILLS, J., stated that he was not prepared to assent to the proposition that rape between married persons was impossible, while FIELD and CHARLES, JJ., expressed doubts. A. L. SMITH, HAWKINS and STEPHEN, JJ., seem to have accepted the traditional view, though their judgments are not entirely clear on the point.[9]

A husband may be convicted as a secondary party to a rape committed by another on his wife; for, as Hale puts it,[10]

> "tho in marriage she hath given up her body to her husband, she is not to be by him prostituted to another."[11]

The basis for the general rule as stated by Hale is plainly fictitious—the wife may in fact have withdrawn her consent and the civil law recognises that she may properly do so in certain circumstances. She is not bound to submit to inordinate or unreasonable demands by her husband[12] and may refuse intercourse because her husband has been guilty of a matrimonial offence, which she does not wish to condone, or because he is suffering from a venereal disease.[13] The criminal law should not be based upon fictions. It may be, however, that the continuance of the rule can be justified on grounds of policy:

> "If the wife is adamant in her refusal the husband must choose between letting his wife's will prevail, thus wrecking the marriage, and acting without

---

[6] *Ibid.* at p. 449.
[7] [1954] 2 Q.B. 282; [1954] 2 All E.R. 529.
[8] (1888), 22 Q.B.D. 23; above, p. 254.
[9] See the discussion by Morris and Turner, *op. cit.*
[10] *Loc. cit.*
[11] See *Lord Castlehaven*'s case (1631), 3 State Tr. 401.
[12] Bromley, *Family Law* (2nd ed.), 154.
[13] *Foster* v. *Foster*, [1921] P. 438.

her consent. It would be intolerable if he were to be conditioned in his course of action by the threat of criminal proceedings."[14]

The law does not, however, leave the wife defenceless against violence by her husband. In *Miller*,[15] LYNSKEY, J., held that though the husband had a right to sexual intercourse, he was not entitled to use force or violence in order to exercise that right:

"If he does so, he may make himself liable to the criminal law, not for the offence of rape, but for whatever other offence the facts of the particular case warrant. If he should wound her, he might be charged with wounding or causing bodily harm, or he may be liable to be convicted of common assault."[16]

(ii) *Sexual Intercourse.*—The phrase "carnal knowledge", formerly favoured in statutes, was replaced in the consolidation by the Sexual Offences Act by "sexual intercourse". Section 44 provides some guidance as to the meaning of that term:

"Where on the trial of any offence under this Act, it is necessary to prove sexual intercourse (whether natural or unnatural), it shall not be necessary to prove the completion of the intercourse by the emission of seed, but the intercourse shall be deemed complete upon proof of penetration only."

While s. 1 does not use the term "sexual intercourse", there can be no doubt that s. 44 applies to the intercourse which must be proved for the purpose of rape. The slightest penetration will suffice and it is not necessary to prove that the hymen was ruptured.[17]

(iii) *The absence of consent.*—The absence of P's consent is an essential part of the *actus reus* and must be proved by the prosecution. Earlier authorities emphasised the use of force; but it is now clear that lack of consent is the crux of the matter and this may exist though no force is used. A subtle change of emphasis occurred in the middle of the nineteenth century in the cases of *Camplin*[18] and *Fletcher*.[19] The test is not "was the act against her will?" but "was it without her consent?" This may seem, as it has to at least one judge,[20] a distinction without a difference; but it emphasises that it is not necessary for the Crown to prove a positive dissent by the woman; it is enough that she did not assent. So convictions were upheld where D had intercourse with a woman whom he had rendered insensible by giving her liquor in order to excite her;[21] and again where D had intercourse with a woman who was asleep.[1]

A similar principle was applied where D had intercourse with a girl of thirteen years of weak intellect and it was held that the jury were rightly told that he was guilty if they were satisfied that the girl was incapable of giving consent or exercising any judgment on the matter.[2] WILLES, J., said[3] that a consent produced by mere animal instinct would be sufficient to prevent the act from con-

---

[14] Morris and Turner, *op. cit.*, at 259, quoting Lord DUNEDIN in *G. v. G.*, [1924] A.C. 349 at p. 357: "It is indeed permissible to wish that some gentle violence had been employed. . . ."
[15] [1954] 2 Q.B. 282: [1954] 2 All E.R. 529; *Cf. Sharmpal Singh*, [1962] A.C. 188.
[16] *Ibid.* at pp. 292 and 534. Miller was convicted of assault occasioning actual bodily harm.
[17] *Russen* (1777), 1 East P.C. 438; *Hughes* (1841), 9 C. & P. 752; *Lines* (1844), 1 Car. & Kir. 393.
[18] (1845), 1 Den. 89.
[19] (1859), Bell, C.C. 63.
[20] LAWSON, J., in *Dee* (1884), 15 Cox C.C. 579 at p. 595 (Irish C.C.R.).
[21] *Camplin* (1845), 1 Den. 89.
[1] *Mayers* (1872), 12 Cox, C.C. 311; *Young* (1878), 14 Cox C.C. 114.
[2] *Fletcher* (1859), Bell, C.C. 63.
[3] *Ibid.*

stituting a rape and this was followed by KEATING, J.,[4] and approved by KELLY, C.B.[5] PALLES, C.B., however, described this as a doctrine

"abhorrent to our best feelings, and . . . discreditable to any jurisprudence in which it may succeed in obtaining a place."[6]

It is submitted that his view that consent must be an intelligent act is the better view.

No doubt it is also rape to have intercourse with a child too young to understand the nature of the act; but there is no fixed age limit below which consent is impossible as a matter of law.[7] It is a question of fact in each case and therefore it is a misdirection to tell a jury that, as a matter of law, a child of six cannot consent. Yet, since

". . . it would be idle for anyone to suggest that a girl of that age had sufficient understanding and knowledge to decide whether to consent or resist"

a conviction may be upheld, notwithstanding such a misdirection.[8] The effect seems to be much the same as if it were a rule of law.

Submission exacted by duress has been held to be no consent:

"There is a difference between consent and submission; every consent involves a submission; but it by no means follows that a mere submission involves consent."[9]

The distinction, however, is by no means clear cut. Moreover, since 1885[10] it has been a specific statutory misdemeanour

"to procure a woman by threats or intimidation to have unlawful sexual intercourse in any part of the world."[11]

Apart from the jurisdictional point (rape is only indictable if committed within the jurisdiction) it is arguable that there is no distinction between this crime and the type of rape now being discussed;[12] that Parliament cannot have intended that the same deed should be both a felony at common law and a statutory misdemeanour and that the common law has been repealed.[13] It is most improbable, however, that it was ever intended that the exaction of consent to intercourse by threats of violence should be punishable only with a maximum of two years' imprisonment; and it is submitted that this is still rape at common law. It may be that the statutory offence may be committed by threats of less gravity than are required for rape.

An apparent consent arising from a fundamental error induced by fraud is no consent. The Act provides, by s. 1 (2), that

---

[4] In *Fletcher* (1866), L.R. 1 C.C.R. 39.
[5] In *Barratt* (1873), L.R. 2 C.C.R. 81.
[6] In *Dee* (1884), 15 Cox C.C. at p. 594.
[7] *Harling*, [1938] 1 All E.R. 307 at p. 308. "It may well be that in many cases the prosecution would not want much evidence beyond the age of the girl to prove non-consent, but in every charge of rape the fact of non-consent must be proved to the satisfaction of the jury": *per* HUMPHREYS, J.
By s. 46 of the Sexual Offences Act 1956 "woman" in that Act includes "girl".
[8] *Howard*, [1965] 3 All E.R. 684 (C.C.A.).
[9] *Day* (1841), 9 C. & P. 722 at p. 724; *per* COLERIDGE, J.
[10] Criminal Law Amendment Act 1885, s. 3, now repealed and replaced by Sexual Offences Act 1956, s. 2.
[11] Below, p. 294.
[12] The statutory offence may be committed either by the person who has intercourse or another.
[13] But *cf. Williams*, [1923] 1 K.B. 340; below, p. 292.

"a man who induces a woman to have sexual intercourse with him by impersonating her husband commits rape."

This provision, re-enacting the Criminal Law Amendment Act 1885, s. 4, reverses a line of decisions[14] culminating in *Barrow*[15] where the Court for Crown Cases Reserved held that the woman's consent to sexual intercourse was a defence even though she was deceived into thinking that D was her husband. However, in *Flattery*[16] four of the five judges in the Court for Crown Cases Reserved thought that *Barrow* ought to be re-considered; and in *Dee*[17] the Irish Court for Crown Cases Reserved dissented from it and upheld the impersonator's conviction. The *Barrow* line of cases might still be of importance where D obtains intercourse by impersonating some person other than a husband. It is submitted that this should be rape. It is true that, where the husband is impersonated, there is also an error as to the nature of the transaction—it is not marital intercourse but adultery—whereas if D impersonates another, the transaction is both understood to be and is adultery or fornication; but such an error has never been held sufficiently fundamental to found an indictment for rape. Sexual intercourse is, however, a relationship in which personality is supremely important and consent to have intercourse with A is not consent to have intercourse with B. The *Barrow* line of cases is presumably authority against this view but it contained a fundamental inconsistency in that it held that D was guilty of an assault; yet consent should have been equally a defence there as in rape and the cases might be treated, as they were in *Dee*, as depending on the narrow view of rape which was rejected in *Fletcher*.[19]

If D had intercourse with P by impersonating, for example, P's fiancé, it is submitted that *Barrow* should be overruled and D convicted of rape at common law.

Where D, by fraud, deceives the woman as to the nature of the transaction, it is well established that this is rape. So in *Flattery*[20] D was convicted where P submitted to intercourse with him under the impression that he was performing a surgical operation.[20] It is a misdemeanour under the Sexual Offences Act 1956, s. 3

"for a person to procure a woman, by false pretences or false representations, to have sexual intercourse in any part of the world."

It seems probable that this section covers conduct such as that of Flattery but that it also extends to a much wider range of frauds of a much less fundamental character; and it has been held by the Court of Criminal Appeal in *Williams*,[1] a case with substantially the same facts as *Flattery*, that such conduct is still indictable as rape.

Probably any fraud which does not go to the nature of the act or the identity of the man is not sufficient to destroy consent. So misrepresentations by a man as to his wealth, social position or freedom to marry would not render inter-

---

[14] *Jackson* (1822), Russ. & Ry. 487 (C.C.R.); *Saunders* (1838), 8 C. & P. 265; *Williams* (1838), 8 C. & P. 286; *Clarke* (1854), Dears. C.C. 397.
[15] (1868), 11 Cox C.C. 191.
[16] (1877), 2 Q.B.D. 410.
[17] (1884), 15 Cox C.C. 579.
[18] *Jackson* (1882), Russ. & Ry. 487.
[19] (1859) Bell, C.C. 63; above, p. 290.
[20] (1877), 2 Q.B.D. 410.
[1] [1923] 1 K.B. 340.

course thereby obtained rape.[2] Even where the woman is induced by fraud to suppose that she is already married to D, her consent to intercourse affords a defence.[3]

(iv) *Fundamental mistake not arising from fraud.*—Though stress in the cases has been laid on the element of fraud it is thought that this is not the crucial matter; and that if D had intercourse with P, knowing that she was under a mistake, not induced by him, either as to his identity or as to the nature of the act, that would be rape.[4]

2 The Mens Rea

According to the general principles of *mens rea* discussed above, it is clear that the *mens rea* of rape is an intention to have sexual intercourse with a woman, knowing that she does not consent or being reckless whether she consents or not. If the act is proved, it is inconceivable that there will ever be any difficulty about proving the intention to have sexual intercourse. It is possible, however, that a man might have intercourse believing that the woman does consent whereas in fact she does not.[5] He might suppose she was consenting whereas in fact she was asleep, in a drunken stupor, or an idiot not capable of giving or withholding consent. In such cases it is submitted that D has no *mens rea* and should be acquitted. As Stephen (later STEPHEN, J.) put it in the 7th edition of Roscoe's *Criminal Evidence*:

> "It is submitted that the true rule must be that where the man is led from the conduct of the woman to believe that he is not committing a crime known to the law, the act of connection cannot under such circumstances amount to rape. In order to commit rape there must, it would appear, be an intent to have connection with the woman notwithstanding her resistance."[6]

This view of the law was approved by the Full Court of the Supreme Court of Victoria in *Burles*,[7] though the point was not, perhaps, strictly necessary to the decision, since it was held that D had not satisfied the evidential burden of mistake which, at least, lay on him. GAVAN DUFFY, J., suggested at one point[8] that there was an onus of proof on D; but that would be contrary to the fundamental principle in *Woolmington* v. *Director of Public Prosecutions*[9] and the suggestion cannot stand with the subsequent decision of the Full Court in *Daly*:[10]

> ". . . the Crown must establish beyond reasonable doubt that the accused either was aware that the woman was not consenting, or else realised she might not be, and determined to have intercourse with her, whether she was consenting or not."

This seems to be inconsistent with any requirement that the mistake be a reasonable one and, though the court seems to have left the question open, it is

---

[2] See STEPHEN, J., in *Clarence* (1888), 22 Q.B.D. 23 at p. 44. *Cf.* Canadian Criminal Code, s. 298.
[3] *Papadimitropoulos* v. *R.* (1958), 98 C.L.R. 249; [1958] A.L.R. 21, where it is pointed out that there is no reported instance of an indictment for rape based on the fraudulent character of the ceremony.
[4] See *Papadimitropoulos* v. *R.* (1958), 98 C.L.R. 249 at p. 260.
[5] *Per* DENMAN, J., in *Flattery* (1877), 2 Q.B.D. 410 at p. 414.
[6] It is now clear that the word "resistance" should be replaced by "lack of consent". Above, p. 290.
[7] [1947] V.L.R. 392.
[8] *Ibid.*, at p. 403.
[9] [1935] A.C. 462 ; above, p. 27.
[10] [1968] V.L.R. 257 at p. 258.

submitted that reasonableness is merely evidence that the mistake was in fact made.[11] In asserting his mistake, D is merely denying the allegation made by the Crown.

3 Boys under Fourteen; and Women

As noted above,[12] there is an irrebuttable presumption that a boy under the age of fourteen is incapable of committing rape, any other crime of which sexual intercourse is an ingredient or sodomy.[13] There are conflicting *dicta* whether he may be convicted of an attempt[14] but it is submitted that, in principle, he should not be so convicted, for, if he completes the act, it is not a crime.[15] This view is supported by the cases which decided that a boy under fourteen cannot be convicted of an assault with intent to commit rape.[16]

It is clear, however, that a boy under fourteen may be convicted of aiding and abetting a rape,[17] as may a woman.[18]

2 OTHER OFFENCES INVOLVING SEXUAL INTERCOURSE

The wide meaning given to "consent" in rape left a number of cases where consent was in some way imperfect, but which were not crimes at common law. The law has therefore been supplemented by several statutory crimes involving sexual intercourse where consent has been improperly obtained by threats, false pretences or the administration of drugs; or where the woman, though consenting in fact, is deemed by the law to be incompetent to consent on account of age or mental deficiency. Except where otherwise stated the offences are punishable with two years' imprisonment.

1 Procurement of Woman by Threats or by False Pretences

By s. 2 (1) of the Sexual Offences Act 1956:[19]

> "It is an offence for a person to procure a woman, by threats or intimidation, to have unlawful sexual intercourse in any part of the world."

By s. 3 (1) of the Sexual Offences Act 1956:

> "It is an offence for a person to procure a woman, by false pretences or false representations, to have unlawful sexual intercourse in any part of the world."[20]

These offences are not committed unless sexual intercourse actually takes place. Persuading a girl to agree to have intercourse and to accompany a man for that purpose is not "procuring" if the intercourse does not take place; but it is

---

[11] See above, pp. 129–131.
[12] See p. 112.
[13] *Groombridge* (1836), 7 C. & P. 582; *Waite*, [1892] 2 Q.B. 600 (C.C.R.); *Cratchley* (1913), 9 Cr. App. Rep. 232; *Tatam* (1921), 15 Cr. App. Rep. 132.
[14] In *Williams*, [1893] 1 Q.B. 320.
[15] Above, p. 171.
[16] *Eldershaw* (1828), 3 C. & P. 396; *Phillips* (1839), 8 C. & P. 736. *Cf.* Williams, C.L.G.P. 634.
[17] *Eldershaw, supra.*
[18] *Ram and Ram* (1893), 17 Cox C.C. 609; above, p. 94.
[19] This replaces the Criminal Law Amendment Act 1885, s. 3 (1).
[20] This replaces the Criminal Law Amendment Act 1885, s. 3 (2), as amended by Criminal Law Amendment Act 1951.

an attempt to procure.[1] Persuasion is an essential element in procuring,[2] but proof of the threats or false pretences will inevitably establish this.

It has been held[3] that s. 3 (1) applies to a man who procures a woman to have intercourse with *himself*, as well as with another. No doubt the same is true of s. 2 (1). Where the intercourse is with the procurer himself, it is clear that the sections apply to some cases which would also be rape at common law. It is established that an indictment for rape will lie although the case falls within s. 3 (1)[4] and is thought that the same rule would probably apply to s. 2 (1).

These offences can be committed by any person, whether male or female, but a boy under fourteen cannot be convicted of procuring intercourse with himself because of the irrebuttable presumption that he is incapable.[5]

Threats.—It is probable that only threats of immediate personal violence to P (or possibly to another such person as her child) will negative consent for the purposes of rape; and it is possible that less grave threats inducing consent will be sufficient for this much less serious offence. Suppose that, for example, D threatens that, if P does not consent, he will (a) tell the police of a theft she has committed; (b) tell her father of her previous immorality; (c) dismiss her from her present employment; (d) not give her a rise in salary; (e) never take her to the pictures again. Clearly, a line must be drawn somewhere before we reach the last case. Once we go beyond the threats of violence, it is not obvious on what principle the line should be drawn. Perhaps it is nothing more precise than that the threats substantially deprived P of freedom of choice.[6]

False Pretences.—There is a similar uncertainty about the meaning of false pretences. In *Williams*,[7] HEWART, C.J., said that "it is obvious" that the words of the section go "far beyond the case of rape". It seems likely that it extends to cases where there is no mistake as to the nature of the act. Certainly cases of impersonation, if they are not rape, will be offences under s. 3. It may be that any false pretence which in fact induces P to give a consent which she would not otherwise have given is enough, though it is arguable that the pretence must be one which would influence a reasonable woman. Suppose, for example, that D tells P that intercourse improves the voice, or is a certain cure for rheumatism? Whether the restricted meaning given to "false pretences" under the Larceny Act 1916 applies to s. 3 does not seem to have been decided. If it does, "false pretences" is confined to misrepresentation of present fact and, for example, it would be no offence for D to procure intercourse with P by misrepresenting that it was his intention to marry her.[8] But the words "or false representations" suggest that the wider meaning should be adopted.

2 Administering Drugs to Obtain or Facilitate Intercourse

By s. 4 (1) of the Sexual Offences Act 1956:[9]

---

[1] *Johnson*, [1964] 2 Q.B. 404; [1963] 3 All E.R. 577, and commentary thereon. See also Glazebrook, [1959] Crim. L.R. 774.
[2] *Christian* (1913), 78 J.P. 112; below, p. 298.
[3] In *Williams* (1898), 62 J.P. 310, by the Recorder, who declined to state a case. *Cf. Cook*, [1954] 1 All E.R. 60; below, p. 298.
[4] *Williams*, [1923] 1 K.B. 340; above, p. 292.
[5] On the question of an attempt to have intercourse by a boy under fourteen see above, p. 294, footnote 15.
[6] See Howard, *Australian Criminal Law*, 132 *et seq.*
[7] [1923] 1 K.B. 340, above, p. 292.
[8] *Cf. Dent*, below, p. 386, footnote 12.
[9] This replaces the Criminal Law Amendment Act 1885, s. 3 (3).

"It is an offence for a person to apply or administer to, or cause to be taken by, a woman any drug, matter or thing with intent to stupefy or overpower her so as thereby to enable any man to have unlawful sexual intercourse with her."

It will be noted that this offence is complete when the drugs, etc., have been applied, administered, etc., with the ulterior intent;[10] and it is not necessary that intercourse should have taken place or been attempted. No doubt this section also applies to the man who seeks to have intercourse himself, and, clearly, the offence can be committed by any person male or female, except a boy under fourteen intending to have intercourse himself.

3 Intercourse with a Girl under Thirteen

By s. 5 of the Sexual Offences Act 1956:[11]

"It is an offence for a man to have unlawful sexual intercourse with a girl under the age of thirteen."

4 Intercourse with a Girl between Thirteen and Sixteen

By s. 6 of the Sexual Offences Act 1956:[12]

"(1) It is an offence, subject to the exceptions mentioned in this section, for a man to have unlawful sexual intercourse with a girl under the age of sixteen.

(2) Where a marriage is invalid under section two of the Marriage Act 1949 or section one of the Age of Marriage Act 1929 (the wife being a girl under the age of sixteen), the invalidity does not make the husband guilty of an offence under this section because he has sexual intercourse with her, if he believes her to be his wife and has reasonable cause for the belief.

(3) A man is not guilty of an offence under this section because he has unlawful sexual intercourse with a girl under the age of sixteen, if he is under the age of twenty-four and has not previously been charged with a like offence, and he believes her to be of the age of sixteen or over and has reasonable cause for the belief.

In this subsection, 'a like offence' means an offence under this section or an attempt to commit one, or an offence under paragraph (1) of section five of the Criminal Law Amendment Act 1885 (the provision replaced for England and Wales by this section)."

The offence under s. 5 is punishable with life imprisonment. Since they were amended by the Criminal Law Act 1967, the offences under ss. 5 and 6, which was formerly mutually exclusive, overlap, so that a man who has intercourse with a girl under thirteen commits both offences. It is clear that these sections must be read in the light of *Prince*.[13] It follows that a belief that the girl is over thirteen, no matter how reasonable it may be, will not afford a defence to a charge under s. 5 and that a belief that the girl is over sixteen is a defence to a charge under s. 6 only if it is reasonable and held by a man under twenty-four who has not previously been charged with a like offence. The defence is available only to one who has an actual belief that the girl was over sixteen; reasonable cause for such a belief does not afford a defence to one who never directed his mind to the

---

[10] *Cf. Shillingford*, [1968] Crim. L.R. 282.
[11] This replaces the Criminal Law Amendment Act 1885, s. 4.
[12] This replaces the Criminal Law Amendment Act 1885, s. 5.
[13] (1875), L.R. 2 C.C.R. 154; above, p. 42; see especially *per* BLACKBURN, J. at p. 171.

question of the girl's age.[14]   A man is "charged" for the purposes of this section when he first appears before a court having jurisdiction to determine the matter.[15] Thus, if the other conditions of the defence are satisfied, D will not be guilty of an offence under the section if he has unlawful sexual intercourse with a girl under sixteen after being committed for trial for a like offence, even though he be convicted of the first offence before the second one comes before the court of trial; otherwise if he appears before the court of trial for the first offence before he commits the second.   Presumably the rationale of the sub-section is that the defence should be available to a young man who has not had brought to his attention in a formal way the serious consequences of a mistake as to the girl's age.   If so, does not the restrictive interpretation of "charge" extend the defence too far? When D has been committed for trial he is well aware of the risks involved in his conduct.

When the present offence was originally enacted in 1885 the age of marriage for a girl was fixed by the common law at twelve and it so remained until the Age of Marriage Act 1929 which raised it to sixteen.[16]   Intercourse with a girl under sixteen is now necessarily unlawful, except in the case of a marriage valid under a foreign law.   In the latter case there is no *actus reus* under s. 5 or s. 6.[17]

The onus of proving (on a balance of probabilities) all the elements of a defence under sub-ss. (2) or (3) of s. 6 is on the accused.[18]   Thus a jury ought to convict a man if they thought that there was an even chance that he believed on reasonable grounds that the girl was his wife or that the conditions of sub-s. (3) were fulfilled.

5   Procuration[19] of Girl under Twenty-One

It is no crime to have unlawful sexual intercourse with a girl over the age of sixteen.   But, by s. 23 (1) of the Sexual Offences Act 1956:

> "It is an offence for a person to procure a girl under the age of twenty-one to have unlawful sexual intercourse in any part of the world with a third person."

As already noted in connection with other sections, procuration implies that there must be some persuasion or invitation by the accused and the offence is not complete until intercourse takes place.[20]   It is likely that the principle of *Prince*[1] is again applicable, so that a reasonable belief that the girl is over twenty-one will afford no defence.

A man who procures a girl under twenty-one to have intercourse with himself commits no offence; but if he agrees with a third person that the third person

---

[14] *Banks*, [1916] 2 K.B. 621;   *Harrison*, [1938] 3 All E.R. 134.   Yet the Criminal Law Amendment Act in terms required only "reasonable cause to believe" and made no mention of actual belief.   *A fortiori*, then, this interpretation must apply to the present statute.
[15] *Rider*, [1954] 1 All E.R. 5, *per* STREATFEILD, J.
[16] See now the Marriage Act 1949, s. 2.
[17] *M. v. K.*, [1968] Crim. L.R. 341 and commentary thereon.
[18] Section 47 of the Act provides: "Where in any of the foregoing sections the description of an offence is expressed to be subject to exceptions mentioned in the section, proof of the exception is to lie on the person relying on it."
[19] The Act uses "procurement" in ss. 2, 3 and 9 and "procuration" in ss. 22 and 23 (*cf.* s. 40); but it does not appear that there is any difference in the meaning of these terms.
[20] *Johnson*, [1964] 2 Q.B. 404; [1963] 3 All E.R. 577;   *Mackenzie* (1910), 6 Cr. App. Rep. 64.
[1] (1875), L.R. 2 C.C.R. 154; above, p. 42.

shall procure the girl for him, then he may be convicted under this section as an abettor and also of conspiracy to commit an offence under this section.[2]

6 Intercourse with a Defective

Section 7 of the Sexual Offences Act 1956, as amended by the Mental Health Act 1959, provides:[3]

> "(1) It is an offence, subject to the exception mentioned in this section, for a man to have unlawful sexual intercourse with a woman who is a defective.
>
> (2) A man is not guilty of an offence under this section because he has unlawful sexual intercourse with a woman if he does not know and has no reason to suspect her to be a defective."

By s. 45 of the Sexual Offences Act 1956, as amended by the Mental Health Act 1959, "defective" means a person suffering from "severe subnormality", that is

> "a state of arrested or incomplete development of mind which includes subnormality of intelligence and is of such a nature or degree that the patient is incapable of living an independent life or of guarding himself against serious exploitation, or will be so incapable when of an age to do so."[4]

The onus of proving a defence under sub-s. (2) is on the accused.[5]

7 Procurement of a Defective

By s. 9 of the Sexual Offences Act 1956:[6]

> "(1) It is an offence, subject to the exception mentioned in this section, for a person to procure a woman who is a defective to have unlawful sexual intercourse in any part of the world.
>
> (2) A person is not guilty of an offence under this section because he procures a defective to have unlawful sexual intercourse, if he does not know and has no reason to suspect her to be a defective."

Procurement (or "procuration")[7] requires an element of persuasion or invitation so that it would seem that a girl is not procured to have intercourse if the initiative comes from her.[8] The problem can hardly arise under s. 2 or s. 3 when false pretences or duress have been proved. But it may arise under s. 9.

It is not clear that this section applies, as do ss. 2, 3 and 23, to the case of a man who procures a defective to have intercourse with himself. In *Cook*[9] STABLE, J., held that D had no case to answer although one morning he asked P to go back to bed and then went and had intercourse with her. The judge pointed out that while the Mental Deficiency Act 1913 made it an offence to have intercourse with a mental defective in an institution or out on licence, there was in that Act no such provision for mental defectives generally. STABLE, J., did not, however, clearly rule that it was no offence for D to procure P to have sexual intercourse with D, but seems rather to have held that the element of persuasion

---

[2] *Mackenzie*, above, p. 297, following *Whitchurch*, above, p. 156.
[3] This replaces the Criminal Law Amendment Act 1885, s. 5, with minor amendments.
[4] Mental Health Act 1959, s. 4 (2).
[5] Sexual Offences Act 1956, s. 47.
[6] This replaces the Mental Deficiency Act 1913, s. 56.
[7] See above, p. 297, footnote 19.
[8] *Christian* (1913), 78 J.P. 112.
[9] [1954] 1 All E.R. 60.

involved in procuration was lacking.[10]   Any gap in the law revealed by this case is now closed by s. 7[11] and any procuration by D of P to have sexual intercourse with himself is an offence under that section.   Only in one situation is the question whether s. 9 applies to this case now of importance; some attempts to procure may not amount to attempts to have intercourse.[12]

It is clear that, under ss. 7 and 9 it would be a defence for D to establish that he reasonably[13] did not advert to the question whether P was defective or not.   It would not be necessary for him to prove that he considered the question and decided she was not.[14]

8   Sexual Intercourse with Mentally Disordered Patients

Without prejudice to s. 7 of the Sexual Offences Act 1956 and subject to a similar exception, it is an offence under s. 128 of the Mental Health Act 1959, punishable with two years imprisonment, for an officer, employee or manager of a hospital or mental nursing home to have sexual intercourse with a woman receiving treatment in the hospital or home or, if the intercourse is on the premises, who is receiving treatment there as an out-patient.   Similarly in the case of a man having intercourse with a woman who is a mentally disordered patient subject to his guardianship or in his custody or care.

9   Permitting Use of Premises for Intercourse

Sections 25, 26 and 27 of the Sexual Offences Act 1956 create offences ancillary to those in ss. 5, 6 and 7 respectively.   Where the owner or occupier of premises, or any person who has or acts or assists in the management or control of any premises, induces or knowingly suffers to resort to or be on those premises, for the purpose of having unlawful sexual intercourse with men or with a particular man—

(i) a girl under thirteen, he is, by s. 25, guilty of an offence punishable with life imprisonment;

(ii) a girl under sixteen or

(iii) a woman who is defective, he is, by ss. 26 and 27 respectively, guilty of an offence punishable with two years' imprisonment.

Although each of these sections uses the expression "induce or knowingly suffer", it is not clear that *mens rea* is required for s. 27 alone provides for an exception:

> "A person is not guilty of an offence under this section because he induces or knowingly suffers a defective to resort to or be on any premises for the purpose mentioned, if he does not know and has no reason to suspect her to be a defective."

It is implicit in this that D may "knowingly suffer" a defective to be on the premises, although he does not know she is a defective if he has reason[14] so to suspect.   It is likely to be held, therefore, that D may likewise "knowingly suffer" girls under thirteen and under sixteen respectively to be on premises for the purpose of intercourse, although he believes them to be over those ages;[15]

---

[10] "He did not get the girl to come into his house.   He did not get her away from her mother."   But surely there was evidence that D procured P *to have intercourse?*

[11] See above, p. 298.

[12] See [1963] Crim. L.R. at p. 861.

[13] But see *Hudson*, [1965] 1 All E.R. 721, and comment at [1965] Crim. L.R. 172.

[14] Contrast the position under s. 6 and *Harrison*, above, pp. 296–297.

[15] *Cf.* above, pp. 73–74.

and, in the absence of the exception which applies to s. 27, it may be immaterial that that belief is perfectly reasonable; that is, *Prince*[16] is applicable.

10 Incest

There remains one offence involving sexual intercourse which does not depend in any way upon a deficiency in the consent of the woman. This is incest, which consists in sexual intercourse between persons within a specified degree of consanguinity. Incest was not a crime at common law or at all until 1908, but was dealt with by the ecclesiastical courts. The Marriage Act 1949 Schedule I sets out the degrees of relationship within which marriage is prohibited and, if celebrated, void but it is only in the case of a much narrower range of relationships that sexual intercourse is a criminal offence. The law is now to be found in ss. 10 and 11 of the Sexual Offences Act 1956:

> "10.—(1) It is an offence for a man to have sexual intercourse with a woman whom he knows to be his grand-daughter, daughter, sister or mother.
>
> (2) In the foregoing subsection 'sister' includes half-sister, and for the purposes of that subsection any expression importing a relationship between two people shall be taken to apply notwithstanding that the relationship is not traced through lawful wedlock.
>
> 11.—(1) It is an offence for a woman of the age of sixteen or over to permit a man whom she knows to be her grandfather, father, brother or son to have sexual intercourse with her by her consent.
>
> (2) In the foregoing subsection 'brother' includes half-brother, and for the purposes of that subjection any expression importing a relationship between two people shall be taken to apply notwithstanding that the relationship is not traced through lawful wedlock."

The statute makes it clear[17] that the prohibition applies equally to illegitimate as to legitimate blood relationships, so that D may be convicted of incest with his illegitimate grand-daughter, etc. Presumably the basis of the law is eugenic.

It would seem that a consent by a woman sufficient to negative a charge of rape will not necessarily amount to a permission to the man for the purpose of this offence. In *Dimes*[18] it was held that D's acquittal of rape on the ground of P's consent did not necessarily mean that P was an accomplice in incest:

> "There is a distinction between submission and permission."[19]

Mens rea must be proved; so D has a defence if he believes that his wife's daughter, P, is the child of an adulterer.[20]

3 INDECENT ASSAULT AND INDECENCY WITH CHILDREN[1]

Under the Sexual Offences Act 1956 it is an offence punishable with two years' imprisonment to commit an indecent assault on a woman[2] and with ten years'

---

[16] (1875), L.R. 2 C.C.R. 154; above, p. 42.
[17] *Cf. Minnis* (1903), 22 N.Z.L.R. 856.
[18] (1911), 7 Cr. App. Rep. 43.
[19] But *cf.* above, p. 291, suggesting that mere submission is not consent for the purpose of rape either.
[20] *Carmichael*, [1940] 1 K.B. 630; [1940] 2 All E.R. 165.
[1] See generally A. N. Macksey, "The Criminal Law and the Woman Seducer", [1956] Crim. L.R. at pp. 453 and 451.
[2] Section 14. In the case of girl under thirteen, the maximum is five years: Indecency with Children Act 1960.

imprisonment to commit an indecent assault on a man.[3] Generally, consent is a defence but, in both cases, it is provided that a person under sixteen or who is a defective cannot give any consent which would prevent an act being an assault for the purposes of these sections. If D does not know and has no reason to suspect that P is a defective, P's consent is a defence, although he is in fact a defective.[4] There is no similar provision with respect to persons under sixteen so, once again it is clear that *Prince*[5] is applicable and that a reasonable belief that P is over that age is not a defence if he or she is in fact under it. As in rape, a consent exacted by force, or by fraud as to the nature of the transaction[6] is not a defence. Nor, according to *Donovan*[7] is consent a defence if the probable consequence of the assault is the infliction of bodily harm; though, as is pointed out above,[8] there are considerable difficulties about that decision.

Where D has gone through a form of marriage with a girl under sixteen and the marriage is invalid, his "wife's" consent to indecent acts is a defence, although she is under sixteen, if D believes on reasonable grounds that she is his wife.[9] There is no similar provision in s. 15 with respect to a woman who has gone through a form of marriage with a boy under sixteen and the implication would seem to be that she would have no defence. Perhaps such a case is unlikely to arise, but it is possible, and the omission of the defence from s. 15 seems to be an oversight.

Where a man under the age of twenty-four is charged under s. 6 with intercourse with a girl under sixteen and establishes a defence on the ground that he reasonably believed her to be over sixteen, he may thus be convicted on a second count for an indecent assault under s. 14.[10] In *Laws*[11] the Court of Criminal Appeal rightly said that

> "it is indeed a grotesque state of affairs that the law offers a defence upon the major charge but excludes that defence if the minor charge is preferred."

Yet the anomaly was re-enacted, after these observations, in the consolidation of the law in 1956.

A not dissimilar curiosity is that boys under fourteen, who must be acquitted of any charge involving sexual intercourse because of their presumed incapacity, may be convicted of indecent assault on evidence that they did in fact have intercourse.[12] This discrepancy seems less objectionable, however, since the acquittal on the major charge is on a "technicality", whereas an acquittal under s. 6 (3) is based on the absence of *mens rea* or even negligence.

1   The Requirement of an Assault

The term "assault" is here used both in its strict sense[13] and to include a battery.[13] So in *Rolfe*[14] D was convicted where he moved towards a woman with

---

[3] Section 15.
[4] Sections 14 (4) and 15 (4); and see *Hudson*, above, p. 299, footnote 13.
[5] (1875), L.R. 2 C.C.R. 154; above, p. 42.
[6] *Case* (1850), 1 Den. 580.
[7] [1934] 2 K.B. 498.
[8] See above, p. 257.
[9] Section 14 (3) which is in similar terms to s. 6 (3), above p. 296.
[10] *Forde*, [1923] 2 K.B. 400; *Keech* (1929), 21 Cr. App. Rep. 125; *Maugham* (1934), 24 Cr. App. Rep. 130.
[11] (1928), 21 Cr. App. Rep. 45 at p. 46.
[12] *Waite*, [1892] 2 Q.B. 600; *Williams*, [1893] 1 Q.B. 320.
[13] Above, pp. 249–250.
[14] (1952), 36 Cr. App. Rep. 4.

his person exposed, inviting her to have connection with him, even though he did not touch her. More frequently there is actual physical contact in cases of indecent assault.

There can be no assault unless D does something to P or acts so as to cause P to apprehend that D is going to do something to him. So in *Fairclough* v. *Whipp*[15] D was acquitted where he invited a girl aged nine to touch his exposed person. The *ratio decidendi* of this case appears to be that an invitation to somebody to touch the invitor cannot amount to an assault. In *Burrows*,[16] where the facts were similar except that the child was a boy, the court followed its earlier decision but added that the invitation could not be an assault

> "because there was no hostile act towards the child, and, unless there is a hostile act there can be no assault."[17]

This causes difficulty. In indecent assaults D's attitude to P will frequently not be "hostile" in the ordinary sense, but unduly affectionate![18] "Hostile", it is submitted, cannot mean more than against the will of P. But, if this is so, how can hostility be an essential element in an offence against a child under sixteen, where consent is irrelevant? Yet in *Director of Public Prosecutions* v. *Rogers*[19] D was acquitted expressly on the ground of the absence of any *hostile* act though he did put his arm around his eleven-year-old daughter and led her upstairs in order that she should masturbate him. Lack of hostility was presumably also the ground of the acquittal in *Williams* v. *Gibbs*,[20] where D took some little girls paddling and, in drying them, was guilty of conduct for which "every right minded person would feel disgust." These cases go well beyond *Fairclough* v. *Whipp*,[1] for something was done by D to P. In holding that the action must be hostile, the court seems, in effect, to ignore the statutory rule that the child's consent is irrelevant.

Where, as in *Burrows*,[2] both the persons concerned are male, a charge of gross indecency under s. 13[3] will lie; but where one of the parties is a female there is no possible charge under the Sexual Offences Act.[4] The Divisional Court pointed out the necessity for an amendment of the law on several occasions and now, by the Indecency with Children Act 1960—

> "Any person who commits an act of gross indecency with or towards a child under the age of fourteen, or who incites a child under that age to such an act with him or another, shall be liable on conviction on indictment to imprisonment for a term not exceeding two years or on summary conviction to imprisonment for a term not exceeding six months, to a fine not exceeding one hundred pounds or to both."

---

[15] [1951] 2 All E.R. 834. It has been argued that this was wrong because "A battery may be committed if the impact is occasioned by the movement of the victim himself against some stationary matter, provided that the accused has intentionally caused that impact . . ."; A. N. Macksey, "The Criminal Law and the Woman Seducer", [1956] Crim. L.R. at pp. 453 and 542. Earlier cases supported this view: *Police* v. *Marchant* (1938), 2 J. Cr. L. 324; *Boxer* (1944) discussed at 8 J. Cr. L. 168–170.

[16] [1952] 1 All E.R. 58, n.; 35 Cr. App. Rep. 180.

[17] 35 Cr. App. Rep. at p. 182.

[18] "Offenders frequently approach their victims with gentleness and there is no doubt, too, that in many cases the child is a willing party to, and in some cases even the instigator of, the act which takes place": Cmd. 247 at p. 36.

[19] (1953), 37 Cr. App. Rep. 137.

[20] [1958] Crim. L.R. 217.

[1] *Supra.*

[2] *Supra.*

[3] Below, p. 322.

[4] It might be indecent exposure at common law or under the Vagrancy Act 1824, below, pp. 317 and 319.

Since this makes mere incitement the offence, it is immaterial that the child does not act on the invitation to touch the accused. The offence would also be committed if D suggested to two children, at least one of whom was under fourteen, that they should commit a gross indecency together.

So far as persons over fourteen are concerned, the law is unchanged and an assault as defined in *Fairclough* v. *Whipp* and its successors must be proved. The problem of the "hostile act" may still arise in relation to children between fourteen and sixteen.

2 Circumstances of Indecency

The assault must be "accompanied with circumstances of indecency on the part of" the prisoner.[5] In *Beal* v. *Kelley*[6] where this definition was approved, D exposed his person to a boy of fourteen and asked him to handle it. The boy refused whereupon D got hold of the boy's arm and pulled him towards himself. D argued that it was not enough to prove an assault with an indecent motive and that it must be established that the assault itself was of an indecent nature. The act of pulling another towards oneself is not, without more, indecent; but no act can be divorced from the circumstances in which it takes place and it was surely right to hold that the circumstances in this case rendered the assault indecent.

It has been questioned whether an indecent motive can make an act "decent in itself" an indecent one. But it is almost as difficult to divorce an act from the intention with which it is done as from the circumstances in which it is done. So, according to BRETT, J.,

"The kisses of young people in seasons of universal gaiety are not indecent, but kisses given by a man under the influence of carnal passion are indecent."[7]

An examination of a woman by a midwife for medical purposes would not be indecent, but the same acts done by her for improper purposes or without consent might be.[8]

In *Beal* v. *Kelley*[9] there was more than an indecent motive. D's act was indecent for there was the indecent exposure with which the assault was accompanied. In Canada it has been held that an assault accompanied by words or circumstances evincing an indecent intention is an indecent assault:[10]

". . . if a man took hold of a woman and attempted to drag her into a brothel that would constitute an indecent assault."

In South Africa, on the other hand, it appears to be clearly established that

"the violence constituting the assault must in itself be indecent; there must be some indecent handling of the complainant";[11]

---

[5] Archbold, § 2981.
[6] [1951] 2 All E.R. 763.
[7] Instruction to the grand jury in the case of Col. Valentine Baker, quoted in Kenny, *Outlines*, 195. *Cf. Leeson*, [1968] Crim. L.R. 283.
[8] *Armstrong* (1885), 49 J.P. 745.
[9] *Supra*.
[10] *Chong* (1914), 23 C.C.C. 250, approved by the Supreme Court in *Quinton*, [1947] S.C.R. 234.
[11] *Abrahams*, [1918] C.P.D. 593.

and that accompanying indecent language or even acts such as exposure will not make the assault an indecent one. A similar view seems to be taken in Australia.[12]

It is thought that if nothing indecent is done, a secret indecent intention is not enough. In *George*[13] D attempted to remove a girl's shoe from her foot because it gave him perverted sexual gratification. STREATFEILD, J., rejecting an argument that the indecent motive made this an indecent assault, held that circumstances of indecency must be proved and that there was no evidence of them in this case. If something indecent is done, there is an indecent *battery*. If P is induced by D's acts to apprehend that D is about to do something indecent, there is an indecent *assault*. Such an apprehension might be induced by words used by P or other circumstances. It is submitted therefore that the Canadian view is to be preferred to that of South Africa and Australia.

3 Assaults by Women

Under ss. 14 and 15 of the Sexual Offences Act 1956 it is an offence for "a person" to commit an indecent assault and it is clear that this includes a woman as well as a man. It was held in *Hare*[14] that a woman who instigated a twelve-year-old boy to have intercourse with her and infected him with venereal disease was guilty of an offence under s. 62 of the Offences against the Person Act 1861, the predecessor of the present s. 15. This was in spite of the fact that ss. 61–63 of the 1861 Act were headed "Unnatural Offences". The court held that the words of the heading could not control the plain meaning of the statute.[15] In the present Act, ss. 14 and 15 fall under the heading "Assaults" and not under "Unnatural Offences."

In *Hare* the court said *obiter* that a woman might be guilty of an indecent assault on another woman. This seems to have been held by LOPES, J., in *Armstrong*[16]; and, indeed, there is no reason for interpreting "person" more narrowly in s. 14 than in s. 15.[17]

It has been suggested that

> "*Hare* is an authority for the proposition that an indecent assault may be committed passively."[18]

It is submitted, however, that this is not so, for a woman's part in voluntary sexual intercourse, particularly where she is the instigating party, may reasonably be presumed to involve the doing by her of acts, which, if done without consent, would be battery.

---

[12] *Culgan* (1898), 19 N.S.W. L.R. 166; *Nisbett*, [1953] V.L.R. 298; *cf. Turner* (1900), 18 N.Z.L.R. 874.

[13] [1956] Crim. L.R. 52.

[14] [1934] 1 K.B. 354.

[15] That headings and sidenotes are not part of the Act and cannot be used as an aid to construction has now been held by the House of Lords in *Chandler* v. *Director of Public Prosecutions*, [1962] 3 All E.R. 142. C. K. Allen criticises the principle of interpretation applied in *Hare* as "the extreme of literalism": *Law in the Making* (7th ed.), 524.

[16] (1885), 49 J.P. 745.

[17] The Wolfenden Committee found no instance of an assault by one female on another "which exhibits the libidinous features that characterise sexual acts between males". In most cases where a woman is convicted under s. 14 it is as aider and abettor of a man in an assault upon another woman: Cmnd. 247, p. 38.

[18] Macksey, [1956] Crim. L.R. at p. 455.

4 ABDUCTION OF WOMEN[19]

1 Classification of Abduction Offences

The Sexual Offences Act 1956 re-enacts five offences of abducting women and girls. There are four offences where the abduction consists in *taking the girl from the possession of her parent or guardian*.[20] Only in the first of these, under s. 20, does the Act provide that the taking must be "without lawful authority or excuse." In each of the other cases there must be proved an unlawful intention of some kind and, if this were proved, it would probably be no defence to show that there was lawful authority for the actual taking.[1] Under s. 20, where the only intention required is that of taking the girl out of the possession of her parents, it is clearly necessary that "lawful authority"—for example, the order of a court—should afford a defence. What is an "excuse" does not clearly appear. But the word might cover the cases where D has no lawful authority, but believes he has; and where it is necessary to take the girl to save her from the commission against her of illegal violence or some other crime. The mere fact that D has admirable religious and philanthropic motives is no excuse.[2]

(i) *Girls under sixteen* (s. 20).—The girl must be (a) unmarried and (b) taken against the will of the parent or guardian. There need be no sexual motive.

(ii) *Girls under eighteen* (s. 19).—In addition to conditions (a) and (b), it must be proved (c) that the girl was taken with intent that she should have unlawful sexual intercourse with men or with a particular man.

(iii) *Girls under twenty-one* (s. 18).—In addition to conditions (a) and (b) it must be proved (c) that the girl has property or expectations of property and (d) that she was taken or detained by fraud and (e) with the intention that she should marry or have unlawful sexual intercourse with the taker or any other person.[3]

(iv) *Defective women of any age* (s. 21).—The woman may or may not be married but must be taken (a) against the will of the parent or guardian; and (b), as in (ii), with the intention that she shall have unlawful sexual intercourse with men or with a particular man.

(v) *Abduction of woman by force or for the sake of her property*.—Under the fifth offence of abduction[4] the woman who is taken away or detained need not have been in anyone's possession. It is an offence to take away or detain a woman of any age (a) against *her* will (b) with the intention that she shall marry or have unlawful sexual intercourse with the taker or any other person, and (c) either by force or for the sake of her property or expectations of property.

Offences (i), (ii) and (iv) are punishable with two years' imprisonment. Offences (iii) and (v) are punishable with fourteen years' imprisonment.

---

[19] *Cf.* the offences of false imprisonment, kidnapping and child-stealing, above, pp. 271–277.

[20] In each case, "guardian" means "any person having the lawful care or charge of the girl".

[1] *Cf. Dadson*, above, p. 29.

[2] *Booth* (1872), 12 Cox C.C. 231.

[3] The Latey Committee recommended the abolition of this offence; Cmnd. 3342, para. 268.

[4] Sexual Offences Act 1956, s. 17.

2 The "Taking"

In offences (i), (ii) and (iv) a *taking* must be proved; in offences (iii) and (v) a *taking*[5] or *detaining*. So in *Alexander*,[6] D's conviction of offence (i) was quashed where the recorder said that the offence consisted in keeping the girl secretly and preventing her parents knowing her whereabouts. While this might have been detaining, it was certainly not taking.

The word "takes" does not imply the use of any force, actual or constructive, and it is irrelevant that the girl freely consents to go.[7] Even if the girl takes the initiative, D is still guilty if he assists her to leave with him; as where D, at the girl's suggestion, brought a ladder to her window so that she might elope with him.[8] If any kind of persuasion is exercised by D, *a fortiori*, he is guilty. If, however,—

> "she was determined to leave her home, and showed prisoner that that was her determination, and insisted on leaving with him—or even if she was so forward as to write and suggest to the prisoner that he should go away with her, and he yielded to her suggestion, taking no active part in the matter . . ."[19]

he would not be guilty.

D need not be present when the girl leaves, if she does so as the result of his persuasion.[10] If she leaves her father's possession without persuasion or assistance from D, then he cannot be guilty of taking, though he may be of detaining. A girl does not, however, leave her father's possession merely because she is out of the house for a particular purpose,[11] unless it is her intention not to return home.[12]

"Taking" does not require a permanent deprivation and so in *Timmins*[13] D was guilty where he took a girl away for three days and slept with her at night. The court's view was that this deprived the father of possession of the girl because it

> "placed her in a situation quite inconsistent with the existence of the relation of father and daughter."[14]

In *Baillie*[15] the girl was absent from her father's house only for a matter of hours but the court seems to have regarded this as a permanent deprivation since in that time D married her so that the father

> "never could have the custody of her in the same sense as before her marriage."[16]

The offence can hardly be committed by a boy who takes a girl for a walk against her father's will. Some more radical infringement of the father's right to control his daughter, as by keeping her away overnight, must surely be proved.

---

[5] Though the cases interpreting this word are mainly on s. 20 (and its predecessors) it is reasonable to assume that they apply to all the offences.

[6] (1912), 107 L.T. 240; *Olifier* (1866), 10 Cox C.C. 402.

[7] *Mankletow* (1853), Dears. C.C. 159. "Suppose you take a person to the Playhouse, does it follow that it is against the will of the person taken ?" *per* ALDERSON, B.

[8] *Robins* (1844), 1 Car. & Kir. 456; *cf. Biswell* (1847), 9 L.T.O.S. 394.

[9] *Jarvis* (1903), 20 Cox C.C. 249 at p. 251, *per* JELF, J. *Cf. Handley* (1859), 1 F. & F. 648.

[10] *Olifier* (1866), 10 Cox C.C. 402; *Frazer* (1861), 8 Cox C.C. 446.

[11] *Mankletow* (1853), Dears. C.C. at p. 165.

[12] *Mycock* (1871), 12 Cox C.C. 28.

[13] (1860), 8 Cox C.C. 401.

[14] *Ibid.*, at p. 404.

[15] (1859), 8 Cox C.C. 238.

[16] *Ibid.*, at p. 239.

The taking must be assumed to be against the will of the father if it appears that, had he been asked, he would have refused his consent.[17] Where, however, the parent permits the daughter to follow a lax course of life[18] or does not take reasonable care of her,[19] this may be evidence of consent to the taking.

3   The Mens Rea

The celebrated case of *Prince*[20] was, of course, decided on the forerunner of s. 20 and the principle of that case applies to all these offences, except where it is expressly modified.   In offences (i) (s. 20) and (iii) (s. 18) a belief even on reasonable grounds that the girl is above the specified age is no defence; but in offence (ii) (s. 19) it is a defence for D to prove, on a balance of probabilities,[1] that he believed on reasonable grounds that the girl was over eighteen.   Similarly, in offence (iv) (s. 21) it is a defence for D to show that he did not know and had no reason[2] to suspect the woman to be a defective.

In all the offences except (i) (s. 20), the ulterior intent described in the section must, of course, be proved by the prosecution.

In offences (i) to (iv) it must be shown that D knew that the girl was in the possession of a parent or guardian.[3]   In principle, it should be enough that D is reckless whether the girl has a father or not, and it would seem that in both *Hibbert* and *Green*[3] D ought to have been convicted on that ground.

5   OFFENCES RELATING TO PROSTITUTION

"... prostitution is proved if it be shown that a woman offers her body for purposes amounting to common lewdness for payment in return."[4]

In so defining prostitution in *Webb*[5] Lord PARKER, C.J., rejected an argument that prostitution is limited to cases in which the woman offers herself for ordinary sexual connection and approved the decision in *de Munck*[6] where a conviction for procuring a girl to become a common prostitute was upheld although it was proved that the girl was *virgo intacta*.   It was enough that the girl had exposed herself to men in order to gratify their passions and that the accused had procured her so to do.   *Webb* went rather farther.   Though the nature of the lewdness was not proved in *de Munck*, it may perhaps be assumed that the men did something to the girl.   In *Webb* the girl was employed as a masseuse and was expected, as part of her employment, to masturbate clients who so desired.   The court rejected an argument that the role of the prostitute must be passive and that active indecency of this nature could not be prostitution.

---

[17] *Handley* (1859), 1 F. &. F. 648, *per* WIGHTMAN, J.
[18] *Primelt* (1858), 1 F. & F. 50.
[19] *Frazer* (1861), Cox C.C. 446.
[20] (1875), L.R. 2 C.C.R. 154.
[1] Sexual Offences Act 1956, s. 47.
[2] See *Hudson*, [1965] 1 All E.R. 721; above, p. 299, footnote 13.
[3] *Hibbert* (1869), L.R. 1 C.C.R. 184; *Green* (1862), 3 F. & F. 274.
[4] *Per* DARLING, J., in *de Munck*, [1918] 1 K.B. 635 at p. 637; cited with approval in *Webb*, [1964] 1 Q.B. 357 at p. 366; [1963] 3 All E.R. 177 at p. 179 (C.C.A.).
[5] Last note.   Application for leave to appeal to the House of Lords in this case was refused: [1963] Crim. L.R. 708 (H.L.).
[6] [1918] 1 K.B. 635.

"Indeed, it can be said with some force that some activity on her part is of the very essence of prostitution. It cannot matter whether she whips the man or the man whips her; it cannot matter whether he masturbates himself on her or she masturbates him."[7]

Prostitution, as such, is not criminal. It is, however, in the opinion of the Wolfenden Committee,[8]

"a social fact deplorable in the eyes of moralists, sociologists and . . . the great majority of ordinary people."

Thus the law actively discourages prostitution in a number of ways. It is criminal to cause or encourage others to become prostitutes; in some circumstances to allow premises to be used for prostitution; to live on the earnings of prostitution; and to loiter or solicit for purposes of prostitution. These crimes require further examination.

1 Causing or Encouraging Women to become Prostitutes

By s. 22 (1) of the Sexual Offences Act 1956:

"It is an offence for a person—

(a) to procure a woman to become, in any part of the world, a common prostitute; or

(b) to procure a woman to leave the United Kingdom, intending her to become an inmate of or frequent a brothel elsewhere; or

(c) to procure a woman to leave her usual place of abode in the United Kingdom, intending her to become an inmate of or frequent a brothel in any part of the world for the purposes of prostitution."

As with the other cases of procuring,[9] the offence is not complete till the woman becomes a common prostitute, or leaves the United Kingdom, or leaves her usual place of abode, as the case may be: and the element of persuasion or invitation must be proved.[10]

Procuration of a girl under twenty-one,[11] though not an offence directly involving prostitution, is also highly relevant. By s. 24, it is an offence to detain a woman against her will in a brothel or in any premises with intent that she shall have unlawful sexual intercourse. And by s. 28:

"(1) It is an offence for a person to cause or encourage the prostitution of, or the commission of unlawful sexual intercourse with, or of an indecent assault on, a girl under the age of sixteen for whom he is responsible.

(2) Where a girl has become a prostitute, or has had unlawful sexual intercourse, or has been indecently assaulted, a person shall be deemed for the purposes of this section to have caused or encouraged it, if he knowingly allowed her to consort with, or to enter or continue in the employment of, any prostitute or person of known immoral character."[12]

---

[7] [1963] 3 All E.R. at p. 179. In the case of *Stephen Ward* (*The Times*, July 31, 1963) MARSHALL, J., cautiously confined his definition of prostitution to normal sexual intercourse. This was because he summed up the day before *Webb* came before the House of Lords and the learned judge no doubt envisaged the possibility that *de Munck* might be overruled.

[8] Report, Cmnd. 247, p. 79.

[9] Above, p. 294.

[10] *Christian*, above, p. 295.

[11] Sexual Offences Act 1956, s. 23; above, p. 297.

[12] Subsections (3) and (4) of this section define the persons who are "responsible" for a girl for the purposes of the section—broadly, a parent or legal guardian or any person having possession or control or custody of her. Sub.-s. (5) provides that a girl who appears to the court to be under sixteen may be presumed to be so, unless the contrary is proved.

This offence seems to overlap to a large extent with ss. 21, 6 and 14. One who caused the prostitution of, or sexual intercourse with, or an indecent assault on, a girl under sixteen would be guilty as an aider and abettor under s. 21 and s. 6 (or s. 5 if the girl was under thirteen) and s. 14 respectively. One who "encouraged" these offences would be guilty of incitement to commit them. Causing or encouraging prostitution will also, in the great majority of cases necessarily involve aiding and abetting or inciting sexual intercourse or indecent assault on the girl, though, owing to the wide definition of prostitution, the section may occasionally cover cases outside these limits.[13] Perhaps the real value of the section lies in the wide meaning given to "cause or encourage" by sub-s. (2). The conduct there described might be insufficient to support a charge of aiding or abetting or incitement.

The section may be wider in one other respect. It may well be that *Prince*[14] governs the section yet again and, if so, a belief even on reasonable grounds that the girl was over sixteen would be no defence. Such a belief would afford a defence to a charge of aiding and abetting or incitement;[15] but it would in any event, be difficult to establish in the case of a person responsible for a girl actually under sixteen.

By s. 29 (1) of the Sexual Offences Act 1956:

> "It is an offence, subject to the exception mentioned in this section, for a person to cause or encourage the prostitution in any part of the world of a woman who is a defective."

Reasonable ignorance that the woman is a defective is a defence under the section.[16]

It seems that very few cases of procuration come to the notice of the police, probably because most women who become prostitutes do so because they want to and the element of persuasion implicit in procuring is lacking.[17]

2   The Use of Premises for Prostitution

(i) *Brothel keeping.*—By s. 33 of the Sexual Offences Act 1956:

> "It is an offence for a person to keep a brothel, or to manage, or act or assist in the management of, a brothel."

By s. 34:

> "It is an offence for the lessor or landlord of any premises or his agent to let the whole or part of the premises with the knowledge that it is to be used, in whole or in part, as a brothel, or, where the whole or part of the premises is used as a brothel, to be wilfully a party to that use continuing."

And by s. 35 (1):

> "It is an offence for the tenant or occupier, or person in charge, of any premises knowingly to permit the whole or part of the premises to be used as a brothel."

---

[13] *Cf. Webb*, above, p. 307.
[14] (1875), L.R. 2 C.C.R. 154; above, p. 42.
[15] Above, pp. 94 and 149.
[16] Sexual Offences Act 1956, s. 29 (2). And *cf. Hudson*, [1965] 1 All E.R. 721; above, p. 299, footnote 13.
[17] Cmnd. 247 at p. 112.

The Act does not define "brothel" but this term has a definite meaning at common law. It is a common law misdemeanour to keep a disorderly house and a brothel or bawdy house is one variety of disorderly house. For the purposes of ss. 33, 34 and 35 of the Sexual Offences Act 1956, it is now provided by the Sexual Offences Act 1967, s. 6, that premises shall be treated as a brothel

> ". . . if people resort to it for the purpose of lewd homosexual practices in circumstances in which resort thereto for lewd heterosexual practices would have led to its being treated as a brothel for the purposes of those sections."

At common law a brothel is

> "a place resorted to by persons of both sexes for the purpose of prostitution;"[18]

and there must be at least two women plying their trade as prostitutes in that place. Now it would seem that a place may be a brothel though persons of only one sex resort to it. It is presumably necessary that two women, or two men, or a man and a woman ply their trade there. If two persons are using the premises for prostitution, the place is a brothel and it is immaterial that one of them is the occupier.[19] But in *Singleton* v. *Ellison*[18] a woman occupied premises at which she alone received a number of men for the purposes of prostitution. It was held that she was rightly acquitted of keeping a brothel. In *Caldwell* v. *Leech*[20] the occupier was acquitted where he permitted a single woman to use the premises for prostitution. Where a building comprised three floors and D let the first and second floors to one woman and the third floor to another, knowing both to be prostitutes, he was acquitted of letting the premises with knowledge that they were to be used as a brothel[1] when it appeared that the two flats were separate premises, each being occupied by one prostitute only[2] But in *Donovan* v. *Gavin*[3] it was held that a brothel may be constituted by rooms independently let for separate occupation, "if they are sufficiently close to each other to constitute in effect what might be called a nest of prostitutes", at least if there is some common management of the business of prostitution or if (as in this case) at least two of the prostitutes are collaborating in their business.

(ii) *Tenant permitting premises to be used for prostitution.*—By s. 36 of the Sexual Offences Act 1956:

> "It is an offence for the tenant or occupier of any premises knowingly to permit the whole or part of the premises to be used for the purposes of habitual prostitution."

A tenant who sub-lets part of the premises to a woman whom he knows to be a prostitute is not guilty of an offence under the section; "tenant" in the section means tenant in occupation.[4] *A fortiori*, it would be no offence if the whole of the premises were sub-let. But if a tenant allowed a mere licensee to use the

---

[18] *Singleton* v. *Ellison*, [1895] 1 Q.B. 607 at p. 608, *per* WILLS, J.

[19] *Gorman* v. *Standen*, [1964] 1 Q.B. 294; [1963] 3 All E.R. 627.

[20] (1913), 109 L.T. 188, RIDLEY, J., dissenting and PICKFORD, J., concurring with regret. RIDLEY, J., would have confined *Singleton* v. *Ellison*, above, to the case where the sole prostitute was also the occupier. PICKFORD, J., regretted that he did not think that case could be so confined.

[1] See s. 34 of the Sexual Offences Act 1956.

[2] *Strath* v. *Foxon*, [1955] 3 All E.R. 398.

[3] [1965] 2 Q.B. 648; [1965] 2 All E.R. 611 (D.C.). *Cf. Durose* v. *Wilson* (1907), L.T. 645; *Abbott* v. *Smith*, [1964] 3 All E.R. 762.

[4] *Siviour* v. *Napolitano*, [1931] 1 K.B. 636, decided under the Criminal Law Amendment Act 1885, s. 13, which used the words "tenant, lessee or occupier . . .". The decision would apply, *a fortiori*, to the present section.

premises for prostitution, he would no doubt be guilty although he was not actually living on the premises himself.

The effect of ss. 33–36, then, is that it is an offence for a landlord to let premises, knowing that they are to be used as a brothel, or to be wilfully a party to their being so used; for anyone to keep a brothel, or to act or assist in the management of one; or for the tenant or occupier knowingly to permit even one woman to use any part of those premises for habitual prostitution. But it is not an offence for a landlord to let premises knowing that they are to be used for prostitution by one woman, or to be a party to the use of the premises by a single prostitute; nor is it an offence for the tenant herself to practise prostitution on the premises.

If D lets a flat to T whom he knows to be a prostitute, and T carries on the business of prostitution in the flat, no offence is committed.[5] If D has let flats to a number of other prostitutes, even within a single building, and they carry on their business there, no offence is committed by anybody, provided only that it is clear that each woman has exclusive possession of her flat so as to constitute it separate premises for legal purposes.[6] But even the landlord of prostitutes who is careful so to arrange his affairs as to fall outside the provisions so far examined may yet fall foul of the rule next to be considered.

3 Living on the Earnings of Prostitution

By s. 30 of the Sexual Offences Act 1956:

> "(1) It is an offence for a man knowingly to live wholly or in part on the earnings of prostitution.
>
> (2) For the purposes of this section a man who lives with or is habitually in the company of a prostitute, or who exercises control, direction or influence over a prostitute's movements in a way which shows he is aiding, abetting or compelling her prostitution with others, shall be presumed to be knowingly living on the earnings of prostitution, unless he proves the contrary."

By s. 4 of the Street Offences Act 1959[7] the maximum penalty for this offence was increased from two to seven years. This provision replaces that in the Vagrancy Act 1898, as amended by s. 7 of the Criminal Law Amendment Act 1912, which in turn replaced a provision in the Vagrancy Act 1824. It has been said by Lord SIMONDS, however, that no assistance in its interpretation is to be derived from its ancestry.[8]

According to the Wolfenden Committee,[9]

> "In its simplest and most usual form, 'living on the earnings of prostitution' consists of an arrangement by which a man lives with a prostitute and is wholly or mainly kept by her. Such a man is commonly known as a 'ponce' or souteneur."

---

[5] T cannot be said to "permit" the flat to be used for prostitution for "permitting" means letting someone else do something: *Mattison* v. *Johnson* (1916), 85 L.J.K.B. 741. *Cf. James* v. *Smee*, above, p. 75.

[6] The neighbours of such premises may have a remedy in the civil courts. In *Thompson-Schwab* v. *Costaki*, [1956] 1 All E.R. 652, the Court of Appeal held that the user of premises for prostitution and the perambulations of the prostitutes and their customers may amount to such an interference with the comfortable and convenient enjoyment of nearby houses as to be an actionable nuisance. An interlocutory injunction was granted.

[7] Below, p. 315.

[8] *Shaw* v. *Director of Public Prosecutions*, [1962] A.C. 220 at p. 263; [1961] 2 All E.R. 446 at p. 449: "The Act of 1824 may be regarded as a convenient peg on which to hang divers offences to which the words 'vagabondage and roguery' would not be entirely appropriate."

[9] Report, Cmnd. 247, p. 99.

There may be difficulties in proving the existence of such a relationship, but, once established, there is no doubt that the offence is proved. It is now clear, however, that the meaning of the section extends beyond this, and difficult questions have arisen as to its limits. In deciding these questions,

> "the second subsection is probative and explanatory of the first but not an exhaustive definition of it."[10]

One view of the words of s. 30 (1) would be that anyone who received money from a prostitute, knowing that she had earned it by practising her profession, is guilty of an offence. It is agreed on all hands that such an interpretation would be far too wide. Its effect would be that no one could receive payment for the supply of food, clothing, lodging or other necessaries to the prostitute.

The opposite view would be that anyone who gives value, whether goods or services to the prostitute and is paid by her, is living on his own earnings, not on hers, and is not guilty. This view too, is generally rejected.

> "To give effect to it would be to exclude from the operation of the Act the very persons, the tout, the bully or protector, whom it was designed to catch. For they would surely claim that they served the prostitute, however despicable their service might seem to others".[11]

Somewhere between these two views a line must be drawn and, in a series of cases since 1954, the courts have attempted to draw it. Two situations must be considered:

1. It is clear that the offence is committed where D, for reward and with the intention of furthering prostitution, supplies goods or services or premises which in their nature are referable to the prostitution and nothing else.[12] In the leading case of *Shaw* v. *Director of Public Prosecutions*[13] the whole object of the *Ladies' Directory* was to facilitate the business of the advertisers and it was agreed by all the judges in that case that D, in receiving payment from the prostitutes for the advertisements, was living on their earnings within the meaning of the section. The majority so held for the reason given above. Lord REID alone thought that the seller of goods, etc., exclusively for prostitution is not necessarily guilty. In his view, it must also appear that D's occupation is "parasitic"—and Shaw's ("He was really no more than a tout . . .") was.[14]

The same principle governs in *Calvert* v. *Mayes*,[15] where D allowed his parked car to be used for prostitution or drove prostitutes and their clients to secluded places in the countryside where they might have intercourse. Slightly more difficult are the further instances alleged in *Mayes* where the intercourse took place in the back of the car while servicemen were being driven to their base; but the fact that free transport was provided satisfied the court that the *sole*

---

[10] *Per* Lord SIMONDS, [1962] A.C. 220 at p. 263; [1961] 2 All E.R. 446 at p. 449.

[11] Lord SIMONDS, [1962] A.C. at pp. 263, 264; [1961] 2 All E.R. at p. 450.

[12] *Cf.* the test suggested by BRAMWELL, B., for civil cases where a prostitute is sued for goods supplied: to afford a defence it must appear that ". . . the thing supplied must be not merely such as would be necessary or useful for ordinary purposes, and might also be applied to an immoral one; but that they must be such as would under the circumstances not be required, except with that view": *Pearce* v. *Brooks* (1866), L.R. 1 Exch. 213, at p. 215. Would not the supplier of the ornamental brougham in that case and the laundress of the clients' nightcaps in *Lloyd* v. *Johnson* (1798), 1 Bos. & P. 340 (who recovered the price!), now be guilty of living on the earnings of prostitution?

[13] [1962] A.C. 220; [1961] 2 All E.R. 446. The facts are set out above, p. 160.

[14] [1962] A.C. at p. 270; [1961] 2 All E.R. at pp. 453, 454.

[15] [1954] 1 Q.B. 342; [1954] 1 All E.R. 41.

reason for hiring the car was the facilitation of prostitution. In such cases it is immaterial that the charge made is reasonable—in *Mayes* the court accepted that D would have been paid the same sum of money if the journey had been a legitimate one and in *Shaw* it was held to be irrelevant that the charges for the advertisements in the *Ladies' Directory* were reasonable.[16]

In *Thomas*,[17] D let a prostitute have the use of a room for prostitution between 9 p.m. and 2 a.m. each night. PILCHER, J., who was upheld by the Court of Criminal Appeal, directed that this amounted to the offence if the rent was grossly inflated. But, as Lord SIMONDS has pointed out,[18] there was strong evidence there that the accommodation was provided for prostitution and nothing else, in which case it should have been irrelevant whether the rent was inflated or not.

2. It seems that the offence is also committed where D receives the price of the supply of goods or services or premises which, though not exclusively referable to the prostitution, will be used to further it in some way but only where D makes an exorbitant charge because the woman is a prostitute. In *Silver*[19] Judge MAUDE directed an acquittal of a landlord who let premises to a woman and charged her an exorbitant rent ("a prostitute rent") because he knew that she intended to practise prostitution there. In *Thomas*, the Court of Criminal Appeal upheld a ruling by PILCHER, J., that, in such circumstances,[20] there was a case to leave to a jury and in *Shaw* the majority were disposed to favour this view. In the latter case Lord SIMONDS (with whom Lords TUCKER, MORRIS and HODSON concurred on this point) distinguished the case where the flat is let only for prostitution, as in *Thomas*, and went on:[1]

> "But, if the flat is let for occupation, I am not prepared to say that the landlord commits an offence merely because he knows that his tenant is a prostitute and must be assumed to know that she will there ply her trade. The prostitute must live somewhere just as she must eat and drink to live. It is, I think, too fine a distinction to say that a grocer supplying her with groceries does not, but a landlord letting her a flat does, commit an offence. It is true that the flat is the scene of her prostitution, but if she did not eat and drink she would not have a body to prostitute. Therefore, in such a case as *Silver* (where the flats appear to have been let for occupation) the landlord can only be convicted of an offence upon the ground that the rent is exorbitant. This may be a tenable view upon the footing that, to the extent to which the rent is in excess of normal, he extorts it from the prostitute upon no other ground than that she is a prostitute."

Lord REID agreed[2] with the majority on this point:

> "In reality he is not then merely acting as landlord; he is making her engage in a joint adventure with him which will bring to him a part of her immoral earnings over and above the rent."

Would it not then follow that a grocer overcharging a prostitute because she was a prostitute would be guilty of the offence? The problem is unlikely to arise.

---

[16] [1962] A.C. 220 at p. 229; [1961] 1 All E.R. 330 at p. 335 (C.C.A.).
[17] [1957] 2 All E.R. 181.
[18] [1962] A.C. 220 at p. 265; [1961] 2 All E.R. 446 at p. 451.
[19] [1956] 1 All E.R. 716.
[20] PILCHER, J., attached no importance to the fact, noted above, that the premises were apparently let for prostitution and nothing else.
[1] [1962] A.C. 220 at pp. 265, 266; [1961] 2 All E.R. 446 at p. 451.
[2] [1962] A.C. at p. 271; [1961] 2 All E.R. at p. 454.

Prostitutes are vulnerable to overcharging for premises, because it is difficult for them to find accommodation; but they can get groceries—and most other goods and services—as easily as anyone else.

Thus, though the matter is not free from doubt,[3] it seems likely that the landlord who lets premises for prostitution commits no offence provided that the rent is the reasonable or normal rent for these premises. The Wolfenden Committee rejected proposals that this loophole in the law should be closed:[4]

> "As long as society tolerates the prostitute, it must permit her to carry on her business somewhere. That she ought not to be allowed to carry it on in public will be apparent . . .; and the law, for a variety of reasons, rightly frowns on the brothel. The only remaining possibility is individual premises. We have therefore reached the conclusion that it would not be right to amend the law in such a way as to make guilty of a criminal offence a person who lets premises to a prostitute who uses them, even to his knowledge, for the purposes of her own habitual prostitution."

This accords with the general attitude of the law towards prostitution. Life is not to be made impossible for the prostitute. She must have food, clothing, clean linen and the other necessaries (or, indeed, luxuries) of life, not exclusively referable to prostitution. The civil courts do not discourage tradesmen from supplying these by refusing to allow them to recover the price and the criminal courts will not construe the statute so widely as to make the supply a criminal offence. As regards premises, the civil law goes farther than the criminal for it is clear that the landlord who lets premises for prostitution[5] cannot recover the rent,[6] however reasonable it might be. But, while it would be intolerable for the civil law to allow recovery of money which, when recovered, would be regarded as the earnings of prostitution for the purposes of the section, it is not unreasonable to use the milder sanction of the civil law to discourage landlords while withholding the bigger guns of the criminal law.

It will have been noted that the offence under s. 30 of the Sexual Offences Act 1956 can be committed only by a man.[7] This continues to be so, as far as female prostitution is concerned; but now, by s. 5 of the Sexual Offences Act 1967, it is an offence punishable with seven years' imprisonment for a man or a woman knowingly to live wholly or in part on the earnings of another man.

4 A Woman Exercising Control over a Prostitute

A closely related offence under s. 31 of the Sexual Offences Act 1956 may be committed only by women:

> "It is an offence for a woman for purposes of gain to exercise control, direction or influence over a prostitute's movements in a way which shows she is aiding, abetting or compelling her prostitution."

As in the case of complicity in suicide,[8] statute here makes it an offence to aid and abet an act which, in itself, is no crime.

---

[3] Professor Goodhart argues that the landlord is guilty even if the rent is reasonable: ". . . rent, however exorbitant, is still rent. Thus if the normal rent of a hotel room is doubled at the time of a coronation, the whole of the payment remains rent. The nature of the services cannot be affected by the amount that is charged for them . . .": 77 L.Q.R at 563.

[4] Cmnd. 247 at p. 104.

[5] Or even for use by a mistress: *Upfill* v. *Wright*, [1911] 1 K. B. 506.

[6] Nor can he recover possession of the premises until the lease is terminated: *Alexander* v. *Rayson*, [1936] 1 K.B. 169 at p. 186.

[7] May a woman aid and abet? *Cf.* pp. 96–97, above.

[8] Above, p. 238.

5 Loitering or Soliciting in Public Places

In all the offences so far considered, the crime is committed not by the prostitute but by another. The legislation now to be considered is aimed at the prostitute herself. Its object is not the suppression or discouragement of prostitution, but the elimination of an offence against public order and decency arising from the activities of prostitutes in public places. The present law is to be found in the Street Offences Act 1959 which provides in s. 1:

"(1) It shall be an offence for a common prostitute to loiter or solicit in a street or public place for the purpose of prostitution.

(2) A person guilty of an offence under this section shall be liable, on summary conviction, to a fine not exceeding ten pounds or, for an offence committed after a previous conviction, to a fine not exceeding twenty-five pounds or, for an offence committed after more than one previous conviction, to a fine not exceeding twenty-five pounds or imprisonment for a period not exceeding three months or both.

(3) A constable may arrest without warrant anyone he finds in a street or public place and suspects, with reasonable cause, to be committing an offence under this section."

This provision was enacted as a result of the report of the Wolfenden Committee[9] and it repeals and replaces a number of earlier enactments. The law is strengthened in a number of respects: (1) It is no longer necessary to establish "annoyance" on the part of any member of the public. This was difficult to prove because men solicited by prostitutes were almost invariably unwilling to give evidence and the standard of proof accepted by the courts was far from uniform. (2) The Act is not limited to urban areas as was the previous legislation. And (3) the penalties have been greatly increased. The terms "common prostitute", "loiter", "solicit" and "in a street or public place" require further examination.

(i) *Common prostitute.*—There is no statutory definition of this term, but it has been commonly used in legislation, and it means simply a woman who offers her body commonly for acts of lewdness for payment.[10] The Wolfenden Committee, rejecting criticisms of this term, observed[11] that it is

"a description of a trade or calling that is not of itself unlawful, and that there are parallels for prohibiting to members of one trade or calling actions which for other persons are not offences;"

and they found no evidence that injustice results from its use in legislation. Its value is said to be that it protects from arrest a respectable woman who, through ignorance or indiscretion, loiters, quite innocently but so as to give rise to reasonable suspicion in the mind of a policeman that she is doing so for the purposes of prostitution. But if a policeman reasonably suspects that D is loitering for the purposes of prostitution, does he not thereby necessarily also suspect that she is a common prostitute?

(ii) *Loiter.*—This word "loiter" has been used in other Acts of Parliament and it is probable that the meaning attributed to it in those Acts dealing with a similar mischief is applicable. Under the Street Betting Act 1906 it was an

---

[9] Cmnd. 247 (1957).
[10] See above, p. 307.
[11] Cmnd. 247 at p. 88.

offence to loiter in a street for the purpose of betting. In *Williamson* v. *Wright*[12] the Court of Session held there was no evidence of loitering when a car slowed down on a single occasion to pick up betting slips. Lord ANDERSON said that loitering

> "is just travelling indolently and with frequent pauses" and "involves an idea of a certain persistence or repetition."

Lord ALNESS thought that loitering "connotes the idea of lingering"—which was absent in that case. Lord HUNTER was inclined to think the word appropriate only to a pedestrian but Lord ANDERSON was quite clear that a person may loiter in a car; and this was accepted by a Divisional Court in *Bridge* v. *Campbell*[13] where it was held that D was loitering for the purpose of the Vagrancy Act 1824 when he followed a vehicle in his van and repeatedly stopped when that vehicle stopped.

(iii) *Solicit.*—Soliciting is conduct amounting to an importuning of prospective customers. The prostitute must be physically present, so that the offence is not committed where she displays a card on a notice board in a street, inviting men to visit her for the purpose of prostitution.[14] If one has regard to the mischief at which the Act is aimed, this limitation upon its effect is clearly right.[15] It is probably not necessary that the prostitute's invitation should ever be received. It is enough that it is made and it is irrelevant that the prospective clients are deaf, blind, or merely day-dreaming and unaware that they are being solicited.[16] There is undoubtedly an attempt to solicit in such cases and this is no less severely punishable, but the point is not academic as magistrates' courts have no power to convict of an attempt on a charge of committing the full offence.[17] Solicitation may be by acts done and it is unnecessary to prove that D used any words. It was enough in *Horton* v. *Mead* that he

> "smiled in the faces of gentlemen, pursed his lips, and wriggled his body."[18]

(iv) *In a street or public place.*—By s. 1 (4) of the Street Offences Act 1959:

> "For the purposes of this section 'street' includes any bridge, road, lane, footway, subway, square, court, alley or passage, whether a thoroughfare or not, which is for the time being open to the public; and the doorways and entrances of premises abutting on a street (as hereinbefore defined), and any ground adjoining and open to a street, shall be treated as forming part of the street."

The meaning of "street" is thus a wide one yet it will be noted that the subsection does not provide an exclusive definition. The term "public place" is not defined at all and is more likely to occasion difficulty. That term is to be found in many statutes and formerly had a meaning at common law as part of the definition of affray.[19] Clearly its meaning may vary according to the context.

---

[12] 1924 S.C. (J.) 57.

[13] [1947] W.N. 223.

[14] *Weisz* v. *Monahan,* [1962] 1 All E.R. 664. *Cf. Burge* v. *Director of Public Prosecutions,* below, p. 324.

[15] It might be noted that a shopkeeper publishing such notices for reward might possibly be convicted of (i) conspiracy to corrupt public morals: *Shaw* v. *Director of Public Prosecutions* (above, p. 160); (ii) publishing an obscene article (*cf.* the *Ladies Directory,* below, p. 490), and (if a man) (iii) living on the earnings of prostitution.

[16] *Horton* v. *Mead,* [1913] 1 K.B. 154, a case under s. 1 (1) of the Vagrancy Act 1898 (see now, Sexual Offences Act 1956, s. 32); below, p. 324.

[17] Above, pp. 176.

[18] [1913] 1 K.B. 154 at p. 157.

[19] See below, p. 540.

Generally, however, it is construed to mean a place to which the public has access in fact, whether as of right or not and whether only on payment or not. Such a construction is supported in the present case by the use of the phrase "for the time being open to the public" in connection with "street"; for "public place" probably must be construed *ejusdem generis* with "street".[20] If so, the term might include privately-owned fields to which the public have access for the purpose of viewing point-to-point racing,[1] a car-park belonging to a dance-hall[2] or public house,[3] the grounds of a hospital to which visitors and their friends are admitted,[4] an omnibus[5] or train, a village hall at which there is a dance open to members of the public,[6] and a public house[7] during licensing hours.

It has been emphasised in recent cases, however, that whether a place is public is a question of degree and fact.

> "If only a restricted class of person is permitted or invited to have access, the case would fall on the side of the place being private. If only a restricted class is excluded the place would be public."[8]

Soliciting takes place *in* a street or public place where the solicitation takes effect there, even though D may be outside the street or public place. In *Smith v. Hughes*[9] D attracted the attention of men in the street by tapping on the window pane, and by gestures invited them in and indicated the price of her services. Applying the "mischief rule" of construction, the Divisional Court dismissed her appeal:[10]

> "Everybody knows that this was an Act intended to clean up the streets, to enable people to walk along the streets without being molested or solicited by common prostitutes. Viewed in that way, it can matter little whether the prostitute is soliciting while in the street or is standing in a doorway or on a balcony, or at a window, or whether the window is shut or open or half open; in each case her solicitation is projected to and addressed to somebody walking in the street."

It does not follow that the result would be the same if the prostitute failed to attract anyone's attention,[11] for HILBERY, J., thought that solicitation was not complete until the signals reached the men.[12]

6 INDECENT EXPOSURE

1 Indecent Exposure at Common Law

(i) *The actus reus.*—It is a common law misdemeanour[13] to commit an act outraging public decency in public and in such a way that more than one person

---

[20] As "public place" is construed *ejusdem generis* with "road" in the Road Traffic Acts: *Elkins* v. *Cartlidge*, [1947] 1 All E.R. 829; below, p. 340.

[1] *Collinson* (1931), 23 Cr. App. Rep. 49.

[2] *Williams* v. *Boyle*, [1963] Crim. L.R. 204.

[3] *Elkins* v. *Cartlidge*, supra; *Waters*, [1963] Crim. L.R. 437.

[4] *Powell*, [1963] Crim. L.R. 511, above, p. 284.

[5] *Holmes* (1853), Dears C.C. 207.

[6] *Morris* (1963), 47 Cr. App. Rep. 202.

[7] *Mapstone*, [1963] 3 All E.R. 930.

[8] *Waters* [1963] Crim. L.R. 437 at p. 438.

[9] [1960] 2 All E.R. 859. What of the opposite case where D, in the street, attracts the attention of men in private premises?

[10] [1960] 2 All E.R. 889 at p. 861.

[11] This is probably immaterial if the prostitute is in the street: *Horton* v. *Mead*, above, p. 316.

[12] *Cf.* the problem arising under the Public Order Act 1936; *Wilson* v. *Skeock* (1949), 113 J.P. 294; *Ward* v. *Holman*, [1964] Crim. L.R. 541; below, p. 542.

[13] *Sidney* (1663), 1 Sid. 168.

sees, or is at least able to see, the act. The most common way of committing this offence is by indecently exposing the body.

A wide view is taken of "in public". In *Wellard*[14] GROVE, J., said that a public place is one where the public go, no matter whether they have a right to or not. But earlier cases seem to go farther than this. D may himself be on private premises, to which the general public do not have access and so may those who see him. In *Bunyan*,[15] D was in the parlour of a public house and was witnessed through the window of another room of the house; and in *Thallman*[16] D was on the roof of a private house and could be seen only from the windows of other houses. These could hardly be described as places "where the public go" yet both were convicted. It is doubtful if "in public" adds anything to the requirement that two or more persons must have been able to see the act.[17]

It has been held to be no offence where only one person was able to see the act;[18] but it has never been held that two persons must have actually seen it. In *Elliot*[19] it was submitted that it was enough that D exposed himself in a place where he might have been seen, although *no one* saw him. The court was evidently divided, three to two (but which way does not appear) and asked for the case to be re-argued. They later changed their minds and no judgment was delivered. In the recent case of *Mayling*[20] the Court of Criminal Appeal did not go farther than to say that it is clear that more than one person must *at least have been able* to see the act; but two persons actually saw it in that case. The point is therefore not settled. It seems artificial to insist on two persons having seen the act; but if this is not required, what is the test? Must two persons have been present? Or is it enough that D exposed himself in a street or at a window where two or more persons might have been expected to pass by and see him though no one did? As a practical matter, of course, there will almost invariably be one witness of the act, for otherwise it would not be provable except by confession.

It is not necessary to prove that anyone was actually disgusted or annoyed. This was decided in *Mayling*,[20] where the court pointed out that a requirement of actual disgust would be incompatible with a rule that the offence could be established by proof that persons could have seen, but did not see the act. But it can hardly be an offence to expose oneself to others who consent to the exposure.[1]

(ii) *The mens rea.*—It is unnecessary to prove any sexual motive or any intention to insult or annoy. Lady Godiva would have been guilty, notwithstanding her admirable motives, at least if there had been two peeping Toms. In *Crunden*[2] D was convicted when he undressed and swam (presumably

---

[14] (1884), 14 Q.B.D. 63.
[15] (1844), 1 Cox C.C. 74.
[16] (1863), 9 Cox C.C. 388.
[17] *Cf.* Lord DENMAN, C.J., in *Watson* (1847), 2 Cox C.C. 376 at p. 377: ". . . a nuisance must be public; *that is*, to the injury or offence of several," and WILLES, J., in *Harris* (1871), 11 Cox C.C. 659 at p. 661. See also Lord COLERIDGE, C.J., and HUDDLESTON, B., in *Wellard* as reported in 15 Cox C.C. 559 at pp. 562, 563.
[18] *Reubegard* (1830), cited in 1 Den. 344; *Webb* (1848), 1 Den. 338; *Watson, supra*; *Farrell* (1862), 9 Cox C.C. 446.
[19] (1861) Le. & Ca. 103.
[20] [1963] 3 Q.B. 717; [1963] 1 All E.R. 687.
[1] Below, p. 319.
[2] (1809) 2 Camp. 89; *Reed* (1871), 12 Cox C.C. 1.

naked) opposite the East Cliff at Brighton in view of a row of houses. It was held irrelevant that his object was to procure health and enjoy a favourite recreation, not to outrage decency or corrupt the public morals.

It is submitted that it must at least be proved that D intended that, or was reckless whether, the exposure might be seen by two or more persons who do not consent to see it. In *Bunyan and Morgan*[3] the recorder seems to have held that negligence would suffice and that, although D had been seeking privacy, it was enough that there was a reasonable probability of his being discovered. This seems to be contrary to principle.

The offence may be committed by a female as well as a male person,[4] and the exposure need not necessarily be to persons of the opposite sex. If, however, three men were to bathe together naked, in a place in which they would reasonably expect not to be observed by anyone else, it is thought that no offence would be committed because this could not be said to outrage public decency. But it is quite otherwise if a man masturbates himself in the view of other men.[5] Is the offence committed if a mixed party of men and women bathe naked together? It is thought not (unless they are liable to be observed by others) because their consent negatives the outraging of decency. If it were not so, nudist camps would be illegal.

2 Indecent Exposure under the Vagrancy Act 1824

By s. 4 of the Vagrancy Act 1824:

". . . every person wilfully, openly, lewdly and obscenely exposing his person with intent to insult any female . . . shall be deemed a rogue and vagabond. . . ."

The offence is punishable summarily by three months' imprisonment or a fine of £25; or, on a second conviction and committal to Quarter Sessions for sentence, by one year's imprisonment.

Unlike the common law offence this crime is limited to exposure by a male to a female and requires a specific intent to insult. It has been suggested, though there is no authority on the point, that there is another limitation on this offence which is not applicable to the common law offence—that is, that "person" means "genital organ" and

"however deliberate be the intent to insult the female, and however great the insult she feels, the exposure of the backside is not within the section."[6]

The section was formerly limited to public places, but this limitation was removed by the Criminal Justice Act 1925 s. 42. The vast majority of charges of indecent exposure are brought under this Act.[7]

Indecent exposure is also an offence under various local acts and byelaws, some of which are set out in *Sexual Offences*.[8]

---

[3] (1844), 1 Cox. C.C. 74.
[4] *Elliot* (1861), Le. & Ca. 103.
[5] For example, *Mayling*, above, p. 318.
[6] *Sexual Offences* (ed. Radzinowicz), 427.
[7] *Ibid.*
[8] *Ibid.*, pp. 358 *et seq.*

7 UNNATURAL OFFENCES

1 **Buggery**

Buggery consists in intercourse *per anum*[9] by a man with a man or woman;[10] or intercourse *per anum* or *per vaginam*[11] by a man or a woman[12] with an animal. It can be committed by a husband with his wife.[13] As in rape, penetration must be proved, but emission need not.[14]

Consent is no defence. Indeed, the consenting party is also guilty of the offence, not merely as an abettor but as a principal offender.[15] The person effecting the intercourse is known as the "agent" and the other party as the "patient".

By s. 12 (1) of the Sexual Offences Act 1956:

> "It is an offence for a person to commit buggery with another person or with an animal."

This is now qualified by the Sexual Offences Act 1967 which provides[16] that it shall not be an offence for a man to commit buggery or gross indecency with another man provided that:

(i) the act is done in private;

(ii) the parties consent and

(iii) the parties have attained the age of twenty-one.

An act is not done in private for this purpose if (i) more than two persons take part or are present; or (ii) the act is done in a lavatory to which the public have or are permitted to have access, whether on payment or otherwise.

A person suffering from severe subnormality[17] cannot consent for the purposes of the Act. It is a defence for D to prove "that he did not know and had no reason to suspect" P to be suffering from severe subnormality. It seems probable that it would be no defence to show that D1 believed D2 to be over twenty-one if he was in fact under that age.[18]

The Act expressly puts on the Crown the onus of proving that the act was

(i) not done in private, or

(ii) without consent or

(iii) that any party was under twenty-one.

An act of buggery or gross indecency continues to be an offence where it is done on a United Kingdom merchant ship by a member of the crew of that ship with another man who is a member of the crew of that or any other United Kingdom merchant ship.[19] The Act does not affect the provisions of the Army

---

[9] Other unnatural forms of intercourse are not within the meaning of the term: *Jacobs* (1817), Russ. & Ry. 331; but may amount to indecent assault or an act of gross indecency; see below, p. 322.

[10] *Wiseman* (1718), Fortes. Rep. 91.

[11] East says "in any manner": 1 P.C. 480.

[12] *Bourne* (1952), 36 Cr. App. Rép. 125; above p. 94. *Cf.* Coke, 3 Inst. 59 ". . . a great lady had committed buggery with a baboon and conceived by it . . ."!

[13] *Jellyman* (1838), 8 C. & P. 604.

[14] *Reekspear* (1832), 1 Mood. C.C. 342; *Cozins* (1834), 6 C. & P. 351. Where penetration is impossible, D may be convicted of an attempt: *Brown* (1889), 24 Q.B.D. 357.

[15] Stephen, *Digest*, Art. 221.

[16] Section 1.

[17] Above, p. 298.

[18] *Cf. Prince* (1875), L.R. 2 C.C.R. 154; above, p. 42.

[19] Section 2.

Act 1955, or the Air Force Act 1955, under which disgraceful conduct of an unnatural kind is punishable with two years' imprisonment,[20] or the Naval Discipline Act 1957[1] under which disgraceful conduct of an indecent kind is similarly punishable.

A consenting party under twenty-one continues to be guilty of an offence but proceedings against him for participating in any buggery or gross indecency may not be instituted except with the consent of the Director of Public Prosecutions.[2]

It continues to be an offence under s. 12 (1) of the 1956 Act for a man to commit buggery with a woman, though both parties consent, or for a man or a woman to commit buggery with an animal, whether in private or not.

It seems to be the law that a person under fourteen whether male or female, cannot be convicted as a principal offender either as agent or as patient.[3] Clearly, as regards the female and the male patient this does not depend upon any presumption of sexual incapacity. Coke,[4] Hale[5] and East[6] put this rule upon the child's want of discretion; but, if this is so, then the child over ten ought to be liable to conviction on proof of mischievous discretion. However, in *Tatam*[7] the Court of Criminal Appeal ruled that three boys under fourteen were not accomplices in buggery, "being unable at law to commit that offence." This presumably means that they could be convicted neither as principals nor as abettors. Yet, somewhat remarkably, it seems that a child under fourteen could be convicted of abetting D to commit buggery upon P. This was held in *Cratchley*,[8] where a boy of under ten, who kept watch, was held not to be an accomplice in the buggery of P by D but only on the ground of lack of evidence of guilty knowledge.[9] If the child's immunity really depends on presumed lack of discretion, the presumption ought equally to be rebuttable, or irrebuttable, whether D is the patient or the abettor of a buggery upon another. The only basis on which the present rule can be justified is that the law is designed to protect the patient[10]—which seems to be contrary to fact. It may well be that the present rule is due to a misunderstanding by the courts and subsequent writers of Hale, Coke and East who probably meant no more than that a person under fourteen is not liable unless a mischievous discretion is proved.

Where the agent is a boy under fourteen, the patient, if over fourteen, may nevertheless be convicted,[11] a result difficult to reconcile with the conclusive presumption of incapacity.

2 Procuring Others to Commit Lawful Homosexual Acts

Section 4 of the Sexual Offences Act 1967 creates a new offence, punishable

---

[20] Section 66 of both Acts.
[1] Section 37.
[2] If consent is not obtained, any proceeding is a nullity: *Angel*, [1968] Crim. L.R. 342; but consent is not required on a charge of incitement to commit the offence: *Ass. Recorder of Hull, ex p. Morgan*, [1969] 1 All E.R. 416.
[3] *Cf.* Hogan, [1962] Crim. L.R. 683; Williams, [1964] Crim. L.R. 686.
[4] 3 Inst. 59.
[5] 1 P.C. 670.
[6] 1 P.C. 480.
[7] (1921), 15 Cr. App. Rep. 132.
[8] (1913), 9 Cr. App. Rep. 232.
[9] The case is distinguishable from *Tatam*, above, only on the assumption that, in the latter case, none of the boys aided and abetted the buggery of another.
[10] *Cf. Tyrrell*, above, p. 96.
[11] *Allen* (1849), 1 Den. 364. It is perhaps not surprising that the court was anxious to uphold the conviction in that case: D induced a boy of twelve to bugger him.

with two years' imprisonment, of procuring another man to commit with a third man an act of buggery which, by reason of s. 1 of the Act, is not an offence.

3   Assault with Intent to Commit Buggery: and Attempts

By s. 16 (1) of the Sexual Offences Act 1956:

> "It is an offence for a person to assault another person with intent to commit buggery."

The offence is punishable with ten years' imprisonment.   An attempt to commit buggery is likewise punishable, though it is no longer[12] a statutory offence. Most cases under s. 16 (1) will also amount to an attempt but there may be occasional instances where the statutory provision is useful, as where D assaults P, intending to carry him off and commit buggery some hours later.[13] Here the act would probably not be sufficiently proximate to be an attempt but would amount to the statutory offence.   On the other hand an attempt covers cases obviously not within the statute, as where D attempts buggery with an animal or, perhaps, approaches a sleeping P and does a sufficiently proximate act which does not amount to an assault or battery.

The necessity for an assault also means that consent must be a defence to a charge under the section, and this even though the other party be under sixteen (for there is here no statutory provision to the contrary) but old enough to understand the nature of the act;[14] but where a charge under s. 16 (1) would fail only because of consent, the act is almost certainly an indecent assault under s. 15 by the one party where the other is under sixteen.   And, whatever the age of the parties, it may amount to a gross indecency under s. 13.[15] Consent would be no defence, however, to a charge of attempt to commit buggery and here both parties might be convicted if their acts were sufficiently proximate.

As a boy under fourteen cannot be convicted of an assault with intent to ravish or attempted rape,[16] presumably no child under fourteen can be convicted either of an offence under s. 16 (1) or of attempted buggery.

4   Indecency between Men

By s. 13 of the Sexual Offences Act 1956:

> "It is an offence for a man[17] to commit an act of gross indecency with another man, whether in public or private, or to be a party to the commission by a man of an act of gross indecency with another man, or to procure the commission by a man of an act of gross indecency with another man."

As noted above[18], this is now qualified by the Sexual Offences Act 1967, s.1. This Act also provides, by s. 4 (3) that it shall not be an offence under s. 13 of the 1956 Act for a man to procure the commission *with himself* of an act of gross indecency by another man where that act, by reason of s. 1 of the 1967 Act, is not an offence.   It continues to be an offence under s. 13 for a man to procure

---

[12] It was formerly included in s. 62 of the Offences against the Person Act 1861.   Now the only statutory reference to attempt is in the Second Schedule to the 1956 Act, providing for the punishment.

[13] And *cf. Lankford*, [1959] Crim. L.R. 209.

[14] *Wollaston* (1872), 12 Cox C.C. 180: consent negatives an assault.   The point seems to have been overlooked in *Cratchley*.

[15] *Infra.*

[16] Above, p. 294.

[17] "Man" includes "boy": s. 46.

[18] See p. 320.

another man to commit with a third man an act of gross indecency, though the act, by reason of s. 1 of the 1967 Act, is not an offence.

The nature of "gross indecency" does not seem to have been further defined by the courts, save that it has been held that[19] there is no need for actual physical contact, if two men concert to behave in an indecent manner. It is enough that

> "two men put themselves in such a position that it can be said that a grossly indecent exhibition is going on."

According to the evidence before the Wolfenden Committee:[20]

> ". . . the offence usually takes one of three forms; either there is mutual masturbation; or there is some form of intercrural contact; or oral-genital contact (with or without emission) takes place. Occasionally the offence may take a more recondite form; techniques in heterosexual relations vary considerably, and the same is true of homosexual relations."

The distinction between "indecency" and "gross indecency" is not clear. It has been suggested, as an example, that if

> "two male persons kissed each other under circumstances which showed that the act was immoral and unnatural",

this would be indecent but not grossly indecent.[1]

Consent is no defence and both parties are guilty. One accused may be convicted, however, if the other party is not consenting: "with" in s. 13 does not mean "with the consent of" but "against" or "directed towards".[2] If two men independently perform acts of gross indecency at the same place and time, but without physical contact, it seems clear that no charge will lie under the section. Here D_1 can be said to be committing the act *with* D_2 only if they are acting in concert.[3] But if D assaults P in a grossly indecent manner, he commits a gross indecency with him. Perhaps this is also true where D commits no assault but masturbates himself in P's sight.

Where the charge is one of *procuring*, the same considerations apply as where that term is used elsewhere in the Act.[4]

5 Penalties for Buggery and Gross Indecency

The Sexual Offences Act 1967, s. 3, provides a new scale of penalties for buggery and gross indecency as follows:—

> *Buggery*
> If with a boy under the age of sixteen or with a woman or an animal—life.
> If with a man who is sixteen or over who did not consent—ten years.
> If with a man between sixteen and twenty-one who consented where D is twenty-one or over—five years.
> If with a man of twenty-one or over who consented (whatever D's age)— two years.
> If with a man of sixteen or over who consented and D is under twenty-one —two years.

---

[19] *Hunt* [1950] 2 All E.R. 291.
[20] Cmnd. 247, p. 38. See also *Sexual Offences* (ed. Radzinowicz), 349.
[1] *The Criminal Law Amendment Act* (4th ed.) (1963), by Mead and Bodkin, cited in *Sexual Offences*, p. 349.
[2] *Hall*, [1963] 2 All E.R. 1075. *Cf. Pearce*, [1951] 1 All E.R. 493 and *Jones*, [1896] 1 Q.B. 4.
[3] *Hornby and Peaple*, [1946] 2 All E.R. 487.
[4] Above, p. 294. See also *Jones*, [1896] 1 Q.B. 4; *Bentley*, [1923] 1 K.B. 403.

Attempted Buggery

If with a boy under the age of sixteen or with a woman or an animal—ten years.[5]

If with a man of sixteen or over—the maximum for the completed offence (above).[5]

Committing or Procuring Gross Indecency

If by a man of or over twenty-one with a man under that age—five years. In other cases two years.

6 Solicitation by Men

By s. 32 of the Sexual Offences Act 1956:

"It is an offence for a man persistently to solicit or importune in a public place for immoral purposes."

There is no distinction between importuning and soliciting.[6] The meaning of "solicit" and "public place" would seem to be the same here as in the Street Offences Act 1959 and has already been sufficiently considered in that connection.[7]

This offence differs from that under the Street Offences Act in that the soliciting must be "persistent". In *Dale* v. *Smith*[8] it was said that the word implies "a degree of repetition, of either more than one invitation to one person or a series of invitations to different people". It was held that it was enough that there were two invitations. It may be that a single act of "continuing solicitation" would be enough. In *Burge*[9] the alleged solicitation consisted in the display of a card. As it was held on appeal[10] that this could not be soliciting since D was not physically present, the point did not, in the end, require decision, but the Chairman of Quarter Sessions thought that a display, even for half an hour, would be persistent.

Although this section is being discussed under "Unnatural Offences", it seems that its original object was to penalise soliciting by men on behalf of female prostitutes.[11] "Immoral purposes" however is not defined, and is clearly wide enough to cover both homosexual and heterosexual behaviour. In *Crook* v. *Edmondson*[12] it was held that a man does not solicit for immoral purposes within s. 32 by soliciting a woman to have intercourse with himself. The court did not define "immoral purposes" but said that a possible view is "such immoral purposes as are referred to in this part of the Act". It is surprising that "unlawful sexual intercourse" should not be regarded as an immoral purpose. The interpretation suggested seems to require that the solicitation be for *criminal* purposes.

---

[5] Sexual Offences Act 1967, s. 3 (1) and Criminal Law Act 1967, s. 7 (2).
[6] *Field* v. *Chapman*, [1953] C.L.Y. 787.
[7] Above, p. 316.
[8] [1967] 2 All E.R. 1133 at p. 1136. *Cf. Barker* v. *Barker*, [1949] P. 219 at p. 221; [1949] 1 All E.R. 247 at p. 248; *Broad* v. *Broad* (1898), 78 L.T. 687.
[9] [1961] Crim. L.R. 412.
[10] *Burge* v. *Director of Public Prosecutions*, [1962] 1 All E.R. 666, n. *Cf. Weisz* v. *Monahan*, above, p. 316.
[11] Cmnd. 247 at p. 42.
[12] [1966] 2 Q.B. 81; [1966] 1 All E.R. 833 (D.C.), Sachs, J., dissenting.

CHAPTER 14

Road Traffic Offences

The advent of the motor vehicle created problems with which the existing law was ill-equipped to deal. The threat of proceedings for manslaughter might deter the motorist from driving with wilful disregard for human life, but where some harm less than death was caused other offences against the person were hardly pertinent at all. These offences, in the main, require that the harm should be caused intentionally or recklessly. It is rare for a motorist to intend harm and almost as rare for him to be reckless as to whether or not he causes harm, at least if recklessness involves a subjective awareness of consequences. Though the motorist who causes harm may often be at fault, the harm he causes is ordinarily both undesired and unforeseen by him.

There were some provisions of some statutes which applied to motorists, but only, as it were, by chance. Under the Highways Act 1835 s. 72, for example, it was an offence to drive any carriage on the pavement and this could be applied to the motor carriage, and under the Town Police Clauses Act 1847 s. 28, the furious driving of any horse or carriage was an offence and this was applied to motorists. In short, the law barely concerned the motorist at all. There were no tests of driving proficiency, no registration requirements, no compulsory insurance, and virtually no driving offences. The common law could not fill gaps like these and the result is that for practical purposes the regulation of road traffic is almost entirely statutory. And the bulk of the legislation is considerable. The principal Act, the Road Traffic Act 1960, runs to two hundred and seventy-one sections and twenty schedules, and that is a large body of law.

It is also worth noting that the inadequacy of the existing law was not merely technical or procedural but substantive. It was not merely a question of modifying some of the common law rules or extending the operation of some statutes: it was a question of a new set of rules for an entirely new problem. There has emerged from this one of the striking features of road traffic law: the imposition of criminal liability for negligence, something unusual at common law. Another significant feature is that under the legislation it is generally unnecessary to prove harm to person or property before the offence is committed. There is sense in this of course: prevention is better than cure. But it would be a mistake to believe that law is the sole, or even the principal agency for solving the serious problems created by road traffic.

1 GENERAL CONSIDERATIONS

1 Road

"Road" is defined in s. 257 of the Road Traffic Act 1960 as

"any highway and any other road to which the public has access, and includes bridges over which a road passes."

The definition, then, requires (a) a road, that is a definable route leading from one place to another, *and* (b) public access.[1] Hence it was held in *Griffin* v. *Squires*[2] that a free public car park was not a road for although the public had access it was not a road. The case does not decide, however, that a car park cannot be a road: merely that this particular car park was not a road. The question, as the courts have frequently emphasised, is pre-eminently one of fact, but like all questions of fact it involves a preliminary question of law: is there evidence to support the conclusion contended for? In *Bugge* v. *Taylor*,[3] therefore, where the forecourt of an hotel was separated from the highway by an island but was open to highways at both ends and was used frequently by traffic, there was evidence upon which the justices could find that the forecourt was a road. But in *Thomas* v. *Dando*[4] the court said that *Bugge* v. *Taylor* was not an authority for the general proposition that a forecourt becomes a road simply because it is not separated from the highway by a wall or fence, and upheld the justices' conclusion that the forecourt of a shop which was used by vehicles to reach the shop was not a road.[5]

In *Bugge* v. *Taylor* the forecourt was privately owned but it had long since been held that a road might fall within the statutory definition even though privately owned so that the public could be excluded at any time: *Harrison* v. *Hill*,[6] where the Court of Justiciary held that a way leading from the highway to a farmhouse which was used by people not having business at the farm was a road. Lord CLYDE said that the definition of road was intended to embrace roads to which the public had access by virtue of some positive right and also any private road to which the public had access by permission or toleration, but did not include roads to which access could be had by trespass. Public, which included both pedestrians and drivers, meant the public generally and would not extend to cover the case where the road was used only by a special class of the public. Hence the car park in *Griffin* v. *Squires*[7] did not become a road because it was used by club members, a special class of the public, to reach their premises situated on the other side of the park.[8]

---

[1] See [1959] Crim. L.R. 326 *et seq.*
[2] [1958] 3 All E.R. 468 (D.C.).
[3] [1941] 1 K.B. 198 (D.C.), a decision under the Road Transport Lighting Act 1927, wherein road is defined as in Road Traffic Acts.
[4] [1951] 2 K.B. 620; [1951] 1 All E.R. 1010; Road Transport Lighting Act 1927.
[5] See also *Bass* v. *Boynton*, [1960] Crim. L.R. 497 (justices clearly wrong in holding that ordinary form cul-de-sac was not a road) and *Heath* v. *Pearson*, [1957] Crim. L.R. 195 (court refused to reverse justices' finding that a yard which had one entrance through which vehicles could and did pass was not a road although ten cottages abutted the yard, which must, in some respects, have resembled a cul-de-sac).
[6] 1932 S.C. (J.) 13. The case has been frequently cited with approval in England.
[7] [1958] 3 All E.R. 468; *supra*.
[8] See also *Newcastle-upon-Tyne Corporation* v. *Walton*, [1957] Crim. L.R. 479, where a quayside which pedestrians and motorists were allowed to use was held to be a road, and *Buchanan* v. *Motor Insurers' Bureau*, [1955] 1 All E.R. 607, where a dock road to which access could be had only with a pass was held not to be a road.

A final point to note is that whereas driving offences are normally confined to roads as so defined, a particular provision may extend the places in which the offence may be committed. Thus the offence of driving while unfit through drink or drugs under s. 6 of the Act may be committed on a road "or other public place". The expression public place here would certainly include, for example, the car park in *Griffin* v. *Squires*.[9] Again, the offence of motor racing under s. 7 may be committed only on public highways, that is roads or ways over which the public are entitled to pass and repass.

2 Driver

By s. 257 of the Act—

"except for the purposes of sections one[10] and eighty-eight.[11] 'driver', where a separate person acts as steersman of a motor vehicle, includes that person as well as any other person engaged in the driving of the vehicle, and 'drive' shall be construed accordingly."

It seems tolerably clear from the terms of this provision that the Legislature intended "driver" to be widely construed, but in practice the courts have tended to construe the word narrowly and somewhat inconsistently. A useful starting-point is provided by *Munning*[12] where a Magistrate's Court held that D was not driving a motor-scooter which he was pushing along a road; it was common sense that pushing was not driving. This conclusion may be one of common sense but it is not easy to reconcile with other cases. In *Wallace* v. *Major*[13] it was held that the person who was steering a vehicle which was being towed was not the driver and was not driving the vehicle. "It is difficult to see," said Lord Goddard, C.J.,[14]

"how a person who is merely at the steering wheel of a car and having nothing to do with the propulsion of the car, having nothing to do with making the car go, is driving the vehicle. The vehicle, in fact, was not being driven; it was being drawn."[15]

In *Saycell* v. *Bool*,[16] on the other hand, it was held that D who released the hand-brake on a lorry and steered it down an incline without starting the engine was driving the lorry since he controlled it by operating the brakes and the steering wheel. And in *Spindley*[17] it was held that where D sat in and steered a car

---

[9] [1958] 3 All E.R. 468; above, p. 326. And see further below, p. 340.
[10] Which deals with causing death by reckless or dangerous driving. This offence can be committed, it seems, only by the driver in the narrow sense, that is, the steersman of the vehicle. But another could aid and abet the steersman to commit the offence. See *Baldessare* (1930), 22 Crim. App. Rep. 70; above, p. 84, and *cf. Du Cros* v. *Lambourne*, [1907] 1 K.B. 40; above, p. 83.
[11] Which deals with offences relating to parking places. Section 88 (2) states that the driver of a vehicle designated in s. 88 (1) (a) shall be construed as a reference to the person driving the vehicle at the time it was left in the parking place. *Cf. Jones* v. *Prothero*, [1952] 1 All E.R. 434, where it was held that D was the driver of a vehicle for the purposes of the offence of failing to report an accident notwithstanding that the car was stopped and he had switched off the engine.
[12] [1961] Crim. L.R. 555.
[13] [1946] K.B. 473; [1946] 2 All E.R. 87.
[14] [1946] K.B. at p. 477; [1946] 2 All E.R. at p. 88.
[15] Lord Goddard defended the restricted interpretation on the ground that penal statutes must be strictly construed but criminal cases are littered with the bones of this particular cliché. It is surprising (*cf.* Singleton, J.'s observations, *ibid.*, at pp. 481 and 490) that the Legislature did not expressly provide for this sort of case in the Act of 1960. The failure to do so would seem to strengthen *Wallace* v. *Major*.
[16] [1948] 2 All. E.R. 83.
[17] [1961] Crim. L.R. 486 (Q.S.).

pushed by E that D was the driver of the vehicle. *Munning*[18] is distinguishable from these last two cases only in that D did not sit astride the scooter. If this is regarded as a valid distinction then D in *Spindley* might have avoided prosecution by walking alongside the car and steering with his hand through the open window—an operation which probably involves significantly more hazards for other road users. Regard being had to the mischief of the statute it is submitted that it would not be unreasonable to hold that anyone exercising any degree of direct control over the motion of a vehicle is driving it for this purpose.

A case falling nicely between *Wallace* v. *Major*[19] and *Spindley*[20] is *Arnold*[1] where D was steering a car which was being pushed from behind by a vehicle driven by E. It was held that D was not driving as there was no evidence that he was making the vehicle go. Perhaps it would be better to say, since in *Spindley* there was no evidence that D was making the vehicle "go", that D did not have effective control over the forward movement of the vehicle.

Driving requires some voluntary conduct on the part of the driver; hence it has been said that a person would not be driving who, by reason of disease or other cause over which he had no control, was unable to govern his actions.[2] But a person sitting in the passenger's seat who did not know how to drive was held to be driving the car which, since it had been left in gear, moved forward a short distance when he pressed the starter.[3] A more remarkable case is *Kitson*.[4] D, who was incapable through drink of having proper control of a vehicle, awoke in the passenger's seat of E's car to find that there was no one in the driver's seat and that the car was moving down an incline. D immediately grabbed the steering wheel and pursued an erratic course down the hill until he steered it into the grass verge; he did not apply the handbrake because of the greasy condition of the road. D's conviction on a charge of driving under the influence of drink was upheld. The case is, of course, distinguishable from *Hill* v. *Baxter*[5] for here D was aware of what he was doing and intended to do it. But the decision seems to be an unduly harsh one,[6] and it is submitted that it would not have been unrealistic to extend the general defence of necessity to such a case.[7]

The definition contemplates that more than one person may be engaged in the driving of a vehicle. In *Wallace* v. *Major*[8] this was construed to refer only to the case where more than one person is engaged in the driving of the same vehicle, and the court regarded the case of towing as involving two separate vehicles. Some vehicles require (for example, locomotives), or are adapted for (for example, dual-control cars), operation by more than one person, and in such cases either or both persons may constitute the driver for the purposes of the Act. Where a vehicle has only one set of controls it is possible for the controls to be shared so that more than one person may be held to be driving the vehicle.[9]

---

[18] Above, p. 327; *cf. Whitlow*, [1965] Crim. L.R. 170.
[19] Above, p. 327.
[20] Above, p. 327.
[1] [1964] Crim. L.R. 664.
[2] *Hill* v. *Baxter*, [1958] 1 Q.B. 277; [1958] 1 All E.R. 193; above, p. 32.
[3] (1956), 20 J. Cr. L. 5.
[4] (1955), 39 Cr. App. Rep. 66 (C.C.A.). *Cf. Brown* v. *Dyerson*, [1968] 3 All E.R. 39 (D.C.).
[5] *Supra*.
[6] D was sentenced to four months' imprisonment and disqualified for three years.
[7] Above pp. 136 *et seq.*.
[8] [1946] K.B. 473; [1946] 2 All E.R. 87; above, p. 327.
[9] *Langman* v. *Valentine*, [1952] 2 All E.R. 803 (D.C.). Instructor who had one hand on handbrake and the other on steering wheel held to be a driver of the car. *Cf. Evans* v. *Walkden*, [1956] 3 All E.R. 64.

Where D steers a vehicle which is pushed by E both could be regarded as "engaged in the driving" of the vehicle, but if *Munning*[10] is accepted E should be regarded as aiding and abetting the driving by D.

3 Motor Vehicle

By s. 253 (1) of the Act—

"In this Act 'motor vehicle' means a mechanically propelled vehicle intended or adapted for use on roads. . . ."[11]

In *Newberry* v. *Simmonds*[12] D was charged with keeping on a road a vehicle for which he had no licence.[13] D alleged that the engine of his car had been stolen and thus it was not at the material time a mechanically propelled vehicle, a contention which was accepted by the justices. On appeal the prosecution, contending for the widest possible interpretation of "vehicle", argued that the words were words of classification, not words of definition,[14] so that a motor car would remain within the classification until it finally reaches the breaker's yard and its registration book is surrendered. The court, neither accepting nor rejecting this submission, held that the mere removal of the engine did not mean that the car ceased to be mechanically propelled at least where

"the evidence admits the possibility that the engine may shortly be replaced and the motive power restored."[15]

However, the court subsequently rejected the wider interpretation and held in *Smart* v. *Allan*[16] that where the car in question lacked engine parts, gearbox, battery and a tyre and there was no reasonable prospect of the car ever being made mobile again, it was not a mechanically propelled vehicle. This case established the somewhat surprising proposition that whether a vehicle is a mechanically propelled vehicle turns not only on the physical state of the vehicle but also on D's intentions with regard to further use.[17] Having regard to the mischief aimed at, it would surely not have been unreasonable to have adopted the wider interpretation. The present position means that if D keeps a broken-down car on a road he may be convicted of using a vehicle without insurance so

---

[10] [1961] Crim. L.R. 555; above, p. 327.

[11] For purposes other than driving offences motor vehicles are sub-divided into various classes. By s. 19 (1) of the Road Traffic Act 1962 hovercraft are to be treated as motor vehicles. Note that by ss. 9–13 of the Act certain driving offences are created for cyclists.

[12] [1961] 2 Q.B. 345; [1961] 2 All E.R. 318 (D.C.).

[13] Vehicles (Excise) Act 1949, s. 15. The court felt that motor vehicles should be given the same meaning as in the Road Traffic Acts. See now the Vehicles (Excise) Act 1962, s. 7.

[14] The heading to s. 1 of the Road Traffic Act 1930 (which formerly defined vehicle) reads, "Classification of Motor Vehicles" and the marginal note to s. 253 (1) of the 1960 Act reads, "Interpretation of expressions relating to motor vehicles and classes or descriptions thereof." *Cf.* the observations of DEVLIN, J., in *Lawrence* v. *Howlett*, [1952] 2 All E.R. 74 at p. 75: "The question is whether this vehicle was a mechanically propelled vehicle within the meaning of s. 1 of the Road Traffic Act 1930 and that section is one of a group of sections which is headed: 'Classification of motor vehicles.' I am, therefore, satisfied, that the words 'mechanically propelled' are intended as words of classification and *prima facie* do not refer to the way in which a vehicle is being propelled at any given moment." But on the use of marginal notes, *cf. Chandler* v. *Director of Public Prosecutions*, [1964] A.C. at p. 777; [1962] 3 All E.R. 142.

[15] *Newberry* v. *Simmonds*, [1961] 2 Q.B. 345 at p. 350; [1961] 2 All E.R. 318 at p. 319 (D.C.).

[16] [1963] 1 Q.B. 291; [1962] 3 All E.R. 893.

[17] *Cf. Maclean* v. *Hall* 1962, S.L.T. (Sh. Ct.) 30. Here the car, which was in working condition when purchased, was clearly a vehicle at the commencement of a journey from Glasgow to Carnbo but it ceased to be a vehicle on route when it broke down so completely that D decided to scrap it.

long as the evidence admits the possibility that the car will be put in working order,[18] but if the evidence does not admit that possibility then D does not commit this offence.[19] Yet both cases create precisely the same hazard to other motorists, particularly at night or in fog, and thus both ought to be insured.

Where the vehicle is *ordinarily* capable of propulsion by more than one means, as with pedal cycles fitted with auxiliary motors, rather different considerations may be applied. In *Lawrence* v. *Howlett*[20] where a cycle was being used as an ordinary pedal cycle and the auxiliary motor was not in working order it was held not to be a motor vehicle although there Was no evidence that the engine might not be repaired. DEVLIN, J., pointed out,[1] that where a vehicle was so designed different questions were raised and regard must be had to its working condition and the use to which it was being put at the material time. But it was subsequently held in *Floyd* v. *Bush*[2] that D was driving a motor vehicle where the auxiliary engine was in working condition even though D was pedalling the cycle at the material time.

(a) *Intended for use on roads.*—In order to comply with the definition the vehicle must also be "intended or adapted for use on roads". It is to be observed, as it was pointed out in *MacDonald* v. *Carmichael*,[3] that the statute does not refer to vehicles which may be used on roads, but to vehicles intended or adapted for such use. It was accordingly held in that case that dumpers used for carrying materials at a building site were not intended for use on roads even though the evidence showed they were in fact used on roads near to the building site; the dumpers were intended to be used by a builder at a building site as part of his plant and not as motor vehicles. This was followed in *Daley* v. *Hargreaves*[4] which also involved the use of dumpers on a building site with some limited use of nearby roads. However, SALMON, J., was not very happy with the result and but for the desirability of conformity might not have followed *MacDonald* v. *Carmichael*. He thought that "intended . . . for use on roads" might mean no more than suitable or apt for such use, and did not refer to the intention of the manufacturer, seller, or owner of the vehicle. This, it is respectfully submitted, makes good sense; the idea must surely have been to bring within the purview of the Acts all vehicles suitable for use on roads, and that a dumper is so suitable, even though it may not be its primary use, seems an obvious conclusion. Nevertheless *MacDonald* v. *Carmichael* and *Daley* v. *Hargreaves* must be considered to have settled the point. But the mischief permitted by the decision, that of uninsured dumpers on the roads, may be severely limited if courts follow the suggestion made by SALMON, J., in *Daley* v. *Hargreaves*[5] that it should not be applied to dumpers generally, and should not be applied where the dumper is reasonably suitable for being driven along roads in transit[6] or is used to carry

---

[18] *Cf. Elliot* v. *Grey*, [1960] 1 Q.B. 367; [1959] 3 All E.R. 733.

[19] But D may commit an offence under the Litter Act 1958, s. 1 (1), see *Vaughan* v. *Biggs*, [1960] 2 All E.R. 473.

[20] [1952] 2 All E.R. 74 (D.C.).

[1] *Ibid.* at p. 75.

[2] [1953] 1 All E.R. 265 (D.C.).

[3] 1941 S.L.T. 81. *Note* that English courts have stressed the desirability of a uniform construction of the Road Traffic Acts in England and Scotland: see *Cording* v. *Halse*, [1955] 1 Q.B. 63; [1954] 3 All E.R. 287.

[4] [1961] 1 All E.R. 552.

[5] *Ibid.* at p. 556.

[6] In the principal case the dumper was not equipped with lamps, reflectors, wings, number-plates or direction indicators, and there was no evidence that it had been used on roads other than in the immediate vicinity of the site.

material from one site to another. The suggestion was acted upon by a magistrates' court which held that a mobile crane lacking speedometer, horn, lights and number-plate was a motor vehicle intended for use on roads because, whatever the owner's intentions, D, who had hired it for the day, intended to use it and did use it on a road.[7] In *Burns* v. *Currell*,[8] however, it was reiterated by the Divisional Court that "intended . . . for use on roads" did not refer to the intention of any particular person, including the user for the time being. Lord PARKER, C.J., preferred the test: would a reasonable person contemplate some general use on a road as one of the uses of this particular vehicle?[9] It was accordingly held that a "Go-Kart" without springs, parking-brake, driving-mirror or wings was not a motor vehicle intended for use on roads even though D had in fact been found driving the vehicle on a road. All that had been proved was an isolated user, nor had it been proved that other people used these vehicles on roads. Thus whether a vehicle is intended for use on roads will depend partly upon its suitability for such use and partly upon the use to which vehicles of that kind are put.

(b) *Adapted for use on roads.*—It was further argued in *Burns* v. *Currell*[10] that the Go-Kart was "adapted" for use on roads. On this point Lord PARKER, C.J., said:[11]

> "The word 'adapted' is used through the Act of 1960 in a number of different contexts. Sometimes it is used as an alternative to 'constructed or adapted', and it seems clear, and, indeed it has been so held for a very long time, that 'adapted' there means altered.[12] On the other hand, as it was pointed out in *Maddox* v. *Storer*,[13] it is used in other contexts in this Act, in particular when it stands alone, as clearly meaning 'apt' or 'fit', in other words in an adjectival sense. Here in this context, my own view is . . . that 'adapted' when used disjunctively with 'intended' and not with the word 'constructed', is used in its adjectival sense. . . . If, of course, it means 'altered', there is no question of (the Go-Kart) having been altered in the present case; but if . . . as I am inclined to feel, it does mean 'fit and apt', again I do not think that it was proved that the Go-Kart was fit or apt. It was undoubtedly capable of being used on the road, but 'adapted' adjectivally means considerably more than that."

2 CARELESS DRIVING

The Road Traffic Act 1960 s. 3 (1) provides—

> "If a person drives a motor vehicle on a road without due care and attention, or without reasonable consideration for other persons using the road, he shall be liable on summary conviction to a fine not exceeding forty pounds, or in the case of a second or subsequent conviction to a fine not exceeding eighty pounds or to imprisonment for a term not exceeding three months or to both such fine and such imprisonment."[14]

---

[7] (1961), 25 J.C.L. 161. See also *Woodward* v. *James Young (Contractors), Ltd.*, 1958 S.L.T. 289, where a tractor was held to be a motor vehicle.

[8] [1963] 2 Q.B. 433; [1963] 2 All E.R. 297 (D.C.).

[9] [1963] 2 All E.R. 297 at p. 300; *Chalgray, Ltd.* v. *Aspley*, [1965] Crim. L.R. 440 (D.C.). *Cf.* the problem arising under the Prevention of Crime Act 1953; above, pp. 282–284.

[10] [1963] 2 Q.B. 433; [1963] 2 All E.R. 297.

[11] [1963] 2 Q.B. at p. 441; [1963] 2 All E.R. at p. 300.

[12] See, for example, *Flower Freight Co., Ltd.* v. *Hammond*, [1963] 1 Q.B. 275; [1962] 3 All E.R. 950.

[13] [1963] 1 Q.B. 451; [1962] 1 All E.R. 831.

[14] Section 10 creates similar offences in respect of cycling.

In order to determine whether the offence of careless driving is committed, the test, as Lord GODDARD, C.J., said in *Simpson* v. *Peat*[15] is: was D exercising that degree of care and attention that a reasonable and prudent driver would exercise in the circumstances? The standard is an objective one and it was accordingly held in *Simpson* v. *Peat* that where D made an error of judgment in turning right so that he collided with an oncoming motor cyclist he was guilty of the offence because the reasonable and prudent driver would not, in the circumstances, have made that error. The standard to be applied is the same for all motorists and no allowance is to be made for the learner-driver on account of his inexperience.[16] It is no defence for D to say that he was doing his best if his best is not good enough. Nor does it matter that the failure to exercise due care arises from a deliberate act of bad driving on D's part.[17] But note that the objective nature of negligence does not necessarily rule out consideration of subjective factors. It may be, for example, that D could be convicted of careless driving where, because of his expertise, he has knowledge of a defect in the braking system of which the ordinary driver would be reasonably unaware.[18]

Section 3 creates two distinct offences, careless driving and inconsiderate driving. In many cases the facts would constitute either offence but they are not identical since the latter, unlike the former, may be committed only where other persons are using the road. Inconsiderate driving is the more appropriate offence where, for instance, D drives his car through a puddle which he might have avoided and drenches pedestrians.

For the purposes of s. 3 "other persons using the road" includes the passengers in a vehicle driven by D.[19]

3 RECKLESS AND DANGEROUS DRIVING

The Road Traffic Act 1960 s. 2 (1) provides—

> "If a person drives a motor vehicle on a road recklessly, or at a speed or in a manner which is dangerous to the public, having regard to all the circumstances of the case, including the nature, condition and use of the road, and the amount of traffic which is actually at the time, or which might reasonably be expected to be, on the road, he shall be liable:

---

[15] [1952] 2 Q.B. 24; [1952] 1 All E.R. 447 at p. 449. Consider whether a driver would be any less likely to exercise the degree of care and attention that a reasonable and prudent driver would exercise if there were no offence of careless driving. Might not the driver still feel equally constrained to drive carefully by a desire to avoid harm to himself or his vehicle, or even to avoid the trouble which an accident would involve?

[16] *McCrone* v. *Riding*, [1938] 1 All E.R. 157; see above, p. 50. Presumably no account would be taken of age although D may lawfully drive a motor cycle at sixteen years and a motor-car at seventeen years and might be expected at these ages not to show the experience of an adult. But what of careless cycling under s. 10 where D may be only ten years? In civil cases generally a child must exercise the care to be expected of a child of his age but where a child engages in an activity such as cycling on a road there is much to be said for holding him to the standard of the reasonably experienced cyclist. *Cf.* Fleming, *Torts* (2nd ed.), at p. 123. But an infant child of ten to fourteen years is criminally liable only if he knows his act to be wrong; above, p. 98. How is this doctrine to be applied in the case of negligent crimes? Inexperience is relevant to sentence: *Mabley* (1964), *The Times*, 2 April.

[17] *Taylor* v. *Rogers*, [1960] Crim. L.R. 271.

[18] See above, p. 54.

[19] *Pawley* v. *Whardall*, [1966] 1 Q.B. 373; [1965] 2 All E.R. 757.

(*a*) on conviction on indictment, to a fine or to imprisonment for a term not exceeding two years or to both a fine and such imprisonment;

(*b*) on summary conviction, to a fine not exceeding one hundred pounds, or to imprisonment for a term not exceeding four months or to both such fine and such imprisonment, or in the case of a second or subsequent conviction to a fine not exceeding one hundred pounds or to imprisonment for a term not exceeding six months or to both such fine and such imprisonment."[20]

The section creates three offences: reckless driving, driving at a dangerous speed and driving in a dangerous manner. If the distinction between the last two is only one of form it might be thought that the distinction between these and reckless driving is one of substance. In fact the courts have not been reported as defining reckless driving, but it is submitted this is the case. Recklessness ordinarily connotes the idea of wanton conduct; it suggests that D is aware of the possible harmful consequences of his conduct but chooses to take the risk involved. If this is so in the case of reckless driving then it is a more serious offence than dangerous driving. Although the maximum punishment is the same for both offences it is likely that where recklessness can be shown (which is probably rarely) the case will be dealt with more severely than a case of dangerous driving.

It is clear that dangerous driving does not require (though it will include) any subjective awareness of possible harmful consequences. Viewed as a matter of principle it might be thought that dangerous driving fell between careless driving on the one hand and reckless driving on the other. It is implicit in this view that there are degrees of negligence.[1] Though objections have been raised to the notion of degrees of negligence,[2] it would seem that as an everyday matter people do draw a distinction between driving which falls short of the standard to be expected of a reasonably competent driver (careless driving) and driving which falls seriously short of that standard (dangerous driving). It is not possible to state the distinction in terms any more precise than that, but the broad distinction may be understood and it might be thought that juries or judges of fact would experience no great difficulties in applying it. Certainly if legislative intent is ever plain, it is surely plain that by making dangerous driving a significantly more serious offence than careless driving, the intent was to require a significantly higher degree of negligence for the former as against the latter.

This view of the distinction between careless and dangerous driving has, however, received little judicial support.[3] In *Hill* v. *Baxter*, Lord GODDARD, C.J., said:[4]

"The first thing to be remembered is that the Road Traffic Act [1960] contains an absolute prohibition against driving dangerously or ignoring 'Halt' signs. No question of *mens rea* enters into the offence; it is no answer to a charge under these sections to say: 'I did not mean to drive dangerously' or 'I did not notice the "Halt" sign.'"

which rules out negligence altogether, but that some negligence is required to support a charge of dangerous driving appeared to be the effect of *Spurge*.[5] Here

---

[20] Section 9 creates similar offences in respect of cyclists.
[1] See above, p. 56.
[2] Above, p. 56.
[3] SELLERS, J., once stated that dangerous driving required some deliberate act as opposed to mere inadvertence: [1955] Crim. L.R. 239.
[4] [1958] 1 Q.B. 277 at p. 282; [1958] 1 All E.R. 193 at p. 195.
[5] [1961] 2 Q.B. 205; [1961] 2 All E.R. 688 (C.C.A.).

D's defence to a charge of dangerous driving was that defective brakes had caused his car to pull to the right into the oncoming lane so that he had collided with a motor-scooter. His appeal against conviction was dismissed because there was evidence that he was aware of the tendency to pull to the right, but it was made clear by the court that D would not have been liable if he had been unaware of the defect and the defect could not have been discovered by the exercise of reasonable care. In such a case D would not be at fault in respect of his driving and thus would not be liable.

Spurge, though requiring negligence, did not indicate that any higher degree of negligence would be required for dangerous driving as against careless driving. The indications were that the same degree of negligence would suffice for either, and this seems also to have been the effect of *Evans*.[6] *Evans* involved a charge of causing death by dangerous driving, and part of the direction of SALMON, J., to the jury was as follows:[7]

> "You have got to make up your minds here whether or not what (D) did was dangerous to the public, that is, dangerous to other road users. If it was, then even although the dangerous driving was caused by slight negligence, the slightest negligence on his part, he is guilty of the offence of driving to the danger of the public."

Dismissing D's appeal against conviction, ATKINSON, J., delivering the judgment of the court, said:[8]

> "It is quite clear from the reported cases[9] that if a driver in fact adopts a manner of driving which the jury think was dangerous to other road users in all the circumstances, then on the issue of guilt it matters not whether he was deliberately reckless, careless, momentarily inattentive or even doing his incompetent best."

Thus D may be guilty of dangerous driving if his driving is negligent without any qualifying epithet. Even so, it *may*[10] be that the court in *Evans* did envisage some distinction between careless and dangerous driving. Counsel complained of SALMON J.'s summing-up that it meant that if a man through the slightest fault on his part has an accident and someone has been killed, then danger has in fact resulted from his driving and he must necessarily be guilty of causing death through dangerous driving. But, the court pointed out[11]

> "That . . . does not follow at all. There is really nothing in this summing-up to lead the jury to suppose that, merely because an accident had happened and somebody had been killed, danger had in that sense arisen, and, therefore,

---

[6] [1963] 1 Q.B. 412; [1962] 3 All E.R. 1086.
[7] See [1963] 1 Q.B. 412 at p. 413; [1962] 3 All E.R. 1086 at p. 1087.
[8] [1963] 1 Q.B. at p. 418; [1962] 3 All E.R. at p. 1088.
[9] The reported cases are hardly "quite clear". The strongest case in favour of this view is *Parker*, [1957] Crim. L.R. 468, where it was held that momentary carelessness might amount to dangerous driving. But "momentary carelessness" is not a term of art and in given circumstances requiring a driver's undivided attention might constitute gross carelessness. *Cf. Johnson*, [1960] Crim. L.R. 430. *Scates*, [1957] Crim. L.R. 406, is equivocal. The courts have frequently stated that a given set of facts would support a conviction for either careless or dangerous driving but this is not a statement that both offences require the same degree of negligence. SELLERS, J. once stated that dangerous driving requires some deliberate act as opposed to mere inadvertence, see [1955] Crim. L.R. 239. In fact ATKINSON, J., in the instant case relied heavily on the questionable proposition given by Lord GODDARD, C.J., in *Hill* v. *Baxter*, [1958] 1 Q.B. 277 at p. 282; [1958] 1 All E.R. 193 at p. 195, cited above, p. 333.
[10] The judgment is not clear on this point.
[11] [1963] 1 Q.B. 412 at p. 418; [1962] 3 All E.R. 1086 at p. 1088.

it must follow that (D) was driving in a manner dangerous to the public. The learned judge here in his summing-up put the issue fairly and squarely to the jury in these terms: 'Look to see what in fact this driver did. You are the judges, you set the standard; are you satisfied that he drove in fact in a manner dangerous to the public? If he did so, then it is no answer to say, "Well, this is only a very slight degree of negligence".' "

In apparently disagreeing with counsel's view that the effect of the trial judge's direction was that a person who killed through the slightest fault would necessarily be guilty of dangerous driving, the court seems to have had in mind some sort of distinction between dangerous and careless driving. Quite what the distinction was remains obscure, but, at the very least, it can be seriously argued that *Evans* required some negligence to support a charge of dangerous driving. In *Ball and Loughlin*,[12] however, the Court of Criminal Appeal treated *Evans* as showing "quite clearly that the test is a purely objective one and that it matters not why the dangerous situation was caused or the dangerous manoeuvre executed".[13]

In *Ball and Loughlin*, D was driving a military scout-car and since this vehicle had restricted vision he was assisted by a commander, E, who stood in the turret and gave directions over the intercom. At a cross-roads D halted and then turned right on being instructed by E that it was safe to do so; in fact a motor-cycle was approaching which collided with the scout-car killing the cyclist. Upholding the conviction of D for causing death by dangerous driving (and that of E for aiding and abetting) the court said:[14]

"It is, in the opinion of this court, perfectly clear that what is meant by 'driving in a manner dangerous' is the manner of the actual driving, which in this case was the coming out of a minor road across a major road. It has been held time and again that an offence under this section is an absolute offence, not a question of the driver being vicariously liable for somebody else's action,[15] but it is a liability on the driver which he cannot get rid of,[16] and if the result of his driving produced what the jury considered to be a dangerous situation, a dangerous manoeuvre, *then even though he had been completely blameless*, he can be held liable."

According to the court "the only possible defence" to a charge of dangerous driving is where the driver is deprived of control of the car owing to some sudden affliction (*Hill* v. *Baxter*[17]), or owing to a mechanical defect suddenly manifesting itself (*Spurge*[18]).[19]

---

[12] (1966), 50 Cr. App. Rep. 266.
[13] *Ibid.*, at p. 270.
[14] *Ibid.*, at p. 270.
[15] On this matter see above, p. 98.
[16] The court considered this an important point and returned it subsequently in its judgment. "Perhaps another way in which the matter could be put is that a driver of a motor-car on a road cannot get rid of his responsibilities by delegating part of the driving to a further person." (1966), 50 Cr. App. Rep. 266 at p. 271. Presumably this means that a driver may be convicted of dangerous driving even where he is following what seems to be the sound advice in the Highway Code (para. 48) in getting help in reversing his vehicle where his view to the rear is restricted. *Cf. Thornton* v. *Mitchell*, [1940] 1 All E.R. 339, above, p. 93; *Liddon* v. *Stringer*, [1967] Crim. L.R. 371, above, p. 65.
[17] [1958] 1 Q.B. 277; [1958] 1 All E.R. 193, above p. 32.
[18] [1961] 2 Q.B. 205; [1961] 2 All E.R. 688, above p. 333.
[19] But presumably the general defences available on a charge of crime would be equally available, in appropriate circumstances, on a charge of dangerous driving. See above, p. 67.

Ball and Loughlin[20] must be taken to have settled the test for dangerous driving so far as the Court of Appeal is concerned.[1] On any view the decision so far as D was concerned, was grossly unjust. The decision does not even have the saving merit of simplifying the court's task in these cases because whether D was

> "reckless, careless, momentarily inattentive or even doing his incompetent best . . . is highly relevant [when] it . . . comes to sentence, and equally relevant in the mind of any person who has to consider whether a prosecution is justified or not."[2]

Yet the jury, most of whom are likely to be drivers and may be expected to be helpful to the court in determining these issues, are excluded from giving their view.[3] An interpretation which may lead to the conviction for dangerous driving (or causing death by dangerous driving) of a driver who has taken all reasonable care, when he could not on the same facts be convicted of careless driving, is manifestly absurd.[4]

D may be convicted of dangerous driving even though his driving creates no danger in fact, since potential as well as actual danger must be considered.[5] Further, although the section requires that D drive *in a manner* which is dangerous it now appears to be settled that D is so driving where he is a *source* of danger even though the *manner* of his driving is unobjectionable.[6] Thus if D knows, or ought to know, that he is frequently subject to epileptic fits he may be guilty of dangerous driving so soon as he takes a vehicle on the road even though the manner of his driving is not ostensibly dangerous until he has a fit. Again, if D continues to drive when feeling drowsy he may be guilty of dangerous driving even though the manner of his driving does not become dangerous until he falls asleep.[7] Since D's driving will become dangerous when he is overtaken by a fit or sleep it might be thought that the point is academic, but there is judicial authority for the view that whenever a driver loses conscious control of his vehicle he is no longer driving.[8] But this view has not been permitted to create a logical trap and D may be convicted of dangerous driving without evidence that the manner of his driving was dangerous before he became unconscious, provided, of course, that D knew, or ought to have known, of the onset of unconsciousness.[9] If it is accepted that in circumstances like these D is driving

---

[20] (1966), 50 Cr. App. Rep. 266.
[1] See also *Scammell*, [1967] 3 All E.R. 97 (C.A.).
[2] *Evans*, [1963] 1 Q.B. 412 at p. 418; [1962] 3 All E.R. 1086 at p. 1088. In *Ball and Loughlin* (1966), 50 Cr. App. Rep. 266, D was given an absolute discharge.
[3] *Cf. Dalas* (1966), *The Times*, 28 Sept., above p. 68.
[4] See Williams, "'Absolute Liability' in Traffic Offences", [1967] Crim. L.R. 142, at pp. 194–205; Elliott & Street, *Road Accidents* (1968), at pp. 21–25.
[5] *Bracegirdle* v. *Oxley*, [1947] K.B. 349; [1947] 1 All E.R. 126.
[6] "Manner" means fashion or way of doing something. Where D is steering an erratic course his manner of driving may properly be described as dangerous. Yet it may not be inapt to say that D's manner of driving is dangerous even though he steers a straight course but is liable because of some defect in himself (for example, liability to epileptic seizure) or his vehicle (for example, defective brakes: *cf. Spurge*, [1961] 2 Q.B. 205; [1961] 2 All E.R. 688; above, p. 333) suddenly to lose control.
[7] *Kay* v. *Butterworth* (1945), 173 L.T. 191.
[8] *Hill* v. *Baxter*, [1958] 1 Q.B. 277; [1958] 1 All E.R. 193. See above, p. 32.
[9] *Sibbles*, [1959] Crim. L.R. 660; *Henderson* v. *Jones*, [1955] Crim. L.R. 318 (D.C.); *Edwards* v. *Clarke* (1951), 115 J.P. 426, which appeared to require some evidence of the manner of driving prior to falling asleep will not now be followed. But perhaps *Edwards* v. *Clarke* does serve to underline the reluctance to disturb justices' decisions on careless driving; there is no such reluctance to disturb them on dangerous driving: see [1956] Crim. L.R. 204 at p. 205.

in a dangerous manner then there is no difficulty about a further conclusion that D may be guilty of causing death by dangerous driving even though the death is caused after D has lost conscious control.

One particular consequence of the view that D is driving dangerously when he is a source of danger has been that the courts may permit evidence to be given of drink taken by D.[10] Since drink slows down the reaction time of a driver, a driver who has taken drink may be a source of danger even though his driving appears to be safe. "Dangerous driving", said the Court of Criminal Appeal in *McBride*,[11]

> "may occur without a collision or, indeed, without any indication from the speed or movement of the vehicle that the driving of it was in the circumstances dangerous."

Nevertheless, as a practical matter, prosecutions for dangerous driving where no collision and no questionable manoeuvre are involved must be extremely rare. Where, as is ordinarily the case, some collision or questionable manoeuvre occurs then, since the test is an objective one, all the jury need consider is whether D's driving was dangerous. It is unnecessary to ask why D did what he did unless he tenders evidence that he was deprived of control by some sudden affliction, or by a mechanical defect of which he was reasonably unaware. Hence if the prosecution adduce evidence that D had been drinking this can be only because the prosecution feels that the manoeuvre is one which is not clearly "dangerous." Evidence of drink may thus be given to bolster up what is otherwise a weak case against D and accordingly is prejudicial rather than probative. The courts have said in these cases that the judge has a disrection to rule evidence of drink inadmissible where it would merely be prejudicial, and yet in one of them[12] the Court of Criminal Appeal upheld D's conviction of dangerous driving although the judge elicited from a passanger in the car that he and D had been visiting public houses and Lord PARKER, C.J., said it was natural the jury's opinion would be influenced by the knowledge gained.

4 CAUSING DEATH BY RECKLESS OR DANGEROUS DRIVING

The Road Traffic Act 1960 s. 1 (1) provides:

> "A person who causes the death of another person by the driving of a motor vehicle on a road recklessly, or at a speed or in a manner which is dangerous to the public, having regard to all the circumstances of the case,, incuding the nature, condition and use of the road, and the amount of traffic which is actually at the time, or which might reasonably be expected to be, on the road, shall be liable. . . ."

At common law, and it is still the law, a motorist who causes death by his driving might be prosecuted for, and convicted of, manslaughter. In practice prosecutions for manslaughter have a dismal record of success owing to the reluctance of juries to convict. Nor would the House of Lords in *Andrews* v. *Director*

---

[10] *Richardson, Fisher,* [1960] Crim. L.R. 135; *McBride,* [1962] 2 Q.B. 167; [1961] 3 All E.R. 6; *Sibley,* [1962] Crim. L.R. 397.
[11] [1961] 3 All E.R. 6 at p. 9; [1962] 2 Q.B. 167 at p. 172.
[12] *Sibley,* [1962] Crim. L.R. 397.

of Public Prosecutions[13] extend the doctrine of constructive manslaughter to the motorist. The legislature therefore introduced the offence of causing death by reckless or dangerous driving punishable with imprisonment up to five years.[14]

Causing death by *reckless* driving is indistinguishable from involuntary manslaughter except in name and the maximum punishment. Manslaughter requires a high degree of negligence and

> "Probably of all the epithets that can be applied 'reckless' most nearly covers the case. It is difficult to visualise a case of death caused by 'reckless' driving, in the connotation of that term in ordinary speech, which would not justify a conviction for manslaughter. . . ."[15]

Causing death by *dangerous* driving, however, is quite clearly distinguishable from manslaughter. It was clear to LORD ATKIN in *Andrews* v. *Director of Public Prosecutions*[16] that dangerous driving might be committed though the negligence would not be of such a degree as to amount to manslaughter if death ensued. From the preceding discussion of dangerous driving[17] it now appears that dangerous driving is an offence of strict liability and may be committed although there is no negligence. Since in dangerous driving no awareness of risk to life, no indifference to the physical safety of others,[18] is involved, then the motorist may be penalised for consequences in which chance plays a large part. Although the offence, especially in view of the courts' interpretation of dangerous driving, has a long reach, it has properly enabled the conviction of those who in the past might have relied upon the jury to acquit them on a charge of manslaughter.

In order to prove the offence of causing death by dangerous driving the prosecution must prove that the dangerous driving caused death. "Cause" here has no unusual meaning; it means that the dangerous driving must be "a substantial cause" of the death[19] though it need not be the sole cause. There is nothing to suggest that causation for this offence differs in any way from causation in homicide generally which is discussed elsewhere.[20]

Where D is charged with causing death by dangerous driving, the jury may return a verdict of dangerous driving if they are not satisfied that D's driving was the cause of death.[1] Such a verdict might properly be returned in circumstances parallel to *Dalloway*,[2] but it is a verdict which juries sometimes return in the teeth of clear evidence that the dangerous driving was the cause of death.[3]

5 DRIVING UNDER THE INFLUENCE OF DRINK OR DRUGS

The Road Traffic Act 1960 s. 6 provides—

> "(1) A person who, when driving or attempting to drive a motor vehicle on a

---

[13] [1937] A.C. 576; [1937] 2 All E.R. 552. See above, pp. 218 and 225.
[14] Originally in Road Traffic Act 1956, s. 8.
[15] *Per* Lord ATKIN in *Andrews* v. *Director of Public Prosecutions*, [1937] A.C. 576 at p. 583; [1937] 2 All E.R. 552 at p. 556.
[16] [1937] A.C. 576 at p. 584; [1937] 2 All E.R. 552 at pp. 556, 557.
[17] Above, pp. 332–337.
[18] *Cf. Lundt-Smith*, [1964] 2 Q.B. 167; [1964] 3 All E.R. 225.
[19] *Gould*, [1963] 2 All E.R. 847. See above, p. 187.
[20] Above, pp. 184–193.
[1] Road Traffic Act 1960; s. 2 (2).
[2] (1847), 3 Cox C.C. 273; above, p. 186.
[3] *Curphey*, [1957] Crim. L.R. 191.

road or other public place, is unfit to drive through drink or drugs shall be liable—

    (*a*) on conviction on indictment, to a fine or to imprisonment for a term not exceeding two years or to both a fine and such imprisonment;

    (*b*) on summary conviction, to a fine not exceeding one hundred pounds or to imprisonment for a term not exceeding four months or to both such fine and such imprisonment, or in the case of a second or subsequent conviction to a fine not exceeding six months or to both such fine and such imprisonment.

A person who, when in charge of a motor vehicle which is on a road or other public place (but not driving the vehicle), is unfit to drive through drink or drugs shall be liable—

    (*a*) on conviction on indictment, to a fine or to imprisonment for a term not exceeding twelve months or to both a fine and such imprisonment;

    (*b*) on summary conviction, to a fine not exceeding one hundred pounds or to imprisonment for a term not exceeding four months, or to both such fine or such imprisonment.

A person shall be deemed for the purposes of this subsection not to have been in charge of a motor vehicle if he proves that at the material time the circumstances were such that there was no likelihood of his driving the vehicle so long as he remained unfit to drive through drink or drugs."

Formerly sub-s. (6) of this section then went on to state that the phrase "unfit to drive through drink or drugs" meant under the influence of drink or a drug to such an extent as to be incapable of having proper control of the vehicle.[4] but this has been amended by s. 1 of the Road Traffic Act 1962 which provides:

". . . a person shall be taken to be unfit to drive if his ability to drive properly is for the time being impaired."

The offences under s. 6 of the Road Traffic Act 1960 are supplemented by (and, so far as offences relating to *drinking* and driving are concerned, may for practical purposes be superseded by) offences under s. 1 of the Road Safety Act 1967 which provides:

"(1) If a person drives or attempts to drive a motor vehicle on a road or other public place, having consumed alcohol in such a quantity that the proportion thereof in his blood, as ascertained from a laboratory test for which he subsequently provides a specimen under s. 3 of this Act, exceeds the prescribed limit at the time he provides the specimen, he shall be liable [to the same penalties as provided by s. 6 (1) of the Road Traffic Act 1960].

(2) Without prejudice to the foregoing subsection, if a person is in charge of a motor vehicle on a road or other public place having consumed alcohol as aforesaid, he shall be liable [to the same penalties as provided by s. 6 (2) of the Road Traffic Act 1960].

(3) A person shall not be convicted under this section of being in charge of a motor vehicle if he proves that at the material time the circumstances were such that there was no likelihood of his driving it so long as there was any probability of his having alcohol in his blood in a proportion exceeding the prescribed limit.

(4) In determining for the purposes of the last foregoing subsection the likelihood of a person's driving a motor vehicle when he is injured or the vehicle is damaged, the jury, in the case of proceedings on indictment, may be directed to disregard, and the court in any other case may disregard, the fact that he had been injured or that the vehicle had been damaged."

---

[4] This is still the criterion on a charge of cycling when under the influence of drink or drugs contrary to s. 11.

Apart from the penalties specified in these sections it should also be noted that where a person is convicted of an offence under s. 6 (1) of the Road Traffic Act 1960 or s. 1 (1) of the Road Safety Act 1967 the court must disqualify him for at least twelve months, unless the court for special reasons thinks fit to disqualify him for a shorter period or not to disqualify him at all.

1   Road or Public Place

The offences under both Acts may be committed "on a road or other public place".[5] In *Elkins* v. *Cartlidge*[6] Lord GODDARD, C.J., said:

> "The section refers to 'a road or other public place.' I emphasise the word 'other.' 'Road' is defined . . . and one must have regard to that definition when considering the meaning of the words 'public place,' because the two things are treated *ejusdem generis*. 'Road' means 'any highway and any other road to which the public has access,' and so includes every road over which the public passes. Having regard to the definition of 'road,' 'public place' for the purposes of this section must be read as meaning a place to which the public have access, that is, have access in fact."

It was accordingly held that a car park at the rear of an inn was a public place because the evidence showed that the public had access and actually parked cars there. It has been held that a field used as a temporary car park to which the public was admitted on payment of a parking fee was a public place.[7]

2   Driving or Attempting to Drive

Both Acts specifically make it an offence to attempt to drive, as well as to drive, a vehicle.[8] D attempts to drive a vehicle when, intending to drive it, he attempts to put the vehicle in motion. D does not cease to be driving though he temporarily leaves his car during his journey, but once he leaves his car upon the completion of his journey he ceases to be driving.[9] If it is doubtful whether D is driving or attempting to drive, it may be that he is guilty of an offence of being in charge.

3   In Charge

(a) *Road Traffic Act* 1960, s. 6 (2).—It is also an offence, though the maximum punishment is less, to be "in charge" of a vehicle while unfit to drive. The reason for this offence, no doubt, was that it was felt desirable that the police should be able to intervene to prevent the unfit driver before he got to the stage of an attempt to drive. Moreover, the expression is apt to cover cases such as *Wallace* v. *Major*[10] where D has been held not to be driving the vehicle although he certainly ought to be guilty of an offence if he is unfit through drink or drugs.

---

[5] For the meaning of "road" see above, p. 326. And for "public place" see above, p. 286.

[6] [1947] 1 All E.R. 829. *Cf. Williams* v. *Boyle*, [1963] Crim. L.R. 204, where there was no evidence that the car park was a public place.

[7] *Collinson* (1931), 23 Cr. App. Rep. 49.

[8] The Road Traffic Act 1960 does not specifically make it an offence to attempt to drive dangerously or carelessly but it would be unwise to conclude that these offences could not be attempted. If D, knowing that his car has defective brakes, were to attempt to drive, it is submitted he would be attempting to drive dangerously or carelessly.

[9] *Price*, [1968] 3 All E.R. 814; *Campbell* v. *Tormey*, [1969] Crim. L.R. (March); *Wall* (1969), *The Times*, February 18.

[10] [1946] K.B. 473; [1946] 2 All E.R. 87; above, p. 327.

There is no definition of "in charge" in any of the Acts, and the courts have held, in effect, that the person who takes out the car on the road remains in charge of it until he puts someone else in charge.[12] Being in charge is not the same thing as owning since being in charge refers to the driving control of the vehicle.

> "When the section goes on to refer also to a person 'in charge of' a car the reference must be to the person in *de facto* control, even though he may not be at the time actually driving or attempting to drive."[13]

Nor, it might be added, even intending to drive. Thus in *Jowett-Shooter* v. *Franklin*[14] D, realising he was unfit to drive, had decided to sleep it off in the passenger seat of his car and not to drive again that night. It was held that he was in charge of the car when unfit to drive through drink. This was not satisfactory, for a man might be convicted when there was no chance of his driving the car at all and, if anything, it gave to the man who found he was drunk an incentive to get the car home before he was found in it by the police.

The law was therefore modified[15] to provide that a person shall be deemed not to have been in charge of a motor vehicle if he proves (and this is one of the exceptional cases where the burden of proof is put on the defendant) that there was no likelihood of his driving so long as he remained unfit.[16] This defence was considered by the Divisional Court in *Morton* v. *Confer*[17] where it was said that the court must be satisfied, not merely that D did not intend to drive again until fit, but that there was no likelihood of D driving until he was fit.[18] It is possible to envisage extreme cases where it is D's intention to drive, but there is no likelihood of his so doing, and in such circumstances it seems clear that D is not guilty of the offence. Apparently it has even been argued before magistrates that D's arrest by the police means that there is no likelihood that he will drive while unfit.[19] The answer to this is that "at the material time", which would be some time before the arrest, there would be a likelihood that D would drive while unfit: there ceases to be a likelihood after D has committed the offence. In

---

[12] *Haines* v. *Roberts*, [1953] 1 All E.R. 344. Friends of D, who was unfit, were arranging to have someone else drive his motor-cycle but had not effected this before the police found D within a few feet of his motor-cycle. D was held to be in charge of the vehicle. Had D been dispossessed of the cycle by his friends it is submitted he would no longer have been in charge.

[13] *Crichton* v. *Burrell*, 1951 S.L.T. 365 at p. 366, *per* Lord Justice-General COOPER. It was held that an owner who was standing by his car and possessed an ignition key was not in charge when the evidence showed he was waiting for his chauffeur to drive him home. See also *Harnett*, [1955] Crim. L.R. 793; *Fisher* v. *Kearton*, [1964] Crim. L.R. 470.

[14] [1949] 2 All E.R. 730 (D.C.).

[15] Originally by the Road Traffic Act 1956. Note that s. 6 (2) (ii) of the Road Traffic Act 1960 has been deleted by s. 1 (5) of the Road Safety Act 1967. The idea behind this amendment (which brings the offences under both Acts into line) was that the law as it stood provided no incentive to the driver who realised while driving that he was unfit to pull off the road and sleep it off.

[16] Although *Jowett-Shooter* v. *Franklin*, above, might now be decided differently it should be noted that the "in charge" cases are still relevant (i) because the prosecution must prove that D was in charge before the evidential burden is shifted to D, and (ii) to prosecutions under s. 16 for leaving vehicles in dangerous positions.

[17] [1963] 2 All E.R. 765.

[18] Thus the justices were wrong in *Morton* v. *Confer*, above, to fail to give consideration to the fact that the first thing D did when awoken by a policeman in his car was to switch on the ignition.

[19] Wilkinson, "Road Traffic 1954–63", [1964] Crim. L.R. 348, 354.

John v. *Bentley*[20] it was held there was evidence on which Quarter Sessions could come to the conclusion that there was no likelihood that D would drive so long as he remained unfit where he was found on the floor of the car so drunk that it was impossible to wake him either during his sojourn at the police station or while he was being medically examined. It was also the fact that D had set out with the intention to get someone to drive him home if he became unfit, and he was not found in the driving seat of the car. But for this it might well have been found that at some stage after he became unfit there was every likelihood that D would drive, and, if that was the case, the fact that he subsequently became comatose, or was subsequently arrested, would not help him.[21]

The material time is any time when D is unfit and there is a likelihood that he will drive the vehicle. It is not enough to show that D was driving shortly before he became unfit; it must be shown that there was a likelihood that he would have driven again after becoming unfit. Accordingly in *Jephcott*,[1] where D claimed that he had taken only a small amount of alcohol before the accident but had also taken brandy after the accident and sought to bring himself within the proviso by showing that his car was so badly damaged that there was no likelihood of his driving it, it was held that the trial judge was wrong to have withdrawn D's defence from the jury.

(b) *Road Safety Act* 1967, s. 1 (2).—Much of what has been said in relation to the offence under s. 6 (2) of the Road Traffic Act 1960 is equally relevant to the offence under s. 1 (2) of the Road Safety Act 1967. But there are some differences.

While under the 1960 Act it is a defence for D to prove that at the material time the circumstances were such that there was no likelihood of his driving "so long as he remained unfit", under the 1967 Act D must prove there was no such likelihood "so long as there was any probability of his having alcohol in his blood in a proportion exceeding the prescribed limit". This difference in wording is explained by the different nature of the tests of "fitness" to drive under the respective sections. Under the 1960 Act the question of D's fitness involves a consideration of a number of factors, one of which may[2] be his blood-alcohol level as determined by scientific analysis. But where the charge is brought (as it would now normally be brought) under the 1967 Act the only relevant consideration on the question of "unfitness" is the blood-alcohol level as determined by scientific analysis.[3] That analysis will normally relate to a sample of blood or urine taken some time (perhaps an hour or two) after he has taken a breath test and been requested or required to go to a police station to provide a sample of blood or urine. The time at which the sample is taken does not necessarily coincide with the time at which there would have been a likelihood that D would have been driving the vehicle. The likelihood may have been that D would have driven the vehicle some time before or after the time when the sample was taken, and when his blood-alcohol level might have been higher or lower. To meet this situation s. 1 (2) of the 1967 Act puts on D the onus of showing that there was no

---

[20] [1961] Crim. L.R. 552; *cf. Northfield* v. *Pinder*, [1969] Crim. L.R. 92.
[21] *Northfield* v. *Pinder*, [1968] 3 All E.R. 854.
[1] [1967] Crim. L.R. 52 (C.A.).
[2] D may refuse to provide a specimen of urine or blood for analysis in which case, if his refusal is unreasonable, this may be used as supporting evidence for the prosecution, see Road Traffic Act, s. 2.
[3] And if D refuses, without reasonable cause, to provide a specimen of breath, blood or urine, he may in any case be convicted of the offence under s. 1 (1), see Road Safety Act 1967, s. 3.

likelihood of his driving so long as there was any *probability* of his having a blood-alcohol level exceeding the prescribed limit.[4]

A further difference between the offences under the Road Traffic Act 1960 and the Road Safety Act 1967 is that s. 1 (4) of the latter provides that for the purposes of determining the likelihood of D's driving the vehicle, the jury, or judge of fact, may disregard the fact that D had been injured or that the vehicle has been damaged.[5]

4 Impairment of Ability to Drive

(*a*) *Road Traffic Act* 1960.—The first formula used by Parliament as the criterion of unfitness to drive was that the driver must be shown to be "drunk while in charge" of any mechanically propelled vehicle.[6] The case of *Presdee*[7] demonstrated the unsatisfactory nature of "drunk in charge" as a test of criminal liability. The jury found—in their own words—that D was

> "guilty of being incapable of driving a motor-car brought about by alcohol, but he was not drunk—not drunk to the extent we should call a drunken man."[8]

In the Court of Criminal Appeal counsel for D argued that a man was not necessarily drunk simply because he was unfit through alcohol to handle a motor car. and this was, in effect, accepted by the court for it was held that the finding of the jury, "he was not drunk", was conclusive. In view of this decision a new formula was introduced by s. 15 (1) of the Road Traffic Act 1930: the driver must be

> "under the influence of drink or a drug to such an extent as to be incapable of having proper control of the vehicle."

This formula, it seems, was never considered by the courts in any reported decision, but perhaps this is hardly surprising in view of the fact that it is readily intelligible. Since the formula is necessarily imprecise it was criticised on the ground that many persons escaped who ought to have been convicted because, in practice, a high degree of intoxication had to be proved. It was commonly said that juries in particular tended to interpret "incapable" as if it meant "drunk and incapable"—a hangover from the old law.

So the present formula was introduced; a person is unfit to drive "if his ability to drive properly is for the time being impaired". This formula was introduced with the avowed object of making it easier to secure a conviction where conviction is justified, but it is not entirely clear how the new formula does this. A possible view is that any impairment of D's ability to drive, however minute, will satisfy the definition, so that, in effect, the formula virtually prohibits drinking before driving at all. Another view, and it is submitted the correct view, is that no offence is committed unless D's ability to drive falls below an objective

---

[4] Note that likelihood has to be considered in the light of the circumstances as they were before a breath test was requested. *Cf. Northfield* v. *Pinder*, [1968] 3 All E.R. 854. Once a breath test has proved positive and D is taken to a police station there ceases to be any further likelihood that D will drive while his blood-alcohol limit exceeds the prescribed limit. Indeed s. 4 of the Road Safety Act authorises the police to detain D until a breath test establishes that his blood-alcohol level has fallen below the prescribed limit.

[5] *Cf. Jephcott*, [1967] Crim. L.R. 52, above p. 342. Note that the relevant time for determining blood-alcohol concentration is when the sample is given, below, p. 345; drinking after an accident but before a sample is given is therefore hazardous.

[6] Criminal Justice Act 1925, s. 40 (1).

[7] [1927], 20 Cr. App. Rep. 95.

[8] See *ibid.*

standard—the ability to drive *properly*. The formula does not say that any impairment of ability to drive is enough, but that the ability to drive *properly* must be impaired. If D is able to drive properly, the fact that he is not able to drive perfectly is immaterial.[9] Against this it may be argued that D is not driving properly unless he is exercising all the skill which he possesses, but this seems to be against the natural meaning of the words.

It follows, if this view is accepted, that the change of formula makes no difference at all in law. If D's ability to drive properly is impaired, he is incapable of having proper control and if he is incapable of having proper control, his ability to drive properly is impaired. But it does not follow that this semantic legerdemain is unjustified. If the previous formula was unsuccessful with juries because of the unfortunate association of "incapable" with "drunk and incapable" any formula which might avoid this association was desirable.

The Road Traffic Act 1962, s. 2, also seeks to deal with the difficulties of proof. It requires the court to have regard to the evidence of the quantity of alcohol in the body as ascertained from a specimen of blood, or urine, or (when it is brought into force) breath, but no guidance is given of the amount which might be considered to impair driving ability and the courts are dependent upon the evidence on this in each case. It is provided that refusal, without reasonable cause, to supply a specimen may be treated as supporting evidence given by the prosecution, or as rebutting any evidence given on behalf of the defence, as to D's condition.[10]

As it turned out, however, neither the introduction of the new formula nor the introduction of scientific evidence resulted in any significant increase in convictions by juries on charges of driving while unfit. Accordingly it was felt necessary to introduce new offences in the Road Safety Act 1967 under which the criterion would be objective. The offence of driving while unfit remains but in practice it is likely to be used only where the alleged unfitness arises through the taking of drugs, or possibly where D is allegedly unfit though his blood-alcohol level does not exceed the prescribed limit for the purposes of the Road Safety Act.[11]

(*b*) *Road Safety Act* 1967, s. 1 (1).—Under this provision[12] it is simply an offence to drive or attempt to drive with a blood-alcohol level in excess of the prescribed limit, a limit presently fixed at 80 mg. of alcohol to 100 ml. of blood. It is not thought necessary to show any impairment of driving ability but there can be little doubt that when this concentration is reached the ability of the vast majority of drivers is seriously impaired. "Most drivers are impaired significantly

---

[9] It should be noted that though these two views of the formula differ, the acceptance of the latter in preference to the former does not involve subscribing to the view that relatively large amounts of alcohol are required to impair the ability to drive properly. In general (though there are variable factors such as tolerance to alcohol, form in which taken, whether accompanied by meals, time taken, etc.), the ability to drive properly is impaired by relatively small amounts of alcohol. See *Relation of Alcohol to Road Accidents*, Report of B.M.A., 1960, London; Havard, *Recent Developments in the Alcohol and Road Traffic Situation* (1963) Brit. Jo. Addiction, 55; *Effect of Small Doses of Alcohol on a Skill Resembling Driving*, H.M.S.O., 1959.

[10] See further Wilkinson, *Road Traffic Offences* (5th ed.), 104.

[11] A successful prosecution in this last case would be unlikely. The limit presently prescribed under the Road Safety Act is 80 mg. *per* 100 ml. and in prosecutions under s. 6 of the Road Traffic Act "convictions are rarely obtained at blood-alcohol concentrations under 150 mg./100 ml."—Havard, "Road Safety Bill—A Medical View", [1967] Crim. L.R. 151, 160.

[12] See Havard, *op. cit.*; Elliott and Street, *Road Accidents* (1967), pp. 25–33.

by the time a concentration of 50 mg. *per* 100 ml. is reached."[13] It is as unnecessary as it is unwise to attempt to convert the concentration into a number of
beers or whiskies. Nor is it necessary to make any kind of back calculation to
determine the concentration at the time of driving or attempting to drive since
the offence is committed where the blood-alcohol level exceeds the prescribed
limit when D provides the specimen of blood or urine.

It will be noted that whereas the Road Traffic Act 1962 allows evidence of the
blood/alcohol concentration to be given to support a charge of unfitness, the
Road Safety Act makes a prescribed blood/alcohol concentration part of the *actus
reus* of the offence. If the concentration is less than that prescribed then D cannot be convicted under the Road Safety Act even though the evidence shows
that he was manifestly unfit to drive through drink. Moreover, s. 1 (1) states
that D commits the offence where his blood/alcohol concentration "as ascertained from a laboratory test for which he subsequently provides a specimen
under s. 3 of this Act" exceeds the prescribed limit. In *Scott* v. *Baker*[14] it was
held that the offence was not made out where the requirements of s. 3 were not
complied with, and accordingly D could not be convicted where it was not shown
that the breath-testing device was of a type approved by the Secretary of State.
The court reasoned that the requirements of s. 3 in relation to the provision of a
specimen were requirements of the offence, that is, part of the *actus reus*. But
in *Brush*,[15] notwithstanding that s. 3 (10) provides that a constable

> "shall . . . warn [D] that failure to provide a specimen of blood or urine may
> make him liable to imprisonment, a fine and disqualification",

the court held that the giving of a warning was not a constituent of the offence.
No doubt this was right because s. 3 (10) goes on to provide that if no warning is
given the court *may* dismiss the charge or direct an acquittal. Since the subsection contemplates that D may be convicted although no warning is given, it
follows that a warning, though otherwise relevant, is not a constituent of the
offence.

5   Mens Rea

(*a*) *Road Traffic Act* 1960, s. 6.—In *Armstrong* v. *Clark*,[16] D, who was a
diabetic, had taken his usual dose of insulin and consumed a regular meal.
Owing to the overaction of the insulin D suffered a hypoglycaemic coma and
drove off the road. It was held by the Divisional Court that he was guilty of
driving while unfit through drugs. LYNSKEY, J., said:[17]

> "It is clear that Parliament in passing this particular section[18] was con-
> cerned about persons driving on the public roads in a state of being either
> under the influence of drugs or drink, because subsection (2) of the same
> section makes it compulsory for the justices who convict of this particular
> offence to disqualify the person from driving for the next 12 months unless
> there are special circumstances. The section was intended to keep off the
> roads, so far as it could, people attempting to take control or having control
> while not having the power to do so through drink or drugs."

---

[13] Havard, *op. cit.*, at p. 161.
[14] [1968] 2 All E.R. 993 (D.C.); [1968] Crim. L.R. 393. *Cf. Withecombe*, [1969]
1 All E.R. 157 (C.A.); *Hoyle* v. *Walsh*, [1969] 1 All E.R. 38 (D.C.).
[15] [1968] 2 All E.R. 467.
[16] [1957] 2 Q.B. 391; [1957] 1 All E.R. 433.
[17] [1957] 2 Q.B. 391 at p. 395; [1957] 1 All E.R. 433 at p. 436.
[18] Then s. 15 (1) of the Road Traffic Act 1933.

14*

It has been argued[19] that *Armstrong* v. *Clark* could be interpreted as imposing liability for negligence but there is other authority indicating that liability is strict. In *Wickins*,[20] the Court of Criminal Appeal held there were special reasons for not disqualifying D where he had consumed a small quantity of beer which would not have effected his driving but for the fact that, unknown to himself, D was suffering from diabetes. The court said that a special reason must be one which did not itself amount to a defence to the charge and that was the case here.

So it seems tolerably clear that the courts favour the imposition of strict liability in connection with offences under s. 6, but, as with many other instances of strict liability, fault has to be assessed for the purposes of punishment. It seems that if D is in fact not negligent this would be a special reason why he should not be disqualified.

(*b*) *Road Safety Act* 1967, *s.* 1.—In view of the objective nature of the requirements of this section it is clear that strict liability will be imposed at least to the extent that it will not be a defence for D to show that he did not intend to exceed the limit. D may have heard that it is "safe" to drink up to a certain amount, but this will not help him. The only real safety lies in not drinking at all before driving. Possibly this is one case where strict liability can be justified, but in truth, though D may not wish to exceed the prescribed limit, there is an element of risk-taking in his conduct which distinguishes it from other instances of strict liability. On this hypothesis D ought not to be convicted where he does not knowingly run the risk as where, for example, he consumes what he reasonably believes to be a fruit drink which, unknown to him, contains alcohol.[21]

6 Drink or Drugs

The unfitness must arise through "drink or drugs". Drug includes a medicant or medicine, something which is given to cure or alleviate or assist an ailing body, and hence has been held to include insulin.[1] Drink means alcoholic drink.[2] The unfitness must arise *through*, that is, be caused by, drink or drugs. So if D has taken drink or drugs but his ability to drive properly is impaired by some illness (not itself caused by the drink or drugs) to which he succumbs when driving he would not be guilty of this offence.

6 OTHER OFFENCES

The foregoing constitute only the principal driving offences; there are many others connected with driving and very many more connected with road traffic generally. Unless the provision creating the offence includes some expression (such as knowingly, permits, allows) indicating that some form of *mens rea* is required then, with isolated exceptions, these offences have been strictly construed by the courts. One of the exceptions is *Harding* v. *Price*[3] where it was held

---

[19] By Williams, "'Absolute Liability' in Traffic Offences", [1967] Crim. L.R. 206.
[20] (1958), 42 Cr. App. Rep. 236.
[21] *Cf. Brewer* v. *Metropolitan Police Commissioner* (1968), 112 S.J. 1022 (D.C.); the the court, while holding that an unwitting absorption of alcohol was a special reason for not disqualifying D, upheld D's conviction under s. 1.
[1] *Armstrong* v. *Clark*, [1957] 2 Q.B. 391; [1957] 1 All E.R. 433.
[2] *Ibid.*
[3] [1948] 1 K.B. 695; [1948] 1 All E.R. 283.

no offence to fail to report an accident where D was unaware that an accident had taken place, and this case is authority for the general proposition that if an offence imposes a duty to do something on the happening of a given event, D must have knowledge of the given event.[4] But there has been no discernible attempt to discriminate between the serious and the minor offences arising under the Road Traffic Acts. It may be understandable that construction and use offences[5] should be strictly construed: it is less understandable that the offence of driving without insurance should be strictly construed.[6]

---

[4] But *cf. Warner* v. *Metropolitan Police Commissioner*, [1968] 2 All E.R. 356, 364.
[5] See the Motor Vehicles (Construction and Use) Regulations 1963 (S.I. 1963 No. 1646).
[6] Wilkinson, *Road Traffic Offences* (5th ed.), 202 and cases there cited.

CHAPTER 15

Offences against Property involving Fraud

The law of theft was codified by the Theft Act 1968.[1] This Act provides a code relating to virtually all offences against property involving fraud, with the notable exception of forgery. On two previous occasions, in the Larceny Acts of 1861 and 1916, the law relating to theft has been the subject of major legislation but the Theft Act 1968 is quite unlike these earlier enactments. In general terms it may be said that the aim of the Acts of 1861 and 1916 was to consolidate the various statutory provisions and to state these in a convenient and accessible form. The Theft Act 1968 proceeds on another basis altogether. Although the Criminal Law Revision Committee, which was charged with the task of reforming the law,[2] saw that there were advantages in retaining the old system with some necessary amendment to repair its defects, they decided that the time had come

> "for a new law of theft and related offences, based on a fundamental reconsideration of the principles underlying this branch of the law and embodied in a modern statute."[3]

The Theft Act 1968 is that modern statute and it is new law in a way in which the Larceny Acts of 1861 and 1916 were not new law. This has consequences of fundamental importance so far as the interpretation of the Theft Act is concerned. Even in the case of a statute which purports to codify the common law:

> "The proper course is, in the first instance, to examine the language of the statute and to ask what is its natural meaning influenced by any considerations derived from the previous state of the law, and not to start with inquiring how the law previously stood, and then, assuming that it was probably intended to leave it unaltered, to see if the words of the enactment will bear an interpretation in conformity with this view."[4]

---

[1] See Smith, *The Law of Theft* (hereinafter Smith, *Theft*); Griew, *The Theft Act* 1968 (hereinafter Griew, *Theft*).

[2] See Eighth Report, *Theft and Related Offences* Cmnd. 2977, H.M.S.O.; hereinafter referred to as Cmnd. 2977.

[3] Cmnd. 2977, para. 7.

[4] *Bank of England* v. *Vagliano Bros.*, [1891] A.C. 107, at p. 144 *per* Lord HERSCHELL. The court was considering the Bills of Exchange Act 1882, but the observation applies to codifying statutes generally.

In practice the Larceny Act 1916 was often construed on the tacit assumption that there was no intention to alter the previous law and the earlier case law lost little or no authority. Such an approach to the Theft Act would be wholly wrong, and any assumption that there was no intention to alter the previous law would be completely misconceived.

Nevertheless reference to earlier cases would be permissible in certain restricted circumstances. A clear instance would be where the Theft Act refers to concepts of the civil law, such as "trust", "equitable interest", or "proprietary right or interest". Obviously civil cases, whether decided before or after the Act, would be authoritative to explain these concepts. Indeed, all offences relating to the appropriation of property can be defined intelligibly only in relation to a law of property.

But while a reference to civil cases to explain civil concepts is generally permissible, reference to prior criminal cases will be rarely permissible. One case where such reference may be made is where the Theft Act uses expressions taken from earlier legislation which have acquired a settled meaning. For example, it would be permissible to refer to earlier decisions to elucidate the meaning of "menaces" in connection with the offence of blackmail under s. 21. Strictly the earlier cases on the meaning of "menaces" are no longer authoritative but reference to them is legitimate and it is most likely they would be followed.[5] The word "menaces" had acquired a special meaning which was rather wider than that which it has in ordinary parlance and accordingly it may be assumed, since the draftsmen could have chosen another word such as "threats", that by retaining "menaces" the intention was to retain its earlier meaning. But this process cannot be carried too far and certainly affords no pretext for any wholesale reference to the earlier law. Before any reference can be made it must be clear from the context in which the expression is used in the Theft Act that it is being used in its special sense. For example, it would not be relevant to consider earlier authorities in the meaning of "robbery" since s. 8 itself defines robbery exhaustively and that definition may or may not accord with the former position.

Beyond this limited point it would not be relevant to refer to previous decisions. If codification of the kind exemplified by the Theft Act is to operate effectively it must be "within its field the authoritative, comprehensive and exclusive source of that law".[6] If a code is not so regarded it is in danger of failing to develop or reform the law.[7]

But earlier cases often provide convenient fact situations in which to consider the effect of the provisions of the Theft Act and for that purpose some reference is made to them in the ensuing pages. It is to be hoped, since no attempt will be made herein to explain the substance of the former law, that the use of these old faces will help those who must translate their old learning into the new, while not misleading those come to the subject for the first time.

1 THEFT

By s. 1 (1) of the Theft Act 1968:

"A person is guilty of theft if he dishonestly appropriates property belonging to another with the intention of permanently depriving the other of it; and 'thief' and 'steal' shall be construed accordingly."

---

[5] See further below p. 404.
[6] Scarman, *Codification and Judge-Made Law* (1966), at p. 7.
[7] *Ibid*, p. 8.

And by s. 7 a person guilty of theft is liable to ten years' imprisonment.

There is much about this definition which is self-explanatory and the vast majority of instances which actually occur will be covered without further elaboration. It is worth noting that before turning to the elaboration.

(1) THE ACTUS REUS

The *actus reus* of theft consists in the appropriation of property belonging to another.

1 Appropriation

By s. 3 (1) of the Theft Act 1968:

> "Any assumption by a person of the rights of an owner amounts to an appropriation, and this includes, where he has come by the property (innocently or not) without stealing it, any later assumption of a right to it by keeping or dealing with it as owner."

Broadly, appropriation, in the context of the Theft Act, conveys the idea of annexing something or treating something as one's own. But while this notion is conveyed by appropriation it is important to keep in mind that s. 3 (1) itself provides the only relevant definition and according to this subsection "*any* assumption by a person of the rights of an owner" amounts to an appropriation and, as will appear, this may have a wider import than that ordinarily conveyed by appropriation.

(*a*) *Appropriation and conversion.*—The Criminal Law Revision Committee took the view that "appropriates" meant the same as "converts" in the former offences of fraudulent conversion under s. 20 (1) (iv) of the Larceny Act 1916.[8] Consequently it would be permissible in this instance to have regard to decisions on the meaning of conversion in the former law though, as it turns out, there are few helpful decisions on the point. There is, however, an obvious affinity between appropriation and conversion as a concept of the civil law of tort; and it may be that civil cases will be helpful to elucidate the meaning of appropriation. But though there is likely to be a substantial correspondence between the concepts of appropriation and conversion it would be a mistake to assume that the expressions are entirely synonymous, and that the one is not capable of conveying nuances not conveyed by the other.[9] In any case the analogy between the criminal and civil wrongs can be pressed only in relation to the nature of acts capable of constituting an assumption of an owner's rights.[10] Beyond this point there are obvious differences and especially in relation to the mental element required for liability. Moreover the policies of the civil and criminal law differ and this may lead to differences of result.[11]

---

[8] Cmnd. 2977, para. 35. The Committee apparently preferred "appropriates" only on the ground that "converts" was a lawyer's word which was not as meaningful to the layman as "appropriates".

[9] In *Jackson* (1864), 9 Cox C.C. 505, MARTIN, B., thought that many acts (none were specified) might amount to the tort of conversion but not the crime of conversion.

[10] But note that in *Rogers* v. *Arnott*, [1960] 2 Q.B. 244 at p. 249; [1960] 2 All E.R. 417 at p. 419, DONOVAN, J., thought an analogy between civil and criminal conversion was "misleading" because the tort is not actionable without proof of damage. But *cf.* Street, *Torts*, at p. 35, n. 7: "The tort [of conversion] appears to be actionable without proof of special damage: *Hiort* v. *London and North Western Ry. Co.* (1879), 4 EX. D. 188."

[11] See below p. 353.

(*b*) *Appropriation and permanent deprivation.*—To a degree the notion of permanent deprivation may be implicit in appropriation as ordinarily understood. In so far as appropriates means to annex or to treat as one's own, the same meaning is conveyed by permanent deprivation, and to this extent appropriation and permanent deprivation might be considered different sides of the same coin. If, for example, D, without permission, borrows P's book for an hour or two he would not be guilty of theft since dishonest borrowing is not generally an offence under the Theft Act.[12] The reason which would ordinarily be given for saying that D had not stolen the book is that he does not intend to deprive P permanently of it. But might it not equally be given as a reason that there is no appropriation of the book? A person who borrows a thing would not ordinarily be said to be appropriating it. But it has to be said that what is ordinarily thought of as appropriation is strictly beside the point since s. 3 (1) defines what is to be considered an appropriation and that definition embraces "*any* assumption . . . of the rights of an owner". Borrowing and using a book may amount to an assumption of the rights of an owner and accordingly to an appropriation. D, however, is still not a thief where he borrows the book for an hour or two because he does not intend permanently to deprive. The argument serves to show that though appropriation as defined in s. 3 (1) may be a wide ranging concept, it is limited in terms of creating criminal liability by the requirement of the intent permanently to deprive.[13]

(*c*) *Appropriation as an unauthorised dealing*—Appropriation will ordinarily involve some act, some dealing in the property. A mere mental resolution to appropriate would not suffice even if it could be proved. If, for example, P lends his lawn mower to D, D would not become a thief merely by making up his mind never to return it. D must do something in pursuance of his intent which can be described as an appropriation.

Section 3 (1) however, may go a little further than this because it states that property may be appropriated by "keeping . . . it as owner". It can be argued[14] in view of this that an appropriation may be constituted by an omission, as by a failure to return property to the owner. Clearly, though, even if an omission may amount to an appropriation, the situation would have to be one where D is under some duty to act[15] and fails so to act. P may have lost his umbrella and D may know where it is, but D would not become a thief merely because he has decided to appropriate the umbrella and accordingly fails to inform P of its whereabouts.[16] It cannot be said here that D "keeps" the umbrella as owner, since keeping necessarily implies that he has at some stage assumed control of it and has failed to relinquish that control. Where, however, D has control of the property his

---

[12] There are, however, certain exceptions; see below, p. 397.

[13] There is no such limitation on civil liability for the tort of conversion. A borrowing may amount to the tort of conversion if it is for a period or in circumstances which are seriously inconsistent with the owner's right to possess, and although there is no intent permanently to deprive; but see further below, p. 377.

[14] *Cf.* Smith, *Theft*, paras. 62, 63.

[15] See above, p. 35.

[16] *Cf. Walters* v. *Lunt*, [1951] 2 All E.R. 645, where D's seven-year-old son brought home a tricycle belonging to P. D took possession of the tricycle and kept it and this would now amount to an appropriation of the tricycle. Had D merely refrained from telling P of the whereabouts of the cycle, or had merely turned a blind eye to his son's use, there would be no appropriation by D. But in such a case comparatively little would be required to show an assumption of possession by D.

failure to return it to the owner may amount to an appropriation and to that extent an appropriation may be constituted by an omission.[17]

But this does not mean that D, in the illustration just given concerning the lawn mower, is now guilty of theft by virtue of his resolution to steal. His *mens rea* must be accompanied by some *actus reus* of appropriation. Suppose, then, that at the time he makes up his mind to steal D is in the process of mowing his lawn and continues to do so. There is now an act done by D after he has determined to steal, but the act is not an act of appropriation. D is authorised to use the mower in this way, and in so dealing with it is not assuming the rights of an owner. Similarly there would be no appropriation where a postman decides to steal a letter which is in his pouch although he thereafter carries it about with him; but his removal of the letter from his pouch to his pocket would amount to an appropriation.[18]

An appropriation is then some unauthorised dealing in the property which shows that D has assumed the rights of an owner. It is something he ought not have done unless authorised by the owner.

(d) Appropriation and possession.—Appropriation is in no way geared to possession as such. A person who is in possession of the property may of course steal it by assuming the rights of an owner, as where the borrower of a book destroys it. Equally a person out of possession may appropriate property by assuming the rights of an owner. The test of appropriation in either case (or indeed in any case) is the same: has D assumed the rights of an owner? No doubt where D is out of possession the most usual form of appropriation will be a taking of possession from P. But a taking of possession is merely one way (though no doubt the most common way) of assuming the rights of an owner.

Perhaps this is perfectly obvious to anyone who has no acquaintance with the former law of larceny, but the point may still be worth making because it serves to emphasize that there may be an appropriation although there is no physical removal of the property from the control of P into the control of D. To destroy P's goods *in situ* would amount to an appropriation. Normally this might not be thought of as an appropriation, but only because normally the motive for theft is to enjoy in some way the property stolen. No doubt in such a case a charge would be brought under the Malicious Damage Act 1861, but there has been a clear assumption of the rights of an owner and consequently an appropriation.

Appropriation therefore does not require an assumption of control over the property—"*any* assumption . . . of the rights of an owner suffices". Accordingly it is arguable[19] that a mere attempt to assume control is an appropriation. Thus if D puts his hand towards P's pocket in order to steal P's watch this might be an appropriation. Clearly the appropriation would be complete in such a case, at the latest, when D puts his hand on the watch and there would be no need of a removal of the watch to complete the appropriation. D has already taken control and thus already assumed the rights of an owner. But on a common sense approach it seems difficult to say that D has assumed the rights of an owner where

---

[17] Whether "keeping" is an act of omission or commission may be purely semantic. See further the discussion in connection with *Wakeman* (1912), 8 Cr. App. Rep. 18; below, p. 355.

[18] *Cf. Poynton* (1862), 9 Cox C.C. 249. D may indeed have appropriated the letter at a stage before it reaches his pocket, see *infra*.

[19] *Cf.* Smith, *Theft*, para. 27; Stuart, "Reform of the Law of Theft" (1967), 30 M.L.R. 609, at p. 626.

he merely puts his hand towards P's pocket; he is trying to assume control and as his act is sufficiently proximate[20] he may be convicted of an attempt.

(e) *Instances of appropriation.*—It should be apparent from the foregoing discussion that appropriation is a broad concept. Obviously it is not possible to catalogue all the forms which appropriation may take since the range of acts capable of amounting to an assumption of ownership is considerable. But there may be some utility in looking briefly at some of the more obvious instances of appropriation. In general terms an owner's rights are to use, enjoy and destroy his property[1] and consequently any such assumption by D may amount to an appropriation.

(i)   *Taking.*—This clearly amounts to an appropriation and is in practice by far the most common form of appropriation. As has been shown,[2] removal is not necessary to complete the appropriation. The appropriation is certainly complete when D has assumed control, and may even be complete when D attempts to take.

(ii) *Destroying.*—To destroy property is clearly to assume the rights of an owner and therefore amounts to appropriation. As has been shown, theft may not be the most appropriate charge and, so far as a charge of theft is concerned, there may be some difficulties here with the intent permanently to deprive.[3]

But merely to damage goods would not ordinarily amount to theft. Of course one of the rights of an owner is to abuse his own property and in damaging P's property D is assuming the rights of an owner. Strictly it seems that there may be an appropriation in such a case,[4] but normally there would be no theft owing to the absence of an intent permanently to deprive.

(iii) *Using.*—To use property in an unauthorised way would amount to an appropriation and would constitute theft if accompanied by the relevant *mens rea*. Thus if D wears pearls which have been deposited with him by P only for safe custody, this would be an appropriation. In this connection it is worth considering the facts of *Jackson*,[5] where D, who had been lent P's coat for the day, was found some days later wearing the coat on a ship bound for Australia. MARTIN, B., held there was no evidence of a conversion of the coat. This holding may be consistent with the civil cases on conversion for there is apparently no case which holds that mere excess of permitted use constitutes a conversion,[6] and certainly it is not a conversion for civil purposes (though it may be a breach of contract) merely to fail to return property

---

[20] See above, p. 166.

[1] The rights of an owner appear to be nowhere authoritatively defined and have to be inferred from cases establishing what constitutes interference with ownership. For a general discussion of an owner's rights see Honoré, *Oxford Essays in Jurisprudence*, pp. 112–120.

[2] Above, p. 352.

[3] See below, p. 375.

[4] It appears that merely to damage goods is not a conversion for the purposes of the civil law; *Simmons* v. *Lillystone* (1853), 8 Ex. 431. But at this point appropriation may be wider than conversion. "*Any* assumption . . . of the rights of an owner" amounts to an appropriation whereas conversion in the civil law requires some *serious* interference with the owner's rights.

[5] (1864), 9 Cox C.C. 505.

[6] Street, *Torts* at 37, n. 4. But there was more than a mere excess of permitted use by Jackson, and it is thought he would be liable in a civil action in conversion.

upon the termination of a bailment.   But whatever Jackson's position
may be under the civil law, it seems clear that the above facts would
now afford evidence that he was "keeping . . . [the coat] as owner"
and there would thus be an appropriation within s. 3 (1) of the Theft
Act 1968.

(*iv*) *Selling and pledging.*—Any unauthorised sale or pledge by D of P's
property amounts to an appropriation since it is an obvious assumption
of the rights of an owner.   Thus if D is authorised to sell P's car at a
certain price and he sells it for less[7] or sells it to persons to whom he is
not authorised to sell,[8] there is evidence of an appropriation of the
goods.   *A fortiori* when D is not authorised to sell at all.   Indeed the
appropriation in such cases is complete so soon as D attempts to sell
or pledge the property, for an attempted sale or pledge is itself an
assumption of the rights of an owner.[9]

Possibly there may be an appropriation where D sells P's property
even though D at no stage has any control of the property.   It has been
pointed out[10] how there may be an appropriation although there is no
assumption of control by D.   Moreover the Criminal Law Revision
Committee took the view that property might be appropriated by D
although at no stage was he in possession if it.[11]   If, then, D sells
P's car to Q, D may be held to have appropriated the car although all
along the car has been standing in P's driveway and has remained
exclusively in P's possession.[12]

It seems, however, that for the purpose of the civil law of conversion
a mere sale which does not involve any transfer of ownership or delivery
of possession is not a conversion.[13]   Appropriation may, however, be a
wider concept than conversion in the civil law as has been pointed out
above;[14] the emphasis of the crime of theft is upon D's conduct and
intentions whereas the emphasis in civil law is upon some serious interference in fact with P's use of the property.

So far as theft is concerned there are really two problems where D,
who is not in possession or control, purports to sell P's car to Q.[15]   One
is whether D appropriates the car and the other is whether he intends
to deprive P permanently of it.[16]   Of course if D intends that Q should

---

[7] *Cf. Wainwright* (1960), 44 Cr. App. Rep. 191.
[8] *Cf. Davies* (1866), 10 Cox C.C. 239.
[9] *Cf. Rogers* v. *Arnott*, [1960] 2 Q.B. 244; [1960] 2 All E.R. 417.
[10] Above, p. 352.
[11] Cmnd. 2977, para. 35.
[12] *Cf. Bloxham* (1943), 29 Cr. App. Rep. 37, where D, employed by the P Urban
District Council, sold a refrigerator belonging to P to Q.   At no stage did D have control
of the refrigerator and at no stage did he take control; nor did Q take control in pursuance
of the "sale".   It was held that D could not be convicted of larceny but his conduct might
now amount to an appropriation of the refrigerator.
[13] *Lancashire Waggon Co.* v. *Fitzhugh* (1861), 6 H. & N. 502; *Consolidated Co.* v
Curtis, [1892] 1 Q.B. 495, *per* COLLINS, J., at p. 498.
[14] Above, p. 350.
[15] The matter might be said to be entirely academic because, whether D is guilty of
theft or not, he is certainly guilty of obtaining, or attempting to obtain, money from Q by
deception contrary to s. 15 of the Act.   But, apart from the possibility (unlikely though it
may be) that a prosecutor will some day charge D with theft on facts such as these, consideration of the problem as one of theft directs attention to the difficulties in the meaning
of appropriation.
[16] This aspect of the problem is taken up below, p. 377.

take away the car in pursuance of the "sale" and Q does so, D may be said to have appropriated the car through the agency of Q.[17] Suppose, as D knows, there is no danger in fact of any interference with P's rights as owner. It may be said that an appropriation is not an *interference with* the rights, but an *assumption of* the rights of the owner; the latter goes further than the former and it may be that merely claiming to be the owner, or to act with the owner's authority, is such an assumption.[18]

(v) *Receiving.*—To receive may amount to an appropriation and, if done with the relevant *mens rea*, will constitute theft. A receiver would normally be charged with handling under s. 22[19] of the Theft Act which carries a higher maximum punishment than theft, but it is worth noting that most forms of handling will also constitute theft because in some circumstances it may not be clear whether the offence under s. 22 is made out.

(vi) *Other acts.*—Any other acts showing that D is assuming the rights of an owner may amount to an appropriation. There may be an appropriation where, for example, D denies P access to his property or refuses to surrender the property upon R's demand. Such acts surely afford evidence that D is "keeping . . . [the property] as owner" and if D has the requisite *mens rea* he may be convicted of theft.

In *Wakeman*,[20] D borrowed a bicycle and failed to return it on demand. Although D was found riding the bicycle two days later, the court treated his refusal as a conversion and did not rely on his use *after* the refusal. No doubt D's refusal would now afford evidence of an appropriation. Theoretically D may have appropriated the bicycle at an even earlier stage. Once the period of loan expired D would be bound to return the bicycle and his failure to return could amount to "keeping . . . it as owner". As a practical matter, though, it would be difficult to prove a dishonest intent from a mere retention of property beyond the time when it ought to have been restored.[1]

At all events it will now be clear that the concept of appropriation is a broad one. So broad that it has been fairly asked,[2] "What about a man who boasts that he owns property which he knows he does not own?" Is a mere assertion of title capable of amounting to an appropriation? Certainly it would seem that if D has borrowed P's bicycle and D subsequently claims it is his, this would afford evidence that he is "keeping . . . it as owner". In *Wakeman*,[3] D had at one stage claimed that he was the owner of the bicycle and had paid P for it, and this seems to have been treated by the court as evidence of a conversion.

But where D is not in possession the position is not quite so straightforward. It might be said the point is entirely academic because no one is going to bring D to court in respect of vain claims to ownership.

---

[17] See above, p. 81.
[18] See further *infra* and p. 377.
[19] See further below, p. 421.
[20] (1912), 8 Cr. App. Rep. 18.
[1] See the discussion in connection with *Jackson* (1864), 9 Cox C.C. 505; above, p. 353.
[2] By Roy Stuart, "Reform of the Law of Theft", (1967) 30 M.L.R. 609, 626.
[3] (1912), 8 Cr. App. Rep. 18; *supra*.

But consider *Bloxham*.[4] Before D sells P's refrigerator to Q, he might well claim to be the owner of the refrigerator. If the sequence stops there, D has not yet sold, or attempted to sell, the refrigerator and consequently there would be no offence under s. 15. This is not a mere boast about ownership, but an essential preliminary to perpetrating a fraud on Q. Has D appropriated the refrigerator? What D has done appears not to amount to the tort of conversion because for the civil wrong

> "there must always be some active assumption of control over goods, a mere assertion of title to goods not in one's possession, unaccompanied by any other act of interference, is not a conversion".[5]

Presumably, however, because the tort requires some "serious" interference with the owner's use and the civil courts prefer to treat a mere claim of title as amounting, at most, to some other tort[6] which permits the award of a small amount of damages while conversion restricts the court to the more drastic remedy of making D pay the full value of the goods. Such considerations do not have the same force in the criminal law of theft and a mere claim of title, even by one not in possession, may amount to an appropriation. But whether in such a case D commits theft depends on whether, in addition, he intends to deprive P permanently of his property.[7]

(*f*) *Appropriation and innocent acquisition.*—It should be clear from the foregoing that the emphasis lies fairly and squarely on the dishonest appropriation of the property. The fact that D acquired the property innocently in the first place constitutes no bar whatever to a conviction of theft if D dishonestly appropriates the property at some subsequent stage. To make the point absolutely clear s. 3 (1) provides that an appropriation includes a later assumption of the rights of an owner where D has "come by the property (innocently or not) without stealing it". Strictly this part of s. 3 (1) may not be necessary but its express incorporation was probably desirable in view of certain limitations in the former law of larceny in favour of persons whose original acquisition of property was innocent.[8]

"Come by" is a convenient expression to embrace any mode of acquisition. D may have come by the property, for example, by delivery from P under a bailment, by finding a banknote in the street, by receiving a letter meant for another which is mistakenly addressed to his house, by his employer mistakenly placing extra sacks of coal on his lorry, or by a friend handing him a £5 note when he intended to deliver a £1 note. In all these cases any dishonest appropriation by D of the property will amount to theft.

(*g*) *The exception in favour of bona fide purchasers.*—Notwithstanding that there is no general limitation on liability for theft in favour of persons acquiring property innocently in the first place, s. 3 (2) of the Act imposes a particular limitation in favour of *bona fide* purchasers. S. 3, (2) provides:

> "Where property or a right or interest in property is or purports to be transferred for value to a person acting in good faith, no later assumption by him of rights which he believed himself to be acquiring shall, by reason of any defect in the transferor's title, amount to theft."

---

[4] (1943), 29 Cr. App. Rep. 37; above p. 354, footnote 12.
[5] Street, *Torts*, at p. 53.
[6] *E.g.* slander of title.
[7] And on this see below, p. 377.
[8] *Cf.* Cmnd. 2977, para. 36.

The Criminal Law Revision Committee explained this exception as follows:[9]

"A person may buy something in good faith, but may find out afterwards that the seller had no title to it, perhaps because the seller or somebody else stole it. If the buyer nevertheless keeps the thing or otherwise deals with it as owner, he could . . . be guilty of theft. It is arguable that this would be right; but on the whole it seems to us that, whatever view is taken of the buyer's moral duty, the law would be too strict if it made him guilty of theft."

The exception is in favour only of a person acquiring his interest in good faith and for value.[10] It would extend to a pledgee or a person acquiring a lien as well as a buyer of property; but if a pledgee, having discovered the pledgor's lack of title, were to, say, destroy the property he might be guilty of theft because he is assuming rights greater than those which he believed he had acquired.

2 Property

The property which may be stolen is defined in s. 4 of the Theft Act 1968, and the broad effect of this section is that all property may be stolen subject to certain exceptions in relation to land, wild growth and wild creatures. Section 4 (1) provides the general definition:

"'Property' includes money and all other property, real or personal, including things in action and other intangible property."

The one limitation on the generality of this definition, apart from the specified exceptions, is that the property must be capable of appropriation. It is easy enough to visualise how tangible property, such as land or goods, may be appropriated, but the definition also extends to intangible property and it may be as well to illustrate how intangible property may be appropriated. The short answer, of course, is that intangible property may be appropriated by any assumption of the rights of an owner in respect of it. Thus a debt might be appropriated by D where he causes P's bank account to be debited and his own credited.[11] D may not yet have withdrawn from his account the money so credited, but he has already appropriated the debt which the bank owes to P. So if D causes the Q company to transfer P's shares into D's name in the company's books, D has appropriated the shares.[12] In cases such as these D will probably be guilty of theft at an earlier stage by appropriating the cheque forms or the share certificates belonging to P, and he may frequently commit forgery or deception to carry out his fraud.

On the face of it all property is capable of appropriation but there seems to be some doubt whether electricity is capable of appropriation since the dishonest use, wasting or diverting of electricity is a separate offence under s. 13 of the Theft Act, and the Criminal Law Revision Committee observed that:

"This has to be a separate offence because owing to its nature electricity is excluded from the definition of stealing in . . . [s.] 1 (1) of the [Act]."[13]

It is not easy to see quite how electricity is excluded from theft under s. 1 (1) because, looked at as a practical rather than a metaphysical problem, the man who puts a "jumper" on his electricity meter is just as much appropriating the property of another as the man who puts a "jumper" on his gas meter.

---

[9] Cmnd. 2977, para. 37.

[10] Suppose that the *bona fide* purchaser, having discovered that the goods were stolen, gives them to E. By virtue of s. 3 (2) he is not guilty of *theft*; but is he guilty of handling contrary to s. 22 (below, p. 431) in disposing of the goods for the benefit of E? The case seems to fall literally within s. 22 unless it can be said that in assuming the rights which he believed himself to be acquiring he does not act dishonestly.

[11] *Cf. Davenport*, [1954] 1 All E.R. 602.

[12] See Smith, *Theft*, para. 133 for further discussion.

[13] Cmnd. 2977, para. 85, below, p. 379.

But this discussion of the appropriation of choses in action and electricity may serve to show that D must appropriate some property of P's. There must be an assumption by D of the rights of an owner in respect of something belonging to P. Suppose, for example, that P lends D £5 and, shortly after receiving the money but before he has spent it, D dishonestly decides that he will never repay the money. In this case, when D spends the notes given him, he does not commit theft for he is using his own money, and not appropriating P's. There remains the chose in action (the debt which D owes to P). But D has not appropriated that. He cannot appropriate P's chose by using his own money and he does not otherwise do anything (except mentally resolve not to repay which is not itself enough[14]) which amounts to an assumption of the rights of an owner in respect of P's chose in action.[15]

(*a*) *Limitations on the theft of land.*—It should be appreciated at the outset that it would have been technically possible to make land stealable in general, since land is just as capable of appropriation as goods ; such limitations as there are arise from policy considerations. Take, for example, the case (which has apparently occurred from time to time) where D moves the boundary fence between his and P's property and thus annexes some of P's land. Supposing this is done dishonestly there are no obstacles in the way of treating this as theft. D has appropriated land belonging to P with intent to deprive him permanently of it. But the Criminal Law Revision Committee, for a number of reasons[16] (such as that appropriating land by encroachment was not so widespread or socially evil that civil remedies were insufficient,[17] the civil law might give D a good title by occupation for twelve years and it would be odd if he remained even theoretically guilty of theft for ever afterwards),[18] felt that such a case ought not to be treated as theft and s. 4 (2) gives effect to this view. Section 4 (2) of the Theft Act 1968 provides:

> "A person cannot steal land, or things forming part of land and severed from it by him or by his directions, except in the following cases, that is to say—
>
> > (*a*) when he is a trustee or personal representative, or is authorised by power of attorney, or as liquidator of a company, or otherwise, to sell or dispose of land belonging to another, and he appropriates the land or anything forming part of it by dealing with it in breach of the confidence reposed in him; or
> >
> > (*b*) when he is not in possession of the land and appropriates anything forming part of the land by severing it or causing it to be severed, or after it has been severed; or
> >
> > (*c*) when, being in possession of the land under a tenancy, he appropriates the whole or part of any fixture or structure let to be used with the land.
>
> For purposes of this subsection 'land' does not include incorporeal hereditaments; 'tenancy' means a tenancy for years or any less period and includes an agreement for such a tenancy, but a person who after the end of a tenancy remains in possession as statutory tenant or otherwise is to be treated as having possession under the tenancy, and 'let' shall be construed accordingly."

(*i*) *Appropriation by trustees etc.*—The rule here is that land, or things forming part of the land, are capable of being stolen. Thus a trustee

---

[14] Above, p. 351.

[15] See further Smith, *Theft*, paras. 136–141.

[16] Cmnd. 2977, paras. 40–44.

[17] But the Committee observed (*ibid.*, para. 42) that moving boundaries was a "real problem, especially in crowded housing estates." *Cf.* the offence under s. 11 (below, p. 398) which seems to owe its origin to *three* known instances of its occurrence.

[18] But a thief of goods may equally acquire a good title after six years yet remains liable to a charge of theft.

may appropriate land held in trust by an unauthorised disposition. Of course an unauthorised dealing is not of itself theft since the other requirements of the offence must be present. If, for example, a trustee is authorised to sell the land only to A and he sells it to B because B is offering a much better price, the unauthorised sale by the trustee may not be dishonest.

(*ii*) *Appropriation by persons not in possession.*—Here, as has been shown,[19] the rule is that land as such cannot be stolen by a person not in possession. However a person not in possession can steal anything forming part of the land by severing it or by appropriating it after it has been severed. Thus it may be theft where D helps himself to the topsoil in P's garden, or to a gate, or to rose bushes, or even to growing grass. In each case the appropriation is complete upon severance,[20] but where the thing is already severed, as where the gate is lying in P's yard for repair, the appropriation would be complete, at the least, when D takes control of it.[1]

(*iii*) *Appropriation by tenants of fixtures.*—A tenant cannot steal the land of which he stands possessed nor things forming part of the land. If D, a tenant, removes topsoil from the demised premises to sell to a neighbout he is appropriating property of another (the landlord) but he is not guilty of theft. But if D's son, who is living with D, removes the topsoil for the same purpose the son would be guilty of theft because he is not "in possession" of the land although he happens to live there.

A tenant may be guilty of theft, however, where he appropriates any fixture or structure let to be used with the land. A fixture here means something annexed to land for use or ornament, such as a washbasin, cupboards or fireplace, and a structure seems to mean some structure of a moveable or temporary character, such as a garden shed or a greenhouse. A house would not be a structure in this sense.

(*b*) *Limitations on the theft of things growing wild.*—Section 4 (3) of the Act provides:

> "A person who picks mushrooms growing wild on any land, or who picks flowers, fruit or foliage from a plant growing wild on any land, does not (although not in possession of the land) steal what he picks, unless he does it for reward or for sale or other commercial purpose.
>
> For purposes of this subsection 'mushroom' includes any fungus, and 'plant' includes any shrub or tree."

In some ways this might be thought that s. 4 (3) is rather an unnecessary provision. It exempts from liability for theft one who picks wild mushrooms, or one who picks flowers, fruit or foliage "*from* a plant" (thus a person who takes the whole plant may be convicted of theft) growing wild on land unless done for sale or other commercial purpose. Picking holly branches round about Christmas time for the purpose of sale may amount to theft as may picking elderberries for making wine if the purpose is to sell the wine. The whole matter might have been left to the common sense of the police who would hardly institute proceedings where the appropriation was trivial. Of course this would leave the

---

[19] Above, p. 358.

[20] Note that if D is caught in the act of severing he is guilty only of an attempt. By attempting to sever D is of course assuming the rights of an owner and in other circumstances, (above, p. 353), this alone constitutes a complete appropriation. But in this case the effect of the subsection is to insist upon severance to complete the theft.

[1] See above, p. 353.

aggrieved landowner free to take proceedings in such trivial cases, but generally under the criminal law the person aggrieved is free to take proceedings in the most trivial case and this does not apparently lead to any serious abuse. However, the Criminal Law Revision Committee thought that

> "a provision could reasonably be criticized which made it even technically theft in all cases to pick wild flowers against the will of the landowner."[2]

(c) *Limitations on the theft of wild creatures.*—Section 4 (4) of the Act provides:

> "Wild creatures, tamed or untamed, shall be regarded as property; but a person cannot steal a wild creature not tamed nor ordinarily kept in captivity, or the carcase of any such creature, unless either it has been reduced into possession by or on behalf of another person and possession of it has not since been lost or abandoned, or another person is in course of reducing it into possession."

Wild animals while at large are not owned by anyone, nor does a landowner have a proprietary interest in such animals even where they constitute game. The landowner has the right to take wild animals and once a wild animal is caught or killed it immediately becomes the property of the landowner where this takes place, but he has no proprietary interest in such animals while at large.[3] Technically the person catching or killing the animal would not, at that precise moment, be guilty of theft since he is not then appropriating the property of another. But since, as has been shown,[4] a person may commit theft, even where he has come by the property innocently, by any subsequent assumption of ownership there would be no difficulty in finding such an assumption at a later stage. Indeed, unless the catcher immediately releases it, or the killer does nothing about appropriating the carcase, each would be guilty of theft.

Though this would be the position under the general law of theft, s. 4 (4) creates an exception which is, substantially, in favour of poaching. Thus if D takes rabbits running wild on P's land he is not guilty of theft, though he may commit an offence in relation to poaching,[5] and in this case it does not become theft though the poacher takes the rabbit for purposes of sale.

It is, however, possible to steal wild creatures where these have been tamed or are ordinarily kept in captivity. A tiger may be stolen from a zoo, and if it has escaped it may be stolen while at large because it is "ordinarily" kept in captivity. Wild animals may also be stolen when they are in process of being reduced into possession by or on behalf of another. A lazy poacher who picks up the pheasants shot from the skies by P is a thief, as is a gamekeeper who keeps for himself a pheasant which he shot for his employer. But if P, having shot a pheasant, cannot find it in the brush and gives up the search, a subsequent appropriation by D does not make D a thief.[6]

3   Belonging to Another

At first sight it is a perfectly obvious proposition that a man may steal only the property of another. But appearances can be deceptive. In the vast majority of

---

[2] Cmnd. 2977, para. 47.
[3] *Cf. Gott* v. *Measures*, [1948] 1 K.B. 234; [1947] 2 All E.R. 609; below, p. 463.
[4] Above, p. 356.
[5] *E.g.* under the Poaching Prevention Act 1862; and as to the taking etc. of deer or fish see Sch. 1 of the Theft Act 1968.
[6] Something is lost when it cannot be found, but something which has been lost has not necessarily been abandoned. *Cf.* Smith, *Theft*, para. 130. As to abandonment, see *ibid.*, para. 72

cases there is of course no difficulty. D snatches P's handbag; the handbag is owned and possessed by P and clearly D has appropriated property belonging to P. In some cases, however, it may not be quite so clear to whom the handbag belongs or whether it belongs to anyone at all.

Moreover property in a given case may belong to both D and P; they may, for example, be joint owners of the property. Obviously there is no reason in principle why D should not be treated as a thief if he dishonestly appropriates P's share, and he is so treated under the Theft Act. It is easy enough to accept the good sense of the idea that D may steal property belonging to himself if it also belongs to another, but the idea is capable of refinement which sometimes leads to difficulty.

Then, again, there are situations in which, though the property in law belongs only to D, it is desirable that his dishonest appropriation of it should be treated as theft. Take a simple illustration suggested by the facts of *Hassall*.[7] There members of a club paid sums of money each week to D, the treasurer, on the understanding that the following Christmas D would return to each member the total sum paid in; but in fact D misappropriated the money. In this situation D becomes the owner of the money (it was never expected that D should return to each member the identical coins given him) and the relationship between D and the members is essentially that of debtor and creditor. Here is a situation where the property in law belongs to D,[8] but it is a situation in which D ought to be treated as a thief and ought not to be allowed to shelter behind his legal ownership. Accordingly, s. 5 provides that in some situations, notwithstanding that D is the owner of the property, the property shall be treated as belonging to another even though that other has no (or only a doubtful) right or interest in the property. Once more the basic idea is simple enough to grasp but it can lead to difficulties in application.

This, in broad outline, explains the purport of s. 5. The section may now be looked at in more detail.

(a) Property belonging to another: the general rule.—Section 5 (1) of the Theft Act 1968 provides:

> "Property shall be regarded as belonging to any person having possession or control of it, or having in it any proprietary right or interest (not being an equitable interest arising only from an agreement to transfer or grant an interest)."

In the ordinary case property is stolen from one who both owns and possesses it by one who has no interest in the property whatever. Section 5 (1) covers this case of course but it goes much further. Suppose that P lends a book to Q and that Q is showing the book to R when D snatches the book from R's hands and makes off with it. Here D has stolen the book from R (who has control of it), and Q (who has possession of it), and P (who also has a proprietary interest —ownership—in it).

As we have just seen it does not matter that the property happens to belong to D in one of these senses if at the same time it also belongs to P and it is D's intention dishonestly to deprive P permanently of his interest. Thus in the above illustration if R were to dishonestly appropriate the book he would steal it from

---

[7] (1861), Le. & Ca. 56.
[8] See further below, p. 364.

both P and Q,[9] and if Q were to dishonestly appropriate the book he would steal it from P.

Conversely P, the owner, may steal the book from Q, his bailee. While the book is in Q's possession it belongs to Q for the purposes of s. 5 (1) which does not place any limitations on the class of persons who may steal from him. Of course the circumstances in which P's appropriation of his own property will amount to theft will not be of common occurrence since P may easily be able to show a claim of right.[10] But consider the facts of *Rose* v. *Matt*.[11] D had left his travelling clock with P as security against the unpaid price of goods purchased from P, on the understanding that if D did not pay within the month P was to be free to sell the clock. Later on D returned to the shop and took back his clock when the attendant was not looking. In this case D was acting dishonestly because he was cheating P of his security for the unpaid purchase money, and he intended to deprive P permanently of his proprietary interest in the clock. It seems clear that this would amount to theft under the Act.

So, too, P might steal this book from R who has only the control of it. In the circumstances of *Rose* v. *Matt*.[12] D steals the clock not only from P but also from the attendant since the attendant would have at least the control of the property in the shop.

(i) *Possession or control.*—To a degree possession and control may overlap, and it is not important to pursue any possible distinction between them because property is treated as belonging to P if he has either possession or control. It is the limits of these concepts which is important, not the difference between them.

Possession requires both an intention to possess and some degree of dominion in fact. If P and D both see a wallet on the pavement, both may have the same intent to possess it, but until one of them seizes it neither has possession. Once P seizes it he has both possession and control. If he hands it to D just to show D wha the has got, it would normally be said that P retains possession while D has control.

Possession and control are not, however, always as clear cut as in this illustration. There P's intent existed in respect of a specific article and he reduced it into his actual control—he had it in his hands. But it is not necessary to have, or ever to have had, control of a thing in this sense in order to have possession. An Electricity Board may have possession of the coins inserted in a domestic meter although the Board does not know at any given moment how many coins, if any, are in the meter.[13] Similarly, a householder normally has possession of the whole contents of his house even though he cannot itemise his goods. He may consign unwanted articles to his attic or cellar and forget about them, but he still retains possession. It is not, then, essential that P's intent should exist in respect of a specific thing: it may be enough for P's intent to exist in respect of all the goods situate about his premises. In *Hibbert* v. *McKiernan*,[14] it was held that a golf club possessed

---

[9] *Cf. Thompson* (1862), Le. & Ca. 225. D made off with a sovereign which P handed him to buy a ticket for her because she was unable to make her way through the crowd before a ticket office. This would be theft by D.

[10] Below, p. 371.

[11] [1951] 1 K.B. 810; [1951] 1 All E.R. 361.

[12] *Supra.*

[13] *Cf. Martin* v. *Marsh*, [1955] Crim. L.R. 781. But see [1956] Crim. L.R. 74.

[14] [1948] 2 K.B. 142; [1948] 1 All E.R. 860. *Cf. Williams* v. *Phillips* (1957), 41 Cr. App. Rep. 5.

golf balls lost by members on the links although the club did not know at any given moment how many balls there were, nor where they were. The club intended to possess the balls and they were in control of them to the extent that they controlled the land upon which they were lying. It follows that anyone dishonestly appropriating the balls would be dishonestly appropriating the property of the club.[15]

(ii) *Any proprietary right or interest.*—Property is also to be regarded as belonging to any person having in it "any proprietary right or interest". Obviously, then, property may be stolen from the owner although at the time of the appropriation the owner is not in possession or control; and even though the owner may never have been in possession or control. If D sells goods to P (ownership passing to P) and D remains in possession, a dishonest appropriation by E will be theft from both D and P. Moreover if D dishonestly appropriates the goods he steals them from P.[16] The section extends to "*any* proprietary right of interest", and whether a person has a proprietary right or interest is a question of civil law. A person who owns, possesses or controls property has a proprietary right or interest in the property, but in what other circumstances a proprietary right or interest may exist is somewhat speculative.[17] In an American case[18] P purchased flowers from D which he laid on the grave of a friend; D entered the cemetery that night and took back the flowers in order to sell them again. It was held that P retained a proprietary interest in the flowers so that D could steal them from P, and it was indicated that Q, the owner of the cemetery, would also have a proprietary interest so that the flowers could be stolen from Q as well. But in this case it could fairly be said that P retained possession of the flowers,[19] and that Q, at least if he looked after the cemetery lot, would have control of them. In *Rose* v. *Matt*[20] Lord GODDARD, C.J., spoke of P as having a "special property" in the clock, but here P's special property was his possession.

D may appropriate property which belongs to P in any of the senses described in s. 5 (1). It does not matter that P's interest is precarious or that it may be short-lived; wild birds reared by P may belong to P although they may "betake themselves to the woods and fields" as soon as they are old enough to fly.[1] It does not matter that someone exists

---

[15] *Cf. Rowe* (1859), 8 Cox C.C. 139, where D, employed to clean out P's canal, was convicted of stealing in appropriating iron found by him on the bed of the canal. For a case holding that P became the owner of coins thrown into his fountain for luck, see *The Times*, 8 August, 1964. But *cf. Bridges* v. *Hawkesworth* (1851), 21 L.J.Q.B. 75, which is authority for the proposition that a person finding property in the public part of a shop is entitled to the property as against the shopkeeper; consequently the property so found does not belong to the shopkeeper and cannot be stolen from him. Presumably the finder of goods on the highway is entitled to the goods as against the highway authority. For a general discussion of the finder's rights as against the landowner see Street, *Torts*, (4th ed.), 39.

[16] And of course (see above, p. 362) P may steal the goods from D by, say, surreptitiously removing them without payment.

[17] Arguably anyone who can sue in trespass, detinue or conversion in respect of the property has a proprietary right or interest. Perhaps anyone who may trace the property at law or in equity has a proprietary right or interest.

[18] *Bustler* v. *State* (1944), 184 S.E. 2d 24 (S.C. of Tennessee). Note that D may be convicted of stealing property belonging to a person unknown.

[19] *Cf. Edwards & Stacey* (1877), 13 Cox C.C. 384.

[20] [1951] 1 K.B. 810; [1951] 1 All E.R. 361, above, p. 362.

[1] *Cf. Shickle* (1868), L.R. 1 C.C.R. 158.

who has a better right to the property than P: a thief may steal from a thief.[2] Any power to exclude others, however small, will suffice.

(*iii*) *Equitable interests:*—"Any proprietary right or interest" extends to both legal and equitable proprietary interests. Where property is subject to a trust it belongs to both the trustee (legal interest) and beneficiary (equitable interest) and it may be stolen from either.[3] But in the case of equitable interests s. 5 (1) introduces a limitation, and property is not to be regarded as belonging to a person who has an equitable interest arising only from an agreement to transfer or grant an interest. The limitation is of no great practical importance. In some circumstances an agreement to sell may give the intending buyer an equitable interest in the property[4] and this provision makes it clear that the seller cannot commit theft by reselling the property to another.

(*b*) *Trust property.*—Section 5 (2) of the Theft Act 1968 provides:

"Where property is subject to a trust, the persons to whom it belongs shall be regarded as including any person having a right to enforce the trust, and an intention to defeat the trust shall be regarded accordingly as an intention to deprive of the property any person having that right."

In the ordinary case appropriation of trust property by a trustee is covered not only by this subsection but also by s. 5 (1) because the beneficiary ordinarily has a proprietary interest and accordingly the trust property belongs to the beneficiary within s. 5 (1). But in some exceptional circumstances there may be no ascertained beneficiary. This occurs in the case of "purpose" trusts whether charitable[5] or private,[6] where the object is to effect some purpose rather than benefit ascertainable individuals. To meet such cases s. 5 (2) goes further than s. 5 (1) by providing that the property is to be treated as belonging to anyone who has a right to enforce the trust.[7]

(*c*) *Property received for a partcular purpose.*—It has already been mentioned[8] that it is in some circumstances right that D should be convicted of theft notwithstanding that he is the legal owner of the property, and the case of *Hassall*[9] was given as an illustration of the kind of situation envisaged. In *Hassall,* though D became the legal owner of the money paid in, it would be clear, even to someone who knew no law, that D was not free to do what he liked with the money. He was under an obligation to deal with the money in a particular way. He might have kept the money in a box or he might have kept it in an account at the bank, but, one way or another, he had to keep the fund in existence. Consequently D's dishonest appropriation of the fund would now amount to theft by virtue of s. 5 (3)[10] which provides:

---

[2] *Cf. Clarke,* referred to at [1956] Crim. L.R. 369–70.

[3] See further s. 5 (2), *infra.*

[4] See Smith, *Theft,* paras. 77–79; Griew, *Theft,* 19.

[5] *E.g.,* where money is given to D in trust for the improvement of schools in a particular locality.

[6] *E.g.,* where money is given to D in trust for the maintenance of a tomb, or for the upkeep of animals.

[7] In the foregoing examples this would be, respectively, the Attorney-General and the person entitled to the residue of the estate.

[8] Above, p. 361.

[9] (1861), Le. & Ca. 56; above, p. 361.

[10] It would seem to be the case that D's appropriation of the money would amount to theft even without s. 5 (3). The depositors surely retain a proprietary right or interest in the money deposited in such circumstances. Indeed in all cases falling within s. 5 (3) it seems clear that the person from, or on whose account, the property is received would have a proprietary right or interest and thus the case would be covered by s. 5 (1). However, s. 5 (3) does make the point explicitly clear.

"When a person receives property from or on account of another, and is under an obligation to the other to retain and deal with that property of its proceeds in a particular way, the property or proceeds shall be regarded (as against him) as belonging to the other."

It is easy enough to appreciate that in *Hassall* D was under an obligation to deal with the money deposited in a particular way but it is more difficult to say, in general terms, when a person "is under an obligation to the other to retain and deal with that property or its proceeds in a particular way." The essential notion is that D must be under a fiduciary obligation with regard to the property which he receives. The idea of fiduciary obligation conveys accurately the essential requirement: the property, though it may be owned only by D, must be earmarked in D's hands for certain purposes of P's.

Take a simple case of loan. P lends D £10—and, having received the money, D dishonestly decides never to repay P and subsequently denies that P made the loan. D is not guilty of theft. Clearly D is acting dishonestly and the view might be taken that his case is indistinguishable from that of a Hassall who misappropriates £10 from his workmates' holiday fund; but he is not a thief under the Theft Act.[11] He does not appropriate property belonging to another, and the property (the £10) cannot under the Act be regarded as belonging to another since he was under no obligation whatever to deal with it in a particular way. It was D's to deal with as he liked.

But suppose that D had agreed to do certain work for P and that P made D an advance of £10 on the agreed price for the job. If D does not do the work, and never intended to do it, it may be that D can be convicted of obtaining the £10 by deception;[12] but he cannot be convicted of stealing the £10. Again the money belongs only to him, and, although it was advanced to him in connection with a particular transaction, it was not received by him to deal with in a particular way. D may again spend the £10 as he likes. However it is just in this sort of situation that D, in order to ensure an advance payment, will tell P that he needs cash in advance in order to procure materials for the job. When this happens D will often be guilty of obtaining the money by deception, but he is also guilty of theft because he is now under an obligation to deal with the money in a particular way.

Sometimes—perhaps less frequently nowadays than used to be the case—an employer requires an employee to pay a sum of money as security for his honesty. When the evidence shows that the money was to be placed as deposit at a bank and to be returnable at the termination of the employment, the employer may be convicted of theft if he appropriates it;[13] but if the evidence shows that this transaction is substantially one of loan, and it is clear that the employer, though he is under an obligation to repay at the termination of the employment, is entitled to use the money deposited with him as his own then the money would not have been received for a particular purpose.[14]

The contract of sale or return is worth noting in this connection. In the ordinary case of sale or return P delivers goods to D on the terms that D will return them within a certain time unless D decides to buy them. Should D sell the goods to a third party he makes himself, *vis à vis* P, the buyer of the goods and must pay the agreed purchase price to P. Suppose then that P delivers jewellery

---

[11] Consider why the law does not treat as a thief a debtor who dishonestly decides to avoid payment.
[12] See below, p. 382.
[13] *Cf. Smith*, [1924] 2 K.B. 194.
[14] *Cf. Hotine* (1904), 68 J.P. 142.

to D which D sells to Q and then absconds with the purchase price. D cannot be convicted of stealing the jewellery for he has not appropriated it.[15] Does D steal the proceeds? It is submitted that he does not because his only obligation is to pay P the agreed purchase price;[16] he is not, when he receives the money from Q, under any obligation to deal with it in any particular way. In other words, the buyer under a sale or return transaction is in the same position as any other purchaser of goods who has not paid the price: he is no more than P's debtor for the price.

It might be thought that another reason why the buyer under a contract of sale or return is not under an obligation to deal with the proceeds in a particular way is that he receives the proceeds from Q and not from P. But this will not do. Section 5 (3) applies when D receives property "from or on account of another" and clearly D may receive property from Q on the account of P.[17]

Thus it is not necessary that the fiduciary duty should arise out of the transaction between D and the person delivering the property to him; it is enough that D's fiduciary duty arises out of a relationship with a person other than the deliveror. To go back to the sale or return illustration: D's immunity there was not based on the fact that he received the money from Q; it was based on the fact that he did not receive the money from Q on P's account. It would be another matter if D had been simply an agent for the sale of the jewellery. Then D would not become the buyer of the jewellery at all, and the money paid by Q would belong to P and not to D. In this situation D might in fact become the owner of the money (as where it is expected that D will account for the money but is not expected to hand over the very coins and notes which he receives); nonetheless D has a duty to keep the fund of money in existence and his appropriation of it may amount to theft.

(d) *Property got by mistake.*—By s. 5 (4):

> "Where a person gets property by another's mistake, and is under an obligation to make restoration (in whole or in part) of the property or its proceeds or of the value thereof, then to the extent of that obligation the property or proceeds shall be regarded (as against him) as belonging to the person entitled to restoration, and an intention not to make restoration shall be regarded accordingly as an intention to deprive that person of the property or proceeds."

This provision may be explained by reference to the facts of *Moynes* v. *Coopper.*[18] In this case D, a labourer employed by P, was given an advance of pay by the site agent amounting to £6 19s. 6½d. Unaware that this advance had been made, P's wages clerk paid D the full weekly wage of £7 3s. 4d. and D dishonestly kept all of the money.

The difficulty with this case is that in law the whole of the £7 3s. 4d. belongs to D. The wages clerk made a mistake of course, but his mistake was not such as would prevent ownership of all the money passing to D. Had the clerk known of the advance he would have paid D only 3s. 9½d; nevertheless the clerk did intend to pay the full amount, and he was authorised as P's wages clerk to pay wages. The case is now covered by s. 5 (4) and D steals the excess payment if he dishonestly appropriates it; although D becomes the owner of the money he is under a legal obligation, at the very least, to repay the value of the excess payment.

But why, it may be asked, is all this trouble taken to deal with this particular

---

[15] "Appropriation" is an unauthorised assumption of ownership; see above, p. 351.
[16] *Cf.* Hughes, "Sale or Return, Agents and Larceny", [1963] Crim L.R. 312, 411.
[17] *Cf. Grubb*, [1915] 2 K.B. 683.
[18] [1956] 1 Q.B. 439; [1956] 1 All E.R. 450

kind of debtor? In terms of moral turpitude only the finest shading separates a Moynes from the ordinary debtor who dishonestly decides not to repay his loan. Under the former law Moynes was in fact acquitted, but in view of the criticism which his acquittal attracted it was no doubt felt necessary to bring such conduct within the net of the criminal law.

Section 5 (4) will cover any situation in which property is got by mistake and D is under an obligation to make restoration of the property, its proceeds or its value. It would cover the well known case of *Cundy* v. *Lindsay*[19] where the rogue Blenkarn, having induced P to believe that he was dealing with Blenkiron & Co., dishonestly appropriated the handkerchiefs which P consigned to Blenkirons. But in this connection two points should be noted. The first is that Blenkarn's fraud would be more naturally treated as obtaining property by deception. There is thus an overlap at this point between the offences of obtaining property by deception and theft. The extent and implications, of this overlap are considered hereafter.[20]

The second point to note is that while s. 5 (4) certainly extends to conduct such as Blenkarn's, Blenkarn may be convicted of theft without resort to s. 5 (4) at all. When P consigned the handkerchiefs, he intended to pass ownership not to Blenkarn, of whom P had never heard, but to Blenkiron & Co., a respectable company with which P had dealt in the past. Consequently ownership remained in P; P thus retained a proprietary interest and Blenkarn could be convicted of theft by virtue of s. 5 (1).

Section 5 (4) then, is not there merely to provide for cases where a mistake has been made; it is there to provide for that kind of case (which will arise only exceptionally in practice) where the mistake does not prevent ownership from passing to D, *and* D is under an obligation (by virtue of the civil law of course) to make restoration of the property, its proceeds or its value. D must be under an obligation. P may sell a valuable antique to D in the mistaken belief, as D well knows, that it is merely a reproduction. D is not a thief merely because he takes advantage of P's ignorance; the contract is binding and D is under no obligation whatever to make restoration.

But when does the law impose upon D such an obligation? The answer to this question involves a consideration of the civil law of unjust enrichment,[1] and no simple answer can be given for the law is by no means straightforward and is not free from considerable subtlety. This may mean that D's liability for theft can turn upon a consideration of fine points of law remote from the central question of D's dishonesty.[2] But to a degree this sort of complexity is inevitable in a law of theft since the law is defined by reference to a law of property which itself is complex. Even so, s. 5 (4) is open to objection in that it artificially treats property as belonging to P when in law it belongs to D and, unlike s. 5 (2),[3] and, possibly, s. 5 (3),[4] which may also artificially treat property as belonging to P although P has no proprietary interest in it, is not so precise in its operation.

(e) Property of corporations.—Property may of course belong to a corporation just as much as an individual, and may be stolen from a corporation.

---

[19] (1878), 3 App. Cas. 459.
[20] Below, p. 388.
[1] See Goff & Jones, *The Law of Restitution* (1966), Ch. 3.
[2] *Cf.* Griew, *Theft*, at p. 23; Smith, *Theft*, para. 99.
[3] See above, p. 364.
[4] See above, p. 364, footnote 10.

Normally the legal personality of a corporation continues, notwithstanding changes of membership, until the corporation is dissolved, but in the case of a corporation sole (a bishop of the Established Church, for example) a vacancy may occur owing to the death of the incumbent. Section 5 (5) accordingly provides:

> "Property of a corporation sole shall be regarded as belonging to the corporation notwithstanding a vacancy in the corporation."

(*f*) *The effect of consent.*—Where P consents to the appropriation of his property by D and D knows this, there can be no theft since D is not acting dishonestly; indeed D does not act dishonestly if he believes that P would have consented had he known of the appropriation and the circumstances of it.[5] But it may happen that, quite unknown to D, P is willing that D should appropriate his property. A typical instance of this is where an employee is approached by D with a plan to steal from the employer which requires the co-operation of the employee. The employee then informs his employer of the plan, and the employer instructs him to go along with it while he calls in the police to help catch D in the act. Here the employer agrees to his employee handing over the property to D, and to that extent he consents to the appropriation of his property by D. But there is nothing in the Act which indicates that P's consent to an appropriation is, as such, a bar to a conviction for theft. Since D knows nothing of P's consent, and clearly does not believe that P would have consented, he is acting dishonestly; and when he takes the property from the employee he is appropriating the property of P because the property still belongs to P.

But if the effect of P's consent is to vest the ownership in the property in D before the appropriation then there can be no theft since the property would no longer belong to P. In the illustration just given it is manifest that P's consent to his employee handing over the property to D does not vest the ownership of that property in D. But there are situations in which it is more difficult to say whether the effect of P's consent is to vest ownership in D, and two in particular are worth a little exploration.

(*i*)   *Consent and fraud.*—Anyone familiar with the civil case on fraud and mistake will know that it is not always easy to determine whether the fraud does or does not have the effect of preventing the passing of ownership from P to D. If the fraud is such that ownership does not pass to D[6] then the property still belongs to P and D may be convicted of stealing it. If, however, ownership passes to D, D may not be convicted of theft unless the case is caught by s. 5 (4) which, as we have seen,[7] treats the property as belonging to P if D is under an obligation to make restoration.

The moral of this exercise is as follows. If D has by fraud caused P to part with his property, the sensible course is to charge D with obtaining by deception contrary to s. 15 of the Theft Act. Under s. 15 these difficulties do not arise for D may be convicted whether ownership in the property passes to him or not.[8]

(*ii*) *Consent and imtimidation.*—Where P is obliged to hand over property because he has been intimidated by D into so doing, P might be said to

---

[5] See s. 2 (1) (b) of the Act, below, p. 371.
[6] *Cundy* v. *Lindsay* (1873), 3 App. Cas 459; above, p. 367, provides an illustration of this. *Cf. Ingram* v. *Little*, [1961] 1 Q.B. 31; [1960] 3 All E.R. 332.
[7] Above, p. 366, and below, p. 388.
[8] See further below, p. 386.

assent to the handing over but he is unlikely in any real sense to assent to the appropriation of his property by D, and accordingly D may be convicted of theft. Difficulty arises where D demands that P transfer ownership to him, as by forcing P to make a gift or sale of the property. It might be thought on principle that P does not in fact transfer owner-ship. There is no real intention on P's part to do so; the property still belongs to him and D may be convicted of stealing it.

It is thought that this is the position in law; but it has to be admitted that the little civil authority there is,[9] and the general opinion of com-mentators[10] seems to show that intimidation renders a transaction voidable rather than void. Accordingly D would not commit theft because ownership would be transferred notwithstanding the intimi-dation, and the property would belong to D, not to P.

Again the problem may be obviated: this time by charging D with blackmail contrary to s. 21 of this Act.[11] In this sort of situation D is making an unwarranted demand with menaces and, so far as blackmail is concerned, it does not matter whether D obtains ownership or not. The problem would not be obviated, however, by charging D with robbery under s. 8 since robbery is merely an aggravated form of stealing. Suppose that D wishes to purchase a particular painting from P but P is unwilling to sell. D thereupon threatens P with violence unless he does sell so P hands over the painting and receives payment. D might now be convicted of blackmail, but can he be convicted of theft or robbery? It is submitted that he can. The civil cases, such as they are, are hardly decisive since the result in them would have been the same whether the contract was considered void or voidable. It is difficult to resist the conclusion that

> ". . . in all contracts it is essential that there should be consent. Not even the officious by-stander would care to testify that a person with a gun to his head appeared to consent to the transaction in hand, whatever kind of contract was involved."[12]

So far it has been assumed that the duress takes the form of physical harm to P, actual or threatened. But what if the threat is not one to use physical violence? Suppose, for example, that D, a newspaper proprietor, tells P that unless P pays him money he will attack the credit-worthiness of P's business in his newspaper, and P pays the money demanded.[13] This is best treated as a case of blackmail, but could D also be convicted of stealing the money? Does D become the owner of the money or does the money still belong to P? Again an earlier case implies that ownership does not pass to D in this situation, but again the particular point was not argued.[14] Much might depend on the nature of the threat; not every threat will necessarily nullify P's assent to the appropriation. The common sense approach would be

---

[9] *Whelpdale's Case* (1604), 5 Co. Rep. 119a.

[10] See, *e.g.*, Cheshire & Fifoot, *The Law of Contract* (6th ed.), 253; Treitel, *Law of Contract* (2nd ed.), 286; but *cf.* Lanham, "Duress and Void Contracts" (1966), 29 M.L.R. 615; Hooper, "Larceny by Intimidation", [1965] Crim. L.R. 532 and 592.

[11] Below, p. 403.

[12] Lanham, "Duress and Void Contracts" (1966), 29 M.L.R. 615, 619. *Cf. McGrath* (1869), L.R. 1 C.C.R. 205; *Lovell* (1881), 8 Q.B.D. 185; and see further Smith, *Theft*, para. 53.

[13] *Cf. Boyle & Merchant*, [1914] 3 K.B. 399.

[14] *Boyle & Merchant*, see last footnote.

15

". . . to pose the question 'was there consent' or perhaps 'would the officious by-stander say that [P] consented to the transaction?' This would be a question of fact in each case, though the nature of the threat would always be a very important factor."[15]

In cases of doubt, however, it would be better, if the facts will support it, to charge blackmail or deception.

(2) MENS REA

An appropriation of property belonging to another amounts to theft if it is done (1) dishonestly, and (2) with the intention of permanently depriving the other of it.

1 Dishonesty

Everyone has some idea of what is honest and what is dishonest conduct. Perhaps no two people would have absolutely identical views, but most people would find that their views substantially coincide. And it may be safely guessed, the views of most other people would substantially coincide with those of the law. After all, the law seeks here only to represent the standards of right thinking members of society generally. Consequently the bulk of cases give rise to no problems whatever. But there is in some cases—as always—room for some difference of view. Everyone would agree that it was dishonest of Hassall[16] to appropriate the savings of his workmates; there is more room for argument where D appropriates money to which he believes himself morally entitled, or where he appropriates money which he intends to repay, or goods which he intends to replace.

"Dishonestly" in the Theft Act 1968 replaces the requirement in the former law that D should act "fraudulently and without a claim of right made in good faith". The Criminal Law Revision Committee felt that "dishonest" was a better word than "fraudulently", being easier for the layman to understand.[17] In this instance some reference to the cases on fraudulent conduct is inevitable in order to elucidate what is dishonest conduct. Such cases are no longer authoritative of course,[18] but in so far as they are indicative of attitudes to the conduct in question it would be hard to gainsay their relevance. It is unlikely that attitudes will change very much on this issue whether the relevant adverb is "fraudulently" or "dishonestly".

The Committee thought that "dishonestly" would probably stand without definition,[19] but decided on a partial definition. Section 2 accordingly provides:

"(1) A person's appropriation of property belonging to another is not to be regarded as dishonest—

(a) if he appropriates the property in the belief that he has in law the right to deprive the other of it, on behalf of himself or of a third person; or

(b) if he appropriates the property in the belief that he would have the other's consent if the other knew of the appropriation and the circumstances of it, or

(c) (except where the property came to him as trustee or personal representative) if he appropriates the property in the belief that the person to whom the property belongs cannot be discovered by taking reasonable steps.

(2) A person's appropriation of property belonging to another may be dishonest notwithstanding that he is willing to pay for the property."

---

[15] Lanham, *op. cit.*, 621. And see above, p. 142.
[16] Above, p. 361.
[17] Cmnd. 2977, para. 39.
[18] See above, p. 349.
[19] *Loc. cit.*

(*a*) *Belief in legal right.*—D does not commit theft where he appropriates property in the belief that he is in law entitled to deprive P of the property. Thus if D mistakenly believes that he owns P's umbrella, his appropriation of it would not be dishonest whether his mistake, or ignorance, is of fact or law. Moreover, s. 2 (1) (a) makes it clear that D will not commit theft where he appropriates P's umbrella in the belief that it belongs to E on whose behalf D is acting.[20] It may be that E dishonestly told D that the umbrella was his; nevertheless if D acts in good faith he will not be guilty of theft though E will be.

Of course it is all very easy and all very reasonable to make mistakes about umbrellas. One umbrella often looks uncommonly like another. But what if D's mistake is unreasonable? D may make an unreasonable mistake of fact or law, or he may unreasonably believe that he has a legal right which the law does not recognise at all. Suppose, for example, that D, honestly believing that upon marriage a wife's property belongs in law to her husband, sells his wife's clothes. His belief is (probably) unreasonable and the law recognises no such claim. It seems clear, however, that he would not be guilty of theft. The Act says that D's appropriation is not to be regarded as dishonest "if he appropriates the property in the belief that *he* has in law the right to deprive the other of it". It would be difficult to read into this any objective requirement of reasonableness.

(*b*) *Belief in the other's consent.*—Obviously D is not acting dishonestly where, as he knows, P is willing that D should appropriate his property and deprive him permanently of it. It may happen, however, that P is not in fact given the opportunity to express assent or dissent, but D believes that he would have done so had he been asked. Section 2 (1) (b) makes it clear that D is not a thief if he believes that D would have assented. Again, the single criterion appears to be the honesty of D's belief and it does not matter that it is in the circumstances unreasonable.

But D must believe not only that P would have consented to the appropriation but that P would have consented to the appropriation in the particular circumstances. D may believe that his next-door neighbour would consent to his appropriating a pint of milk from his doorstep when D himself had forgotten to leave an order for the milkman; but may believe that his neighbour would not consent to D's appropriating the milk in order to sell it at a profit to a thirsty hitch-hiker who is passing by.

(*c*) *Belief that property has been lost.*—Property which has been lost, as opposed to abandoned,[1] continues to belong to the loser and accordingly anyone appropriating lost property would normally be appropriating property belonging to another. But where the owner of lost property cannot be found by taking reasonable steps, no one regards the appropriation of that lost property as dishonest; better that D should have the use of it rather than it be put to no use at all. Section 2 (1) (c) provides accordingly.

Here again it seems clear enough that if D honestly believes that the person to whom the property belongs cannot be traced by taking reasonable steps, he is not a thief although any reasonable person would have appreciated that the owner could be traced by taking the most simple measures. D may be stupid in not appreciating that the owner of the wig he finds on the floor of the law court

---

[20] *Cf. Knight & Roffey* (1781), 2 East P.C. 510.
[1] *Cf. Hibbert* v. *McKiernan*, [1948] 2 K.B. 142; [1948] 1 All E.R. 860.

cannot be traced by taking reasonable steps, but stupidity is no substitute for dishonesty. What are reasonable steps would depend on the circumstances, including of course the value of the thing found and the place where it is found. It may be that when D finds, say, a number of banknotes he believes that the owner cannot be traced, but some days later learns of facts which lead him to believe that the owner can be traced. If D now appropriates the money he is acting dishonestly and may be convicted of theft. If, however, D is fortunate enough to have spent the money before he learns that the owner might be traced he cannot be convicted of theft. His appropriation when it took place was not dishonest and now, when he might have acted dishonestly, there is nothing left to appropriate.

(*d*) *Other cases.*—Section 2 (1) contains only a partial definition and conduct is not to be regarded as dishonest simply because it cannot be brought within the subsection. Two further subsections touch on the question of dishonesty. One is s. 1 (2) which provides:

> "It is immaterial whether the appropriation is made with a view to gain or is made for the thief's own benefit."

Normally, of course, people steal to gain something for themselves,[2] but this subsection makes it clear that an appropriation may amount to theft although this motive is lacking.

> "The subsection will prevent argument that it is not theft to take something which is useless to the taker or to take something with the intention of immediately destroying it."[3]

Thus it may be theft for D to destroy or hide away ledgers belonging to P because the ledgers provide evidence that D's friend had been misappropriating P's money.[4]

The other provision is s. 2 (2) which states:

> "A person's appropriation of property belonging to another may be dishonest notwithstanding that he is willing to pay for the property."

This subsection meets a possible argument that an appropriation cannot amount to theft by virtue only of the fact that D is willing to pay for the property. Obviously all the circumstances must be considered along with D's willingness to pay. In an old case[5] a traveller met a fisherman and, upon the latter's refusal to sell him any fish, took some from him by force and threw down money much above its value. It was doubted whether the traveller was acting dishonestly but it is thought that in circumstances such as these the traveller would now be convicted of theft or of robbery. Certainly it would be an undesirable principle that D should be able to take what he wants from another without fear of any criminal sanction provided only that he is willing to pay. Nevertheless, as will appear, it is possible to imagine circumstances in which it is arguable that D's intention to pay, or to repay, shows that he is not acting dishonestly.

The Theft Act does not, then, provide an exhaustive definition of dishonesty.[6] As a practical matter the definition covers virtually all situations of any common

---

[2] As to gain see s. 34 (2) of the Act, below, p. 406. Note that where s. 4 (3) applies (above, p. 359) D commits theft only where in effect, he has a view of gain.
[3] Cmnd. 2977, Annex. 2.
[4] *Cf. Cabbage* (1815), Rus. & Ry. 292.
[5] *The Fisherman's Case* (1584), 2 East P.C. 661.
[6] For an argument that "dishonestly" might have been exhaustively defined, see MacKenna, "The Undefined Adverb in Criminal Statutes", [1966] Crim. L.R. 548, 553.

occurrence, but it may be worth considering two instances where the question of dishonesty may be said to be at large.

The first is where D acts under a moral claim of right. D might appropriate property belonging to P believing that he is morally entitled to it; in such a case D might know that he has no legal right or simply not consider whether he has any legal right. In either event it would seem that he may be convicted of theft.[7] Under the former law it was held that D was acting fraudulently where he appropriated money belonging to his employer in the honest belief that he ought to have been promoted and was thus entitled to a higher salary.[8] It seems unlikely in the extreme, though the matter is now theoretically open, that the courts will hold[9] that a person acting merely under a moral claim of right is not acting dishonestly.

The second instance arises where D appropriates money or goods intending to return equivalent money or goods at a later stage. In the recent case of *Sinclair v. Neighbour*,[10] a civil action for wrongful dismissal, D had "borrowed" money from his employer's till to place a bet and returned the money the following day. He left his I.O.U. in the till and made no secret of the fact among his fellow employees that he had borrowed the money. But he did not ask his employer's permission since he knew it would not have been given. It was held that D had been properly dismissed since his conduct was inconsistent with his duty towards his employer.

But did D steal the money from the till? Was he acting dishonestly?[11]

There is an initial matter to be disposed of. Although many might say in common parlance that D had "borrowed" the money (and borrowing is not in general theft because there is no permanent deprivation), D did not, strictly, borrow the money. He deprived P permanently of it because it must have been the case that the money he took was passed on to the bookmaker with whom he placed the bet, and he would have replaced it with *other* money the following day. There is then no difficulty here in showing permanent deprivation. Consequently D has appropriated property belonging to P intending to deprive him permanently of it; he does not act under a legal claim of right and he knows that P would not have consented to the appropriation. All the elements of theft are thus present unless it can be said that "dishonestly" imports some further requirement.

It is clear from s. 2 (2)[12] that an intention on D's part to repay does not, as such, mean that he is not acting dishonestly. *Williams*,[13] provides a good illustration. In this case D was the proprietor of a shop and E, his wife, was sub-postmistress of a post office conducted on the premises. D's business did not prosper so from time to time E, abetted by D, took sums of money belonging

---

[7] *Cf.* blackmail, below, p. 403.

[8] *Harris* v. *Harrison*, [1963] Crim. L.R. 497.

[9] What does or does not amount to dishonesty appears to be a question of law for the judge: *cf.* Smith, *Theft*, paras. 168–169. Although the jury (or judge of fact) must decide whether D was in fact acting dishonestly, the relevant criteria of dishonesty must be given them by the judge. It cannot be supposed that whether D was acting dishonestly is at large in every case for each particular jury to express its own view.

[10] [1966] 3 All E.R. 988 (C.A.).

[11] See Lowe, "The Fraudulent Intent in Larceny", [1965] Crim. L.R. 78; Smith, "Fraudulent Intent in Larceny", [1956] Crim. L.R. 238.

[12] Above, p. 372.

[13] [1953] 1 Q.B. 660; [1953] 1 All E.R. 1068.

to P (the Postmaster-General) from the till, and used it to subsidise D's business. D and E said they intended to repay the money, in part from E's earnings and in part from the profits of D's business. The jury found that D and E, with regard to the sums first taken, intended to repay and honestly believed that they would be able to do so, and with regard to the sums last taken they intended to repay but had no honest belief that they would be able to do so.

Counsel[14] for D submitted that "fraudulently" required an intention on D's part to act to the detriment of P against P's wishes. Even on this view (and as counsel conceded) a person may be so acting although he intends to repay, if in so acting he intends to put the owner's money at risk because then he could be acting to the detriment of the owner and against his wishes.

The Court of Criminal Appeal held that all the takings were fraudulent and, it is submitted, rightly so. Even in respect of the earlier takings, which D and E honestly believed they would be able to repay, they had no present ability to repay. Their ability to repay was, in part at least, dependant upon the contingency of D's business doing better and making the necessary profits. They were thus clearly putting P's money at risk and therefore acting to P's detriment.

In *Sinclair* v. *Neighbour*,[15] of course, D speculated with P's money, but there is an essential difference. The restoration of P's money did not depend on the contingency of D's backing the winner (as in *Williams* it depended upon an improvement in D's business); D was going to repay the money, and had the ability to repay the money, even if the horse lost. It is then arguable that D did not intend to act to the detriment of P and that his conduct should not be accounted dishonest.[16] But in *Cockburn*[17] the Court of Appeal held that D was acting fraudulently where he took £50 from his employer's till on a Saturday intending to repay on the Monday following by means of a cheque which he would receive from his daughter. The court said that D's intention to repay and his ability to do so would be relevant to the mitigation of sentence, but nevertheless:

> "If coins, half a crown, a 10s. note, a £5 note, whatever it may be, are taken . . . with the intention of spending or putting away somewhere those particular coins or notes, albeit not only hoping but intending and expecting reasonably to be able to replace them with their equivalent, nevertheless larceny has been committed because with full appreciation of what is being done, the larcenous person, the person who commits the offence, has taken something which he was not entitled to take, without the consent of the owner, and is in effect trying to force on the owner a substitution to which the owner has not consented."[18]

It is perhaps probable that *Cockburn* expresses the prevailing judicial attitude

---

[14] J. H. Buzzard.

[15] Above, p. 373.

[16] The trial judge thought that D's action was reprehensible but not dishonest. While the C.A. did not think it necessary to pass upon the point, SELLERS, L.J., said ([1966] 3 All E.R. 988, 989) "On these facts a jury might have taken the view that they would not convict . . . Views might differ." DAVIES, L.J., expressed no opinion, and SACHS, L.J., said (at p. 991):
> "For my part, I go a little further . . . As between the employer and the employee (and that seems to me the cardinal matter) when the former (*sic*) deliberately takes money illicitly behind the back of his employer and appropriates it, even temporarily, for his own use, knowing that the employer would disapprove, that is sufficient, to my mind, to establish that as between the employer and the employee that conduct is dishonest."
See MacKenna, "The Undefined Adverb in Criminal Statutes", [1966] Crim. L.R. 548, at pp. 550–553.

[17] [1968] 1 All E.R. 466.

[18] *Ibid.*, at p. 468.

and that similar conduct will now be accounted dishonest for the purposes of theft. But consider the more recent case of *Sinclair*.[19] Here D and E, directors of P. Co. Ltd., were charged with conspiracy to defraud the company and its shareholders and creditors. They had transferred money belonging to the company to F against a "vague promise" by F that he would put assets of an equivalent or greater value into the company. The trial judge directed the jury thus:

> "To prove fraud it must be established that the conduct was deliberately dishonest. In the circumstances of this case what sort of test should be applied as to whether the conduct was dishonest? It is fraud if it is proved that there was the taking of a risk which there was no right to take which would cause detriment or prejudice to another."[20]

This direction was approved by the Court of Appeal in upholding the conviction of D and E. But suppose that D and E, having the ability to do so, intended to make good the assets of the company in the event of F failing to do so. In such a case there might be "the taking of a risk which there was no right to take" but the risk would not be one "which would cause detriment or prejudice" to the company if D and E intended, and were able, to make good any loss. Yet D and E, though they might not be guilty of a conspiracy to defraud the company, would, if *Cockburn* is followed, have stolen the company's property.

2 Intention Permanently to Deprive

Theft requires an intention permanently to deprive the other of his property, and while the Theft Act contains provisions making it an offence in certain cases to use the property of another,[1] it should be noted that even in these instances the offence created is not theft. Theft always requires an intention permanently to deprive, and s. 6 provides:

> (1) A person appropriating property belonging to another without meaning the other permanently to lose the thing itself is nevertheless to be regarded as having the intention of permanently depriving the other of it if his intention is to treat the thing as his own to dispose of regardless of the other's rights, and a borrowing or lending of it may amount to so treating it if, but only if, the borrowing or lending is for a period and in circumstances making it equivalent to an outright taking or disposal.

> (2) Without prejudice to the generality of subsection (1) above, where a person, having possession or control (lawfully or not) of property belonging to another, parts with the property under a condition as to its return which he may not be able to perform, this (if done for purposes of his own and without the other's authority) amounts to treating the property as his own to dispose of regardless of the other's rights."

There need not, of course, be any permanent deprivation in fact; D may be guilty of theft even though P is never in any danger of losing his property so long as D appropriates with the intent.[2] Conversely, the fact of permanent deprivation is insufficient if there was no intent. But it must be clear that the facts— the history of what D did with the goods—will often have an important bearing on the proof of D's intent. If, for instance, D was found respraying the car which he took from P without his permission, the jury is likely to favour the inference that D's intent was to deprive P permanently of it. If, on the other hand, D had taken P's lawn-mower without permission and left it in full view of P's house

---

[19] [1968] 3 All E.R. 241.
[20] [1968] 3 All E.R. 241, 246.
[1] See below, p. 397.
[2] *Cf. Egginton* (1801), 2 Leach 913.

after he had used it to mow his own lawn, the jury is likely to favour the inference that it was not D's intent to deprive P permanently of it.   In every case it is for the jury to determine, on the evidence, whether D did so intend, so that where the evidence as to D's intent is circumstantial the judge will instruct the jury that they *may* infer the intent from evidence pointing to that conclusion, but it would be an error of law for the judge to direct that because the evidence points to that conclusion they *must* infer the intent, and the conviction may be quashed on appeal.   The meaning of the intent to deprive permanently and its relation to the accompanying problem of proof may be illustrated by reference to the situation in which D takes P's goods and then abandons them.   Suppose, for instance, that D takes P's car and subsequently abandons it.   If D's intention was to use the car for some temporary purpose then he does not steal it.   Nor need D take any steps to return the car, so it follows that as a matter of fact it is often difficult to make out a case of car stealing because it will be difficult for P to show (even if D has been apprehended in possession) that it was D's intent to steal the car rather than to use it temporarily.[3]   It is less difficult where what D has taken is P's umbrella.   If D takes P's car in Nottingham and abandons it in London it would be virtually impossible to get a conviction of theft; if D does the same with P's umbrella a conviction of theft is a virtual certainty.   It is not a case of treating cars and umbrellas differently for the jury will be asked to apply the same test to both.   Everyone knows that if an umbrella is borrowed in Nottingham and abandoned in London that it will be lost forever to its owner, and ordinarily D will know and intend this.

(*a*) *Disposal regardless of the other's rights.*—In the foregoing illustration concerning the umbrella it is assumed that D knows the umbrella will be lost forever to P and that he intends this.   D thus means P permanently to lose the thing and there is no problem whatever concerning intent.   But it might be that when D disposes of P's property he is merely indifferent as to whether it will be recovered by P;   D might even hope that the property will somehow be restored to P, but realises that in the circumstances this is unlikely.   Where D is thus indifferent it may be difficult to say that he is "meaning the other permanently to lose the thing itself".   However s. 6 (1) provides that D is nevertheless to be regarded as having the intention of permanently depriving P of it if "his intention is to treat the thing as his own to dispose of regardless of the other's rights".

Note that it is not enough that D is treating the property as his own.   In borrowing P's property without P's consent and using it there is an appropriation of the property and D is treating it as his own; but he does not steal the property unless he intends, in addition, to treat it as his own to dispose of regardless of P's rights.   Any such disposal will suffice.

Suppose, for example, that D appropriates property belonging to P intending all along to sell it back to P.[4]   He will certainly be guilty of obtaining by deception if he carries through his fraud, but it is necessary to decide whether he is a thief when he appropriates the property.   It seems clear enough that he is, for he intends to treat the property as his own to dispose of regardless of P's rights.   It can hardly be argued that he is not treating the property as his own to dispose of since D proposes to represent to the true owner himself that he is the owner or

---

[3] Hence it was made a statutory offence merely to take P's car without P's consent; see below, p. 400.

[4] *Cf. Hall* (1849), 1 Den. 381.

is authorised by the owner to sell. Nor can it be seriously argued that he is not acting regardless of the owner's rights. D is of course aware of the owner's rights and it is his very awareness which shows that he is acting regardless of them.

To take another example, D would have an intention permanently to deprive where he pawns P's property and sends P the pawn ticket; he might know that P is in law entitled to recover the goods pawned, and he has informed P of the whereabouts of the goods, but he has treated the goods as his own to dispose of regardless of P's rights.

A case worth considering at this point is *Holloway*.[5] D, who was employed by P to dress skins and was paid by the piece, took some already dressed skins from P's warehouse and then claimed payment for dressing them. Here, D though guilty of obtaining or attempting to obtain by deception, does not steal the skins. He does not mean P to be permanently deprived of them nor does he treat them *as his own* to dispose of regardless of P's rights; all along D acknowledges that the skins belong to P.[6]

It seems that where D treats the thing as his own to dispose of regardless of P's rights, he is to be regarded as having the intention of permanently depriving P even though he does not in fact intend that P should be permanently deprived of his property and there is in fact no danger that P will be so deprived. Section 6 (1) states that D "*is to be* regarded" not "may be regarded". Consequently in circumstances such as those of *Bloxham*,[7] D, in selling P's refrigerator to Q, was treating the thing as his own to dispose of regardless of P's rights, and "is to be regarded" as having the intention of permanently depriving P of it, notwithstanding that D does not intend that Q should ever deprive P in fact of the refrigerator.

(*b*) *Borrowing or lending.*—Where D merely borrows P's umbrella and uses it without P's consent there is an appropriation, but if D intends to return the umbrella to P at some future date—definite or indefinite—he would not be "meaning" P permanently to lose it. Nor, by merely intending to use the umbrella indefinitely, does he intend to treat it as his own *to dispose of* regardless of P's rights. However s. 6 (1) provides that a borrowing or lending may amount to so treating it "if, but only if, the borrowing or lending is for a period and in circumstances making it equivalent to an outright taking or disposal".

Suppose, then, that D intends to return the property in a year's time, ten years' time or fifty years' time. Would the borrowing in any or all of these cases amount to an outright taking? On the whole it would seem that this provision was not inserted to leave it to the judges to determine how long a period of borrowing is equivalent to an outright taking. If D intends to return the property at some future stage then, without more, it is difficult to see how this could be equivalent to an outright taking—it necessarily falls short of an outright taking. Moreover this sort of problem is not merely academic, it is almost fanciful. People do not ordinarily borrow property for one, five or fifty years as the case may be; property is either borrowed (*i.e.* D intends to return it) or it is appropriated permanently.

---

[5] (1849), 1 Den. 370.
[6] It may be there is a more fundamental reason why Holloway would not now be guilty of stealing the skins; there may be no appropriation of the skins. *Cf.* Smith, *Theft*, para. 61.
[7] (1943), 29 Cr. App. Rep. 37; above, p. 354.

So it is reasonable to suppose that the draftsman had some other sort of case in mind. This is borne out by the fact that the borrowing or lending must be "for a period *and* in circumstances" making it equivalent to an outright taking or disposal. Perhaps the intended meaning can be divined,[9] and the provision appears to be aimed at the sort of case where D borrows P's theatre season ticket and uses it to gain admission to a series of performances. It would thus apply to the case where D takes a railway ticket in order to get a free ride; he intends that the ticket should be restored to P at the end of his journey, but the ticket is now worthless and his borrowing of it has been for a period and in circumstances making it equivalent to an outright taking.

But there are difficulties. Suppose, for example, that D uses the season ticket for nineteen out of the twenty performances[10] for which it is valid and then returns it to P for the last performance. Is this use by D equivalent to an outright taking?[11] If it is so treated then the courts would again be faced with considerable difficulties in drawing the line. More important, if it is admitted that something short of an intention to use the ticket to view all twenty performances will suffice (say ten or fifteen) then dishonest use will in some circumstances amount to theft. A principle that was firmly kept out at the front door will have been allowed in at the back.

(*c*) *The thing.*—Rather curiously s. 6 (1) speaks of "the thing" where it might have been expected to use "the property". The explanation may be that the draftsman sought to make it clear that the kind of case provided for was one where P is to get the thing itself, in a literal sense, restored to him but it is D's intention that the thing shall be worthless in the real sense. The thing (the cancelled season ticket) is restored to P but the season ticket as property of value is not restored to him.

(*d*) *Parting with property under a condition as to its return.*—Section 6 (2) is meant to provide for the case where D (who will most often be a bailee of the property though the position is the same here even if D has taken the property in the first place without P's consent) pledges P's property without P's authority. If D intends to redeem the property and return it to P in due course he would not ordinarily be said to mean to deprive P permanently of the property. The difficulty with such cases arises because it may be uncertain whether D will be able to redeem the goods—the very fact that he has pawned them tends to show that he is lacking in funds. Accordingly s. 6 (2) provides that D is to be treated as having an intention permanently to deprive P if he parts with the property under a condition "which he *may* not be able to perform".

The subsection clearly infers that if D parts with the property, by pledging or otherwise, under a condition as to its return which he knows he can perform then D would not be guilty of theft. Yet in such a case D, by pledging P's property without authority, is treating the property as his own to dispose of regardless of P's rights within s. 6 (1) and s. 6 (2) is expressed to be without prejudice to the generality of s. 6 (1). Presumably, though, s. 6 (1) is to be read subject to s. 6 (2) to this extent otherwise s. 6 (2) would be devoid of any worthwhile meaning.

---

[9] Though a reference to the Parliamentary Debates (H.C. Vol. 769, cols. 470–473) helps in making this deduction.

[10] The example given at H.C. Vol. 769, col. 472.

[11] *Cf.* Smith, *Theft*, para. 188; Griew, *Theft*, 38.

(e) *Deprivation of the owner's interest*—Normally a thief intends to deprive permanently in the fullest sense, that is, he intends to make the property his own. In such a case it does not matter that the person from whom the property is stolen is the owner or a person, such as a bailee, who has a limited interest. But it might happen that D, while not intending to deprive the owner permanently of the property, nevertheless intends to deprive, say, a bailee of his interest. For example, knowing that P has hired a car for the duration of his holiday D appropriates the car for the period of that holiday intending to return it to the owner. Since theft is the dishonest appropriation of property belonging to another with the intention of depriving that other permanently of it, and since the property belongs to the bailee, it seems that D will be guilty of theft if, knowing of P's limited interest as bailee, he dishonestly deprives him permanently of it.

2 ABSTRACTING ELECTRICITY

It has been shown[12] why the Criminal Law Revision Committee thought it necessary to make special provision for electricity, and s. 13 accordingly provides:

> "A person who dishonestly uses without due authority, or dishonestly causes to be wasted or diverted, any electricity shall on conviction on indictment be liable to imprisonment for a term not exceeding five years."

No doubt this provision will ordinarily be applied to the case where D dishonestly uses some device to by-pass his electricity meter, but it is in fact capable of some curious applications.[13] Strictly there might be an offence under this section where D borrows an electrically driven, hand-operated, milk float, though there would be no theft of the float nor an offence of taking a conveyance under s. 12.[14] But proceedings under s. 13 in such a case are perhaps very unlikely; there might be some reluctance to prosecute when the substance of what D does is not criminal even though there is technically some incidental offence.[15] Moreover, in this sort of situation, it may be that D does not at all advert to the fact that he is causing the electricity to be wasted.

It was perhaps for these reasons that the Post Office Act 1953, s. 65, is amended by the Theft Act[16] to create a specific offence of dishonestly using a public or telex system with intent to avoid payment.[17] This gets at the substance of the mischief and avoids any difficulty.

It is enough under s. 13 that D dishonestly causes electricity to be wasted or diverted; he need not be shown to have made any use of the electricity for himself. An employee who out of spite for his employer leaves on all the lighting and heating appliances in the office over the weekend would commit the offence.

---

[12] Above, p. 357.

[13] *Cf.* Smith, *Law of Theft*, paras. 403–405.

[14] See below, p. 402.

[15] Prosecutions have been brought for stealing the petrol consumed where D has borrowed a motor vehicle, but this was never regarded as satisfactory and the offence of taking motor vehicles was introduced; see below, p. 400. In the case of the removal of the Goya portrait (below, p. 398) D was acquitted of stealing the painting but convicted of stealing the frame.

[16] Sched. 2., para. 8. But this does not cover 999 calls since no payment is involved; see p. 517 below.

[17] Punishable, on summary conviction, by three months' imprisonment and/or a fine of £100; and, on indictment, by two years' imprisonment.

3 ROBBERY[18]

By s. 8 of the Theft Act 1968:

"(1) A person is guilty of robbery if he steals, and immediately before or at the time of doing so, and in order to do so, he uses force on any person or puts or seeks to put any person in fear of being then and there subjected to force.

(2) A person guilty of robbery, or of an assault with intent to rob, shall on conviction on indictment be liable to imprisonment for life."

As defined robbery is essentially an aggravated form of theft; and if there is no theft, or attempted theft, there can be no robbery or attempted robbery. So it would not be robbery where D by force takes a car from P in the belief that he has the legal right to it;[19] or where D by force takes a car from P not intending to deprive P permanently of it. In the first case D may be guilty of an assault, and in the latter of both an assault and an offence under s. 12 of the Theft Act, but in neither case is he guilty of robbery.

The offence of robbery is complete when the theft is complete, that is when the appropriation is complete. In the case of robbery the appropriation must normally be by taking,[20] since it is difficult to imagine realistic situations in which robbery might be affected by other modes of appropriation.[1]

1 Use or Threat of Force

Any use or threat of force against the person suffices. To pick a pocket would not normally amount to robbery although there might be some degree of physical contact. "Force on any person" must involve more than mere physical contact. The Criminal Law Revision Committee said they would "not regard mere snatching of property, such as a handbag, from an unresisting owner as using force for the purpose of the definition."[2] This seems acceptable since in an ordinary case of handbag-snatching D certainly does not seek to put P in fear of being subject to force, and it may fairly be said that he does not use force "on any person". But it requires very little to turn such a case of theft into one of robbery. As the Committee recognised,[3] it might amount to robbery if the owner resisted. It is presumably enough that P resists only to the extent that she takes hold of the handbag and it is pulled by D from her grasp. In an old case[4] D snatched P's ear-ring and tore through the lobe of her ear; this would certainly amount to a use of force on the person for the purposes of s. 8.

2 On Any Person

In most cases of robbery D will use or threaten force against the person to whom the property belongs.[5] But the offence is not so limited. Provided the force is used or threatened *in order* to steal it will be robbery.

"If, for example, the only force used at the time of the [Great Train Robbery]

---

[18] See Andrews, "Robbery", [1966] Crim. L.R. 524.
[19] *Cf. Skivington*, [1968] 1 Q.B. 166.
[20] See above, p. 353.
[1] See Andrews, *op. cit.*, 527, for possible instances.
[2] Cmnd. 2977, para. 65.
[3] *Loc cit.*
[4] *Lapier* (1784), 1 Leach 320.
[5] Above, p. 360.

in 1963 had been on a signalman, this would under the [Act] have been sufficient."[6]

It does not matter that the person against whom the force is used or threatened
has no interest whatever in the property; it would be robbery to overpower the
same signalman because his signal-box overlooks a factory from which the thieves
wish to steal and they fear that he will notice them and raise the alarm. It would
seem to amount to robbery where D threatens to use force on Q in order to overcome P's reluctance to part with his money, as where D holds P's child over a
river and threatens to throw her in unless P hands over his wallet.[7] Such a case
is more naturally treated as one of blackmail under s. 21 of the Act, but it seems
to fall literally within s. 8.[8]

3 Immediately Before or At the Time of Stealing and In Order to Steal

Robbery is naturally thought of as stealing *accomplished* by force, and s. 8 gives
expression to this idea. The point may perhaps still be illustrated by reference
to *Harman's Case* (1620)[9] where D, who was on horseback, so deftly picked P's
pocket that P did not realise his purse was gone till he saw it in D's hands. P's
remonstrations brought from D a threat to pull down P's house about his ears
and drive him out of the country if he spoke a word about the matter. It was
held that this was not robbery then, and it would not be robbery under the Act
since the threats were not used in order to steal the purse.

Even if force is used in order to steal, it will not be robbery unless the force is
used or threatened "immediately before or at the time of" the theft. This
expression gives rise to some difficulties.[10] On one view "the time of" the theft
might mean no more than the time taken to begin and complete the *actus reus* of
theft. Suppose, for example, that D enters a post office, grabs money from the
counter and makes for the door; P, the postmistress, intervenes and is knocked
down by D. Here the appropriation is complete, at the latest, when D takes
control of the money and it is after this that P is assaulted. On the view that the
time of the theft is the time taken to complete the *actus reus*, P is not assaulted at
the time of, but after, the theft. But this view may seem unduly technical and it
may be that a common-sense view has to be taken of "the time of" the theft;
and in the above illustration it seems perfectly sensible to say that the assault
took place at the time of the theft. The technical argument might, however, be
reinforced by pointing out that not only does s. 8 require the force to be used or
threatened "immediately before or at the time of" the theft, but it adds "*and* in
order to" steal. D might argue (at least if he knew his law) that he had already
stolen the money and knocked down the postmistress in order to escape with it.
But again this argument might be met by the common-sense view that the assault
was part and parcel of the stealing.

But a line has to be drawn somewhere. If, having taken the money from the
post office, without using or threatening force, D is stopped by a police officer in
the street outside and knocks him down in order to avoid arrest, this would not

---

[6] Cmnd. 2977, para. 65. *Cf. Smith* v. *Desmond & Hall*, [1965] A.C. 960; [1965] 1 All
E.R. 976.

[7] *Cf. Reane* (1794), 2 Leach 616.

[8] *Cf.* Smith, *Theft*, paras. 213, 214.

[9] 2 Roll Rep. 154.

[10] *Cf.* Smith, *Theft*, paras. 208–210; Griew, *Theft*, 49.

amount to robbery. Even on a broad view the use of force is neither at the time of, nor in order to commit, the theft.[11]

"Immediately before" must add something to "at the time of" the theft. Clearly if a gang overpower P, the nightwatchman, at the main gate of a factory, this would be a use of force immediately before the theft, although some minutes must elapse before the gang reaches the part of the factory where the safe is housed.[12] And it can make no difference, as such, that P is not present in the factory at all; it would be robbery where some members of the gang by force detain P at his home while their confederates open the safe in the factory.

It is not enough that D gets P to part with property by threatening to use force on another, and future, occasion. This may well amount to blackmail but the fact that P is intimidated or frightened is not in itself enough for robbery unless he is "then and there" put in fear of being subject to force. But suppose a gang by threats of force persuade P, the factory nightwatchman, to stay away from work the following evening, and on that evening they steal from the factory uninterrupted. At the time of the theft the threat of force still operates on P's mind; he stays at home because he is afraid of what will happen if he goes to work. But this does not seem to amount to robbery. At the time of the theft P is not put in fear of being "then and there" subjected to force.

It does not seem to be possible to put any particular temporal limit on "immediately". All the circumstances have to be considered including the time when, and the place where, the force was used or threatened in relation to the theft. Force converts theft into robbery only when its use or threat is in a real sense directly part of the theft, and is used in order to accomplish the theft.

4 Mens Rea

Obviously robbery requires at least an intent to steal. But it seems to require more than this. It could be argued that if D intends to steal it will be robbery if in fact there is some use of force, or if in fact he puts someone in fear, whether he intends to do so or not. But it seems clear that D must use or threaten force *in order* to steal, and a merely accidental use of force would not be done in order to steal.[13] It is enough that D seeks to put another in fear of being subjected to force. Fear here means to apprehend, and it would be no less a robbery because P was not afraid. Even if P does not apprehend that he will be subjected to force (because, perhaps, plain-clothes policemen are present and D has walked into a trap), it will be robbery if D sought to make him fear. But it would not be enough that P is in fact put in fear unless D intended to put P in fear. A timorous witness to a smash and grab raid might well fear that the thieves will turn on him, but if the thieves do not intend to put him in fear of being there and then subjected to force the offence cannot amount to robbery.

4 DECEPTION

At common law it was never an offence, as such, to obtain property by deception. In more robust—or less sophisticated—times, it was not apparently

---

[11] *Cf.* Cmnd. 2977, para. 65.
[12] Possibly the force in this illustration is used "at the time of" the theft. If a broad view is taken of "at the time of" it might well extend back to the moment when the thieves enter the premises.
[13] *Cf. Edwards* (1843), 1 Cox C.C. 32.

regarded as particularly grave to obtain property by swindling. In a case in 1704,[14] HOLT, C.J., holding that it was not stealing where D obtained £20 from P by pretending that he was authorised by Q to collect it, observed, "Shall we indict one man for making a fool of another?" But by 1757 a statutory offence of obtaining property by false pretences had been created. The law is now contained in s. 15 of the Theft Act 1968 which provides:

"(1) A person who by any deception dishonestly obtains property belonging to another, with the intention of permanently depriving the other of it, shall on conviction on indictment be liable to imprisonment for a term not exceeding ten years.

(2) For purposes of this section a person is to be treated as obtaining property if he obtains ownership, possession or control of it, and 'obtain' includes obtaining for another or enabling another to obtain or to retain.

(3) Section 6 above shall apply for purposes of this section, with the necessary adaptation of the reference to appropriating, as it applies for purposes of section 1.

(4) For purposes of this section 'deception' means any deception (whether deliberate or reckless) by words or conduct as to fact or as to law, including a deception as to the present intentions of the person using the deception or any other person."

(1) THE DECEPTION

Deception is defined in s. 15 (4) and the following matters arise for consideration.

1 Deliberate or Reckless Deception

In line with general theory concerning criminal liability[15] D may be convicted not only where he knows that what he represents as true is untrue, but also where he represents as true that which, as he is aware, may or may not be true. Of course D cannot be convicted of deception should what he represents to be true turn out to be true[16] because P would not have been deceived though on one view it may be that D can be convicted of an attempt.[17] Clearly there would be no offence where D represents as true that which he believes to be true but which, as he ought as a reasonable man to have known, is false. Recklessness ordinarily involves a subjective awareness which is absent from negligence.[18] Moreover the offence of deception requires dishonesty and negligence is no substitute for dishonesty.[19]

2 Words or Conduct

The deception may take the form of either words or conduct but it does seem that something more than mere acquiescence by D in P's self-deception is required. If, for example, D merely offers a boat for sale it is not his duty to

---

[14] *Jones* (1704), 2 Ld. Raym. 1013.
[15] See above, p. 41.
[16] *Cf. Deller* (1952), 36 Cr. App. R. 184 (C.C.A.); above p. 29.
[17] Above, p. 171.
[18] See above, p. 39.
[19] *Cf. Derry* v. *Peek* (1889), 14 App. Cas. 337. And see below, p. 390. The Prevention of Fraud (Investments) Act 1958, s. 13, as amended by s. 21 (1) of the Protection of Depositors Act 1963, imposes criminal liability for "the reckless making (dishonestly or otherwise)" of statements in certain circumstances. But under s. 15 of the Theft Act dishonesty is of course required in all cases.

point out that its hull is rotting below the water-line and he may lawfully accept an extravagant price from P who has failed to inspect it thoroughly. But for D to represent that the hull was sound would be a deception.

Conduct alone[20] will suffice and it would seem to be enough that D, with the intention of concealing the state of the hull from P, were to move it from the slipway into the water.[1] A more difficult case is where during the negotiations D honestly represents the hull to be sound but discovers on taking the boat from the water that it is rotten. Is he guilty of deception if he goes through with the sale without informing D that his earlier representation is untrue?[2] D has acted dishonestly and P has in fact been deceived[3] but there are real difficulties here.[4] But it would seem reasonable to regard D's representation as a continuing one[5] which operates up to the time of the obtaining. Suppose P says: "I take it from what you said the other day that the hull is sound and there is no need to have her taken from the water."; and then, supposing assent to his statement because D does not deny it, concludes the sale. D's "conduct" here surely falls within s. 15, and, if it does, the position ought to be the same although P does not in terms call D's attention to his earlier representation.

3   Fact or Law

The deception will nearly always be one of fact but s. 15 (4) makes it clear that a deception as to law suffices. So a lawyer might commit the offence where, dishonestly intending to prefer one beneficiary to another, he represents to the executors that "heirlooms" in the testator's will means all the personal chattels of the testator.

A statement of fact is not the same thing as a statement of opinion but as a practical matter it is often difficult to distinguish the two. Regard has to be had, so far as the offence of deception is concerned, to D's knowledge and intentions, and the effect produced in the mind of P. If D says in a testimonial concerning X that X is honest this would normally be taken as a statement of opinion, but it is a statement of fact to the extent that it will be taken to imply that D knows of no circumstances which show X to be dishonest. Thus if D knows that X is dishonest his statement is untrue in point of fact,[6] and it can make no difference that he expresses himself in the form, "It is my opinion that X is honest."

But in ordinary commerce people are given to making extravagant claims about the quality of property in order to induce its sale. It may often happen that D knows that (or does not care whether) his claim is untrue. Take, for example, the case of *Bryan* (1857),[7] where D obtained money from P by pledging

---

[20] *Cf. Barnard* (1837), 7 Car. & P. 784. D, knowing it was the practice for Oxford shops to extend credit to students, obtained goods on credit by stating that he was a student. BOLLAND, B., said that even if nothing had passed in words the jury might find a pretence in the fact that D wore a cap and gown.

[1] *Cf. Schneider* v. *Heath* (1813), 3 Camp. 506.

[2] *Cf. Incledon* v. *Watson* (1862), 2 F. & F. 841.

[3] *Cf.* Cmnd. 2977, para. 87: "The word 'deception' seems to us . . . to have the advantage of directing attention to the effect that the offender deliberately produced in the mind of the person deceived . . . "

[4] See above p. 46. *Cf.* Smith, *Theft.*, paras. 271–276; Griew, *Theft.*, 81, 82. Cross & Jones, *Introduction to Criminal Law* (6th ed.), would apparently regard a failure to undeceive as falling outside s. 15.

[5] *Cf. With* v. *O'Flanagan*, [1936] Ch. 575.

[6] *Cf. Smith* v. *Land & Property Corporation* (1884), 28 Ch. D. 7.

[7] Dears. & B. 265.

with him certain spoons which D represented as being of the best quality, equal to Elkington's A (this being a high quality silver spoon manufactured by Elkington), and to have as much silver on them as Elkington's A. D's spoons were in fact of very inferior quality, and were not worth the sum advanced. D was convicted of obtaining by false pretences, the jury finding that he knew his representations to be untrue. It was held, quashing D's conviction, that dishonestly to exaggerate the quality of goods was not within the offence; in so far as there was a representation of fact—that the spoons pledged were silver spoons—this was true, even though they did not have the quality represented.

But there is much force in the dissenting judgment of WILLES, J., in this case.[8] He regarded as crucial the fact that D's representation was dishonestly made with intent to defraud P, and to the extent that D claimed his spoons had on them as much silver as Elkington's A it could be demonstrated as D well knew, that they had not. To the more general argument that to uphold D's conviction might interfere with the course of trade, WILLES, J., replied that the court ought to prevent trade being carried out in this fashion.

It would seem to be quite open to a court to uphold a conviction for deception under s. 15 of the Theft Act on facts like these. D knew perfectly well, as the jury found, that his spoons were not as good as Elkington's A and to that extent there was an assertion of fact. WILLES, J., might have been ahead of the commercial morality of his time but there is no reason to suppose that standards of fair dealing might not have improved.[9]

This is not to say that any person who knowingly exaggerates the quality of his goods will commit the offence of deception. Regard must be had to the effect produced in the mind of P. There is a deal of give and take in commercial transactions and P is unlikely to be deceived by mere puffs. On the sale of a car it is thought that D would not be guilty of deception when he asserts that the car is "a good runner" for no one is really deceived by puffs of this kind.

4 Statements of Intention

In the tort of deceit it has long been the rule that a false statement of intention is actionable. In *Edgington* v. *Fitzmaurice*,[10] where the directors of a company were held liable for falsely stating in a prospectus that the company was raising money to improve buildings when the real object was to use the money to discharge existing liabilities, BOWEN, L.J., said:

> "There must be a misstatement of an existing fact; but the state of a man's mind is as much a fact as the state of his digestion. It is true that it is very difficult to prove what the state of a man's mind at a particular time is, but if it can be ascertained it is as much a fact as anything else. A misrepresentation as to the state of a man's mind is therefore a misstatement of fact."[11]

In view of this it might be thought unnecessary to provide expressly in s. 15 that deception included "a deception as to the present intentions of the person using the deception or any other person", but it was probably necessary to do so

---

[8] *Ibid.*, p. 280.
[9] *Cf. Jeff & Bassett* (1966), 51 Cr. App. Rep. 28. Note that the Trade Descriptions Act 1968 deals in a comprehensive way with false description applied to goods and services "in the course of a trade or business".
[10] (1885), 29 Ch. D. 459 (C.A.).
[11] *Ibid.*, at p. 483.

because, under the former law it had been held[12] that a false statement of intention was not a false pretence. The directors in *Edgington* v. *Fitzmaurice*[13] would thus now be liable under the criminal as well as the civil law; and, it might be noted, the case provides an example of a deception as to the intentions of another person, namely, the company.

Sometimes the words or conduct of D may be intended by D to imply certain facts although there is no express assertion of those facts. An obvious case is where D obtains goods or services by giving a cheque in payment. The giving of a cheque does not imply that D then has funds in the bank to meet it, for he may have the right to overdraw his account; but he does represent, as a fact, that it is a valid order for the payment of its amount at the bank on which it is drawn.[14] So there is clearly a deception where D knows he does not have funds in the bank to meet the cheque and knows that he does not have authority to overdraw his account.[15] But note in this connection that it is not enough to show merely that certain facts may reasonably be inferred from D's words or conduct. P, a wholesaler, might, for example, reasonably come to the conclusion from his dealings with D that D is a retailer in business, and for that reason allow D to have goods on credit. But in such a case D would be guilty of deception only if he intended that (or was reckless whether) P should draw this inference, and the inference that D is in business as a retailer is an effective cause of D's obtaining goods on credit.

Of course where, as in this last case, D obtains goods on credit he may be convicted simply upon the basis that he makes a deception as to his present intentions: he promises to pay having no intention of so doing. But it will often be difficult to prove that, at the time he ordered the goods, D did not intend to pay for them,[16] and it would still be relevant, as evidence tending to prove D's dishonesty, that at that time he deliberately gave P the impression that he was a retailer.

(2) THE OBTAINING

The offence is committed whether D obtains ownership, possession or control. Frequently D will obtain both ownership and possession but either suffices. If D by deception induces P to sell goods to him the offence is complete when ownership is transferred which may occur before the goods are delivered. If D by deception obtains a loan of goods the offence is complete, if all other requirements of the offence are present, when D gets possession or control of them. Most often D will obtain the goods for himself but it suffices under s. 15 (2) that D obtains for another or enables another to obtain or retain. Thus the offence might be committed where, for example, D by deception induces P to sell goods to E, or where D by deception induces P to continue a loan of goods to E. In such cases E may be a confederate, but D may commit the offence, provided he has the necessary intent, although E is acting innocently.

D must by his deception obtain the property or enable another to obtain or retain. The offence would not be committed, though there would be an attempt,[17]

---

[12] *Dent*, [1955] 2 Q.B. 590; [1955] 2 All E.R. 806 (C.C.A.).
[13] *Supra*.
[14] *Cf. Hazelton* (1874), L.R. 2 C.C.R. 134.
[15] *Ibid*.
[16] See below, p. 390.
[17] *Cf. Hensler* (1870), 11 Cox C.C. 570; above, p. 33.

where P knows the true facts and is not deceived and even though P should in fact deliver the property to D or allow E to retain it. The deception must, then, be the cause of the obtaining or retention. It is not necessary that the deception should be addressed personally to P and it would be enough that it is contained in a newspaper or prospectus and causes members of the public to part with money.

In many cases D obtains property by making both true and false representations, and here D may be convicted of the offence if the representations which are false are an effective, though not necessarily the exclusive, cause of the obtaining. If, for example, D obtains money from P by representing, falsely, that he holds high military rank, and by representing, truly, that the money is required for investment in a company,[18] his deception may be held to be an effective cause of P's parting with his money since he parts with it on the basis that D is a man of standing. But it does not follow that the deception is an effective cause of the obtaining simply because P would not have parted with his property had he been aware that a representation made by D was false. In *Clucas*,[19] D and E falsely represented to P, a bookmaker, that they were acting as commission agents on behalf of several other persons and in that way P was induced to take from them a bet on credit; the horse backed won and P paid on the bet. It was held under the former law that D and E did not obtain the winnings by their false pretence and it seems that they would not now obtain the winnings by deception.[20] It was quite clear in this case that P would not have paid on the bet had he known that D and E were not acting for others—indeed at one stage P suspected that all was not as it appeared and was unwilling to pay without further assurances—but the reason why he paid up was because they had backed a winning horse.

With the facts of *Clucas* it is instructive to contrast the facts of *Button*.[1] D had entered races, for which prizes were offered, in the name of E and gave particulars of former running performances which were true of E and which were only modest; on the basis of this D was given a favourable handicap and he romped home in both his races. So much so that suspicion was aroused and the upshot was that D did not stay to take the prize. It was held that D could be convicted under the former law of an attempt to obtain by false pretences, and it seems that he would now be convicted of an attempt to obtain by deception. Here the deception was the effective cause of D winning the race and thereby qualifying for the prize, whereas the deception in *Clucas* in no way improved D's chances of picking the winner. Similarly, where D gets employment by deception he cannot be convicted of obtaining his salary by deception because the salary is paid in respect of work done and not in respect of the appointment.[2]

The deception is no less the cause of the obtaining though it would not have deceived a reasonably prudent person so long as it in fact deceives P. D cannot escape the consequences of his dishonesty by showing his victim to have been unusually gullible.[3]

It will be appreciated that where D by deception obtains merely possession or

---

[18] *Cf. Hamilton* (1845), 1 Cox C.C. 244
[19] [1949] 2 K.B. 226; [1949] 2 All E.R. 40 (C.C.A.).
[20] But they would commit an offence under s. 16 of the Act, below p. 394.
[1] [1900] 2 Q.B. 597.
[2] *Cf. Lewis* (1922), Somerset Assizes, ROWLATT, J.: Russell, at 1186n. But D commits an offence under s. 16; below, p. 394.
[3] *Cf. Giles* (1865), Le & Ca. 502.

control of the property he may be convicted of theft as well as deception. If, for example, D by deception induces P to make him a loan of his car, dishonestly intending to deprive P of it, the offences of both theft and deception are committed. Although the case is more naturally treated as one of deception (since this is what it looks most like) D has in fact appropriated the property of another and may be convicted of theft.

But in most cases of deception D induces P to part with ownership of the property (most commonly by inducing a sale of the property) ,and here it seems, on the face of it, that while D may be convicted of deception, he cannot ordinarily be convicted of theft. The reason is that theft requires an appropriation of property "belonging to another"[4] and where D by deception induces P to transfer ownership to him then—by virtue of the transfer of ownership—D does not appropriate property which belongs to P. It is true of course that D has only a voidable title to the property; it is good only until P discovers the deception and takes steps to have it set aside. But until that moment in time D, not P, is the owner of the property.

But an argument can be advanced to the effect that D may be guilty of theft in this situation notwithstanding that he has obtained ownership.[5] Under s. 5 of the Act,[6] property may be treated as belonging to P although D is in point of law the owner of it. Of particular relevance here is s. 5 (4)[7] which provides that where a person gets property by another's mistake, and is under an obligation to make restoration, then the property is to be regarded as belonging to the person entitled to restoration. A person who obtains property by deception might fairly be said to get property by another's mistake.[8] If so, and if he "is under an obligation to make restoration" then the way is clear to treating all cases of deception as cases of theft. The answer to this argument[9] appears to be that a person who by deception induces a transfer of ownership is not—at the time of the transfer—under an obligation to make restoration. He may subsequently become under an obligation when the transaction is set aside by P, but s. 5 (4) says that a person may be guilty of theft who "is," not who may become, under an obligation to make restoration. It is after all possible that when P becomes aware of the deception he may decide to take no action, or he may not take action until it is too late to be legally effective, and in either event D's title is indefeasible.

Yet it might seem odd if a court were to hold, for example, that where D obtains a car by deception that he is under no obligation to make restoration unless and until P discovers the fraud and chooses to set the contract aside. Is it to be accepted that an employee, like Moynes,[10] receives an overpayment owing to a mistake on his employer's part is under an obligation to make restoration of the overpayment, but that a man who obtains a car by deception is under no obligation to make restoration of the car?

This whole problem need never trouble the courts if in practice D is always charged with deception where he has by deception obtained property from P. The discussion does perhaps serve to show that the distinction between theft and

---

[4] Above, p. 360.
[5] Stuart, "Reform of the law of Theft" (1967), 30 M.L.R. 609.
[6] Above, pp. 361–368.
[7] Above, p. 366.
[8] *Cf.* Griew, *Theft*, 23, who suggests that the word "mistake" in s. 5 (4) might in the context of the Act be read as a mistake *not* induced by the dishonest deception of D.
[9] *Cf.* Smith, *Theft*, paras. 100–106.
[10] See above, p. 366.

deception is at best somewhat technical and that a further simplification might have been achieved by the incorporation of deception in theft.[11]

(3) PROPERTY BELONGING TO ANOTHER

The offence may be committed in respect of any "property belonging to another". By s. 34 (1) of the Theft Act, s. 4 (1)[12] and s. 5 (1)[13]—which contain the primary definitions of "property" and "belonging to another"—are applied generally for the purposes of the Act.

Consequently "money and all other property, real or personal, including things in action and other intangible property" may be obtained by deception, and the limitations imposed by s. 4 on property which may be stolen do not apply to deception. So far as land is concerned the most obvious case is that of an imposter claiming trust property or a deceased person's estate,[14] but it would extend to any case where D by deception obtains any interest in land of another. So far as things in action are concerned D might commit the offence where, for example, by deception he induces P to transfer or assign a debt, a copyright or patent.

Since "property belonging to another" is to be given the same meaning it has for theft under s. 5 (1),[15] it follows that D may commit an offence under s. 15 where by deception he obtains property of which he is the owner. If, for example, in circumstances such as occurred in *Rose* v. *Matt*,[16] D had by deception induced P to part with possession of the clock, he could be convicted of the offence under s. 15.

But D would commit no offence under s. 15 where, for example, owing P £10, he dishonestly tells P that he has paid him and that P must have forgotten about it. Here D does not obtain any property belonging to P.[17] Nor would D commit this offence where he enables himself to retain property belonging to P, as where he tells P that he has lost a book which P lent him.[18] He might commit deception by telling P that E has lost the book which P lent to E, for this might enable E to retain the book; but not by telling P that E has repaid a loan which P made to E because this does not enable E to retain property belonging to P.[19]

(4) MENS REA

Presumably D must in the first place intend by deception to obtain, for himself or another, the property which is in fact obtained. In the course of negotiations for the purchase of goods on credit, for example, D might tell what to him is an inconsequential lie (*e.g.*, that he is an old Etonian) but, as it turns out, this is the substantial reason why P allows him to have the goods on credit. It is thought that D would not be guilty of obtaining by deception although he has in fact deceived P and this deception in fact caused P to part with the property.

---

[11] *Cf.* Cmnd. 2977, para. 38.
[12] Above, p. 357.
[13] Above, p. 361.
[14] Cmnd. 2977, para. 91.
[15] Above, p. 361.
[16] Above, p. 362.
[17] But D commits an offence under s. 16; below, p. 392.
[18] But D would be guilty of stealing the book.
[19] Again D would commit an offence under s. 16. See below, p. 392.

Certainly D must act dishonestly and with intent permanently to deprive P of his property. So far as "intention of permanently depriving" is concerned s. 6 of the Act[20] applies to s. 15 with the necessary adaptation of the reference to appropriating. So far as "dishonestly" is concerned, however, there is no adaptation of the definition of "dishonestly" in s. 2. But it does seem that "dishonestly" ought to be given the same meaning in deception so far as possible, as it has for theft. Accordingly:

> "Owing to the words 'dishonestly obtains' a person who uses deception in order to obtain property to which he believes himself entitled[1] will not be guilty; for though the deception may be dishonest, the obtaining is not. In this respect . . . the offence will be in line with theft, because a belief in a legal right to deprive an owner of property is for the purpose of theft inconsistent with dishonesty and is specifically made a defence by the partial definition of 'dishonestly' in [s.] 2 (1) (a). (The partial definition in [s.] 2 (1) is not repeated in [s. 15 (1)]. It would be only partly applicable to the offence of criminal deception, and it seems unnecessary and undesirable to complicate the [Act] by including a separate definition in [s.] 15.)"[2]

It would seem, following the analogy of dishonesty in theft, that D may act dishonestly for the purposes of deception although he does not obtain the property with a view to gain, or notwithstanding that he intends to pay for the property. The directors in *Edgington* v. *Fitzmaurice*[3] would have been acting dishonestly even if they had honestly believed that the company would get over its difficulties and would have been able to repay the loans; they were acting dishonestly because they knew that the lenders might not have subscribed for the debentures had they known the real facts.[4]

It will be appreciated that owing to the definition of deception (which includes the case where D simply makes a statement of intention, such as a promise to pay, not intending to fulfil it) that this offence—and the same is true of the offence of obtaining a pecuniary advantage by deception under s. 16—might easily give disappointed creditors a criminal remedy against debtors. But the purpose of ss. 15 and 16 is not to provide criminal sanctions against debtors; it is to proscribe dishonesty in the obtaining of property or pecuniary advantage. It does not follow that because D fails to pay or repay that therefore he never intended to do so. Here failure to pay or repay is not proof of a dishonest intent and the jury must be carefully directed on the point.[5]

5 OBTAINING A PECUNIARY ADVANTAGE BY DECEPTION

The offence of deception under s. 15 requires an obtaining of property belonging to another. Although property is widely defined for the purpose, and includes

---

[20] Above, p. 375.
    [1] In view of the subsequent context this must refer to a belief in legal entitlement. A belief in moral right would not suffice, see above, p. 373.
    [2] Cmnd. 2977, para. 88. *Cf. Williams* (1836), 7 C. & P. 354. See *Parker* (1910), 74 J.P. 208; below, p. 450.
    [3] (1885), 29 Ch. D. 459; above, p. 385.
    [4] *Cf. Carpenter* (1911), 22 Cox 618. And see *Williams*, [1953] 1 Q.B. 660; [1953] 1 All E.R. 1068; above, p. 373.
    [5] *Cf. Brownlow* (1910), 4 Cr. App. Rep. 131; *Carpenter* (1911), 76 J.P. 158. In *Ingram*, [1956] 2 Q.B. 424 at 431; [1956] 2 All E.R. 639 at p. 641, DONOVAN, J., said: "Mere delay in paying a debt . . . however, is not a criminal offence, and courts who try to assess these cases will, no doubt, be on their guard against any attempt to abuse . . . by bringing proceedings . . . where there is no real evidence of fraud, but merely of procrastination."

things in action, it has been shown[6] that deception cannot be committed unless some specific property is obtained. D might of course commit an offence under s. 15 where by deception he induces P to assign to him a debt which Q owes to P, because here D has obtained property (the chose in action) from P. But there are many common frauds where, though D does not obtain any specific property belonging to P, he does obtain some pecuniary advantage from P. D might, for example, by deception obtain credit from P, or induce P to postpone the payment of a debt, or get better terms under a policy of life insurance. In none of these cases does D obtain property belonging to P so there would be no offence under s. 15. Section 16 accordingly provides:

"(1) A person who by any deception dishonestly obtains for himself or another any pecuniary advantage shall on conviction on indictment be liable to imprisonment for a term not exceeding five years.

(2) The cases in which a pecuniary advantage within the meaning of this section is to be regarded as obtained for a person are cases where—

(a) any debt or charge for which he makes himself liable or is or may become liable (including one not legally enforceable) is reduced or in whole or in part evaded or deferred; or

(b) he is allowed to borrow by way of overdraft, or to take out any policy of insurance or annuity contract, or obtains an improvement of the terms on which he is allowed to do so; or

(c) he is given the opportunity to earn remuneration or greater remuneration in an office or employment, or to win money by betting.

(3) For purposes of this section 'deception' has the same meaning as in section 15 of this Act."

(1) DECEPTION

By s. 16 (3) "deception" is given the same meaning it has for the offence of deception under s. 15.[7] Deception includes of course a deception as to the present intentions of D and it would be enough, for example, that D books a night's lodgings intending to leave early the following morning without paying his bill. But deception there must be in the obtaining of the pecuniary advantage. No offence is committed where D simply fails to meet his obligations even if he has dishonestly decided not to meet them; there must be deception in the obtaining of the pecuniary advantage.[8] Equally the deception must be an effective cause in the obtaining of the pecuniary advantage.[9] A woman taking out a policy of insurance could not commit an offence in misstating her weight on the proposal by a pound or two.

(2) PECUNIARY ADVANTAGE

The forms which a pecuniary advantage may take are exhaustively defined in s. 16 (2).

The court's power to award costs against a prosecutor may usefully be borne in mind in this connection." DONOVAN, J., was referring to the repealed s. 13 of the Debtors Act 1869, but the observation is equally applicable to the offences under s. 15 and s. 16 of the Theft Act 1968.

[6] Above, p. 389.
[7] See above, pp. 383–386.
[8] See above, p. 390.
[9] See above, p. 387.

1 Reduction, Evasion or Deferment of a Debt or Charge

The following general matters arise for consideration.

(*a*) *Debt or charge.*—It is not clear what "charge" adds to "debt" in s. 16 (2) (a).[10] A debt is a sum of money owed by one person to another. So if D by deception seeks to reduce the amount owing (as by falsely telling P that he has already paid £5 into P's bank account), or seeks to defer its payment (as by falsely telling P that they had agreed on repayment in July and not in June), he may commit the offence. But what if D is under a liability to P not to pay money, but to render services? Suppose D promises to do gardening work for P and is paid in advance. If D never intended to do the work there is no problem because he has then obtained the money paid in advance by deception contrary to s. 15. But it may be supposed that D intended to act honestly at the time he made his contract and subsequently seeks to reduce or defer his obligation to do the work by dishonestly telling P that he agreed only to mow the lawns but not to do the weeding, or that he now has acute lumbago and must postpone the work. D is not now seeking to reduce or defer a debt; but is he seeking to reduce or defer a charge? Prima facie "charge" must add something to "debt", and it cannot be lightly assumed of a modern statute such as the Theft Act that it was meant to convey precisely the same as "debt". On one view it could mean a liability other than a liability to pay money. If this is the case then the jobbing gardener would commit an offence where by deception he seeks to reduce or defer his liability to do the work. But if this was the meaning intended it has to be conceded that "charge" is not the happiest word to choose for the purpose.[11] It may be that charge is used in the sense of incumbrance so that D might commit an offence under the section where he dishonestly tells P, to whom D has mortgaged goods by way of a bill of sale, that the bill is void for want of form. It is possible to imagine circumstances in which "charge" is a more appropriate term than "debt". Suppose, for example, that by deception D obtains a reduction in the rent which he pays for his house. Liability to pay rent is not a debt but may be said to be a charge and consequently D has obtained a reduction in a charge rather than a debt. But this still seems to add little of substance because the rent will become a debt when it falls due, and "any debt . . . for which he . . . *may become* liable" is expressly included in s. 16 (2) (a).

(*b*) *Reduction, evasion, deferment.*—D commits this offence where, by deception he obtains goods on credit since a "debt . . . for which he makes himself liable . . . is . . . deferred". In such a case D also obtains *the goods* by deception and may be convicted of the offence under s. 15. But s. 15 can have no application when D by deception obtains only services on credit. D would commit no offence under s. 15 where, by deception, he induces a jobbing gardener to do certain work for him on credit but since a "debt . . . for which he makes himself liable . . . is . . . deferred" there would be an offence under s. 16.

Section 16 goes further than s. 15 in that D may be convicted where by his deception he obtains only a deferment. For example, D may have purchased goods, without any deception, on cash-on-delivery terms, and when goods are

---

[10] See Smith, *Theft*, paras. 321–324; Griew, *Theft*, 94.

[11] "Liability" might have been the obvious candidate but under the previous law (*cf. Fisher* v. *Raven*, [1964] A.C. 210; [1963] 2 All E.R. 389) "liability" had been held substantially to mean "debt".

delivered he induces P, by deception, to defer payment. Here a "debt . . . for which he . . . is . . . liable . . . is . . . deferred". And if in such a case D contacts P before delivery and by deception induces P to postpone payment then a "debt . . . for which he . . . may become liable . . . is . . . deferred".

Similarly D would commit an offence where by deception any debt or charge for which he is, or makes himself, or may become, liable is reduced. The offence may be committed where by deception D obtains a reduction in his rent, or where he represents himself to a barber as an old age pensioner to get a lower rate for a haircut. Equally it may be said in both these cases that the debt or charge is in part evaded. Reduction, evasion and deferment are not mutually exclusive.

No doubt D may be convicted although the reduction or deferment is not binding on P. It would be enough that D in fact gets a reduction or in fact gets a deferment; that in law D remains liable to pay the full amount or to pay on the due day cannot mean that D commits no offence. Similarly it is enough that D in fact evades payment in whole or in part and it cannot matter that D's legal liability is not evaded. If, for example, D returns to the Inland Revenue an income tax demand, which has been correctly addressed to him, with the legend "Not known at this address" it would seem that a debt for which he is liable is evaded (or possibly deferred) although he still remains legally liable to meet the demand.

(*c*) *Unenforceable debts and charges.*—D may commit the offence of obtaining a pecuniary advantage by deception notwithstanding that the debt for which he makes himself liable is not legally enforceable against him. For example, a debt for which D makes himself "liable" may be unenforceable in civil law because D is under age. But it seems right that a creditor should be protected by the criminal law against the fraudulent practices of an infant[12] as he is against those of an adult. Moreover it is no defence to a charge of obtaining by deception under s. 15 (or any other charge under the Act for that matter) that D is under age.

It would not seem to matter for what reason the debt or charge is not legally enforceable.[13] It might be unenforceable because of D's infancy, or for want of a legally prescribed form, or because it is illegal,[14] or because it is void.[15]

2 Overdrafts and Insurance Policies

D may commit an offence, by virtue of s. 16 (2) (b), where by deception he is allowed to borrow by way of overdraft; as where he tells his banker that he requires the credit to enable him to sell goods abroad when he intends to purchase a car. Where D is so allowed to borrow no debt is created until D draws on his overdraft, but since from the outset a "debt . . . for which he . . . may become liable . . . is . . . deferred" it would seem that the case is already covered by s. 16 (2) (a).[16]

Where, however, D by his deception is allowed to take out an insurance policy or annuity contract, or gets better terms for the same, there would not necessarily

---

[12] Excepting, of course, children under 10; see above, p. 110.
[13] *Cf.* Smith, *Theft*, paras. 325–328.
[14] *Cf. Garlick* (1958), 42 Cr. App. Rep. 141: (illegal contract of hire-purchase).
[15] *Cf. Leon*, [1945] K.B. 136; [1945] 1 All E.R. 14: (void wagering debt).
[16] *Cf.* Smith, *Theft*, para. 331.

be an offence by virtue of s. 16 (2) (a). If by virtue of his deception D is required to pay lower premiums than would otherwise be the case then a debt or charge for which he makes himself liable has been reduced; but if D's deception merely results in an extension of the risks insured against there would be an offence only by virtue of s. 16 (2) (b).

3   Opportunity to Earn by Employment or Win by Betting

As has been shown[17] the offence of obtaining by deception contrary to s. 15 is not committed unless the deception is an effective cause of the obtaining of the property. Consequently that offence is not committed where D by deception induces a bookmaker to take bets on credit since it is the backing of the winning horse that is the effective cause of the obtaining.[18] The case is now expressly covered by s. 16 (2) (c). In so far as D by his deception is allowed to bet on credit a debt for which he may become liable is deferred and the case falls within s. 16 (2) (a); but s. 16 (2) (c) also covers the case where D by his deception is allowed to bet on cash terms.

Again, where D by his deception is given employment there would be no offence under s. 15 since D is paid for work done. The case is now covered by s. 16 (2) (a), as is the case where D is given the opportunity to earn greater remuneration. A schoolteacher who falsely represents that he holds certain qualifications in order to obtain the increments paid to holders of those qualifications would commit an offence under the section.

(3)   MENS REA

What has been said in relation to the *mens rea* of deception[19] seems to be equally applicable to obtaining a pecuniary advantage by deception. On principle, therefore, D does not commit the offence where he acts under a claim of legal right, though, as a practical matter, the circumstances in which D might so act in obtaining a pecuniary advantage are not easily visualised.

6   CHEATING

Cheating was a misdemeanour at common law punishable by imprisonment. The offence was developed most vigorously during the eighteenth century and it appears to require a large and liberal definition to encompass the authorities. Hawkins[20] defined cheating as

> ". . . deceitful practices, in defrauding or endeavouring to defraud another of his own right by means of some artful device, contrary to the plain rules of common honesty."

The common law offence of cheating still retains some importance because though s. 32 (1) of the Act abolishes cheating (along with other common law offences against property) it does so only "except as regards offences relating to the public revenue".

As a practical matter the offence of cheating has been used, on any scale at all, only in connection with frauds against the public revenue. In *Hudson*[21] the Court

---

[17] Above, p. 387.
[18] *Cf. Clucas*, [1949] 2 K.B. 226; [1949] 2 All E.R. 40; above, p. 387.
[19] Above, p. 389.
[20] 1 P.C. 318.
[21] [1956] 2 Q.B. 252; [1956] 1 All E.R. 814, discussed by "Watchful", [1956] B.T.R. 119.

of Criminal Appeal upheld D's conviction on a charge of making false statements to the prejudice of the Crown and the public revenue with intent to defraud where it appeared that D had falsely stated to the Inland Revenue the profits of his business. It was argued that the indictment disclosed no offence known to the law, but the court, relying on *dicta* of Lord MANSFIELD, C.J., in *Bembridge*,[1] and statements by Hawkins[2] and East,[3] held that it was an offence for a private individual as well as a public officer, to defraud the Crown and public.

Hudson's conduct would now be covered by the offence under s. 16 of the Act of obtaining a pecuniary advantage by deception since a debt for which he might become liable is reduced or evaded. It is not easy to see in what circumstances D might commit the offence of cheating without also committing one of the defined offences in the Theft Act. Perhaps this is just why the organs of the public revenue sought its retention.

7 FALSE ACCOUNTING AND OTHER FRAUDS

(1) FALSE ACCOUNTING

By s. 17 of the Theft Act:

"(1) Where a person dishonestly, with a view to gain for himself or another or with intent to cause loss to another,—

(a) destroys, defaces, conceals or falsifies any account or any record or document made or required for any accounting purpose; or

(b) in furnishing information for any purpose produces or makes use of any account, or any such record or document as aforesaid, which to his knowledge is or may be misleading, false or deceptive in a material particular;

he shall, on conviction on indictment, be liable to imprisonment for a term not exceeding seven years.

(2) For purposes of this section a person who makes or concurs in making in an account or other document an entry which is or may be misleading, false or deceptive in a material particular, or who omits or concurs in omitting a material particular from an account or other document, is to be treated as falsifying the account or document."

Where D falsifies any document or record made for an accounting purpose he might often commit offences independently of this section. He might, for example, commit forgery or he might obtain, or attempt to obtain, a pecuniary advantage by deception. But the offence under s. 17 is wider than forgery or obtaining a pecuniary advantage in some respects.

1 Actus Reus

The offence may be committed by any person who makes or is required to make an account for an accounting purpose. Most frequently, no doubt, it will be committed by persons who are employed or engaged to make accounts but it may be committed, for example, where D falsifies his return of income to be submitted to the Inland Revenue. "Any account or any record or document" is wide enough to include mechanical devices for accounting such as a taximeter[4] or a computer.

---

[1] (1783), 22 St. Tr. 1 156.
[2] 1 P.C. 322.
[3] 2 P.C. 821.
[4] *Cf. Solomons*, [1909] 2 K.B. 980.

The offence is also committed where, though D may not himself have falsified the account, he uses the account knowing that it may be misleading, false or deceptive in a material particular. D might then commit the offence where his wife prepares his statement of income for taxation purposes and D uses it knowing that his income is incorrectly stated therein. If in such a case D does not check the account prepared by his wife too closely because he believes that she will have overlooked certain income received by him (and she has in fact done so) then he uses an account which he knows "*may* be" false in a material particular.

2 Mens Rea

The *mens rea* of the offence requires that D act dishonestly and with a view to gain for himself or another, or with intent to cause loss to another.

So far as dishonesty is concerned reference may be made to the discussion elsewhere.[5] No doubt dishonesty should be interpreted here so as to accord with the meaning given it in other sections of the Act.

So far as view to gain and intent to cause loss are concerned "gain" and "loss" are defined in s. 34 (2) (a)[6] which is discussed elsewhere.[7] In this context it may be worth emphasising that there might be a view to gain or an intent to cause loss in falsifying the account although the gain or loss has already taken place. "Gain", for instance, includes a gain by keeping what one has, so it is clear that D would commit an offence under s. 17 where, having already appropriated property of P's, he destroys, defaces, conceals or falsifies an account so that he will not be found out.

In this connection it is worth considering the facts of *Wines*,[8] where D falsified accounts to exaggerate the profit which the radio department, of which he was in charge, was making in order to induce his employer to continue his employment. In such a case there may be no appropriation, or intended appropriation, of any money or goods belonging to the employer, but clearly D is acting dishonestly, and it seems he has both a view to gain (he does this to keep his job and its salary) and an intent to cause loss (in so far as he realises that his employer would make greater profits with an efficient manager).

(2) FALSE STATEMENTS BY COMPANY DIRECTORS

Section 19 of the Act provides:

"(1) Where an officer of a body corporate or unincorporated association (or person purporting to act as such), with intent to deceive members or creditors of the body corporate or association about its affairs, publishes or concurs in publishing a written statement or account which to his knowledge is or may be misleading, false or deceptive in a material particular, he shall on conviction on indictment be liable to imprisonment for a term not exceeding seven years.

(2) For purposes of this section a person who has entered into a security for the benefit of a body corporate or association is to be treated as a creditor of it.

(3) Where the affairs of a body corporate or association are managed by its members, this section shall apply to any statement which a member publishes or concurs in publishing in connection with his functions of management as if he were an officer of the body corporate or association."

---

[5] See above, p. 370 and p. 389.
[6] Set out below, p. 406.
[7] See below, p. 406.
[8] [1953] 2 All E.R. 1497 (C.C.A.).

In two senses the offence created by this section is a narrow one. Firstly, it may be committed only by an officer[9] of a body corporate or unincorporated association. Secondly, it may be committed only where the intent is to deceive members or creditors of the corporation or association about its affairs. But in another sense the offence is a wide one for it extends to the publication of any written statement or account which may be misleading in a material particular. It is not necessary to show that there is any view to gain or intent to cause loss in publishing the statement or account, though no doubt either or both will often be present. The offence might be committed where an officer, in order to inspire confidence in the company, falsely publishes that a well known person has been appointed to the board. Possibly the offence might be committed where an officer publishes in the accounts a payment as having been made to the Conservative Party where it has in fact been paid to the Labour Party.

(3) SUPPRESSION OF DOCUMENTS

By s. 20:

"(1) A person who dishonestly, with a view to gain for himself or another or with intent to cause loss to another, destroys, defaces or conceals any valuable security, any will or other testamentary document or any original document of or belonging to, or filed or deposited in, any court of justice or any government department shall on conviction on indictment be liable to imprisonment for a term not exceeding seven years.

(2) A person who dishonestly, with a view to gain for himself or another or with intent to cause loss to another, by any deception procures the execution of a valuable security shall on conviction on indictment be liable to imprisonment for a term not exceeding seven years; and this subsection shall apply in relation to the making, acceptance, indorsement, alteration, cancellation or destruction in whole or in part of a valuable security, and in relation to the signing or sealing of any paper or other material in order that it may be made or converted into, or used or dealt with as, a valuable security, as if that were the execution of a valuable security.

(3) For purposes of this section 'deception' has the same meaning as in section 15 of this Act, and 'valuable security' means any document creating, transferring, surrendering or releasing any right to, in or over property, or authorising the payment of money or delivery of any property, or evidencing the creation, transfer, surrender or release of any such right, or the payment of money or delivery of any property, or the satisfaction of any obligation."

Despite its length this provision is not likely to be of great practical importance.

"It seemed to us that it might provide the only way of dealing with a person who, for example, suppressed a public document as a first step towards committing a fraud but did not get so far as attempting to commit the fraud. In accordance with the scheme of the [Act] the offence is limited to something done dishonestly[10] and with a view to gain or with intent to cause loss[11] to another."[12]

8 TEMPORARY DEPRIVATION

In general, as has been seen,[13] it is not an offence dishonestly to use the property of another unless there is an intention to deprive the other permanently

---

[9] The officers of a body corporate are frequently defined in the articles or by-laws of a corporation.
[10] See above, p. 370.
[11] See below, p. 406.
[12] Cmnd. 2977, para. 106.
[13] Above, p. 375.

of the property. There is a case to be made out for creating a general offence (which need not necessarily be termed theft) of dishonest use, but the Criminal Law Revision Committee decided against any such course and their view, though subject to vigorous assault in Parliament, was accepted, The Committee were of the opinion—and, it is submitted, were quite rightly of the opinion—that such a considerable extension of the criminal law was not called for by any existing serious evil.[14] But there are particular cases in which temporary deprivation of property is a serious evil. The taking of motor vehicles (which was first made an offence by s. 28 of the Road Traffic Act 1930) is one obvious instance; and the taking of vessels (which was first made an offence by s. 1 of the Vessels Protection Act 1967) is another. These offences are now dealt with in s. 12 of the Theft Act which extends the prior law by making it an offence to take a much wider range of conveyances.

To the offence of taking conveyances the Theft Act adds a further and new offence of temporary deprivation; that of removing articles from places open to the public. Over recent years there have been a number of notorious "removals" such as the removal from the National Gallery of Goya's portrait of the Duke of Wellington, and the Committee thought the problem "serious enough to justify the creation of a special offence".[15]

(1) REMOVAL OF ARTICLES FROM PLACES
OPEN TO THE PUBLIC

Section 11 of the Theft Act 1968 provides:

> "(1) Subject to subsections (2) and (3) below, where the public have access to a building in order to view the building or part of it, or a collection or part of a collection housed in it, any person who without lawful authority removes from the building or its grounds the whole or part of any article displayed or kept for display to the public in the building or that part of it or in its grounds shall be guilty of an offence.
>
> For this purpose 'collection' includes a collection got together for a temporary purpose, but references in this section to a collection do not apply to a collection made or exhibited for the purpose of effecting sales or other commercial dealings.
>
> (2) It is immaterial for purposes of subsection (1) above, that the public's access to a building is limited to a particular period or particular occasion; but where anything removed from a building or its grounds is there otherwise than as forming part of, or being on loan for exhibition with, a collection intended for permanent exhibition to the public, the person removing it does not thereby commit an offence under this section unless he removes it on a day when the public have access to the building as mentioned in subsection (1) above.
>
> (3) A person does not commit an offence under this section if he believes that he has lawful authority for the removal of the thing in question or that he would have it if the person entitled to give it knew of the removal and the circumstances of it.
>
> (4) A person guilty of an offence under this section shall, on conviction on indictment, be liable to imprisonment for a term not exceeding five years."

1 Actus Reus

On the face of it the offence under s. 11 is one of some complexity. As we have

---

[14] Cmnd. 2977, para. 56.
[15] Cmnd. 2977, para. 57 (ii).

seen[16] the intention was to deal with a specific mischief and care has been taken to confine the operation of the section to that michief. The following points arise for consideration.

(*a*) *Public access to a building in order to view.*—The public must have access to the building and the access must be *in order* to view the building (or part of the building or a collection (or part of a collection) housed in it. The public might have access to a building (a shopping precinct or arcade for example) where collections are from time to time exhibited in the lanes connecting the shops; but here access exists in order to shop and it is only incidental to access that the public may view the collection. If, however, the collection is housed in a part of the precinct and access is given to that part so that a collection may be viewed, it would be within the section.

Access must be public access; access limited to a particular section of the public will not suffice. It does not matter that the public are required to pay for the privilege of access, whether the purpose of imposing the charge is merely to cover expenses or to make a profit.[17] But the access must be to a building or part thereof. So if D removes a statuette displayed in the open in a municipal park this would not be within the section. If, however, the park consists of a building and its grounds, and the public have access to the building in order to view, D's removal of the statuette would be within this section.

Normally, no doubt, D will have entered in consequence of the owner's invitation to the public to view. But, so long as the public have access to view, D may commit the offence although he entered as a trespasser, or although he is the owner's guest and is temporarily residing in the building.

(*b*) *Articles displayed or kept for display.*—The offence proscribes the removal of any articles displayed or kept for display, and is not confined to works of art. The coronation stone in Westminster Abbey (something which the Committee expressly considered[18]) is clearly for this purpose an article displayed to the public though it is not a work of art. The criterion is only whether the article, which may be priceless in either sense of the term, is displayed or kept for display to the public.

"Display" here is presumably used in the sense of exhibit and not merely in the sense of able to be seen; the article must be displayed or exhibited *to the public*. Consequently the removal of a fire extinguisher would not be within the section even though it can be seen by members of the public,[19] but it would be within the section if the fire extinguisher was exhibited as an example of an early type of extinguisher, or was in fact an up-to-date extinguisher which was exhibited as an example of good design.

It is enough that the article, though not displayed, is "kept" for display, as where a painting is kept in the gallery's store-room.

(*c*) *Removal.*—To complete the offence the article must be removed from the building or from its grounds. But the removal, as s. 11 (2) makes clear, need not be during the times at which the public have access. If the collection is permanently exhibited (which would be the case, for example, with municipal

---

[16] Above, p. 398.
[17] But see below, p. 400.
[18] Cmnd. 2977.
[19] *Cf.* Smith, *Theft*, 369.

galleries and museums) removal at any time, even on a bank holiday when the building is closed to the public, may amount to an offence. But if the exhibition is temporary only, the removal must take place on a day when the public have access to the building in order to view.

(*d*) *Commercial exhibitions.*—As has been seen,[20] s. 11 applies notwithstanding that the owner charges the public for admission, and even though he admits the public only to make profit. But, whether the owner charges for admission or not, the section does not apply where the owner admits the public only to view a collection,[1] where the collection is "made or exhibited for the purpose of effecting sales or other commercial dealings".

It may seem odd that the law draws this distinction between exhibitions for commercial and non-commercial purposes. The reason given for it is that, but for this restriction upon the offence, the offence would be very wide indeed, and would have created a very substantial exception to the general principle that temporary deprivation should not be a criminal offence.[2] It would have meant, for example, that a removal from the premises of the ordinary commercial book-seller would have been an offence.

As it stands the limitation applies only where the collection is made or exhibited *for the purpose* of sale or other commercial dealings. If then a commercial bookseller, for the purpose of encouraging local art, arranges exhibitions in a room of his bookshop to which the public are admitted, the removal by D of the paintings, or of any other article displayed or kept for display in his premises, would fall within the section. Nor can it make any difference that the artists themselves hope that the exhibition of their work will lead to its sale.

2 Mens Rea

D must intend to remove the article from the building or its grounds. Dishonesty is not required but D would not be guilty of an offence if he removed an article in the belief (and clearly the test of D's belief is here subjective) that he had lawful authority or that the person entitled to give consent would have done so.[3] Strictly it would be an offence for D to remove a statuette from the house to the garden because he thinks the setting better, provided he believes the person entitled to give consent would not have done so.

(2) TAKING CONVEYANCES

S. 12 of the Theft Act 1968 provides:

"(1) Subject to subsections (5) and (6) below, a person shall be guilty of an offence if, without having the consent of the owner or other lawful authority, he takes any conveyance for his own or another's use or, knowing that any

---

[20] Above, p. 399.
[1] Note that if the owner admits the public to view the building as well as the collection D may commit the offence by removing anything displayed (including articles forming part of the collection) although the collection is exhibited for commercial purposes. *Cf.* Smith, *Theft.*, para. 374.
[2] The clause as originally drafted would have excluded not only the case where the public was invited to view the contents for a commercial object, but also where the public was invited to view the building for a commercial object. The latter limitation was removed; *cf.* last footnote.
[3] See further in connection with the offences under s. 12; below, p. 403.

conveyance has been taken without such authority, drives it or allows himself to be carried in or on it.

(2) A person guilty of an offence under subsection (1) above shall on conviction on indictment be liable to imprisonment for a term not exceeding three years.

(3) Offences under subsection (1) above and attempts to commit them shall be deemed for all purposes to be arrestable offences within the meaning of section 2 of the Criminal Law Act 1967.

(4) If on the trial of an indictment for theft the jury are not satisfied that the accused committed theft, but it is proved that the accused committed an offence under subsection (1) above, the jury may find him guilty of the offence under subsection (1).

(5) Subsection (1) above shall not apply in relation to pedal cycles; but, subject to subsection (6) below, a person who, without having the consent of the owner or other lawful authority, takes a pedal cycle for his own or another's use, or rides a pedal cycle knowing it to have been taken without such authority, shall on summary conviction be liable to a fine not exceeding fifty pounds.

(6) A person does not commit an offence under this section by anything done in the belief that he has lawful authority to do it or that he would have the owner's consent if the owner knew of his doing it and the circumstances of it.

(7) For purposes of this section—

(a) 'conveyance' means any conveyance constructed or adapted for the carriage of a person or persons whether by land, water or air, except that it does not include a conveyance constructed or adapted for use only under the control of a person not carried in or on it, and 'drive' shall be construed accordingly; and

(b) 'owner', in relation to a conveyance which is the subject of a hiring agreement or hire-purchase agreement, means the person in possession of the conveyance under that agreement."

1 Taking for Own or Another's Use

It would seem that a conveyance is taken whenever D assumes possession or control of it; it does not seem to be necessary that the conveyance should in fact be removed or taken *away*.[4] Normally D will take a conveyance from the possession of P, but it may happen that D is already lawfully in possession or control of the conveyance. In such a case the question may arise whether D can be said to "take" the conveyance by using it in an unauthorised way. Suppose, for example, that D, authorised to use P's van in the course of P's business, uses the van to take his family to the seaside. It seems clear that under this section[5] he may commit the offence for he now "takes [the van] for his own ... use". D does not have the consent of P for the taking for his own use. But there is an exception in the case of a hirer under a hire-purchase agreement. His unauthorised use could not be an offence under the section because by s. 12 (7) he is treated as owner for the purposes of the section.

There must, however, be a taking of a conveyance for one's own or another's use. A hitch-hiker would not commit the offence where, unknown to the driver, he jumps into a passing lorry and "steals" a ride.

---

[4] Section 217 of the Road Traffic Act 1962, which is repealed by the Theft Act, provided that the offence was committed where D "takes and drives away" the vehicle.

[5] As to the position under R.T.A. 1962, s. 217, *cf. Mowe* v. *Perraton*, [1952] 1 All E.R. 423; *Wibberley*, [1965] 3 All E.R. 718.

16

But, subject to the requirement of taking, the offence does seem, in essence, to consist in stealing a ride.[6] This seems implicit in the requirement that the taking be for "his own or another's *use*". Thus if D releases the handbrake of a car so that it runs down an incline, or releases a boat from its moorings so that it is carried off by the tide, this would not, as such, be an offence within the section. The taking must be for D's use or the use of another, and if he intends to make no use of the car or boat there would be no offence under s. 12. But it would be enough if D were to release the boat from its moorings so that he would be carried downstream in the boat.

D might commit an offence of malicious damage in either of the foregoing illustrations. But if he intends merely to inconvenience the boat owner, and neither intends nor foresees that the boat may be damaged, it seems that he would commit no offence. This is a curious limitation on the offence though it may be that as a practical matter the gap at this point between the Theft Act 1968 and the Malicious Damage Act 1861 is very small.

2 Conveyance

In line with the idea that the essence of the offence in stealing a ride, conveyance is defined, in effect, to exclude conveyances which are not meant for riding.[7] Thus, though it would be an offence to take an aircraft, hovercraft or railway engine, it is not an offence within this section to take a handcart or certain kinds of milk-float which, though power driven, are operated by a person who is not carried in or on it. A bath chair might fall within the definition but not a perambulator.

3 Driving or Being Carried

Where D takes a conveyance without consent or other lawful authority, it is an offence for E, knowing the conveyance has been so taken, to drive it or allow himself to be carried in or on it. A hitch-hiker would not be guilty of an offence where, unknown to him, the driver is using his employer's van, contrary to his instructions, to go to Blackpool for the day. If the driver tells the hitch-hiker that he is so using the van then the hitch-hiker will be liable if he allows himself to be carried further.

It could happen that D believes he has authority to take the conveyance but E knows he has not. In such a case E would be guilty of an offence since he knows[8] it was taken without authority. And no doubt E knows the conveyance has been taken without authority, and may be convicted under this provision, though he knows that D has in fact stolen the conveyance.[9]

---

[6] But it may be possible to envisage cases falling within the section although D does not intend to steal a ride; *e.g.*, where D *tows* away P's vintage car in order to exhibit the car at his showrooms to attract customers.

[7] *Cf.* Cmnd. 2977, para. 84. Earlier (para. 82) the Committee seemed to have viewed the mischief of the offence as the danger, loss and inconvenience which often result from it. See Hansard, H.L. Vol. 290, col. 141.

[8] See above, p. 73 and below, p. 403.

[9] *Cf. Tolley* v. *Giddings*, [1964] 2 Q.B. 354; [1964] 1 All E.R. 201.

4 Pedal Cycles

Section 12 (5) creates an offence of taking pedal cycles which is broadly similar in its incidents to the offence under s. 12 (1). A small difference is that the offence under 12 (5) is not committed by one who allows himself to be carried on the cycle knowing that it has been taken without authority. And, of course, the offence is summary only.

5 Mens Rea

Section 12 (6) provides that a person does not commit an offence by anything done in the belief that he has lawful authority to do it or that the owner would have consented. The test of belief appears to be subjective so that an honest but unreasonable belief in authorisation would suffice.[10] If D takes a conveyance not caring whether the owner would or would not have consented, it would seem that he may be convicted for, in such a case, he does not *believe* that the owner would have consented. But where E is charged with driving or allowing himself to be carried in a conveyance taken by D, it must be shown that E *knew* that D had taken the conveyance without authority; presumably wilful blindness on E's part will suffice but it may be[11] that nothing short of actual knowledge will suffice. Hence E would be acquitted where he thinks it quite possible that D might have taken the vehicle without authority but makes no inquiries to ascertain whether this is so or not.

9 BLACKMAIL[12]

Originally the word blackmail was used to describe the tribute paid to Scottish chieftains by landowners in the border counties in order to secure immunity from raids on their lands. In the early stages of its development the crime of black-mail seems to have been pretty well coextensive with robbery and attempted robbery,[13] but over the years the definition has been extended to embrace more subtle methods of extortion. The law is now set out in s. 21 of the Theft Act:

> "(1) A person is guilty of blackmail if, with a view to gain for himself or another or with intent to cause loss to another, he makes any unwarranted demand with menaces; and for this purpose a demand with menaces is unwarranted unless the person making it does so in the belief—
>
> (a) that he has reasonable grounds for making the demand; and
> (b) that the use of the menaces is a proper means of reinforcing the demand.
>
> (2) The nature of the act or omission demanded is immaterial, and it is also immaterial whether the menaces do or do not relate to action to be taken by the person making the demand.
>
> (3) A person guilty of blackmail shall on conviction on indictment be liable to imprisonment for a term not exceeding fourteen years."

1 The Demand

A demand may take any form, and, no doubt, may be implicit as well as

---

[10] *Cf.* R.T.A. 1960, s. 217 (2), under which the test was objective.
[11] *Cf. Tolley* v. *Giddings*, [1964] 2 Q.B. 354; [1964] 1 All E.R. 201. *Cf.* the offence of handling; below, p. 432.
[12] MacKenna, "Blackmail", [1966] Crim. L.R. 467; Hogan "Blackmail", [1966] Crim. L.R. 474.
[13] Winder, "The Development of Blackmail" (1941), 5 M.L.R. 21.

explicit. D may be guilty of blackmail where, for example, he apprehends P in the act of stealing and conveys to P, without any formal demand, that if P pays him money he will hear no more of the matter.[14] The humblest form of request may be a demand if it contains a menace which is to materialise on failure to to comply with the request.[15] But, whether express or implied, there must be a demand. If, having caught P in the act of stealing, D receives and accepts an offer to buy his silence, D might commit the offence of withholding for gain information relating to an arrestable offence[16] but he would not be guilty of blackmail.

Normally the demand will be for money or other property but s. 21 (2) provides that "the nature of the act or omission demanded is immaterial". This is not as far reaching as may appear at first sight because in any event the offence can be committed only if D has a view to gain or an intent to cause loss, and this refers to gain or loss in money or other property.[17] The provision seems to have been included[18] to forestall a possible argument that D's demand must be for some specific property. D might, for example, demand with menaces that he be given employment; in such a case he may be guilty of blackmail if he acts with a view to gain although he does not demand any property of P.

2 Menaces

The word "menace" is capable of a variety of connotations. On one view it might connote only threats of violence to persons or property, but under the former law relating to blackmail "menace" was given a much wider meaning. In this case it seems clear that it was intended to retain the former law; the Criminal Law Revision Committee was of course well aware of the meaning "menace" had acquired and deliberately chose to use this word when they might have chosen some other.[19]

In *Thorne* v. *Motor Trade Association*,[20] Lord WRIGHT said[1] that a menace was a threat of "any action detrimental to or unpleasant to the person addressed". This is of course to define menace very widely. The Committee chose menaces in preference to threats because, "notwithstanding the wide meaning given to "menaces" in *Thorne's Case* . . . we regard that word as stronger than "threats", and the consequent slight restriction on the scope of the offence seems to us right". In view of Lord WRIGHT's definition of menaces it might be thought that any distinction between menaces and threats is wholly illusory, but it does perhaps serve to emphasise that the law will not treat as a menace words or conduct which would not intimidate or influence anyone to respond to the demand. This is not to say that there can be no menace unless P is intimidated. D may be guilty of blackmail where he threatens to assault P unless P pays him money, though P is in no way frightened and squares up to D with the result that D runs

---

[14] *Cf. Collister & Warhurst* (1955), 39 Cr. App. R. 100.

[15] *Cf. Robinson* (1796), 2 East P.C. 1110, where the words "Remember, Sir, I am now only making an appeal to your benevolence" were held in the circumstances capable of importing a demand.

[16] Below, p. 521.

[17] Theft Act, s. 34; below, p. 406.

[18] *Cf.* Cmnd. 2977, Annex 2.

[19] Cmnd. 2977, para. 123.

[20] [1937] A.C. 797; [1937] 3 All E.R. 157.

[1] [1937] A.C. at p. 817; [1937] 3 All E.R. at p. 167.

away.[2] Here D intends to intimidate P when he makes the demand and it can make no difference that P is unmoved. D's intention seems to be the crucial factor here.[3] D may make what is literally a demand with menaces ("give me that book or I'll knock your block off"), but if he believes that in the circumstances his threat will not be taken seriously by P there is no intention to use the threat to reinforce the demand. It may be, of course, that P is an unusually timid soul and promptly parts with the book in the belief that D will assault him if he does not. There will still be no offence unless D knows of P's timidity and believes that in the circumstances P will part with the book because of the threat. D must intend that his threat should operate on the mind of P to cause P to comply with his demand, and this must involve a consideration of D's knowledge of all the circumstances[4] including his knowledge as to whether P is courageous or cowardly.

3 Unwarranted Demand

Not every demand accompanied by a menace will amount to blackmail. It will be appreciated at once that it ought not to be blackmail to demand payment of a debt and to threaten civil proceedings in the event of failure to comply. There is a menace (a threat of action detrimental to or unpleasant to the person addressed) but it is in the circumstances a perfectly lawful demand accompanied by a justifiable threat. At the other extreme a demand by D for property to which he is not legally entitled accompanied by a threat to kill P would be thought of as an obvious instance of blackmail.

But between these two extremes less clear cut cases emerge. D may threaten to post P as a defaulter unless he pays a gaming debt;[5] D may threaten to publish memoirs which expose discreditable conduct of P's unless P buys them from her;[6] or D may threaten to expose P's immoral relationship with her unless P pays money which he had promised her.[7] Whether the conduct in any or all of these cases *ought* to be blackmail might give rise to a good deal of argument, but the solution provided in s. 21 (1) of the Theft Act is that D's demand will be unwarranted unless made in the belief (a) that there are reasonable grounds for making it, *and* (b) that the use of the menaces is a proper means of enforcing the demand.

The test is then essentially a subjective one. Suppose that D has had an immoral relationship with P and P promises that he will pay D £100 for the favours which he has received; P fails to keep his promise whereupon D threatens to expose the relationship to P's wife unless he pays.[8] D's liability would now turn upon whether she believed that she had reasonable grounds for demanding the £100, *and* believed that her threat to expose P's immorality was a proper way of enforcing the demand. All the circumstances have to be taken into account in so far as they are relevant as tending to show or negative that her belief was genuine. D might have believed (wrongly) that she was legally entitled to the £100 and that it was lawful for her to threaten to expose P to get it; if that were her belief she would surely believe the demand reasonable and the menace proper.

[2] *Cf. Moran*, [1952] 1 All E.R. 803 (C.C.A.).
[3] *Cf. Clear*, [1968] 1 All E.R. 74 (C.A.).
[4] *Cf. Clear*, [1968] 1 All E.R. 74, 80.
[5] *Cf. Norreys* v. *Zeffert*, [1939] 2 All E.R. 187.
[6] *Cf.* the case discussed in Lord DENNING's *Report*, Cmnd. 2152, 31–36.
[7] *Cf. Bernhard*, [1938] 2 K.B. 264; [1938] 2 All E.R. 140.
[8] *Cf. Bernhard*, [1938] 2 K.B. 264.

She might have believed she was morally entitled to enforce payment in this way, and this would be enough provided she believed in fact that this was reasonable and proper. One person (a lawyer for example) might feel that he was morally entitled to something and yet recognise that his moral claim would not afford him reasonable grounds for making the demand. Another person might genuinely think that his moral right affords him reasonable grounds. In practice, it may be thought, D does not think precisely in terms of the legality or morality of his conduct, but more in terms whether it is, in a broad way, reasonable.

It has been argued[9] that it is not right that D's own moral standards should determine the rightness or wrongness of his conduct; that the law should give "efficacy to the defendant's moral judgments whatever they may be". The answer to this may be that as a practical matter most people do act according to generally accepted legal and moral standards, and the cases must be rare where D can *genuinely* rely on his own moral standards where these are seriously at odds with accepted standards. Of course there will be such cases,[10] but they will be extremely rare and, given that D honestly believes that his demand was reasonable and his threat a proper way to enforce it, it seems right that he should not be treated as a blackmailer.

Conversely, and because of the subjective nature of the test, D may be guilty of blackmail where he thinks he has no reasonable grounds for his demand or that the use of the menaces is improper, even though, viewed objectively, his demand is perfectly reasonable and his threat perfectly proper. Concentrating to this extent on D's state of mind as the criterion of criminality may be something of an innovation in English criminal law, but cases where the matter arises must inevitably be rare.

Section 21 (2) provides that it is immaterial that the menaces relate to action to be taken by the person making the demand. Consequently if D makes a demand of P and threatens that E will assault P if he does not comply, this may amount to blackmail. Perhaps this was clear enough without express provision for it, but the provision was included to prevent any possible argument.[11]

4 View to Gain or Intent to Cause Loss

It has been noted above[12] that the requirement of a view to gain or intent to cause loss operates as a limiting factor on the offence of blackmail. Many might describe as blackmail a threat by D to prosecute P for theft unless she has sexual intercourse with him, but this, though it may constitute some other offence,[13] would not amount to blackmail under s. 21 (1) of the Act. The Theft Act is concerned with invasions of economic interests, and gain and loss are defined accordingly in s. 34 (2) (a):

> ..."'gain' and 'loss' are to be construed as extending only to gain or loss in money or other property, but as extending to any such gain or loss whether temporary or permanent; and—
>
> (i) 'gain' includes a gain by keeping what one has, as well as a gain by getting what one has not; and

---

[9] By MacKenna, J., "Blackmail", [1966] Crim. L.R. 467, 469.
[10] Hogan, "Blackmail", [1966] Crim. L.R. 474, 479.
[11] Cmnd. 2977, Annex 2.
[12] At p. 404.
[13] See above, p. 294.

(ii) 'loss' includes a loss by not getting what one might get, as well as a loss by parting with what one has.''

In the ordinary case of blackmail D will have both a view to gain and an intent to cause loss; by demanding money from P by threats D will ordinarily wish to gain the money for himself and cause the loss of it to P. But either suffices. D may commit the offence where he intends to cause loss to P without making a gain for himself; as where, by threats, he demands that P destroy property belonging to Q. And clearly in this case D intends to cause loss to "another" though the person threatened is not the person to whom the loss is caused.

Conversely there may be a view to gain although there is no intent to cause loss. D might demand that P appoint him a director in P's company; here D has a view of gain for himself but it may well be that, far from intending to cause P loss, he intends to bring him increased profits.

Most often D's view of gain will be transparently obvious since a blackmailer's prime objective is normally to get money or other property from P. And normally D will intend to deprive P permanently of the property. Section 34 (2) (a) makes it clear, however, that gain and loss extend to a temporary, as well as a permanent, gain or loss. D might be guilty of blackmail, for example, where by threats he demands that P makes a loan of property. But will any view of gain—no matter how remote—suffice?[14] Clearly there may be a view to gain although the gain is not to materialise for a period of time, or even though the gain may never materialise.

D might by threats cause P to destroy Q's will on the assumption that this will be to D's financial advantage; it can make no difference that Q is on his death bed or is in the best of health, or that Q has made another will revoking the one destroyed. The essence of blackmail is the demand with menaces and the offence is then complete whether D succeeds thereafter in making a gain or not.[15] What seems to be important is that D should have the view of gain in his mind when he makes the demand; the fact that it has crossed his mind at some stage that there may be a gain involved might not be enough. One of his objectives in making the demand (though he may well have others) must be to make a gain for himself. Equally where it has to be shown that D *intended* to cause loss to another, it would not be enough that D foresaw some likelihood of loss unless he also intended to cause the loss.[16]

Sub-paragraphs (i) and (ii) of s. 34 (2) (a) were introduced to meet a possible argument that D would not be acting with a view to gain, or with intent to cause loss, where the gain or loss had already taken place. For example, D, who owes P £10, might by threats demand that P forgoes his claim; it is now quite clear that D is acting with a view to gain.

A further problem is whether D can be said to have a view to gain or intent to cause loss where he acts under a legal claim of right to the property demanded. Suppose that D, who is in fact owed £10 by P, threatens to expose to P's employers the fact that P is a homosexual unless P pays the debt. Obviously D can satisfy the requirement that he believes he has reasonable grounds for making the demand, but it may be supposed (as must almost invariably be the case) that

---

[14] See Smith, *Theft*, paras. 441–443.
[15] *Cf. Moran*, [1952] 1 All E.R. 803n.
[16] See above, p. 379.

D does not believe that the use of the menace is a proper means of reinforcing the demand.

It was clearly intended by the Criminal Law Revision Committee that D might be guilty of blackmail if he failed to meet either of the criteria in paragraphs (a) and (b) of s. 21 (1), and irrespective of whether D acted under a legal claim of right to the property demanded:

> "The essential feature of the offence will be that the accused demands something with menaces when he knows either that he has no right to make the demand or that the use of the menaces is improper. This, we believe, will limit the offence to what would ordinarily be thought should be included in blackmail. The true blackmailer will know that he has no reasonable grounds for demanding money as the price of keeping his victim's secret: *the person with a genuine claim will be guilty unless he believes that it is proper to use the menaces to enforce his claim.*"[17]

The offence of blackmail is, however, governed in all cases by the requirement of view to gain or intent to cause loss, and it can be argued[18] that where D demands property to which he is *legally* entitled, he has no view to make a gain for himself or to cause loss to another; D makes no gain in getting what he is legally entitled to, and P sustains no loss in paying his lawful debts. In other statutory contexts gain is sometimes treated as economic gain or profit, but it has also been said to mean acquisition and is not necessarily to be equated with profit.[19] To give it the latter meaning in the context of the Theft Act would certainly be consistent with the Committee's intentions. The point is, perhaps, an open one.

10 BURGLARY AND AGGRAVATED BURGLARY

(1) BURGLARY

Section 9 of the Theft Act provides:

"(1) A person is guilty of burglary if—

(a) he enters any building or part of a building as a trespasser and with intent to commit any such offence as is mentioned in subsection (2) below; or

(b) having entered any building or part of a building as a trespasser he steals or attempts to steal anything in the building or that part of it or inflicts or attempts to inflict on any person therein any grievous bodily harm.

(2) The offences referred to in subsection (1) (a) above are offences of stealing anything in the building or part of a building in question, of inflicting on any person therein any grievous bodily harm or raping any woman therein, and of doing unlawful damage to the building or anything therein.

(3) References in subsections (1) and (2) above to a building shall apply also to an inhabited vehicle or vessel, and shall apply to any such vehicle or vessel at times when the person having a habitation in it is not there as well as at times when he is.

(4) A person guilty of burglary shall on conviction on indictment be liable to imprisonment for a term not exceeding fourteen years."

---

[17] Cmnd. 2977, para. 121, italics supplied.

[18] Hogan, "Blackmail", [1966] Crim. L.R. 474, 476. *Cf.* Smith, *Theft*, paras. 428–434. *Cf.* Griew, *Theft*, 118.

[19] *Cf.* Smith, *Theft.*, para. 432 and authorities there cited. *Cf. Blazina*, [1925] N.Z.L.R. 407 on the meaning of "extort or gain" in the New Zealand Crimes Act 1908.

1   The Actus Reus

(a) Enters

In the vast majority of cases the proof of an entry will present no problems; but there are bound to be borderline cases where difficulties arise. Suppose that D climbs up a drainpipe and puts his arm through a window in order to pull himself inside. Has he entered? If not, is it necessary that his entire body should be within the building? The man with his arm through the window was not "in" a building for the purposes of "being found" there, under s. 28 of the Larceny Act 1916;[20] but he had made a sufficient entry for the purposes of burglary at common law and under the Larceny Act 1916. As the Theft Act gives no express answer to these problems, it is possible that the courts will resort to the common law cases in the interpretation of "enters"; and, indeed, it seems to have been assumed in Parliament[1] that the common law rules would apply.

The common law rule is that the insertion of any part of the body, however small, is a sufficient entry. So where D pushed in a window pane and the forepart of his finger was observed to be inside the building, that was enough[2]. But the common law goes farther than that. If an instrument is inserted into the building *for the purpose of committing the ulterior offence*, there is an entry even though no part of the body is introduced into the building. So it is enough that hooks are inserted into the premises to drag out the carpets[3] or that the muzzle of a gun is introduced with a view to shooting someone inside[4]. It would amount to an entry if the holes were bored in the side of a granary so that wheat would run out and be stolen by D,[5] provided that the boring implement emerged on the inside. On the other hand, the insertion of an instrument *for the purpose of gaining entry* and not for the purpose of committing the ulterior offence, is not an entry if no part of the body enters.[6] If D bores a hole in a door with a centre bit for the purpose of gaining entry, the emergence of the point of the bit on the inside of the door is not an entry.

Even if the courts are willing to follow the common law in holding that the intrusion of any part of the body is an entry, they may be reluctant to preserve these technical rules regarding instruments, for they seem to lead to outlandish results. Thus it seems to follow from the common law rules that there may be an entry if a stick of dynamite is thrown into the building or if a bullet is fired from outside the building into it.[7] What then if a time bomb is sent by parcel post? Has D "entered", even though he is not on the scene at all?—perhaps even abroad and outside the jurisdiction? Whether D enters or not can hardly depend on how far away he is and the case seems indistinguishable from the others put.

There is, however, a cogent argument in favour of the common law rules which may be put as follows. If D sends a child, under the age of ten, into the building to steal, this is obviously an entry by D,[8] through an "innocent agent", under

---

[20] *Parkin*, [1950] 1 K.B. 155.
[1] Parl. Debates, Official Report (H.L.) Vol. 290, cols. 85–86.
[2] *Davis* (1823), R. & R. 499.
[3] (1583), 1 Anderson 114.
[4] 2 East P.C. 49.
[5] *State* v. *Crawford* (1899), 46 L.R.A. 312 (Alabama).
[6] *Hughes* (1785), 1 Leach 406; but *cf. Tucker* (1844), 1 Cox C.C. 73.
[7] 1 Hawk. P.C., c. 17, s 11; 2 East P.C., 490; *contra*, Hale, 1 P.C. 554.
[8] Hale, 1 P.C. 555; see *supra*, p. 81.

16*

ordinary principles. Suppose that, instead of a child, D sends in a monkey. It is hard to see that this should not equally be an entry by D. But if that point be conceded, it is admitted that the insertion of an *animate* instrument is an entry; and are we to distinguish between animate and inanimate instruments? Unless we are, the insertion of the hooks, etc., must also be an entry.[9]

If D puts a child under ten through the window, so that child may open a door and admit D who will himself steal, it is by no means so clear that the innocent agency argument is open; and the common law rule regarding instruments would suggest it is not an entry; since the child is being used to gain entry and not to commit the ulterior offence. But D has probably attempted to commit burglary.

(b)   As a trespasser

Trespass is a legal concept and we must resort to the law of tort in order to ascertain its meaning.[10] It would appear that any intentional, reckless or negligent entry into a building is a trespass if the building is in fact in the possession of another who does not consent to the entry. Mistake is no defence to an action in tort; so that, if D on a very dark night were to enter the house next door in mistake for his own, this would be regarded as an intentional entry and a trespass. This would apparently be so even if D's mistake was a reasonable one, *a fortiori* if it were negligent as, for example, if he made the mistake because he was befuddled with drink.

If D's entry is involuntary, he is not a trespasser and cannot be guilty of burglary, so if he is dragged against his will into P's house and left there by his drunken companions and he steals P's vase and leaves, this is not burglary. If, however, D had intentionally entered the building, believing it to be his own house and committed theft on discovering the truth he would have committed theft after entering as a trespasser and thus committed the *actus reus* of burglary. It is submitted that in this case D should be acquitted on the ground of lack of *mens rea*. Though, under the civil law, he entered as a trespasser, it is submitted that he cannot be convicted of the criminal offence unless he knew of the facts which caused him to be a trespasser or, at least, was reckless.[11] If that be so, D's entry into the house next door in the belief that it is his own, though a trespass for the purposes of the law of tort, is not such a trespass as will found liability for burglary. It might be different if D were reckless as where, for example, being fuddled with drink, he is not sure whether he is on the threshold of his own house or the house next door, and decides to enter, either hoping that it is his own house, or not caring whether it is or not. A merely negligent entry, as

---

[9] Griew suggests that, while entry might be effected through an innocent agent (in which he would include an animal), the intrusion of an instrument should never be regarded as an entry. In such cases D will usually be guilty of an attempt either to commit burglary or to commit the ulterior offence; *op. cit.*, 54. It would be odd that D should be held to have entered if he took the goods out of the shop window with his hand but not if he did so with a rake; but a line has to be drawn somewhere and, wherever it is drawn, there will be some pretty curious results.

[10] Salmond on *Torts* (14th ed.) 67; Winfield on *Tort* (8th ed.) 323; Street, *Law of Torts* (4th ed.) 13, 63. It is submitted that the doctrine of trespass *ab initio*, even if it survives in the law of tort (see *Chic Fashions (West Wales) Ltd.* v. *Jones*, [1968] 2 Q.B. 299 at p. 313 and p. 320; [1968] 1 All E.R. 229 at p. 236 and p. 239) has no relevance in the law of burglary.

[11] The absence of the word "knowingly" should not deter the court from importing a requirement of *mens rea*: *Roper* v. *Taylor's Central Garage Exeter, Ltd.*, [1951] 2 T.L.R. 284 at 288, *per* DEVLIN, J.; above, p 62.

where D enters another's house, unreasonably but honestly believing that it is his own, should not be enough.

Where consent to entry is obtained by fraud, there is no doubt that the entry is a trespass. If D, intending to steal, gains admission to P's house by falsely pretending that he has been sent by the B.B.C. to trace disturbances in transmission, he commits burglary.[12] If D has been given permission to enter for a specific purpose and he enters for some other purpose, it seems that, on the balance of the authorities,[13] he does so as a trespasser so that, if the other conditions of the offence are satisfied, he may be convicted of burglary. That is it is enough to negative a licence to enter, that entry is made with a secret unlawful intent, even though no false pretence is made. If this is right, D, who enters a shop for the purpose of shoplifting, is a burglar. This is perhaps fair enough. Few would object to the conviction of burglary of intending bank robbers who enter the bank flourishing pistols; yet banks are no more and no less open to the public than shops—that is, an invitation is extended by both to those members of the public who wish to enter for the transaction of the business for which the premises exist—the sale of goods, the cashing of cheques, the opening of an account and so on.

This is not to say that all shoplifters now become burglars. In order to convict of burglary, it will be necessary to prove that D entered with intent to steal and this will often be difficult or impossible. If D entered the shop in order to make a purchase or to look at the stock in order to decide whether to make a purchase, he is not a trespasser. If he then yields to temptation and steals, he probably becomes a trespasser but it remains a fact that he did not *enter* as a trespasser. Where there is evidence that the shoplifting was premeditated, as a previous conspiracy, or system, or preparatory acts, as the wearing of a jacket with special pockets, then a conviction for burglary may be possible.

Trespass is an interference with possession. Burglary is therefore committed against the person in possession of the building, or part of the building, entered. Where the premises are let, the burglary is committed against the tenant and not against the landlord. Even if the tenant is only a tenant at will, he may maintain trespass. So may a deserted wife, even if she has no proprietary interest in the matrimonial home.[14] The guest at a hotel does not usually have possession of his room,[15] nor does a lodger.[16] Where D breaks into the hotel bedroom, or the lodger's room he commits burglary against the hotelier or the landlord, not against the guest or lodger. If the hotelier enters the guest's room, or the landlord the lodger's, with intent to steal, this is not burglary because there is no trespass. Depending on the terms of the contract, the posititition may be similar where a servant occupies premises belonging to his master for the more convenient performance of his duties as servant.[17]

---

[12] *Boyle*, [1954] 1 Q.B. 292.

[13] *Taylor* v. *Jackson* (1898), 78 L.T. 555; *Hillen and Pettigrew* v. *I.C.I. (Alkali), Ltd.*, [1936] A.C. 65; *The Carlgarth*, [1927] P. 93 at p. 110, *per* SCRUTTON, L.J.; *Gross* v. *Wright*, [1923] 2 D.L.R. 171; *Farrington* v. *Thomson and Bridgland*, [1959] V.R. 286. *Contra*, *Byrne* v. *Kinematograph Renters Society Ltd.*, [1958] 2 All E.R. 579. Smith, *Theft*, paras. 465–475; Griew, *Theft*, 51–52.

[14] *National Provincial Bank Ltd.* v. *Ainsworth*, [1965] A.C. 1175, but see now Matrimonial Homes Act 1967.

[15] Street, *Torts* (3rd ed.), 67.

[16] It is necessary to look at the particular contract; it *may* give the lodger possession.

[17] *Mayhew* v. *Suttle* (1854), 4 E. & B. 347; *White* v. *Bayley* (1861), 10 C.B.N.S. 227.

(c) Any building or part of a building

The meaning of "building" in various statutes has frequently been considered by the courts.[18] Clearly the meaning of the term varies according to the context and many things which have been held to be buildings for other purposes will not be buildings for the purpose of the Theft Act—for example, a garden wall, a railway embankment or a tunnel under the road. According to Lord ESHER, M.R., its "ordinary and usual meaning is, a block of brick or stone work, covered in by a roof".[19] It seems clear, however, that it is not necessary that the structure be of brick or stone to be a building within this Act. Clearly all dwelling houses are intended to be protected and these may be built of wood; while "the inhabited vehicle or vessel" which is expressly included is likely to be built of steel or of wood.

To be a building, the structure must have some degree of permanence and it seems clear that it would not include a tent even though the tent was someone's home. The outbuildings of a house seem to be buildings for the purposes of the Act so that burglary may now be committed in a detached garage, a wooden toolshed or a greenhouse. Similarly, farm buildings such as a stable, cow-byre, pig-stye, barn or silo and industrial buildings such as factories, warehouses and stores. Other cases are more difficult. It is not uncommon for trespassers to enter unfinished buildings and do damage. If they enter with intent to cause damage are they now guilty of burglary? An unfinished building is a building within s. 6 of the Malicious Damage Act 1861.[20] Why not for the purposes of burglary? Clearly there is a difficult question as to the point in its erection at which a structure becomes a building. In *Manning and Rodgers*[18], LUSH, J., said:

"... it is sufficient that it should be a connected and entire structure. I do not think four walls erected a foot high would be a building."

In that case all the walls were built and finished and the roof was on. It may be that a roof will be thought necessary for a structure to be a building under the present Act, for it clearly is not intended to extend to a walled garden, yard or paddock. What if there is a roof but no walls, as in the case of a bandstand?[19] There is no obvious answer to borderline cases such as this but they are likely to be rare.

(i) *The extent of a "building".*—Under the old law, the entry had to be into a particular dwelling house, office, shop, garage, etc. A single structure might contain many dwelling houses—for example a block of flats—many offices, shops or garages. If D got through the window of Flat 1 with intent to pass through it, go upstairs and steal in Flat 45, the breaking and entering of Flat 1 was neither burglary nor housebreaking for D did not intend to commit a felony therein.[1] It was probably not even an attempt, not being sufficiently proximate to the intended crime. If D broke into a flat about a jeweller's shop with intent to break through the ceiling and steal in the shop, he could be convicted of burglary in the flat only if it could be said that he broke and entered the flat with intent to commit a felony therein, namely to break and enter the shop.[2]

---

[18] See (1871), L.R. 1 C.C.R. 338.
[19] *Moir* v. *Williams*, [1892] 1 Q.B. 264.
[20] (1871), L.R. 1 C.C.R. 338.
[1] *Cf. Wrigley*, [1957] Crim. L.R. 57.
[2] *Cf.* comment on *Wrigley* above at [1957] Crim. L.R. 58. An intention to break through the floor would not be a sufficient ulterior intent if damage to the building was contemplated.

The difficulty about this argument is that while the breaking may reasonably be said to have occurred in the flat, the entering, strictly speaking, took place in the shop. On that view, there was no intent to commit a felony in the flat and it was not, therefore, burglary or house-breaking to break and enter it.

It is not entirely clear how this situation is affected by the Theft Act. It really depends on what is the extent of a "building".[3] In its ordinary natural meaning, this term could certainly include a block of flats. If that meaning be adopted, D's getting into the window of Flat 1 as a trespasser with intent to pass through it, go upstairs and steal in Flat 45 is an entry of a building as a trespasser with intent to steal therein—that is, it is burglary. Similarly the intending jewel thief would be guilty of burglary when he entered the flat above the jeweller's shop as a trespasser. The effect would be to make the full offence of what was previously, at the most, an attempt, and probably was only an act of preparation. There seems no good reason, however, why the law should not be extended in this way. On the contrary, there is everything to be said for enabling the police to intervene at the earliest possible moment to prevent such offences; and for forestalling defences such as "I had no intention to steal in the flat—I was only using it as a passage to another flat which I never reached". It is submitted therefore that the word "building" should be given its natural meaning.

(ii) *Part of a building.*—It is sufficient if the trespass takes place in part of a building so that one lodger may commit burglary by entering the room of another lodger within the same house, or by entering the part of the house occupied by the landlord. A guest in a hotel may commit burglary by entering the room of another guest. A customer in a shop who goes behind the counter and takes money from the till during a short absence of the shopkeeper would be guilty of burglary even though he entered the shop with the shopkeeper's permission. The permission did not extend to his going behind the counter.

What is "a part" of the building may be a difficult and important question. Take a case put by the Criminal Law Revision Committee.[4] D enters a shop lawfully[5] but conceals himself on the premises until closing time and then emerges with intent to steal. When concealing himself he may or may not have entered a part of the building to which customers are not permitted to go; but even if he did commit a tres-pass at this stage, he may not have done so with intent to commit an offence in that part of the building into which he has trespassed. For example, he hides in the broom cupboard of a supermarket, intending

---

[3] In *Hedley* v. *Webb*, [1901] 2 Ch. 126, Cozens-Hardy, J., held that two semi-detached houses were a single building for the purpose of determining whether there was a sewer within the meaning of the Public Health Act 1875, s. 4. In *Birch* v. *Wigan Corporation*, [1953] 1 Q.B. 136, the Court of Appeal (Denning, L.J., dissenting) held that one house in a terrace of six was a "house" within the meaning of s. 11 (1) and (4) of the Housing Act 1936 and not "part of a building" within s. 12 of that Act. But, since the sections were mutually exclusive, the house could not be both a "house" and "part of a building" for the purpose of the Act. Otherwise, Denning, L.J., would have been disposed to say that the house was both and Romer, L.J., also though that "for some purposes and in other contexts two 'houses' may constitute one building". *Cf.* Smith, *Theft*, paras. 489–490.

[4] Cmnd. 2977, para. 75.

[5] *I.e.*, without intent to steal; above, p. 411.

to emerge and steal tins of food. Entering the broom cupboard, though a trespass committed with intent to steal, is not burglary, for he has no intent to steal in the part of the building which he has entered as a trespasser. When he emerges from the broom cupboard after the shop has closed, he is a trespasser and it is submitted that he has entered a part of the building with an intent to steal. He is just as much a trespasser as if he had been told in express terms to go, for he knows perfectly well that his licence to remain on the premises terminated when the shop closed.[6] Suppose, however, having entered lawfully, he merely remained concealed behind a pile of tins of soup in the main hall of the supermarket. This was not a trespass because he had a right to be there. When he emerged and proceeded to steal, still in the main hall of the supermarket, was he entering another part of the building? It is submitted that every step he took was "as a trespasser", but it is difficult to see that he entered any part of the building as a trespasser; the whole transaction took place in a single part of the building which he had lawfully entered.

The word "part" has no precise meaning in relation to buildings. Its significance for the purpose of the section is that a man may lawfully enter one part of a building, yet be a trespasser if he sets foot upon another. It is submitted that there need be no physical division. A line across the floor and a notice, "No customers beyond this line", would be sufficient to divide a shop into two parts. The distinction is between that part into which one is permitted to go, and that part into which one is not. This is the only relevance of the distinction for present purposes; and it is submitted that there is much to be said for the view that a building falls into only two parts; first, that part of the building in which D is lawfully present and, second, the remainder of the building.[7]

If D is lawfully in Flat 1 and, without leaving the building, he enters Flat 2 as a trespasser with intent to pass through it into Flat 3 and steal therein, his entry into Flat 2 does not constitute burglary if each flat is regarded as a separate part. He has not entered *Flat 2*, with intent to steal *therein*. Yet, as we have seen, if he had entered Flat 2 from outside the building as a trespasser, there would have been no problem; he would have entered the *building* as a trespasser with intent to steal *therein*. If the section will bear a construction which will avoid this absurd result, it is submitted that that construction should be adopted.[8] If the view put forward in the previous paragraph be adopted, D has trespassed in the part of the building into which he is not allowed to go, with intent to steal in that part and he is guilty of burglary.

(*iii*) *Inhabited vehicle or vessel.*—The obvious cases which are brought within the protection of burglary by this provision are a caravan or a

---

[6] The Criminal Law Revision Committee thought "The case is not important, because the offender is likely to go into a part of the building where he has no right to be, and this will be a trespassory entry into that part". But he has no right to be in any part of the building after closing time and the only question, it is submitted, is whether he went into *another* part.

[7] *Contra*, Griew, *Theft*, 55, who thinks the construction proposed "desirable but strained".

[8] For further consideration of this problem see Smith, *Theft*, para. 492; Griew, *Theft* 56–57.

houseboat which is someone's home. There seems to be no reason whatever why a home should lack the ordinary protection of the law because it is mobile and this extension is welcome. Its limits should be noted. "Inhabited" implies, not merely that there is someone inside the vehicle, but that someone is *living* there. My saloon car is not an inhabited vehicle because I happen to be sitting in it when D enters against my will. The caravan or houseboat which is a man's home is, however, expressly protected, whether or not he is there at the time of the burglary. He may, for example, be away on his holidays.

The provision is not free from difficulty. Many people now own "dormobiles" or motorised caravans which they use for the ordinary purposes of a motor car during most of the year but on occasions they live in them, generally while on holiday. While the vehicle is being lived in, it is undoubtedly an inhabited vehicle. When it is being used for the ordinary purposes of a motor car it is submitted that it is not an inhabited vehicle. The exact moment at which the dormobile becomes an inhabited vehicle may be difficult to ascertain.

Very similar problems will arise in connection with boats with living accommodation. Ships where the passengers or crew sleep abroad, are clearly covered. The person who trespasses into a passenger's cabin on the *Queen Elizabeth II* in order to steal is clearly guilty of burglary.[9]

Difficult problems of *mens rea* may arise. According to ordinary principles, D should not be convicted unless he knew of the facts which make the thing entered "a building" in law. Suppose D enters a dormobile parked by the side of the road. If he knew that P was living in the vehicle, there is no problem. But what if he did not know? In principle it would seem that he ought to be acquitted of burglary, unless it can be shown that he was at least reckless whether anyone was living there or not; and this seems to involve showing that the possibility was present to his mind.

2 Mens Rea

(a) Intention to enter as a trespasser

As argued above,[10] it is submitted that it must be proved that D intended to enter, knowing of the facts which, in law, made his entry trespassory; or, at least, being reckless whether such facts existed.

(b) The ulterior offence

It must be proved that D, *either*—

    (i) entered with intent to commit one of the following offences:
        (*a*) stealing,
        (*b*) inflicting grievous bodily harm,
        (*c*) rape,
        (*d*) unlawful damage to the building or anything therein;
        or

---

[9] Presumably, in such a case, the trespass is committed against the owners since, under modern conditions, they, and not the master, are in possession of the ship: *The Jupiter* (*No.* 3), [1927] P. 122 at p. 131; affd., [1927] P. 250. The passengers would seem to be in the same situation as the guests in a hotel. See above, p. 411.

[10] See p. 410.

ii) entered and committed or attempted to commit one of the following offences:

(*a*) stealing,

(*b*) inflicting grievous bodily harm.

(*i*)   *Stealing.*—This clearly means theft, contrary to s. 1.[11] So S is not guilty if he enters with intent to commit an offence contrary to s. 15 or s. 16 of the Act. The old distinction between larceny by a trick and obtaining by false pretences becomes important here. Thus D gains admission to P's house or place of business by pretending to be E, the agent of a person well-known to P. This is an entry as a trespasser.[12] D then induces P to sell goods to E, and departs, taking the goods and leaving a forged cheque. There is, of course, no contract with E, the ownership in the goods remains in P, and D has dishonestly appropriated property belonging to another with the intention of permanently depriving the other of it. He is guilty of theft (as well, of course, as obtaining by deception) and, therefore, he is guilty of burglary. But the position is different were D gains admission to P's building by pretending that her (D's) husband is ill and then, by the same pretence, induces P to lend her £20 intending to deprive P permanently of it. Here too D enters as a trespasser but the offence committed inside is only obtaining by deception and not theft (because the ownership in the money passes to D) and therefore burglary is not committed. The difference lies in whether the property passes or not. If D goes into P's shop and induces P to let him have a television set on credit by giving a false address and false references, the nature of D's crime depends on the nature of the transcation in the civil law. If it is hire or hire-purchase, the ownership does not pass and D is guilty of theft as well as obtaining by deception; if it is a credit sale, the ownership passes and D is guilty only of obtaining by deception. Thus, it is burglary in the former case[13] but not in the latter.

(*ii*)   *Grievous bodily harm.*—Though s. 9 (1) (b) does not so provide in express terms, it is clear that, in the context, the infliction of grievous bodily harm must be an "offence".[14] There are three offences of inflicting grievous bodily harm which are likely to be significant for this purpose. These are the offences which have been considered above under ss. 18, 20 and 23 of the Offences against the Person Act 1861.[15] Section 18 requires an actual intent to do grievous bodily harm, s. 20 is satisfied if there is recklessness as to slight bodily harm, whereas s. 23 requires no more *mens rea* than a malicious administration of a poison or noxious thing. Section 9 (1) (a) of the Theft Act clearly requires an intent. One who enters as a trespasser with the *mens rea*

---

[11] See s. 1 (1).

[12] Above, p. 411.

[13] Assuming that entry with intent to commit a fraud of this nature is a trespass: see above, p. 411.

[14] The bill as drafted by the Criminal Law Revision Committee, and as introduced into Parliament did so expressly provide. That the Act does not, is an accidental result of an amendment.

[15] Above, pp. 264–271. See also s. 28 of the same Act. *Cf. Woodburne and Coke* (1722), 16 State Tr. 53; 1 East P.C. 400.

of s. 20 or s. 23 does not, therefore, necessarily commit burglary; but if he then puts his plan into execution and grievous bodily harm actually results, he has committed burglary. Suppose D enters as a trespasser intending to shoot himself or gas himself, knowing that there is risk that, in so doing, he might injure another. This is not burglary. But if he attempts to carry out his intention and survives but causes grievous bodily harm to another, he is a burglar.

It is submitted that an intention to murder should be regarded as an intention to cause grievous bodily harm on the ground that the greater includes the less.

(*iii*) *Rape.*—This offence has been sufficiently considered above. Entry with intent to rape is a species of burglary which might produce some rather odd-looking examples of that crime. For example, D drags P into a barn or persuades her to go into the barn with him, with intent to rape her. If D is trespassing in the barn, this is burglary.

(*iv*) *Unlawful damage to the building or anything therein.*—Again the causing of the damage must amount to an offence. It might be any of the offences created by the Malicious Damage Act 1861.[16] In the case of every one of the offences which is likely to be invoked under this provision, the *actus reus* must be committed "unlawfully and maliciously".

Where the charge is one of entering with intent, it follows that an actual intent at the time of entry to cause the harm in question must be proved. If nothing more can be established than that the damage was caused negligently, then the offence of burglary is not made out.

(2) AGGRAVATED BURGLARY

By s. 10 of the Theft Act:

"(1) A person is guilty of aggravated burglary if he commits any burglary and at the time has with him any firearm or imitation firearm, any weapon of offence, or any explosive; and for this purpose—

(a) 'firearm' includes an airgun or air pistol and 'imitation firearm' means anything which has the appearance of being a firearm, whether capable of being discharged or not; and

(b) 'weapon of offence' means any article made or adapted for use for causing injury to or incapacitating a person, or intended by the person having it with him for such use; and

(c) 'explosive' means any article manufactured for the purpose of producing a practical effect by explosion, or intended by the person having it with him for that purpose.

(2) A person guilty of aggravated burglary shall on conviction on indictment be liable to imprisonment for life."

The reason given by the Criminal Law Revision Committee for the creation of this offence is that "burglary when in possession of the articles mentioned . . . is so serious that it should in our opinion be punishable with imprisonment for life. The offence is comparable with robbery (which will be so punishable). It must be extremely frightening to those in the building, and it might well lead to loss of life."[17]

---

[16] Below, p. 455.

[17] Cmnd. 2977, para. 80.

1   The Articles of Aggravation

"Firearm" is not defined in the Act, except to the extent that it includes an airgun or air pistol. The term is given a very wide meaning by the Firearms Act 1968,[18] but since that statutory definition has not been incorporated in the Theft Act it is submitted that the word should not be given a meaning any wider than that which it naturally bears; and that, therefore, the term "imitation firearm" be similarly limited.

The definition of "weapon of offence" is wider than that of "offensive weapon" in s. 1 (4) of the Prevention of Crime Act 1953,[19] in that it includes (as well as everything within the 1953 Act) any article made for *incapacitating* a person, any article adapted for *incapacitating* a person, and any article which D has with him for that purpose. Articles *made* for incapacitating a person might include a pair of socks made into a gag, and articles *intended* for incapacitating a person might include sleeping pills to put in the night-watchman's tea, a rope to tie him up, a sack to put over his head, pepper to throw in his face, and so on.

The definition of "explosive" closely follows that in s. 3 (1) of the Explosive Substances Act 1875 which, after enumerating various explosives, adds:

> ". . . and every other substance, whether similar to those above mentioned or not, used or manufactured with a view to produce a practical effect by explosion or by a pyrotechnic effect . . ."

It will be observed that the definition in the Theft Act is narrower. The Explosive Substances Act, if read literally, is wide enough to include a box of matches—these produce a "pyrotechnic effect; but it seems clear that a box of matches would not be an "explosive" under the Theft Act. The main difficulty about the definition—and this is unlikely to be important in practice—lies in determining the meaning of "practical effect". Perhaps it serves to exclude fireworks which, so it has been said in connection with another Act, are "things that are made for amusement".[20]

2   "At the Time" of Commission of Burglary

It must be proved that D had the article of aggravation with him *at the time* of committing the burglary. Where the charge is one of entry with intent this is clearly at the time of entry. Where the charge is one of committing a specified offence, having entered, it is at the time of commission of the specified offence.

3   "Has with Him"

This again closely follows the wording of the Prevention of Crime Act 1953. As appears above, the words in that Act mean "*knowingly* has with him",[1] in the sense that D must be proved to have known that he had the thing which is an offensive weapon. It may be predicted with some confidence, therefore, that proof will be required that D knew that he had the article of aggravation with him at the appropriate time. It is submitted that, in principle, proof should also be necessary that he knew the thing had the characteristics of an article of aggravation.

Suppose D enters P's house by using a jemmy, with intent to steal. While he is in the act of stealing he is interrupted by P and attacks him with the jemmy.

---

[18] Above, p. 279.
[19] Above, p. 282.
[20] *Bliss* v. *Lilley* (1832), 32 L.J.M.C. 3, *per* COCKBURN, C.J., and BLACKBURN, J.; but WIGHTMAN, J., thought that a fog-signal was a "firework".
[1] *Cugullere*, [1961] 2 All E.R. 343 at p. 344; above, p. 286.

If the more recent interpretation of the Prevention of Crime Act[2] is followed in construing the Theft Act, the jemmy will be held to be a weapon of offence on the ground that D had it with him for the purpose of causing injury, even though he had no thought of using it for causing injury until that moment. If so, it follows that what is initially a simple burglary may develop into aggravated burglary.[3] In such a case, however, it is submitted that aggravated burglary will lie only if D is charged with entering and committing and not if he is charged with entering with intent.

In the case put, D was in the act of stealing and was therefore guilty of burglary under s. 8 (1) (b) because he had committed or was attempting to commit a specified offence. Suppose, however, that D had been interrupted after entry and before he had reached the stage of an attempt to steal. Even though the jemmy becomes a weapon of offence when it is used against P, D is not guilty of aggravated burglary, if the above submission is correct, because he can now be charged only under s. 8 (1) (a) and the jemmy was not a weapon of offence at the time he committed that burglary. The courts may be tempted, however, to regard burglary as a continuing offence and to hold that it continues to be committed from the time D enters with intent until, he leaves the building. This would extend "aggravated burglary" to the case where D has entered and committed the specified offence, all without thought of using his jemmy as an offensive weapon, but is intercepted as he is about to leave and strikes a blow with it. It is impossible not to sympathise with a desire so to construe the statute so as to avoid the anomalies envisaged above. These anomalies, however, arise from an excessively wide construction of the term "offensive weapon" which, it is feared, will be followed in construing "weapon of offence". To redress the anomalies by adopting a wide interpretation of burglary would result in the statute being given an unduly extended meaning. It is submitted that a better course would be to reconsider the interpretation of "offensive weapon" adopted in *Woodward* v. *Koessler*[4] or not to follow it in construing "weapon of offence". It is submitted that aggravated burglary is really aimed at the criminal who sets out armed with a firearm, etc. It is not aimed at the burglar who sets out unarmed with any aggravating article but happens to make use of such an article in the course of the burglary.[5] If it were, the Act would have said "uses" rather than "has with him". The effect of the *Woodward* v. *Koessler* construction is that if D is interrupted in the course of stealing after a trespassory entry and he picks up an inkstand[6] (or any other object) and throws it with intent to cause injury, he becomes guilty of aggravated burglary. It is submitted that this goes beyond the purpose of this offence.

---

[2] In *Woodward* v. *Koessler*, [1958] 3 All E.R. 557 (D.C.); *Powell*, [1963] Crim. L.R. 511 (C.C.A.); above, p. 284.

[3] Griew argues that, if D enters with a specified intent and so is guilty of burglary under s. 9 (1) (a), he cannot thereafter become guilty under s. 9 (1) (b): *op. cit.*, 61. The effect is that if D1 and D2 enter as trespassers, D1 but not D2 having a specified intent and neither carrying a weapon of offence, and, D2 having fallen in with D1's intent to steal, they use their jemmies, in the course of theft, as weapons, D2 is guilty of aggravated burglary but D1 is not. This is difficult to defend.

[4] Above, p. 284.

[5] It is true of course that these arguments are equally applicable to the Prevention of Crime Act where they do not at present appear to be accepted.

[6] *Cf. Harrison* v. *Thornton*, [1966] Crim. L.R. 388; above, p. 283.

11 POSSESSION OF HOUSEBREAKING IMPLEMENTS, ETC.

By s. 25 (1) and (2) of the Theft Act:

"(1) A person shall be guilty of an offence if, when not at his place of abode, he has with him any article for use in the course of or in connection with any burglary, theft or cheat.

(2) A person guilty of an offence under this section shall on conviction on indictment be liable to imprisonment for a term not exceeding three years."

This provision is expressed to be directed against acts preparatory to:

(i) burglary contrary to s. 9
(ii) theft contrary to s. 1
(iii) criminal deception contrary to s. 15[1]
(iv) taking and driving away a conveyance, contrary to s. 12[2]

(1) THE ACTUS REUS

The *actus reus* consists in the accused's having with him any article. Clearly the article need not be made or adapted for use in committing one of the specified offences. It is sufficient that the *mens rea* is proved in respect of the article, that is, that the accused intended to use it in the course of, or in connection with, one of the specified offences. Thus, it might be a tin of treacle, intended for use in removing a pane of glass, a pair of gloves to be worn so as to avoid leaving finger-prints; a collecting box marked "Oxfam" when the possessor did not represent that organisation; and so on.

The offence is thus very wide in its scope. But there must be some limits. Thus D can hardly be committing an offence by wearing his shoes or any other item of everyday apparel. Yet it was argued above that gloves for the avoidance of fingerprints would entail liability. This suggests that the article must be one which D would not be carrying with him but for the contemplated offence. If it is something which he would carry with him on a normal, innocent expedition, it should not fall within this section. So there might be a difference between a pair of rubber gloves and a pair of fur-lined gloves which D was wearing to keep his hands warm on a freezing night, even though he did intend to keep them on so as to avoid leaving fingerprints. The latter pair of gloves is hardly distinguishable, for this purpose, from D's overcoat which seems to fall into the same category as his shoes. If D is carrying a pair of plimsolls in his car to facilitate his cat-burgling, this seems a plain enough case; but what if he has simply selected his ordinary crepe-sole shoes for wear because they are less noisy than his hob-nails?

The expression "has with him"[3] is the same as in s. 9 (1) (b) of the Act. Questions as to D's knowledge of the nature of the thing can hardly arise here, since it must be proved that he intended to use it in the course of or in connection with a specified offence. No doubt D has an article with him if it is in his immediate possession or control; so that he will be guilty if the article is only a short distance away and he can take it up as he needs it; as where a ladder has been left in a garden by an accomplice and D enters the garden intending to use the ladder to make an entry. If the article is found in D's car some distance from the scene of the crime this will be evidence that D was in possession of the article when driving the car. It is probable that, as under s. 9 (1) (b), mere momentary

---

[1] By s. 21 (5), "cheat" means an offence under s. 15.
[2] By s. 25 (5), "theft" in this section includes an offence under s. 12 (1).
[3] See above, p. 418.

possession will suffice,[4] as where D is apprehended on picking up a stone which he intends to use to break a window in order to commit burglary.

No offence is committed by being in possession of house-breaking implements in one's own home. There is no similar exemption for possession at one's place of work. The offence is committed as soon as D steps from his house into the street carrying the article with intent.

(2) MENS REA

The *mens rea* for the offence would appear to consist in:

(i) knowledge that one possesses the article; and

(ii) an intention to use the article in the course of or in connection with any of the specified crimes.

Section 25 (3) provides:

"Where a person is charged with an offence under this section, proof that he had with him any article made or adapted for use in committing burglary, theft or cheat shall be evidence that he had it with him for such use."

This is probably no more than enactment of the general rules regarding proof of intent.[5] It puts upon D an evidential burden. If he offers no explanation then the jury may be told that there is evidence upon which they may find that he had the necessary intent; but it is submitted that they should be told so to find only if satisfied beyond reasonable doubt that he in fact had that intent.[6] If D does offer an explanation then the jury should be told to acquit if they think it may reasonably be true and to convict only if satisfied beyond reasonable doubt that the explanation is untrue.[7]

Where the article in question is not made or adapted for use in any specified offence, mere proof of possession without more will not amount to *prima facie* evidence—i.e., the case will have to be withdrawn from the jury. It is a question of law for the judge, at what point proof of other incriminating circumstances amounts to a case fit for submission to the jury.

It is not necessarily a defence that D did not intend to use the article while actually committing the contemplated crime. If, for example, he intended to use it only in the course of making his escape after the commission of the offence, this would be enough, being use "in connection with" the offence. Similarly if he intended to use the article while doing preparatory acts. The string used by D to tie himself up in *Robinson*[8] would seem to come within the provision, though it was to be used only in the course of a preparatory act and not in the course of the commission of the proposed criminal deception. Any insurance claim form he might have had, on the other hand, would have been for use in the course of commission of the offence.

12 HANDLING STOLEN GOODS

By s. 22 of the Theft Act:

"(1) A person handles stolen goods if (otherwise than in the course of the

---

[4] Above, p. 418.

[5] *Cf.* Criminal Justice Act 1967, s. 8; above, p. 52.

[6] *Cf.* the case where the alleged receiver is proved to have been in possession of recently stolen property and offers no explanation: *Abramovitch* (1914), 11 Cr. App. Rep. 45.

[7] The decision in *Patterson*, [1962] 2 Q.B. 429 that the onus of proof under Larceny Act 1916, s. 28 was on the accused, was based on the express wording of that section and is entirely inapplicable to the new provision.

(1915), 11 Cr. App. Rep. 124; above, p. 168.

stealing) knowing or believing them to be stolen goods he dishonestly receives the goods, or dishonestly undertakes or assists in their retention, removal, disposal or realisation by or for the benefit of another person, or if he arranges to do so.

(2) A person guilty of handling stolen goods shall on conviction on indictment be liable to imprisonment for a term not exceeding fourteen years."

(1) THE ACTUS REUS

The questions which require consideration are: what are "goods"? when are they "stolen"? and what is "handling"?

1 Stolen Goods

By s. 34 (2) (b):

"... 'goods', except in so far as the context otherwise requires, includes money and every other description of property except land, and includes things severed from the land by stealing."

It will be noted that this definition differs from and is narrower than the definition of "property" for the purposes of theft in s. 1 (1).[9] Since, however, land generally is excluded from theft by s. 4 (1), the effect seems to be that, with small exceptions to be discussed below, the property which can be the subject of handling is co-extensive with that which can be the subject of theft.

(a) Things in action

Things in action are expressly mentioned in s. 4 (1) and not in s. 34 (2) (b). They must however be included in the words "every other description of property except land". The remaining question is whether the context of s. 22 *requires* the exclusion of things in action. If s. 22 were confined, like the old law, to *receiving*, no doubt the context would so require. Receiving connoted taking possession or control of a physical thing and was wholly inapplicable to a thing in action. "Realisation" and "disposal", on the other hand, are words which are perfectly apt to include dealings with a thing in action. Since s. 34 (2) (b) contemplates the possibility of a variable meaning for "goods", it is conceivable that the word excludes things in action for purposes of receiving but includes it for purposes of other methods of handling. It is submitted, however, that a better view would be that things in action are included for all purposes. There is no reason why the assignee of a thing in action should not be held to have received it.

(b) Land

"Land" which is stolen contrary to s. 4 (2) (b)[10] can always be the subject of handling since the stealing necessarily involves severance of the thing in question. A fixture or structure which is stolen contrary to s. 4 (2) (c), on the other hand, may or may not be severed from the land. Only if it is severed can it be the subject of handling. If E, an outgoing tenant, dishonestly sells to D, the incoming tenant, a fixture belonging to P, D cannot be guilty of handling (whether or not his act is in the course of stealing) if the fixture is not severed; nor, of course, is F guilty of handling if he, knowing all the facts, takes over the premises, including the fixture, from D; yet he has knowingly taken possession of a stolen fixture.

Land which is stolen contrary to s. 4 (2) (a) will rarely be capable of being handled since the kind of conduct contemplated by 4 (2) (a) will not normally involve severance.

Land may be the subject of both obtaining by deception and blackmail both of

---

[9] Above, p. 357.
[10] Above, p. 358.

which are stealing for this purpose.[11] Again, severance may or may not take place and handling is possible only if it does so.

(*c*) *Meaning of "stolen"*

By s. 24 (4):

"For purposes of the provisions of this Act relating to goods which have been stolen (including subsections (1) to (3) above) goods obtained in England or Wales or elsewhere either by blackmail or in circumstances described in section 15 (1) of this Act shall be regarded as stolen; and 'steal', 'theft' and 'thief' shall be construed accordingly."

By s. 24 (1):

"The provisions of this Act relating to goods which have been stolen shall apply whether the stealing occurred in England or Wales or elsewhere, and whether it occurred before or after the commencement of this Act, provided that the stealing (if not an offence under this Act) amounted to an offence where and at the time when the goods were stolen; and references to stolen goods shall be construed accordingly."

Thus goods are "stolen" for the purposes of the Act if:

  (i) they have been stolen contrary to s. 1;

  (ii) they have been obtained by blackmail contrary to s. 21.

  (iii) they have been obtained by deception contrary to s. 15 (1);

  (iv) they have been the subject of an act done in a foreign country which was (a) a crime by the law of that country and which (b), had it been done in England, would have been theft, blackmail or obtaining by deception contrary to s. 1 or s. 21 or s. 15 (1) respectively.

(*d*) *The "thief" must be guilty*

If the alleged thief is not guilty, then the handler cannot be convicted for there are no *stolen* goods for him to handle. So if the alleged thief turns out to have been under the age of ten at the time of the alleged theft, then the goods appropriated cannot be stolen goods and there can be no conviction for handling them.[12] In such circumstances, however, the receiver is now guilty of theft.[13]

If the appropriator of the goods is guilty of theft, it is submitted that the goods appropriated may be the subject of handling although the appropriator is immune from prosecution by reason, for example, of diplomatic immunity.[14] The thief could be prosecuted for the theft if diplomatic immunity were waived. The handler may be convicted whether that immunity is waived or not—unless, of course, he too is entitled to diplomatic immunity.

It is submitted that the question whether the thief was guilty must be decided on the evidence of that fact produced at the trial of the handler. Thus the fact that the "thief" has been acquitted is no bar to the prosecution of an alleged handler of the goods which he has been acquitted of stealing and should not even be admitted as evidence that the goods were not stolen.[15] Similarly, the fact that the "thief" has been convicted, far from being conclusive against the alleged handler, is not even admissible evidence that the goods were stolen.[16]

---

[11] Below, p. 423.

[12] *Walters* v. *Lunt*, [1951] 2 All E.R. 645, thus remains good law.

[13] Above, p. 351.

[14] *Cf. Dickinson* v. *Del Solar*, [1930] 1 K.B. 376; *A.B.*, [1941] 1 K.B. 454; *Madan*, [1961] 2 Q.B. 1.

[15] The rule in *Hollington* v. *Hewthorn*, [1943] K.B. 587; [1943] 2 All E.R. 35, though abolished for civil proceedings by s. 11 of the Civil Evidence Act 1968, continues to apply in criminal cases.

[16] *Hollington* v. *Hewthorn*, [1943] K.B. 587; [1943] 2 All E.R. 35; *cf. Humphreys and Turner*, [1965] 3 All E.R. 689; *Remillard* v. *R.* (1921), 62 S.C.R. 21; above, p. 91.

2   When Goods Cease to be Stolen

By s. 24 (3) of the Act:

> "But no goods shall be regarded as having continued to be stolen goods after they have been restored to the person from whom they were stolen or to other lawful possession or custody, or after that person and any other person claiming through him have otherwise ceased as regards those goods to have any right to restitution in respect of the theft."

It is obvious that goods which have once been stolen cannot continue to be regarded as "stolen" so long as they continue to exist thereafter. A line must be drawn somewhere; and the Act draws it in the same place as did the common law. So if the stolen goods are taken from the thief by the owner or someone acting on his behalf, or by the police, and subsequently returned to the thief so that he may hand them over to a receiver, the receiver will not be guilty of handling because the goods are no longer stolen goods.[17] Difficult questions may continue to arise whether goods have in fact been "restored to the person from whom they were stolen or to other lawful possession or custody". Thus in *King*[18] a parcel containing the stolen goods (a fur coat) was handed by E, the thief, to a policeman who was in the act of examining the contents when the telephone rang. The caller was D, the proposed receiver. The policeman discontinued his examination, D was told to come along as arranged, he did so and received the coat. It was held that D was guilty of receiving stolen goods on the ground that the coat had not been reduced into the possession of the police— though it was admitted that there was no doubt that, in a very few minutes, it would have been so reduced, if the telephone had not rung. It is possible that the same result would follow under the Theft Act but it may be that, even if the policeman was not in possession, he had custody of the coat.[19] The case has, moreover, been subjected to criticism. It is easy to see that if the police are examining a parcel to see whether it contains stolen goods they do not take possession of the contents until they decide that this is what they are looking for.[20] In *King*, however, E had admitted the theft of the coat and produced the parcel. One might have expected, therefore, that the policeman had in fact made up his mind to take charge of it before the telephone rang. The decision presumably proceeds on the assumption that he had not done so. It is now quite clear that the goods cease to be stolen in the case where the police are acting without the authority of the owner for they are clearly in "other lawful possession or custody of the goods."[1] Indeed, it would seem to be enough that the goods fall into the possession of any person who intends to restore them to the person from whom they were stolen. If, however, the thief makes a present of the goods to E who does not know that they are stolen, E's possession, though not unlawful in the criminal law, is not a sufficient "lawful possession or custody". Goods may "belong to" more than one person for purposes of the Act; and it is not necessarily enough that they are delivered to an "owner" other than him from whom

---

[17] *Cf. Dolan* (1855), Dears. 436; *Schmidt* (1866), L.R. 1 C.C.R. 15; *Villensky*, [1892] 2. Q.B. 597.

[18] [1938] 2 All E.R. 662, C.C.A.

[19] It is also possible that an "arrangement to receive" had been made before the goods ceased to be stolen.

[20] *Cf. Warner* v. *Metropolitan Police Commissioner*, [1968] 2 All E.R. 356.

[1] *Cf.* the dictum of CRESSWELL, J., in *Dolan* (above footnote 17) that goods retained their stolen character in this situation. Presumably the police in *King* were acting with the owner's authority. The point is not discussed, but it would seem likely that the theft had been reported to the police by the owner.

the goods were stolen. O lets goods on hire to P for a year. E appropriates the goods from P's possession. This is theft from both O and P. If, during the year, the goods are delivered to O who does not intend to restore them to P, they cease to be stolen as against O but can hardly do so as against P.[2] If the goods had been restored to O after the lapse of the year, they would presumably cease to be stolen as against both O and P.

Section 24 (3) also provides that the goods lose their character of stolen goods if the person from whom they were stolen has ceased to have any *right to restitution* in respect of theft. Whether a "right to restitution" exists is a question of civil law. A right to literal restitution is rather rare in English law. The owner of a chattel which has been wrongfully appropriated may sue, according to the circumstances, in conversion or in detinue or both. In an action of conversion he cannot obtain the specific restitution of his chattel and in detinue the court has a discretion which will normally be exercised against specific restitution.[3] Generally the owner will have to be content with damages. It is quite clear that the phrase, "right to restitution", in s. 24 (3) is not intended to be confined to those cases in which the owner would be able to obtain specific restitution in a civil court and it is submitted that it extends to all cases in which he could succeed in an action based upon his proprietary rights in the thing in question, whether in conversion or in detinue or for the protection of an equitable interest.

The provision seems to have been intended to bear a still wider meaning. The Criminal Law Revision Committee explained it as follows:[4]

> "This is because, if the person who owned the goods when they were stolen no longer has any title to them, there will be no reason why the goods should continue to have the taint of being stolen goods. For example, the offence of handling stolen goods will ... apply also to goods obtained by criminal deception under [s. 15]. If the owner of the goods who has been deceived chooses on discovering the deception to ratify his disposal of the goods he will cease to have any title to them."

It is clear that "title" is here used in a broad sense to include a right to rescind. The Committee clearly has in mind a case where property passes from P to D at the moment when the goods are obtained by deception. In such a case, P, strictly, has no "title" and his right to recover the goods (or, much more likely, their value) will only arise on his rescinding the contract.[5] Such a potential right it is submitted, is clearly a "right to restitution" within the Act.

3 Goods Representing those Originally Stolen may be Stolen Goods

By s. 24 (2) of the Act:

> "For the purposes of those provisions references to stolen goods shall include, in addition to the goods originally stolen and parts of them (whether in their original state or not),—
>
> (a) any other goods which directly or indirectly represent or have at any time represented the stolen goods in the hands of the thief as being the proceeds of any disposal or realisation of the whole or part of the goods stolen or of goods so representing the stolen goods; and

---

[2] P retains a right to restitution; below, p. 436.
[3] *Whiteley v. Hilt*, [1918] 2 K.B. 808 at 819, *per* SWINFEN EADY, M.R.
[4] Cmnd. 2977, para. 139.
[5] *Cf.* Smith, *Theft*, paras. 100–104, where it is argued, in relation to s. 5 (4) that a person holding property under a voidable title is not "under an obligation to make restoration"; above, p. 388.

(b) any other goods which directly or indirectly represent or have at any time represented the stolen goods in the hands of a handler of the stolen goods or any part of them as being the proceeds of any disposal or realisation of the whole or part of the stolen goods handled by him or of goods so representing them.''

The Criminal Law Revision stated[6] of this provision:

"It may seem technical; but the effect will be that the goods which the accused is charged with handling must, at the time of the handling or at some previous time, (i) have been in the hands of the thief or of a handler, and (ii) have represented the original stolen goods in the sense of being the proceeds, direct or indirect, of a sale or other realization of the original goods.''

The effect is best explained by an example. If D steals an Austin car, exchanges it with B for a Bentley, exchanges the Bentley with C for a Citroen and sells the Citroen to E for £500; the Austin, Bentley, Citroen and £500 are now all stolen. Although only one car was actually stolen there are now in circulation three stolen cars and five hundred stolen pounds. The position would be exactly the same if D were not the thief but a receiver of the Austin. Clearly this provision can lead to indefinite multiplication of the stolen goods. Whenever any article which is actually stolen or notionally stolen under s. 24 (2) is exchanged for another, that other article is stolen *unless* the person to whom it is delivered is neither the thief nor a handler. So, if in the above example, B knew the Austin to be stolen, anything which he might receive for it would also be stolen; whereas, if C was an innocent receiver of the Bentley, anything which he received for it would lack the taint of stolen goods.

Goods which are notionally stolen, like goods which are actually stolen, continue to bear that taint until the conditions laid down in s. 24 (3) of the Act are satisfied.[7]

4 Forms of Handling

The term "handling" has been adopted because "receiving"—the only way of committing the offence under s. 33 (1) of the 1916 Act—is now one of several ways in which the new offence can be committed. These are:

(i) *Receiving* the goods.

(ii) *Undertaking* the retention, removal, disposal or realisation of the goods by or for the benefit of another person.

(iii) *Assisting* in the retention, removal disposal or realisation of the goods by or for the benefit of another person.

(iv) *Arranging* to do (i), (ii) or (iii).

It is submitted that, in spite of the variety of forms of the offence, there is only one crime, that created by s. 18 (2): "A person guilty of handling stolen goods shall on conviction on indictment be liable . . .". The fact that the offence can be committed in four or six or even eighteen ways is irrelevant since the offence defined as a single one.[8] To hold otherwise would have a disastrously complicating effect on the section, giving wide scope to possible objections on the ground of duplicity.

---

[6] Cmd. 2977 at p. 66.
[7] Smith, *Theft*, paras. 583–587.
[8] See Williams, "The Count System and the Duplicity Rule", [1966] Crim. L.R. 255 at p. 265.

(a) Receiving

All forms of handling other than receiving or arranging to receive are subject to the qualification that it must be proved that D was acting "for the benefit of another person". If there is no evidence of this—as will frequently be the case— then it must be proved that D *received* or *arranged to receive* the goods and evidence of no other form of handling will suffice. The Act does not define receiving in any way and it must be assumed that all the old authorities remain valid.

To establish receiving, it must be proved, then, that D took possession or control of the stolen property or joined with others to share possession or control of it. "Receiving" the thief who has the goods in his possession does not necessarily amount to receiving the goods. If the thief retains exclusive control, there is no receiving.[9] There may, however, be a joint possession in thief and receiver, so it is unnecessary to prove that the thief ever parted with possession—it is sufficient that he shared it with the alleged receiver. In *Smith*[10] it was held that a recorder had correctly directed a jury when he told them that if they believed "that the watch was then in the custody of a person with the cognizance of the prisoner, that person being one over whom the prisoner had absolute control, so that the watch would be forthcoming if the prisoner ordered it, there was ample evidence to justify them in convicting..." Lord CAMPBELL, C.J., said that if the thief had been employed by D to commit larceny, so that the watch was in D's control, D was guilty of receiving. In such a case D was an accessory before the fact to larceny and today he would be guilty of theft. If the facts were as put by Lord CAMPBELL, when did D become a receiver? As soon as the theft was committed? If so, we have the extraordinary result that D became guilty of both theft and receiving at the same moment. But, if this moment is not selected, it is difficult to see what other is appropriate. This may, however, appear less anomalous under the new law than under the old. Virtually all handling is now theft, so it is the general rule that the two offences are committed simultaneously. In the ordinary case, however, the offence is handling because there has been a previous theft. The peculiarity of the present problem is that there has been no *previous* theft.

As is clear from *Smith*, actual manual possession or control by D need not be proved. It is enough if the goods are received by his servant or agent with his authority.[11] The receipt may be for a merely temporary purpose such as concealment from the police.[12] It is unnecessary that the receiver should receive any profit or advantage from the possession of the goods. If D took possession of the goods from the thief without his consent, this was formerly only larceny (from the thief) and not receiving.[13] There seems to be no reason why it should not be both theft and handling under the Act, since it is clear that the two offences can be committed by one and the same act.

It continues to be essential for the judge to give a careful direction as to possession or control.[14] If the only evidence against D is that he ran away on being found by the police in a house where stolen property had been left, there would

---

[9] *Wiley* (1850), 2 Den. 37.
[10] (1855), Dears. 494.
[11] *Miller* (1854), 6 Cox C.C. 353.
[12] *Richardson* (1834), 6 C. & P. 335.
[13] *Wade* (1844), 1 C. & K. 739.
[14] *Frost & Hale* (1964), 48 Cr. App. Rep. 284.

appear to be no case to leave to a jury. Likewise where the evidence is consistent with the view that D went to premises where stolen goods were stored with the intention of assuming possession, but had not actually done so[15] or where the only evidence of receiving a stolen car is that D's finger-print was found on the driving mirror.[16] The mere fact that the stolen goods were found on D's premises is not sufficient evidence. It must be shown that the goods had come either by invitation or arrangement with him or that he had exercised some control over them.[17] D is not necessarily in possession of a stolen safe simply because he assists others in trying to open it.[18]

(b) *Arranging to receive*

Where it is impossible to prove an actual receipt, the evidence may show that D has arranged to receive the goods. Where D has merely made preparations to receive and has not yet reached the stage of an attempt to do so, the preparations may constitute a sufficient arrangement. The difficulties in a case like *King*[19] will be overcome if it appears that the arrangement to receive was concluded before there was a possibility of the goods ceasing to be stolen. Presumably it is enough if the proposed receipt is by a servant or agent. It must be made after the theft, since D must know or believe the goods to be stolen when he makes the arrangement.

Though there is no such express requirement, it is difficult to envisage an arrangement which does not involve an agreement with another. Such an agreement will almost always amount to a conspiracy to receive, so the extension of the law effected by this provision is less far-reaching than might appear. Clearly, however, an arrangement made with an innocent person is enough, as is an arrangement which does not involve another party at all, if that can be envisaged.

The offence of handling is complete as soon as the proposed receipt is arranged. It is immaterial (except as to sentence) that D repents or does nothing in pursuance of the arrangement.

(c) *Undertaking and assisting*

The provisions of the Act relating to handling by *undertaking* and *assisting* extend the law to cover cases which were formerly not criminal at all. They are far-reaching and overlapping. "Undertaking" presumably covers the case where D sets out to retain, etc., the stolen goods, on his own initiative and "assisting", the case where he joins the thief or another handler in doing so. Some examples drawn from the old law will illustrate the kind of case to which the law has been extended.

D negotiates the sale to F of goods which he knows to have been stolen by E. D is never in possession or control of the goods.[20] He would appear to have undertaken or assisted in the disposal of stolen goods. D assists E to lift from a van a barrel of gin which he knows to have been stolen by E or another. Even if he never has possession or control[1] he has, assisted or undertaken the removal

---

[15] *Freedman* (1930), 22 Cr. App. Rep. 133. But this might be sufficient evidence of an arrangement to receive.
[16] *Court* (1960), 44 Cr. App. Rep. 242.
[17] *Cavendish*, [1961] 2 All E.R. 856.
[18] *Tomblin*, [1964] Crim. L.R. 780.
[19] Above, p. 424.
[20] *Cf. Watson*, [1916] 2 K.B. 385.
[1] *Gleed* (1916), 12 Cr. App. Rep. 32; *Hobson* v. *Impett* (1957), 41 Cr. App. Rep. 138.

of the stolen goods. D's fifteen year-old son, E, brings home a bicycle which he has stolen. D assists in its retention if (i) he agrees that E may keep the bicycle in the house, or (ii) he tells the police there is no bicycle in the house, or (iii) he gives E a tin of paint so that he may disguise it. Is D guilty if, knowing that E is keeping the stolen bicycle there, he says and does nothing? Probably some positive act must be proved.[2]

D lights the way for E to carry stolen goods from a house to a barn, so that he may negotiate for the purchase of them.[3] D has assisted in the removal of the goods and would be no less liable to conviction (though his sentence might be lighter) if that was the full extent of his intended dealing with the goods.

(d) Arranging to undertake or assist

The extension of the law to undertaking and assisting is far-reaching, but the Act goes still further. The mere arrangement to do any of the acts amounting to undertaking or assisting amounts to the complete offence of handling. So it would presumably be enough that D agreed to negotiate the sale of the stolen goods, to lift down the barrel of stolen gin or to do any act for the purpose of enabling E to retain, remove or dispose of the stolen goods.

5   Otherwise than in the Course of the Stealing

Whatever the form of handling alleged, it must be proved it was done "otherwise than in the course of the stealing". This provision was obviously necessary if a great many instances of perfectly ordinary theft were not automatically to become handling as well. Thus, without the provision, virtually every instance of theft by two or more persons would have been handling by one or other or, more likely, both of them, since they would inevitably render mutual assistance to one another in the removal of the goods. Given the decision to keep handling as a separate crime, the provision was, then, necessary—but it adds further unfortunate complications to an already complicated offence.

The position was in fact much the same under the old law of receiving because of the rule that a principal in the felony of larceny could not be guilty of receiving as a principal in the first degree.[4] If D received the goods in the course of the stealing, it followed that he was a principal in the larceny and this necessarily meant that he could not be convicted of receiving. If a servant stole money from his master's till and handed it to an accomplice in his master's shop, the accomplice was guilty of larceny and not guilty of receiving,[5] Similarly, if a man committed larceny in the room in which he lodged and threw a bundle of stolen goods to an accomplice in the street, the accomplice was guilty of larceny and not guilty of receiving[6]. "If one burglar stands outside a window", said ALDERSON, B., "while another plunders the house and hands out the goods to him, he surely could not be indicted as a receiver".[7] It seems clear enough that in cases such as these, the same result must be reached under the Theft Act—*i.e.*, in each case D is guilty of theft and not guilty of handling. This result necessarily follows from the words, "otherwise than in the course of the stealing", whether or not

---

[2] But *cf.* the cases in which inactivity has been held to amount to aiding and abetting: above, p. 83.
[3] *Wiley* (1850), 2 Den. 37.
[4] See Smith, *Theft*, paras. 611–616.
[5] *Coggins* (1873), 12 Cox C.C. 517.
[6] *Perkins* (1852), 5 Cox C.C. 554.
[7] *Ibid.* at 555.

the rule survives (under which the cases cited were decided) that a principal in larceny cannot be a principal in the first degree in receiving.[8] These cases show that larceny was a continuing offence. As soon as the thief moved the thing a fraction of an inch the larceny was complete in the sense that, if he had been stopped at that moment, he could have been successfully indicted for the complete crime. The commission of the offence nevertheless continued at least until the point, in those cases, where the goods were put into the accomplice's hands. It has already been seen[9] that it is arguable that theft is not a continuing offence in the way that larceny was. If this argument were accepted, it might well follow that the receipt, on the facts of these cases, is not "in the course of the stealing". On the whole, however, it is thought that such an argument is unlikely to be accepted. If theft were an instantaneous act, the words "in the course of the stealing" would be rendered virtually nugatory. They clearly contemplate that the offence may continue for at least some period of time and it is thought that the authorities on the law of larceny will continue to afford guidance on the matter.[10] These indicate that there is some difficulty in establishing precisely where the line is to be drawn. So where E broke into a warehouse, stole butter and deposited it in the street some thirty yards from the warehouse door, D who then came to assist in carrying it off was not guilty of larceny as a principal offender.[11] Similarly where D waited half a mile from the scene of a proposed larceny and there received a horse stolen by E.[12] Doubtless, in these cases, D was guilty of receiving and would be so guilty on similar facts under the Theft Act.

These cases suggest that the theft continues at least while the thief is on the premises in which he perpetrates it and while "the job" is incomplete. But is E still in the course of theft as he walks down the garden path with the swag? as he drives home? and as he shows it to his wife in the kitchen? On the other hand, is the theft necessarily in the course of commission because the stolen property has not yet been removed from the premises on which it was stolen, if E has completed "the job" and all that remains is for others to take possession of the goods? It is thought that, in such a case, E is no longer in the course of stealing. If so, some of the old cases on larceny are no longer in point. Thus in *Atwell and O'Donnell*[13] goods were left in the warehouse in which they had been stolen for *some time thereafter* and the court held that it was a continuing transaction as to those who joined in the plot *before the goods were finally carried away from the premises*. Presumably until this occurred, the asportation was incomplete. It does not necessarily follow that the course of stealing under the Theft Act continues so long. If E appropriates goods in his employer's warehouse and conceals them so that they may be taken by D who comes to the warehouse a week later, is it to be said that D's taking is in the course of stealing? Surely not. It is thought that E must still be "on the job"—vague though that phrase may be— if the receipt is to be "in the course of the stealing".

6   For the Benefit of Another Person

The undertaking, assisting or arranging (except where it is an arrangement

---

[8] As to which, see Smith, *Theft*, paras. 611–618.

[9] Above, p. 177.

[10] See also s. 5 (1) (a) of the Homicide Act 1957 and *Jones*, [1959] 1 Q.B. 291; *H.M. Advocate* v. *Graham*, 1958 S.L.T. 167.

[11] *King* (1817), R. & R. 332; *cf. Gruncell and Hopkinson* (1839), 9 C. & P. 365.

[12] *Kelly* (1820), R. & R. 421.

[13] (1801), 2 East P.C. 768.

to *receive*) must be shown to be *for the benefit of another person*. If it were not for this qualification almost all thieves would be handlers as well. As it is, the thief may be guilty of handling (by undertaking) if he himself retains, removes, etc., the goods for the benefit of another person. It would seem to be immaterial that the third person is guilty of no offence and even unaware of what is going on.

If D steals goods, sells them to E, a bona fide purchaser, and keeps the purchase price for himself he is not guilty of handling. He is acting solely for his own benefit. D sells the goods to E, a bona fide purchaser, and instructs E to pay the purchase price to F. D is guilty of handling the stolen goods. He has undertaken the disposal of the goods for the benefit of another person. Presumably D is guilty when he sells the goods and receives the purchase price from E with the intention of paying it over to F. Thus an inquiry into D's motives may be necessary.

7 Innocent Receipt and Subsequent Retention with Mens Rea

If D receives the stolen goods innocently, either, that is, believing them not to be stolen or knowing them to be stolen but intending to return them to the true owner, of course, he commits no offence. Suppose he subsequently discovers the goods to be stolen or decides not to return them to the true owner or disposes of them. He has dishonestly undertaken the retention of or has disposed of stolen goods knowing them to be stolen. Whether he is guilty of an offence depends on a number of factors.

1. Where D does not get ownership of the goods. (The normal situation where goods are stolen.):

(i) D gives value for the goods

(*a*) D retains or disposes of the goods for his own benefit. This is not theft because of s. 3 (2);[14] nor is it handling by undertaking, assisting or arranging since it is not for the benefit of another. D might be guilty of handling by aiding and abetting the receiving by the person to whom he disposes of the goods, if that person has *mens rea*.

(*b*) D retains or disposes of the goods for the benefit of another. This is not theft (s. 3 (2)) but is handling.

(ii) D does not give value.

(*a*) D retains or disposes of the goods for his own benefit. This is theft but not handling unless it amounts to aiding and abetting receipt by another.

(*b*) D retains or disposes of the goods for the benefit of another. This is theft and handling.

2. Where D gets ownership of the goods. (Because the rogue obtained them by deception and acquired a voidable title or because of some exception to the *nemo dat* rule.)

(*a*) D gives value for the goods.

Retention or disposal of the goods cannot be theft since P has no property in the goods, nor handling since P has lost his right to restitution,[15] his right to rescind being destroyed on the goods coming into the hands of D who was a bona fide purchaser for value.

---

[14] Above, p. 365.
[15] Above, p. 425.

(*b*) D does not give value.

Again this cannot be theft, since P has no property in the goods, but it may be handling since P's right to rescind and secure restitution of his property is not extinguished by the goods coming into the hands of one who does not give value. It will be handling if this is so *and* D either aids and abets a guilty receipt by another or disposes of the goods for the benefit of another.

8 Handling by the Thief

The common law rules regulating the liability of a thief to a charge of receiving goods feloniously stolen by him were complicated.[16] The better view probably is that these rules were technicalities of the old law of receiving or of felonies and that they have died with it. The effect is that any thief may be convicted of handling the goods stolen by him by receiving them—if the evidence warrants this conclusion. In the majority of cases the thief can only be guilty of handling by receiving where he is abetting the receipt by another because he is already in possession or control and therefore cannot receive as the principal offender. In some circumstances, however, a thief might be convicted of handling the stolen goods by receiving them as the principal offender. For example, D steals goods and, in the course of the theft, delivers them to E. Two days later E returns the goods to D.

It seems clear that there is no reason why the old rules about receiving should be extended to handling by retention, removal, disposal or realisation of the goods and it would be unsatisfactory to have one set of rules for handling by receiving and another set for handling by other acts. The section should be construed so as to preserve, as far as possible, the unity of the offence.

(2) THE MENS REA

1 Knowledge or Belief

It must be proved that D handled the goods, "knowing or believing them to be stolen goods". The Criminal Law Revision Committee thought that this provision would extend the law:

> "It is a serious defect of the present law that actual knowledge that the property was stolen must be proved. Often the prosecution cannot prove this. In many cases indeed guilty knowledge does not exist, although the circumstances of the transaction are such that the receiver ought to be guilty of an offence. The man who buys goods at a ridiculously low price from an unknown seller whom he meets in a public house may not *know* that the goods were stolen, and he may take the precaution of asking no questions. Yet it may be clear on the evidence that he believes that the goods were stolen. In such cases the prosecution may fail (rightly, as the law now stands) for want of proof of guilty knowledge."[17]

The Act now settles beyond any doubt what, it must be assumed, was previously at least a doubtful matter. There will no doubt be general agreement with the committee that such cases ought to be covered by the law of handling. A possible and undesirable side effect of the provision would be an unduly narrow construction of other provisions[18] which use only the word "knowing" and not "believing". It will be possible to point to the Theft Act and to urge

---

[16] See Smith, *Theft*, paras. 611–618.
[17] Cmnd. 2977, 64.
[18] See, for example, s. 12; above, p. 403; and the Criminal Law Act 1967, ss. 4 and 5; below, pp. 517 and 521.

that the omission of "believing" in the other provision means that wilful blindness is not enough. The present provision should, it is submitted, be regarded as a clarification of a doubtful point in a particular case and not as having any bearing in the interpretation of the requirement of knowledge in other statutes.

2 Dishonesty

Dishonesty was an essential ingredient of the old crime of receiving though it was not expressed in the statute. The inclusion of the word "dishonestly" thus makes no change in the law. D may receive goods knowing or believing them to be stolen and yet not guilty if, for example, he intends to return them to the true owner or the police.[19] A claim of right will amount to a defence, but it will be difficult to establish such a claim where D knows or believes the goods to be stolen except in the case put above, where he intends to return the goods to the owner.

3 Proof of Mens Rea

The common law rules concerning proof of *mens rea* on a receiving charge hold good under the Act. Accordingly, where D is found in possession of recently stolen property the judge may direct the jury that they *may* infer guilty knowledge or belief if D offers no explanation of his possession or if they are satisfied beyond reasonable doubt that any explanation he has offered is untrue. The onus of proof remains on the Crown throughout, and, whether D offers an explanation or not, he should be convicted only if the jury are satisfied beyond reasonable doubt that he had the guilty knowledge or belief.[20]

Because of the difficulty of proving guilty knowledge, the Larceny Act provided for the admission of certain evidence on a receiving charge which would not be admissible in criminal cases generally. The Theft Act has corresponding provisions. By s. 27 (3):

> "Where a person is being proceeded against for handling stolen goods (but not for any offence other than handling stolen goods), then at any stage of the proceedings, if evidence has been given of his having or arranging to have in his possession the goods the subject of the charge, or of his undertaking or assisting in, or arranging to undertake or assist in, their retention, removal, disposal or realisation, the following evidence shall be admissible for the purpose of proving that he knew or believed the goods to be stolen goods:
> (a) evidence that he has had in his possession, or has undertaken or assisted in the retention, removal, disposal or realisation of, stolen goods from any theft taking place not more than twelve months before the offence charged; and
> (b) (provided that seven days' notice in writing has been given to him of the intention to prove the conviction) evidence that he has within the five years preceding the date of the offence charged been convicted of theft or of handling stolen goods."

13 MISCELLANEOUS MATTERS

(1) HUSBAND AND WIFE

For many purposes husband and wife occupy a special position under the law and have special rules relating to themselves. This was so under the former law of larceny but now s. 30 of the Theft Act 1968 provides:

---

[19] *Cf. Matthews*, [1950] 1 All E.R. 137.
[20] *Abramovitch* (1914), 11 Cr. App. Rep. 45; *Aves*, [1950] 2 All E.R. 330; *Hepworth*, [1955] 2 Q.B. 600.

17

"(1) This Act shall apply in relation to the parties to a marriage, and to property belonging to the wife or husband whether or not by reason of an interest derived from the marriage, as it would apply if they were not married and any such interest subsisted independently of the marriage.

(2) Subject to subsection (4) below a person shall have the same right to bring proceedings against that person's wife or husband for any offence (whether under this Act or otherwise) as if they were not married, and a person bringing any such proceedings shall be competent to give evidence for the prosecution at every stage of the proceedings.

(3) Where a person is charged in proceedings not brought by that person's wife or husband with having committed any offence with reference to that person's wife or husband or to property belonging to the wife or husband, the wife or husband shall be competent to give evidence at every stage of the proceedings, whether for the defence or for the prosecution, and whether the accused is charged solely or jointly with any other person:

Provided that—

(a) the wife or husband (unless compellable at common law) shall not be compellable either to give evidence or, in giving evidence, to disclose any communication made to her or him during the marriage by the accused; and

(b) her or his failure to give evidence shall not be made the subject of any comment by the prosecution.

(4) Proceedings shall not be instituted against a person for any offence of stealing or doing unlawful damage to property which at the time of the offence belongs to that person's wife or husband, or for any attempt, incitement or conspiracy to commit such an offence, unless the proceedings are instituted by or with the consent of the Director of Public Prosecutions:

Provided that—

(a) this subsection shall not apply to proceedings against a person for an offence—

　(i) if that person is charged with committing the offence jointly with the wife or husband; or

　(ii) if by virtue of any judicial decree or order (wherever made) that person and the wife or husband are at the time of the offence under no obligation to cohabit; and

(b) this subsection shall not prevent the arrest, or the issue of a warrant for the arrest, of a person for an offence, or the remand in custody or on bail of a person charged with an offence, where the arrest (if without a warrant) is made, or the warrant of arrest issues on an information laid, by a person other than the wife or husband."

The substantial effect of s. 30 (1) is to make spouses liable in respect of offences against each other's property as though they were not married. Consequently either spouse may, for example, steal property belonging to the other. It may just be worth pointing out here that while it is clear that a spouse may steal property belonging exclusively to the other, it is equally clear that a spouse may steal property jointly owned with the other spouse since one co-owner may steal from another.[1]

1 Procedure

By s. 30 (2) one spouse may prosecute the other, subject to s. 30 (4), for *any* criminal offence whether that offence is committed by a spouse on the person or property of the other, or whether by a spouse against a third party. A wife,

---

[1] Above, p. 361.

might, for example, prosecute her husband for stealing property belonging to a child of the marriage or for assaulting his mother-in-law.

While it is desirable that a spouse should have the general protection of the criminal law from depredations by the other, it will be appreciated that an over readiness to institute proceedings by the one against the other, or by a third party against one spouse for an offence on the other spouse, can only be divisive, and hardly conducive to the continuation of a satisfactory domestic relationship. It is for this reason that s. 30 (4) provides that proceedings may not be instituted except by or with the consent of the Director of Public Prosecutions. But note that the Director's consent need only be sought where the offence consists of "stealing or doing unlawful damage to property which at the time of the offence belongs to that person's wife or husband". Neither a wife nor a police officer, then, would need the Director's leave to institute proceedings for an assault on the wife by the husband, nor to prosecute the husband in respect of *any* offence committed by him on a third party.

Moreover, the Director's leave is not required in the two cases excepted by s. 30 (4) (a). The idea behind these exceptions is that in neither case does the risk of vexatious or divisive proceedings—which is the basis for the Director's control—exist. Thus a husband may, without the Director's leave, bring proceedings in respect of an appropriation of his property at a time when he was no longer bound to cohabit. And a third party may similarly bring proceedings where the spouses are jointly charged in respect of an offence relating to property belonging to one of them;[2] an example of this might be where H sets fire to his house in order to defraud insurers[3] and W aids him in the enterprise.

2 Evidence

Under the general law of evidence it is not always clear how far a spouse is competent or compellable to give evidence against the other. It is made clear by s. 30 (2) and s. 30 (3) that spouses shall be competent to give evidence against each other whether proceedings are brought by a spouse or by a third party. The subsections, in effect, leave open the question of compellability which is left to be resolved by reference to the pre-existing law.[4]

(2) CORPORATIONS AND THEIR OFFICERS

So far as offences under the Theft Act generally are concerned, the liability of corporations for them falls to be determined in accordance with the general principles applicable to the liability of corporations for crime.[5] Where a corporation commits a crime it must be the case that the crime has been committed by a person, or persons, in control of the corporation's affairs.[6] Such persons are of course liable in accordance with the ordinary principles governing liability for crime. In this particular s. 18 contains a special provision relating to the offences of obtaining property by deception, obtaining a pecuniary advantage by deception, and false accounting. The section provides:

---

[2] *Cf.* Smith, *Theft*, paras. 679, *et seq.*
[3] See below, p. 459.
[4] *Cf.* Smith, *Theft*, paras. 668–675; Griew, *Theft*, 133.
[5] See above, p. 105.
[6] A corporation may of course be vicariously liable for crimes even though the crime is not committed by a person in control of its affairs: see above, p. 105. But vicarious liability would not apply in connection with offences under the Theft Act.

"(1) Where an offence committed by a body corporate under section 15, 16 or 17 of this Act is proved to have been committed with the consent or connivance of any director, manager, secretary or other similar officer of the body corporate, or any person who was purporting to act in any such capacity, he as well as the body corporate shall be guilty of that offence, and shall be liable to be proceeded against and punished accordingly.

(2) Where the affairs of a body corporate are managed by its members, this section shall apply in relation to the acts and defaults of a member in connection with his functions of management as if he were a director of the body corporate."

This provision was explained by the Criminal Law Revision Committee as follows:[7]

"The [section] follows a form of provision commonly included in statutes,[8] where an offence is of a kind to be committed by bodies corporate and where it is desired to put the management[9] under a positive obligation to prevent irregularities, if aware of them. Passive acquiescence does not, under the general law, make a person liable as a party to the offence, but there are clearly cases (of which we think this is one) where the director's responsibilities for his company require him to intervene to prevent fraud and where consent or connivance amount to guilt."

The inference from this seems to be that, but for some such provision, the director might not in some circumstances be liable under the general principles governing liability for crime. Suppose, for example, that D, a director, learns that E, a fellow director, proposes to raise an overdraft from a bank by stating that it is required to enable the company to purchase plant when it is required to pay off creditors, but that D does nothing about it and the overdraft is authorised by the bank. The effect of s. 18 appears to be that D incurs criminal liability in respect of the obtaining of the pecuniary advantage by deception because the offence has been committed with his consent. There would be no need to show that D communicated to E his approval of the deception. Possibly, however, D would be liable under general principles for he has a clear duty to control the actions of E in this situation and his deliberate failure to perform his duty may make him an abettor.[10]

(3) RESTITUTION[11]

Section 28 of the Theft Act provides:

"(1) Where goods have been stolen, and a person is convicted of any offence with reference to the theft (whether or not the stealing is the gist of his offence), the court by or before which the offender is convicted may on the conviction exercise any of the following powers:—

    (a) the court may order anyone having possession or control of the goods to restore them to any person entitled to recover them from him; or

    (b) on the application of a person entitled to recover from the person convicted any other goods directly or indirectly representing the first-mentioned goods (as being the proceeds of any disposal or realisation of the whole or part of them or of goods so representing them), the court may order those other goods to be delivered or transferred to the applicant; or

---

[7] Cmnd. 2977, para. 104.
[8] See further, above, p. 108.
[9] Note that s. 18 imposes criminal liability only on the management; this may include (s. 18 (2)) any member who is in fact in control even though he may not formally hold a managerial post.
[10] See above, p. 83.
[11] Macleod, "Restitution under the Theft Act 1968", [1968] Crim. L.R. 577.

(c) on the application of a person who, if the first-mentioned goods were in the possession of the person convicted, would be entitled to recover them from him, the court may order that a sum not exceeding the value of those goods shall be paid to the applicant out of any money of the person convicted which was taken out of his possession on his apprehension.

(2) Where under subsection (1) above the court has power on a person's conviction to make an order against him both under paragraph (b) and under paragraph (c) with reference to the stealing of the same goods, the court may make orders under both paragraphs provided that the applicant for the orders does not thereby recover more than the value of those goods.

(3) Where under subsection (1) above the court on a person's conviction makes an order under paragraph (a) for the restoration of any goods, and it appears to the court that the person convicted has sold the goods to a person acting in good faith, or has borrowed money on the security of them from a person so acting, then on the application of the purchaser or lender the court may order that there shall be paid to the applicant, out of any money of the person convicted which was taken out of his possession on his apprehension, a sum not exceeding the amount paid for the purchase by the applicant or, as the case may be, the amount owed to the applicant in respect of the loan.

(4) The court shall not exercise the powers conferred by this section unless in the opinion of the court the relevant facts sufficiently appear from evidence given at the trial or the available documents, together with admissions made by or on behalf of any person in connection with any proposed exercise of the powers; and for this purpose 'the available documents' means any written statements or admissions which were made for use, and would have been admissible, as evidence at the trial, the depositions taken at any committal proceedings and any written statements or admissions used as evidence in those proceedings.

(5) Any order under this section shall be treated as an order for the restitution of property within the meaning of sections 30 and 42 of the Criminal Appeal Act 1968 (which relate to the effect on such orders of appeals).

(6) References in this section to stealing are to be construed in accordance with section 24 (1) and (4) of this Act."

On the face of it this is a formidable provision, but the idea behind it (and its anticipated operation) is simple enough. Suppose a straightforward case (and most of them are straightforward) where D has stolen P's watch. Here D is liable to be prosecuted in respect of the crime and proceeded against in respect of the tort. Obviously it would be convenient if the whole matter could be disposed of in one action, and s. 28 provides a procedure for doing this.[12] Equally obviously criminal courts (and especially magistrates' courts where most criminal cases are dealt with) are unsuitable for the trial of complex issues which may arise where goods have been dishonestly obtained and transferred to third parties. It is not intended that they should; and

"In practice the power will be exercisable only where there is no real dispute as to ownership. It would seriously hamper the work of the criminal courts if at the end of a trial they had to investigate disputed titles."[13]

Consequently s. 28 provides that the court *may* exercise the powers thereby conferred, and s. 28 (4) provides that the court *shall not* exercise any such power unless the relevant facts sufficiently appear.

---

[12] *Cf.* Criminal Justice Administration Act 1914, s. 14 (1); below, p. 469.
[13] Cmnd. 2977, para. 164.

(i) *Circumstances in which Order may be made.*—The goods[14] must have been stolen at some stage, and goods obtained by blackmail or deception are stolen for this purpose.[15] The goods need not have been stolen by D, but D must be convicted of an offence with reference to the theft whether or not stealing is the gist of *his* offence. An order might be made, for example, where the gist of D's offence lies in giving assistance to E knowing that E has stolen the goods;[16] stealing is not the gist of D's offence here, but he has been convicted of an offence with reference to the theft.

(ii) *Contents of an Order.*—Upon D's conviction the court may order *any* person (the order might, for example, be made against a person who has in good faith purchased the goods from the thief, or against the police) having possession or control of the goods to restore them to any person entitled to recover them from him (para. (a)).[17]

The court may in addition, though this time only on the application of the person entitled to recover from the person convicted, order any goods, which directly or indirectly represent the stolen goods, to be restored to the applicant. For example, D may have stolen P's gold watch which he exchanges for a necklace which he then sells to E, a handler; P may recover the necklace from E upon E's conviction for handling (para. (b)). Similarly upon P's application, and where for instance E has in turn sold the necklace, the court may order E to pay P the value of the watch out of any money taken from E upon his apprehension (para. (c)).

It might happen that when D is apprehended he has both the necklace and money in his possession but the necklace is worth less than the watch. In this sort of case the court is empowered to order D to give up the necklace to P along with money to make up the difference between the value of the necklace and the value of the watch: s. 28 (2).

Where, as the result of an order under para. (a), a bona fide purchaser or pledgee from the person convicted (D) with respect to the theft is ordered to restore the goods to P, that person may in turn recover from D, out of money in D's possession on apprehension, the amount he paid D for, or lent D upon, the goods.

(iii) *Effect of Order.*—In practice the powers conferred by s. 28 will be exercised in only the clearest cases and ordinarily the goods will be restored to the person who is the owner of them. It might happen, however, that the court has, in pursuance of s. 28, restored the goods to P and later Q claims the goods from P. It seems clear that Q is free to do so and is in no way prejudiced by the order restoring the goods to P. Certainly the fact of a conviction for theft does not affect civil rights for by s. 31 (2)

> "Notwithstanding any enactment to the contrary, where property has been stolen or obtained by fraud or other wrongful means, the title to that or any other property shall not be affected by reason only of the conviction of the offender."

---

[14] See s. 34 (2) (b); above, p. 422.
[15] Section 28 (6): see s. 24 (4); above, p. 422.
[16] See below, p. 517.
[17] The person entitled to recover would be the person with the best right to possess: *cf*. Smith, *Theft*, para. 644. And see below, p. 439, footnote 19.

(iv) *Police (Property) Act* 1897.—Quite apart from the new procedure for restitution introduced by s. 28 of the Theft Act there exists a similar procedure under the Police (Property) Act 1897. Section 1 (1) of that Act provides:

> "When any property has come into the possession of the police in connection with any criminal charge . . . a court of summary jurisdiction may, on application, either by an officer of police or by a claimant of the property, make an order for the delivery of the property to the person appearing to the magistrate or court to be the owner thereof, or, if the owner cannot be ascertained, may make such order with respect to the property as to the magistrate or court may seem meet."

So far as stolen property[18] is concerned, it may well be that the procedure under the Police (Property) Act 1897 will be largely superseded by the procedure now available under the Theft Act. However, there are important, if small, differences which may ensure that, even in connection with stolen property, the Police (Property) Act is not a dead letter. Firstly an owner[19] may get an order for delivery of his property although the thief is never apprehended, much less convicted. Secondly, s. 1 (2) of the 1897 Act provides:

> "An order under the section shall not affect the right of any person to take within six months from the date of the order legal proceedings against any person in possession of property delivered by virtue of the order for the recovery of the property, but on the expiration of those six months the right shall cease."

If, then, an order has been made under the Police (Property) Act delivering the property to P, it *seems* that no third party may take legal proceedings against P after the expiration of six months.[20] On the other hand the powers conferred by the Police (Property) Act may be exercised only by a magistrate's court, and are exercisable only on application.

(v) *The Forfeiture Act* 1870, *s.* 4.[1]—This provides that a court[2] may "upon the application of any person aggrieved" award up to £400 as compensation for any loss of, or damage to, property. Thus where an order for restitution cannot be made under the Theft Act or the Police (Property) Act, the court may award P compensation for his loss of the goods, and the order is enforceable as a judgment debt.

14 FORGERY

Forgery was an offence at common law but, as Lord GODDARD, C.J., said in delivering the judgment of the court in *Hopkins and Collins*,[3]

> "What might have been the position at common law, it is not necessary for us to discuss. Forgery no longer depends on the common law, nor does it

---

[18] The Police (Property) Act applies to property which has come into police possession connection with *any* criminal charge.

[19] The owner, for the purposes of the Act, appears to be the person with the best right to possess the goods: *Marsh* v. *Commissioner of Police*, [1945] K.B. 43 (D.C.).

[20] But it may be that an order under the 1897 Act only bars a claimant who might have asserted his right in the original proceedings: *cf.* Smith, *Theft*, para. 661. However, even on this view, an order under the 1897 Act would be marginally preferable to an order under the Theft Act since the latter would not bar a subsequent claim even by one who might have asserted his right in the original proceedings.

[1] As amended by the Criminal Law Act 1967.

[2] Including a magistrates' court: Magistrates' Court Act 1952, s. 34.

[3] (1957), 41 Cr. App. Rep. 231 at p. 235 (C.C.A.). And see the observations of Lord RADCLIFFE in *Welham* v. *Director of Public Prosecutions*, [1961] A.C. 103 at p. 123; [1960] 1 All E.R. 805 at p. 807.

depend on . . . statutes which have been passed from time to time.[4] It depends simply on the statute of 1913. . . ."

And by s. 1 of that statute, the Forgery Act 1913:

"(1) For the purposes of this Act, forgery is the making of a false document in order that it may be used as genuine, and in the case of the seals and dies mentioned in this Act the counterfeiting of a seal or die, and forgery with intent to defraud or deceive, as the case may be, is punishable as in this Act provided.

(2) A document is false within the meaning of this Act if the whole or any material part thereof purports to be made by or on behalf or on account of a person who did not make it nor authorise its making; or if, though made by or on behalf or on account of the person by whom or by whose authority it purports to have been made, the time or place of making, where either is material, or, in the case of a document identified by number or mark, the number or any distinguishing mark identifying the document, is falsely stated therein; and in particular a document is false:

(a) if any material alteration, whether by addition, insertion, obliteration, erasure, removal, or otherwise, has been made therein;

(b) if the whole or some material part of it purports to be made by or on behalf of a fictitious or deceased person;

(c) if, though made in the name of an existing person, it is made by him or by his authority with the intention that it should pass as having been made by some person, real or fictitious, other than the person who made or authorised it.

(3) For the purposes of this Act—

(a) it is immaterial in what language a document is expressed . . .;

(b) forgery of a document may be complete even if the document when forged is incomplete, or is not or does not purport to be such a document as would be binding or sufficient in law . . ."

(1) THE MEANING OF DOCUMENT

Forgery, as the definition makes clear, may be committed only in respect of documents, and the seals and dies mentioned in the Act. The latter present no problem since the relevant seals and dies are enumerated in s. 5 of the Forgery Act 1913 and it is an offence, punishable by imprisonment for life, to forge these with intent to defraud or deceive. The Act lists a large number of documents in ss. 2 and 3. Under s. 2 (1) it is an offence, punishable by imprisonment for life, to forge wills, deeds, bank notes etc. with intent to defraud; and under s. 2 (2) it is an offence, punishable by fourteen years' imprisonment, to forge valuable securities, documents of title, powers of attorney, insurance policies etc. with intent to defraud. Section 3 is concerned with documents of a public nature and in each case the offence may be committed with an intent to defraud or deceive. Under s. 3 (1) it is an offence, punishable by imprisonment for life, to forge any document bearing the Great Seal or certain other seals; by s. 3 (2) it is an offence, punishable by fourteen years' imprisonment, to forge registers of births, marriages and deaths etc.; and by s. 3 (3) it is an offence, punishable by seven years' imprisonment, to forge a variety of official documents such as documents

---

[4] In fact certain provisions of the Forgery Act 1861 are still in force but this does not affect the validity of this *dictum*. There are a number of statutes which contain provisions creating special offences of forgery, and the practice is still continued although, in view of the comprehensive provisions in the Act of 1913, it seems only to create a proliferation of particular offences.

belonging to a court. But the lists in ss. 2 and 3 do not purport to be exhaustive, and s. 4 accordingly provides, by sub-s. (1), that forgery of any document with intent to defraud shall be an offence punishable by two years' imprisonment; and, by subsection (2), that forgery of any public document with intent to defraud or deceive shall be an offence punishable by two years' imprisonment.

There is, however, no definition of document in the Forgery Act 1913, and it is therefore legitimate in this case to refer to decisions at common law or under earlier statutes.[5] Some things are obviously documents, as wills or deeds, and some things are obviously not documents, as statues and paintings. It is, of course, common usage to speak of a faked painting as a forgery but it would not be a forgery for the purposes of the Act: no one would call a painting a document. At common law it was usual to use the word "writing" and nothing has happened to suggest that writing is not a perfectly good synonym for document. The words "document" and "writing" communicate a good deal of their meaning[6] but they cannot speak entirely for themselves as *Closs*[7] and *Smith*[8] show.

In *Closs* D had sold to P a painting representing it as the work of John Linnell, a celebrated artist. In fact, as D knew, the painting was a copy, as was the signature of John Linnell which appeared upon it. Clearly the painting alone was not a forgery but the prosecution argued that the signature did constitute a forgery as being a certificate which stated that John Linnell was the painter of this painting and such a certificate could be forged. The court rejected this argument, holding that,

> "A forgery must be of some document or writing; and this was merely in the nature of a mark put upon the painting with a view of identifying it, and was no more than if the painter put any other arbitrary mark as a recognition of the picture being his."[9]

There can be no doubt but that it is possible to forge a certificate relating to the authenticity of a painting. In *Pryse-Hughes*[10] D removed the name Watts from a painting and tried to sell it to P as a Constable. Since P doubted whether the painting was a genuine Constable, D gave him a forged authentication certificate purporting to come from an authority on Constable. It was held that D was guilty of forgery and the case lends some substance to the argument that the artist's signature alone is but a short form of authentication certificate.[11] In truth any definition of a document must draw a line which involves a certain element of arbitrariness, and perhaps the real gravamen of the court's decision in *Closs* is expressed in COCKBURN, C.J.'s interjection:

> "If you go beyond writing where are you to stop? Can sculpture be the subject of forgery?"[12]

The substance of the forgery in *Closs* was the painting—the signature was part

---

[5] See Williams, "What is a document?" (1948), 11 M.L.R. 150; Turner, " 'Documents' in the Law of Forgery" (1946), 32 *Virginia Law Review*, 939.

[6] These days progressively more information is stored on punched cards and magnetic tape for use in computers. Punched cards appear to satisfy any relevant definition of document. There may be a difficulty in saying that a magnetic tape upon which information is recorded is a document but at some stage the information will usually be translated into documentary form.

[7] (1858), Dears. & B. 460.

[8] (1858), Dears. & B. 566.

[9] (1858), Dears. & B. 460 at p. 466.

[10] (1958), *The Times*, May 14.

[11] See Turner, *op. cit.*, 949, and in Russell, 1222.

[12] (1858), Dears. & B. 460 at p. 466.

of the painting.[13]   Of course, had it been Linnell's practice to write out a certificate in respect of his paintings and to paste these to the backs of his canvasses then the faking of such a certificate would be forgery.   It might appear arbitrary to draw the line between this and a signature which appears on the face of the painting since the latter gives rise to the same implication as the former, but, in the final analysis, this is where *Closs* holds the line is to be drawn.   Although arbitrary—inevitably—it does not seem to be entirely unrealistic and must now be considered to have settled the point.

In *Smith*[14] D sold his baking powder and egg powder in printed wrappers resembling the wrappers used by P for similar products.   The wrapper for the baking powder reproduced exactly the get up of P's wrapper except that the legend

> "The public are requested to see that each wrapper is signed GEORGE BORWICK without which none is genuine"

was omitted from D's wrappers.   In the case of the egg powders there was no such legend on P's wrappers and D's wrappers were in all respects identical. The jury found that D's wrappers were calculated to deceive persons of ordinary observation, that it was D's intention to defraud and he was convicted of forgery. The conviction was quashed.   POLLOCK, C.B., held that the wrappers were not documents; if they were, it might just as well be said that if one tradesman used brown paper for his wrappers of the same description as the brown paper used by another tradesman, he could be convicted of forging the brown paper.

Although this decision has been generally accepted by commentators, this acceptance has been based on the alternative ground given in the judgments that the wrappers did not tell a lie about themselves[15] and the view of POLLOCK, C.B., and WILLES, J., that the wrappers were not documents has received little support.[16]   However, this view has the support of Williams[17] who, it is respectfully submitted, offers the most satisfactory solution with his test: does the thing have utility apart from the fact that it conveys information or records a promise ? The wrapper had utility (to wrap up baking powder) apart from the fact that it conveyed information hence it was not a document.   As Williams realises, his test is not entirely satisfactory.   For one thing it would mean, presumably, that if Borwicks had packed the baking powder in tins on which were glued labels carrying the same information as the wrappers, the labels would be documents and could be forged since they now have no utility apart from conveying information.   If this test is thought to introduce too much subtlety then, again adopting the view of Williams, it is possible to limit it by requiring the writing to be an instrument as well.[18]   Although "instrument" might be thought to spawn just as many difficulties as "document", the word is of some help in conveying the idea of a document which is made for the purpose of creating or modifying or terminating a right.   A wrapper or a label would not usually be

---

[13] WILLIAMS, J., said in argument, *ibid.*, at p. 465, "It is consistent with all the allegations that (D) may have sold the picture without calling attention to the signature."
[14] (1858), Dears. & B. 566.
[15] See below, p. 443.
[16] See Turner, *op. cit.*, at 952, and in Russell, at p. 1223; Gooderson, (1952), 15 M.L.R. 11 at p. 18; Cross and Jones, *An Introduction to Criminal Law* (6th ed.), 252.
[17] (1948), 11 M.L.R. 150 at p. 160.
[18] (1948), 11 M.L.R. *loc. cit.* As Williams notes, POLLOCK, C.B., had said in *Smith* that the wrapper was not an instrument.

considered an instrument in this sense but a certificate testifying to the authenticity of a painting, or to a man's competency to drive a vehicle[19] or even a football pools coupon[20] would be considered instruments.[21]

(2) THE FORGERY

1 Making a False Document in order that it may appear Genuine

The forgery itself, according to s. 1 (1) of the Act, consists in the making of a false document in order that it may be used as genuine.[1] Section 1 (2), set out above, details a number of circumstances in which the document will be considered false. Section 1 (2) will cover the ordinary run of case but it may not be exhaustive, and to remove any doubts it was provided by the Criminal Justice Act 1925, s. 35 (1), that

> "a document may be a false document for the purposes of the Forgery Act 1913 notwithstanding it is not false in such a manner as is described in subsection (2) of section 1 of that Act."[2]

It was always the rule at common law that forgery involved something more than a mere lie in a document. In *Re Windsor*[3] D, a teller at a bank, fraudulently entered in his books, as assets of the bank, a sum which was higher than the actual assets and it was held this was not forgery. "Forgery," said BLACKBURN, J.,

> "is the falsely making or altering a document to the prejudice of another, by making it appear as the document of that person. Telling a lie does not become forgery because it is reduced to writing. Here this man has not made any false statement purporting to be on behalf of any other person, but a statement purporting to be what it is."[4]

Hence the aphorism: the document must not only tell a lie, it must tell a lie about itself.[5] This was the alternative ground for the decision in *Smith*[6] and is the one commonly accepted: the wrappers, it is said, did not tell a lie about themselves. In the case of the baking powder wrappers at least, the public was

---

[19] *Potter*, [1958] 2 All E.R. 51.
[20] *Butler* (1954), 38 Cr. App. Rep. 57.
[21] See further below, p. 453.
Note: many of the difficulties created by the definition of a document may be circumvented by charging some other offence such as deception or cheating.
[1] See Gooderson, "When is a Document False in the Law of Forgery" (1952), 15 M.L.R. 11.
[2] In *Hopkins and Collins* (1957), 41 Cr. App. Rep. 231 at p. 234, Lord GODDARD, C.J., said that s. 35 (1) was introduced on account of it having been held in a case that s. 1 (2) was exhaustive. The case does not appear to have been reported.
In *Potter*, [1958] 2 All E.R. 51, D took a driving test in the name of E (D's brother) and a certificate of competence to drive made out by the examiner in E's name was given to D who signed it in E's name. PAULL, J., thought that the document was not false within s. 1 (2) but that it was caught by s. 35 (1). The learned judge does not say why the document was not false within s. 1 (2) and, with respect, it seems clearly to fall within the subsection: the signature was surely a material part and the signature purported to be made by E when it was in fact made by D.
[3] (1865), 6 B. & S. 522.
[4] (1865), 6 B. & S. 522 at p. 529. In so far as this *dictum* apparently confines forgery to cases where the document purports to be the document of some person other than the maker, it is misleading. If, supposing it had been material, D had altered the date in his books with intent to defraud this would have been forgery: *Ritson* (1869), L.R. 1 C.C. . 200.
[5] Kenny, *Outlines*, 375.
[6] (1858), Dears. & B. 566; above, p. 442. See above, p. 442, footnote 15.

warned to see that each wrapper bore the signature of George Borwick without which "none is genuine" and D had taken care to omit the warning and the facsimile signature. But this seems altogether too refined.

> "Most people would take a label bearing the words 'Borwick's Baking Powder' as asserting that the label itself (as distinct from the contents of the package) emanated from the house of Borwick."[7]

Further, there was no such signature or warning on the egg powder labels and here D's wrappers were *exactly* the same as P's.

In *Hopkins and Collins*,[8] however, the Court of Criminal Appeal apparently parted company with the common law on the rule that a document must tell a lie about itself. D and E, the secretary and treasurer respectively of a football supporters club, received monies raised by members of the club and made disbursements on behalf of the club. Over a period of time they (i) entered in the books amounts less than were paid in by members, (ii) entered amounts in excess of what was in fact paid out, and (iii) altered certain of the entries. D and E naturally relied on *Re Windsor*[9] as showing that inaccurate entries did not constitute forgery but a full court held they had been rightly convicted of forgery. Whatever was the position at common law, the court said, it had now to decide only whether the document was false within s. 1 (2) of the Act and held that it was.

The only provision of s. 1 (2) which could be relevant to these facts is s. 1 (2) (a) and it is fairly clear that the court relied on this so that D and E were convicted of forgery in respect of (iii)—the alterations.[10] That leaves the way clear to distinguish *Re Windsor*[11] (where there were no alterations) but it does not end the difficulties of *Hopkins and Collins*.[12] The books which D and E made up were, on the face of it, false within s. 1 (2) (a) but s. 1 (1) requires something more than a false document: forgery is there defined as the making of a false document *in order that it may be used as genuine*. If this definition was meant to express the notion that the document must tell a lie about itself then *Hopkins and Collins* is a step ahead, not only of the common law, but of the Act as well. The accounts made by D and E may have been false but, *qua* the accounts of D and E, they were perfectly genuine accounts.

What the court in *Hopkins and Collins* appears to have done is to reason that if the document was *false* within s. 1 (2) it was therefore *forged* within s. 1 (1).

---

[7] Williams (1948), 11 M.L.R. 150 at p. 159.

[8] (1957), 41 Cr. App. Rep. 231.

[9] (1865), 6 B. & S. 522; above, p. 443.

[10] But this submission is not made with complete confidence. It is a perfectly possible interpretation of the judgment that (i) and (ii) were also considered forgery. Neither the report at 41 Cr. App. Rep. 231, nor the report in *The Times*, October 11, 1957, specify the actual charges so it is not possible to draw firm conclusions. The headnote at 41 Cr. App. Rep. 231 indicates that the insertion of false entries in a cashbook amounts to forgery but there is nothing in the judgment which *directly* substantiates this proposition. It is submitted that the judgment ultimately bases the conviction on (iii) alone. *Cf.* Lord GODDARD, C.J., at p. 235, "For the purpose of this case it has been proved that [D and E] made false entries, writing in that they had received so much money when in fact they had received so much more and that on the other side they had altered sums. *Now that we have seen the books, the difficulties which the court felt have been cleared up, because one can see in the plainest way that the totals and individual items have been altered*, with the result that the document gives a wholly false impression of the amount that ought to have been in the hands of [D and E]." Italics supplied.

[11] Above, p. 443.

[12] *Supra.*

On the face of it this seems attractive reasoning because the instances detailed in s. 1 (2) *look* like instances of forgery. The first instances mentioned in the sub-section—where the document purports to be made by one who did not make it—*looks* like the classic case of forgery. But this reasoning ignores the fact that it is quite possible to make a false document which is not a forgery. Suppose that D owns an antique charter which is so shrivelled with age that the process of un-rolling it is likely to damage it; he therefore makes an exact copy of the charter for display purposes. In such a case D has made a false document but it is not a forgery because it was not made false *in order that it may be used as genuine*: it was made to pass *as a copy* of the genuine charter. It might be said that the real reason why D is not guilty of forgery here is that he does not intend to defraud. But this is merely an *additional* reason why D is not guilty of forgery. Section 1 (1) plainly requires both (a) an intent to deceive or defraud as the case may be, *and* (b) the making of a false document in order that it be used as genuine. Some meaning must be given to the expression "in order that it may be used as genuine" beyond the requirement of fraud.[13]

Suppose, for instance, in the illustration given, that at some later stage D decides to pass off his copy as the genuine charter with intent to defraud P. There is now an intent to defraud but there is still no forgery. D is now *using* the false document as the genuine document but it was not *made* false in order that it be used as genuine.

In these illustrations it is assumed that D has made a copy of a genuine charter. Would it make any difference if the charter itself had been forged? Suppose that D, who owes money to P, acquires a receipt to which P's signature has been forged. He tells P that he has paid the debt and when P questions this he sends P a photostat copy of the forged receipt. Clearly the original document is a forgery, but is the photostat a forgery? In *Harris*,[14] where the facts were substantially those of the illustration, the Court of Criminal Appeal did not closely consider whether the photostat was a forgery and the issue was treated as turning on whether D had uttered the original document by making the photo-stat and sending it on.[15] In *Chow Sik Wah*,[16] the Ontario Court of Appeal held that a photostat copy of a forged letter was not a forgery since it did not tell a lie about itself; it would have been a forgery only if made with the intention of being passed off, not as a copy, but as the letter itself. In *Tait*,[17] the New Zealand Court of Appeal, without deciding the point, thought that a submission that a photostat copy of a forged letter was not itself a forgery might well be correct. It is submitted, though the matter is not free of difficulty, that these cases are correct in principle. Suppose that D manages to find the celebrated Zinoviev letter in the Government's archives and makes a photostat copy which he passes off *as a copy* of the Zinoviev letter. It never seems to have been affirmatively settled whether the Zinoviev letter was or was not a forgery. If the letter was not a forgery then clearly the photostat does not tell a lie about itself. If the letter was a forgery the copy still fails to tell a lie about itself because it is still a true copy of the so-called Zinoviev letter. Nor is the copy any less true, as a copy,

---

[13] This was clearly the view of the draftsmen of the Act: see *Reports of Committees* (1913), Vol. 6, p. 40.
[14] [1965] 3 All E.R. 206.
[15] On this point see below, p. 452.
[16] [1964] 1 Can. Crim. Cas. 313.
[17] [1968] 2 N.Z.L.R. 126.

because D happens to know all along that the Zinoviev letter was a forgery, though this factor may be relevant when considering whether D has an intent to defraud. On the other hand, if D passes off his copy as the original Zinoviev letter, this is a forgery whether the Zinoviev letter was forged or not. But it should not be thought, even if it is the case that a photostat of a forged document is not a forgery, that this opens up a gap in the law which the forger may exploit with impunity. The photostat copy may not be a forgery, but in using the photostat to perpetrate fraud D will almost certainly commit the offence of uttering under s. 6 of the Act, not by using the photostat but by virtue of the use which he has made of the original document which is a forgery.[18]

Why then, it might be asked, did Parliament go to all the trouble of enacting the elaborate definition of falsity in s. 1 (2) when this is but "half" of the definition of forgery? The answer is not difficult to find: there were in fact many contradictory decisions, and many uncertain decisions, on the question of falsity and the aim of the Act was to resolve these problems and to put the law on a certain footing. In *Woodward*,[19] for example, it was held not to be forgery where D, a soldier, signed a promissory note in his own name and subsequently passed off the note as coming from his sergeant-major. The court said, immediately on it appearing that D had signed the note in his own name, that he must be acquitted *for the instrument was not false.* Section 1 (2) (c) of the Act clearly overrules *Woodward on this point,* but it does not follow that Woodward would now be guilty of forgery. He may be, but whether he is, it is submitted, turns upon his intent at the time he put his signature to the note. If he then intended to pass it off as his sergeant-major's signature it would be a forgery,[20] but if he then intended to pass it off as his own signature and subsequently changed his mind and passed it off as the signature of another, there would still be no forgery.[1]

It is submitted, therefore, that s. 1 (2) was intended to do what it expressly purports to do, namely, provide a definition of falsity which the cases failed clearly to enunciate, and there is no warrant for a view that s. 1 (2) was intended to define instances of forgery. There is a forgery, as the definition in s. 1 (1) makes perfectly clear, only where a false document is made in order that it appear as genuine.

If, then, s. 1 does not modify the principle that the document must tell a lie about itself, *Hopkins and Collins*[2] should be reconsidered for it is inconsistent with this principle.

2 Omissions

A point left open in *Hopkins and Collins*[2] was whether D and E would have been guilty of forgery if they had omitted to make entries. It is submitted that

---

[18] See below, p. 452.

[19] (1796), 2 Leach 782.

[20] The fact that D uses his own signature (that is, makes no attempt to disguise his hand) cannot help him for it is obvious law that a forgery is no less a forgery where it is of the poorest quality. What matters is that the hand of A passes as the hand of B and is intended so to pass at the time the instrument is made.

[1] *Cf.* Gooderson, *op. cit.* at 23: "It is submitted that [*Woodward*] is in accord with the old principle that to be false a document must tell a lie about itself, but this principle is ignored by s. 1 (2) (c) of the Forgery Act 1913 which clearly overrules this case." On the argument advanced in this text, of course, there is nothing inconsistent in s. 1 (2) (c) with the principle that the document must tell a lie about itself. It is still not forgery to pass off a true instrument by a false representation *dehors* the instrument.

[2] Above, p. 444.

they would not. In the particular circumstances the failure to make an entry would not have made the document tell a lie about itself any more than the entry of false statements. Either way the statement of accounts is an inaccurate statement of accounts, but it would be what it purported to be: a statement of accounts prepared by D and E.

In principle, however, it is possible to predicate cases of forgery by omission, as where P, a blind man, dictates his will to D and D fraudulently omits certain directions given by P. Yet there is some authority[3] for saying it is not forgery for D fraudulently to procure the signature of P to a document by misrepresenting the contents of the document to P. Strictly, at least where the case is one of *non est factum*,[4] the document would seem to tell a lie about itself,[5] but the problem now is to determine the position under the Act. It is submitted that where, for instance, D fraudulently adds a legacy in P's will and P executes the will in ignorance of the fact, the case appears to be one of forgery within s. 1 (2) since a material part of the will purports to be made by a person who did not make it. Where D fraudulently omits a legacy, since there is no express provision for omissions in s. 1 (2), the case is one of forgery only if it can be said D has made a false document in order that it may be used as genuine within s. 1 (1)—and there seems to be no insuperable difficulty in the way of so holding.

3 Materiality of the Falsity

Forgery may be complete even if the document when forged is incomplete, or is not or does not purport to be such a document as would be binding in law.[6] Thus if D forges the attestation clause to a will and, erroneously believing it suffices in law, forges the signature of only one witness, this will be forgery even though the document, as forged, is of no legal effect. The rule was otherwise at common law: it was no forgery unless the document, as forged, was of apparent legal effect.[7] In view of the difficulties lurking in such a rule it is just as well it has been abolished by the Act. There is, however, a possibility of conflict between s. 1 (3) (b) and s. 1 (2) (a) in so far as the latter requires a *material* alteration. Suppose that D, erroneously believing that P's will is validly executed, alters the name of a beneficiary. Now there may be a forgery even though the will is of no legal effect, but could D argue that the alteration is not a material alteration? It is submitted the argument would be unsuccessful. Section 1 (3) (b) surely embraces such a case and to this extent s. 1 (2) (a) must be read subject to s. 1 (3) (b). This does not involve leaving the word "material" in s. 1 (2) without meaning. If D alters the date[8] on P's will (D not realising the

---

[3] *Collins* (1843), 2 M. & R. 461; *Chadwick,* (1844), 2 M. & R. 545. Both are decisions of ROLFE, B.

[4] See Cheshire and Fifoot, *Law of Contract* (6th ed.), 218 *et seq.*

[5] Hawkins, 1 P.C. 265, considered the will illustration given in the text to be a case of forgery. ROLFE, B., expressly disagreed with Hawkins. The American cases accord with ROLFE, B.'s view; see Perkins, *Criminal Law*, 300, but Perkins considers that cases of *non est factum* are strictly cases of forgery.

[6] Forgery Act 1913, s. 1 (3) (b) above, p. 440.

[7] *Wall* (1800), 2 East P.C. 953. D had forged a will and the signatures of two attesting witnesses where the law required three: held not to be a forgery.

[8] A material alteration of the date on a document is forgery. In *Wells* (1939), 27 Cr. App. Rep. 72, D was convicted of forgery where he altered the date on a settlement so as to ante-date the provisions of an Act of Parliament in order to avoid payment of tax on the settlement. The case also shows that the relevant time to determine whether the alteration is material is the time when the alteration was made.

will is invalid for lack of attestation) so that it shall appear to post-date a later will of P, but fails to make it post-date the later will then this would not be forgery. Not because the will is invalid, but because, even if the will had been valid, the alteration would be immaterial.

Herein, perhaps, lies the explanation of *Martin*.[9] D, whose name was Robert Martin, purchased a pony and trap from P, to whom he was well known, and gave in payment a cheque, drawn on a bank with which he had no account, which he signed in the presence of P in the style of William Martin. Ordinarily it is forgery to sign a document in a fictitious name[10] but it was held that D had not forged the cheque. The judgment in the case is obscure and the decision has been justified on the ground that D did not intend to defraud by means of the forged signature.[11] Another permissible interpretation is that the cheque was not false in a material particular. P could have been under no misapprehension as to who was the maker of the cheque since he knew D and watched him draw up the cheque. P had been swindled, of course, and had he observed the false signature he would in all probability have refused to take the cheque,[12] but he would not have refused it because he thought it was not the cheque of D.[13] It is clear that if D uses an alias, E, by which he is known to P, his signing a cheque in the name E will not constitute forgery although he knows the cheque will be dishonoured and he intends to defraud.[14] The cheque does not purport to be made by one who did not make it. Similarly in *Martin*,[15] *in the particular circumstances*, the cheque did not purport to be made by one who did not make it.

4 Instances of Forgery

It is not, of course, possible to anticipate every case of forgery, but typical instances of forgery include the following.

The most common instance is where the document, or some material part thereof, purports to be made by, or with the authority of, one who did not make it or authorise its making. It is forgery, then, where D, without authority, signs P's name to a cheque, or where D, without authority, alters the amount payable on the cheque, or where D, given a signed blank cheque, enters an amount higher than he is authorised to enter as payable on the cheque.[16]

---

[9] (1879), 5 Q.B.D. 34.
[10] *Sheppard* (1782), 1 Leach 226. In payment for goods D gave a banker's draft signed in the name of E, a fictitious person. Held to be a forged draft although P did not know D and assumed from the circumstances that D was called E and that he was giving his own draft. The situation is now expressly provided for by s. 1 (2) (b). See further Gooderson, *op. cit.*, at 11 *et seq.*
[11] Gooderson (1952), 15 M.L.R. 11, 14, 15 and 16.
[12] (1879), 5 Q.B.D. 34 at p. 36.
[13] Kenny (*Outlines* (5th ed.), 259) always regarded *Martin* as a case where the document did not tell a lie about itself and this would seem to be a satisfactory explanation in so far as the cheque did not tell a lie about itself to P; however D had signed the cheque, P would always know whose cheque it was.
[14] *Hadjimitsis*, [1964] Crim. L.R. 128. *Bontien* (1813), Russ. & Ry. 260; 168 E.R. 791.
[15] *Supra.*
[16] *Bateman* (1845), 1 Cox C.C. 186. *Davenport* [1954], 1 All E.R. 602. *Cf. Butler* (1954), 38 Cr. App. Rep. 57, which indicates that where P does not in fact limit D's authority (in that case with respect to the amount to be wagered in a football pools coupon) D does not commit forgery by entering an amount which he knows to be more than P could afford to pay.

It is forgery for D to sign a document in his own name intending to pass his signature off as the signature of another person, real or fictitious.[17] It is also forgery where D procures P, who is unaware of D's fraud, to sign his own name, D intending to pass off P's signature as that of another person of the same name.[18]

(3) MENS REA: THE INTENT TO DEFRAUD OR DECEIVE

The intent required for forgery is an intent to defraud, or, in the case of public documents[19] and seals and dies, an intent to defraud or deceive. The Act contains no definition of public document and so far the courts have not been called upon to define it in this context. In another context a public document has been defined as one made by a public officer so that the public may use it and refer to it[20] and this would probably provide the criterion to be applied in the context of the Act.[1] The distinction between the intent to defraud required for private documents and the intent only to deceive for public documents represents another innovation of the Act for it was unknown at common law.[2]

The classic analysis of defrauding and deceiving belongs to BUCKLEY, J.:

> "To deceive is, I apprehend, to induce a man to believe that a thing is true which is false, and which the person practising the deceit knows or believes to be false. To defraud is to deprive by deceit: it is by deceit to induce a man to act to his injury. More tersely it may be put, that to deceive is by falsehood to induce a state of mind: to defraud is by deceit to induce a course of action."[3]

This definition is not altogether beyond the reach of criticism but

> "it was at once appreciated that it expressed briefly and with felicity the significant distinction between the two kinds of intent when they were referred to together or apart in statutes dealing with criminal offences."[4]

Usually when a person is defrauded he is made to suffer some economic loss, as where he is made to part with money or goods, but defrauding is not confined to cases of economic loss. The point was finally settled, though controversy continues, by the House of Lords in *Welham* v. *Director of Public Prosecutions*.[5] D, who was the sales manager of a firm of motor dealers, had witnessed forged

---

[17] Section 1 (2) (c). *Woodward*, [1796] 2 Leach 782; above p. 472; *Cooper* v. *Vesey* (1882), 20 Ch. D. 611; Gooderson, *op. cit.* pp. 22–24.

[18] *Mitchell* (1844), 1 Den. 282. Gooderson, *op. cit.*, 19, considers this a doubtful case (*sed quaere*) but recognises that s. 1 (2) (c) puts the matter beyond doubt.

[19] Forgery Act 1913 ss. 3 and 5. While s. 3 specifies certain public documents, the forgery of any public document is now covered by s. 4 (2).

[20] *Sturla* v. *Freccia* (1880), 5 App. Cas. 623 at p. 643; *Sealby*, [1965] 1 All E.R. 701.

[1] But *cf.* Goodhart (1947), 63 L.Q.R. 271. Section 3 enumerates certain documents which would not be prepared so that the public might use or refer to them but then s. 3 does not contain the expression "public document" and would hardly prejudice any definition of the expression appearing elsewhere in the Act.

[2] *Contra* Russell, 1238 but see *Welham* v. *Director of Public Prosecutions*, [1961] A.C. 103; [1960] 1 All E.R. 805, *per* Lord RADCLIFFE at pp. 127 and 810, and *per* Lord DENNING at pp. 132 and 815. In jurisdictions following the common law in the United States the distinction is apparently unknown, see Perkins, *Criminal Law*, 303. A New Zealand court concluded that common law required an intent to defraud, *Stewart*, [1908] 27 N.Z.L.R. 682. See below, p. 452, footnote 4.

[3] *Re London & Globe Finance Corporation, Ltd.*, [1903] 1 Ch. 728 at p. 732. BUCKLEY, J., was concerned with provisions of the Larceny Act 1861 and the Companies Act 1862 and his observations were in any event *obiter*.

[4] *Welham* v. *Director of Public Prosecutions*, [1961] A.C. 103 at p. 127; [1960] 1 All E.R. 805 at p. 810, *per* Lord RADCLIFFE.

[5] Last note.

hire-purchase agreements upon which finance companies had advanced money to the firm. His defence to a charge of uttering a forged document was that he believed these agreements were being used to make it appear to the authorities that the finance companies were not avoiding certain credit restrictions then in force. It was held, affirming D's conviction, that in intending to induce the authorities to do something they would not have done but for the deceit, D intended to defraud the authorities. The House of Lords approved earlier cases holding there was an intent to defraud where papers were forged to secure the release of a prisoner from jail,[6] where a seaman forged a certificate of good conduct so that the Trinity House examiners would allow him to sit for his master's certificate,[7] where a testimonial was forged to gain admission to the police force,[8] and where a student forged papers to gain admission to the Inner Temple.[9]

Pressed to its logical conclusion this view of defrauding might mean that if D sent a forged letter to P giving P a fictitious appointment, D would be guilty of forgery. Such a case is strictly one of forgery at least if it can be said that D induced P to act to his injury, for without some prejudice to P it cannot, in fairness, be said he has been defrauded.[10] In *Geach* D[11] forged the acceptance to a bill of exchange and when charged with uttering a forgery he argued he had no intent to defraud since he intended all along to meet the bill himself, and that he had in fact paid off the bankers who had honoured the bill so that no actual loss had been sustained by anyone. In directing the jury PARKE, B., said he had no doubt there was an intent to defraud because D induced the bankers to do something they would not otherwise have done and it could make no difference that D subsequently paid off the bankers. The point is that D put the bankers in a worse position than they would have been had they not been deceived by the forgery, since the bankers were in the position of having advanced money on a bill without the usual security of an acceptor. Clearly the bankers would not have advanced the money had they known this.[12] But if in *Geach* D had honestly believed he had authority to accept the bill in the acceptor's name there would have been no intent to defraud.[13] It seems clear from the cases that if D in fact makes a false document, as by signing it where he has no authority to do so or by entering a larger amount where he is authorised only to enter a smaller amount, the document is not a forgery if D honestly believes he is authorised to act as he does.[14] It might be thought it could be said as a general proposition that a man who is acting honestly cannot be guilty of forgery but such a proposition may go too far on the present state of the authorities. In *Parker*,[15] D, who had made a

---

[6] *Harris* (1833), 1 Mood C.C. 393.

[7] *Toshack* (1849), 1 Den. 492.

[8] *Moah* (1858), Dears. & B. 550.

[9] *Bassey* (1931), 22 Cr. App. Rep. 160.

[10] *Welham* v. *Director of Public Prosecutions*, [1961] A.C. 103 at p. 127; [1960] 1 All E.R. 805 at p. 810, *per* Lord RADCLIFFE. And see Gooderson, "Prejudice as a Test of Intent to Defraud" [1960], C.L.J. 199, who, while approving *Welham* v. *Director of Public Prosecutions*, would adopt a definition of defrauding which would apparently exclude the example given.

[11] (1840), 9 C. & P. 499.

[12] See Stephen's account of *Dr. Dodd's* case: 2 H.C.L. 122. *Cf. Williams*, [1953] 1 Q.B. 660; [1953] 1 All E.R. 1068; above, p. 373.

[13] *Forbes* (1835), 7 C. & P. 224.

[14] *Forbes, supra; Clifford* (1845), 2 Car. & Kir. 202.

[15] (1910), 74 J.P. 208.

loan of £3 to P and was unable to get payment, sent to P (a) a demand for payment and (b) a letter, purporting to emanate from the War Office, which asked P to give the demand his best attention without delay. D was charged with demanding money under a forged instrument with intent to defraud contrary to s. 38 of the Forgery Act 1861,[16] and RIDLEY, J., ruled that there was evidence of an intent to defraud to go to the jury. Arguably this decision confuses the making of a false document and the intent to defraud. Document (b) which D sent to P was unquestionably false since it purported to be made by one who did not make it; but the requirement of an intent to defraud is a requirement additional to the making of a false document and is not satisfied merely by the making of a false document.[17] Yet in *Parker* there was nothing, other than the making of a false document, which would support an intent to defraud since he had a legal claim of right to the debt.[18] So it may be that *Parker* ought to be reconsidered, but it has to be pointed out that this case does not stand alone in holding that D may be convicted of forgery although he has a legal claim of right to the property sought, and there is even the authority of the Court of Criminal Appeal for this view.[19] The cases seem to show, then, that it is not enough that D has a claim of right to the property; he must also believe he is authorised to falsify the document.

Williams says of *Welham* v. *Director of Public Prosecutions*[20] that it leaves it impossible to state a perfectly clear rule for distinguishing between the concepts of defrauding and deceiving.[1] In *Moon*,[2] however, a conviction for forging a document with intent to defraud contrary to s. 4 (1) of the Forgery Act 1913 was quashed because the trial judge had told the jury that either an intent to defraud or deceive would suffice. The Court of Appeal sympathised with Williams's view and conceded that in certain cases it was difficult to draw a distinction between the two types of intent, but concluded that an attempt must be made to distinguish the two. Unfortunately the court did not say how this was to be done. Perhaps the best that can be done is to give an illustration of a case where there might be an intent to deceive without an intent to defraud. In *Hodgson*[3] D altered a diploma of the Royal College of Surgeons to make it appear it had been granted to him. It was not shown that D forged the diploma for any purpose other than inducing others to believe that he was a surgeon and it was accordingly held he had no intent to defraud. If, however, the document had been a public document he would now be guilty of forgery under the Act for he did intend to deceive. What is really hard to understand is not so much the distinction between defrauding and deceiving, but why it should have appeared necessary to make criminal the faking of a public document with intent only to deceive. If, for instance, D forges a birth certificate with intent *only* to

---

[16] Now s. 7 of the 1913 Act; see below, p. 452.
[17] See above, p. 445.
[18] Of course defrauding is not confined to causing economic loss and extends to causing P to do something which he would not otherwise have done, or to refrain from doing something which he would otherwise have done. But in cases like *Welham Harris, Toshack* and *Moah*, above, P had a duty to do, or refrain from doing, otherwise; whereas in *Parker* D was trying to cause P to do that (pay the debt) which it was his duty to do. Consider whether on the facts of *Parker*, D could now be convicted of deception and/or blackmail.
[19] *Smith* (1919), 14 Cr. App. Rep. 101; and see *Wilson* (1847), 2 Car. & Kir. 527.
[20] [1961] A.C. 103; [1960] 1 All E.R. 805.
[1] C.L.G.P., 87.
[2] [1967] 3 All E.R. 962.
[3] (1856), Dears. & B. 3.

make himself appear legitimate and not intending anyone to act on it, this is forgery, although it hardly seems a criminal enterprise.[4]

A final point settled by *Welham* v. *Director of Public Prosecutions* is that there is an intent to defraud where, as in that case, D presents the document to one party, not to defraud him, but to defraud some other party. A general intent to defraud will suffice even if there is no intention to defraud the recipient of the document.[5]

(4) UTTERING

Under s. 6 (1) of the Forgery Act 1913 any person who utters a forged document, seal or die is guilty of an offence and is liable to the same punishment as if he had himself forged the document, seal or die. A person utters a document, seal or die when, knowing that the same is forged, and with the intent to defraud or deceive as the case may be he

> "uses, offers, publishes, delivers, disposes of, exchanges, tenders in evidence, or puts off the said forged document, seal or die."[6]

This sub-section is widely phrased and covers virtually any use by D of the forged document, seal or die. In the case of a forged bill, for instance, the offence of uttering would be complete so soon as D tendered the bill, and on facts like those in *Hodgson*[7] D would utter the forged diploma simply by hanging it on the wall of his sitting room and exhibiting it to his friends. Merely to possess a forgery is not to utter it.[8] To utter (offer, publish, deliver, tender or put off) a forged document seems to require a transaction whereby D in some way communicates the document to another. But it is also enough that D "uses" the document and in *Harris*[9] it was held that the mere *sending* of a photostat copy of an allegedly forged receipt constituted a use of the forged receipt. This interpretation of "uses" leaves little or no room for any meaning to be given to any of the verbs following "uses" which is not covered by "uses" itself.[10] But in any case the verbs overlap in meaning to a considerable extent and it would be impossible to give any of the verbs a meaning which is not substantially conveyed by the other verbs.

In *Harris* the court left open the question whether the mere taking of a photostat copy of a forged document is itself a use of the forged document. If this were to be held a use it would involve giving "uses" a meaning quite out of line with the remaining verbs in the sense that the remaining verbs all connote the notion of communication, or attempted communication, to another.

(5) DEMANDING PROPERTY ON FORGED INSTRUMENTS

The offence of demanding property on forged instruments, punishable by fourteen years' imprisonment, under s. 7 of the Forgery Act 1913, unlike other

---

[4] The draftsmen of the Act apparently thought that at common law forgery of a public document required only an intent to deceive, and relied for this proposition on remarks made by Jervis, C.J., in *Hodgson*. In fact *Hodgson* does not go that far and the Earl of Loreburn, L.C., asked the draftsmen to reconsider the point: *Reports of Committees* (1913), Vol. 6, pp. 21–27. Hadden, "Intent in Forgery" (1965), 28 M.L.R. 154, 286.

[5] [1961] A.C. 103 at p. 134; [1960] 1 All E.R. 805 at p. 816. And see Forgery Act 1913, s. 17 (2).

[6] Forgery Act 1913, s. 6 (2).

[7] (1856), Dears. & B. 3; above, p. 451.

[8] There may be an offence under s. 8; see below, p. 454.

[9] [1965] 3 All E.R. 206; above p. 445.

[10] Except, perhaps, "disposes of". D might dispose of a document without making use of it, as by putting it in his wastebasket. But in the context of s. 6 "dispose" appears to be used in the sense of distribute or deal.

provisions of the Act, restricts the intent to defraud to cases of economic loss. Here D's intent must be to obtain money, security for money or other property, real or personal. The offence is complete when D obtains, or endeavours to obtain, such property for himself or for another

> "(a) under, upon, or by virtue of any forged instrument whatsoever, knowing the same to be forged; or (b) under, upon, or by virtue of any probate or letters of administration, knowing the will, testament, codicil, or testamentary writing on which such probate or letters of administration shall have been obtained to have been forged. . . ."

In paragraph (a) here the word "instrument" is used and not "document". On the face of it this seems to invite some distinction between the two but so far the courts have not articulated any clear distinction. In *Riley*,[11] a case decided under a similar provision in s. 38 of the Forgery Act 1861, it was held that a telegram which D had ante-dated in order to defraud a bookmaker was an instrument. WILLS, J., thought that, in its context, instrument was here synonymous with document or writing and rejected D's view that it was confined to writings which would directly lead to business relations with another. HAWKINS, J., did not specify any distinction between instrument and document but he did not expressly reject the view that it was confined to writings leading to business relations. In the Forgery Act 1861, however, the word "instrument" was used frequently and in a variety of senses, and the point was taken in *Cade*[12] that in the Forgery Act 1913 the words document and instrument were used in such sharp contrast that some distinction must have been intended,[13] and it was suggested that instrument should be confined to deeds and other documents of title. Holding that a forged letter containing a request for money was an instrument the Court of Criminal Appeal rejected the view that instrument was confined to documents of title but it did not expressly reject the view that there might be some distinction, and the court appeared to favour the idea that an instrument was a document which would lead to business with another.[14]

It is submitted that instrument is merely a synonym for document. In *Smith*,[15] it will be recalled, both POLLOCK, C.B., and WILLES, J., said that the wrappers were not documents, *inter alia*, because they were not instruments,[16] and if they were not instruments they could not be documents for the purposes of the law of forgery.[17]

The offence under both pagragraphs (a) and (b) is committed if the money or property is obtained "under, upon, or by virtue of" the forgery and this expression was considered for the first time in *Hurford*.[18] In order to obtain a

---

[11] [1896] 1 Q.B. 309 (C.C.R.).

[12] [1914] 2 K.B. 209.

[13] The word instrument appears twice in the Act. It is used in s. 9 (b) as meaning implement or tool.

[14] See also *Howse* (1912), 23 Cox C.C. 135, where it was held under s. 38 of the Forgery Act 1861 that an envelope ante-dated in order to defraud a bookmaker was an instrument. Note that here it was the envelope which contained the forgery and an envelope is something which has a use other than that of conveying information; see above, p. 442. But in civil cases at least the envelope is always read together with the enclosed writing as part and parcel of one document and it seems only proper so to regard it for the purposes of forgery.

[15] (1858), Dears. & B. 566; above, p. 442.

[16] Above, p. 442.

[17] The draftsmen used "instrument" because it was used in the provision (s. 38 of 24 and 25 Vict. c. 98) which was replaced by s. 7; there was no suggestion it meant anything other than document: *Reports of Committees* (1913), Vol. 6, pp. 104, 105.

[18] [1963] 2 Q.B. 398; [1963] 2 All E.R. 254 (C.C.A.). See [1963] Crim. L.R. 432.

lorry D and E went to P, a dealer, but as they did not have enough capital P sent them to Q, a finance company, to arrange a hire-purchase of the lorry. D there signed a proposal form in the name of R, R being a credit-worthy individual which D was not. Having satisfied itself as to the credit of R, Q then confirmed the proposal with P and P delivered the lorry to D and E. Appealing against their conviction under s. 7, D and E argued that the section applied only if P knew of the forged instrument and relied upon it when handing over the lorry. Upholding the conviction the court said that the expression "by virtue of" following as it did the words "under" and "upon" must be given the widest possible meaning, and was apt to cover a case like the present where D and E used a forged instrument to start a chain of events whereby they obtained the lorry. The expression requires that there be some causal connection between the use of the forged instrument and the obtaining, hence D and E would have been entitled to an acquittal if the jury had believed their story that the lorry was delivered to them by P before Q had communicated his confirmation of the proposal to P, but the expression may be wide enough to cover a case where, on the same facts, a charge of false pretences would fail for lack of a sufficient causal connection. The expression would also cover the case where D receives money or property by virtue of the use of the forged instrument by E.

(6) POSSESSION OF FORGED DOCUMENTS AND IMPLEMENTS OF FORGERY

The mere possession of forged documents, seals or dies is not an offence, as such, under the Forgery Act 1913. However s. 8 makes it an offence, punishable by fourteen years' imprisonment, knowingly to possess forged bank notes, and certain specified stamps, dies and labels, and s. 9 makes it an offence, punishable by seven years' imprisonment, knowingly to possess, make or use certain kinds of paper and certain kinds of implements commonly used in the forgery of bank notes, bills, shares and the like. Under s. 10 it is an offence, punishable by two years' imprisonment, knowingly to purchase, receive or possess certain kinds of paper. These sections provide for the defence of lawful authority or excuse but the proof of this is expressly placed on D.[19]

In order to prove these offences the prosecution is not required to prove that the possessor has some fraudulent or deceitful purpose in mind. Accordingly the offence is made out once possession plus knowledge is proved unless D can then show lawful authority or excuse. It has been held, under a provision *in pari materia*, that there was no lawful authority or excuse where the proprietor of a philatelist newspaper made a die of a stamp in order to produce black and white illustrations of the stamp in his paper.[20] It would seem then that to possess a forged bank note as a curio would constitute an offence. Possession for these purposes is defined in s. 15 of the Act. It should also be noted in this connection that in *Gurmit Singh*,[1] it was held that it is an offence at common law to procure an implement with intent to use the same to forge a document.

---

[19] *Cf. Patterson*, [1962] 2 Q.B. 429; [1962] 1 All E.R. 340.
[20] *Dickins* v. *Gill*, [1896] 2 Q.B. 310, a case under the Post Office Protection Act 1884, s. 7.
[1] [1965] 3 All E.R. 384; above p. 167.

CHAPTER 16

Offences against Property involving Malice

1 GENERAL CONSIDERATIONS

Most of the offences involving damage to property, real or personal, arise under the Malicious Damage Act 1861. Perhaps the most striking feature of this Act is the proliferation of particular offences[1] and the absence of broadly-based offences. There are, for example, six sections creating offences of setting fire to buildings. Sections 1–5 create offences, all punishable with imprisonment for life, of setting fire to specified kinds of buildings, and it is only where the building is not one of the kinds specified that the offence under s. 6, which is confined to "any building other than such as are in the Act before mentioned", and is punishable with imprisonment for fourteen years, is committed. Similarly s. 51 makes it an offence, carrying two years' imprisonment, to damage any property, real or personal, but only if the damage is of a kind "for which no punishment is herein-before provided".[2] The oddities of the Act are perhaps most felt in magistrates' courts. Where the amount of damage does not exceed £100[3] the position is straightforward for this is a summary offence, whatever the nature of the property, under s. 14 (1) of the Criminal Justice Administration Act 1914.[4] The maximum punishment under this provision is, if the damage exceeds £5, imprisonment for three months or a fine of £100; otherwise it is two months or a fine of £5. Although D may be tried summarily under other provisions where the amount of the damage does not exceed £100, it seems unlikely, in view of the complexity of the situation, that any provision other than s. 14 (1) would be used where the damage does not exceed £100. But where the amount of the

---

[1] Many of which carry maximum punishments which are hopelessly out-of-date, for example, life for destroying goods in process of manufacture (s. 14), fourteen years for destroying hopbinds (s. 19). And under the Dockyards Protection Act 1772 it is still a capital offence to set fire to H.M. ships or even to ship's materials in H.M. dockyards.

[2] Thus s. 51 covers those offences in the Act for which no punishment is provided (s. 13 and s. 34) and any case of damage to property not provided for elsewhere in the Act.

[3] Malicious Damage Act 1964, s. 1.

[4] Replacing s. 52 of the Malicious Damage Act 1861. But see further below, p. 468.

damage exceeds £100 some other provision must be used for summary trial. The Act itself provides for summary jurisdiction under s. 22 (damaging trees wheresoever growing), s. 23 (destroying fruit and vegetables in gardens), s. 24 (destroying vegetables not growing in gardens), s. 25 (destroying fences and walls), s. 38 (attempting to injure telegraphs), s. 41 (killing and maiming animals other than cattle), and further provides under s. 37 (injuries to telegraphs) for summary trial if the court deems it inexpedient to the ends of justice to proceed by indictment. And now under the Magistrates' Courts Act 1952, s. 19, summary trial is available, if D consents, for offences under s. 16 (setting fire to crops of corn), s. 20 (damaging trees growing in a pleasure ground), s. 21 (damaging trees elsewhere than in a pleasure ground) and s. 51.[5]

It follows from the terms of s. 51 that D cannot be tried summarily under that section for causing damage which constitutes one of the specified summary offences. If, for instance, D maims P's cat, the only provision of the Act under which he may be prosecuted is s. 41. Moreover, summary trial is not available at all under s. 51 if the damage caused falls within the rag-bag of other offences created by preceding sections. Hence D may be tried summarily for setting fire to a crop of corn whatever the amount of the damage (s. 16), but not for setting fire to a stack of corn where the amount of the damage exceeds £100 (since this is punishable under s. 17). He may be tried summarily for setting fire to P's car whatever its value (since this is nowhere punishable except under s. 51), but not for destroying P's reaping machine (since this is punishable under s. 15).

(1)　MEANING OF UNLAWFULLY AND MALICIOUSLY

Almost all the provisions in the Malicious Damage Act 1861[6] require that the act constituting the offence be caused "unlawfully and maliciously".

1　Maliciously

"In our opinion," it was said by the Court of Criminal Appeal in *Cunningham*,[7]

"the word 'maliciously' in a statutory crime postulates foresight of consequences."

It is submitted, though the matter is not altogether free from doubt, that this is the case under the Malicious Damage Act 1861.

What is quite clear is that D is not acting maliciously simply because he has it in mind to commit some other crime. Thus it was held in *Pembliton*[8] that a finding that D threw a stone with the intention of hitting another person would not support an indictment for maliciously damaging a window broken by the stone. Nor was D acting maliciously simply because he was engaged in the commission of a felony. In *Faulkner*[9] D, bent on stealing rum stored in the hold of a

---

[5] Which has the effect of incorporating the offences under ss. 13 and 41 since no punishment is provided for these.

[6] In one case, that of obstructing engines or carriages on railways under s. 36, the offence may be committed "by any wilful omission or neglect". In two cases, under ss. 11 and 12, it is an offence for persons "riotously and tumultuously assembled" to destroy specified buildings, or to damage specified buildings or machinery; an intent to destroy or damage appears to be required (see Russell (4th ed.) (1865), Vol. 1, pp. 382–385). As to "riotously and tumultuously" cf. *Dwyer (J. F.) Ltd.* v. *Metropolitan Police Receiver District*, [1967] 2 Q.B. 970; [1967] 2 All E.R. 1051; below, p. 538. Note that many statutes (relating, *e.g.*, to railways, tramways, gas, water) contain provisions creating offences of damage to property; note especially the Protection of Animals Acts 1911–64 where the basis of liability for offences often rests in negligence.

[7] [1957] 2 Q.B. 396 at p. 400; [1957] 2 All E.R. 412 at p. 414. See above, pp. 74–270.

[8] (1874), L.R. 2 C.C.R. 119. See above, p. 45.

[9] (1877), 13 Cox C.C. 550.

ship, broke open a cask and then struck a match to see what he was about; the rum ignited and the ship was completely destroyed by fire. On a prosecution under s. 42 of the Act for setting fire to a ship the trial judge directed the jury, in terms, that D was acting maliciously if the fire took place when D was stealing rum. The Irish Court for Crown Cases Reserved held that the direction was wrong and quashed D's conviction.

It is equally clear that the expression does not connote ill-will or hatred. This much is explicitly made clear by s. 58 which provides it shall not be necessary to prove that D committed the offence from malice conceived against the owner of the property or otherwise. D may be convicted though he bears the owner no ill-will and does not wish to do him harm:[10] equally D may not be convicted though he acts out of spite if he does not act maliciously. In *Child*[11] D, from ill-will and malice against P, broke up P's furniture, piled it and P's clothing on the stone floor of a dwelling-house and set it alight, and but for prompt intervention the house itself would almost certainly have been burned. D was charged with unlawfully and maliciously setting fire to the furniture "under such circumstances that if the building were thereby set fire to the offence would amount to felony" contrary to s. 7.[12] The jury found D guilty "but not so that if the house had caught fire the setting fire to the house would have been wilful and malicious." Interpreting this finding as meaning that D did not intend to set fire to the house and that he was not aware of the risk of fire to the house, the court quashed D's conviction.

It was the court's considered opinion in *Pembliton*,[13] and it was part of the *ratio* in *Child*,[14] that the expression "maliciously" required intentional or reckless conduct with regard to the *actus reus* of the crime. In *Faulkner*,[15] on the other hand, most of the judges felt that negligence in regard to the *actus reus* would suffice.[16] But no subsequent English case has cast doubts on the correctness of *Pembliton* and *Child*, and it is submitted, notwithstanding that "maliciously"may be given a different interpretation in other contexts,[17] that in the context of the Malicious Damage Act 1861 "maliciously" has acquired a definite meaning which requires foresight of the very consequences defined in the *actus reus* of the offence in question.

In this text "maliciously" and "unlawfully" are treated separately. Under "maliciously" the mental element in the narrow sense has been discussed; that is, the extent to which liability in offences of malicious damage is founded in intention, recklessness, or negligence. Under "unlawfully" there is a discussion of various circumstances of exculpation or justification, such as self defence and defence of property.

This dichotomy of treatment is, however, largely (or even entirely) one of convenience. It has the merit that it appears to ascribe a specific function to the two adverbs and it is possible that the draftsman of the Act had some such dichotomy in mind. Certainly it seems likely that the draftsman thought that these

---

[10] *Salmon* (1802), Russ. & Ry. 26; *Regan* (1850), 4 Cox C.C. 335.
[11] (1871), L.R. 1 C.C.R. 307.
[12] Section 7 is now amended by the Criminal Law Act 1967, Sch. 2, to read, ". . . thereby set fire to he would be guilty of an offence under any of the preceding sections . . .".
[13] Above, p. 456.
[14] *Supra*.
[15] Above, p. 456.
[16] Only BARRY, J., came out clearly in favour of intention and recklessness.
[17] *Cf. Mowatt*, [1968] 1 Q.B. 421; [1967] 3 All E.R. 47 (C.A.); above, p. 267.

two adverbs were not entirely synonymous. But viewed strictly it seems that the two adverbs may be entirely synonymous, and it is certainly arguable that "unlawfully" conveys nothing that is not already conveyed by "maliciously".

Suppose, for example, that D kills P's dog in the mistaken belief that it is about to savage him. This kind of problem, since it involves consideration of issues of self defence, is treated here under the heading "unlawfully", and it seems more natural to consider this problem from the point of view of the lawfulness or unlawfulness of the measures taken by D to protect his person. But the problem could be equally treated under the heading of "maliciously" and the same result would be reached. If D intends to act in self defence, not only does he not act "unlawfully", but he does not act "maliciously"; that is, he does not intend to bring about the consequences which the law makes penal.

In practice the judges have refrained (perhaps intuitively but probably quite rightly) from attempting to ascribe particular and exclusive meanings to "unlawfully" and "maliciously". The important question is whether in a given case a crime of malicious damage is made out; it is of less importance to attempt to explain the exact relationship, if any, of "unlawfully" to "maliciously". From the student's point of view it may seem untidy, but he should not be misled by the apparent tidiness in this text. *Gott* v. *Measures*[18] for example, is here treated as raising the question whether D acted unlawfully. Lord GODDARD, however, considered whether D was acting maliciously.[19] Either way, essentially the same issue is raised.

2   Unlawfully

In the context of the Malicious Damage Act 1861 the expression "unlawfully" appears to be an explicit recognition of the ordinarily implicit principle that an act is not criminal, even if intentionally done, where there exists some lawful excuse (mistake, necessity, etc.) for its commission. It is no offence, for instance, for D to kill a dog when this is the only way he can prevent it from savaging him. Damage is not done unlawfully simply because it may be described as immoral or barbaric. D may wantonly destroy works of art which he owns, for as a general proposition a man may abuse in any way that which he owns.[20] Where, however, D abuses animals owned by him there is authority for saying that he may commit an offence under the Act, for in *Parry*[1] it was held by RUSSELL, C.J., that an indictment under s. 40 would lie where D, in a fit of temper, kicked and stabbed his horse. The argument that the Act nowhere states that it is an offence to destroy one's own property except where there is some additional requirement (such as an intent to defraud) was rejected, but it is submitted that the argument was essentially sound and that *Parry* was wrongly decided. The Act, which draws no apparent distinction between animate and inanimate objects, can hardly be said to give rise to the proposition that a man cannot destroy his own goods unless some good reason appears for the destruction.

In *Parry* D's act of injuring the horse was unlawful in one sense: it constituted an offence under the Prevention of Cruelty to Animals Act 1849.[2] But it does

---

[18] [1948] 1 K.B. 234; [1947] 2 All E.R. 609, below p. 463.
[19] [1948] 1 K.B. 234, 239; [1947] 2 All E.R. 609, 611.
[20] "A man may do what he will with his own": PHILLIMORE, J., in *Rutter* (1908), 73 J.P. 12 at p. 13.
[1] (1900), 35 L. Jo. 456.
[2] See now Protection of Animals Act 1911.

not follow that therefore D injured the horse "unlawfully" within s. 40 of the Malicious Damage Act. It would be a strange interpretation which declared that "unlawfully" meant "constituting some *other* crime" when the purpose of these provisions is to create substantive crimes.

It seems, however, that the Act does place some general limitation on the proposition that a man may do what he likes with his own. Section 59 of the Act provides:

> "Every provision of this Act not herein-before so applied shall apply to every person who, with intent to injure or defraud any other person, shall do any of the acts herein-before made penal, although the offender shall be in possession of the property against or in respect of which such act shall be done."

The effect of this section seems to be that D may be convicted of any offence under the Act in respect of his own property if his intention in damaging the property is to injure or defraud any person. Thus, for example, if D destroys a valuable painting owned by him in order to defraud P, with whom he has insured it, D would be guilty, by virtue of s. 59, of an offence under s. 51 of the Act.

In order fully to understand s. 59 it is necessary to take account of the position at common law. At common law it was the rule that D could not be convicted of arson in respect of a dwelling *possessed* by him, even though it was *owned* by another; conversely the owner of the dwelling could be convicted of arson if he set fire to it when in the possession of another. Thus at common law there was never any limitation on the offence of arson in favour of ownership as such, but there was a limitation in favour of possession. This limitation was removed by statute and now s. 3 of the Act—which is the one section which "herein-before" applies the principle of s. 59—provides:

> "Whosoever shall unlawfully and maliciously set fire to any house, stable, coach-house, outhouse, warehouse, office, shop, mill, malthouse, hop-oast, barn, storehouse, granary, hovel, shed or fold, or to any farm building, or to any building or erection used in farming land, or in carrying on any trade or manufacture, or any branch thereof, whether the same shall then be in the possession of the offender or in the possession of any other person, with intent thereby to injure or defraud any person, shall be guilty of an offence, and being convicted thereof shall be liable . . . to imprisonment for life."

It is clear that this section removes the limitation in favour of possession. The possessor may be convicted if he "unlawfully and maliciously" sets fire to one of the specified buildings "with intent thereby to injure or defraud any person". Obviously a person in possession of a building owned by another who sets fire to it will normally intend to injure that other. It might be said that the requirement of an intent to injure is superfluous in this case because it adds nothing to that which is already implicit in "unlawfully and maliciously". But it was necessary to add the intent to injure because at common law the act of setting fire to a dwelling in one's own possession was not unlawful, at least not criminally so.

Section 3 keeps the rule that an owner may commit arson in respect of one of the specified buildings where it is in the possession of another—"whether the same shall then be in the possession of the offender or in the possession of any other person". So a landlord may still be convicted of arson in respect of his tenant's house if he intends to injure or defraud. Again, if he sets fire to the house maliciously he will normally intend to injure his tenant, though, since the house is owned by the landlord, he may the more easily be able to make out a defence of claim of right.[3]

---

[3] See below, p. 461.

Arguably s. 3 was intended to go no further than remove this restriction in favour of possession, but the section is now understood[4] to extend to the case where D both owns and possesses the building which he sets fire to with intent to injure or defraud.   Where D both owns and possesses the building the question arises in what circumstances he might injure another by setting fire to it.   Certainly D may injure another where that other has an interest in the building of which D is aware.   Thus D may have an intent to injure where the building is owned jointly by himself and others[5] or where the property is mortgaged to another. But may there be an intent to injure another who has no interest in the property? In *Newill*[6] D was charged with setting fire to a stack of straw with intent to injure P, the owner, but the jury found that D intended to injure Q by throwing the blame for the crime on him.   GASELEE, J., was apparently not disposed to accept this as sufficient and persuaded the jury to find that there was in law an intent to injure P since D knew the stack belonged to P and maliciously set fire to it.   It is submitted that "injure" means to injure P in respect of some interest which P has in property.[7]

The intent to defraud is more easy to define,[8] and the most obvious instance in this context is where D sets fire to his dwelling or business premises with intent to defraud insurers.   Yet "defraud" goes beyond "injure" in a significant way. If the view expressed above concerning "injury" is accepted, D may be convicted of arson with intent to injure under s. 3 only where he sets fire to property in which another has an interest.   But if he has an intent to defraud he may be convicted although no one other than himself has any interest in the property.   In effect, an act preparatory to the offence of deception (punishable, if carried out, by ten years' imprisonment) is elevated to the status of arson (punishable by imprisonment for life).

Section 3, then, appears to impose a particular limitation upon the freedom of an owner to do what he likes with his own.   The *raison d'être* of the section may have been only to remove the immunity of a possessor who did not own the building, but it is taken in addition to impose liability on one who both owns and possesses if there is an intention to injure or defraud.   This limitation on an owner's freedom to do what he likes with his own is applied to all other offences of malicious damage by virtue of s. 59, and for much the same reasons.   At common law it appears to have been the case that the limitation in favour of possession in respect of arson also applied to malicious injuries to property generally.   Certainly there was one case[9] which suggested that a tenant could not be convicted of maliciously damaging trees on the demised premises because the trees were in the possession of the tenant and there could be no trespass. Section 59 was introduced to make it clear that any such restriction no longer applied where there was an intent to injure or defraud.[10]   It seems to follow from

---

[4] *Cf. Ellicombe* (1833), 1 Mood. & R. 260; *Doran* (1791), 1 Esp. 127; *Gillson* (1807), R. & R. 138; *Newboult* (1872), L.R. 1 C.C.R. 344; *Fitzaucher*, [1956] Crim. L.R. 118.
[5] *Cf. Philp* (1830), 1 Mood. C.C. 263.
[6] (1836), 1 Mood. C.C. 458.
[7] Where D sets fire to his house with intent to kill his wife who is inside, he intends, in a very real sense, to injure his wife, but it is thought that the charge lies under s. 2 (setting fire to a dwelling house, any person being therein) and not under s. 3. See below, p. 472.
[8] See above, p. 449.
[9] *Mills* v. *Collett* (1829), 6 Bing. 85.
[10] *Cf.* Greaves' note in Russell (4th ed.) (1865), Vol. 2, at p. 1021, footnote (j).

the effect given by s. 3 that even an owner in possession may be convicted of an offence under the Act provided he maliciously damages the property with intent to injure or defraud, so that it would be just as much an offence under s. 51, punishable in this instance with two years' imprisonment, to destroy a painting with intent to defraud insurers as it is an offence under s. 3 to set fire to a building with the same intent.

This view of ss. 59 and 3 creates difficulties regarding the meaning of "unlawfully". This requirement is in addition to the intent to injure or defraud, yet where D damages property of his own and in his own possession the act is not unlawful except by virtue of the intent to injure or defraud. It has been pointed out[11] that it was necessary to provide that an act might be unlawful notwithstanding that D had possession because of the prior common law position, but it is a significant step forward from this to say that a person acts unlawfully in destroying property of which he is in possession and in which no person other than himself has an interest. The point has not apparently been raised in any case,[12] but the decisions under s. 3 assume that an act is unlawful if done with an intent to injure or defraud any person.

In any event s. 59 would not extend to a case such as *Parry*.[13] There D owned the horse which he injured, but in injuring it he did not intend to injure or defraud any person.

Where D, without lawful excuse, damages the property of another the above difficulties do not arise and he acts unlawfully. There is no need to show that D had no intention in damaging P's property to injure P in any way or to cause him economic loss; it is enough to show that D acted without lawful excuse.[14] Conversely, damage causing serious economic injury to P may be justified; it has always been accepted, for instance, that a house may be pulled down if this is necessary to prevent the spread of fire.[15] In practice the issue whether D is acting unlawfully is most commonly raised in cases where D believes he owns (or has some interest in) the property which he destroys, or where D believes that in order to protect his own property (or person) he may destroy that of others. It may be thought that these two situations are essentially the same so that where D destroys something in the mistaken belief that he is entitled to do so, his conduct is not unlawful, and thus not criminal, whether arising from a mistaken belief in ownership or a mistaken belief in what is permissible to protect ownership. Theoretically there is much to be said for treating both cases in the same way, but the courts do not now appear to do so. There are also cases where D causes damage to P's property in vindicating some other right of his (real or imagined) and, finally, cases arising under s. 14 (1) of the Criminal Justice Administration Act 1914 require special mention in this regard.

(a) *Belief in ownership: claim of right.*—Where D commits no offence under the Malicious Damage Act 1861 in destroying his own property, it follows, in principle, that he ought to be guilty of no offence where he destroys P's property

---

[11] Above, p. 459.
[12] Turner raises the point in relation to s. 3 but concludes that "it is quite probable that if this point were raised the courts would nonetheless disregard the word 'unlawfully' as surplusage introduced by the draftsman *per incuriam*."—Russell, 1339.
[13] (1900), 35 L. Jo. 456; above, p. 458.
[14] *Weich* (1875), 1 Q.B.D. 23 (mare injured for sexual gratification). *Cf. Roper* v. *Knott*, [1898] 1 Q.B. 868; below, p. 471.
[15] Above, p. 137.

under the mistaken impression that it is his own. D may be liable to P in a civil
action but he commits no criminal offence for he lacks *mens rea*. This is so
whether the mistake is one of fact or law. There is, in fact, not a great deal of
authority on the matter but what there is supports this view. It was apparently
accepted in *Rutter*[16] that it was no offence for a tenant to cut down trees belonging to his landlord under the erroneous belief that they were his own trees. But
a clearer case is *James*[17] where the principle was extended to an employee acting
under his employer's instructions. It was held that D had not unlawfully
obstructed an airway in a mine[18] which his employer, who claimed the airway
belonged to him, had ordered him to brick up. It was quite unnecessary to
determine whether the airway did belong to the employer because D could not
be criminally liable if he believed his employer had such a right. Further, it
was said that even if the employer had known he had no such right, D would
still not be liable so long as he believed his employer had the right.

It is clear that for a claim of right to be a defence to a charge of malicious
damage it must be one which is honestly held. Authority is hardly needed for
such an obvious proposition but there are explicit statements in the cases cited.
What is not so clear is whether the claim must be reasonable. The above cases
make no assertion that the claim must be reasonably grounded as well as honestly
held, but it is perhaps unwise to draw a firm conclusion from this in view of the
fact that in none of them was the claim obviously unreasonable. A stronger case
is *Langford*.[19] D, who had married P's daughter, went to live in P's cottage;
it was proposed that P should sell the cottage to D although P would be allowed
to live out his life there and be looked after by D and his wife. No formal
agreement was ever made. Some time later D demanded possession and when
this was refused sought the assistance of E, a sheriff's bailiff, and others. Possession was again refused and, on E telling D he could do what he liked with his
own, they proceeded to demolish the cottage. On a charge of riotously demolishing a house[20] the jury was directed to acquit the defendants if D and E really
thought it was D's house and that they demolished it in a *bona fide* assertion of
D's right.

It is submitted, therefore, that when a claim of right in this sense is asserted
the sole criterion of its validity is its honesty. It would be a singularly harsh
rule which rendered criminal a dealing with property which D honestly believes
to be his own. The analogy of the belief in legal right is theft in apposite for it is
of essentially the same character as the claim of right in this context. It seems
that a belief in legal right is a defence to a charge of theft if it is honestly held,
without any qualification that it should be reasonable.[1]

(b) *Self-defence.*—Just as D may adopt measures of self-defence against
aggression by P, he may adopt such measures where they are necessary to ward
off an attack by animals belonging to P.[2] What is not clear is whether it is

---

[16] (1908), 73 J.P. 12. *Cf. Twose* (1879), 14 Cox C.C. 327; below, p. 463.
[17] (1837), 8 C. & P. 131. And see *Matthews and Twigg* (1876), 14 Cox C.C. 5.
[18] Contrary to 7 & 8 Geo. IV, c. 30, s. 6. See now s. 28 of the 1861 Act.
[19] (1842), Car. & M. 602.
[20] Contrary to 7 & 8 Geo IV, c. 30, s. 8; see now s. 11 of the Act.
[1] See above, p. 371. The statement by Lord GODDARD, C.J., in *Gott* v. *Measures*,
[1948] 1 K.B. 234 at p. 239; [1947] 2 All E.R. 609 at p. 611; below, p. 463, that "one
cannot have a *bona fide* claim of right if the right is one which the law does not recognise"
cannot apply in this situation.
[2] *Hanway* v. *Boultbee* (1830), 4 C. & P. 350.

sufficient that D honestly acts in self defence or whether the objective requirement of reasonableness must be met as well. Since in the general law of defence
of the person[3] D's conduct must ordinarily meet an objective standard of reasonableness, there is no reason to believe that this instance would be treated differently.

It has been submitted above, however, that in defence of the person a *bona fide*
belief that the conditions necessary to found the defence existed ought to suffice,
even if the belief is objectively unreasonable. It is submitted here, *a fortiori*,
that if D honestly believes he is being attacked by P's dog, he ought to be guilty
of no offence under the Act although his belief is unreasonable in the circumstances.

(c) Defence of property.—Where D damages the property of another in defence
of his own property it is clear, at the very least, from the cases that if (i) D has in
law a right to take action in defence of his property, and (ii) the measures taken
are reasonable having regard to the harm threatened, then D cannot be guilty of
an offence of malicious damage. Thus if P unlawfully builds a structure on D's
land, D may dismantle it and remove it from his property;[4] or if D's chickens
are being attacked by P's dog, D may shoot and kill the dog.[5]

So much is clear, but what is not clear is the position where (i) D does not have
in law a right but honestly believes that he has; and the position where (ii) the
measures taken by D in pursuance of his right (or supposed right) are unreasonable.

On the first matter the cases, with one exception, show that it is enough that
D honestly believes that he has in law the right he claims without any qualification that his belief be a reasonable one. In *Day*,[6] it was held that D was not
guilty of an offence in maiming sheep belonging to P which he had distrained
where he did so in the honest belief that he was entitled to do so upon P's refusal
to pay compensation for the damage done by the sheep. In *Twose*[7], where it
appeared that persons living near a common had occasionally burnt the furze to
improve the growth of the grass, it was accepted by LOPES, J., that D's belief in
a right to burn the furze would be a good defence even though there was no such
right. These cases are not concerned with defence of property but the principle
is a general one which applies equally to cases of defence of property. In
Clemens,[8] D, believing he had rights over a common, tore down a wooden hut
which P had erected there and threw it into the sea. While it was held that D's
conviction must be affirmed because he had done more damage than was necessary,[9] it was clearly assumed that had D acted reasonably in removing the hut
he would not have committed an offence although the right of common which he
claimed did not exist.[10] The one exception is *Gott* v. *Measures*.[11] In this case

---

[3] Above, pp. 230 and 232.
[4] *Dyer* (1952), 36 Cr. App. Rep. 155; *Webb* v. *Stansfield*, [1966] Crim. L.R. 449 (forcing
car quarter-light to remove it when causing obstruction).
[5] *Goodway* v. *Becher*, [1951] 2 All E.R. 349 (D.C.). In *Heard* v. *Coles* (1891), 7 T.L.R.
496 (D.C.), where P's clothes line overhung D's land so that soapy water from the
washing dripped on D's broccoli plants, it was held that D was entitled to cut the line.
[6] (1844), 8 J.P. 186.
[7] (1879), 14 Cox C.C. 327.
[8] [1898] 1 Q.B. 556 (D.C.).
[9] This aspect is pursued below, p. 464.
[10] *Cf. Miles* v. *Hutchings*, [1903] 2 K.B. 714 (D.C.).
[11] [1948] 1 K.B. 234; [1947] 2 All E.R. 609 (D.C.). But *cf. Heaven* v. *Crutchley* (1903),
68 J.P. 53 (D.C.), where WILLS, J., supported a conviction on the ground that the right
claimed was unreasonable in point of law.

D, on land over which he had the full sporting rights, shot and killed P's dog which was chasing and killing game.   It was held that D could be convicted of an offence under s. 41 of the Act; his belief that he had any property to protect was unreasonable because a claim of property in game not reduced into possession was one which the law did not recognise.   This decision conflicts with the tenor of the earlier authorities, and it is difficult to see the sense of it.   A claim may appear perfectly reasonable to the most intelligent layman and yet not exist in law.   From the way in which the case was stated by the justices, it seems that not only did D believe he had a right of property to protect, but the justices also concluded that he had, for they dismissed the information on the ground that D had acted reasonably in defence of his property.[12]   It is submitted that *Gott* v. *Measures* was wrongly decided and that D ought to have been treated as though he had the right which he honestly claimed.

On the second problem, where the measures taken by D in pursuance of his right or supposed right) are excessive, the modern cases tend to favour the view that it is not enough that D honestly believed that he was entitled to take those measures, but that D's conduct must conform to an objective standard of reasonableness.   *Clemens*[13] appears to have been the first case to import an objective requirement at this stage.   Lord RUSSELL, C.J., said:[14]

> "It seems to me that the proper direction to give a jury in such a case is that they should ask themselves this question: Did the defendants do what they did in the exercise of a supposed right? adding that if, on the facts before them, the jury come to the conclusion that the defendants did more damage than they could reasonably suppose to be necessary for the assertion or protection of that right, then the jury may properly and ought to find the defendants guilty of malicious damage under s. 51."

But in the subsequent case of *Miles* v. *Hutchings*[15] there is a clear statement that the test is subjective.   There D had shot a dog which was near his employer's aviary and the court held that the important question was whether D *bona fide* believed that the only way of protecting his employer's property was to have shot the dog.   Again, in *Gott* v. *Measures*,[16] although the court held that D could be convicted because he did not have in law the right which he claimed, Lord GODDARD, C.J., said:[17]

> "It seems to me that the law is really not in any doubt here, and that is that a person may be justified in shooting a dog if he honestly believes that it is necessary as being the only way in which he can protect his property."

The next case which needs to be considered for its bearing on the subsequent

---

[12] And what of the case where it is not even clear to lawyers whether the claim is one which the law recognises or not?   If the court has considerable difficulty in determining whether the claim is one recognised by law, it is harsh to brand D's claim as unreasonable because the court ultimately decides against it.   See also *Crick* v. *Crick* (1858), 6 W.R. 594, where D broke into a house to retake *his* furniture; CROMPTON, J., said: "Such a man might very likely think it legal thus to get his wife and furniture."

[13] [1898] 1 Q.B. 556; above, p. 463.

[14] At p. 559.

[15] [1903] 2 K.B. 714 (D.C.).

[16] [1948] 1 K.B. 234; [1947] 2 All E.R. 609, above, p. 458.

[17] [1948] 1 K.B. at p. 239; [1947] 2 All E.R. at p. 610.

criminal cases is the civil case of *Cresswell* v. *Sirl*.[18] Here the Court of Appeal stated the relevant principles of civil law and said that in order to justify killing a dog in defence of property the defendant must show (i) that at the time of the killing the dog was either (a) actually attacking D's animals, or (b) would renew the attack if left at large, *and* (ii) that either (a) there were no practicable means other than killing the dog by which to stop an attack or prevent its renewal, or (b) that the defendant acted reasonably in the circumstances in considering the killing to be necessary for the protection of his animals.

For present purposes the importance of *Cresswell* v. *Sirl* lies in the fact that it was subsequently accepted by the Divisional Court in *Goodway* v. *Becher*[19] as applicable to a prosecution for unlawfully and maliciously killing a dog under s. 41 of the Act. Lord GODDARD said that *Cresswell* v. *Sirl* ought to be followed although it was a civil case, and added that the question now was whether D "was acting reasonably in doing what he did".[20] In its total and uncritical acceptance of the civil law *Goodway* v. *Becher* is open to serious criticism. Clearly its acceptance in the criminal law must be subject to some qualifications,[1] but more important the court did not consider at all whether the objective test which is proper in the context of the civil law might not be out of place in the context of the criminal law. It is unfortunate that Lord GODDARD's attention was not called to his own observation, set out above,[2] in *Gott* v. *Measures*.

Nor were these various conflicting trends clearly brought out in *Workman* v. *Cowper*,[3] where the Divisional Court again applied *Cresswell* v. *Sirl*.[4] In *Workman* v. *Cowper*, D had shot a foxhound, the owner of which was unknown at the time of the shooting, and which was running wild on common land. There was no evidence that the dog was attacking, or likely to attack, sheep but it was the lambing season and D thought it best, attempts to catch it having failed, to shoot it. The justices dismissed a charge under s. 41 of the Act, holding that D acted reasonably in the circumstances. The Divisional Court appeared to feel some sympathy for the justices' conclusion but held there was no evidence indicating that D was acting in defence of his property since the dog was not attacking any property. "The law in regard to the right of a man to shoot a dog for the protection of his own property", said Lord PARKER, C.J., "has been settled by *Cresswell* v. *Sirl*".[5]

This importation of an objective requirement into the law of malicious damage has been criticised by Williams.[6] Furthermore, Williams apparently rejects any distinction between the right claimed and the measures taken to protect the right and would apply the same subjective test to both. Indeed

---

[18] [1948] 1 K.B. 241; [1947] 2 All E.R. 730 (C.A.).
[19] [1951] 2 All E.R. 349.
[20] *Ibid.*, at p. 351.
[1] *E.g.*, the onus of proof in criminal proceedings would be on the prosecution. Again, if D reasonably, but mistakenly, considered that P's dog was attacking his animals this would be a defence to a criminal charge though it might not be a defence in civil proceedings—yet in *Workman* v. *Cowper*, [1961] 1 All E.R. 683, at p. 686, Lord PARKER, C.J., apparently denies this since he says that the test of reasonableness is relevant only in considering the second of the two propositions (set out in the text above) in *Cresswell* v. *Sirl*.
[2] Above, p. 464.
[3] [1961] 2 Q.B. 143; [1961] 1 All E.R. 683.
[4] [1948] 1 K.B. 241; [1947] 2 All E.R. 730; *supra*.
[5] [1961] 2 Q.B. at p. 149; [1961] 1 All E.R. at p. 685.
[6] C.L.G.P., pp. 305–317.

18

Williams would adopt a single test: did D honestly believe the damage to be legally justifiable?[7]

There is much to be said for this view which judges D for the purposes of the criminal law by the single criterion of his honest belief in legal right to do the act complained of. After all, if D does overstep the mark of what is reasonable in defence of his property he would remain liable in a civil action to pay compensation.[8] But there is perhaps a case for the criminal law to limit the measures taken to protect a right by the imposition of an objective standard of reasonableness. Such a limitation may be more in accord with modern developments. For example, s. 3 of the Criminal Law Act 1967 provides that D may use "such force as is reasonable in the circumstances" in the prevention of crime, and this appears to import an element of objectivity.[9] It would be odd if D's use of force in the prevention of crime was subject to an objective standard while his use of force in defence of property was not. Again, it seems that self defence is not available, or is at best a limited defence,[10] where D uses more force than is necessary, and again it would be odd if D's use of force in defence of property was not subject to a similar limitation.

(*d*) *Other cases.*—In *Workman* v. *Cowper*[11] Lord PARKER, C.J., asked whether there were any cases under the Act where the excuse for the damage complained of was other than defence of property. Counsel was unable to cite any case but he suggested certain possible instances, such as killing a dog which had been run over to put it out of pain, or to kill a mad dog though it was not presently attacking person or property. These suggestions are surely sound in principle[12] and there are some miscellaneous cases where damage to the property of others may be justified other than in defence of person or property. Property which is unlawfully obstructing a highway may be removed and D will not be criminally liable in respect of damage which is incidental to the removal, and damage to P's property incidental to the use of reasonable force in retaking chattels detained by P may be justified though this may be regarded as an instance of defence of property.

But more generally it may be said that any general defence available on a charge of crime would be equally available on a charge arising under the Malicious Damage Act 1861. Thus it would be a defence if D destroyed property under duress provided the requirements of the defence of duress are met.[13]

---

[7] *Op. cit.*, 309.

[8] In *Dyer* (1952), 36 Cr. App. Rep. 155, where D's conviction under s. 51 for removing a notice board and its scaffolding from a common was quashed, Lord GODDARD, C.J., said, at p. 161: "The court cannot refrain from expressing regret that this occurrence was made the subject of a criminal prosecution. We are told that [P] complained to the police and the police started these proceedings. It would have been much better if [P] had been left to take civil proceedings if [he] had been so advised, and in that case they would have been liable for the costs if their proceedings failed. As it is, the costs of the prosecution have to be paid by the ratepayers of Somerset, who have also to pay for the costs of the defence as [D was] quite properly granted [legal aid]. The same is true with regard to this appeal. The whole costs, therefore, of the prosecution and the defence have to fall upon the ratepayers. . . ."

[9] See above, p. 230.

[10] See above pp. 232–234.

[11] [1961] 2 Q.B. 143; [1961] 1 All E.R. 683 (D.C.).

[12] In fact many cases of this kind are covered by express statutory authority. It is, for example, permissible to destroy dangerous dogs, destroy injured animals, destroy diseased animals. See generally Halsbury, Vol. 1, tit. Animals.

[13] *Crutchley* (1831), 5 C. & P. 133; and see above, p. 144.

Workman v. *Cowper* suggests a particular problem in respect of ownerless property. At the time of the shooting the owner of the dog was unknown, but there was nothing to suggest it was ownerless so the point did not directly arise. Had the dog been ownerless it is submitted that D would have committed no offence. Although the Act does not expressly require the property destroyed to be the property of another, and the usual form of information or indictment need not contain an allegation of ownership,[14] it would be curious if D could commit an offence in respect of property of which he is legally entitled to assume ownership —unless, perhaps, there was an intent to injure or defraud and the case was caught by s. 59 of the Act.[15] The dog in the principal case, however, was merely a stray, and strays may be owned. There is a procedure under which its destruction would have been justified seven days after capture if efforts to trace the owner failed,[16] but there is no provision for the case, as here, where the dog evades capture. So long as such a dog remains peaceable and healthy it is, it seems, entitled to its days.

(e) *Cases arising under s. 14 (1) of the Criminal Justice Administration Act 1914.*—This subsection, which replaces with amendments s. 52 of the Malicious Damage Act 1861,[17] and has in turn been amended by the Malicious Damage Act 1964, reads:

"If any person wilfully or maliciously commits any damage to any real or personal property whatsoever, either of a public or private nature, and the amount of the damage does not, in the opinion of the court, exceed one hundred pounds, he shall be liable on summary conviction—

(a) if the amount of the damage, in the opinion of the court, exceeds five pounds, to imprisonment for a term not exceeding three months or to a fine not exceeding one hundred pounds; and

(b) if the amount of the damage is, in the opinion of the court, five pounds or less, to imprisonment for a term not exceeding two months or to a fine not exceeding five pounds;

and in either case to the payment of such amount as appears to the court reasonable compensation for the damage so committed which last-mentioned amount shall be paid to the party aggrieved:

Provided that this provision shall not apply where the alleged offender acted under a fair and reasonable supposition that he had a right to do the act complained of."

Before this subsection is examined it is necessary to note the rules relating to ouster of jurisdiction of justices of the peace.[18] It has long been a rule of common law that where a title to real property[19] is in question the exercise of

---

[14] See Archbold, §2382 for specimen indictments. The information in *Workman* v. *Cowper* contained an allegation that the dog was the property of a person unknown. In fact after the killing it was discovered that the dog belonged to a pack of foxhounds and one of the joint masters of the pack gave his approval to the action taken, but consent given by an owner after the event could not of course affect the criminality of this act at the time of the event.

[15] See above, p. 459.

[16] Dogs Act 1906, s. 3.

[17] Which replaced s. 24 of 7 & 8 Geo. IV, c. 30, 1827. The amount was formerly £20 and was raised to £100 by the Malicious Damage Act 1964.

[18] See generally: Russell, App. 2; "Claim of Right before Justices" (1892), 56 J.P. 179, 195, 211; Gooderson, "Claim of Right and Dispute of Title" [1966], C.L.J. 90, at 216.

[19] On this see Gooderson, *op. cit.*, pp. 94–105.

jurisdiction by justices is ousted. The rule is one which applies in all cases unless it is excluded by a statute conferring summary jurisdiction.[20] It is sometimes said that justices' jurisdiction is ousted whenever a claim of right is involved, but this is seriously misleading since the expression "claim of right" is apt to describe claims other than title to real property, and it is only where the latter is involved that jurisdiction is ousted at common law. A convenient, and more accurate, label is "dispute of title".[1]

If, for example, D is tried summarily for destroying P's fence contrary to s. 25 of the Malicious Damage Act 1861, or for digging a ditch through P's land contrary to s. 51, and D claims that the land in question is owned by him, then a dispute of title is involved and the court's jurisdiction is ousted. The jurisdiction is not, however, ousted by a mere claim on D's part: there must be some real foundation for D's claim that he is the owner or that he acted on behalf of the owner. But once it is shown that there is a real foundation for D's claim of title the court cannot try the issue even though, in particular circumstances, the issue may be a simple one.

If, on the other hand, D does not dispute P's title to the land and seeks to justify destroying the fence or digging the ditch on some other ground then the jurisdiction of the magistrates is not ousted. The case now falls to be decided by the principles ordinarily applicable to the offence of malicious damage.

This is clearly the position where D is tried summarily under any of the relevant provisions[2] except, it seems, s. 14 (1) of the 1914 Act. The enigmatic proviso to that subsection has been interpreted to produce a curious anomaly. In *White* v. *Feast*[3] it was held that this proviso[4] completely superseded the implied restriction of dispute of title, and consequently the jurisdiction of justices was ousted whenever D acted under a fair and reasonable supposition that he had a right to do the act complained of.[5] Although there is much to be said, both historically[6] and logically, for the view that the proviso was inserted to provide a defence and was not intended to concern ouster of jurisdiction, *White* v. *Feast* has been taken to settle the point that where a fair and reasonable claim of right is made out, the jurisdiction of justices is thereby ousted.[7] It follows that if D is tried summarily for an offence under, say s. 51 of the 1861 Act and D claims that he acted in defence of his goods, the magistrates have jurisdiction either to convict or acquit. But if D is charged in respect of the same act under s. 14 (1) of the Criminal Justice Administration Act 1914 and D claims he acted in defence of his property, the magistrates, though they may convict D, may not acquit him for they must hold, if D acted under a fair and reasonable supposition of right to do the act, that their jurisdiction is ousted. They may convict D if they find he acted under an unreasonable supposition of right. Unless the Legislature misunderstood the rule of ouster it is difficult to accept that this was the intended result.

---

[20] Sometimes a statute, for example, Offences Against the Person Act 1861, s. 46, expressly incorporates the rule but this is strictly unnecessary.
[1] The expression is taken from Williams, C.L.G.P., 306.
[2] Set out above, pp. 455–456.
[3] (1872), L.R. 7 Q.B. 353.
[4] Then the proviso to s. 52 of the Malicious Damage Act 1861.
[5] Which would, of course, cover most cases of dispute of title.
[6] Russell, 1314.
[7] *Mussett* (1872), 26 L.T. 429; *Usher* v. *Luxmore* (1889), 61 L.T. 110.

Whenever the charge is brought under s. 14 (1) of the Criminal Justice Administration Act 1914 the test of D's claim of right is an objective one. "As the proviso expressly says that the claim of right must be founded on reasonable grounds, the ordinary proviso, usually applied to mere *bona fides*, is superseded."[8]

This leads to some curious anomalies. Suppose that D destroys P's bicycle in the honest but unreasonable belief that it is his own. D may now be prosecuted under s. 51 of the Malicious Damage Act 1861 or under s. 14 (1) of the Criminal Justice Administration Act 1914. If D is tried summarily under the former provision he would be entitled to an acquittal since, as has been shown,[9] an honest belief, even if unreasonable, affords a defence. If D is charged under the latter provision, however, he may be convicted since his claim is unreasonable.[10] Another possible anomaly may arise where D believes he has a legal right but there exists no basis in law for his claim. In *Croydon R.D.C.* v. *Crowley*[11] it was held that a claim cannot be "fair and reasonable" where there exists no legal foundation for it. It has been argued above[12] that an honest belief in legal right affords a good defence to charges under the Malicious Damage Act notwithstanding there exists no legal basis for the claim. *Gott* v. *Measures*[13] is against this argument of course, and, in favour of that case, it may be said that at least it tends to consistency of result with s. 14 (1) of the 1914 Act.

But it may be that there is (or rather was) a reason why s. 14 (1) should impose an objective test while the test for other offences of malicious damage may be subjective. In *White* v. *Feast*,[14] BLACKBURN, J., thought that the reason for the objective test was to be found in the quasi civil purpose of the section.[15] As he saw it, damage might be caused to the property of persons of poor means who could not afford to bring a civil action. The aim of this provision, therefore, was to enable a criminal prosecution to be brought, but one which gave the justices power to award compensation to the injured party. This also explained why D was liable unless his action was both honest and reasonable; if the usual requirement of honesty alone sufficed, the party injured would often be denied compensation when it was proper that he should be recompensed for the harm done. "The real substance of the enactment", concluded BLACKBURN, J.,[16]

> "is the power given to justices to award compensation to a small amount and that power ought to be given and exercised whether the act causing the injury be done under a *bona fide* claim or not, if it is not founded on a fair and reasonable ground."

Whether this explanation holds good today in view of the extension of legal aid is another matter. At all events it serves to show that s. 14 (1) of the Criminal Justice Administration Act 1914 is exceptional in the scheme (such as it is) of offences of malicious damage, and provides no general guidance on claim of right as a defence to other charges under the Malicious Damage Act 1861.

---

[8] *White* v. *Feast* (1872), L.R. 7 Q.B. 353, *per* BLACKBURN, J., at p. 359. *Cf. Brooks* v. *Hamlyn* (1899), 19 Cox C.C. 231, 236.

[9] Above, p. 461.

[10] Thus on essentially the same facts a subjective test was applied in *James* (1837), 8 C. & P. 131 (a prosecution under s. 6 of the Act of 1827) and an objective test in *French* (1873), 37 J.P. 404 (a prosecution under s. 52 of the Act of 1861).

[11] (1909), 22 Cox C.C. 22, (D.C.).

[12] Above, p. 463.

[13] [1948] 1 K.B. 234; [1947] 2 All E.R. 609; above, p. 463.

[14] (1872), L.R. 7 Q.B. 353.

[15] Then, of course, s. 52 of the Malicious Damage Act 1861.

[16] (1872), L.R. 7 Q.B. 353, 359.

Section 14 (1) is also exceptional in that it uses the formula "wilfully or maliciously" in sharp contradistinction to the more general formula "unlawfully and maliciously".[17] The subsection appears to contemplate a distinction between "wilful" and "malicious" but it is not easy to determine wherein this distinction lies. Ordinarily "wilfully" suggests intentional conduct and it may also embrace reckless conduct.[18] If that is the case here then it is merely a synonym for "maliciously" since "maliciously", in this context, must surely be given the meaning it bears under the 1861 Act. Sometimes, however, "wilfully" is held to do no more than impose a requirement that D's conduct must be voluntary and not to extend to his knowledge of circumstances or foresight of consequences.[19] There is some authority for saying that the expression bears this restricted meaning in this context,[20] so that, for instance, D wilfully destroys P's coat although D believes the coat to be his own. But if this is so the balance is partly restored by the proviso because, one way or another, it must be shown that D did not act under a fair and reasonable supposition of right to do the act complained of. D would so act if he reasonably believed the coat to be his.

(2) MEANING OF DAMAGE

Whenever the Act uses the expression "damage" what is contemplated is actual damage. It is not enough to show that what D has done amounts to a civil trespass to goods or land for neither requires proof of actual damage. Accordingly it was held in *Eley* v. *Lytle*[1] that D was guilty of no offence when, during a game of football, he ran over P's land and the only evidence of actual damage was that he had committed a trespass. But in such circumstances actual damage may not be difficult to show and a conviction was upheld where D walked through a field of long grass, trampling it down.[2]

A thing is ordinarily damaged by impairing its utility. A machine may be damaged not only by breaking some part, but by removing some essential part,[3] or by tampering with some part so that it will not work although no part is removed or broken,[4] or by running it in an improper fashion so that impairment will result.[5] But a thing may also be damaged, though there is no signi-

---

[17] "We are unable to give the reason, nor has any been given at the bar, why the phraseology of s. 52 should have been altered from 'unlawfully *and* maliciously,' which is that used . . . in many other sections, to 'wilfully *or* maliciously' ": *Gardner* v. *Mansbridge* (1887), 19 Q.B.D. 217 at p. 221, *per* A. L. SMITH, J. "But while s. 51 follows the wording of other sections in using the expression 'unlawfully and maliciously,' s. 52 says, 'whosoever shall *wilfully or maliciously* commit any damage. . . .' It is quite clear, therefore, that the Legislature intended to draw in this section a distinction between acts which are unlawful *and* malicious, and acts which are merely wilful *or* malicious": *Roper* v. *Knott*, [1898] 1 Q.B. 868 at p. 871, *per* Lord RUSSELL, C.J.

[18] As in *Cotterill* v. *Penn*, [1936] 1 K.B. 53; above, p. 75.

[19] As in *Cotterill* v. *Penn*, [1936] 1 K.B. 53; above, p. 75.

[20] WILLS, J., appears to have understood it in this sense in *Hamilton* v. *Bone* (1888), 16 Cox C.C. 437, at p. 439. For a further judicial comment see BLACKBURN, J., in *White* v. *Feast* (1872), L.R. 7 Q.B. 353.

[1] (1885), 50 J.P. 308.

[2] *Gayford* v. *Chouler*, [1898] 1 Q.B. 316. Or breaking a stalagmite: (1964), *The Times*, September 12.

[3] *Tacey* (1821), Russ. & Ry. 452.

[4] *Fisher* (1865), L.R. 1 C.C.R. 7; *cf. Getty* v. *Antrim County Council*, [1950] N.I. 114 (dismantling).

[5] *Norris* (1840), 9 C. & P. 241.

ficant interference with its performance, if it is made less valuable.[6] Food and drink is damaged if it is spoiled in any way, as where milk is watered.[7]

The expression "destroy" is used in the Act even more frequently than "damage". Clearly destruction goes well beyond damage and it does not contemplate half measures. To destroy, of structures means to pull down or demolish, of crops and growing things, means to lay waste, of machines to break up, and of animals to deprive of life.

2 PARTICULAR INSTANCES OF DAMAGE: DAMAGE TO BUILDINGS

The Malicious Damage Act 1861 creates offences in respect of damage to a wide variety of property, real and personal. Broadly, the Act creates particular offences of damage to buildings, machines and goods in process of manufacture, growing things, mines, animals, railways and ships, and general offences of malicious damage are created by s. 51 of the Act and s. 14 (1) of the Criminal Justice Administration Act 1914. The net result is that any property may be the subject of a charge of malicious damage provided it is tangible property.[8] But to this rule an exception was acknowledged in *Gardner* v. *Mansbridge*[9] where it was held that D was not guilty of an offence under s. 52 of the 1861 Act (replaced by s. 14 (1) of the 1914 Act) in picking uncultivated mushrooms off P's land. The court reasoned that "real" in s. 52 meant the realty itself and did not include things growing on the realty since express provision was made elsewhere for things growing on the realty. Since these other sections do not extend to mushrooms growing wild it follows that it is no offence to pick them (or wild fruits and flowers) under this Act.

Damage to buildings is governed by both particular and the general provisions. At common law arson was defined as

> "maliciously and voluntarily burning the house of another by night or by day,"[10]

but the expression "arson", which is nowhere used in the Act, is now merely a term of convenience to describe damaging property by fire.

As a general proposition it is an offence to set fire to any building of another, but some care must be taken to select the appropriate section.[11] Thus, for instance, D can be charged only under s. 1 for setting fire to a church, and only under s. 5 for setting fire to a university library. If he sets fire to a dwelling-house when some person is inside he would be prosecuted under s. 2 but he could be prosecuted under s. 3 if there is an intent to injure or defraud. If there is no person in the house then he must be prosecuted under s. 3 unless there is no intent to injure or defraud in which case he must be prosecuted under s. 6.

---

[6] *Foster* (1852), 6 Cox C.C. 25. *Cf. King* v. *Lees* (1949), 65 T.L.R. 21 (passenger urinating in taxi held to have caused injury for purposes of s. 41 of the London Hackney Carriage Act 1831).

[7] *Roper* v. *Knott*, [1898] 1 Q.B. 868.

[8] *Laws* v. *Eltringham* (1881), 8 Q.B.D. 283. Held that a right of herbage was not "any real or personal property whatsoever" within s. 52 of the Act. The section applies to tangible property and not to incorporeal rights.

[9] (1887), 19 Q.B.D. 217; *cf.* Theft Act 1968, s. 4, above, p. 359.

[10] Hawkins, 1 P.C. 137.

[11] See above, p. 455.

Although ss. 1–5 specify particular buildings there is no definition of a building for the purposes of s. 6. But it may be that the buildings specified afford some assistance for the generic definition of building in this context. If this is so then what is contemplated is an edifice designed to stand more or less permanently on one site which is meant for the use and shelter of man, beast, or goods. It has been held by a magistrates' court that a caravan—a typical gypsy caravan on wheels meant to be drawn by a horse—was not a building within s. 6 of the Act.[12] But it would seem that some caravans may be buildings, at least where they are on a permanent site and are not ordinarily moved from place to place. A structure is not a building merely because it will be a building when completed, but it may become a building before it is completed; it is a question of fact in each case.[13]

Setting fire to a building requires that some part of the structure of the building be burnt; once this has occurred the crime is committed although the fire might be dowsed so that the actual damage is negligible. It is not enough that some part of the structure is blackened by smoke from burning materials set near to it,[14] but it suffices that some part of the structure has been consumed by fire even though there is no blaze.[15]

All the offences of setting fire to the buildings use the formula "unlawfully and maliciously".[16] Section 3 is exceptional in additionally requiring an intent to injure or defraud.[17] Under s. 2 it is an offence unlawfully and maliciously to set fire to any dwelling house "any person being therein". This offence may also have exceptional features and needs further comment.

Section 2 was considered in *Pardoe*[18] where Lord COLERIDGE, C.J., ruled that D might be convicted under the section although he was the only person in the house when he set fire to it. In view of the mischief aimed at by the section— the danger created to human life—this seemed a questionable decision and it was not followed by HOWARD, J., in *Arthur*.[19] HOWARD, J., reasoned that while it was at first sight difficult to read s. 2 as though it read "any *other* person being therein" this was a more reasonable construction; moreover, although s. 18 of the Offences against the Person Act 1861 makes it an offence unlawfully and maliciously to wound or cause any grievous bodily harm "to any person", no one had ever heard of a prosecution under that section where D caused harm to himself.

A narrow view of s. 2 might lead to the conclusion that so long as D unlawfully and maliciously sets fire to the dwelling house he may be convicted of the offence although he was not aware that any person was therein. It is submitted, on principle and in view of the mischief aimed at by the section and the gravity of the offence, that it must be shown that D was aware of the presence of another in the house, or was reckless as to the presence of another.

---

[12] *Hawkins* v. *Wilson*, [1957] Crim. L.R. 320. See 93 J.P. 293.
[13] *Manning and Rogers* (1871), 12 Cox C.C. 106.
[14] *Russell* (1842), Car. & M. 541. Burning faggot placed on wooden floor which was scorched but not burnt.
[15] *Parker* (1839), 9 Car. & P. 45. Held it would be enough to show that floor had been scorched and charred even though there was no blaze. Note that "scorched" may be used to mean blackened by smoke (which is not enough) or very slightly burnt (which is enough).
[16] See above, pp. 456–470.
[17] See above, pp. 459–461.
[18] (1894), 17 Cox C.C. 715.
[19] [1968] 1 Q.B. 810.

Arguably the offence under s. 2 cannot be committed where D sets fire to his own house, since in setting fire to his own house he would not be acting unlawfully. By virtue of s. 59 of the Act[20] D could be convicted under s. 2, even though the house is his own, if he has intent to injure or defraud;[1] but unless the intent to injure extends to injury to the person[2] s. 59 does not cover the case. But it may be that s. 2 does extend to the case where D sets fire to his own house. The section makes it an offence to set fire to "*any* dwelling house", and clearly the danger to human life is the same whether the house is D's or another's.

Apart from these provisions dealing with setting fire to buildings there is in the Act a miscellaneous assortment of specific offences concerned with damage to, or destruction of, buildings,[3] but these are limited in scope and most other kinds of damage would in practice fall under the residuary provisions of s. 51 of the Malicious Damage Act 1861 and s. 14 (1) of the Criminal Justice Administration Act 1914.

---

[20] See above, pp. 459–461.
[1] Above, p. 461.
[2] See above, p. 460, footnote 7.
[3] For example, s. 9 (damaging or destroying houses with explosives); s. 13 (tenants of houses maliciously damaging them).

CHAPTER 17

Offences against Public Morals

1 BIGAMY

Bigamy was originally only an ecclesiastical offence but it was declared to be a capital felony by statute in 1603.[1] Now, by s. 57 of the Offences against the Person Act 1861,[2] it is an offence punishable with seven years' imprisonment. The offence is committed by:

> "Whosoever, being married, shall marry any other person during the life of the former husband or wife, whether the second marriage shall have taken place in England or Ireland or elsewhere . . ."

The section goes on, however, to provide that it does not extend to:

> 1. "any second marriage contracted elsewhere than in England and Ireland by any other than a subject of Her Majesty"; or

> 2. "to any person marrying a second time, whose husband or wife shall have been continually absent from such person for the space of seven years then last past and shall not have been known by such person to be living within that time"; or

> 3. "any person who, at the time of such second marriage, shall have been divorced from the bond of the first marriage"; or

> 4. "any person whose former marriage shall have been declared void by the sentence of any court of competent jurisdiction."

(1) "BEING MARRIED"

Obviously a person who is unmarried is incapable of committing bigamy[3] and the prosecution must prove that D was validly married at the time of the second ceremony. For most purposes a marriage may be presumed from evidence that the parties co-habited with the reputation of being husband and wife; but

---

[1] 1 Jac. 1, c. 11.
[2] Re-enacting, with minor modifications, s. 22 of the Offences against the Person Act 1828 which repealed the Act of 1603.
[3] *Cf.* above, p. 94.

according to a *dictum* of Lord MANSFIELD in *Morris* v. *Miller*,[4] a case of criminal conversation, this is not sufficient on a charge of bigamy:

> "Perhaps there need not be strict proof from the register or by a person present, but strong evidence must be had of the fact: as by a person present at the wedding dinner, if the register be burnt and the parson and clerk are dead."

There must be evidence of the celebration of the marriage and of the identity of the parties; but it is sufficient to call a witness who was present and can describe the ceremony and identify the parties, without any proof of the registration of the marriage or of any licence or publication of banns.[5] The formal validity of the marriage will be presumed, for *omnia praesumuntur rite esse acta*. Thus, where the building in which the marriage was celebrated has been habitually used for divine service, the prosecution need not prove that it was licensed unless D introduces credible evidence that it was not.[6]

Where there is cohabitation and repute, it is almost inevitable that D will have acknowledged that W is his wife;[7] and it has been held[8] that the production of a certificate of marriage coupled with an acknowledgment is sufficient evidence of the first marriage. Since 1914 the injured spouse has been a competent, but not compellable witness for the prosecution on a bigamy charge;[9] and, where she is willing to give evidence, the problem of proof of the first marriage is obviously greatly simplified.

If evidence is introduced suggesting that the first marriage is invalid, then the better view is that the onus is on the prosecution to establish its validity beyond any reasonable doubt.[10]

Evidence that one of the parties to the first marriage had, before that marriage, cohabited with a third party with the reputation of being husband and wife, is sufficient to establish a *defence*[11] on the ground of the invalidity of the first marriage.[12]

In the light of these principles the decision in *Naguib*[13] seems a harsh one. D, an Egyptian by birth, being charged with marrying C in the lifetime of B, gave evidence that, before "marrying" B, he had married A in Egypt according to the rites and ceremonies of that country. Where the prosecution relies on a foreign marriage, it must prove the requirements of the foreign law. The Court held that it followed that there was a similar onus on D with regard to his marriage with A. Although D may have described the ceremony, he had no expert knowledge of Egyptian law and there was no evidence that the ceremony was valid. It is, however, surely fallacious to equate the duties of the prosecution and defence in this respect. The prosecution must prove the first marriage

---

[4] (1767), 1 Wm. Bl. 632.
[5] *Allison and Wilkinson* (1806), Russ. & Ry. 109; *Manwaring* (1856), 7 Cox C.C. 192.
[6] *Cresswell* (1876), 1 Q.B.D. 446 (C.C.R.).
[7] The acknowledgment is admissible *against* D; but it was not, of course, admissible *in favour* of the plaintiff in an action for criminal conversation: East, 1 P.C. 471.
[8] *Birtles* (1911), 6 Cr. App. Rep. 177; *cf. Umanski*, [1961] V.L.R. 242.
[9] Criminal Justice Administration Act 1914, s. 28 (3); *Leach* v. *R.*, [1912] A.C. 305.
[10] *Willshire* (1881), 6 Q.B.D. 366 (C.C.R.); *Morrison*, [1938] 3 All E.R. 787 (C.C.A.) and *Kay* (1887), 16 Cox C.C. 292. *Thomson* (1905), 70 J.P. 6 and *Kircaldy* (1929), 167 L.T. Jo. 46 seem to go the other way. *Shaw* (1943), 60 T.L.R. 344 (C.C.A.) is inconclusive, as D introduced no evidence of invalidity. See *Naguib, infra*, and Williams, C.L.G.P., 906 and Cross, *Evidence*, (3rd ed.) 124, n. 7.
[11] Contrast the case where the prosecution are relying on similar evidence; above, pp. 474–475.
[12] *Wilson* (1862), 3 F. & F. 119.
[13] [1917] 1 K.B. 359.

alleged in the indictment beyond reasonable doubt. If the defence can establish a reasonable doubt whether there was a prior valid marriage, the prosecution case is not made out; and surely the description of the earlier ceremony should be evidence from which a jury might feel such a doubt. It is, of course, easy for a defendant who has lived abroad to go into the witness box and say he was married already and correspondingly difficult for the prosecution to rebut this; but that is not a good reason for upholding a conviction where there are real doubts about D's guilt.

1   Void and Voidable Marriages

A marriage which is defective is either void or voidable. The expression "a void marriage" is a contradiction in terms; but it is a convenient way of describing the situation where the parties have gone through a ceremony of marriage which is utterly ineffective in law, so that they have never acquired the status of husband and wife. In such a case, therefore, neither party is "married" for the purposes of s. 57 of the Offences against the Person Act 1861 and, without going through any formality, either may proceed to a second ceremony with impunity. The most obvious example of a void marriage is where, at the time of the marriage, one of the parties is already married to a third party. A marriage may also be void on the ground of lack of juristic capacity—for example, where the marriage is governed by English law, because the parties are related within the prohibited degrees or one of them is under sixteen; or on the ground of the lack of true consent arising from a mistake as to the identity of the other party or as to the nature of the ceremony, or from duress[14] or because one of the parties was a lunatic, so found.[15]

A voidable marriage, however, is entirely different.

> "Until it has been avoided at the suit of the aggrieved party it will be regarded by every court as valid and subsisting. The parties are husband and wife till a decree has been pronounced . . ."[16]

The fact that a marriage is *voidable* is, therefore, irrelevant for the purposes of the law of bigamy[17] and the grounds on which a marriage may be voidable require no consideration here.[18] Where a voidable marriage has actually been *avoided* by a decree of nullity, however, an entirely different situation arises, which is considered below.

The first marriage need not have been celebrated in England.[19] Even before 1828, when it was probably necessary, even in the case of British subjects, that the second marriage should be within the jurisdiction, this was so; for it is the second marriage alone which constitutes the offence.[20]

---

[14] But, according to one view duress makes a marriage *voidable* only. See the authorities collected in Webb and Bevan, *Source Book*, 82 *et seq.*

[15] Marriage of Lunatics Act 1811, repealed by the Mental Health Act 1959. Since the 1959 Act came into effect the test in all cases is whether D understood the nature of the ceremony.

[16] *Algar*, [1954] 1 Q.B. 279 at p. 287; [1953] 2 All E.R. 1381 at p. 1384, *per* Lord GODDARD, C.J.

[17] Co. 3 Inst. 88.

[18] See Bromley, *Family Law* (3rd ed.), 73 *et seq.*; Webb and Bevan, *loc. cit.*

[19] Hale, 2 P.C. 692; East, 1 P.C. 465; *Topping* (1856), 7 Cox C.C. 103 (both marriages in Scotland).

[20] East, *loc. cit.*

2 A Polygamous First Marriage

According to the recent decision in *Sarwan Singh*,[21] a valid polygamous or potentially polygamous marriage is not such a first marriage as will found an indictment for bigamy. The Chairman was strongly influenced in his ruling by the fact that bigamy by a citizen of the United Kingdom and Colonies is now indictable wherever committed,[1] so that a contrary ruling would have rendered criminal polygamous marriages celebrated abroad which are otherwise entirely valid. Thus:

". . . if a citizen of the United Kingdom and Colonies whose personal law permitted polygamy married two wives in the colony where he was domiciled, it is inconceivable that he would be prosecuted for bigamy in England. His conduct was lawful by his personal law and by the law of the place where he acted, and there would be strong reasons of a public nature against a prosecution."[2]

It is submitted that, if there is a reasonable construction of the Act which will avoid such an absurd result, it should be adopted. The immunity from prosecution of a citizen whose acts are entirely lawful by his personal law and the law of the place where he acts ought not to depend on the benevolent exercise of a discretion.[3]

While the civil courts do not recognise a polygamous or potentially polygamous marriage for the purposes of matrimonial relief, they do regard it as effective to nullify a subsequent marriage in England.[4] Thus, the second marriage in *Sarwan Singh*[5] was invalid, though not an offence. The same would be true of any subsequent marriage D might have contracted while his first marriage continued. The effect is that one who has contracted a valid potentially polygamous marriage is incapable of committing bigamy so long as that marriage lasts. Since a person domiciled in England lacks capacity to contract a polygamous marriage,[6] this means of evading the law is limited in scope.

The decision in *Sarwan Singh* is supported by *dicta* of LUSH, L.J., in *Harvey* v. *Farnie*[7] and of AVORY, J., in *Naguib*,[8] and, extra-judicially but powerfully, by the Criminal Code Commissioners.[9] Pointing out that in half a century[10] no attempt had been made to apply the Act to such cases as that of a Hindu with two wives, they presumed that the reason was that " 'marriage' in these statutes

---

[21] [1962] 3 All E.R. 612 (T. R. Fitzwalter Butler, West Bromwich Quarter Sessions) See Andrews, "A Licence for Bigamy", [1956] Crim. L.R. 261.

[1] Below, p. 479.

[2] Dicey and Morris, *Conflict of Laws* (8th ed.), 287.

[3] Bartholomew, "Polygamous Marriages and English Criminal Law" (1954), 17 M.L.R. 344, would avoid the difficulty in another way; he argues that a valid potentially polygamous first marriage will found an indictment—but that a *valid* second polygamous marriage would not be indictable; below, p. 479, footnote 4.

[4] *Baindail* v. *Baindail*, [1946] P. 122; [1946] 1 All E.R. 342, where the Court of Appeal left open the question of criminal liability.

[5] *Supra.*

[6] It is generally considered that *Re Bethell, Bethell* v. *Hildyard* (1888), 38 Ch. D. 220, is authority for this but see Bartholomew (1964), 13 I.C.L.Q. at p. 1052, n. 16.

[7] (1880), 6 P.D. 35 at p. 53 (on appeal (1882), 8 App. Cas. 43).

[8] [1917] 1 K.B. 359 at p. 360. But the *dicta* go too far in that they assert that a prior polygamous marriage would be insufficient to invalidate the first marriage alleged in the indictment. This is inconsistent with *Baindail* v. *Baindail* and must be considered wrong.

[9] Lord BLACKBURN and BARRY, LUSH and STEPHEN, JJ.

[10] That is, since 1825 when bigamy abroad by a British subject was made indictable.

means the union of one man with one woman to the exclusion of all others, as is well expressed by Lord PENZANCE in *Hyde* v. *Hyde and Woodmansee*".[11]

While it is true that the attitude of English law to polygamous marriages has changed since *Hyde* v. *Hyde*, it is legitimate to construe the 1861 Act in the light of the law as it was then believed to be.

3 Subsistence of the First Marriage

It is necessary to prove not only that the first marriage was validly celebrated but that it was subsisting at the time of the second ceremony. In effect, this means that it must be proved that the wife was alive at that time, for the prosecution do not have to prove that there has been no decree of divorce or nullity unless some evidence of such a decree is first tendered by the defence.

If there is direct evidence that the first spouse was alive at the time of the second ceremony, there is no problem. Difficulty may arise where there is evidence only that she was alive at some time before the second ceremony. It is then a question of fact for the jury taking into account all the circumstances of the case whether they are satisfied beyond reasonable doubt that she was alive at the crucial time.[12] There is no presumption of law that life continues for any time; but if the wife were proved to be alive and in good health only an hour, or a day beforehand, the jury could hardly fail to be so satisfied, in the absence of any evidence to the contrary. If she has not been heard of for say, two years, the result of the jury's assessment of the probabilities would be less predictable.

(2) THE SECOND CEREMONY

The second "marriage" in bigamy is, in the nature of things, void; and it is immaterial that there are other grounds for voidness in addition to its bigamous nature:

> "It is the appearing to contract a second marriage and the going through the ceremony which constitutes the crime of bigamy, otherwise it could never exist in the ordinary cases."[13]

So where D, being married, went through a ceremony of marriage with his niece, he was guilty notwithstanding his lack of capacity to contract such a marriage.[14] The words, "shall marry another person", were taken to mean "shall go through the form and ceremony of marriage with another person"; but:

> ". . . . in thus holding it is not at all necessary to say that forms of marriage unknown to the law, as was the case in *Burt* v. *Burt*,[15] would suffice to bring a case within the operation of the statute. We must not be understood to mean that every fantastic form of marriage to which parties might think proper to resort,[16] or that a marriage ceremony performed by an unauthorised person, or in an unauthorised place would be a marrying within the meaning of the 57th section . . ."

---

[11] (1866), L.R. 1 P. & D. 130.

[12] *Lumley* (1869), L.R. 1 C.C.R. 196.

[13] *Brawn* (1843), 1 Car. & Kir. 144; *per* Lord DENMAN (D "married" deceased sister's widower in lifetime of her own husband).

[14] *Allen* (1872), L.R. 1 C.C.R. 367, followed in *Robinson*, [1938] 1 All E.R. 301.

[15] (1860), 2 Sw. & Tr. 88; where D married a woman in Australia according to the form of the kirk of Scotland, but there was no proof that the form in question was recognised as legal by the local law.

[16] Consider the pretended marriage ceremony in *Kemp and Else*, [1964] 2 Q.B. 341; [1964] 1 All E.R. 649; below, p. 486; and *Ali Mohammed*, [1964] 1 All E.R. 653, n. (2).

It must be "a form of marriage known to and recognised by the law[17] as capable of producing a valid marriage." Thus, a polygamous form of marriage celebrated in England without a civil ceremony would appear to be insufficient.[18]

It is probably no defence that the law of D's domicile permits polygamy if, having married in England,[19] he goes through a second ceremony in England in a form recognised by English law.[20] Thus in *Naguib* D, an Egyptian by birth and a Mohammedan by religion, went through two ceremonies of marriage in England and was convicted, the court apparently not considering it relevant to inquire where he was domiciled.

Is a polygamous form of marriage a sufficient second ceremony if it is valid by the law of the place where it is celebrated and D's domicile? D, a citizen of the United Kingdom and Colonies, marries in England, returns to the colony where he is domiciled, and marries a second wife according to a polygamous form recognised by the law of the colony. If a polygamous form of marriage is enough, D is clearly guilty of bigamy; yet it seems that the English civil courts would recognise the second marriage as valid.[1] It would be preposterous that a marriage should be regarded as valid in one English court and an offence in another. On the other hand, if a polygamous ceremony will not found an indictment for bigamy, it must follow that D, domiciled in England, may marry there and then with impunity proceed to go through a polygamous ceremony in a country where that is recognised as a valid form of marriage. But why should this be regarded as criminal in England? A polygamous ceremony is not "the solemn ceremony" which it was the object of the legislators of 1603 and 1861 to protect from prostitution.[2]

It is submitted that the most convenient and consistent course would be to regard polygamous forms of marriage as irrelevant for the law of bigamy, wherever they be celebrated. This view seems to be supported both by that of the Criminal Code Commissioners[3] and by the general attitude of the law to polygamous ceremonies at the time of the enactment of the 1861 Act and its predecessors.[4]

1 Proviso (1): the Place of the Second Marriage

The second marriage, in the case of a British subject who is a citizen of the United Kingdom and Colonies,[5] may take place anywhere[6] in the world.[7] A

---

[17] Presumably, the law of the place where it is celebrated: *Burt* v. *Burt*, above.

[18] Dicey and Morris, *Conflict of Laws* (8th ed.), 280 and Illustration 2, p. 291. *Cf. Bham*, below, p. 486 and *Attorney General of Ceylon* v. *Reid*, [1965] A.C. 720 where D, domiciled and resident in Ceylon, contracted a Christian marriage and later, having embraced the Muslim faith, went through a second Muslim ceremony. He was held not guilty of bigamy under the Ceylon Penal Code; the second marriage was valid by the law of Ceylon.

[19] Or, presumably, anywhere else, provided that it is a valid monogamous marriage.

[20] *Naguib*, [1917] 1 K.B. 359.

[1] Dicey, *op. cit.*, Rule 36 and authorities there cited.

[2] Below, p. 485.

[3] Above, p. 477.

[4] Bartholomew, "Polygamous Marriages and the English Criminal Law" (1954), 17 M.L.R. 344, argues that a polygamous second ceremony in this country is indictable; but that the polygamous marriage abroad of a British subject whose personal law permits polygamy is not. *Cf. Attorney-General of Ceylon* v. *Reid*, [1965] A.C. 720.

[5] British Nationality Act 1948, s. 3 (1).

[6] The 1603 Act was limited to second marriages in England and Wales. This extension in respect of British subjects was made in the 1828 Act.

[7] In *Earl Russell*'s case, [1901] A.C. 446, the argument that the words, "or elsewhere", should be limited to elsewhere within the King's dominions was rejected.

British subject who is not a citizen of the United Kingdom and Colonies can only be guilty of bigamy if the second ceremony takes place in a part of the Commonwealth other than one of the independent countries mentioned in s. 1 (3) of the British Nationality Act 1948. In the case of an alien, the second ceremony must have taken place in England or Northern Ireland.

In the case of a citizen of the United Kingdom and Colonies, then, both marriages may take place outside the ordinary jurisdiction of the court. This was decided in *Topping*,[8] where both marriages were in Scotland.

2 Proviso (2): Continual Absence for Seven Years

The period of seven years was used in the original statute of 1603[9] and was subsequently adopted[10] by analogy in the common law rule that a person may be presumed dead when he has not been heard of for seven years by those who would be likely to hear of him if he were alive. But the statutory defence does not depend upon any presumption of death; indeed, D need not rely on the statutory defence unless the prosecution can prove that his wife was alive at the time of the second ceremony. Nor does the defence depend upon any belief by D that his wife was dead.[11] It is enough that he did not, at any period during the relevant seven years, know her to be alive.[12] If D did not know his wife to be alive during the seven years, it is irrelevant that he had the means of knowledge but did not take advantage of them.[13] Indeed, it would seem that if D hid himself in the Outer Hebrides for seven years for the purpose of not knowing his wife to be alive during that time, he would have a defence, for he comes within the plain words of the statute. It has been held[14] that the defence is available though the absence is due to D's own wilful desertion; and this result could hardly be altered by his motives in so absenting himself.

It is settled that, when seven years' absence is proved, the onus is on the Crown to prove beyond reasonable doubt that D knew his wife to be living during that time.[15] It is also settled that the burden of adducing evidence of seven years' absence is on D;[16] but whether he has to go further and *prove*, on a balance of probabilities, that the absence occurred is not so clear. The Australian cases suggest that he must;[17] but it is submitted that the principle of *Woolmington* v. *Director of Public Prosecutions*[18] requires that, once D has introduced some evidence of seven years' absence, the onus should be on the Crown to prove

---

[8] (1856), 7 Cox C.C. 103. D was usually resident in England at the time of both marriages, but this was irrelevant to his conviction—though it may be relevant in deciding whether to prosecute in England.

[9] But under that Act it seems that D had a defence (i) if his spouse had been *beyond* the *seas* for seven years, even if D *knew* her to be alive; and (ii) if she were absent from him for seven years, but in England or Wales, and D did not know her to be alive.

[10] See *Doe* d. *Knight* v. *Nepean* (1833), 5 B. & Ad. 86 at p. 94.

[11] *Tolson* (1889), 23 Q.B.D. 168 at p. 183, *per* CAVE, J.; *Gould* [1968] 1 All E.R. 849 at p. 853, *per* DIPLOCK, J.

[12] *Cullen* (1840), 9 C. & P. 681.

[13] *Briggs* (1856), Dears. & B. 98.

[14] *Faulkes* (1903), 19 T.L.R. 250.

[15] *Curgerwen* (1865), L.R. 1 C.C.R. 1; *Lund* (1921), 16 Cr. App. Rep. 31.

[16] *Jones* (1883), 11 Q.B.D. 118.

[17] *Bonnor*, [1957] V.L.R. 227, where a full court of five judges of the Supreme Court of Victoria, by a majority of three to two rejected the contrary view of the majority (two to one) in *Broughton*, [1953] V.L.R. 572. But *Bonnor* was concerned with the onus of proof of a defence of mistaken belief in the dissolution of his first marriage, below, p. 484. See Norval Morris (1955), 18 M.L.R. 452 and MacDougall (1958), 21 M.L.R. 510.

[18] [1935] A.C. 462; above, p. 27.

beyond reasonable doubt either (a) that there was no such absence or (b) D knew his wife to be living during it.[19]

Proof of seven years' absence is only a defence to a criminal charge; it does not affect the validity of the first marriage.

The words in the proviso, "marrying a second time", refer to the second of the two "marriages" charged in the indictment and it is irrelevant that D has in fact gone through other ceremonies of marriage in the interval between the two referred to in the indictment. It is necessary to make this obvious point because the Court of Criminal Appeal had held in *Treanor*[20] that the defence was not available where the "second marriage" charged in the indictment was in fact the third ceremony he had gone through. Happily this decision was overruled in *Taylor*[1] where D was charged in two counts with "marrying" W4 in 1946 and W5 in 1948, both in the lifetime of his wife W1. He had not seen W1 since 1927, but did not raise the statutory defence because he had "married" W2 in 1927 and W3 in 1942 and thus the marriages charged were the fourth and fifth ceremonies. His convictions were quashed, for each of those marriages was the second marriage in the indictment in which it was charged.

3 Proviso (3): Divorce

The third proviso seems to be entirely unnecessary for a person who goes through a ceremony of marriage after being divorced does not do so "being married", if that expression is given its natural meaning as, so it has recently been held, it should.[2] The explanation[3] probably is that, in the original Act of 1603, the divorce referred to was a divorce *a mensa et thoro* pronounced by the Ecclesiastical Court which did not dissolve a marriage; and that the draftsman of the 1861 Act retained the proviso for the benefit of persons so divorced.[4]

To afford a defence, the divorce must have been granted by a court[5] which is recognised by the English civil law as having jurisdiction over the marriage in question—that is, in general, (i) a court[6] of the country in which the parties are domiciled at the commencement of the proceedings;[7] (ii) a court of some other country whose decree will be recognised as valid by the courts of the country where the parties are domiciled at the date of the decree;[8] (iii) a court exercising jurisdiction on a basis similar to that of s. 40 (1) (a) and (b) of the Matrimonial Causes Act 1965;[9] and (iv) courts having jurisdiction over marriages of British subjects in England, Scotland or Northern Ireland under the Colonial and Other Territories (Divorce Jurisdiction) Acts 1926–1950.[10]

---

[19] See Williams, C.L.G.P., 909.

[20] [1939] 1 All E.R. 330.

[1] [1950] 2 K.B. 368; [1950] 2 All E.R. 170.

[2] *Gould*, [1968] 1 All E.R. 849 at p. 852.

[3] The courts sometimes say that they are bound to give meaning to every word in a statute if they can possibly do so: *Williams*, [1953] 1 Q.B. 660 at p. 666; [1953] 1 All E.R. 1068 at p. 1070; above, p. 373.

[4] *Cf.* the discussion by Williams, C.L.G.P., 178–182.

[5] It is curious that the draftsman expressly requires the annulment to be by a "court of competent jurisdiction" and yet makes no such express requirement in the case of dissolution.

[6] But a divorce may be effected by the law of the domicile without court proceedings: *Cf. Har-Shefi* v. *Har-Shefi*, [1953] P. 161; [1953] 1 All E.R. 783.

[7] Dicey and Morris, *Conflict of Laws* (8th ed.), 308.

[8] *Ibid.*, 311.

[9] *Ibid.*, 312.

[10] *Ibid.*, 315.

In *Lolley*'s case, D,[11] being domiciled in England, obtained a divorce in Scotland and remarried in England. He was held guilty of bigamy. The grounds given by the court—that "no sentence or act of any foreign country or state could dissolve an English marriage"—were far too wide[12] but the decision appears to be correct. The Scottish divorce was invalid, not because the marriage was celebrated in England, but because D was domiciled in England. The position was similar in *Earl Russell*'s case,[13] where D, being a British subject domiciled in England, obtained a decree of divorce in Nevada, U.S.A., and there remarried. In neither case was the question of *mens rea* discussed.[14]

The decree of divorce must, of course, have been made absolute before the second marriage. To marry after the decree nisi and before it is made absolute is bigamy, for the decree nisi does not dissolve the first marriage.[15]

4   Proviso (4): Marriage declared Void

Where D's first "marriage" is void, as distinct from voidable, this proviso is unnecessary, for he has a defence whether he has obtained a decree absolute or not. Where the first marriage is voidable, however, D is liable unless he has obtained a decree absolute. If he has obtained a decree absolute before the second marriage, he need not rely on the proviso; he is not a person who, *being married*, marries. But this proviso is not, in terms, limited, as is the third one, to a decree obtained before the second marriage. It would seem, *prima facie*, to apply to a decree obtained at any time before the criminal case is brought. This has the rather remarkable result that D, who was guilty of bigamy when he went through the second ceremony, becomes retrospectively innocent when he obtains his decree absolute.[16] This result is, however, a logical consequence of the curious concept of a voidable marriage which is in every way a good marriage until a decree has been obtained, whereupon the parties are deemed never to have been husband and wife.[17]

While there may have been in recent years

> "an obvious judicial tendency to regard decrees of nullity where the marriage is voidable more like decrees of divorce,"[18]

the plain meaning of the 1861 Act is consistent with the view taken of voidable marriages at the time of its enactment and for many years afterwards.[19] But what is the position if D, *having been convicted* of bigamy, obtains a decree of nullity of his first and voidable marriage?

The decree must have been granted by "a court of competent jurisdiction" if it is to afford a defence under the proviso. Reference should be made to works on the Conflict of Laws for elucidation of this phrase.[20] In general, it appears

---

[11] (1812), Russ. & Ry. 237.

[12] *Cf.* the rules stated in the preceding paragraph; and see *Bater* v. *Bater*, [1906] P. 209 at pp. 229–30 and 235, 236.

[13] [1901] A.C. 446.

[14] According to H. A. D. Philips (1885), 1 L.Q.R. at p. 475, Lolley was assured by several lawyers that his divorce was valid before he married again.

[15] *Wiggins* v. *Wiggins*, [1958] 2 All E.R. 555.

[16] But the second marriage remains "bigamous" for the purposes of the law of nullity: *Wiggins* v. *Wiggins*, [1958] 2 All E.R. 555.

[17] The marriage is declared "to have been and to be absolutely null and void to all intents and purposes in the law whatsoever . . .": Rayden, *Divorce* (9th ed.), 1778.

[18] Bromley, *Family Law* (3rd ed.), 65.

[19] See *Newbould* v. *A.G.*, [1931] P. 75.

[20] For example, Dicey and Morris, *op. cit.*, 344–358, 371–379.

that a decree will be effective if it is granted by (i) the court of the parties' common domicile; (ii) the courts of another country whose jurisdiction is recognised by the courts of the common domicile; (iii) (probably) the courts of the parties' common residence, or those of the respondents' residence, or (in the case of *void* marriages only) the courts of the country in which the marriage was celebrated.

What is the position if the marriage is annulled under the law of D's domicile otherwise than by the decree of a court?—as under the Turkish legal rule that if a Christian woman takes up the Mohammedan religion and marries a Moslem, her prior marriage is automatically annulled.[1] It is submitted that such a prior marriage would not thereafter be a valid first marriage so as to found an indictment for bigamy. Though the case is not within proviso (4), D did not "being married, marry".

(3) MENS REA

Section 57 of the Offences against the Person Act 1861 gives no indication of the requirement of *mens rea* and the question has caused a good deal of controversy and difficulty. In other sections of this Act[2] the word "maliciously" is found, and its absence from s. 57 has been used as an argument for the imposition of strict liability.[3] But this argument is weakened by the fact that the 1861 Act[4] was primarily a consolidating act and simply brought together a number of crimes from other acts. It is not surprising that the word is not to be found in the 1603 Act and no conclusion could properly be drawn from its omission from such an early statute.[5] Moreover, though it is now clear that "maliciously" has a technical meaning, it was not always so, and a legislator may well have jibbed, even in 1861, at the notion of "maliciously marrying"!

As a result of the recent case of *Gould*,[6] the position is now clear. If D reasonably believes in the existence of facts which, if true, would preclude his conviction, he is not guilty, though his belief be mistaken; and no distinction is to be drawn

> "... between facts the result of which would be that he was innocent because he did not come within the enacting words at all, and facts the result of which would be that he was excluded from the enacting words by the proviso."

The position, as the law now stands, appears to be that, in the first instance, the prosecution need prove no more *mens rea* than that D intended to go through the second ceremony of marriage. D may then establish a defence if he introduces evidence that, at the time of that marriage, he believed, on reasonable grounds (a) that his first wife was dead, or (b) that his first marriage had been dissolved, or (c) that his first marriage was void or had been annulled.

In *Tolson*,[7] the Court for Crown Cases Reserved, by a majority of nine to five, held that D was not guilty when she re-married, five years after being deserted by her husband, believing wrongly, but in good faith and on reasonable grounds,

---

[1] *Cf. Kapigian* v. *Der Minassian* (1962), 212 Mass. 412; 99 N.E. 264.
[2] See above, Ch. 12.
[3] *Tolson* (1889), 23 Q.B.D. 168 at p. 199, *per* MANISTY, J.
[4] Like its predecessor of 1828.
[5] Yet the preamble, with its reference to "evil disposed persons" who "run out of one county into another or into places where they are not known" indicates that the statute was directed at persons with *mens rea*.
[6] [1968] 2 Q.B. 65; [1968] 1 All E.R. 849.
[7] (1889), 23 Q.B.D. 168; above, p. 129.

that he was dead. The majority rejected the argument that the seven-year rule in the proviso excluded by implication the defence raised. The argument would have been valid if the proviso had covered less ground, or the same ground, as the defence raised; but the proviso is, in one respect, of far wider application, not requiring an honest and reasonable belief in death;[8] and it would be "monstrous to say that seven years' separation should have a greater effect in excusing a bigamous marriage than positive evidence of death."[9] Indeed Lord COLERIDGE, C.J.,[10] who had at first been disposed to dissent, ultimately concurred with the majority precisely because of the presence of the proviso.

It was not strictly necessary in *Tolson* to decide that an *unreasonable* belief would not afford a defence for such a case was not before the court. But this point was directly in issue in *King*,[11] where D's defence, that he believed in good faith and on reasonable grounds that the first marriage alleged was void,[12] was rejected because the evidence showed no reasonable grounds for such a belief. It was accepted, however, that the defence would have been good if only there had been reasonable grounds for the belief.[13]

Between *Tolson*[14] and *King* was decided the unsatisfactory case of *Wheat*.[15] D, a man of little education, who had consulted solicitors about divorce proceedings, received from them a letter telling him they hoped to send him papers for signature in a day or two. He jumped to the erroneous conclusion that he was already divorced and married again. The jury, in answer to a question left to them by the judge, found that D believed in good faith and *on reasonable grounds* that he was divorced. The judge directed a verdict of guilty and D's conviction was upheld by the Court of Criminal Appeal, on the grounds (i) that there was no evidence to support the jury's finding;[16] and (ii) that a belief in good faith and on reasonable grounds was no defence.

The decision was based on fallacious reasoning and a misinterpretation of the judgment in *Tolson*. It was widely criticised and has now been overruled by *Gould*.[17] This is a most welcome decision; and the only criticism to be advanced is of the courts' consistent insistence that the mistake must be a reasonable one.[18]

Where "mistake" is a defence, it is sufficient, it is submitted, if D introduces such evidence of it as might raise a reasonable doubt; and the onus is then on the Crown to establish *mens rea*. The Victorian case of *Bonnor*[19] is to the contrary, but this seems to be inconsistent with *Woolmington* v. *Director of Public Prosecutions*.[20]

---

[8] See, for example, *per* CAVE, J., *ibid.*, at p. 183.
[9] *Per* STEPHEN, J., *ibid.*, at p. 192.
[10] *Ibid.*, at p. 201.
[11] [1964] 1 Q.B. 285; [1963] 3 All E.R. 561. See notes at (1963), 27 M.L.R. 222; (1964), 80 L.Q.R. 14.
[12] Because, he said, he thought that an earlier marriage had not been dissolved at the time.
[13] A number of earlier rulings at first instance are to the same effect: *Thomson* (1905), 70 J.P. 6; *Connatty* (1919), 83 J.P. 292; *Weiwow* (1945) referred to in Archbold, § 3802; *Dolman*, [1949] 1 All E.R. 813; and the Australian High Court so held in *Thomas* v. *R.* (1937), 59 C.L.R. 279. *Kircaldy* (1929), 167 L.T. Jo. 46 and *Johnston* (1940), 5 J. Cr. L. 185, are to the opposite effect and must be considered wrong.
[14] Above, p. 483.
[15] [1921] 2 K.B. 119.
[16] The propriety of this ruling is questioned by DEVLIN, J., in *Trial by Jury*, 174, n. 35.
[17] [1968] 1 All E.R. 849.
[18] See above, p. 129. An insistence that Lord DIPLOCK reiterated in *Sweet* v. *Parsley*, above, p. 64.
[19] [1957] V.R. 227, criticised by MacDougall (1958), 21 M.L.R. 516.
[20] [1935] A.C. 462; above, p. 27.

(4) THE RATIONALE OF BIGAMY[1]

The traditional rationale of bigamy is well stated by COCKBURN, C.J., in *Allen*:[2]

"... it involves an outrage on public decency and morals, and creates a public scandal by the prostitution of a solemn ceremony, which the law allows to be applied only to a legitimate union, to a marriage at best but colourable and fictitious, and which may be made and too often is made, the means of the most cruel and wicked deception."

Bigamy clearly had its origin in religious concepts, being at first only an ecclesiastical offence. The Act of 1603 recited that men had been committing bigamy

"to the great dishonour of God, and utter undoing of divers honest men's children . . ."

Today the second marriage may, of course, take place in a registry office but this makes no difference to the gravity of the offence. To make the "prostitution" of this ceremony an offence punishable with seven years' imprisonment seems altogether out of proportion. The justification is hardly greater where the ceremony is performed in a church, for there are sound objections to the use of the criminal law to uphold religious beliefs. The bigamy which is likely to be severely punished today is that where the other party is innocent and is deceived into taking a highly detrimental course of action.[3] Such conduct should certainly be severely discouraged by the criminal law. But where both parties know the facts and marry to make their co-habitation appear respectable the offence is a relatively minor one:

"The only anti-social consequences that are necessarily involved in the mere celebration of a bigamous marriage are (1) the falsification of the State records, and (2) the waste of time of the Minister of Religion or Registrar."[4]

Bigamy may still fulfil a useful purpose as a crime in the type of case with grave social consequences; but it cannot be regarded as satisfactory that a grave offence should extend so far beyond this to cases no longer regarded as really serious offences.

It might be answered that the law provides for extremely severe penalties for offences against the Marriage Acts;[5] but these, also, seem excessively severe.

2 OTHER OFFENCES RELATING TO MARRIAGE

(1) OFFENCES RELATING TO SOLEMNISATION OF MARRIAGES

By s. 75 (1) of the Marriage Act 1949 it is an offence, punishable with fourteen years' imprisonment, knowingly and wilfully to solemnise a marriage,

(1) at any time other than between 8 a.m. and 6 p.m. (subject to certain exceptions); or

(2) according to the rites of the Church of England,

    (a) where banns have not been duly published (except in the case of a special licence, etc.); or

---

[1] See Williams (1945), 61 L.Q.R. at pp. 76–78.
[2] (1872), L.R. 1 C.C.R. 367 at pp. 374–375; above, p. 478, footnote 14.
[3] *Cf. King*, [1964] 1 Q.B. 285; [1963] 3 All E.R. 561; above, p. 484.
[4] Williams (1956), 72 L.Q.R. at pp. 77–78.
[5] *Infra.*

(b) in any place other than a church or other building in which banns may be published; or

(c) falsely pretending to be in Holy Orders.

By s. 75 (2) of the Act, it is an offence, punishable with five years' imprisonment, knowingly and wilfully to solemnise a marriage,

(1) in a place other than those specified in the Act; or

(2) in the absence of a registrar or "authorised person" (s. 43); or

(3) within twenty-one days of, or after the expiration of three months from, the day on which the notice of marriage was entered in the marriage notice book.

By s. 75 (3) of the Act it is an offence, punishable with five years' imprisonment if a superintendent registrar,

(1) issues a certificate for marriage within twenty-one days of, or after the expiration of three months from, the day on which notice of marriage was entered in the marriage book;

(2) issues a certificate where the issue has been forbidden under s. 30 of the Act by any person whose consent to the marriage is required under s. 3;

(3) solemnises or permits to be solemnised in his office any marriage void under Part III of the Act.

1   A Marriage

It was held, in *Bham*[6] that the Marriage Act 1949 is concerned only with marriage as known and permitted by English domestic law and has no application to a ceremony which does not purport to be a marriage of the kind allowed by that law. Accordingly D who performed a ceremony of nichan, a potentially polygamous marriage in accordance with the Islamic law, in a private house was not guilty of an offence under s. 75 (2) of the Act.

2   Knowingly and Wilfully

These words seem clearly to require that D shall know of the circumstances which make the solemnisation of the marriage an *actus reus*—that the time is not between 8 a.m. and 6 p.m., that the banns have not been duly published, that the place is not one in which banns may be published, and so on. In one instance at least, the requirements of *mens rea* go further. Where the charge is one of solemnising a marriage, falsely pretending to be in holy orders, it is not enough that D deliberately dressed up as if he were a clergyman, and officiated as a clergyman, reading out the words of the marriage service. He must also have intended to deceive. This seems to be the effect of *Kemp and Else*.[7] D1, who was married, wished to go through a ceremony of marriage with E. He persuaded D2, who was not and never had been in Holy Orders, to dress up as a clergyman and to officiate at a marriage ceremony according to the rites of the Church of England in a church. He told D2 that he was already married to E and that, as E and F knew, this was merely a re-enactment of the ceremony for the benefit of E's mother, F, who had been unable to be present at the real ceremony. E and F, however, believed, as D1 intended them to believe, that

---

[6] [1966] 1 Q.B. 159; [1965] 3 All E.R. 124 (C.C.A.).
[7] [1964] 2 Q.B. 341; [1964] 1 All E.R. 649 and commentary.

this was a genuine marriage ceremony. The Court of Criminal Appeal held[8] that D2 was not "knowingly and wilfully falsely pretending" to be in Holy Orders." "A pretender is one who claims to be what he is not." If D

> "believes that he is only taking part in what everyone present knows to be a charade, the foundation of the offence must go."[8]

Though this decision might be confined to the crime charged because of the presence of the word, "falsely" which does not appear in other parts of the section, it is thought more likely that it does apply to the other offences. D2's conduct was equated with that of one taking part in a play. If this analogy is accepted the defence would seem to be equally applicable to the other offences in the section—for example, it would not be an offence to enact a marriage ceremony in a play after 6 p.m.

(2) OFFENCES RELATING TO THE REGISTRATION OF MARRIAGES

By the Marriage Act 1949, s. 76:

(1) A registrar who knowingly and wilfully registers any marriage which is void under Part III of the Act commits an offence punishable with five years' imprisonment (s. 76 (3)).

(2) Any person who refuses, or without reasonable cause omits, to register any marriage which he is required by the Act to register[9] is liable on summary conviction to a fine of £50 (s. 76 (1)).

(3) Any person who carelessly loses or injures or allows to be injured, any marriage register book or certified copy of a marriage register book which is in his custody is liable on summary conviction to a fine of £50 (s. 76 (1)).

(4) A person who is required to make quarterly returns under s. 57 to the superintendent registrar commits an offence punishable summarily with a fine of £10 if he fails to do so (s. 76 (2)).

3 OBSCENE PUBLICATIONS[10]

Obscenity was originally an ecclesiastical offence but it was held in *Curl*[11] that the publication of an obscene libel was a common law misdemeanour. The law is now to be found in the Obscene Publication Acts 1959 and 1964.

(1) WHAT IS OBSCENITY?

The 1959 Act, s. 1 (1), provides the test of obscenity:

> "For the purposes of this Act an article shall be deemed to be obscene if its

---

[8] D1's conviction was also quashed, apparently as a necessary consequence of the quashing of D2's. According to the view advanced above, p. 94, this was unnecessary. D2's conviction was quashed for lack of *mens rea*; but there was certainly an *actus reus* and D1 had abundant *mens rea*. The point does not seem to have been argued.

[9] See ss. 53 and 69.

[10] N. St. John Stevas, *Obscenity and the Law* and [1954] Crim. L.R. 817; C. H. Rolph, *The Trial of Lady Chatterley*; Street, *Freedom, the Individual and the Law*, Ch. 5; D.G.T. Williams, "The Control of Obscenity", [1965] Crim. L.R. 471, 522.

[11] (1727), 2 Stra. 788; following *Sidney* (1663), 1 Sid. 168; *sub nom. Sydlyes'* case. 1 Keb. 620, a case of an indecent exhibition.

effect or (where the article comprises two or more distinct items) the effect of any one of its items is, if taken as a whole, such as to tend to deprave and corrupt persons who are likely, having regard to all relevant circumstances, to read, see or hear the matter contained or embodied in it."

This retains, in substance, the test applied at common law and laid down by COCKBURN, C.J., in *Hicklin*:[12]

". . . I think the test of obscenity is this, whether the tendency of the matter charged as obscenity is to deprave and corrupt those whose minds are open to such immoral influences, and into whose hands a publication of this sort may fall."

Until recently the law of obscenity was only invoked in relation to sexual depravity. The prosecutions invariably concerned publications of an erotic and pornographic kind. The words "deprave and corrupt" are clearly capable of bearing a wider meaning than this; and it has now been held that depravity and corruption is not confined to sexual depravity and corruption. In *Calder (John) Publications Ltd.* v. *Powell*[13] it was held that *Cain's Book* might properly be found obscene on the ground that it

". . . highlighted, as it were, the favourable effects of drug-taking, and, so far from condemning it, advocated it, and that there was a real danger that those into whose hands the book came might be tempted at any rate to experiment with drugs and get the favourable sensations highlighted by the book."

The difficulty about extending the notion of obscenity beyond sexual morality is that it is not now apparent where the law is to stop. It seems obvious that an article with a tendency to induce violence is now obscene;[14] and, if taking drugs is depravity, why not drinking, or, if evidence of its harmful effects accumulates, smoking? Whether the conduct to which the article tends amounts to depravity would seem to depend on how violently the judge (in deciding whether there was evidence of obscenity) and the jury (in deciding whether the article was obscene) disapproved of the conduct in question. It has never been made clear whether depravity and corruption consist merely in thoughts[15] or in action of some kind;[16] nor, for example, whether it relates to all sexual thoughts or sexual acts, or only to immoral or perverted sexual acts. It is usually left to a jury—or bench of magistrates—to put its own interpretation on the words with little or no elucidation of these questions. Thus in *Penguin Books*[17] BYRNE, J., told the jury:

"to deprave means to make morally bad, to pervert, to debase, or corrupt morally. The words 'to corrupt' mean to render morally unsound or rotten, to destroy the moral purity or chastity of, to pervert or ruin a good quality, to debase, to defile."

---

[12] (1868), L.R. 3 Q.B. 360 at p. 371. This was an appeal from a decision of a recorder quashing an order of the justices for the destruction of certain pamphlets under the Obscene Publications Act 1857; below, p. 497.

[13] [1965] 1 Q.B. 509; [1965] 1 All E.R. 159.

[14] Cf. *D.P.P.* v. *A. and B.C. Chewing Gum Ltd.*, [1968] 1 Q.B. 159; [1967] 2 All E.R. 504; *Calder and Boyars Ltd.*, [1968] 3 W.L.R. at p. 984.

[15] As COCKBURN, C.J., seems to have thought in *Hicklin*, L.R. 3 Q.B. at p. 371.

[16] As Gardiner, Q.C., submitted in *Penguin Books*: Rolph, *op. cit.*, 28. In *John Calder (Publications), Ltd.* v. *Powell*, above, the principal ground given for holding that *Cain's Book* was obscene was that, in effect, it advocated drug taking and that "there was a real danger that those into whose hands the book came might be tempted at any rate to experiment with drugs and get the favourable sensations highlighted by the book": *per* Lord PARKER, C.J., [1965] 1 All E.R. at p. 162.

[17] Rolph, *op. cit.*, 227, 228.

Nevertheless, much may depend on the tone of the judge's direction to the jury. In the case of *Martin Secker and Warburg*,[18] concerning the publication of *The Philanderer*, STABLE, J., gave a direction to a jury which was acclaimed in the press for its enlightened attitude and was thought to be reassuring to those who fear that the criminal law as applied by the judges is out of touch with public opinion.[19] The learned judge told the jury:[20]

"... the charge is a charge that the tendency of the book is to corrupt and deprave. The charge is not that the tendency of the book is either to shock or to disgust. That is not a criminal offence. The charge is that the tendency of the book is to corrupt and deprave. Then you say: 'Well, corrupt and deprave whom?' to which the answer is: those whose minds are open to such immoral influences and into whose hands a publication of this sort may fall. What, exactly, does that mean? Are we to take our literary standards as being the level of something that is suitable for the decently brought up young female aged fourteen? Or do we go even further back than that and are we to be reduced to the sort of books that one reads as a child in the nursery? The answer to that is: Of course not. A mass of literature, great literature, from many angles, is wholly unsuitable for reading by the adolescent, but that does not mean that a publisher is guilty of a criminal offence for making those works available to the general public."

Dealing with the particular book, he said:[1]

"... the book does deal with candour or, if you prefer it, crudity with the realities of human love and of human intercourse. There is no getting away from that, and the Crown say: 'Well, that is sheer filth.' Is it? Is the act of sexual passion sheer filth? It may be an error of taste to write about it. It may be a matter in which, perhaps, old-fashioned people would mourn the reticence that was observed in these matters yesterday, but is it sheer filth? That is a matter which you have to consider and ultimately to decide."

Other directions to juries in recent times, however, have been a good deal less liberal and it has been suggested that STABLE, J.'s is not the typical judicial attitude.[2] Nor is it so clear that the law does not require us to take our standards from "the decently brought up young female aged fourteen". The article is obscene if it has a tendency to deprave "persons who are likely ... to read, see or hear the matter contained or embodied in it". It would not, apparently, necessarily be sufficient that there existed two persons who were likely to read the book and who might be depraved by it. It is obscene only if it has a tendency to deprave "a significant proportion" of those likely to read it.[3] It would not be obscene, simply on the ground that it might tend to deprave "a minute lunatic fringe of readers".[4] If, however, a significant, though comparatively small, number of the likely readers were decently brought up fourteen year-old girls, then whether the book was obscene would turn on whether it was likely to deprave them.

The questions for the jury are of a highly speculative nature. How, for example, is the jury to say whether a significant proportion of the readers will be fourteen year-old girls? The answer seems to depend on all kinds of matters of which the jury can, at best, have imperfect knowledge. The same article may or

---

[18] [1954] 2 All E.R. 683.
[19] See (1954), 17 M.L.R. 571.
[20] [1954] 2 All E.R. at p. 686.
[1] *Ibid.*, at pp. 687, 688.
[2] Street, *op. cit.*, 135.
[3] *Calder and Boyars Ltd.*, [1968] 3 W.L.R. 974 at p. 983.
[4] *Ibid.*, at p. 984.

may not be obscene depending on the manner of publication. If it has a tendency to deprave fourteen year-old girls, a bookseller who sells a copy to a club for fourteen year-old girls is obviously publishing an obscene article; but if he sells the same book to the Conservative Club or a working men's club, this may not be so. The fact that the publisher (in the sense of the producer) of the book is acquitted of publishing an obscene libel, does not mean, then, that other subsequent "publishers" of the book do not commit an offence.

The actual intention of the author is irrelevant. If the article has a tendency to deprave a significant proportion of the readership, it does not matter how pure and noble the author's intent may have been;[5] the article is obscene. In *Martin Secker and Warburg* STABLE, J., told the jury:[6]

> "You will have to consider whether the author was pursuing an honest purpose and an honest thread of thought, or whether that was all just a bit of camouflage . . ."

This was too favourable to the defence, unless the jury were to take account of the author's intention, as it appeared in the book itself, as a factor which would have a bearing on whether people would be depraved.

It is now made perfectly clear by the Act that an "item" alleged to be obscene must be "taken as a whole" so that the jury must judge a book on a reading of the whole article[7] and not merely by looking at selected passages.

If depravity and corruption means merely thinking impure thoughts or imagining violent or other depraved acts, then no doubt many books are obscene; but if it implies the causation of some change in the reader's character or behaviour, then there is very little evidence on which to found the law of obscenity. It has been questioned whether there is any evidence that anyone was ever depraved or corrupted by reading a pornographic or erotic book. As Gardiner, Q.C., said in argument in *Penguin Books*:[8]

> "In a case like this one is perhaps permitted to reflect that nobody suggests that the Director of Public Prosecutions becomes depraved or corrupted. Counsel read the book; they do not become depraved or corrupted. Witnesses read the book; they do not become depraved or corrupted. Nobody suggests the Judge or the Jury become depraved or corrupted. *It is always somebody else; it is never ourselves.*"

Perhaps the publication in *Shaw* v. *Director of Public Prosecutions*[9] fell into a rather different category. It was *The Ladies' Directory* which was designed to facilitate the carrying on of their trade (including sexual perversion) by prostitutes. While this publication may not have been obscene in the popular understanding of that word, it perhaps satisfied the legal test more clearly than any pornographic or erotic literature. Similarly, it seems at least plausible that the effect of a book describing the delights of taking drugs might encourage drug-taking. The evidence of psychiatrists is admissible to show what sort of effect an article would have on children of certain ages and what it would lead them to do.[10] Such expert evidence may not be admissible when the question

---

[5] *Calder and Boyars Ltd.*, [1968] 3 W.L.R. at p. 983–984.
[6] [1954] 2 All E.R. at p. 688.
[7] As to the meaning of "article", see below, p. 498.
[8] Rolph, *op. cit.*, 37.
[9] [1962] A.C. 220; [1961] 2 All E.R. 446; above, p. 160.
[10] *D.P.P.* v. *A. and B.C. Chewing Gum Ltd.*, [1968] 1 Q.B. 159; [1967] 2 All E.R. 504.

is as to the effect of the article on an adult, since the court may take the view that the witness is no better equipped to answer this question than the jury.[11]

(2) OFFENCES

It is an offence if D:

(1) publishes an obscene article whether for gain or not;[12] or

(2) "has" an obscene article for publication for gain (whether gain to himself or gain to another).[13]

1 Publication

Section 1 (3) of the Obscene Publications Act 1959 provides:

"For the purposes of this Act a person publishes an article who—

(a) distributes, circulates, sells, lets on hire, gives, or lends it, or who offers it for sale or for letting on hire; or

(b) in the case of an article containing or embodying matter to be looked at or a record, shows, plays or projects it:

Provided that paragraph (b) of this subsection shall not apply to anything done in the course of a cinematograph exhibition (within the meaning of the Cinematograph Act, 1952), other than one excluded from the Cinematograph Act 1909 by subsection (4) of section seven of that Act (which relates to exhibitions in private houses to which the public are not admitted) or to anything done in the course of television or sound broadcasting."

If the article has a tendency to deprave and corrupt P, the person to whom it is published by D, then of course D is guilty.

If it does not have a tendency to deprave and corrupt P, then D will be guilty only if either—

(1) (a) there are "persons who are likely, having regard to all the relevant circumstances, to read see or hear the matter contained in it" (whether they have done so or not) and (b) it will have a tendency to deprave and corrupt those persons;[14] or

(2) it has in fact been published to a person whom it is likely to deprave and corrupt, and this publication could reasonably have been expected to follow from publication by D.[15]

In *Barker*,[16] where D published certain photographs to P and the judge told the jury that the fact that P kept them under lock and key was unimportant, the conviction was quashed. If the jury had been told that they were to consider the tendency of the article to deprave and corrupt only P, the direction would seem to be unobjectionable. If, however, they were directed or left to suppose that they should consider its tendency to deprave and corrupt others, then the direction was clearly wrong. The fact that P kept the articles under lock and key

---

[11] *Ibid.*, at p. 506.
[12] Obscene Publications Act 1959, s. 2 (1).
[13] *Ibid.*, s. 2 (1) as amended by the 1964 Act, s. 1 (1).
[14] *Ibid.*, s. 1 (1).
[15] Obscene Publications Act 1959, s. 2 (6).
[16] [1962] 1 All E.R. 748.

was not *conclusive,* for he may have intended to produce them at some future time; but it was certainly *relevant* to the answer to proposition 1 (a) above.

If the article has no tendency to deprave and corrupt the person to whom it is published and neither of the conditions specified above is satisfied, then D must be acquitted. So in *Clayton and Halsey*[17] where P was an experienced police officer who testified that he was not susceptible to depravity or corruption and there was no evidence of publication, or likelihood of publication, to a third party, the Court of Criminal Appeal held that the case should have been withdrawn from the jury.[18] Lord PARKER, C.J., said:[19]

> ". . . while it is no doubt theoretically possible that a jury could take the view that even a most experienced officer, despite his protestations, was susceptible to the influence of the article yet, bearing in mind the onus and degree of proof in a criminal case, it would, we think, be unsafe and therefore wrong to leave that question to the jury."

2   Having an Obscene Article for Publication for Gain

This second type of offence was introduced by amendments made by the 1964 Act and was intended to deal with the difficulties arising from *Clayton and Halsey.* In fact the accused in that case were convicted of *conspiracy* to publish the articles, so, from the prosecution's point of view, no harm was done in that particular instance. But the implications of the case were serious; for, where there was no evidence that D had conspired with another, it made it virtually impossible to get a conviction on the evidence of a policeman that the articles had been sold to him. Under the amendment it is now possible to charge D with *having* the article for publication for gain; and the incorruptibility of the particular police officer who purchases it will be irrelevant. The jury is unlikely to suppose that D kept these articles solely for sale to police officers; and they need only be satisfied that, having regard to all the relevant circumstances, (i) D contemplated publication to such a person as the article would have a tendency to deprave and corrupt; or (ii) that he contemplated publication from which a further publication to susceptible persons could reasonably be expected to follow (whether D in fact contemplated that further publication or not). By s. 1 (3) (b) of the 1964 Act:

> "the question whether the article is obscene shall be determined by reference to such publication for gain of the article as in the circumstances it may reasonably be inferred he had in contemplation and to any further publication that could reasonably be expected to follow from it, but not to any other publication."

The meaning of "having" an article is elucidated by s. 1 (2) of the 1964 Act:

> ". . . a person shall be deemed to have an article for publication for gain if with a view to such publication he has the article in his ownership, possession or control."

---

[17] [1963] 1 Q.B. 163; [1962] 3 All E.R. 500.
[18] D, of course, did not know that he was dealing with an incorruptible police officer. He had *mens rea.* According to the theory advocated by some writers (above, p. 173), therefore, he could have been convicted of an attempt.
[19] [1963] 1 Q.B. at p. 168; [1962] 3 All E.R. at p. 502.

Thus the owner of the shop in which the article is stocked may be convicted as the owner of the article, as well as his servant who has possession or control of it. The van driver who takes it from wholesaler to retailer may also be thought to be in control of it for the purposes of gain.

This overcomes another difficulty which arose under the 1959 Act. It was held[20] that a person who displays an obscene article in a shop window is not guilty of publishing it. Of the various ways of publishing referred to in s. 1 (3), the only one which could conceivably have been applicable was "offering for sale"; and it was held that "offer" must be construed in accordance with the law of contract,[1] under which the display of goods in a shop window is an "invitation to treat" and not an offer.[2] This decision, of course, remains good law; but now a charge might successfully be brought of having the obscene article for publication for gain, whether it had been displayed or not.

(3) DEFENCES

1 No Reasonable Cause to Believe Article Obscene

By s. 2 (5) of the 1959 Act and s. 1 (3) (a) of the 1964 Act, it is a defence for D to prove that (i) he had not examined the article and (ii) had no reasonable cause to suspect that it was such that his publication of it, or his having it, as the case may be, would make him liable to be convicted of an offence against s. 2. Both conditions must be satisfied; so if D has examined the article, his failure to appreciate its tendency to deprave and corrupt is no defence under these sections.

2 Public Good

Section 4 of the 1959 Act provides a defence of "public good":

"(1) A person shall not be convicted of an offence against section 2 of this Act . . . if it is proved that publication of the article in question is justified as being for the public good on the ground that it is in the interests of science, literature, art or learning, or of other objects of general concern.

(2) It is hereby declared that the opinion of experts as to the literary, artistic, scientific or other merits of an article may be admitted in any proceedings under this Act either to establish or negative the said ground."

The defence becomes relevant only when the jury has decided that the book is obscene—that it has a tendency to deprave a significant proportion of those likely to read it. The Act assumes that this harm to a section of the community might be outweighed by the other considerations referred to in the section. The jury's task is then to

". . . consider, on the one hand, the number of readers they believe would tend to be depraved and corrupted by the book, the strength of the tendency to deprave and corrupt, and the nature of the depravity or corruption; on the other hand, they should assess the strength of the literary, sociological or

---

[20] *Mella* v. *Monahan*, [1961] Crim. L.R. 175, following *Fisher* v. *Bell*, [1961] 1 Q.B. 394; [1963] 3 All E.R. 731.
[1] For a criticism of this ruling, see [1961] Crim. L.R. at p. 181; *cf. Partridge* v. *Crittenden*, [1968] 2 All E. R. 421.
[2] *Pharmaceutical Society of Great Britain* v. *Boots (Cash Chemists), Ltd.*, [1953] 1 Q.B. 401; [1953] 1 All E.R. 482.

ethical merit which they consider the book to possess. They should then weigh up all these factors and decide whether on balance the publication is proved to be justified as being for the public good."[3]

This defence was relied on in the case of *Penguin Books*[4] where the jury found that D Ltd. were not guilty of an offence under s. 2 in publishing *Lady Chatterley's Lover*. The acquittal may have been either on the ground that the book was not obscene or, under s. 4, that it was obscene but that it was for the public good that it should be published.

The onus of establishing the defence is on the accused and the standard required is proof on a balance of probabilities.[5]

The "other merits" referred to in s. 4 (1) include merit

"from a sociological point of view, from an ethical point of view, and from an educational point of view."[6]

In *Penguin Books*, the Bishop of Woolwich, who had made a special study of ethics, was permitted to give evidence as an expert on the ethical merits of the book. No doubt "other merits" must be *ejusdem generis* with "literary, artistic, scientific . . ." and clearly must be such as to tend to establish that the publication is for the public good. The experts may also, it seems, testify that publication is for the public good, although that is the very question the jury has to decide.[7]

In *Reiter*,[8] the jury were asked to look at a large number of other books in order to decide whether the books which were the subject of the charge were obscene. The Court of Criminal Appeal held that this was wrong. It appears that it is still not permissible, under the Act, to prove that other books, which are just as obscene as the one in issue, are freely circulating;[9] but evidence relating to other books may now be admitted to establish the "climate of literature" in order to assess the literary merit of the book.[10]

In *Penguin Books*,[11] Crown counsel conceded in argument that the intention of the *author* in writing the book is relevant to the question of literary merit. If this is right, it must again[12] refer only to the intention as it appears in the book itself.

(4) MENS REA

1 At Common Law

In *Hicklin*[13] it was held that it was not necessary to establish that D's motive was to deprave and corrupt; and that, if he knowingly published that which had a tendency to deprave and corrupt, it was no defence that he had an honest and laudable intention in publishing the work in question. D, a member of the

---

[3] *Calder and Boyars*, [1968] 3 W.L.R. at p. 986.

[4] [1961] Crim. L.R. 176. The rulings of the judge and the summing-up are reported in some detail in *The Trial of Lady Chatterley* by C. H. Rolph.

[5] [1968] 3 W.L.R., at p. 985.

[6] *Penguin Books* (1961), Rolph; *op. cit.*, at p. 234; *Calder and Boyars Ltd.*, [1968] 3. W.L.R. at p. 986; *John Calder, Ltd. v. Powell*, [1965] 1 All E.R. at p 161.

[7] *D.P.P. v. A. and B.C. Chewing Gum Ltd.*, [1968] 1 Q.B. 159; [1967] 2 All E.R. 504.

[8] [1954] 2 Q.B. 16; [1954] 1 All E.R. 741.

[9] *Penguin Books* (1961), Rolph, *op. cit.*, 127.

[10] *Ibid.*

[11] Rolph, *op. cit.*, 87 and 123.

[12] As with the question whether the book is obscene. Above, p. 490.

[13] (1868), L.R. 3 Q.B. 360.

Protestant Electoral Union, sold[14] copies of *The Confessional Unmasked*. He argued that he did so with the intention, not of prejudicing good morals, but of exposing what he deemed to be the errors of the Church of Rome and, particularly, the immorality of the confessional. To this COCKBURN, C.J., answered:

> "Be it so. The question then presents itself in this simple form: May you commit an offence against the law in order that thereby you may effect some ulterior object which you have in view, which may be an honest and even a laudable one? My answer is, emphatically, no."[15]

The case did not decide, as is sometimes supposed, that no *mens rea* is required. The argument was not that D did not know the nature of the thing published nor even that he did not know that its natural consequence was to tend to deprave and corrupt; but that the publication was justified by his predominant intention of exposing the errors of the Church of Rome. COCKBURN, C.J., indeed, assumed that D *did* know what the effect of the publication would be:

> ". . . it is impossible to suppose that the man who published it must not have known and seen that the effect upon the minds of many of those into whose hands it would come would be of a mischievous and demoralising character."[16]

A man who knows that a certain result will follow may properly be said to intend it[17] or, at the very least, to be reckless. BLACKBURN, J., relied particularly upon *Vantandillo*,[18] which lays down that it is a misdemeanour to carry a person with a contagious disease through the street, though no intent to infect anyone be alleged; but in that case the court insisted that D should have "full knowledge"[19] of the fact of the contagious disease. *Hicklin*,[20] then, need not be taken to have decided more than that, if D publishes that which he knows will have a tendency to deprave and corrupt, it is no defence that he did so with the best of motives.

No case before the Act of 1959 decided anything to the contrary. In *Thomson*[1] the Common Serjeant admitted evidence of other books found on D's premises as tending to show that

> "she sold this book with the intention alleged in the indictment [to corrupt morals], and not accidentally."

In *Barraclough*,[2] it was held unnecessary (but desirable) that the indictment should contain an allegation of intent, because the intent was implicit in the allegation of publishing obscenity.[3] In *De Montalk*,[4] D handed to a printer some poems he had written, intending to circulate about 100 copies, mostly to young people of both sexes ("literary people"). The printer sent the poems to the police and D was convicted. His appeal on the ground that there was not

---

[14] For the price he paid for them and not "for gain".
[15] (1868), L.R. 3 Q.B. at pp. 371, 372.
[16] *Ibid.*, at p. 372. If the law requires knowledge, this is now clearly a question for the jury: Criminal Justice Act 1967, s. 8; above, p. 52.
[17] Above, p. 38.
[18] (1815), 4 M. & S. 73; below, p. 543.
[19] *Ibid.*, at p. 77.
[20] Above, p. 494.
[1] (1900), 64 J.P. 456 at p. 457.
[2] [1906] 1 K.B. 201 (C.C.R.).
[3] ". . . intent . . . is still part of the charge or the publication would not have been unlawful": *per* DARLING, J., *ibid.*, at p. 212.
[4] (1932), 23 Cr. App. Rep. 182.

sufficient direction on intent was dismissed; but the headnote goes farther than the judgment in asserting that the jury should not be directed that they must find an intent to corrupt public morals. Crown counsel (later BYRNE, J.) submitted merely that intention *was to be inferred* from the act of publication and that no affirmative evidence of intention need be given; and the Court dismissed the appeal, saying that the law was accurately stated in *Barraclough*.[5] But in *Penguin Books*,[6] BYRNE, J., held that, if D publishes an article which is obscene, the inference that he intends to deprave and corrupt is irrebuttable. Such an approach today would seem to be inconsistent with s. 8 of the Criminal Justice Act 1967;[7] but, though BYRNE, J., used the language of proof, he was probably saying, in substance, that intent to deprave was not a constituent of the offence.[8] He conceded that the judgment in *De Montalk* was not very clear, but stated that the court came to the conclusion that there was nothing in the argument that the presumption was rebuttable, and that he was bound by that decision.

2   Under the Obscene Publications Act

In *Shaw* v. *Director of Public Prosecutions*[9] D was charged with publishing an obscene article in the form of the *Ladies' Directory*. His appeal to the Court of Criminal Appeal[10] on the ground that the judge did not direct the jury to take into account D's "honesty of purpose" was dismissed. ASHWORTH, J., said:[11]

> "If these proceedings had been brought before the passing of the Obscene Publications Act 1959, in the form of a prosecution at common law for pub-lishing an obscene libel, it would no doubt have been necessary to establish an intention to corrupt. But the Act of 1959 contains no such requirement and the test of obscenity laid down in s. 1 (1) of the Act is whether the effect of the article is such as to tend to deprave and corrupt persons who are likely to read it. In other words obscenity depends on the article and not on the author."[12]

This, of course, is inconsistent with the view of BYRNE, J., who, in *Penguin Books*,[13] conceived that he was applying the common law rule. According to the Court of Criminal Appeal view, he was wrong about the common law, but reached the right result by accident, the common law having been revised by the Act! As a matter of fact, it seems that this was not the intention of Parliament.[14] It was not necessary to the decision to decide that no *mens rea* was required. To rule that "honesty of purpose" is irrelevant is one thing and no more than was done in *Hicklin*; to decide that no *mens rea* with reference to depravity and corruption is necessary, is another. D's motives of benevolence towards the prostitutes whom he was assisting to ply their trade may have been wholly admirable but if he knew (as he must have done!) that the inevitable result would be what the law regards[15] as depravity and corruption, he intended that

---

[5] Above, p. 495.
[6] Above, p. 488.
[7] Above, p. 52.
[8] See the discussion of s. 8; above, pp. 52 and 198.
[9] [1962] A.C. 220; [1961] 2 All E.R. 446; above, p. 490.
[10] He was refused leave to appeal to the House of Lords on this count.
[11] [1962] A.C. at p. 227; [1961] 1 All E.R. at p. 333 (C.C.A.).
[12] The reference to the author is puzzling. Presumably "the publisher" is meant. They were one and the same in Shaw.
[13] *Supra*.
[14] Street, *Freedom, the Individual and the Law*, 141.
[15] Whether he knew the law so regarded it, is irrelevant.

result. Moreover, the test laid down in s. 1 (1) is not decisive, for this merely defines the *actus reus* and says nothing about *mens rea*. It is difficult, however, to dispute the conclusion of the Court of Criminal Appeal in the light of the defence provided by s. 2 (5).[16] If *mens rea* in the sense described above were required, this provision would be quite unnecessary. But the clear implication of s. 2 (5) is that D would be guilty (i) although he had examined the article and concluded that it had no tendency to deprave and corrupt if there were reasonable grounds on which he might have suspected that it would; (ii) although the jury thought it as likely as not that he did not suspect the article's tendency;[17] and (iii) although he had examined the article and failed to appreciate its tendency. Thus, it appears likely that the Act, perhaps inadvertently, has restricted the requirement of *mens rea*.

(5) FORFEITURE OF OBSCENE ARTICLES

The Obscene Publications Act 1857 provided a summary procedure for the forfeiture of obscene articles. That Act is replaced by s. 3 of the Obscene Publications Act 1959. The procedure is that an information on oath must be laid before a magistrate that there is reasonable ground for suspecting that obscene articles are *kept* in any premises, stall or vehicle in the justice's area *for publication for gain*.[18] The justice may then issue a warrant authorising a constable to search for and seize any articles which he has reason to believe to be obscene and to be kept for publication for gain.

Any articles seized must be brought before a justice for the same area. If the justice, after looking at the articles, decides they are not obscene, then the matter drops and the articles are, no doubt, returned.[19] But if he thinks they may be obscene (and he need not come to a decided opinion at this stage) he may issue a summons to the occupier of the premises, etc., to appear before the court and show cause why the articles should not be forfeited. If the court is satisfied[20] that the articles, at the time they were seized, were obscene articles kept for publication for gain, it must order the articles to be forfeited.

The owner, author or maker of the articles, or any other person through whose hands they had passed before being seized, is entitled to appear and show cause why they should not be forfeited; and any person who appeared or was entitled to appear to show cause against the making of the order has a right of appeal to Quarter Sessions.

The defence of "public good" is available in proceedings for forfeiture;[21] but the decision is, of course, now in the hands of the justices and not in the hands of a jury. Thus, if proceedings for forfeiture are brought instead of an indictment, the author or publisher of a book can, in substance, be deprived of a right to jury trial.

---

[16] Above, p. 493.

[17] The onus of proof on a balance of probabilities is on D.

[18] *Hicklin*'s case might thus now fall outside the Act. He sold the pamphlets for the price he paid for them and this was evidently considered not to be selling for gain: (1868), L.R. 3 Q.B. at pp. 368 and 374.

[19] *Thomson* v. *Chain Libraries, Ltd.*, [1954] 2 All E.R. 616.

[20] In *Thomson* v. *Chain Libraries*, [1954] 2 All E.R. at p. 618, HILBERY, J., said that the onus of proof is on the person who appears to show cause. *Sed quaere?* The magistrate must be *satisfied* that the article is obscene.

[21] Obscene Publications Act 1959, s. 4 (1).

There is not necessarily any uniformity of decision. One bench may pass a magazine or picture, while another condemns it.[22] In practice, it seems that the advice of the Director of Public Prosecutions is usually taken by the police before applying for a warrant. His advice is not *necessary* for it is thought undesirable that he should be in the position of a literary or moral censor.[1]

(6) THE COMMON LAW OF OBSCENE LIBEL

The 1959 Act did not, in terms, abolish the common law misdemeanour of obscene libel, but provided in s. 2 (4):

> "A person publishing an article shall not be proceeded against for an offence at common law consisting of the publication of any matter contained or embodied in the article where it is of the essence of the offence that the matter is obscene."

It might be thought that the intention was that, in future, all proceedings in respect of obscene publications should be brought under the Act. The subsection has not been so interpreted. In *Shaw* v. *Director of Public Prosecutions*[2] it was relied on by the defence in relation to the first count alleging a common law conspiracy to corrupt public morals by the publication of the *Ladies' Directory*; that is, as was held, the publication of an obscene article. The answer to this argument, accepted by the Court of Criminal Appeal[3] and the House of Lords,[4] was that the conspiracy did not "consist of the publication" of the booklet; it consisted in the agreement to corrupt public morals by publishing it.

It thus appears that it would still be possible to bring a prosecution for conspiracy to publish an obscene libel (and possibly an incitement or attempt to do so). The publishers of *Lady Chatterley's Lover* might have been indicted for conspiracy to publish an obscene libel or, indeed, conspiracy to corrupt public morals. On such charge, the statutory defence of public good would not be available, and the expert evidence, which played such an important part in the *Penguin Books* case,[5] would be inadmissible.

(7) WHAT IS AN ARTICLE?

The 1959 Act provides by s. 1 (2):

> "In this Act 'article' means any description of article containing or embodying matter to be read or looked at or both, any sound record, and any film or other record of a picture or pictures."

In *Straker* v. *Director of Public Prosecutions*[6] it was held that while a negative *might* be within this definition, it was not kept for "publication" as described in s. 3 (1) since it was not to be shown, played or projected, but to be used for

---

[22] The same thing could of course occur in relation to proceedings on indictment. If another publisher were to be prosecuted for publishing *Lady Chatterley*, the decision in *Penguin Books* (above, p. 488) would not be relevant in evidence, let alone an estoppel; and another jury, hearing different expert evidence, might well arrive at a different conclusion.

[1] Under the Prosecution of Offences Regulations 1946, reg. 6 (2) (d), a chief officer of police must report to the Director any alleged commission of an *offence* of obscenity.

[2] [1962] A.C. 220.

[3] [1962] A.C. at pp. 235, 236.

[4] [1962] A.C. at pp. 268, 269, 290, 291.

[5] Above, p. 494.

[6] [1963] 1 Q.B. 926; [1963] 1 All E.R. 697 (D.C.).

making prints. It could not, therefore, be forfeited under s. 3. This gap is closed by s. 2 of the 1964 Act which provides

"(1) The Obscene Publications Act 1959 (as amended by this Act) shall apply in relation to anything which is intended to be used, either alone or as one of a set, for the reproduction or manufacture therefrom of articles containing or embodying matter to be read, looked at or listened to, as if it were an article containing or embodying that matter so far as that matter is to be derived from it or from the set."

By s. 2 (2) of the 1964 Act an article is had or kept for publication

"if it is had or kept for the reproduction or manufacture therefrom of articles for publication".

The negatives in *Straker* clearly fall within this provision.

(8) POSTING INDECENT OR OBSCENE MATTER

It is an offence under the Post Office Act 1953, s. 11, punishable summarily by a fine of £10 and, on indictment, by imprisonment for twelve months, to

". . . send or attempt to send or procure to be sent a postal packet which:
(b) encloses any indecent or obscene print, painting, photograph, lithograph, engraving, cinematograph film, book, card or written communication, or any indecent or obscene article whether similar to the above or not . . ."

It was held in *Stanley*[7] that the words "indecent or obscene" in this section:

"convey one idea, namely offending against the recognised standards of propriety, indecent being at the lower end of the scale and obscene at the upper end of the scale . . .
. . . an indecent article is not necessarily obscene, whereas an obscene article must almost certainly be indecent."

Therefore the verdict of a jury holding that certain cinematograph films were not obscene (for the purposes of the Obscene Publications Act but were indecent (for the purposes of the Post Office Act) was upheld.

If "indecent" comprehends everything which is obscene and more, the word "obscene" in the Act is redundant. But it is not certain that this is so, for obscenity may include matter advocating drug-taking or violence[8] which would not ordinarily be described as "indecent".[9] On the other hand, such articles might well be said to offend against "recognised standards of propriety"; and, for the purposes of other legislation, abusive language and shouts in church alleging hypocrisy against the reader of the lesson[10] have been held to be "indecent". It is possible therefore that "indecent" is not confined to sexual indecency, but extends to other improper matter.

The test of indecency is objective and the character of the addressee is immaterial.[11] It is not clear whether similar tests should be applied to "obscene" but probably they should. The word seems to bear a wider meaning than in the

---

[7] [1965] 2 Q.B. 327; [1965] 1 All E.R. 1035.
[8] Above, p. 488.
[9] *Lees* v. *Parr*, [1967] All E.R. 181 n. (By-law).
[10] *Abrahams* v. *Carey*, [1967] 3 All E.R. 179 (Ecclesiastical Courts Jurisdiction Act 1860, s. 2).
[11] *Straker*, [1965] Crim. L.R. 239.

Obscene Publications Act; for an article may offend grossly against "recognised standards of propriety" without any tendency to deprave and corrupt.

(9) OBSCENITY IN THE THEATRE

The Theatres Act 1968, which abolished censorship of the theatre, makes it an offence, punishable under s. 2, summarily with six months, and on indictment with three years' imprisonment, to present[12] or direct an obscene performance of a play. The definition of obscenity is the same as in s. 1 (1) of the Obscene Publications Act 1959,[13] except that attention is directed to the effect of the performance on the persons who are likely to *attend* it instead of "read, see or hear it". A defence of "public good" is provided which is the same as that under s. 4 of the 1959 Act,[14] except that the interests which may justify the performance are those of "drama, opera, ballet or any other art or of literature or learning".

A performance given "on a domestic occasion in a private dwelling" is excepted by s. 7 from the provisions of s. 2; and, by s. 8, proceedings may not be instituted except by or with the consent of the Attorney General.

If proceedings are to be brought in respect of the alleged obscenity of the performance of a play, they must be brought under the Act; for, by s. 2 (4), it precludes proceedings at common law (including conspiracy) or under the Vagrancy Act 1824. A prosecution on indictment under s. 2 must be commenced within two years of the commission of the offence: s. 2 (3).

(10) OTHER STATUTES

There are a number of other statutes under which summary proceedings may be, and are instituted, where the safeguards of the Obscene Publications Acts do not apply. These include the Vagrancy Act 1824, s. 4, the Metropolitan Police Act 1839, s. 54, the Town Police Clauses Act 1847, s. 28, the Indecent Advertisements Act 1889 and the Children and Young Persons (Harmful Publications) Act 1955. No doubt there are also many local Acts and by-laws which may be invoked.

4 BLASPHEMY[15]

(1) ACTUS REUS

It is a common law misdemeanour to publish blasphemous matter whether orally or in writing. Matter is blasphemous if it denies the truth of the Christian religion[16] or of the Bible[17] or the Book of Common Prayer,[18] or the existence of God. The earlier cases required no more than this for, as Stephen says, they

---

[12] *Cf. Grade* v. *Director of Public Prosecutions*, [1942] 2 All E.R.; above, p. 103.
[13] Above, p. 487–488.
[14] Above, p. 493.
[15] G. D. Nokes, *History of the Crime of Blasphemy*. Stephen, 2 H.C.L. 469–476. Street, *Freedom, the Individual and the Law*, 193–198.
[16] *Taylor* (1676), 1 Vent. 293.
[17] *Hetherington* (1841), 4 St. Tr. N.S. 563.
[18] According to Russell, 1519; Archbold, § 3401.

"all proceed upon the plain principle that the public importance of the Christian religion is so great that no one is allowed to deny its truth."[19]

The gist of the offence is

"a supposed tendency to shake the fabric of society generally."[20]

Yet, while the law was stated in these broad terms, there is no recorded instance of a conviction for blasphemy where an element of contumely and ribaldry was absent.[21] In the course of the nineteenth century it came to be held that matter denying the truth of Christianity, etc., will not be held criminal if it is expressed in decent and temperate language and not in such terms as are likely to lead to a breach of the peace. "If the decencies of controversy are observed, even the fundamentals of religion may be attacked without the writer being guilty of blasphemy."[22]

Stephen found himself unable to accept this milder view of the law because of the weight of the earlier authorities;[23] but the milder view found favour with the House of Lords in *Bowman* v. *Secular Society, Ltd.*[1] In that case it was held that a company formed to promote the secularisation of the state was not unlawful although one of its objects was to deny Christianity. Blasphemous words are punishable

"for their manner, their violence, or ribaldry, or, more fully stated, for their tendency to endanger the peace then and there, to deprave public morality generally, to shake the fabric of society and to be a cause of civil strife."[2]

It may now be taken as settled that a publication denying the truth of Christianity, etc., will not be indictable unless it is expressed in such violent or ribald language as to tend to endanger the peace.

ALDERSON, B., has held that it is only the Christian religion and, indeed, only the established church which is protected by the law of blasphemy.[3] The difference, it appears is that the established church alone is part of the constitution of the country so that an attack on other religions was not thought to have the supposed tendency to shake the fabric of this society. This was characterised as "a strange *dictum*" by Lord SUMNER who pointed out that

"After all, to insult a Jew's religion is not less likely to provoke a fight than to insult an episcopalian's . . ."[4]

It is perhaps conceivable, though not likely, that the protection of blasphemy could be extended to other branches of Christianity and non-Christian religions held by substantial numbers of people in this country.[5]

---

[19] 2 H.C.L. 475.

[20] *Per* Lord SUMNER in *Bowman* v. *Secular Society, Ltd.*, [1917] A.C. 406 at p. 459.

[21] This was common ground in *Bowman* v. *Secular Society, Ltd.*, see, for example, *per* Lord SUMNER, [1917] A.C. 406 at p. 460. Stephen says that the placards held to be blasphemous in *Cowan* v. *Milbourn* (1867), L.R. 2 Exch. 230 "could hardly have been expressed in less offensive language": 2 H.C.L. at 474; but that was a civil action, and Lord SUMNER and the Court of Appeal thought the decision wrong: [1917] A.C. at p. 463.

[22] *Ramsay and Foote* (1883), 15 Cox C.C. 231 at p. 238, *per* COLERIDGE, C.J.

[23] 2 H.C.L. 474, 475 and *Digest* (4th ed.), Art. 161.

[1] [1917] A.C. 406.

[2] *Per* Lord SUMNER, [1917] A.C. at p. 466.

[3] *Gathercole* (1838), 2 Lew, C.C. 237.

[4] [1917] A.C. at p. 460.

[5] *Cf.* Street, *op. cit.*, 197.

(2) MENS REA

There seems to be no clear modern authority on the nature of the *mens rea* required, but it ought to follow in principle from the nature of the *actus reus* that there must be proved at least an intention so to ridicule the Christian religion, etc., as to tend to provoke ordinary Christians (or, possibly, those actually addressed[6]) to violence. It may be that the prosecution would have to go further and prove an actual intention to provoke.[7] If D's intention was to propagate sincerely held opinions on religious subjects and not to ridicule or provoke, he should have a defence even if the matter in fact provoked some people to violence.

(3) REFORM OF THE LAW

Prosecutions for blasphemy have been extremely rare for over a hundred years[8] but several attempts to abolish the blasphemy laws have failed.[9] There is a strong case for their abolition. It is highly illogical that scurrilous attacks on the established church should be punishable as blasphemy because of their tendency to cause civil strife, while similar attacks on other religions held by persons in this country are not. Moreover, since the law appears now to be limited to cases where the peace is endangered there are other provisions adequate and more apt for use to preserve public order.[10]

It should be noted, finally, that the common law of blasphemy is supplemented by a number of statutes,[11] but these are not invoked in practice.

---

[6] *Cf.* Seditious Libel, below, p. 557.
[7] *Cf. Burns*, below, p. 558.
[8] *Pooley* (1857), 8 St. Tr. N.S. 1089; *Ramsay* (1883), 15 Cox C.C. 231; *Boulter* (1908), 72 J.P. 188; and *Gott* (1922), 16 Cr. App. Rep. 87.
[9] R. S. W. Pollard, *Abolish the Blasphemy Laws*, 7.
[10] See below, pp. 533 *et seq.*
[11] See Archbold, §§ 3402–3404; Russell, 1520–1524.

CHAPTER 18

Offences relating to the Administration of Justice

1 PERJURY

In the early days of the common law, the only false swearing which was punished was that of compurgators and jurymen. The jury originally fulfilled the function of the modern witness, for it was expected to know the facts. When witnesses in the modern sense began to be called, there was at first probably no offence of which they could be convicted for giving false evidence. Then a series of decisions in the Star Chamber[1] created the common law misdemeanour of perjury.[2]

At common law, perjury, strictly so-called, consisted in giving false evidence on oath in a material matter in a judicial proceeding. But it was also a misdemeanour to swear falsely outside a judicial proceeding where the statement was one required to be made by law, as, for example, for the purpose of obtaining a marriage licence.[3] A very large number of statutes also made criminal the making of false statements in a wide variety of circumstances.

The law is now to be found in the Perjury Act 1911 which codified and modified the common law and swept away the relevant sections of more than 130 statutes.[4]

Perjury is defined by s. 1 (1) of the Act:

> "If any person lawfully sworn as a witness or as an interpreter in a judicial proceeding wilfully makes a statement material in that proceeding, which he knows to be false or does not believe to be true, he shall be guilty of perjury, and shall on conviction thereof on indictment, be liable to imprisonment for a term not exceeding seven years, or to a fine or to both such imprisonment and fine."

---

[1] *Rowland ap Eliza* (1613), 3 Co. Inst. 164.
[2] Stephen, 3 H.C.L. 241.
[3] *Foster* (1821), Russ. & Ry. 459; *De Beauvoir* (1835), 7 C. & P. 17.
[4] See the Schedule to the Act.

1   Lawfully Sworn as a Witness

Perjury originated as a spiritual offence and at common law the only oath recognised is one "calling Almighty God to witness that his testimony is true."[5]   It is not necessary that the oath be in accordance with the Christian religion; it is sufficient that the witness believes in God by whom he swears in accordance with the particular religion he professes.[6]   The common law is modified by the Oaths Act 1888 which permits a witness to affirm if he objects to being sworn on the ground that (i) he has no religious belief; or (ii) the taking of an oath is contrary to his religious belief.   By the Oaths Act 1961 this is extended to (iii) a person to whom it is not reasonably practicable to administer an oath in the manner appropriate to his religious belief.   A person who has affirmed is subject to the law of perjury as if he had taken the oath.[7]   The common law position, as modified by the Oaths Acts, is preserved by s. 15 of the Perjury Act which provides:

> "(1) For the purposes of this Act, the forms and ceremonies used in administering an oath are immaterial, if the court or person before whom the oath is taken has power to administer an oath for the purpose of verifying the statement in question, and if the oath has been administered in a form and with ceremonies which the person taking the oath has accepted without objection, or has declared to be binding on him.
>
> (2) In this Act—
>> "The expression 'oath' in the case of persons for the time being allowed by law to affirm or declare instead of swearing, includes 'affirmation' and 'declaration', and the expression 'swear' in the like case includes 'affirm' and 'declare'. . . ."[8]

In a criminal case, a child of tender years who does not understand the nature of an oath but is of sufficient intelligence to justify the reception of his evidence and does understand the duty of speaking the truth, may be allowed to give unsworn evidence.   Such a child, wilfully giving false evidence in such circumstances that it would be perjury if he had taken the oath is, if of the age of ten or above,[9] liable to punishment on summary conviction.[10]

A person who is not a competent witness but is sworn by mistake cannot be indicted for perjury.   This was decided in *Clegg*[11] where D, the accused in a criminal case, tricked the court into receiving his evidence by pretending to be his own son, and was held not indictable for perjury.   Since 1898, of course, an accused person is competent to give evidence for the defence at every stage of the proceedings and may be convicted of perjury even if the false evidence is given after verdict in mitigation of punishment but on oath.[12]

It is a defence to a charge of perjury that D was not lawfully sworn.   So in *Pritam Singh*[13] the case was withdrawn from the jury where D, a Sikh, had given evidence on affirmation although the taking of an oath was not contrary to his religious belief, because the copy of the holy book of the Sikhs was not available

---

[5] Co. 3 Inst. 165.
[6] *Omychund* v. *Barker* (1744), 1 Atk. 21.
[7] Oaths Act 1888, s. 1.
[8] On declarations, see below, p. 511.
[9] Above, p. 110.
[10] Children and Young Persons Act 1933, s. 38.
[11] (1868), 19 L.T. 47.
[12] *Wheeler*, [1917] 1 K.B. 283.
[13] [1958] 1 All E.R. 199.

in the magistrates' court. If the same situation arose today, D, having been affirmed, would be "lawfully sworn" for the purpose of the perjury trial by virtue of the Oaths Act 1961.

2 A Judicial Proceeding

By s. 1 (2) of the Perjury Act 1911:

"The expression 'judicial proceeding' includes a proceeding before any court, tribunal, or person having by law power to hear, receive, and examine evidence on oath."

Clearly, proceedings in all the ordinary courts of law, courts-martial and tribunals appointed under the Tribunals of Inquiry (Evidence) Act 1921 are judicial proceedings. Two Special Commissioners of Income Tax sitting to hear an appeal against an assessment to sur-tax constitute a judicial tribunal;[14] but where licensing justices held a special preliminary meeting, for which there was no statutory authority, they had no power to administer an oath, and thus the proceeding was not a judicial one.[15] Even though the oath be properly administered by the person having power to receive evidence on oath, there can be no perjury if that person should withdraw. This was decided in *Lloyd*,[16] where D was sworn in a bankruptcy proceeding before a county court registrar, but examined in another room in the absence of the registrar, no person having power to receive evidence on oath being present.

If the court before which the proceeding is brought lacks jurisdiction to deal with it, perjury is impossible. So where D gave false evidence against E on an information for furious *riding* contrary to the Highway Act 1835 his conviction for perjury was quashed, since only furious *driving* was an offence under the Act.[17] But D's conviction was affirmed where he swore falsely in an action brought by him in a fictitious name against defendants.[18] This was primarily because the Commissioners for Oaths Act 1889,[19] under which the prosecution was brought extended to

"every case where, *if he had so sworn in a judicial proceeding* before a court of competent jurisdiction, he would be guilty of perjury;"

but the court also thought that the proceedings were judicial proceedings.

The statement need not have been made before the tribunal itself. It is enough that it is made for the purposes of the judicial proceedings before a person authorised to administer an oath and to record or authenticate the statement.[20] A statement so made in England for the purposes of a judicial proceeding anywhere abroad[21] is treated as a statement made in a judicial proceeding in England. Where a person is sworn outside England for the purposes

---

[14] *Hood-Barrs*, [1943] 1 K.B. 455; [1943] 1 All E.R. 665.
[15] *Shaw* (1911), 6 Cr. App. Rep. 103.
[16] (1887), 19 Q.B.D. 213.
[17] *Bacon* (1870), 11 Cox C.C. 540; and see cases in 15 *English and Empire Digest* (Repl.) 817–819. Presumably it is perjury to give false testimony in an inquiry by the court to ascertain whether it has jurisdiction, whatever the outcome of that inquiry.
[18] *Castiglione and Porteous* (1912), 7 Cr. App. Rep. 233.
[19] Repealed by the Perjury Act 1911.
[20] Perjury Act 1911, s. 1 (3).
[21] This seems to be the effect of s. 1 (4).

of a judicial proceeding in England the statement is to be treated as if made in that proceeding, only if the person,

> ". . . . is lawfully sworn under an Act of Parliament—
>
> > (a) in any other part of His Majesty's dominions; or
> >
> > (b) before a British tribunal or a British officer in a foreign country, or within the jurisdiction of the Admiralty of England."[1]

3 "A Statement Material in that Proceeding"

The doctrine that the statement must be material goes back to Coke:[2]

> "For if it be not materiall, then though it be false, yet it is no perjury, because it concerneth not the point in suit, and therefore in effect it is extra-judiciall. Also this act[3] giveth remedy to the party grieved, and if the deposition be not materiall, he cannot be grieved thereby."

According to Stephen[4] the doctrine is based on a misunderstanding of Bracton but, however, this may be, it became an established part of the common law, which is preserved by the Act. Settling a disputed point, the Act provides:[5]

> "The question whether a statement on which perjury is assigned was material is a question of law to be determined by the court of trial."

The rule exempting immaterial statements from the sanctions of perjury has been very narrowly construed—so narrowly that clear illustrations of its operation are not very easy to find. In *Townsend*[6] a statement was held to be immaterial where it was made in the course of a preliminary inquiry by magistrates into the truth of an alleged criminal libel, truth being irrelevant to such a charge at common law.[7] Similarly, in *Tate*,[8] D was acquitted of perjury where, at a trial for assault, he said that he had seen the defendant's wife committing adultery. The wife's adultery could affect neither the fact of the assault nor the defendant's liability for it and was therefore held immaterial.

The Court of Criminal Appeal has said[9] that it could not accept everything that COCKBURN, C.J., said in *Tate*; but it may be that this refers to the fact that COCKBURN, C.J., apparently considered that it made no difference that the adultery might have been relevant to the *punishment* of the defendant in the assault case, as affording provocation. It is now clear that evidence on oath directed solely to the issue of punishment—and even where given by the accused after conviction—is material.[10] But just as provocation might be relevant to punishment on a charge of assault, so might the truth of a statement in a charge of libel even if it were no defence in law. If this is an objection to *Tate*, it is equally an objection to *Townsend*.[6]

A statement is obviously material if it bears directly on the result of the case. So D was guilty of perjury where he falsely swore that his Christian name was

---

[1] Perjury Act 1911, s. 1 (5); But see *O'Mealy* v. *Newell* (1807), 8 East, 364 at p. 372 below, p. 514, footnote 5.
[2] 3 Inst. 167.
[3] 5 Eliz. 1, c. 9.
[4] 3 H.C.L. 248.
[5] Section 1 (6).
[6] (1866), 4 F. & F. 1089.
[7] Below, p. 548.
[8] (1871), 12 Cox C.C. 7.
[9] In *Hewitt* (1913), 9 Cr. App. Rep. 192 at p. 195.
[10] *Wheeler*, [1917] 1 K.B. 283; above, p. 504.

"Edward" and not, as was in fact the case, "Bernard Edward" with the result that the judge struck out the case because it had been brought against him in the latter name.[11]

Equally, circumstantial evidence is material, as where D, testifying to E's alibi, says not only (i) that E was in a certain house at the time of the crime (which is the matter directly in issue) but (ii) that he has lived there for two years and (iii) that he has never been absent during that time. All three statements are material,[12] for the second and third are circumstantial evidence supporting the first.

In *Phillpotts*[13] it was held that false testimony directed to procuring the admission of evidence which may be inadmissible on another ground is perjury. D swore falsely that he had examined a copy of a document with the original, with the object of having the copy admitted in evidence. It was held that he was guilty, notwithstanding that the copy would have been inadmissible even though it *had* been examined with the original. The argument to the contrary, said CAMPBELL, C.J.,[14] had the effect of

> "making the offence of perjury to depend upon whether a judge were right or wrong in his direction on a question of law, and upon the decision of some nice point in a bill of exceptions, which might ultimately go to the House of Lords."

The evidence must be material "in that proceeding", not necessarily in the main issue which falls for decision. So it seems clear that an answer to a question going solely to the witness's credit and not at all to the question to be decided, is material.[15] In *Baker*[16] Lord RUSSELL, C.J., held that

> "the defendant's answers would affect his credit as a witness, and all false statements wilfully and corruptly made, as to matters which affect his credit, are material."

So in *Lavey*[17] D brought an action for goods sold and, in answer to a question put in cross-examination to test her credit, said that she had never been tried at the Old Bailey. This was untrue and Lord CAMPBELL, C.J., told the jury that it was material if it might have influenced the County Court judge in believing or disbelieving her other statements.[18]

Where a matter is put to a witness in cross-examination which goes solely to his credit and he denies it, the general rule is that his answer is final and evidence is not admissible to rebut his denial. It was, no doubt, for this reason that the court held in *Murray*[1] that D was not indictable for false statements made when he was permitted to testify in rebuttal of a witness's denial under cross-examination. On similar facts, however, the opposite result was reached in *Gibbons*[2]

---

[11] *Mullany* (1865), Le. & Ca. 593. ERLE, C.J., said that his inclination was to hold that any false swearing in a judicial proceeding with intent to mislead should be perjury whether it was material or not. But this was obviously not necessary to the decision and the Perjury Act settles the matter to the contrary.

[12] *Tyson* (1867), L.R. 1 C.C.R. 107.

[13] (1851), 2 Den. 302.

[14] *Ibid.*, at p. 309.

[15] *Griepe* (1697), 1 Ld. Raym. 256 at p. 259, *per* HOLT, C.J.; *Overton* (1842), 2 Mood. C.C. 263 at pp. 266, 267, *per* Lord DENMAN, C.J. *Worley* (1849), 3 Cox C.C. 535, seems to be an indulgent decision.

[16] [1895] 1 Q.B. 797 at p. 799.

[17] (1850), 3 Car. & Kir. 26.

[18] Today the question of materiality would be wholly for the judge; above, p. 506.

[1] (1858), 1 F. & F. 80.

[2] (1862), 9 Cox C.C. 105.

where eleven judges (MARTIN, B., and CROMPTON, J., *dubitantibus*) held that D was guilty, apparently because his statement, though inadmissible in law, was logically relevant to the question to be decided—that is the witness's credibility. The court relied upon Hawkins:[3]

> ". . . . though the evidence signify nothing to the merits of the cause and is immaterial, yet, if it has a direct tendency to corroborate the evidence concerning what is material, it is equally criminal in its own nature, and equally tends to abuse the administration of justice, and there does not seem to be any reason why it should not be equally punishable."

But what value is "tendency to corroborate", if the court is bound in law to ignore the evidence? The case goes farther than any other[4] and there is force in the objection of MARTIN, B.:[5]

> "I cannot conceive how the error of the magistrates can make that evidence material in the sense in which it should be material to support an assignment of perjury upon it."

If *Gibbons* is correctly decided, this is another reason for doubting *Tate*,[6] though the decisions may be technically distinguishable—in *Gibbons* the evidence was directed to an issue which the magistrates were entitled to try—the veracity of the witness; in *Tate*, it was directed to an issue that was not before them at all.

Stephen thought that the interpretation of the law relating to materiality by MAULE, J., in *Phillpotts*[7] "would practically get rid of the doctrine altogether."[8] MAULE, J. said of the evidence in dispute:

> ". . . it is material to the judicial proceeding, and it is not necessary that it should have been relevant and material to the issue being tried."

This is substantially the doctrine adopted by the Perjury Act. As Stephen said:

> "It is difficult to imagine a case in which a person would be under any temptation to introduce into his evidence a deliberate lie about a matter absolutely irrelevant to the matter before the court."[9]

Perhaps the statement is only immaterial where

> "it is so irrelevant that it is no longer made by a person in the character of participant in the proceedings;"[10]

as if in answer to a question, "Were you at York on a certain day?", the witness were to reply, "Yes, and A.B. picked my pocket there", such statement having nothing whatever to do with the inquiry in hand. It was such a case that HOLT, C.J., used as an example in *Griepe*:[11]

> ". . . if A being produced as a witness to prove that B was *compos mentis* when he made his will, swears that such a day he left his own house and went to C and lay there, and the next day lay at D, etc., if he swears falsely in these circumstances immaterial to the point of the issue, it will not be perjury."

---

[3] 1 P.C., c. 69.

[4] There was no question of the admissibility of the evidence turning on a nice point of law as in *Philpotts*, above, p. 507.

[5] 9 Cox C.C. at p. 109.

[6] Above, p. 506.

[7] (1851), 2 Den. 302 at p. 306; above, p. 507.

[8] 3 H.C.L. 249.

[9] *Ibid.* An example might be that of a woman who, out of motives of vanity, lies about her age when that is irrelevant to any issue before the court.

[10] Street, *Torts*, 316, stating the rule under which a witness loses his privilege for the purposes of defamation. It would not be inappropriate that the extent of the privilege should be co-extensive with the liability to perjury.

[11] (1697), 1 Ld. Raym. 256 at p. 259.

4 The Statement may be True

It was no defence at common law that the statement was in fact true, if D believed it to be false, or was reckless whether it be true or false.[12] This rule appears to be preserved by the wording of s. 1 of the Perjury Act 1911. This has the curious result that every material statement made on oath in a judicial proceeding is the *actus reus* of perjury; for, beyond the making of such a statement, nothing more need be proved than that D made it with *mens rea*.[13]

5 The Statement may be an Opinion

It is often said in the older authorities that it is not perjury unless the matter be stated "absolutely and directly".[14] Of course, the statement must be one which is sufficiently precise[15] to be capable of being proved false. If the statement is ambiguous, being true in one sense and false in the other, the Crown must prove that D used it in the false sense:[16] that is, that he intended it to be understood in the false sense. It is not clear that more than this is required. Thus it used to be said that an expression of opinion or belief was not enough but in *Schlesinger*[17] the Queen's Bench held that an expression of opinion, when that opinion is not genuinely held, is perjury.[18] The witness had stated that he "thought" a certain writing was not his, whereas in truth, he thought it was. The court recognised that this may be very difficult to prove; but that was not a good reason for holding it not to be perjury where it could be proved.

6 Mens Rea

The statement must be one which D "knows to be false or does not believe to be true." That is, either intention or recklessness will suffice. Negligence, of course, is not enough.

> "It seemeth that no one ought to be found guilty thereof without clear proof, that the false oath alleged against him was taken with some degree of deliberation; for if, upon the whole circumstances of the case, it shall appear probable, that it was owing rather to the weakness than perverseness of the party, as where it was occasioned by surprise, or inadvertency, or a mistake of the true state of the question, it cannot but be hard to make it amount to voluntary and corrupt perjury . . ."[19]

---

[12] Co. 3 Inst. 160; Hawkins, 1 P.C., c. 27, §§ 3, 6; *Ockley and Whitlesbye's* case (1622), Palm. 294; *Allen* v. *Westley* (1629), Het. 97; Stephen, *Digest* (4th ed.), 95, 96.

[13] Where D has made contradictory statements on oath he cannot be convicted of perjury unless it is proved which of the statements is the false one and that D knew it to be false; or that, *on a specified occasion*, D made a statement which he did not believe to be true. It may, therefore, be quite clear that D has committed perjury on one occasion or the other but not possible to establish which. In that case, D must be acquitted. The Criminal Law Revision Committee has reluctantly but unanimously decided not to recommend legislation aimed at persons who dishonestly contradict their evidence: Sixth Report (Cmnd. 2465).

[14] Co. 3 Inst. 166; Hawkins, 1 P.C., c. 27, § 7.

[15] In *Crespigny* (1795), 1 Esp. 280, Lord KENYON directed an acquittal apparently because the statement was as to the effect of a deed; but why should not this be perjury if D stated the effect to be other than he believed it to be? The true construction of the deed is immaterial. *Supra*.

[16] *Hayford* (1922), 62 D.L.R. 90.

[17] (1867), 10 Q.B. 670.

[18] The propositions to the contrary in Coke and Hawkins, above, must be considered wrong.

[19] Hawkins, 1 P.C., c. 27, § 2, p. 429.

The presence of the word, "wilfully", emphasises that a degree of deliberation is required. Thus,

> "the attention of a witness ought to be called to the point upon which his answer is supposed to be erroneous before a charge for perjury can be founded upon it."[20]

If a man states that which he believes to be true, he is not guilty of perjury though he knows that the court may draw from his assertion a conclusion that he knows to be untrue, and though the statement is in fact false.[1]

7 Subornation of Perjury

Section 7 of the Perjury Act provides:

> "(1) Every person who aids, abets, counsels, procures, or suborns another person to commit an offence against this Act shall be liable to be proceeded against, indicted, tried and punished as if he were a principal offender."

This seems to add nothing to the general law.[2]

Subornation of perjury was an independent misdemeanour at common law. It consisted in procuring another to commit perjury. It was regarded as a separate offence apparently because the suborner was considered to be more blameworthy than the actual perjurer: *"plus peccat author quam actor."*[3]

Subornation is no longer of any importance, as such, and the reference to it in the section seems to be entirely unnecessary, as its meaning is comprehended in "procures."

2 OFFENCES AKIN TO PERJURY

1 Statements on Oath not in Judicial Proceedings and False Statements with reference to Marriage

By s. 2 of the Perjury Act 1911:

> "If any person—
>
> (1) being required or authorised by law to make any statement on oath for any purpose, and being lawfully sworn (otherwise than in a judicial proceeding) wilfully makes a statement which is material for that purpose and which he knows to be false or does not believe to be true; or
>
> (2) wilfully uses any false affidavit for the purposes of the Bills of Sale Act 1878, as amended by any subsequent enactment,
>
> he shall be guilty of a misdemeanour, and, on conviction thereof on indictment shall be liable to imprisonment for a term not exceeding seven years."

By s. 3 (1) of the Perjury Act 1911:

> "If any person—
>
> (a) for the purpose òf procuring a marriage, or a certificate or licence for marriages, knowingly and wilfully makes a false oath, or makes or signs a false declaration, notice or certificate required under any Act of Parliament for the time being in force relating to marriage; or

---

[20] *London* (1871), 24 L.T. 232 at p. 233, *per* WILLES, J.; *Stolady* (1859), 1 F. & F. 518
[1] *Penn*, [1966] Crim. L.R. 681.
[2] Above, p. 80.
[3] Co. 3 Inst. 167.

(b) knowingly and wilfully makes, or knowingly and wilfully causes to be made, for the purpose of being inserted in any register of marriage, a false statement as to any particular required by law to be known and registered relating to any marriage; or

(c) forbids the issue of any certificate or licence for marriage by falsely representing himself to be a person whose consent to the marriage is required by law knowing such representation to be false,

he shall be guilty of a misdemeanour, and, on conviction thereof on indictment shall be liable to imprisonment for a term not exceeding seven years or to a fine or to both such imprisonment and fine.

It will be observed that a person who commits bigamy in England could hardly fail to be guilty of one of these offences. But where D, who had been divorced, described himself as "a bachelor", it was held that he committed no offence under s. 3 (1) (b); for "bachelor" means "an unmarried man" and D was then unmarried.[4]

If the statement is not required to be made by law, no offence can be committed under ss. 3 (a) or 3 (b). So the use of a forged document, purporting to be the parents' consent to D's marriage, was held to be no offence under s. 3 (1) (a).[5] The document was a form used for the convenience of superintendent registrars but there was no statutory authority for it.[6]

2 False Statements as to Births or Deaths

Section 4 (1) of the Perjury Act 1911 creates offences, punishable with seven years' imprisonment on conviction on indictment, or with a fine of £50 on summary conviction, of wilfully[7] making false statements, etc., relating to the registration of births and deaths or to the live birth of a child.

3 False Statutory Declarations and Other False Statements without Oath

By s. 5 of the Perjury Act 1911:

"If any person knowingly and wilfully makes (otherwise than on oath) a statement false in a material particular, and the statement is made—

(a) in a statutory declaration; or

(b) in an abstract, account, balance sheet, book, certificate, return, or other document which he is authorised or required to make, attest, or verify, by any public general Act of Parliament for the time being in force; or

(c) in any oral declaration or oral answer which he is required to make by, under, or in pursuance of any public general Act of Parliament for the time being in force,

---

[4] *Peters*, [1955] Crim. L.R. 712 (London Q.S.).

[5] *Frickey and Frickey*, [1956] Crim. L.R. 421 (Southampton Q.S.).

[6] But D was no doubt guilty of forgery. The comment in [1956] Crim. L.R. 422 asserts that there was no intent to defraud, but see *Welham* v. *Director of Public Prosecutions*, above, p. 449.

[7] *Cf.* the problem which may arise where a woman who has been artificially inseminated with the seed of a donor gives birth to a child. "If the informant does not believe that there is a real possibility that the husband may be the father, then we think the law is being broken. If, on the other hand, he is, rightly or wrongly, under the impression that there is genuinely such a possibility we cannot see how he can be found guilty of the offence of perjury": Report of the Departmental Committee on Artificial Insemination (Cmnd. 1105), para. 94.

he shall be guilty of a misdemeanour and shall be liable on conviction thereof on indictment to imprisonment for any term not exceeding two years or to both such imprisonment and fine.

By s. 15 (2):

> The expression 'statutory declaration' means a declaration made by virtue of the Statutory Declarations Act 1835, or of any Act, Order in Council, rule or regulation applying or extending the provisions thereof;"

Before 1835, oaths were taken in a great number and wide variety of circumstances in the ordinary course of business. For example, an oath was required by the Bank of England of one who sought replacement of a mutilated banknote; of a churchwarden or sidesman on entering upon his office; and by the statutes regulating the business of pawnbrokers. The widespread use of the oath was not only very inconvenient, but also caused the oath to be regarded very lightly. The Act of 1835, therefore, provided that a "statutory declaration" in the form prescribed in the schedule to the Act should, or might, be substituted for an oath except in the case of an oath of allegiance and in the courts of justice. It will be noted that the false statutory declaration is much less severely punishable than the false statement on oath.

Under s. 5 (b) the written statement must be one which D is "authorised or required" to make, whereas under 5 (c) the oral statement must be "required" and it is not enough that it is authorised.[8]

4   False Declarations to Obtain Registration for Carrying on a Vocation

Section 6 of the Perjury Act 1911 makes it an offence, punishable with one year's imprisonment, to attempt to become registered on any statutory roll of persons qualified by law to practise any vocation or calling, by any written *or oral* representation known to be false or fraudulent.

3   PERVERTING THE COURSE OF JUSTICE

An attempt to pervert the course of justice, though most commonly indicted as a conspiracy, may be committed by only one person.[9] It has been used in cases where false evidence has been fabricated and where false statements have been made to officers of justice.

1   Fabrication of False Evidence

It was held by the Court for Crown Cases Reserved in *Vreones*[10] that the fabrication of false evidence for the purpose of misleading a judicial tribunal is a misdemeanour. Samples had been taken from a cargo of wheat and sealed with the seals of the buyer and seller for use, in the event of a dispute between the parties, in any arbitration which might take place. D opened the bags, substituted wheat of a different quality and forwarded them to the London Corn Trade Association. His conviction was affirmed and it was held irrelevant that the evidence was never tendered and that there was no tribunal in existence—for no arbitrator had been appointed. Lord COLERIDGE, C.J., with whom STEPHEN, CHARLES and LAWRENCE, JJ., agreed, seems to have regarded the offence as an *attempt* to pervert the course of justice. He stressed[11] that

"All that the defendant could do to commit the offence he did."

---

[8] See *Mailey*, [1957] Crim. L.R. 328, and comment thereon.
[9] *Grimes*, [1968] 3 All E.R. 179 (Judge KILNER BROWN).
[10] [1891] 1 Q.B. 360.
[11] On four occasions, *ibid.*, at pp. 367, 368.

In *Vreones* the bags were intended to be put in evidence. *Smalley*[12] goes a little farther in that there, statements of evidence fabricated by a police constable could not have been put in evidence but, (i) they might have led to D's superior officer applying for summonses, as he would not otherwise have done; (ii) on a plea of guilty, the accused might have been dealt with on the basis of the fabricated statements and (iii) on a plea of guilty, the case for the prosecution might have been opened falsely. D was convicted, apparently[13] on two counts: (i) fabricating evidence with intent to mislead a judicial tribunal; (ii) fabricating evidence with intent to pervert the course of justice. The case more clearly falls within the latter than the former.

As in *Vreones*, so in *Smalley*, D's conduct was sufficiently proximate to be an attempt,[14] for when he handed the "statements" to his superiors he had done all he could. It does not seem to be clear whether the fabrication of evidence with intent to pervert the course of justice is an offence if it is only a preparatory act. Suppose *Smalley* had been detected, or had changed his mind, after fabricating the statements and before giving them to his supervisors ?[15]

The course of justice is perverted if the court is misled by false evidence, even though that evidence be directed to the establishment of the truth. D perverts the course of justice by tendering false evidence to prove that he has not committed adultery even though, in fact, he has not committed adultery.[16]

2   Making or Using False Statements

Conspiracy to make false statements to officers of justice with a view to perverting the course of, or preventing, judicial proceedings is a misdemeanour. In *Field*,[17] D1 and D2 were convicted of conspiracy to pervert the course of justice by concealing the identity of a certain person by making false statements to the police.[18] In *Sharpe*,[19] the conspiracy was to procure a third person to make an untrue statement. All the cases are of conspiracy,[20] and it cannot be taken as settled that the same acts done by an individual would be indictable; but analogy with *Vreones*[1] suggests that they would. In Australia it was held to be a common law misdemeanour to send false and forged documents to a judge in support of a petition for an enquiry (which the judge has a statutory power to order) into D's conviction.[2] But a similar petition supported by nothing other than D's own false statement was held not indictable.[3]

---

[12] [1959] Crim. L.R. 587 (Leeds Assizes, Mr. Commissioner G. C. Baker, Q.C.). *Cf.* *Bailey*, [1956] N.I. 15.
[13] The report is not absolutely clear about this.
[14] Above, pp. 163 *et seq.*
[15] See also *Eddols* (1910), Bristol Assizes, cited in Archbold, § 3544; *White* (1906), 4 C.L.R. 153. Report of the Criminal Code Commission (1879), 21, cited in Williams, C.L.G.P. 416.
[16] *Senat* (1968), 52 Cr. App. Rep. 282.
[17] [1964] 2 All E.R. 269. See also the cases discussed by Williams, C.L.G.P. 417.
[18] No doubt it was then a conspiracy to commit misprision of felony.
[19] [1938] 1 All E.R. 48.
[20] The Criminal Procedure Act 1851, s. 29, refers to "any *conspiracy* . . . to obstruct, prevent, pervert or defeat the course of public justice. . . ."
[1] Above, p. 512 and see *Grimes*; above, footnote 9.
[2] *White* (1906), 4 C.L.R. 152.
[3] *Ibid.* Similarly in New Zealand: *Cane* v. *R.*, [1968] N.Z.L.R. 787. *Cf. King*, [1965] 1 All E.R. 1053.

A false affidavit made out of the jurisdiction is not indictable as perjury unless it falls within the terms of s. 1 (5) of the Perjury Act 1911;[4] but, if it is used in an English court, the user commits a common law misdemeanour and may be committed for contempt of court.[5]

3   Interfering with Witnesses

It is a common law misdemeanour to attempt to dissuade or prevent a witness from appearing or giving evidence,[6] or to alter evidence previously given in a preliminary enquiry.[7]

This is so whether the proceedings in view are to be in an inferior court or a superior court of record; but, in the latter case, the offence is a contempt punishable summarily.[8]

4   Personating a Juryman

It is a misdemeanour at common law to personate a juryman even though D has no intention of perverting the course of justice or any dishonest intention other than of answering to the name of the juror summoned and taking his place on the jury.   This was decided in *Clark*,[9] where D who took the place of his employer, "under a kind of blind obedience" to the employer's behests, was held guilty.

5   Disposal of Corpse with Intent to Prevent an Inquest

If a person destroys or otherwise disposes of a dead body with intent to prevent an inquest being held, he is guilty of a common law misdemeanour, if the inquest intended to be held is one that might lawfully be held.[10] An inquest may lawfully be held if the coroner honestly believes information to be true which, if it were true, would make it his duty to hold an inquest.[11] It is not enough that the corpse has been concealed; the jury must be directed to convict only if satisfied of the intent.[12]

6   Embracery[13]

Embracery is a common law misdemeanour which consists in any attempt to influence a juror in the giving of a verdict otherwise than by evidence and arguments in open court.   It is, of course, committed if a bribe is offered to a juror, but it is not necessary to prove that D went to these lengths.   Conduct amounting to embracery is more likely to be dealt with today as a contempt of court.[14]

---

[4] Above, p. 506, footnote 1.
[5] *O'Mealy* v. *Newell* (1807), 8 East, 364 at p. 372.
[6] Co. 3 Inst. 139; *Shaw* v. *Shaw* (1861), 31 L.J.P.M. & A. 35.
[7] *Greenberg* (1919), 121 L.T. 288.
[8] Russell, 312, 313; below, p. 531.
[9] (1918), 82 J.P. 295 (AVORY, J.).
[10] *Stephenson* (1884), 13 Q.B.D. 331 (C.C.R.).
[11] *Ibid.*
[12] *Purcy* (1933), 149 L.T. 432.
[13] Russell, 357; Archbold, § 3452; Halsbury, Vol. 10, 622.
[14] Below, p. 531.

7 Prison Breaking, Escape and Rescue[15]

It is an offence at common law for one who is lawfully confined in connection with a criminal offence (whether before or after trial):

(1) To break out of the prison or other building in which he is confined. Unlike "breaking" under the common law of burglary,[16] an actual breaking must be proved and merely getting over the walls or passing through a door will not suffice.[17] An accidental breaking in the course of escape is enough. But if the breaking is effected by others without D's consent he does not commit the offence by escaping through the breach. If D is acquitted of the crime for which he was imprisoned he may not, thereafter, be convicted of prison breach.

(2) To escape from confinement without any breaking as, for example, where the doors are left open by the consent or negligence of the gaoler, or where D escapes through a breach made by others without his consent or connivance.[18]

The *mens rea* is an intention to escape from lawful custody and it must coincide with the act of withdrawing from lawful custody. One who withdraws from custody without intention to escape (because, for example, he has lost his memory) and thereafter deliberately remains at large does not commit the offence.[19]

It is a distinct offence for an officer of the law or a private person voluntarily to permit a prisoner to escape. If the prisoner was guilty of treason, so too is the officer who permits him to escape.[20] If the escape is through the *negligence* of the officer or private person, a misdemeanour punishable by a fine is committed.

Escaping or attempting to escape from prison is also an offence under the Prison Rules 1949, rule 44. Since this is technically not a criminal offence and is dealt with by the Visiting Committee and not a court, the imposition of punishment under the Rules is no bar to a subsequent charge either of prison breach or escape.[1]

By the Prison Act 1952, s. 39 it is an offence punishable with five years' imprisonment to aid the escape or attempted escape of a prisoner, or with intent to facilitate escape, to convey anything into or leave it outside a prison with a view to its coming into the possession of a prisoner.

Rescue is a common law misdemeanour consisting in forcibly liberating a prisoner from lawful custody. If the prisoner was gaoled for treason, the rescuer is also guilty of treason. The prisoner must be tried before the rescuer; and if the prisoner is acquitted, the rescuer can be convicted only of misdemeanour, whatever the nature of the charge against the prisoner.[2]

---

[15] Russell, Chs. 19–21; Archbold, §§ 3421–3445; Halsbury, Vol. 10, 635–640.

[16] See the first edition of this book at p. 398; and above, p. 409.

[17] *Burridge* (1735), 3 P. Wms. 439 at p. 484, *per* Lord HARDWICKE, C.J.; Archbold, § 1263; Russell, 332.

[18] Russell, 339; *Hinds* (1957), 41 Cr. App. Rep. 143; [1956] Crim. L.R. and commentary thereon.

[19] *Scott*, [1967] V.R. 276.

[20] Hale, 1 P.C. 593.

[1] *Hogan and Tompkins*, [1960] 2 Q.B. 513; [1960] 3 All E.R. 149; [1960] Crim. L.R. 775 and commentary thereon.

[2] For other similar offences see Prisoners of War Escape Act 1812, s. 1; Mental Health Act 1959, ss. 129, 139.

8 Public Mischief and Wasteful Employment of Police

In *Manley*[3] D reported to the police that she had been attacked and robbed and described her attacker. The story was entirely false. The police wasted their time in the investigation of her allegations and members of the public answering to the description she had given were put in peril of suspicion and arrest. She was convicted of committing a public mischief and her appeal to the Court of Criminal Appeal on the ground that there was no such offence known to the law was dismissed. The court relied upon decisions in conspiracy cases[4] and approved the statement of LAWRENCE, J., in *Higgins*[5] that

> "All offences of a public nature, that is, all such acts or attempts as tend to the prejudice of the community are indictable."

It is obvious that this proposition is immensely wide and could be used to make criminal any conduct which a prosecutor and the judges happened to concur in thinking undesirable. The case was severely criticised as a piece of judicial legislation which opened up "a gloomy vista of indefinite criminal liability."[6] In *Newland*[7] Lord GODDARD accepted the criticism of *Manley* that

> "In effect, it would leave the judges to declare new crimes and enable them to hold anything which they considered prejudicial to the community to be a misdemeanour. However beneficial that may have been in the days when Parliament met seldom, or at least only at long intervals, it surely is now the province of the legislature and not of the judiciary to create new criminal offences."[8]

and he concluded that "the safe course is no longer to follow it."[9] However, in other passages, the Lord Chief Justice admitted that the Court of Criminal Appeal is bound by *Manley*[10] so it may be that this amounted to no more than advice to prosecutors and *Manley* has never been overruled.[11] On the contrary, in *Shaw* v. *Director of Public Prosecutions* the Court of Criminal Appeal held that there is a substantive misdemeanour consisting in conduct calculated or intended to corrupt public morals—a concept which, though perhaps narrower than public mischief, is closely akin to it. While the House of Lords decided the case on a different ground, they did not disapprove of the decision of the Court of Criminal Appeal and it therefore presumably remains good law. The corruption of public morals would seem to be one variety of public mischief and, until *Manley* is overruled, it seems that public mischief exists as an independent misdemeanour.

It is convenient to deal with *Manley* here because of the particular facts of that case and most of those which have followed it;[13] but clearly the offence of public

---

[3] [1933] 1 K.B. 529.
[4] *Higgins* (1801), 2 East 5; *Brailsford*, [1905] 2 K.B. 730, and *Porter*, [1910] 1 K.B. 369; above, pp. 160–161.
[5] (1801), 2 East at p. 21.
[6] Stallybrass, "Public Mischief" (1933), 49 L.Q.R. 183; M.A.C.L. 66.
[7] [1954] 1 Q.B. 158; [1953] 2 All E.R. 1067; *cf. Joshua* v. *R.*, [1955] A.C. 121; [1955] 1 All E.R. 22 (P.C.).
[8] [1954] 1 Q.B. at p. 167.
[9] *Ibid.*, at p. 168.
[10] *Ibid.*, at pp. 167, 168. But see *Taylor*, [1950] 2 K.B. 368; *Gould*, [1968] 2 Q.B. 65; [1968] 1 All E.R. 849.
[11] See the criticism of the decision in *Bailey*, [1956] N.I. 15.
[12] [1962] A.C. 220; [1961] 1 All E.R. 330 (C.C.A.); [1962] A.C. at p. 237; [1961] 2 All E.R. 446 (H.L.); above, p. 160.
[13] See Stallybrass, M.A.C.L. at p. 75.

mischief defies classification for it could embrace any offence discussed in this book. Thus, it was used in a case where the offence consisted in publishing articles attacking those of the Jewish faith.[14]

Section 5 (2) of the Criminal Law Act 1967 has created a new offence aimed at the kind of conduct which was the subject of the prosecution in *Manley.* The section provides:

> "Where a person causes any wasteful employment of the police by know-ingly making to any person a false report tending to show that an offence has been committed, or to give rise to apprehension for the safety of any persons or property, or tending to show that he has information material to any police inquiry, he shall be liable on summary conviction to imprisonment for not more than six months or to a fine of not more than two hundred pounds or to both."

The Criminal Law Revision Committee, when proposing this provision stated:[15]

> "We considered including a provision that the conduct in question should not in future be prosecuted as a public mischief (if that offence exists) but only as a summary offence under the clause; but we decided that a provision was unnecessary because, having regard to the creation of the new offence and to the observations in *Newland's* case, no prosecution for the public mischief offence would be likely to be instituted."

The new provision is, however, relatively narrow. Public servants other than the police may have their time wasted by false reports—for example, fire brigades, ambulance men and social workers and it might be thought appropriate to bring a prosecution for public mischief in such cases. The consent of the Director of Public Prosecutions is required for a prosecution under s. 5 (2), and any allega-tion of the commission of the common law offence must be reported to him by the police under the Prosecution of Offences Regulations 1946.

4   IMPEDING THE APPREHENSION OR PROSECUTION OF ARRESTABLE OFFENDERS

At common law anyone who gave to any party to a felony any assistance whatever, tending to and having the object of, enabling him to evade arrest, trial or punish-ment, was guilty of the felony as accessory after the fact. The whole of the law relating to accessories after the fact is repealed by the Criminal Law Act 1967 and is replaced by a new offence under s. 4 of that Act:

> "(1) Where a person has committed an arrestable offence, any other person who, knowing or believing him to be guilty of the offence or of some other arrestable offence, does without lawful authority or reasonable excuse any act with intent to impede his apprehension or prosecution shall be guilty of an offence.
>
> (2) If on the trial of an indictment for an arrestable offence the jury are satisfied that the offence charged (or some other offence of which the accused might on that charge be found guilty) was committed, but find the accused not guilty of it, they may find him guilty of any offence under subsection (1) above of which they are satisfied that he is guilty in relation to the offence charged (or that other offence).
>
> (3) A person committing an offence under subsection (1) above with intent to impede another person's apprehension or prosecution shall on conviction

---

[14] *Leese and Whitehead* (1936), *The Times*, September 19 and 22.
[15] Cmnd. 2659, para. 45.

on indictment be liable to imprisonment according to the gravity of the other person's offence, as follows:—

    (a) if that offence is one for which the sentence is fixed by law, he shall be liable to imprisonment for not more than ten years;

    (b) if it is one for which a person (not previously convicted) may be sentenced to imprisonment for a term of fourteen years, he shall be liable to imprisonment for not more than seven years;

    (c) if it is not one included above but is one for which a person (not previously convicted) may be sentenced to imprisonment for a term of ten years, he shall be liable to imprisonment for not more than five years;

    (d) in any other case, he shall be liable to imprisonment for not more than three years.

(1) THE ACTUS REUS

There are two elements in the *actus reus*: (i) an arrestable offence must have been committed by the person (O) whose apprehension or prosecution D is charged with impeding; and (ii) D must have done "any act" with the appropriate intent.

Once the arrestable offence has been proved, the remaining element in the *actus reus*—any act—is almost unlimited. There must be an *act*—an omission will not suffice—but it need not be an act having a natural tendency to impede the apprehension or prosecution of an offender. Where the act does not have such a tendency, however, it will be difficult to prove the intent, in the absence of a confession. The common instances of the offence will undoubtedly correspond to the typical ways of becoming an accessory after the fact under the old law—by concealing the offender, providing him with a car, food or money to enable him to escape, or destroying evidence against him. According to the Criminal Law Revision Committee,[16] "The requirement that there should be an attempt to 'impede' a prosecution will exclude mere persuasion not to prosecute". Yet words are no doubt a sufficient act; so that the offence would be committed by intentionally misdirecting police who were pursuing an offender, or making a false statement to a detective.[17]

An act done through an agent would be sufficient. Indeed, the mere authorisation of the agent would be a sufficient act, when done with intent to impede, to constitute the offence, though the agent never acted on it.

(2) THE MENS REA

There are two elements in the *mens rea*: (i) D must know or believe the offender to be guilty of the arrestable offence which he has actually committed, or some other arrestable offence; and (ii) D must intend to impede the apprehension or prosecution of the offender.

"Some other arrestable offence" must refer to an offence which O has not committed, for otherwise the words are redundant. If D thinks he has seen O commit a robbery and acts with intent to conceal this, he will be guilty, though O had in fact committed a murder and not a robbery. This is obviously as it should be, where, as in this example, D's belief relates to the transaction which constituted the actual offence. Suppose, however, that unknown to D, O committed murder last week. D believes, wrongly, that O committed bigamy two

---

[16] Cmnd. 2659, para. 28.
[17] This would amount to other offences as well; see above, pp. 258–263.

years ago. If D does an act with intent to impede O's prosecution for bigamy—such as burning O's letters—it would seem very odd indeed that he should be liable only because O committed murder last week—the murder has nothing to do with the case. This suggests that the supposed offence must arise from the same transaction as the actual offence (and, undoubtedly, this will normally be the case) but so to hold would require the imposition of some limitation on the express words of the section.[18]

If D thinks he sees R committing an arrestable offence and acts, intending to impede his apprehension or prosecution, is he guilty under s. 4 if it was in fact O whom he observed? Perhaps the question should be answered by making a distinction. If D does an act which he intends to assist the person whom he in fact observed, his mistake of identity should be immaterial. For example, he sends a constable, who is pursuing the offender, in the wrong direction. Here D knows that the *person he is assisting* has committed an arrestable offence, and that person has in fact done so. Suppose, on the other hand, that D fabricates evidence the following day so as to prove an alibi for R and this evidence could not, and was of course not intended to assist O, of whom D has never heard. Here he does not intend to assist the person whom he in fact observed. An indictment charging D with doing an act, knowing O to be guilty of an arrestable offence and with intent to impede his prosecution is plainly bad. If R has never committed an arrestable offence, it would seem that D is not guilty under the section;[19] if R once did commit an arrestable offence, then D is guilty unless the limitation tentatively suggested in the previous paragraph be imposed.

D must *know or believe*. "... some other arrestable offence" must be governed only by "believing" since, *ex hypothesi*, the offence has not been committed and, therefore, D cannot "know" it has. "... the offence"—the arrestable offence which has actually been committed—is probably governed both by "knowing" and "believing". "Believing" is probably intended to cover the case of the man who is reckless—who has a pretty shrewd idea that O is an arrestable offender and assists him regardless. If the word "believing" had not been included "knowing" might well have been construed to include wilful blindness.[20] Conceivably, it might still bear that broader meaning: D has a mere suspicion that O is an arrestable offender and, shutting his eyes to an obvious means of knowledge, assists him. He can hardly be said to "believe" in O's guilt—but it is arguable that he should be guilty.

In order to know or believe that an arrestable offence has been committed, D need know no law. It will be enough that he believes in the existence of facts which, whether he knows it or not, amount in law to an arrestable offence.[1] His ignorance of the law cannot afford a defence.[2] The position is, perhaps, not quite so obvious where D has a positive mistaken belief. D knows that there is a duty not to conceal arrestable offenders, but, knowing what O has done, is wrongly informed that it does not constitute an arrestable offence. Arguably, he now

---

[18] *Cf.* the discussion of s. 5, below, p. 522.
[19] Can D be convicted of an attempt to commit the offence? See above, p. 173.
[20] Above, p. 73.
[1] *Cf. Sykes* v. *Director of Public Prosecutions,* [1962] A.C. at p. 563; [1961] 3 All E.R. at p. 42.
[2] Above, p. 48.

has no *mens rea* on the ground that he has made a mistake of civil law,[3] whether there is a right to arrest being a civil and not a criminal matter.

The act must be done with intent to impede the arrestable offender's apprehension or prosecution. It seems that it must be proved that D's *purpose* was to impede, and that it is not enough that he knew his act would certainly impede if that was not his object or one of his objects; or, as it has been put above, that a "direct" and not merely an "oblique" intention is required.[4] At all events, this seems to be the Criminal Law Revision Committee's view of the clause which became s. 5. Discussing the case of harbouring, they wrote:

> "If the harbouring is done with the object of impeding apprehension or prosecution . . . it will be within the offence; if it is done merely by way of providing or continuing to provide the criminal with accommodation in the ordinary way, it will not; and juries will be able to tell the difference."[5]

If this be the correct interpretation of the section, then, as under the old law of accessories after the fact, a handler of stolen goods will not be guilty of an offence under s. 4, even where he knows that his conduct has the effect of impeding the apprehension or prosecution of the thief, if that is not his object.[6] Nor is D guilty if, by acts done with the object of avoiding his own arrest or prosecution, he knowingly impedes the arrest or prosecution of another.[7] If, however, D has the dual object of saving himself and the other from arrest or prosecution then, no doubt, he is guilty.

Under the old law, D was guilty as an accessory after the fact if he assisted a felon to evade his punishment by enabling him to escape or to remain at large. It is clearly not an offence under s. 5 to enable a convicted arrestable offender (as opposed to one awaiting trial) to escape from gaol; but this is not important as such acts will amount to other offences.[8] Whether it is an offence to assist such an arrestable offender who has escaped to remain at large depends on the interpretation of "apprehension". Does it extend beyond its obvious meaning of apprehension with a view to prosecution and include the re-arrest of the escaped convicted prisoner? There seems to be no reason why it should not be so interpreted.

Even though the act is done with intent to impede, it is not an offence if there is "lawful authority or reasonable excuse" for it. According to the Criminal Law Revision Committee:[9]

> "The exception for 'lawful authority' will cover an executive decision against a prosecution, and that for 'reasonable excuse' will avoid extending the offence to acts such as destroying the evidence of an offence (for example a worthless cheque) in pursuance of a legitimate agreement to refrain from prosecuting in consideration of the making good of loss caused by that offence."

It is possible that the exception may have some application outside this situation. As with the Prevention of Crime Act,[10] it enables the courts to afford a defence in circumstances in which they think it reasonable to do so.

---

[3] Above, p. 50.
[4] Above, p. 39.
[5] Cmnd. 2659, para. 30.
[6] *Andrews and Craig*, [1962] 3 All E.R. 961.
[7] *Jones.*, [1949] 1 K.B. 194; [1948] 2 All E.R. 964.
[8] See above, p. 515.
[9] Cmnd. 2659, para. 28.
[10] Above, p. 285.

(3) THE SENTENCE

Section 4 (3)[11] provides for a sliding scale of sentences which is related to the arrestable offence which has actually been committed. Where D believes that some other arrestable offence has been committed, the punishment to which he is liable is fixed according to the *actus reus*, not according to the *mens rea*. If D acts with intent to impede the apprehension of O whom he believes to have committed malicious wounding[12] (maximum, five years), he is liable to three years' imprisonment if his belief is correct; but if O has in fact committed murder, he is liable to ten years. This is another instance of the penalty being related to the harm, rather than the fault of the offender.[13]

It is clear that the arrestable offence which fixes the maximum under s. 4 must have been committed when the act of impeding takes place. D, rightly believing O to be guilty of malicious wounding, acts to impede his arrest. Subsequently, O's victim, P, dies, and O becomes guilty of murder. D is liable to only three and not ten years' imprisonment.

5 COMPOUNDING AN ARRESTABLE OFFENCE

The abolition of felonies by the Criminal Law Act 1967 eliminated two common law misdemeanours known respectively as compounding a felony and misprision of felony.[14] The former consisted in an agreement for consideration not to prosecute, or to impede a prosecution for, a felony. The latter consisted simply in an omission to report a felony to the police. In place of these offences s. 5 (1) of the Criminal Law Act enacts as follows:

> "Where a person has committed an arrestable offence, any other person who, knowing or believing that the offence or some other arrestable offence has been committed, and that he has information which might be of material assistance in securing the prosecution or conviction of an offender for it, accepts or agrees to accept for not disclosing that information any consideration other than the making good of loss or injury caused by the offence, or the making of reasonable compensation for that loss or injury, shall be liable on conviction on indictment to imprisonment for not more than two years."

This provision is much less far-reaching than the previous law. It is narrower than misprision in that the offence is committed only if D accepts or agrees to accept a consideration for not disclosing the information relating to the arrestable offence. It is narrower than compounding in that it is not now criminal to accept or agree to accept consideration for not disclosing information relating to the arrestable offence, if the consideration is no more than the making good of loss or injury caused by the offence or the making of reasonable compensation for that loss or injury.

(1) ACTUS REUS

There are two elements in the *actus reus*: (i) an arrestable offence must actually have been committed; and (ii) D must accept or agree to accept consideration for not disclosing information which he knows or believes to be material.

---

[11] Above, p. 517.
[12] Above, p. 264.
[13] Above, p. 8.
[14] See the first edition of this book, pp. 539–544.

The offence is committed only where D "accepts or agrees to accept" the consideration. The situation envisaged is that where an offer is made to D. If the offer comes from D, then he would seem to be guilty also of the much more serious offence of blackmail.[15] Consideration presumably bears much the same meaning as in the law of contract and extends to money, goods, services, or any act or forbearance.[16]

The new offence is wider than misprision and compounding in that it extends to all arrestable offences which, of course, include some crimes which were not felonies; but it is provided by s. 5 (5):

> "The compounding of an offence other than treason shall not be an offence otherwise than under this section."

It is thus clear that it is not an offence to agree to accept any consideration for not prosecuting a non-arrestable offence, though whether the resulting contract is enforceable is another matter.

The Act makes no provision for any privileged relationships (such as may have existed under the law of misprision) but proceedings may not be instituted without the consent of the Director of Public Prosecutions.[17]

(2) MENS REA

There are two elements in the *mens rea*. It must be proved that (i) D knew or believed that an arrestable offence had been committed and (ii) D intended to accept or to agree to accept consideration other than the making good of loss or the making of reasonable compensation.

Where D's knowledge or belief relates to the arrestable offence which has actually been committed, the application of the section seems quite straightforward. But D's belief may relate to some other arrestable offence which, *ex hypothesi*, has not been committed. Here D's acceptance, or agreement to accept consideration must relate to the offence which he believes to have been committed and thus not to the offence which has actually been committed since they are different. Under this section D's belief need not—as, under s. 4, it probably must[18]—be that an arrestable offence has been committed by the same person who has in fact committed such an offence. If D wrongly supposes that he has seen an arrestable offence committed by R and accepts consideration for not disclosing what he saw, he will be guilty if in fact he saw O committing an arrestable offence.

The result is that the argument advanced in connection with s. 4, that D's belief must relate to the transaction which resulted in the actual offence, is much stronger in relation to s. 5. If D wrongly supposes that R has committed an arrestable offence and accepts consideration for not disclosing that fact, his guilt can hardly be established by proving that some time, somewhere, someone committed an arrestable offence—for example, that Dr Crippen committed murder.[19] The offence which D supposes to have been committed must have something to do with the offence which has actually been committed. The most

---

[15] Above, p. 403.
[16] See Cheshire and Fifoot, *Law of Contract* (6th ed.), Chapter 2.
[17] Section 5 (3).
[18] See above, p. 519.
[19] Can D be convicted of an attempt to commit the offence? See above, p. 173.

obvious point of connection is that the real and the supposed offence must both arise out of the same transaction. An alternative view might be that it is sufficient if either (a) the two offences arise out of the same transaction or (b) they both relate to the same person. Unknown to D, O committed murder last week. D believes, wrongly, that O committed bigamy two years ago. O offers money to D "to keep his mouth shut". D, believing that O is talking about the bigamy, accepts. According to the first view put above, D is not guilty; according to the alternative view, he is. It is submitted that the first view is better; according to the second, D's liability depends entirely on chance.

If D's acceptance of consideration relates to the transaction in question, then it seems that it will be immaterial that is mistaken as to both (i) the nature of the arrestable offence; (ii) the identity of the perpetrator. He supposes he was saw R perpetrating a robbery. Actually, he saw O committing murder. If he accepts consideration for not disclosing what he saw he should be guilty.

The Criminal Law Revision Committee stated [20]

". . . the offence will not apply to a person who refrains from giving information because he does not think it right that the offender should be prosecuted or because of a promise of reparation by the offender. It would be difficult to justify making the offence apply to those cases."

It is difficult to see, however, how it can be a defence for D simply to say that he did not "think it right that the offender should be prosecuted", if he has accepted consideration for not disclosing information. Even if he convinces the court of his views as to the impropriety of the contemplated prosecution he still falls within the express words of the section. He could be acquitted only if the section were interpreted so as to require that D's object or motive be the acquisition of the consideration. As we have seen,[1] on a charge under s. 4, it is probable that a *purpose* of impeding must be proved, but this may be justified by giving a narrow meaning to the ulterior intent specified in that section. No ulterior intent is specified in s. 5 and, consequently, it is difficult to see how the section can be limited in the same way.

In the light of the new rules about compounding, it is perhaps a little surprising that the offence of advertising rewards for the return of goods stolen or lost has been retained.[2] Section 23 of the Theft Act provides:

"Where any public advertisement of a reward for the return of any goods which have been stolen or lost uses any words to the effect that no questions will be asked, or that the person producing the goods will be safe from apprehension or inquiry, or that any money paid for the purchase of the goods or advanced by way of loan on them will be repaid, the person advertising the reward and any person who prints or publishes the advertisement shall on summary conviction be liable to a fine not exceeding one hundred pounds.'

In so far as an advertisement states that "no questions will be asked", it is only proposing what is perfectly lawful under s. 5 (1) of the Criminal Law Act.[3] It is not clear why this should be an offence because it is done through a public advertisement. Nor is it clear why it should be an offence to offer a reward for

---

[20] Cmnd. 2659, para. 41.

[1] Above, p. 520.

[2] The section replaces s. 102 of the Larceny Act 1861 which provided for a penalty of £50 recoverable by a common informer. This was changed to a fine of £100 by the Common Informers Act 1951. The Criminal Law Revision Committee hesitantly recommended the retention of the provision "as advertisements of this kind may encourage dishonesty": Cmnd. 2977, para. 144.

[3] Above, p. 521.

the return of stolen goods, even their return by the thief. The promise to pay the reward might be unenforceable for lack of consideration but, if it were actually paid, there would be nothing unlawful about that. Possibly the theory is that, if such advertisements were common, theft might be encouraged in that thieves would have an easy and safe way of disposing of the stolen goods for reward. This cannot apply to an advertisement addressed to the bona fide purchaser offering to recompense him if he will return the stolen goods; this seems quite a reasonable thing to do, especially since the bona fide purchaser commits no offence by retaining the goods for himself.[4]

"Stolen" bears the wide meaning given to that word by s. 24 (4) of the Theft Act so the bona fide purchaser may indeed have become the absolute owner of the goods where, for example, they have been obtained by deception and the property passed.

6 CONTEMPT OF COURT[5]

Contempts are of two kinds:

(1) Criminal contempt, which consists in acts tending to obstruct the due administration of justice.

(2) Civil contempt,[6] which consists in disobedience to the judgments, orders or other process of the superior courts.[7]

The distinction between the two types of contempt is not always by any means clear-cut; but certain important differences in the nature of the proceedings flow from it.

Criminal contempt is a common law misdemeanour which may be dealt with either on indictment in accordance with ordinary criminal procedure or under the jurisdiction of the superior courts to punish contempt by the summary process of attachment or committal.[8] The object of the proceeding is punitive, and a fine[9] or a sentence for a definite term of imprisonment may be imposed. The court has no power to release D before the expiration of that term, even though satisfied that he has purged his contempt.[10] As it is a criminal proceeding, the sentence may be remitted by the Crown.

Civil contempt, on the other hand, may be dealt with only by summary process and an indictment will not lie. The object of the proceedings is not punitive but coercive and a sentence for a definite term need not be imposed. D

---

[4] Above, p. 356.

[5] Fox, *Contempt of Court*; Street, *Freedom, the Individual and the Law*, Ch. 6; Fischer "Civil and Criminal Aspects of Contempt of Court" (1956), 34 Can. Bar. Rev. 121; Beale, "Contempt of Court, Civil and Criminal" (1908), 21 Harv. L.R. 161; Goodhart "Newspapers and Contempt of Court in English Law" (1935), 48 Harv. L.R. 885; D. G. T. Williams, [1961] Crim. L.R. at 92 *et seq.*; Miller, "Contempt of Court: the Sub Judice Rule", [1968] Crim. L.R. 63, 137 and 191.

[6] Sometimes called "contempt in procedure": Halsbury, Vol. 10, p. 20.

[7] Disobedience to the orders of justices of the peace is a common law misdemeanour: *Robinson* (1759), 2 Burr. 799 at p. 804. And see the Magistrates Courts' Act 1952, s. 54.

[8] See Halsbury, Vol. 8, p. 30. Contempt seems invariably to be dealt with by summary process, the last case of trial by indictment apparently being *Tibbitts*, [1902] 1 K.B. 77; D. G. T. Williams, [1961] Crim. L.R. at p. 93.

[9] *Davison* (1821), 4 B. & Ald. 329.

[10] *A.G.* v. *James*, [1962] 2 Q.B. 637; [1962] 1 All E.R. 255.

may be released by the court when he has purged his contempt; but the Crown never interferes.[11]   Where D intentionally disobeys an order of the court, the proceedings may have the dual purpose (i) of enforcing the order for the benefit of the person in whose favour it was awarded and (ii) of punishing D for having "contumaciously set at naught" the order of the court.[12]   In this case the proceeding is civil and it therefore seems that if D2 aids and abets D1 in disobeying an order of the court made against D1 only, D2's contempt is criminal, whereas D1's is civil.[13]

While there has always been a right of appeal to the Court of Appeal from a committal for civil contempt,[14] no appeal lay from a committal[15] for criminal contempt until the Administration of Justice Act 1960.[16]   By s. 13 of this Act, a right of appeal to the Court of Appeal is provided for all cases of contempt, both civil and criminal.

This book is concerned only with criminal contempts.   These take various forms which are considered below.

1   Contempt in the Face of the Court

Contempt in the face of the court consists in words or action in the presence of the court which interferes or tends to interfere with the course of justice.[17]

It is obviously a contempt to make a physical attack on the judge,[18] jury, counsel, witnesses or potential witnesses[19] or to use threatening language against them.   Language which is merely insulting to the judge[20] or jury[1] may amount to a contempt; but this is said to be "very different" from an insult to counsel or to the opposing litigant.[2]   It may be enough, however, that the language used of the opposing litigant is so outrageous and provocative as to be likely to lead to a brawl in court.[3]

Defiance of the proper order of the court is a contempt, as where a person persists in the use of language or a line of conduct against the ruling of the judge; or a witness refuses to be sworn, or to answer,[4] or does not leave the court when told to do so.[5]

---

[11] According to the Attorney General (Sir Charles Russell), *arguendo*, ". . . though the Crown could interfere, it would be unconstitutional to do so": *Re Special Reference from the Bahama Islands*, [1893] A.C. 138 at p. 145 (P.C.); *Seaward* v. *Paterson*, [1897] 1 Ch. 545 at p. 559 (C.A.), *per* RIGBY, L.J.

[12] *Seaward* v. *Paterson*, [1897] 1 Ch. at pp. 555, 556 (C.A.), *per* LINDLEY, L.J.

[13] *Ibid.* But Lord ATKINSON thought there was an absurdity in holding that D2 was a criminal because he did what he was *not* prohibited from doing, yet D1 was not a criminal though he did the same thing, which he *was* prohibited from doing: *Scott* v. *Scott*, [1913] A.C. 417 at pp. 456–460.

[14] *Scott* v. *Scott*, [1912] P. 241 at p. 285, *per* FLETCHER MOULTON, L.J.

[15] As distinct from a conviction on indictment where, of course, there was an appeal to the Court of Criminal Appeal.

[16] See D. G. T. Williams, [1960] Crim. L.R. 87, at pp. 92–100.

[17] *Parashuram* v. *R.*, [1945] A.C. 264 at p. 268, *per* Lord GODDARD, C.J.

[18] *Re Cosgrave*, Seton's *Judgments and Orders* (7th ed.), 457, discussed in 38 L.Q.R. at 185 (throwing an egg at the judge).

[19] *Re. B. (J.A.) (an infant)*, [1965] Ch. 1112; [1965] 168 at p. 174, *per* CROSS, J.

[20] *Davison* (1821), 4 B. & Ald. 329.

[1] *Ex parte Pater* (1864), 5 B. & S. 299.

[2] [1945] A.C. at p. 269 *per* Lord GODDARD, C.J.

[3] *Ibid.*

[4] *Ex parte Fernandez* (1861), 10 C.B.N.S. 3.

[5] *Chandler* v. *Horne* (1842), 2 Mood. & R. 423.

2 Contempt out of Court in relation to Future Proceedings

Any action which may have the effect, or which is intended to have the effect[6] of prejudicing the fair trial of a pending proceeding, whether civil or criminal, is a contempt. Threatening or intimidating parties, witnesses or jurors, or offering bribes are obvious examples. To offer a witness a fee for his story would almost certainly be a contempt if the fee were contingent on the case being decided in a particular way.[7] Any private communication to a judge for the purpose of improperly influencing his decision is a contempt, whether it is accompanied by a bribe or not.[8] A juror who discusses the case (except with his fellow-jurors) before verdict and anyone not on that jury who discusses it with him is guilty. The problem has arisen principally, however, in relation to comment, particularly in newspapers and magazines, on the pending case or the parties to it.

(a) Proceedings which are "pending or imminent".—Criminal proceedings are pending for this purpose at the latest from the moment the accused has been arrested and is in custody, though he has not yet been brought before any court.[9] It now appears clear that contempt may be possible at a still earlier stage.[10] The Administration of Justice Act 1960, s. 11,[11] appears to assume that contempt can be committed when proceedings are "pending *or imminent*". In reliance on this wording, it has been held in Northern Ireland[12] to be contempt to publish information about a man who was at the time suspected but not yet arrested or charged. The Australian High Court, on the other hand, has recently held that there can be no contempt unless proceedings have commenced (as by arrest and charging) and that it is not enough that they are imminent.[13] WINDEYER, J., suggested the possibility that the Act might have effected a change in English law.[14] The object of the Act was, however, to afford new defences to charges of contempt,[15] not to extend the law; and it is submitted that it should not be so construed as to increase the scope of criminal liability by a side-wind. At all events—whether because of the Act or because of its interpretation of the common law—the Court of Appeal has made it very clear in its most recent decision that the protection of the law extends to proceedings which are not yet pending. In *Savundranayagan*.[16] SALMON, L.J., said:

> "It must not be supposed that proceedings to commit for contempt of court can be instituted only in respect of matters published after proceedings have actually begun. No one should imagine that he is safe from committal from contempt of court if, knowing or having good reason to believe that criminal proceedings are imminent, he chooses to publish matters calculated to prejudice a fair trial."

---

[6] *Skipworth and Castro* (1873), L.R. 9 Q.B. 230; and see C. J. Miller, *op. cit.*, at p. 191.

[7] See Parliamentary Debates, Official Report (H.C.) Vol. 728, col. 400.

[8] *Per* COTTENHAM, L.C., *Re Ludlow Charities, Lechmere Charlton's* case (1837), 2 My. & Cr. 316 at p. 319; *Re Dyce Sombre* (1849), 1 Mac. & G. 116 at p. 122. It would not, of course, be contemptuous to write to a judge drawing attention to relevant evidence or to an authority on a point of law involved in the case.

[9] *Clarke, ex parte Crippen* (1910), 103 L.T. 636; *Stirling* v. *Associated Newspapers, Ltd.*, 1960 S.L.T. 5.

[10] "It is possible very effectually to poison the fountain of justice before it begins to flow": *Parke*, [1903] 2 K.B. 432 at p. 438 *per* WILLS, J. And see *Daily Mirror, ex parte Smith*, [1927] 1 K.B. 845 at p. 851, *per* Lord HEWART.

[11] Below, p. 528.

[12] *Beaverbrook Newspapers, Ltd.*, [1962] N.I. 15.

[13] *James* v. *Robinson* (1963), 37 A.L.J.R. 151.

[14] *Ibid.*, at p. 159.

[15] Below, p. 528.

[16] [1968] 3 All E.R. 439, at p. 441.

It was a case in which the Court took the view that, at the time of the publication (a television interview) "it was obvious to all" that D was about to be arrested
on charges of fraud. This development adds to the uncertainty of the law; for
while it is reasonably clear when proceedings are "pending", "imminent" is
much less precise;[17] and opinions might well differ about whether it is "obvious
to all" that proceedings are about to begin.

Criminal proceedings continue to be pending at least until an appeal to the
Court of Appeal has been determined or the time for appealing has run out.[18]
A statement which would be a contempt before the jury heard the case will not,
however, necessarily be one if made while the appeal is pending; for a judge is
trained to exclude irrelevant matter from his mind and it is not enough that the
publication puts on the judge, quite unnecessarily, the task of dismissing
the offending matter from his mind. It is a contempt only if there is a real, as
distinct from a remote possibility that the publication might prejudice a fair
hearing of the appeal.[19]

Contempt in respect of civil proceedings may now be possible when they are
merely imminent. They are pending immediately the writ is issued and are
apparently at an end when judgment is given,[20] even though an application for a
new trial[1] or an appeal[2] is pending. But it has been held to be contempt to comment after a jury has disagreed and the writer knows that a new trial is probable.[3]

The court has held that it will not issue a writ of attachment unless it is satisfied that the proceedings are genuine and that the writ has not been issued simply
in order to enable a party to gain immunity from criticism.[4]

(*b*) *Examples of contempt.*—Examples of statements amounting to contempt
are any comment suggesting that an accused person is guilty of the offence
charged,[5] or has confessed, or that he has been guilty of other offences; and
adverse comment on the character of a party to civil proceedings, though not
referring to the subject-matter of the proceedings, if it may in fact prejudice the
trial.[6] Tendency to prejudice is enough, and it is not necessary to show that the
trial was in fact prejudiced. It is a contempt for a newspaper to carry out, and
publish the results of, an independent investigation into a crime for which a man
has been arrested;[7] or to publish the photograph of the accused where it is
reasonably clear that the question of his identity with the criminal has arisen
or may arise.[8] The publication of photographs and "Identikit" pictures to

---

[17] It has been suggested that proceedings are imminent when no one has been charged
but an arrest is expected hourly: 40 Halsbury's Statutes (2nd ed.), 218.

[18] *Davies, ex parte Delbert Evans,* [1945] K.B. 435; *Duffy, ex parte Nash,* [1960] 2 Q.B.
188; [1960] 2 All E.R. 891. Presumably proceedings are still pending until the time for
appealing to the House of Lords has run out; but the court left that point open in *Duffy,*
[1960] 2 Q.B. at p. 196; [1960] 2 All E.R. at p. 893.

[19] *Duffy,* last note.

[20] *Dunn* v. *Bevan,* [1922] 1 Ch. 276.

[1] *Dallas* v. *Ledger, Re Ledger* (1888), 4 T.L.R. 432; 52 J.P. 328.

[2] *Ibid., per* FIELD, J., 4 T.L.R. at p. 433.

[3] *Re Labouchère, ex parte Columbus Co., Ltd.* (1901), 17 T.L.R. 578.

[4] *Daily Mail (Editor), ex parte Factor* (1928), 44 T.L.R. 303.

[5] After a revolver had been dropped near the King's horse and a man was arrested, the
publication in a cinema of a news film of the arrest with the caption, "Attempt on the
King's Life", was a contempt: *Hutchinson, ex parte McMahon,* [1936] 2 All E.R. 1514.

[6] *Higgins* v. *Richards* (1912), 28 T.L.R. 202.

[7] *Evening Standard* (1924), 40 T.L.R. 833.

[8] *Daily Mirror, ex parte Smith,* [1927] 1 K.B. 845.

enable the police to apprehend a suspected person is presumably justifiable, even where it might cause prejudice, if the public interest in the apprehension of the suspect outweighs that in the complete fairness of criminal trials.

It is primarily to protect juries from prejudice that the law of contempt is invoked; a judge sitting alone is not in the least likely to be influenced in his decision by statements published in the press.[9] So a full discussion of the merits of a case pending in the Chancery Division has been held not to be a contempt.[10] But it may be a contempt, even in such a case, to publish injurious misrepresentations against a party, for it might cause a plaintiff to discontinue an action, or a defendant to agree to a compromise from fear of public dislike;[11] and it might deter other persons with good causes of action from taking proceedings. Similarly if the publication has a tendency to deter witnesses from coming forward.[12]

(c) *Mens rea.*—In *Odhams Press, Ltd., ex parte A.-G.*[13] the Divisional Court held that contempt of court is an offence of strict liability. D Ltd. had published a newspaper article containing conspicuous allegations of crime against E. Unknown to D Ltd., E had not only been arrested and charged but had been committed for trial at the time of publication. While the court was clearly disposed to think that D Ltd. had in fact been negligent in not knowing of E's committal, the decision does not depend on that ground:

> "The test is whether the matter complained of is calculated to interfere with the course of justice, not whether the authors and printers intended that result, just as it is no defence for the person responsible for the publication of a libel to plead that he did not know that the matter was defamatory and had no intention to defame."[14]

The *Odhams* case was followed by the Divisional Court in *Griffiths*.[15] D distributed in England an American magazine which contained prejudicial comments on a murder trial then proceeding in England. D was unaware of the existence of these comments. He was held to be guilty whether he was negligent or not. This time, the analogy of libel was rejected and the court held that the defence of innocent dissemination[16] was not available:

> "Cases of contempt by the publication of matter tending to prejudice a fair trial stand in a class of their own and are not truly analogous to defamation."[17]

Both these decisions are modified by the Administration of Justice Act 1960. By s. 11 (1) it is a defence to a charge of publishing, if D proves, that at the time of publication,

---

[9] *Re William Thomas Shipping Co., Ltd.*, [1930] 2 Ch. 368 at p. 373, *per* MAUGHAM, J.; *cf. Duffy*, above, p. 527.
[10] *Vine Products Ltd.* v. *Mackenzie & Co., Ltd.*, [1966] Ch. 484; [1965] 3 All E.R. 58.
[11] [1930] 2 Ch. 368 at p. 376.
[12] *Re Labouchère, ex parte Columbus Co., Ltd.* (1901), 17 T.L.R. 578.
[13] [1957] 1 Q.B. 73; [1956] 3 All E.R. 494.
[14] [1957] 1 Q.B. at p. 80; [1956] 3 All E.R. at p. 497, *per* Lord GODDARD, C.J. The court followed *Roach* v. *Garvan* (1742), 2 Atk. 469; and *ex parte Jones* (1806), 13 Ves. 237, and distinguished the more recent cases of *Metropolitan Music Hall Co.* v. *Lake* (1889), 58 L.J.Ch. 513, and *Re Marquis Townshend* (1906), 22 T.L.R. 341, as cases in which the court did not consider that the matter complained of was sufficiently serious to call for action.
[15] [1957] 2 Q.B. 192; [1957] 2 All E.R. 379.
[16] *Emmens* v. *Pottle* (1885), 16 Q.B.D. 354.
[17] [1957] 2 Q.B. at p. 204.

". . . (having taken all reasonable care) he did not know and had no reason to suspect that the proceedings were pending, or that such proceedings were imminent as the case may be."

By s. 11 (2) it is a defence to a charge of distributing if D proves that, at the time of distribution,

". . . (having taken all reasonable care) he did not know that it contained [any matter calculated to interfere with the course of justice in connection with any proceedings pending or imminent at the time of publication] and had no reason to suspect that it was likely to do so."

Thus, if the facts of the *Odhams* case[18] were to recur, D would have a defence only if he were able to prove that he had taken all reasonable care to find out whether proceedings were pending or imminent. If the facts of the *Griffiths* case[19] were to recur, D would have a defence only if he were able to prove that he had taken all reasonable care to find out whether the publication contained offensive matter.

Subject to these modifications, the basic rule of strict liability stands.[20] It is no defence to either the editor or the proprietor that the editor has devised, "so far as humanly possible", a system to prevent the publication of prejudicial matter, if he knows, or has reason to suspect, that proceedings are pending.[1] The Act would have no effect on the decision in the *Evening Standard* case.[2] A reporter telephoned an inaccurate report of the evidence in a criminal trial and the defendant newspaper published it. The jury at the trial might thus have read of matters of which in fact no evidence had been given. It was held that the newspaper was liable for contempt. The responsible officers of the paper did not know, and had no reason to suspect, that the report was in any way inaccurate, but of course they knew that the proceedings were pending, and they were not mere distributors of the paper.

The *Evening Standard* case is sometimes said to establish that contempt is also a crime of vicarious liability and, indeed, the court itself said that this was the law,[3] the editor and proprietors being liable for the act of the reporter. But surely the contempt was the *publication* and surely this was the act of the company, through its responsible officers.[4] The company is clearly a principal offender and the editor, because of the very special position of responsibility for the published matter which he occupies,[5] should perhaps be regarded as a joint principal. The journalist, however, committed no contempt of court in sending the material to his superiors. His liability, on a true analysis, was, if any, that of a counsellor or abettor. Yet the court did not believe "that the reporter for a moment deliberately or intentionally sent out false information". No doubt he

---

[18] Above, p. 528.
[19] *Supra.*
[20] But see the remarks of Lord DENNING in *A.-G.* v. *Butterworth*, [1963] 1 Q.B. 696 at p. 722; [1962] 3 All E.R. 326 at p. 331; below, p. 531.
[1] *Thomson Newspapers Ltd., ex p. Att.-Gen.*, [1968] 1 All E.R. 268.
[2] [1954] 1 Q.B. 578; [1954] 1 All E.R. 1026.
[3] [1954] 2 Q.B. at p. 585; [1954] 1 All E.R. at p. 1029.
[4] See above, p. 105.
[5] See *Steiner* v. *Toronto Star Ltd.*, [1956] 1 D.L.R. 297; and *cf.* the peculiar position of the holder of a justices' licence who is a servant: *Goodfellow* v. *Johnson*, [1965] 1 All E.R. 941.

was negligent, but negligence is not enough to found liability as a secondary party.[6] Thus it seems very doubtful whether the reporter was rightfully convicted.[7]

3 Contempt out of Court otherwise than in relation to Future Proceedings

(a) *Scandalising the court.*—Even though the proceedings have terminated it may be contempt to publish scurrilous personal abuse of a judge's conduct in them. In *Gray*[8] such an attack was published in a newspaper circulating in the town where the judge was still sitting. Lord RUSSELL, C.J., said:

> "Any act done or writing published calculated to bring a court or a judge of the Court into contempt or to lower his authority is a contempt of court. Further, any act done or writing published calculated to obstruct or interfere with the due course of justice or the lawful process of the Courts is a contempt of court."[9]

The former class of contempt, with which this section is concerned, (but not the latter[10]) is subject to the qualification that:

> "Judges and Courts are alike open to criticism, and if reasonable argument or expostulation is offered against any judicial act as contrary to law or the public good, no court could or would treat that as contempt of court."[11]

But scurrilous abuse is not "reasonable argument or expostulation" and D was convicted. On the other hand, the Privy Council allowed an appeal where the alleged contempt consisted of a reasoned argument about inequalities in sentencing, under the heading "The Human Element". Lord ATKIN said:

> ". . . provided that members of the public abstain from imputing improper motives to those taking part in the administration of justice, and are genuinely exercising a right of criticism, and not acting in malice or attempting to impair the administration of justice, they are immune."[12]

Applying these principles, the Divisional Court held[13] that the editor of the *New Statesman* was guilty of contempt in publishing a statement that

> ". . . an individual owning to such views as those of Dr. Stopes [favouring birth-control] cannot apparently hope for a fair hearing in a court presided over by Mr. Justice Avory—and there are so many Avorys."

The court rejected the argument that this was permissible criticism, being intended only to convey that the subject of birth-control was so controversial that no one who held strong views on one side or the other could prevent his judgment from being unconsciously influenced by his personal views. Lord HEWART, C.J.,[14] said:

---

[6] *Callow v. Tillstone* (1900), 19 Cox C.C. 576; above, p. 95.
[7] In *Griffiths, ex parte A.-G.*, [1957] 2 Q.B. 192 at p. 202; [1957] 2 All E.R. 379 at p. 382, Lord GODDARD, C.J., said that it had never been held that the reporter who supplied the material was liable. This overlooks the *Evening Standard* case, above; but it seems that the reporter *ought* not to be convicted unless he has *mens rea*.
[8] [1900] 2 Q.B. 36 (D.C.).
[9] *Ibid.*, at p. 95.
[10] Which is discussed above, pp. 526–530.
[11] *Ibid.*
[12] *Ambard v. A.G. for Trinidad and Tobago*, [1936] A.C. 322 at p. 335; [1936] 1 All E.R. 704 at p. 709.
[13] (1928), 44 T.L.R. 301.
[14] *Ibid.*, at p. 303.

"[The article] imputed unfairness and lack of impartiality to a Judge in the discharge of his judicial duties. The gravamen of the offence was that by lowering his authority it interfered with the performance of his judicial duties."

More recently, the Court of Appeal has held a vigorous and, in some respects, inaccurate criticism of itself not to amount to a contempt. SALMON, L.J., said:[15]

". . . no criticism of a judgment, however vigorous, can amount to contempt of court, providing it keeps within the limits of reasonable courtesy and good faith. The criticism here complained of, however rumbustious, however wide of the mark, whether pressed in good taste or in bad taste, seems to me to be well within these limits."

It is contempt only when the judge is attacked in his capacity as such: The power of committal

"is not to be used for the vindication of the judge as a person. He must resort to action for libel or criminal information."[16]

So where a letter was published containing sarcastic allusions to the refusal by the Chief Justice of the Bahamas of a gift of pineapples, the Privy Council held that, while the letter might have been the subject of an action for libel, it was not a contempt because it was not calculated to obstruct or interfere with the course of justice or the due administration of the law.[17]

(b) Intimidation of a juror or witness.—It is contempt to intimidate, threaten or punish a juror or witness with respect to his part in the proceedings, whether they are pending[18] or terminated It was so held in the case of a juryman in *Martin*.[19] D called on the foreman of a jury which, the previous day, had convicted D's brother of a crime, and challenged him to mortal combat "for having bullied the jury." He was committed for contempt and PIGOT, C.B., said[20] that jurors must be protected:

"from all interference with them in the discharge of their duties, from all attempt to assail their characters or reputations, and from the imputation of motives other than those which should actuate men having such solemn and important duties to discharge: if it is necessary to guard their reputation how much more necessary is it to guard their persons from outrage, and the consequences of threats of outrage to their persons or their homes."

This rule was extended to witnesses by the Court of Appeal, reversing the Restrictive Practices Court, in the case *A.-G.* v. *Butterworth*.[1] D and others, members of a trade union, disapproving of evidence which E, another member, had given before the Restrictive Practices Court, censured him for his conduct and purported to relieve him of his position as branch treasurer. It was held that those of the defendants whose motives included that of punishing E for giving evidence in the way he did were guilty of contempt, whether this was their predominant motive or not. Defendants whose motives were not established were acquitted. While there was no precedent directly in point, there were a

---

[15] *R.* v. *Commissioner of Police of the Metropolis, ex. p. Blackburn,* [1968] 2 Q.B. 150 at p. 155; [1968] 2 All E.R. 319, at p. 321.
[16] *McLeod* v. *St. Aubyn,* [1899] A.C. 549 at p. 561, *per* Lord MORRIS.
[17] *Re Special Reference from Bahama Islands,* [1893] A.C. 138.
[18] Above, p. 526.
[19] (1848), 5 Cox C.C. 356.
[20] *Ibid.,* at p. 359.
[1] [1963] 1 Q.B. 696; [1962] 3 All E.R. 326. See also *Wright,* [1968] V.R. 164 (assault on witness after trial).

number of persuasive authorities, and the decision is supported by the general principles governing contempt cases.

> "If this sort of thing could be done in a single case with impunity, the news of it would soon get round. Witnesses in other cases would be unwilling to come forward to give evidence, or, if they did come forward, they would hesitate to speak the truth for fear of the consequences."[2]

It was immaterial that the accused did not have any future proceedings in mind and had no intention to interfere with the course of justice. But, according to DONOVAN, L.J.:[3]

> ". . . in this kind of case it must be proved by the Crown that knowledge of the revenge taken upon one who has given evidence is likely to come to the knowledge of potential witnesses in future cases."

The question of motive is crucial in such cases because it is only if the motive is to punish the witness, as such, that there is a tendency to obstruct the administration of justice; that is, if E had been removed from his position by the accused because, for example, he was inefficient or corrupt in his discharge of his duties, this could hardly have affected witnesses in future cases. Lord DENNING, M.R., was prepared to go further:[4]

> ". . . contempt of court is a criminal offence, punishable summarily by the court itself, and, like all criminal offences, it requires in general, a guilty mind. I do not think that *Odhams Press, Ltd., ex parte A.-G.* warrants the large proposition that has been drawn from it; and in any case it has since been reversed by s. 11 (1) of the Administration of Justice Act 1960."

DONOVAN, L.J., on the other hand, did not appear disposed to question the correctness of the *Odhams* case and it was certainly not necessary to the decision to do so. It must be assumed that the propositions in *Odhams* case remain good law;[5] though the observation of the Master of the Rolls suggests that they might in future be reconsidered and, perhaps, narrowed by the Court of Appeal.

(c) *Obstructing an officer of the court.*—It is a contempt to obstruct an officer of the court when he is carrying out his duties, as by assaulting or threatening a process server,[6] a sheriff, a receiver, a bailiff, or a solicitor when leaving a judge's chambers after the hearing of an application:[7]

> "The principle is that those who have duties to discharge in a court of justice are protected by the law and shielded on their way to the discharge of such duties, while discharging them, and on their return therefrom, in order that such persons may safely have resort to courts of justice."[8]

---

[2] [1963] 1 Q.B. at p. 719; [1962] 3 All E.R. at p. 329, *per* Lord DENNING, M.R.
[3] [1963] 1 Q.B. at p. 726 ; [1962] 3 All E.R. at p. 333.
[4] [1963] 1 Q.B. at p. 722; [1962] 3 All E.R. at p. 331. But see above, p. 528.
[5] Subject, of course, to the 1960 Act.
[6] *Williams* v. *Johns* (1773), 1 Mer. 303 n. (process server compelled to eat writ and beaten).
[7] *Re Johnson* (1887), 20 Q.B.D. 68.
[8] *Ibid.*, at p. 74, *per* BOWEN, L.J.

CHAPTER 19

Offences against Public Order[1]

1 UNLAWFUL ASSEMBLY, ROUT AND RIOT[2]

Unlawful Assembly, Rout and Riot are three separate misdemeanours at common law. The Criminal Law Commissioners in 1840 thought[3] this division unnecessary and inconvenient, the point of the offence in all being the unlawful assembly. The constituents of an unlawful assembly, according to the authorities,[4] are:

(1) An assembly of three or more persons;

(2) A common purpose (a) to commit a crime of violence or (b) to achieve some other object, whether lawful or not, in such a way as to cause reasonable men to apprehend a breach of the peace.

The unlawful assembly becomes a rout as soon as some act has been done "moving towards" the execution of the common purpose; and the rout becomes a riot when some act is done in part execution of this common purpose. As the Commissioners pointed out, the distinction between an act "moving towards" the execution of a common purpose and an act done in part execution of it is extremely subtle; but it is of small importance at the present day in the criminal law. Rout requires no further consideration. Prosecutions for unlawful assembly and riot are not generally brought today;[5] but the recent history of the criminal law shows that it is by no means impossible that they will be brought into use again; and it is, therefore, worthwhile to examine them in more detail.

---

[1] D.G.T. Williams, *Keeping the Peace.*
[2] See Brownlie, *The Law Relating to Public Order*, Chapter 4.
[3] XX Parl. Papers, Vol. I; Russell, 243.
[4] Dalton, *Country Justice*, Ch. 136, § 1; Hawkins, 1 P.C. 1, c. 28, §§ 9 and 10; Blackstone, *Commentaries*, iv, 146; Stephen *Digest*, Art. 90, and 2 H.C.L. 385.
[5] But D. G. T. Williams refers to some modern instances at [1963] Crim. L.R. 156. Note the observations of LAWTON, J., there referred to.

(1) UNLAWFUL ASSEMBLY

1 Actus Reus

The mere assembly—the coming or being together—with the necessary intent constitutes the offence and the parties are guilty notwithstanding that they change their minds and disperse without doing anything.[6] The meeting may be initially lawful, but if three or more of the persons assembled then form the appropriate common purpose, it becomes an unlawful assembly.[7] Of course, not everyone present is necessarily guilty, but only those who share in the common purpose.[8] If three persons are assembled, and two resolve to set upon the third, this is not an unlawful assembly;[9] but if the three of them resolve to attack a fourth, it is.

The essence of the offence is the disturbance, or the probability of the disturbance of, the public peace. If the meeting is to effect some unlawful purpose not likely to cause a breach of the peace—for example, "A, B and C meet for the purpose of concerting an indictable fraud"[10]—this is probably a conspiracy but not an unlawful assembly. But a prize-fight at which one spectator is guilty of aiding and abetting the two combatants in their assault upon one another is.[11] Russell[12] equates assemblies to witness a bull-fight, cock-fight or badger-baiting with prize-fights; but it is not clear that these exhibitions constitute a breach of, or danger to the peace.

The assembly need not be in a public place; so HOLROYD, J., held that a meeting of sixteen people in a private house, in order to go out, armed and with faces disguised for night poaching, was unlawful.[13]

It is not necessary that the persons assembled should have any intention to commit a crime; but

> ". . . wherever a body of persons met together in great numbers, in such a manner and under such circumstances as reasonably to excite terror and alarm in the neighbourhood . . . that was an unlawful assembly."[14]

All the circumstances may be taken into account[15] by the jury—that the assembly was at night and by torchlight, that the accused carried inflammatory banners,[16] the language used, the appearance of being drilled, or actual drilling[17] and so on. It is not enough that a merely foolish or timid person would be alarmed. The question is whether

> "firm and rational men having their families and property there would have reasonable ground to fear a breach of the peace."[18]

---

[6] *Birt* (1831), 5 C. & P. 154, *per* PATTESON, J.

[7] *Burns* (1886), 16 Cox C.C. 355; *cf. Graham and Burns* (1888), 16 Cox C.C. 420 at p. 433.

[8] *Burns* (*supra*); *Graham, loc. cit.*

[9] But it is a breach of the peace and might amount to the crime of affray, below, p. 539.

[10] Stephen, *Digest*, Art. 90, Illustration 2.

[11] *Billingham* (1825), 2 C. & P. 234; *Perkins* (1831), 4 C. & P. 537; *Coney* (1882), 8 Q.B.D. 534.

[12] *Crime*, 257.

[13] *Brodribb* (1816), 6 C. & P. 571.

[14] *Stephens* (1839), 3 State Tr. N.S. 1189 at p. 1234 (PATTESON, J.).

[15] *Hunt* (1820), 1 State Tr. N.S. 171.

[16] *Ibid.*

[17] *Hunt* (*supra*). Probably also, the known characters of those assembled: *Goodall* v. *Te Kooti* (1890), 9 N.Z.L.R. 26.

[18] *Vincent* (1839), 9 C. & P. 91, *per* ALDERSON, B.

The assembly may have the object of putting one of its members in possession of land to which he is entitled; but if this is to be done by such force as would excite apprehension of a breach of the peace, the assembly is unlawful.[19]

> "You have no business to redress private grievances by a dangerous disturbance of the public peace."[20]

Even the right of self-defence appears to be limited:

> "If one be menaced—that if he come to such a market, or to such a place, he will be beaten—in this case he cannot assemble people to assist him to go there in safeguard of his person, because there is no necessity to go there, and he may have his remedy by surety of the peace."[1]

The only concession made is that a man may assemble his friends to defend the possession of his house or the safety of his person against those who would break in and dispossess him or beat him.[2] But even this has been held to be limited to the house itself and not to allow an armed assembly in defence of a man's close.[3]

Where there is no other means of preserving the peace, magistrates and police are entitled—and bound—to call upon even a lawful assembly to disperse; and if those assembled then decline to do so, they are guilty of unlawful assembly[4] as well as of obstructing police officers in the execution of their duty.[5]

2 Mens Rea

It must be proved that D intended to use or to abet the use of violence; or to do or abet acts which he knows to be likely to cause a breach of the peace.[6] When, for example, the likelihood of a breach of the peace depends on the display of a banner.

> ". . . it is not necessarily illegal on that account as to every man present at the meeting, but would only be illegal as to that particular man or as to those particular persons, who had adopted the banner, or who, with full knowledge of the existence of the banner, had given their co-operation and countenance to the meeting."[7]

If D is doing a lawful act, he does not intend to cause a breach of the peace merely because he knows that E will unlawfully breach the peace to impede or prevent D doing that which he may lawfully do.[8] It may be different, however, if D's *object* is to provoke a breach of the peace.

In *Beatty* v. *Gillbanks*,[9] members of the Salvation Army marched through the street of Weston-super-Mare, knowing that they would be opposed, as they had

---

[19] Hawkins, 1 P.C., c. 28, § 7.
[20] *Graham and Burns* (1888), 16 Cox C.C. at p. 428, *per* CHARLES, J.
[1] FINEUX, C.J., Y.B. Hen. 7, 39 (a); And see *Semayne's* case (1604), 5 Co. Rep. 91A; Hawkins, 1 P.C., c. 28, § 10; Stephen, 2 H.C.L. 385; *Goodall* v. *Te Kooti* (1890), 9 N.Z.L.R. at p. 45.
[2] See authorities cited in previous note.
[3] *Bishop of Bangor* (1796), 26 St. Tr. 463 at p. 525 (HEATH, J.). *Cf. Beatty* v. *Gillbanks, infra.*
[4] *O'Kelly* v. *Harvey* (1883), 14 L.R. Ir. 105; Dicey, *Law of the Constitution*, 278.
[5] *Duncan* v. *Jones*, [1936] 1 K.B. 218; above, p. 258.
[6] *Stephens* (1839), 3 St. Tr. N.S. at 1234.
[7] *Hunt* (1820), 1 State Tr. N.S. 171.
[8] *Cf. Steane* and other cases discussed above, p. 38. If Steane had refused to make the broadcasts and, in consequence, his wife had been grievously harmed by the enemy, it could hardly have been contended that he had caused her grievous bodily harm. See Williams, C.L.G.P., § 19.
[9] (1882), 9 Q.B.D. 308. See Dicey, *op. cit.*, Ch. VII; D. G. T. Williams, *Keeping the Peace*, pp. 101 *et seq.*

been in the past, in a riotous and tumultuous manner by an organisation called the Skeleton Army, and intending to force their way to the terror of the peaceful inhabitants through the streets as they had done on previous occasions.[10] On a complaint alleging unlawful assembly,[11] the members of the Salvation Army were bound over by the justices to keep the peace and be of good behaviour.

The Divisional Court quashed the order, FIELD, J., saying,[12]

"... the finding of the justices amounts to this, that a man may be convicted for doing a lawful act if he knows that his doing it may cause another to do an unlawful act. There is no authority for such a proposition ..."

The case was distinguished in *Wise* v. *Dunning*[13] where D, a Protestant lecturer, held meetings in public places in Liverpool, at which he used gestures and language, highly insulting to the faith of the large body of Roman Catholic inhabitants of that city. At these meetings, both D's opponents and his supporters committed breaches of the peace though he himself did not. It was held that D was properly bound over to keep the peace and be of good behaviour. Lord ALVERSTONE, C.J., thought it important that it was an offence under the Liverpool Improvement Act to use any threatening or abusive or insulting words or behaviour with intent to provoke a breach of the peace (which, he thought, was not this case) or *whereby a breach of the peace may be occasioned*. But no charge had been made under that Act nor, apparently, at all;[14] and the Chief Justice was, it seems, prepared to hold that D was properly bound over even if his act was lawful, because the breach of the peace was a natural consequence of it; while DARLING and CHANNELL, JJ., expressly put their decision on that ground.

In *Beatty* v. *Gillbanks* it was held that there was no unlawful assembly; in *Wise* v. *Dunning* the question was not raised. If, however, a breach of the peace was the natural consequence of D's conduct in the latter case, that would seem to be evidence that D intended it;[15] and therefore (if he had two "aiders and abettors")[16] that it was an unlawful assembly. The cases are certainly not indistinguishable. The Draft Criminal Code defined an assembly as unlawful, *inter alia*, where the assembly will

"needlessly and without any reasonable occasion provoke other persons to disturb the peace tumultuously."[17]

---

[10] Williams suggests the Divisional Court attached insufficient importance to the fact of their intention to overcome resistance: [1954] Crim. L.R. at 581; and see *O'Kelly* v. *Harvey* (1883), 14 L.R. Ir. 105 at p. 111.

[11] But it was not a *charge* of unlawful assembly, for the justices had no jurisdiction to try such a charge; and *cf.* the Attorney-General, *arguendo*, in *Graham* as reported in (1888), 4 T.L.R. at p. 222.

[12] (1882), 9 Q.B.D. at p. 314.

[13] [1902] 1 K.B. 167; and see *Londonderry JJ.* (1891), 28 L.R. Ir. 440; *Patterson*, [1931] 3 D.L.R. 267.

[14] Appeal by way of case stated lay from a binding over order: *cf. Lansbury* v. *Riley*, [1914] 3 K.B. 229; but there was at that time no appeal on a question of fact: *London County Quarter Sessions, ex parte Metropolitan Police Comrs.*, [1948] 1 K.B. 670; [1948] 1 All E.R. 72. But now, by the Magistrates' Courts (Appeal from Binding Over Orders) Act 1956, an appeal lies to quarter sessions against a binding-over order where there has been no conviction.

[15] Curiously, Lord ALVERSTONE seems to have thought he did not.

[16] All three would be principal offenders.

[17] Stephen said that this part of the definition had not been the subject of a specific decision in any case: 2 H.C.L. 385; but subsequently HAWKINS, J., so directed the jury in *Clarkson* (1892), 17 Cox C.C. 483. The jury convicted but, on a case reserved, it was held that the conviction was not supported by the evidence. And see *Goodall* v. *Te Kooti* (1890), 9 N.Z.L.R. 26: ".... there can never be reasonable occasion that a man should incur risk of a breach of the Queen's Peace by visiting his relatives with a train of three hundred men."

It may be that there was "a reasonable occasion" for the procession in *Beatty* v. *Gillbanks* and none for the meetings, as they were conducted, in *Wise* v. *Dunning*. It may be objected that such a solution puts too large a discretion in the hands of the court; but a high proportion of legal disputes turn on what is reasonable.

(2) RIOT

In *Field* v. *Metropolitan Police Receiver*[18] the Divisional Court, after reviewing the authorities, declared that there are five necessary elements of a riot:

> "(1) number of persons, three at least:
> (2) common purpose;
> (3) execution or inception of the common purpose;
> (4) an intent to help one another by force if necessary against any person who may oppose them in the execution of their common purpose;
> (5) force or violence not merely used in demolishing, but displayed in such a manner as to alarm at least one person of reasonable firmness and courage."[19]

In that case more than three youths carried out their common purpose of demolishing a wall; but, as they ran away as soon as a solitary caretaker approached, there was no evidence of elements (4) and (5). The caretaker's wife was frightened by the noise of the falling wall, but not by the youths; and, the court found, the conduct of the youths was not such as would alarm persons of reasonable firmness and courage.

Elements (4) and (5) may be present although the people assembled go about their purpose quietly and in good humour. Thus in *Ford* v. *Metropolitan Police District Receiver*[20] on peace night, 1919, an amiable crowd tore out the woodwork and floorboards of an unoccupied house to make a bonfire. But it was found that there was no doubt that anybody who had interfered with them would have been subjected to very rough usage and that the man next door did not interfere as he was afraid of being killed had he done so.

1 The Common Purpose

It is submitted that either the common purpose must be unlawful or, if it is lawful, the force or violence must be displayed "needlessly and without any reasonable occasion."[1] If three police officers, in pursuance of the common purpose of arresting a dangerous criminal, use such violent measures as are necessary to do so and thereby alarm one or more bystanders, they can hardly be guilty of a riot. And in *Beatty* v. *Gillbanks*[2] the members of the Salvation Army executed their common purpose of marching through the streets, forcing their way through the opposition, to the terror of the peaceful inhabitants, but were evidently not rioters.

---

[18] [1907] 2 K.B. 853.
[19] *Ibid.*, at p. 860.
[20] [1921] 2 K.B. 334; followed in *Munday* v. *Metropolitan Police District Receiver* [1949] 1 All E.R. 337.
[1] *Cf.* Unlawful assembly, above, p. 534, footnote 17.
[2] Above, p. 535.

2 The Requirement of Alarm

In *Langford*[3] it was held that it was *enough* that one person was terrified; and this case was the basis of element (5) of the definition in *Field*'s case.[4] But while it is enough to call evidence that one person was terrified, even that may not be necessary. In *Sharp*,[5] Lord GODDARD thought, *obiter*, it would be enough that the natural tendency of the conduct would be to cause alarm to members of the public; and that element (5) in *Field*'s case might require reconsideration at some future time.

3 Suppression of Riot

Riot is a misdemeanour at common law, but the Riot Act 1714 provided that, in certain circumstances, it became a felony. The reason for this enactment was that it was supposed that greater force was permissible in preventing a felony than in preventing a misdemeanour. The Riot Act has been repealed by the Criminal Law Act 1967. Consequently, it is now lawful to use "such force as is reasonable in the circumstances" in suppressing a riot.[6]

4 The Riot (Damages) Act 1886

Prosecutions for riot are not normally brought nowadays, and the crime is mainly important for its effect on powers of arrest and the civil remedies it affords to persons injured by riots under the Riot (Damages) Act 1886. All the modern reported cases involving riot were brought under this Act. It provides that where a house, shop or building[7] in any police district, or property inside it, has been injured, stolen or destroyed by rioters, the owner shall be compensated out of the police rate. The amount may be appropriately reduced where he has contributed to his loss by taking inadequate precautions or by offering provocation, or otherwise.

Many ordinary robberies amount to riot:

"... if three persons enter a shop and forcibly or by threats steal goods therein, technically they are guilty not only of larceny or robbery, but of riot."[8]

The victim of a robbery is not entitled to be compensated out of the police rate merely on the ground that the robbery amounted to a riot. The Act uses the words, "riotously and tumultuously" and the word "tumultuously" was added:

"... for the specific reason that it was intended to limit the liability of compensation to cases where the rioters were in such numbers and in such a state of agitated commotion, and were generally so acting, that the forces of law and order should have been well aware of the threat which existed, and, if they had done their duty, should have taken steps to prevent the rioters from causing damage."[9]

Where a robbery amounted to a riot and there was commotion and noise in the shop but the attention of persons outside it was not attracted and the whole

---

[3] (1842), Car. & M. 602.
[4] *Supra.*
[5] [1957] 1 Q.B. 552 at p. 560; [1957] 1 All E.R. 577 at p. 579; below, p. 539.
[6] Criminal Law Act 1967, s. 3; above, p. 229.
[7] Thus, the victims of the Great Train Robbery could not have recovered compensation under the Act.
[8] *Sharp*, [1957] 1 Q.B. at p. 560; [1957] 1 All E.R. at p. 579 *per* Lord GODDARD, C.J.
[9] Case cited in next footnote at p. 539.

activity was on too small a scale to be described as a tumult it was held that the plaintiff was not entitled to compensation.[10]

(3) AFFRAY

Affray is a common law misdeamour which, after a long period of desuetude, has not only been brought back into regular use, but greatly expanded in scope by judicial decision. Its elements are

(1) fighting by one or more persons: or
a display of force by one or more persons without actual violence;

(2) in such a manner that reasonable people might be frightened or intimidated.

1 Fighting, by One or More Persons

Until recently, it was held that this type of affray was a joint offence requiring evidence that at least two people unlawfully fought, the one against the other.[11] If one was acting only in self-defence, he had to be acquitted; and it followed that his attacker must also be acquitted of this crime.[12] In *Scarrow*[13] it was held that there was no need for any such "reciprocity of violence;" and that three men were guilty of affray where they attacked others who did not resist or retaliate. The court thought that a single attacker might by guilty of affray, though his victim acted only in self-defence.[14] Presumably it would be the same if the victim did not resist at all.

2 Display of Force

For affray otherwise than by fighting, there is no clear modern authority. Lord PARKER has said that it is not any disturbance in public which will make an affray and all the recent cases have involved fighting. Hawkins,[15] however, says,

"in some cases there may be an affray where there is no actual violence; as where a man arms himself with dangerous and unusual weapons, in such a manner as will naturally cause a terror to the people, which is said to have been always an offence at common law . . ."

and this seems to be accepted by the Court of Criminal Appeal in *Sharp*.[16]

3 A Continuing Offence

A single affray may continue for a considerable period of time and over a wide area; so an indictment was not bad for duplicity where it alleged an affray on August 31 and September 1 "in divers streets".[17] It appeared in evidence that the accused were milling about, armed, uttering threats and fighting, from

---

[10] *Dwyer (J.W.), Ltd.* v. *Metropolitan Police District, Receiver for the,* [1967] 2 Q.B. 970; [1967] 2 All E.R. 1051 (LYELL, J.).
[11] *Sharp,* [1957] 1 Q.B. 552; [1957] 1 All E. R. 577 (C.C.A.).
[12] *Ibid.,* at p. 561.
[13] (1968), 52 Cr. App. Rep. 591.
[14] *Ibid.,* at p. 596.
[15] 1 P.C., c. 28, §. 4, p. 488.
[16] [1957] 1 Q.B. at p. 559; [1957] 1 All E.R. at p. 579.
[17] *Woodrow* (1959), 43 Cr. App. Rep. 105.

8.30 p.m. until 12.30 a.m., over a radius of a quarter of a mile. This was held to be a single affray.

4 Public Alarm

Where the fight is in a public place, it is not necessary to offer any evidence that any individual was frightened or intimidated or, indeed, that anyone was present.[18] It is enough that the natural consequence would be that reasonable people would be frightened or intimidated if they saw the acts in question. As in unlawful assembly and riot, the question concerns a reasonably firm and constant person:

> ". . . if two lads indulge in a fight with fists no one would dignify that as an affray, whereas if they used broken bottles or knuckledusters and drew blood a jury might well find that it was, as a passer-by might be upset and frightened by such conduct."[19]

It was assumed in *Sharp* that the offence could only be committed in a public place. The House of Lords in *Button* v. *Director of Public Prosecutions*,[20] affirming the Court of Criminal Appeal held that this is not so. In that case a fight took place in a hall hired by a local darts league. The public were not admitted, but it was held that this was immaterial. "The essence of the offence is that two or more fight together to the terror of the Queen's subjects."[1] In so deciding, the House was conscious that it was removing a defence which an accused person would, in practice, have had at any time during the last hundred years; but the fact that Blackstone, Archbold and the judges, following them, had made an error was no reason for not restoring the true rule of the common law.

A distinction must still be drawn between public and private places;[2] for a fight on private premises cannot be an affray unless at least one person other than those fighting is present. The House approved[3] Hawkins's statement that:

> ". . . there may be an assault which will not amount to an affray; as to where it happens in a private place out of the hearing or seeing of any except the parties concerned; in which case it cannot be said to be the terror of the people . . ."[4]

The Solicitor General argued[5] that one person is enough; whereas in the Court of Criminal Appeal it was said[6] that it does not matter whether few or many persons are present—"the few are entitled to the same protection as the many"—that this, perhaps suggests that there must be more than one person.

5 The Utility of Affray

In *Button's Case* the House rejected an argument that no purpose was to be served by re-establishing the law relating to affray since the crime of assault

---

[18] *Mapstone*, [1963] 3 All E.R. 930.
[19] [1957] 1 Q.B. at p. 559; [1957] 1 All E.R. at p. 579, *per* Lord GODDARD, C.J.
[20] [1966] A.C. 591; [1965] 3 All E.R. 587.
[1] [1966] A.C. at p. 626; [1965] 3 All E.R. at p. 590.
[2] See *Morris* (1963), 47 Cr. App. Rep. 202; *Clark* (1963), 47 Cr. App. Rep. 203.
[3] [1966] A.C. at p. 626.
[4] 1 P.C. 134.
[5] [1966] A.C. at p. 621.
[6] [1966] A.C. at p. 609; [1965] 1 All E.R. at p. 974.

affords sufficient protection to the public. The House appears to have accepted the argument that, because evidence is difficult to obtain in the mêlée of a fight, there are situations in which it would be possible to convict of affray on evidence which would not justify a conviction for assault.[7] Since D can be convicted of affray only if he is proved to have fought or abetted fighting, it is difficult to see how this can be so. There may be another reason of expediency; in *Sharp*, Lord GODDARD said:[8]

"... in this class of case each prisoner throws the blame on the other and there is danger that perhaps being disgusted with both and thinking each only got his deserts, a jury will acquit both if the charges are of the one wounding the other."

This assumes that the jury has regard to the mischief of the offence—the injury to the person attacked in assault, the injury to the bystander in affray—in arriving at its verdict. If this is really so, then affray is justified; but is it so? There is one very practical reason why the prosecutor may prefer affray to assault: common assault is punishable on indictment with one year's imprisonment; affray, being a common law misdemeanour, is punishable with fine or imprisonment at the discretion of the court.

(4) PUBLIC ORDER ACT 1936, SECTION 5

By s. 5 of the Public Order Act 1936, as amended by the Race Relations Act 1965, s. 7:

"Any person who in any public place or at any public meeting—
  (a) uses threatening, abusive or insulting words or behaviour, or
  (b) distributes or displays any writing, sign or visible representation which is threatening, abusive or insulting,
with intent to provoke a breach of the peace or whereby a breach of the peace is likely to be occasioned, shall be guilty of an offence."[10]

The penalty may now[11] be three months' imprisonment or a fine of £100 or both, on summary conviction; and twelve months' imprisonment or a fine of £100, or both, on conviction on indictment.

Such conduct with such an intent is also an offence punishable with a fine of forty shillings under the Metropolitan Police Act 1839, s. 54 (13), if committed "in any thoroughfare or public place" within the limits of the metropolitan police district.

1 Actus Reus

The Public Order Act is inapplicable where one neighbour shouts abuse at another, each being on his own premises.[12] The obvious reason is that the act is not done in a public place; but the court seemed, in one passage, to put its decision on the more general ground that the Public Order Act was not passed to deal with disputes between neighbours, but with a quite different sort of

---

[7] [1966] A.C. at p. 628; [1965] 3 All E.R. at p. 592.
[8] [1957] 1 Q.B. at p. 561; [1957] 1 All E.R. at p. 580.
[9] D. G. T. Williams, "Threats, Abuse, Insults" [1967] Crim. L.R. 287.
[10] For the statutory definition of "public place" and "public meeting" see above, p. 287.
[11] Public Order Act 1963.
[12] *Wilson* v. *Skeock* (1949), 65 T.L.R. 418.

mischief—the riotous behaviour arising from political meetings. Yet Lord GODDARD's *dicta* clearly contemplated that, if the person addressed had been in a public place, the offence might have been committed.[13]   Recently, in *Ward* v. *Holman*,[14] the court held that the offence was committed when D shouted abuse at his neighbour, P, both being on the highway; the words of the Act are completely unambiguous and, therefore, it was not proper to look, as Lord GODDARD had looked, at the long title.[15]

2 Mens Rea

D must have intended to use the words or behaviour he did use.   There can be no problem about that.   He must also, it is submitted, have intended the words to be threatening, abusive or insulting to the audience, or been reckless whether they were so.   If D was convinced on reasonable grounds that his audience consisted entirely of anti-semitic persons, words insulting to Jews would not, it is submitted, come within the Act.   But, since the offence is only committed if the words are used in a public place or at a public meeting, such a situation can hardly ever arise.   D will almost invariably be reckless as to the effect of his words if they are insulting to a section of the community.

If D has an actual intention to cause a breach of the peace, he is guilty under the first branch of the section.   If he has no such ulterior intent, then he may be guilty under the second branch.   A breach of the peace probably includes any act involving danger to the person.[16]

Under the second branch of the section, no ulterior intent need be proved; the speaker who intentionally or recklessly uses threatening, abusive or insulting words in a public place must take his audience as he finds them.   The only remaining question is whether the audience actually present was likely to be provoked to a breach of the peace.   It is no defence that the audience were hooligans, bent on preventing D from speaking.[17]   D is not entitled to assume that his audience consists of reasonable men.

2 PUBLIC NUISANCE AND OBSTRUCTION OF THE HIGHWAY

(1) PUBLIC NUISANCE

Public nuisance is a misdemeanour at common law.   It consists in,

> ". . . an act not warranted by law or an omission to discharge a legal duty, which act or omission obstructs or causes inconvenience or damage to the public in the exercise of rights common to all His Majesty's subjects."[18]

---

[13] This suggests that language is used in a public place if it is *heard* in a public place, though spoken on private premises.   *Cf. Smith* v. *Hughes,* above, p. 317.   What of the opposite case where D uses language in a public place, which is heard on private premises ? Both cases might be thought to fall within the mischief of the Act.

[14] [1964] 2 Q.B. 580; [1964] 2 All E.R. 729 (D.C.).   For similar provisions regulating the public performance of plays, see Theatres Act 1968, ss. 5 and 6.

[15] See further D. G. T. Williams in (1963), 26 M.L.R. 425.

[16] Williams, [1954] Crim. L. R. 578 and C.L.G.P. 714–715; Brownlie, *Public Order*, 4.

[17] *Jordan* v. *Burgoyne*, [1963] 2 Q.B. 744; [1963] 2 All E.R. 225.

[18] Stephen, *Digest*, 184.

A person who has suffered particular damage as the result of a public nuisance can maintain an action for damages in tort;[19] and the major importance of public nuisance today is in the civil remedy which it affords.

1 Nature of Nuisance

The most common and important instance of a public nuisance is obstruction of the highway and this is more particularly considered below. But it also includes a wide variety of other interferences with the public; for example, the carrying on of an offensive trade which impregnates the air "with noisome offensive and stinking smoke" to the common nuisance of the public passing along the highway;[20] polluting a river with gas so as to destroy the fish and render the water unfit for drinking;[1] unnecessarily, and with full knowledge of the facts, exposing in a public highway a person infected with a contagious disease;[2] taking a horse into a public place knowing that it has glanders and that that is an infectious disease;[3] sending food to market, knowing that it is to be sold for human consumption and that it is unfit for that purpose;[4] burning a dead body in such a place and such a manner as to be offensive to members of the public passing along a highway or other public place;[5] keeping a fierce and unruly bull in a field crossed by a public footway;[6] discharging oil into the sea in such circumstances that it is likely to be carried on to English shores and beaches;[7] and by causing excessive noise and dust in the course of quarrying operations.[8]

A great many varieties of nuisance are now the subject of special legislation[9] and proceedings are unlikely to be brought at common law where there is a statutory remedy. But the common law may still be useful where no statute has intervened or where the penalty provided by statute is too slight.[10]

A public nuisance may be committed by omission, as by permitting a house near the highway to fall into a ruinous state[11] or by allowing one's land to accumulate filth, even though it is deposited there by others for whom D is not responsible.[12]

Whereas private nuisance always involves some degree of repetition or continuance,[13]

> "an isolated act may amount to a public nuisance if it is done under such circumstances that the public right to condemn it should be vindicated."[14]

---

[19] See Street, *Torts*, 238 *et seq.*
[20] *White and Ward* (1757), 1 Burr. 333.
[1] *Medley* (1834), 6 C. & P. 292.
[2] *Vantandillo* (1815), 4 M. & S. 73.
[3] *Henson* (1852), Dears. C.C. 24.
[4] *Stevenson* (1862), 3 F. & F. 106; otherwise if D did not intend it for human consumption: *Crawley* (1862), 3 F. & F. 109; 176 E.R. 49.
[5] *Price* (1884), 12 Q.B.D. 247.
[6] Archbold, § 3831.
[7] *Southport Corporation* v. *Esso Petroleum Co., Ltd.,* [1954] 2 Q.B. 182 at p. 197; [1954] 2 All E.R. 561 at p. 571, *per* DENNING, L.J. (C.A.; reversed [1956] A.C. 218; [1955] 3 All E.R. 864).
[8] *A.-G.* v. *P.Y.A. Quarries, Ltd.,* [1957] 2 Q.B. 169; [1957] 1 All E.R. 894.
[9] See, for example, *Archbold*, §§ 3825–3834.
[10] *Cf.* obstruction of the highway, below, p. 546.
[11] *Watts* (1703), 1 Salk. 357.
[12] *A.-G.* v. *Tod Heatley,* [1897] 1 Ch. 560.
[13] *Per* DENNING, L.J., [1957] 2 Q.B. at p. 192.
[14] *Ibid.* In *Mutters* (1864), Le. & Ca. 491, a conviction was upheld where the indictment alleged that D, on a particular day, caused an explosion which scattered pieces of rock on to neighbouring dwelling-houses and the highway; but the indictment did allege that D allowed the stones to remain on the highway for several hours.

The interference with the public's rights must be substantial and unreasonable. Not every obstruction of the highway is a public nuisance:

> "If an unreasonable time is occupied in the operation of delivering beer from a brewer's dray into the cellar of a publican, this is certainly a nuisance. A cart or wagon may be unloaded at a gateway; but this must be done with promptness. So as to the repairing of a house;—the public must submit to the inconvenience occasioned necessarily in repairing the house; but if this inconvenience is prolonged for an unreasonable time, the public have a right to complain and the party can be indicted for a nuisance."[15]

The interference with the public's rights must be caused by some unnecessary and unreasonable act or omission by D. In *Dwyer* v. *Mansfield*[16] it was held that, when queues formed outside D's shop because he was selling only 1 lb. of potatoes per ration book in view of the wartime scarcity, he was not liable because he was carrying on his business in a normal and proper way without doing anything unreasonable or unnecessary. The nuisance, if there was one, had been created not by D's conduct, but by the short supply of potatoes.[17] The result would be different if D sold ice-cream through the window of a shop, causing a crowd to gather on the pavement, because this is not a normal and proper way of carrying on business.[18]

2 The Public

Blackstone says that a public nuisance must be an annoyance to all the King's subjects.[19] This is obviously too wide for, if it were so, no public nuisance could ever be established. DENNING, L.J., declared that the test is,

> ". . . that a public nuisance is a nuisance which is so widespread in its range or so indiscriminate in its effect that it would not be reasonable to expect one person to take proceedings on his own responsibility to put a stop to it, but that it should be taken on the responsibility of the community at large."[20]

Whether an annoyance or injury is sufficiently widespread to amount to a public nuisance is a question of fact. In *Lloyd*,[1] where D's carrying on his trade caused annoyance to only three houses in Clifford's Inn, Lord ELLENBOROUGH said that this, if anything,[2] was a private nuisance, not being sufficiently general to support an indictment. But in the *P.Y.A. Quarries* case the nuisance was held to be sufficiently general where the inhabitants of about thirty houses and portions of two public highways were affected by dust and vibration.

3 Mens Rea

It has been held that it is not necessary to establish that it was D's object to create a public nuisance. In *Moore*,[3] D was held liable where he organised

---

[15] *Jones* (1812), 3 Camp. 230, *per* Lord ELLENBOROUGH. And see *Cross* (1812), 3 Camp. 224: "A stage-coach may set down or take up passengers in the street, this being necessary for the public convenience; but it must be done in a reasonable time": *per* Lord ELLENBOROUGH. For a similar statutory rule, see Public Service Vehicles Regulations 1936, reg. 7, and *Ellis* v. *Smith*, [1962] 3 All E.R. 954.

[16] [1946] K.B. 437; [1946] 2 All E.R. 247.

[17] *Sed quaere.* Would it be a defence to obstructing a pavement that D's strip-tease club was the only one in town.?

[18] *Fabbri* v. *Morris*, [1947] 1 All E.R. 315 (Highway Act 1835, s. 72).

[19] *Commentaries*, iii, 216.

[20] *A.-G.* v. *P.Y.A. Quarries, Ltd.*, [1957] 2 Q.B. at p. 191; [1957] 1 All E.R. at p. 908.

[1] (1802), 4 Esp. 200.

[2] The annoyance could be avoided by shutting the windows.

[3] (1832), 3 B. & Ad. 184.

pigeon-shooting on his land and, in consequence, great numbers of persons collected on the highway to shoot at pigeons as they escaped. Apparently this result (in 1832) was one which "the experience of mankind must lead anyone to expect."[4] Similarly the proprietor of a club[5] and of a theatre[6] have been held liable when the natural consequence of the nature of the entertainment provided within was to cause crowds or queues to gather outside and substantially to interfere with the public's use of the highway.

Although the authorities, on their face, suggest that D may be criminally liable in public nuisance for negligence, it would be dangerous to assume that this is necessarily and invariably so. References to "natural and probable consequences" are frequently ambiguous and may amount to no more than a finding of intention or recklessness. Modern civil cases on public nuisance certainly suggest that negligence is enough to establish civil liability. As the civil action involves establishing that the crime has been committed, this might be thought to settle the question. But it is not conclusive. While the plaintiff certainly has to establish the *actus reus* of public nuisance, it may well be that it is not necessary to prove the same degree of culpability as would be required in a criminal case. The rules in the civil action and the criminal prosecution are not necessarily the same. Thus DENNING, L.J., tells us:

> "In an action for a public nuisance, once the nuisance is proved, and the defendant is shown to have caused it, the legal burden is shifted to the defendant to justify or excuse himself."[7]

But in a criminal prosecution the principle of *Woolmington* v. *Director of Public Prosecutions*[8] surely requires that, at most, there is only an evidential burden on D who sets up justification or excuse.[9] Similarly, it may be that, in some types of nuisance at least, a higher degree of culpability—intention or recklessness—must be proved. It is true that BLACKBURN, J., has said that

> "the evidence which would maintain the action would also support the indictment";[10]

but that was a case where the proceedings were regarded as substantially civil in character.

Public nuisance covers a wide variety of different offences and it may be a mistake to assume that the same rules apply to all of them. In some of the cases, knowledge of the facts has been insisted upon.[11]

4 Vicarious Liability

In at least some types of public nuisance a master is liable for the acts of his servant, performed within the scope of employment, even though the mode of performance which creates the nuisance is contrary to the master's express

---

[4] *Per* LITTLEDALE, J.
[5] *Bellamy* v. *Wells* (1890), 60 L.J. Ch. 156.
[6] *Lyons, Sons & Co.* v. *Gulliver*, [1914] 1 Ch. 631.
[7] *Southport Corpn.* v. *Esso Petroleum Co., Ltd.*, [1954] 2 Q.B. at p. 197; [1954] 2 All E.R. at p. 571.
[8] [1935] A.C. 462; above, p. 26.
[9] Another obvious difference is that the civil case may be made out on a balance of probabilities, but the criminal case must be proved beyond reasonable doubt.
[10] *Stephens* (1866), L.R. 1 Q.B. 702 at p. 710; *infra*.
[11] Above, p. 543, footnotes 2, 3 and 4.

18—C.L.

orders. Thus in *Stephens*,[12] D was held liable for the obstruction by his servants of the navigation of a public river by depositing rubbish therein. The reason given was that the proceeding was, in substance, civil, the object being not to punish D but to prevent the continuation of the nuisance.[13] But MELLOR and SHEE, JJ., thought that there may be nuisances of such a character that this rule would not be applicable. Baty[14] criticises the ground of this decision and pertinently asks:

> "who is to decide whether [the] prosecution is 'substantially civil' or tinged with criminology ?"[15]

Certainly, prosecutions for obstructing the highway are by no means always civil in substance: frequently the object is the punishment of the offenders.[16] In *Chisholm* v. *Doulton*[17] FIELD, J., said that *Stephens* "must be taken to stand upon its own facts";[18] and the court held that, in a charge under the Smoke Nuisance (Metropolis) Act 1853 D was not criminally liable for the negligence of his servant in creating a nuisance. In cases of statutory nuisance D is vicariously liable only if the words of the statute require it.[19]

The rule imposing vicarious liability for public nuisance may thus be neither so firmly established nor so all-embracing as is sometimes supposed.

(2) OBSTRUCTION OF THE HIGHWAY[20]

1 By Public Nuisance

The highway can be used by members of the public for passing and re-passing and purposes reasonably incidental thereto.[1] It follows from this that there is a fundamental distinction between a public meeting on the highway and a public procession on the highway.[2] The public meeting is a civil trespass against the person or body in whom the surface of the highway is vested. Not every trespass on the highway is necessarily a public nuisance; it is so only if it interferes in an appreciable way with the public's right of passage and an impediment may be too trifling to be properly called a nuisance.[3] So a coffee stall erected in the middle of the highway, but between a public convenience and a fountain, is not necessarily a nuisance.[4] This is the explanation of *Burden* v. *Rigler*,[5] where it

---

[12] (1866), L.R. 1 Q.B. 702; see also *Medley* (1834), 6 C. & P. 292.
[13] Does this involve an inquiry into the motives of the prosecutor ? Or does it reflect the courts' own view of what is the proper remedy for the wrong in question ?
[14] *Vicarious Liability*, 204.
[15] In *Russell* (1854), 3 E. & B. 942, Lord CAMPBELL thought that the obstruction of navigation by building a wall was "a grave offence."
[16] See below, p. 547.
[17] (1889), 22 Q.B.D. 736.
[18] *Ibid.*, at p. 740.
[19] *Cf. Armitage, Ltd.* v. *Nicholson* (1913), 23 Cox C.C. 416.
[20] Brownlie, *Public Order*, Ch. 7.
[1] *Harrison* v. *Duke of Rutland*, [1893] 1 Q.B. 142; *Hickman* v. *Maisey*, [1900] 1 Q.B. 752.
[2] See Goodhart, "Public Meetings and Processions" (1937), 6 C.L.J. 161; E. C. S. Wade, "The Law of Public Meeting" (1939), 2 M.L.R. 177; Ivamy, "The Right of Public Meeting" (1949), 2 C.L.P. 183.
[3] *Ward* (1836), 4 Ad. & El. 384 at p. 387.
[4] *Bartholomew*, [1908] 1 K.B. 554.
[5] [1911] 1 K.B. 337.

was held that a public meeting on the highway is not necessarily unlawful;[6] and that it does not follow that, simply because a public meeting is on the highway, it can be freely interrupted, notwithstanding the provisions of the Public Meeting Act 1908.[7] There was no evidence of any obstruction in that case and a small group of persons might—like the coffee-stall—be so placed on the highway as not to interfere appreciably with the public's right of passage. But any appreciable interference by a public meeting will amount to nuisance.

The procession, on the other hand, is *prima facie* lawful, even though it inevitably interferes to some extent with the rights of others to use the highway, for those taking part in it are using the highway for its proper purpose. The rights of any individual or group to use the highway, even for passage, must however be exercised reasonably. If they are exercised so as *unreasonably* to interfere with the rights of other members of the public, then the user ceases to be lawful and becomes a nuisance. A procession is a nuisance only if it is an unreasonable interference. Thus, a conviction will be quashed if the judge fails to direct the jury that the user must be unreasonable.[8]

2   Statutes relating to Obstruction of the Highway

There are many statutory rules relating to obstruction of the highway. The more important are briefly considered below.

By s. 121 of the Highways Act 1959,

> "If a person without lawful authority or excuse, in any way wilfully obstructs the free passage along a highway he shall be guilty of an offence and shall be liable in respect thereof to a fine not exceeding fifty pounds."

By s. 28 of the Town Police Clauses Act 1847,

> ". . . every person who, by means of any cart, carriage, sledge, truck or barrow, or any animal or other means wilfully interrupts any public crossing, or wilfully causes any obstruction in any public footpath or other public thoroughfare . . ."

is guilty of an offence punishable with a fine of twenty pounds.

The essence of these offences is that the obstruction of the highway must be intentional. It is not enough to prove that D wilfully opened a car door which in fact obstructed the passage of a cyclist. Thus in *Eaton* v. *Cobb*[9] D looked in his mirror and reasonably, but mistakenly, concluded that the opening of the door would obstruct no one. As under the common law relating to public nuisance, it is not every obstruction which will amount to an offence under these sections. There must be some unreasonable user of the highway.[10] It appears to be irrelevant that no one was impeded in his usage of the highway.[11]

Under the Highways Act it would seem that any unreasonable obstruction would suffice. So D was convicted where he made a speech in the highway

---

[6] But it is *prima facie* a nuisance for a group of demonstrators to sit down in the highway: *Moule*, [1964] Crim. L.R. 303.
[7] Which makes it an offence to act in a disorderly manner at any *lawful* public meeting for the purpose of preventing the transaction of business.
[8] *Clark*, [1963] 3 All E.R. 884 (incitement to public nuisance).
[9] [1950] 1 All E.R. 1016 (Highway Act 1835).
[10] *Dunn* v. *Holt* (1904), 73 L.J.K.B. 341; *Gill* v. *Carson and Nield*, [1917] 2 K.B. 674.
[11] *Gill* v. *Carson, supra,* (obiter).

causing a crowd to assemble;[12] but it may be that a narrower interpretation should be put upon the Town Police Clauses Act and "other means" be construed *ejusdem generis* with the preceding list, and therefore not to include obstruction by a crowd[13] or by walking four abreast on a pavement causing the public to step into the road.[14]

Obstruction by motor vehicles is likely to be dealt with under the Motor Vehicles (Construction and Use) Regulations 1963, reg. 90 which is punishable with a fine of twenty pounds:[15]

> "No person in charge of a motor vehicle or trailer shall cause or permit the motor vehicle or trailer to stand on a road so as to cause any unnecessary obstruction thereof."

The test here is whether the obstruction is "necessary" not whether it is reasonable, though whether there is any difference between the two has not been decided. If parking is unreasonable then it is certainly unnecessary.[16] But Lord PARKER, C.J., has said that he wished to keep open the question whether reasonable parking could be held to be an unnecessary obstruction.[17] Whether there has been an unnecessary obstruction or not is a question of fact and the considerations likely to be taken into account seem to be much the same as those which would decide whether it was reasonable.[18]

3 LIBEL

(1) ACTUS REUS

A libel is traditionally described as a writing[19] which tends to injure the reputation of another by exposing him to hatred, ridicule and contempt. This definition has been found inadequate in the law of tort and the test which is more likely to be applied today is that proposed by Lord ATKIN:

> "Would the words tend to lower the plaintiff in the estimation of right-thinking members of society generally?"[20]

The publication of a libel is a common law misdemeanour but by s. 5 of the Libel Act 1843, it is now punishable by no more than one year's imprisonment. It is also a tort and the tortious aspect of libel is much more important. Criminal proceedings for libel are rare and are not encouraged by the courts. While it is not necessary in a criminal proceeding to prove that libel was likely to result in a breach of the peace, the proceeding should not be brought if the libel was unlikely either to disturb the peace or seriously to affect the reputation of the person defamed.[21] Consequently the subject is best studied as a branch of the

---

[12] *Horner* v. *Cadman* (1886), 55 L.J.M.C. 110.
[13] *Ball* v. *Ward* (1875), 33 L.T. 170.
[14] *Long* (1888), 59 L.T. 33; *Williams* (1891), 55 J.P. 406.
[15] S.I. 1963 No. 1646. Road Traffic Act 1960, s. 239.
[16] *Solomon* v. *Durbridge* (1956), 120 J.P. 231.
[17] *Worth* v. *Brooks*, [1959] Crim. L.R. 855.
[18] *Police* v. *O'Connor*, [1957] Crim. L.R. 478 and comment.
[19] Defamatory words published in the course of the performance of a play amount to a criminal libel unless the performance is given on a domestic occasion in a private dwelling: Theatres Act 1968, ss. 4 and 6.
[20] *Sim* v. *Stretch*, [1936] 2 All E.R. 1237 at p. 1240.
[21] *Wicks* (1936), 25 Cr. App. Rep. 168.

law of torts and the reader is referred to the books on that subject for the details.[1]

It is necessary here, however, to note the differences which exist between the crime and the tort. In the first place, libel is the only form of defamation which is indictable. Slander is not a crime.[2] The crime of libel is wider than the tort in three respects.

(1) Publication to the person defamed is sufficient in crime but not in tort.[3] In tort, the gist of the matter is the loss of the plaintiff's reputation and this only occurs through publication to a third party; but libel is said to be indictable because of the danger to the public peace[4] and this may obviously be even greater where the publication is to the prosecutor himself than where it is to another.

(2) The truth of the defamatory statement affords a complete defence (justification) in tort but in crime the defendant must prove not only that the statement is true but that it is for the public benefit that it be published. This is the effect of s. 6 of the Libel Act 1843, modifying the common law under which it is probable that truth was not a defence to an indictment.

(3) A libel on a class of persons is not *actionable* unless the words used are such as to lead persons acquainted with the plaintiff to believe that they refer to him as an individual;[5] but it may be indictable. Though no individual's reputation be harmed yet the libel may tend to a breach of the peace by or against members of the class. So a libel on the clergy of Durham or the Justices of the Peace of Middlesex is indictable[6] though probably not actionable. A libel on a small class, like a body of trustees or directors would probably be actionable as well, since it might be taken to refer to each member individually.

There is a fourth respect in which it has been thought that the criminal libel may be wider. It is not actionable to defame a dead person, but according to Coke[7] it is indictable, again because of a tendency to cause strife. Later decisions, however, suggest that this is so only if the libel is designed to bring the surviving relations of the deceased person into hatred or contempt[8]—in which case it seems to be a libel on them—or was actually intended to provoke or annoy the surviving relatives.[9]

(2) VICARIOUS LIABILITY

In other respects, the crime is narrower than the tort. In accordance with general principle, a master is liable in tort for libels published by his servant in the

---

[1] See Salmond, Ch. 9, Street, Ch. 16 and Winfield, Ch. 22.
[2] *Burford* (1669), 1 Ventr. 16; *Langley* (1704), 6 Mod. Rep. 124. But note that blasphemous or seditious spoken words, or words likely to cause a breach of the peace are indictable.
[3] *Adams* (1888), 22 Q.B.D. 66.
[4] *Holbrook* (1878), 4 Q.B.D. 42 at p. 46; but *cf. Wicks*, above, p. 548.
[5] *Knuppfer* v. *London Express Newspapers, Ltd.*, [1944] A.C. 116; [1944] 1 All E.R. 495.
[6] *Williams* (1822), 5 B. & Ald. 595.
[7] *De Libellis Famosis*, 5 Co. Rep. 125a.
[8] *Topham* (1791), 4 Term Rep. 126.
[9] *Ensor* (1887), 3 T.L.R. 366; and see Stephen, *Digest* (4th ed.), 208 n.

course of his employment.[10]   It may be that vicarious liability also extended at
common law to a criminal charge against the proprietor of a newspaper in respect
of libels published by his servant.[11]   However that may be, by the Libel Act
1843, s. 7 it is a defence to prove that the publication was made without D's
authority, consent or knowledge and that the publication did not arise from want
of care or due caution on his part.   It seems clearly to follow from this provision that D is liable for the acts of his servants within the scope of their authority
unless the statutory conditions are satisfied.

(3) MENS REA

Under s. 7 of the 1843 Act the master may be liable because of his negligence.   It
is not clear to what extent *mens rea* is required generally.   In principle, it ought to
be necessary to prove that D either knew of all the facts which make his statement defamatory of P, or was reckless whether such facts existed.   It is clear that
in tort it is not necessary to prove that D knew of all such facts.[12]   But even in
tort, it seems that in no case has it been decided that D may be liable where he has
taken all possible care to ensure that his statement is not defamatory[13]—that is,
though liability is said to be "absolute", yet it is still possible to hold that negligence is required.   While negligence is enough in tort, intention or recklessness
should be required in crime at common law.[14]

(4) PUBLICATION OF LIBEL KNOWN TO BE FALSE

The publication of a libel *known to be false* is a misdemeanour under s. 4 of
the Libel Act 1843 punishable with two years' imprisonment.   If it is not proved
that D knew the libel to be false or if it is true, D may be convicted of the common
law offence and sentenced to not more than one year's imprisonment.[15]

---

[10] Above, p. 98.
[11] *Walter* (1799), 3 Esp. 21; *Gutch, Fisher and Alexander* (1829), Mood. & M. 433. But
cf. Holbrook (1877), 13 Cox C.C. 650.
[12] *Cassidy* v. *Daily Mirror Newspapers, Ltd.*, [1929] 2 K.B. 331.
[13] Street, *Torts*, 303.
[14] Williams, C.L.G.P., § 29.
[15] *Boaler* v. *R.* (1888), 21 Q.B.D. 284.

CHAPTER 20

Offences against the Security of the State

1 TREASON

The law of treason, which is a capital offence, still stems from the Treason Act 1351. The Act was passed to clarify the uncertainty and arbitrariness of the common law which it supersedes. It declares that it is treason:

(1) to "compass or imagine the death of our lord the King or our lady his Queen or of their eldest son and heir."

(2) To "violate the King's companion [wife] or the King's eldest daughter unmarried or the wife [of] the King's eldest son and heir "

(3) To "levy war against our lord the King in his realm".

(4) To "be adherent to the King's enemies in his realm giving to them aid and comfort in the realm, or elsewhere".

(5) To slay "the chancellor, treasurer, or the King's justices . . . being in their places, doing their offices."

In addition it is treason by the Treason Act 1702, s. 3:

(6) By overt act to attempt to deprive or hinder the person next in succession to the Crown from succeeding.

The first, third and fourth of these forms of treason require some further consideration.

1 Compassing the King's Death

It is established that, despite the words of the Act, this requires more than a mental operation and that an overt act at least manifesting the intention, and perhaps intended to further it,[1] must be proved. Words used in conspiring or

---

[1] *Thistlewood* (1820), 33 State Tr. 681.

inciting to kill the sovereign are a sufficient overt act.[2] The Act was broadly construed by the judges to include conspiracies to imprison the King, to endanger his life and to depose him as well as actually to kill him. Certain of these "constructive treasons" are confirmed by the Treason Act 1795 which, by s. 1, provides that it is treason for any person to,

> "within the realm or without, compass, imagine, invent, devise or intend death or destruction or any bodily harm tending to death or destruction, maim or wounding, imprisonment or restraint, of the person of . . . the King,"

such compassing, etc., being expressed by

> "publishing any printing or writing or by any overt act or deed."

Other constructive treasons which were formerly in the 1795 Act were made felony by the Treason Felony Act 1848 and are now simply offences akin to treason.[3]

2 Levying War against the King in his Realm

The obvious form of treason under this head would be an insurrection against the authority of the sovereign. Enlisting and marching are sufficient overt acts without coming to an actual engagement. "War" has been interpreted in a wide sense and this type of treason was extended constructively to include forcible resistance to authority of the government in some public or general respect. So war is levied,

> "when an insurrection is raised to reform some national grievance, to alter the established law of religion, to punish magistrates, to introduce innovations of a public concern, to obstruct the execution of some general law by an armed force, or for any other purpose which usurps the government in matters of a public and general nature."[4]

It is only in the generality of its object that this form of treason differs from an ordinary unlawful assembly or riot. Treason might consist in

> "an assembling together for the purpose of destroying all meeting houses or all bawdy houses, under colour of reforming a public grievance; or an insurrection to reduce by force the general price of victuals, to inhance the common rate of wages, to level all inclosures, to expel all foreigners, or to reform by numbers or an armed force any real or imaginary grievance, of a public and general nature, in which the insurgents have no peculiar interest."[5]

If the object of the uprising is of a private or local nature, then it is not treason.[6]

> "As if the rising be, only against a particular market or to destroy particular inclosures, to remove a local nuisance, to release a particular prisoner, unless imprisoned for high treason, or even to oppose the execution of an act of parliament, if it only effect the district of the insurgents; as in the case of a turnpike act."

Such an uprising would, of course, be a riot. The distinction is of no practical importance today, for such disturbances, amounting technically to treasons, would certainly be dealt with as riots.

---

[2] See the list of overt acts in Archbold, §§ 3019, 3020.
[3] Below, p. 555.
[4] East, 1 P.C. 72.
[5] *Ibid.*, 73. *Dammaree* (1710), Fost. 214.
[6] *Ibid.*

3 Being Adherent to the King's Enemies

This is the most important form of treason, being that which is invoked to deal with acts of disloyalty in wartime. The Queen's enemies are foreign states in actual hostility against her, whether there has been a declaration of war or not.[7] Whether there is war or not is a question of fact for a jury but a certificate from a Secretary of State is conclusive evidence.[8] To incite a foreign state to make war would not amount to adherence until the incitement was successful[9] as, until then, there would be no "enemy" to adhere to; but it might be "constructive" compassing of the Queen's death. Assisting rebels within the realm is not adhering to the Queen's enemies—though it may be levying war against the Queen in her realm.

The offence is *being adherent to* the King's enemies. The words "giving aid and comfort to the King's enemies" are to be read in apposition, to explain what is meant by being "adherent to." D is guilty if he adheres to the King's enemies in his realm—that is, gives them aid and comfort in his realm; or if he adheres to them elsewhere—that is, gives them aid and comfort elsewhere. The Court of Criminal Appeal so held in *Casement*,[10] rejecting the argument that the vital words "or elsewhere" govern only "giving aid and comfort" and not "being adherent". According to the rejected argument the person being adherent must be in the realm, though he may be giving aid and comfort in the realm or elsewhere. This is certainly a possible interpretation of the rather curious language of the statute; but the opinions of Coke, Hale, Hawkins and Stephen supported the wider view which found favour. The phrase, "the King's enemies *in his realm*", is not explained by the court. Pollock suggested that it excluded from the law of treason adherence to enemies of the King, not in his capacity as King of England, but as Lord (in the fourteenth century) of provinces abroad.[11]

The effect of the decision in *Casement* was that D could be convicted of treason, although all the overt acts alleged were committed in Germany.[12]

4 Who may Commit Treason

The common law rule is that anyone who owes allegiance to the Crown at the time of the act may commit treason. It follows that:

(1) British subjects who are citizens of the United Kingdom and Colonies, who owe allegiance wherever they may be, may commit treason (under English law) in any part of the world.[13] A British subject cannot cast off his allegiance to the Crown in time of war by becoming a naturalised citizen of an enemy state. Indeed the act of becoming naturalised is itself an overt act of treason.[14]

(2) A British subject or a citizen of the Republic of Ireland who is not a citizen of the United Kingdom and Colonies may commit treason (under English law) only if the act be done in the United Kingdom or in any country of the

---

[7] East, 1 P.C. 77. As to the position of persons assisting enemies of a United Nations force, including British troops, see Bowett, *United Nations Forces*, pp. 53–54.

[8] *Bottrill, ex parte Kuechenmeister*, [1947] K.B. 41; [1946] 2 All E.R. 434.

[9] East, 1 P.C. 78.

[10] [1917] 1 K.B. 98.

[11] (1917), 33 L.Q.R. 110. Serjeant Sullivan's rejected explanation, [1917] 1 K.B. at pp. 101, 102 (see also *The Last Serjeant*, 269–270), was thought by Pollock "more ingenious than convincing."

[12] The indictment is set out in full in Archbold, § 3029.

[13] For an examination of the position in Rhodesia after the Unilateral Declaration of Independence, see [1966] Crim. L.R. 5 and 68.

[14] *Lynch*, [1903] 1 K.B. 444.

Commonwealth which is not self-governing; unless he owes allegiance under the rules stated in 3 (b) and 3 (c), below. At common law, all British subjects were governed by the rule stated in paragraph 1, above; but now, by s. 3 of the British Nationality Act 1948, a British subject who is not a citizen of the United Kingdom and Colonies is not guilty of an offence against English law by reason of anything done or omitted in a foreign country, or in any self-governing country of the Commonwealth[15] unless the act or omission would be an offence against English law if he were an alien acting in a foreign country. Since aliens may not commit treason unless they either are on British territory at the time of the act, or owe allegiance under 3 (b) or 3 (c) below, the position appears now to be as stated at the beginning of this paragraph.

If the facts of *Casement*[16] were to recur today D, not being a citizen of the United Kingdom and Colonies would not, *prima facie*, be guilty of treason because the acts done would not be an offence against English law if done by an alien in Germany. The position would be the same if the acts had been done, not in Germany, but in one of the independent countries of the Commonwealth, for example, Canada.

(3) An alien, even an alien enemy, may be guilty of treason if he has accepted the protection of the Crown, for this carries with it a correlative duty of allegiance. An alien is under the protection of the Crown:

(a) if he is voluntarily[17] on British territory (whether in one of the independent countries of the Commonwealth or not) at the time of the act, otherwise than as a foreign diplomatic representative or member of an invading or occupying force:[18] or

(b) if, having been within British territory, he leaves with a British passport which he still possesses at the time of the treasonable act.

Proposition (b) is the *ratio decidendi* of *Joyce* v. *Director of Public Prosecutions*[19] where it was held immaterial that D obtained the passport by false pretences. The basis of the decision is that by possession of the passport, D was enabled to obtain in a foreign country the protection extended to British subjects; and, therefore, that he owed a corresponding duty of allegiance. It was immaterial that he had never availed himself, and had no intention of availing himself, of the protection of the Crown. If he had surrendered the passport or taken any overt step (other than the act of treason itself) to withdraw his allegiance, this would have been effective; but there was no evidence that he had done so.[20]

(c) Where an alien after residing in British territory, goes abroad without a British passport, but leaving behind a family and "effects", his duty of allegiance may continue so long as his family and effects remain under the protection of the Crown. According to Foster[21] it was so resolved by an assembly of all the judges

---

[15] As specified in s. 1 (3) of the British Nationality Act 1948.

[16] Above, p. 553.

[17] It is assumed that a prisoner-of-war on British territory could not commit treason.

[18] Such an alien's duty of allegiance does not cease merely because the protection of the Crown is temporarily withdrawn owing to the occupation by the enemy of the area in which the alien resides: *De Jager* v. *A.-G. of Natal*, [1907] A.C. 326.

[19] [1946] A.C. 347; [1946] 1 All E.R. 186. And see *Re P. (G.E.) (an infant)*, [1964] 3 All E.R. 977.

[20] Lord PORTER dissented on the ground that the jury had not been properly directed that they must be satisfied that the passport remained in Joyce's possession at the relevant date.

[21] *Crown Law*, 185.

in 1707, and he and other writers of authority[1] accept this as law. The resolution, being made extra-judicially, was in no sense a binding precedent,[2] but, having been emphatically approved by the House of Lords in *Joyce*, it must probably be accepted as law. But its extent is uncertain.

> "Does 'family' mean wife or children or both?[3] Does the term include a wife living apart from her husband by judicial or voluntary separation? At what age, if any, do children cease to belong to the family?"[4]

The resolution seems to have been limited to the case where D had himself been in British territory and it could very reasonably be limited to that where D has his home in the realm at the time of the act.[5]

Joyce has been severely criticised.[6] Joyce had no *right* to protection while abroad; there was, at most, a possibility that he might have obtained protection through the passport. This makes the capital offence turn on the merest technicality.[7]

5 Procedure in Treason Trials

Certain special rules of procedure and evidence were enacted by Parliament for treason trials

> "for the safeguard of the subject under the weight of a state prosecution and the popular odium of so detestable a charge."[8]

It was, for example, necessary, in the absence of an admission, for the prosecution to produce at least two witnesses swearing to the same overt act or one witness to one and a second witness to another overt act of the same treason.

These complexities were swept away by the Treason Act of 1800 for cases where the overt act was directed against the person of the King. They continued to be applicable, however, to all other cases of treason until the Treason Act 1945 which extended the operation of the Act of 1800 to all cases of treason and misprision of treason. Now, by the Criminal Law Act 1967, s. 12 (4):

> ". . . the procedure on trials for treason or misprision of treason shall be the same as the procedure as altered by this Act on trials for murder."

2 OFFENCES AKIN TO TREASON

1 Under the Treason Felony Act 1848

The statute of 1351 made it treason to compass the King's death and to levy war against the King: but it did not, in terms, make it treason to conspire to levy war. It was established doctrine, however, that a conspiracy to levy war might

---

[1] Hawkins, 1 P.C., c. 2, § 5; East, 1 P.C. 52; Chitty on the *Prerogatives of the Crown*, 12, 13; Holdsworth in Halsbury (2nd ed.), Vol. 6, 146, n. (*t*).

[2] *Entick* v. *Carrington* (1765), 19 State Tr. 1029 at p. 1071, *per* Lord CAMDEN.

[3] Lord JOWITT said he regarded parents or brothers or sisters as a family for this purpose: [1946] A.C. at p. 368.

[4] Williams (1948), 10 C.L.J. at 62. See *Re P. (G.E.) (an infant)*, [1964] 3 All E.R. 977.

[5] *Cf.* Pitt Cobbett's *Cases on International Law* (6th ed.), 199, 200.

[6] Biggs, "Treason and the Trial of William Joyce" (1947), 7 Toronto L.J. 162; Williams, "The Correlation of Allegiance and Protection" (1948), 10 C.L.J. 54; Pitt Cobbett, *loc. cit.*

[7] On the position of British Protected Persons, see Williams, *op. cit.* and *cf. Re Mwenya*, [1960] 1 Q.B. 241; [1959] 3 All E.R. 525.

[8] East, 1 P.C. 106.

be given in evidence as an overt act of compassing the King's death.   The notion of compassing death was broadened by judicial construction to include conspiracies to do acts whereby the King's life might be endangered and to depose or imprison him; for, as Foster says,

> "experience hath shown that between the prisons and the graves of Princes the distance is very small."[9]

Other, perhaps less reasonable, constructions of the 1351 Act were adopted to extend its effect to conspiracies directed not at the royal person but at the overthrow of the government.   This judicial extension of the 1351 Act led to the same kind of uncertainty as had brought about the enactment of that statute itself; and in 1795 Parliament passed an "Act for the Safety and Preservation of His Majesty's Person and Government" which enacted that certain of these "constructive treasons" were indeed treason.   The part of that Act which remains in force has been set out above;[10]   but the remainder of its substantive provisions were repealed by the Treason Felony Act 1848[11] which enacted that certain constructive treasons were to be *felonies*, punishable with life imprisonment.   The offence is committed by one who shall,

> "within the United Kingdom or without, compass, imagine, invent, devise or intend",

any of the acts enumerated below:

> (1) "to deprive or depose . . . the Queen, from the style, honour, or royal name of the imperial crown of the United Kingdom, or of any other of Her Majesty's dominions and countries,"

> (2) "to levy war against her Majesty within any part of the United Kingdom, in order by force or constraint to compel her to change her measures or counsels, or in order to put any force or constraint upon or in order to intimidate or overawe both Houses or either House of Parliament,"

> (3) "to move or stir any foreigner or stranger with force to invade the United Kingdom or any other of her Majesty's dominions or countries under the obeisance of her Majesty;"

and shall,

> "express, utter or declare" [his compassing, etc.], "by publishing any printing or writing, or by open and advised speaking or by any overt act or deed,".

The Act specifically provides that

> "nothing herein contained shall lessen the force of or in any manner affect any thing enacted by the Treason Act 1351"[12]

and that an indictment for an offence under the Act is valid although the facts alleged and proved at the trial in law to treason.[13]

> "The result is, that the judicial construction of the statutes of treason has been adopted by the legislature, making, however, many of the offences which they

---

[9] *Crown Law*, 196.
[10] See p. 552.
[11] See the explanation of this legislation by the Attorney-General in *Mitchel* (1848), 6 St. Tr. 599 at pp. 636–639; and see *Mulcahy* v. *R.* (1868), L.R. 3 H.L. 306 at pp. 317–321.   See also Woodham-Smith, *The Great Hunger*, 340; and [1966] Crim. L.R. 7.
[12] Section 6.
[13] Section 7.

included felonies . . . so that in cases of positive proved design to overthrow the Queen's government by armed force, there is, it seems a choice of remedies."[14]

That is, the same act may now be both treason punishable by death under the construction put upon the 1351 Act and an offence punishable by life imprisonment under the 1848 Act.

2 Misprision of Treason

Misprision of treason is a common law misdemeanour and is committed when any person who knows, or has reasonable cause to believe, that another has committed treason, omits to disclose this information or any material part of it to the proper authority within a reasonable time.[15]

Conviction entails forfeiture to the Crown of all the offender's goods and the profits of his lands during his life. Stephen thought that misprision of treason was overlooked when forfeiture for felonies was abolished.[16]

3 Seditious Words and Libels

Sedition is closely related to the form of treason consisting in "levying war" against the Queen in her realm and may be a preliminary step towards that crime. There is probably no offence properly described as "sedition" in English law,[17] but the oral or written publication of words with a seditious intention is a common law misdemeanour and an agreement to further a seditious intention by doing any act is a conspiracy. The question, then, is what is a seditious intention? Stephen[18] defined it as:

> ". . . an intention to bring into hatred or contempt, or to excite disaffection against the person of, Her Majesty, her heirs or successors, or the government and constitution of the United Kingdom, as by law established, or either House of Parliament, or the administration of justice, or to excite Her Majesty's subjects to attempt, otherwise than by lawful means, the alteration of any matter in Church or State by law established, or to raise discontent or disaffection amongst Her Majesty's subjects, or to promote feelings of ill-will and hostility between different classes of such subjects.
>
> An intention to shew that Her Majesty has been misled or mistaken in her measures, or to point out errors or defects in the government or constitution as by law established, with a view to their reformation, or to excite Her Majesty's subjects to attempt by lawful means the alteration of any matter in Church or State by law established,[19] or to point out, in order to their removal, matters which are producing, or have a tendency to produce, feelings of hatred and ill-will between classes of Her Majesty's subjects, is not a seditious intention."

This definition was approved by the criminal code Commissioners and followed by CAVE, J., in his direction to the jury in *Burns*.[20]

---

[14] *Mulcahy* v. *R.* (1868), L.R. 3 H.L. at p. 320, *per* WILLES, J., delivering the opinion of the judges.

[15] *Cf.* the discussion of Misprision of Felony in the first edition of this book at p. 539; Stephen, *Digest*, Art. 209 and p. 489.

[16] *Digest*, p. 489.

[17] Stephen, 2 H.C.L. 298.

[18] *Digest* (3rd ed.), Art. 93. See now 9th ed., Art. 114.

[19] In the fourth and subsequent editions, Stephen inserted at this point ". . . or to incite any person to commit any crime in disturbance of the peace . . . ."

[20] (1886), 16 Cox C.C. 335 at p. 360.

21

(*a*) *Real or presumed intention?*—The most important and difficult question in the law of sedition is whether the "intention" which must be proved is a genuine intention or whether, as Stephen himself put it:[1]

> "In determining whether the intention with which any words were spoken, any document was published, or any agreement was made, was or was not seditious, every person must be deemed to intend the consequences which would naturally follow from his conduct at the time and under the circumstances in which he so conducted himself.

There is some authority[2] in favour of this objective test, which would require no more *mens rea* than an intention to publish the words which were published. In the Scottish case of *Grant*,[3] five judges held that the use of word "calculated" (that is, "likely") to produce disaffection, etc. was enough and that it was not necessary to prove an actual intention to produce that result. The court found support in the English authorities. But Lord COCKBURN, who dissented, thought that there had been confusion between (a) the meaning of the libel and (b) the intention of the writer;[4] and that while the former is very cogent evidence of the latter, it is not the only evidence. Similar confusion has been found in other branches of the criminal law[5] and it would not be surprising that it should exist here also.

Lord COCKBURN's view was that the true meaning of the English (as well as the Scottish) authorities was that either intention or recklessness as to the consequences must be proved. This would be in accordance with principle. One judge at least has gone even further and held that recklessness is not enough and that intention must be proved. In *Burns*,[6] CAVE, J., told the jury that it was not enough that the natural consequence of the words used was disorder but:

> ". . . although it is a good working rule to say that a man must be taken to intend the natural consequences of his acts, and it is very proper to ask a jury to infer, if there is nothing to show the contrary, that he did intend the natural consequences of his acts, yet, if it is shown from other circumstances, that he did not actually intend them, I do not see how you can ask a jury to act upon what has then become a legal fiction."

and that

> "It is one thing to speak with the distinct intention to produce disturbances, and another thing to speak recklessly and violently of what is likely to produce disturbances."[7]

In so directing the jury, CAVE, J., said he again had the authority of STEPHEN, J. This is remarkable, since he had just read out Article 93 of the *Digest*, and in Article 94 Stephen says the opposite! But CAVE, J., was at this point relying on the *History of the Criminal Law*[8] and this work does indeed support his direction. Stephen there appears to argue, in effect, that the law *was* as stated

---

[1] *Digest* (4th ed.), Art. 94.
[2] *Burdett* (1820), 1 State Tr. N.S. 1; *Harvey* (1823), 2 B. & C. 257; *Cobbett* (1804), 29 State Tr. 1, as reported in Archbold (12th ed.), 607; see 7 State Tr. N.S. at p. 621 n. (a); *Lovett* (1839), 9 C. & P. 462.
[3] (1848), 7 State Tr. N.S. 507.
[4] Where it is the writer who is charged. If it is not, his intention is irrelevant; below, p. 560.
[5] Above, pp. 51–52.
[6] (1886), 16 Cox C.C. 355 at p. 364.
[7] *Ibid*.
[8] Vol. 2, 359.

in his Article 94[9] before the Libel Act 1792 but that that Act enlarged the definition

"by the addition of a reference to the specific intention of the libeller—to the purpose for which he wrote."

Thus Stephen seems to have been inconsistent. CAVE, J.'s adoption of the view in the *History* in preference to that in the *Digest* can hardly have been accidental.

The ruling in *Burns* was, in effect, followed by BIRKETT, J., in *Caunt*,[10] where he expressly adopted the proposition in *Steane*,[11] under which nothing less than a *desire* to cause the disorder etc., would suffice.

One modern authority which is out of tune with these cases is *Aldred*,[12] where COLERIDGE, J., stated the test to be

"was the language used calculated, or was it not, to promote public disorder . . .";

and that the innocence of the motive with which it may have been published was no defence. The irrelevance of motive may be conceded—a man may conceivably have admirable motives for wishing to overthrow the government by violence—but COLERIDGE, J.'s language seems also to exclude the necessity for proof of an intention to overthrow the government. It is submitted that the better view is that stated in *Burns*[13] and in *Caunt*.[14]

(b) *Intention to cause violence.*—There is a further qualification to be made to the rule as stated by Stephen. It is not sufficient that D used words with the intention of achieving one of the objects specified; he must have intended to achieve that object *by violence*. In *Collins*,[15] LITTLEDALE, J., according to Stephen,

"states the modern view of the law plainly and fully. . . . In one word nothing short of direct incitement to disorder and violence is a seditious libel."[16]

In *Burns*,[17] CAVE, J., told the jury that the question was, did D incite the people whom he was addressing to redress their grievances *by violence*?[18] In *Aldred*, COLERIDGE, J., though not requiring proof of intention, did require language calculated to incite others to

"public disorders, to wit, rebellions, insurrections, assassinations, outrages, or any physical force or violence of any kind."[19]

In *Caunt*,[20] BIRKETT, J., said:

"It is not enough to provoke hostility or ill-will . . . sedition has always had implicit in the word public disorder, tumult, insurrections or matters of that kind."

---

[9] 4th ed.
[10] (1947), reported in *An Editor on Trial* (Morecambe Press, Ltd.).
[11] Above, p. 38.
[12] (1909), 22 Cox C.C. 1.
[13] Above, p. 558.
[14] *Supra.* Consider the effect of s. 8 of the Criminal Justice Act 1967, above, p. 52.
[15] (1839), 9 C. & P. 456 at p. 461.
[16] 2 H.C.L. 374, 375.
[17] Above, p. 558.
[18] In holding that an intention to cause violence was not a necessary ingredient of sedition under the Criminal Code of the Gold Coast, the Privy Council was concerned solely with the construction of the relevant section and cast no doubt on the authority of *Burns*: *Wallace-Johnson* v. *R.*, [1940] A.C. 231 at p. 239; [1940] 1 All E.R. 241 at pp. 243, 244.
[19] (1909), 22 Cox C.C. at p. 4.
[20] *Supra.*

(*c*) *Actus reus.*—It cannot be enough that the words are used with a seditious intention. There must also be an *actus reus*. That is, the words must have a tendency to incite public disorder. In deciding whether the words have this tendency, it is proper to look at all the relevant surrounding circumstances—the state of public feeling, the place, the mode of publication, and so on. Most important of all, the jury is entitled

> ". . . to look at the audience addressed, because language which would be innocuous practically speaking, if used to an assembly of professors or divines, might produce a different result if used before an excited audience of young and uneducated men."[1]

On the other hand if the tendency of the words is to incite ordinary people to violence, it is no defence that the audience addressed was unaffected by the incitement:

> "A man cannot escape from the consequences of uttering words with intent to excite people to violence solely because the persons to whom they are addressed may be too wise or too temperate to be seduced into that violence."[2]

Thus words are seditious (i) if they are likely to incite ordinary men whether likely to incite the audience actually addressed or not; or (ii) if, though not likely to incite ordinary men, they are likely to incite the audience actually addressed.

D need not have himself written the libel. The crime may consist in the publication of the words of another with the appropriate intent. If the publisher has *mens rea* it is immaterial that the writer of the libel did not.[3]

Whether publication is necessary is not settled. In *Burdett*,[4] HOLROYD, J., and ABBOTT, C.J., thought that the mere composition of the libel without publishing it was an offence. Earlier cases[5] supported this view but their authority was forcefully attacked by Sir James Scarlett, afterwards Lord ABINGER.[6]

(*d*) *Sedition and freedom of speech.*—It is common for the judge to stress the importance of freedom of speech and of the press. In *Burns*,[7] CAVE, J., said

> "You will recollect how valuable a blessing the liberty of the press is to all of us, and sure I am that that liberty will meet no injury—suffer no diminution at your hands.

and in *Caunt*,[8] BIRKETT, J.'s last words to the jury were:

> "Two matters would seem to emerge over all others in this case.
> First of all it is in the highest degree essential that nothing should be done in this court to weaken the liberty of the press; and secondly, remember at all times that it is the duty of the prosecution to prove this case beyond all reasonable doubt."[9]

---

[1] *Aldred* (1909), 22 Cox C.C. at p. 3, *per* COLERIDGE, J.
[2] *Burns* (1886), 16 Cox C.C. at p. 365, *per* CAVE, J. In *Cohen* (1916), 34 W.L.R. 210, it was held that, if the words were likely to be an incitement to an ordinary man, D was not entitled to the benefit of the steadfast loyalty of the person actually addressed.
[3] (1789), 22 St. Tr. 300, *per* EYRE, C.B., delivering the unanimous opinion of the judges.
[4] (1820), 1 St. Tr. N.S. at pp. 122, 123 and 128, 139.
[5] They are cited in argument, *ibid.*, at 57.
[6] *Ibid.*
[7] (1886), 16 Cox C.C. at p. 362.
[8] Above, p. 559.
[9] See also COLERIDGE, J., in *Aldred* (1909), 22 Cox C.C. at p. 4.

4 Unlawful Oaths

By the Unlawful Oaths Act 1797, s. 1, it is an offence punishable with seven years' imprisonment (i) to administer or (ii) to assist in, or (iii) even to be present at and consenting to the administration of an oath (a) to engage in any mutinous or seditious purpose or (b) to disturb the public peace or (c) to be of any association formed for such purpose or (d) to obey the orders of any body not lawfully constituted or any person or body not having authority by law for that purpose or (e) not inform or give evidence against any associate, confederate or other person or (f) not to reveal any illegal combination or act or any illegal oath.

Notwithstanding a reference in the preamble to the Act to mutinous and seditious purposes, the Act is not confined to such cases but extends to any oaths of the nature set out above. So an oath not to reveal a combination was held to be unlawful although the purpose of the combination was not mutinous or seditious but to raise the wages and make regulations in a certain trade[10] and where a party of men about to engage in night poaching took the oath not to "peach upon each other" they were held guilty.[11]

5 Incitement to Mutiny and Disaffection[12]

By the Incitement to Mutiny Act 1797 it is an offence punishable with life imprisonment "maliciously and advisedly" (a) to endeavour to seduce any member of the forces from his "duty *and* allegiance" to the Crown or (b) to incite to mutiny or (c) to make a mutinous assembly or (d) to commit "any traitorous or mutinous practice whatsoever . . ."

By the Incitement to Disaffection Act 1934, s. 1, it is an offence punishable with two years' imprisonment "maliciously and advisedly" to endeavour to seduce any member of the forces from his "duty *or* allegiance" to the Crown.

It is not necessary to prove that the endeavour was directed against any named individuals; it may be addressed to the forces generally.[13]

It is clear that these offences require *mens rea*. The word "advisedly" appears to be equivalent to "knowingly"[14] and D cannot be convicted unless it is proved that he knew P to be a member of the forces. "Maliciously" requires that the D should be intentional or reckless as to the seduction, etc. The 1934 Act is clearly very much wider in its scope since an endeavour to seduce from either "duty" or "allegiance" is enough, whereas under the 1797 Act the endeavour must be to seduce from both. A relatively trivial offence, such as persuading a soldier to overstay his leave is thus within the later Act, but not the earlier.[15]

It is also an offence under s. 2 of the 1934 Act to be in possession of a document, the dissemination of which would be an offence under s. 1, with intent to commit or to aid and abet or counsel the commission of such an offence.

By the Police Act 1964, s. 53, it is an offence punishable with two years' imprisonment if any person

"causes or attempts to cause or does any act calculated to cause disaffection"

---

[10] *Marks* (1802), 3 East 157.
[11] *Brodribb* (1816), 6 C. & P. 571. See also Unlawful Oaths Act 1812; Seditious Meetings Act 1817.
[12] Street, *Freedom, the Individual and the Law*, 211–218.
[13] *Bowman* (1912), 76 J.P. 271.
[14] *Fuller* (1797), 2 Leach 790.
[15] See Street, *op. cit.*, at 216.

amongst members of any police force, or does any act calculated to induce a policeman to withhold his services or commit breaches of discipline. It is by no means so clear that *mens rea* is necessary here: there are no such words as "maliciously and advisedly" and an "act calculated" may well mean no more than an act the probable consequence of which is disaffection, etc.

3 OFFICIAL SECRETS[16]

1 Spying and Sabotage

By s. 1 (1) of the Official Secrets Act 1911 it is an offence punishable with fourteen years' imprisonment,

> "If any person for any purpose prejudicial to the safety or interests of the State—
>
> (a) approaches, inspects, passes over or is in the neighbourhood of, or enters any prohibited place within the meaning of this Act; or
>
> (b) makes any sketch, plan, model, or note which is calculated to be or might be or is intended to be directly or indirectly useful to an enemy; or
>
> (c) obtains, collects, records, or publishes or communicates to any other person any secret official code word or pass word or any sketch, plan, model, article, or note, or other document or information which is calculated to be or might be or is intended to be directly or indirectly useful to an enemy; . . ."

A "prohibited place" is defined by s. 3 and includes such places as naval, military and air force establishments, munitions factories and depots belonging to or occupied by the Crown, or used under contract with the Crown; and any place belonging to or used by the Crown which a Secretary of State may declare to be a prohibited place for the time being, on the ground that information with respect to it, or damage to it, would be useful to an enemy.

(*a*) *Scope of the section.*—The section is clearly directed against spying; and the marginal note reads "Penalties for spying". But it has been held by the House of Lords that the marginal note is no part of the Act and cannot be used as an aid to construction.[17]

The literal meaning of the section clearly extends beyond spying. A person may, for example, approach an airfield or munitions factory with the object of causing an explosion, so as to impede the defence of the realm against an enemy. If this is a purpose prejudicial to the safety or interests of the state, his conduct falls within the plain meaning of s. 1.

In *Chandler*,[17] the accused, members of an organisation supporting nuclear disarmament, approached an airfield with the admitted object of grounding all aircraft, immobilising the airfield and reclaiming it for civilian purposes. The Court of Criminal Appeal and the House of Lords held that this conduct was an offence against the Act. This interpretation was fortified by the fact that the definition of "prohibited place" included not only places where "information

---

[16] D. G. T. Williams, *Not in the Public Interest*; Street, *Freedom, the Individual and the Law,* 218 *et seq.*

[17] *Chandler* v. *Director of Public Prosecutions,* [1964] A.C. 763; [1962] 3 All E.R. 142.

with respect thereto" would be useful to an enemy, but also places where "damage thereto" or the "destruction or obstruction thereof or interference with" would be useful to an enemy. This suggests that

> "The saboteur just as much as the spy in the ordinary sense is contemplated as an offender under the Act."[18]

Apart from the rejected marginal note, there was nothing in the Act to support the narrow construction which the defence sought to put upon it and the decision on this point seems clearly correct, according to the established rules of statutory interpretation. It has, however, been clearly demonstrated[19] that the actual intention of Parliament was to legislate only against spying. The restrictive rules of statutory interpretation allowed by our law prevented the court from looking at the Parliamentary Debates on the subject; but whether a prosecution should, in these circumstances, have been brought on the facts of *Chandler* is a different matter. It has been suggested[20] that it was

> "indefensible on the part of the Attorney General to press arguments upon the courts to give the section a wider meaning"

than, as he knew, or ought to have known, was intended by Parliament.

(*b*) *Mens rea.*—Clearly D must intend an *actus reus* as defined in s. 1 and he must have a "purpose prejudicial to the safety or interests of the state". The meaning of this latter element in the *mens rea* provided the most difficult problem in *Chandler*. D argued unsuccessfully that his purpose was not prejudicial to the safety or interests of the State because he believed that it was in the interests of the State that these aircraft, which he believed to contain nuclear weapons, should be immobilised. It appears from the speeches of their Lordships:

(i) That the term "purpose" requires a subjective element. It must be proved at least that D, when he acts, knows that "certain objects will probably be achieved by the act whether he wants them or not."[1] This proposition perhaps understates the requirements of "purpose" and was wider than was necessary for the decision for, as Lord REID said:

> "The accused both intended and desired that the base should be immobilised for a time, and I cannot construe purpose in any sense that does not include that state of mind."[2]

(ii) When it has been proved that D had certain objects for his purpose, the further question, whether those objects are prejudicial to the safety or interests of the State, is an objective one. D's opinion on this issue is irrelevant to his liability. D's purpose was the immobilisation of the airfield. His opinion whether that was beneficial or prejudicial to the interests of the State was irrelevant. Of course, he knew that he was acting contrary to the policy of the State. The answer might be different if the accused was unaware that this was so.

---

[18] [1964] A.C. at p. 794; [1962] 3 All E.R. at p. 148, *per* Lord RADCLIFFE.
[19] By D. Thompson, "The Committee of 100 and the Official Secrets Act 1911", [1963] *Public Law* 201.
[20] *Ibid.*
[1] [1964] A.C. at p. 805; [1962] 3 All E.R. at p. 155, *per* Lord DEVLIN.
[2] [1964] A.C. at p. 790; [1962] 3 All E.R. at p. 146.

(iii) The disposition of the armed forces of the Crown is within the exclusive discretion of the Crown.[3] Whether the policy of the Crown is right or wrong is not an issue capable of trial in a court of law and, accordingly evidence is not admissible on it.[4]

It followed necessarily that D's intention to obstruct the operations of the armed forces of the Crown was a purpose prejudicial to the safety or interest of the state.

Though the decision has been vigorously criticised,[5] it is submitted that it arrived at the only sensible interpretation of the Act. If it were necessary to prove that D believed his object to be prejudicial to the interests of the state, a man would have had a defence if, during the world wars, he believed that it was in Britain's interests that Germany should win the war. Such an interpretation would obviously defeat the object of the Act. If the question were whether the policy of the Crown which D obstructed was in the interests of the state, the court would be presented with an issue which it could not properly try; and, if the Act can reasonably be read so as to avoid raising such an issue, then it should be so read.[6]

The result, nevertheless, is that the Act appears to be uncomfortably far-reaching: Does it now follow, as defending counsel suggested in argument, that,

> "a workman on strike who approached a government establishment, for example Woolwich Arsenal, in order to induce workers there to come out on strike would be guilty under this Act . . ." ?[7]

2   Wrongful Communication of Information

Section 2 of the Act of 1911 is designed to prevent the misuse of any sketch, plan, model, article, note, document or information to which the section applies. It is a misdemeanour for a person who has a sketch, etc., or information, within the meaning of the section—

(1) To communicate it to any person except (a) a person to whom he is authorised to communicate it; (b) a person to whom it is, in the interest of the State, his duty to communicate it.

(2) To use it for the benefit of any foreign power or in any other manner prejudicial to the safety or interests of the State.

(3) To retain it when he has no right to do so.

(4) To fail to take reasonable care of it, or so to conduct himself as to endanger its safety.

A person who receives the article or information knowing or having reasonable cause to believe that it is given in contravention of the Act, is likewise guilty of an offence punishable by two years' imprisonment.[8]

---

[3] "Those who are responsible for the national security must be the sole judges of what the national security requires", *per* Lord PARKER OF WADDINGTON in *The Zamora*, [1916] 2 A.C. 77 at p. 107, quoted with approval by Lord PARKER, C.J., in the Court of Criminal Appeal and Lords HODSON and DEVLIN in the House of Lords in *Chandler*.
[4] Lord DEVLIN differed from the remainder of the House in holding that, while it might be presumed that the immobilisation of the airfield was prejudicial to the interest of the state, the presumption was not irrebuttable.
[5] By Thompson, *op. cit.*
[6] See Lord REID, [1964] A.C. at p. 791; [1962] 3 All E.R. at p. 147.
[7] [1964] A.C at p. 778.
[8] Section 2 (2).

The section is very far-reaching since it includes any of the specified articles or any information which D has obtained, "owing to his position as a person who holds or has held office under her Majesty". The article or information need not be of a secret character or even confidential. In *Crisp and Homewood*[9] AVORY, J., held that the section was applicable to the case of D, a clerk in the War Office, who handed to the director of a firm of tailors copies of documents containing particulars of contracts between the War Office and contractors for army officers' clothing.

Under this section, no *mens rea* beyond an intention to cause the *actus reus* is required, and it is no defence that D did not intend to do anything to prejudice the safety or interests of the State.[10]

3 False Pretences to Gain Admission to Prohibited Places

By s. 1 of the Official Secrets Act 1920 it is an offence to practise various specified false pretences for the purpose of gaining admission to a prohibited place. These include using the uniform of a member of the forces, or one so nearly resembling it as to be calculated to deceive, forging a pass, personating one holding office under the Crown, using the die, seal or stamp of a government department, or one like it; and making a false statement or omission, orally or in writing in any declaration or application.

4 Obstruction of Guards in Prohibited Places

By s. 3 of the 1920 Act it is an offence for a person in the vicinity[11] of any prohibited place to "obstruct, knowingly mislead or otherwise interfere with or impede" any police officer or member of the forces who is "on guard, sentry, patrol or other similar duty" in relation to the prohibited place.

Offences under ss. 1 and 3 of the 1920 Act are punishable with two years' imprisonment.

5 Acts Preparatory, Incitement and Attempt

By s. 7 of the 1920 Act, to attempt to commit an offence under that Act or the Act of 1911, or to solicit or incite or endeavour to persuade another to commit such an offence; or to aid and abet or[12] to do any act preparatory to the commission of such an offence is an offence and is punishable as if the offence attempted, etc., had been committed. This provision goes further than the common law in that it includes "acts preparatory" which would not be offences at all at common law.

Thus, an act preparatory to the commission of an offence under s. 1 of the 1911 Act is an offence punishable with fourteen years' imprisonment. For example, D buys paper and pencils with a view to making a sketch of a military installation. In such a case it will, of course be necessary to establish *mens rea* that is (it is submitted) an intention to complete the offence as defined in the section.

---

[9] (1919), 83 J.P. 121.
[10] *Fell*, [1963] Crim. L.R. 207.
[11] It has been held that the words "in the vicinity of" mean "*in*, or in the vicinity of"; so that D could be convicted where he obstructed a member of the R.A.F. actually on an R.A.F. Station: *Adler* v. *George*, [1964] 2 Q.B. 7; [1964] 1 All E.R. 628.
[12] The Act says "aids abets *and* does any act preparatory"; but it has been held that, in order to produce an intelligible result, the words quoted must be read as if "or" were substituted for "and": *Oakes*, [1959] 2 Q.B. 350; [1959] 2 All E.R. 92 (C.C.A.). See comment at [1959] Crim. L.R. 457.

21*

Index

A

E

ELECTRICITY,
abstraction of, 379
EMBRACERY,
misdemeanour of, 514
EMPLOYMENT,
earning by, obtaining by deception, 394
ENTERING. *See* BURGLARY
ESCAPE,
offence of, 515
EVIDENCE,
false, fabrication of, 512, 513
And see PERJURY
EXHIBITIONS,
articles, removal from, 398–400

F

FALSE ACCOUNTING,
elements of offence, 395, 396
gain and loss, meaning, 396
mens rea, 396
statutory provision, 395
FALSE DECLARATIONS. *See under*
PERJURY
FALSE EVIDENCE,
fabrication of, 512, 513
And see PERJURY
FALSE IMPRISONMENT,
area of confinement, 272
arrest—
arrestable offence, where, 274–276
breach of peace, 276
constable, by, 274–276
private person, by, 274–276
statutory powers, 274–275
valid warrant, under, 274
assault unnecessary, 272
child-stealing, 277
consciousness of, relevance, 272, 273
crime and tort, as, 271
direction, free to go in other, 272
indirect means, 273
innocent agent, 273
kidnapping, 276, 277
meaning of imprisonment, 271, 272
mens rea, 276
omission, by, 273, 274
unlawful, must be, 274
FALSE PRETENCES,
obtaining by. *See* DECEPTION
procurement of women by. *See under*
SEXUAL OFFENCES
prohibited place, to gain entry, 565
FALSE STATEMENTS,
making or using, 513, 514
And see PERJURY
FELONY,
misdemeanours and, distinction abolished, 23, 24
FIREARMS. *See also* OFFENSIVE
WEAPONS
aggravated burglary, 417, 418
arrest, use to resist—
additional offence, as, 278, 279
statutory provision, 279
strict liability, 280
carrying, with intent, 281, 282
imitation, 279

FIREARMS—*continued*
meaning, 279
offensive weapons. *See* OFFENSIVE
WEAPONS
possessing with intent, 280, 281
prohibited weapons, 278
public place, having in, 282
statutory definition, 281
regulations, 278
trespassing with, 281
unlawful possession—
offences, in relation to, 279
other offence, commission necessary, 280
statutory provision, 279
strict liability, whether, 280
FORGERY,
authority, fictitious, 448
cheque, false signature, 448
common law obsolete, 439, 440
defraud or deceive, intent to—
definition, 449
distinction, drawbacks of, 451, 452
economic loss, 449, 450
honest belief, 450, 451
prejudice to recipient, 450
public documents, 449, 451
third party, 452
documents—
instruments distinguished, 453
meaning—
examples, 440, 441
information, giving, other use, 442
instrument, 442, 443
painting, 441
wrappers for baking powder, 442,
writing, 441
no legal effect, 447, 448
possession of, 454
public, 449, 451
uttering, 452
false document—
accounts, false entries, 444
circumstances making, 443
copy of—
forged document, 445, 446
genuine document, 444, 445
falsity and forgery distinguished, 446
genuine, to be used as, 444, 445
intent, relevance of, 445
lie about itself, 443
omission, by, 446, 447
photostat copies, 445, 446
forged instruments, demanding on—
"by virtue of", meaning, 453, 454
causal connection, 454
economic loss, 452, 453
instruments and documents, 453
money or property, 452, 453
statutory provision, 453
implements of, possession, 454
instances of, 448, 449
materiality of falsity, 447, 448
mens rea, 449–452
omission, by, 446, 447
public documents, 449, 451
signature, same name, 449
statutory provision, 440
uttering forged document, 452

OBSTRUCTION—*continued*
  highway, of—
    appreciable interference, 546, 547
    processions and meetings, 547
    public nuisance, 543, 546, 547
      And see PUBLIC NUISANCE
    statutory provisions—
      motor vehicles, 548
      unreasonable, must be, 548
      wilful obstruction, 547
    unreasonable user, 547
  meaning, 261, 262
  mens rea, 263,
  refusal to answer questions, 262, 263
  warning to escape, 261, 262
OBTAINING,
  deception, by. *See* DECEPTION
OFFENSIVE WEAPONS,
  aggravated burglary, 417, 418
  burden of proof, 283
  injury—
    carrying for purpose, 283, 284
    made or adapted for, 283, 284
  lawful—
    authority, 285
    possession originally, 284
  meaning—
    categories, 283
    injury to person, for causing, 282
  mens rea, 286
  poaching, night, 287
  public meetings, etc., at, 286, 287
    place, 286
  purpose, meaning of, 283, 284
  reasonable excuse, 285
  smuggling, when, 287
  statutory defence, 285
    provisions, 282
  weapon of offence distinguished, 283
OFFICIAL SECRETS,
  attempt, 565
  incitement, 565
  information, communication of—
    elements of offence, 564
    far reaching scope, 565
    mens rea, 565
    person receiving, 564
  preparatory acts, 565
  prohibited place—
    false pretences to gain entry, 565
    guards, obstruction of, 565
    meaning, 562
  spying and sabotage—
    far reaching scope, 564
    interpretation of provision, 563
    mens rea, 563, 564
    obstructing Crown forces, 564
    purpose prejudicial to State, 563, 564
    scope beyond spying, 562, 563
    statutory provision, 562
OMISSION,
  actus reus, as element of. *See under*
    ACTUS REUS
  false imprisonment by, 273, 274
  forgery by, 446, 447
  public nuisance by, 543
  rarely punished, 35

OVERDRAFTS,
  deception, obtaining by, 393

P

PARENTS,
  abduction of girls from, 305
  child, reasonable chastisement, 257
    stealing, 277
PARTIES,
  accomplices. *See* ACCOMPLICES
  principal offender, 81
  victims as, 96, 97
PECUNIARY ADVANTAGE,
  deception, obtaining by. *See* DECEP-
    TION
PEDAL CYCLES,
  taking, 403
PERJURY,
  affirmation, 504
  births or deaths, false statements, 237,
    511
  child, unsworn testimony, 504
  common law offence, origins of, 503
  defence, not lawfully sworn, 504, 505
  false statements, and, 503
  God, belief in, 504
  homicide by, 194, 195
  judicial proceeding—
    jurisdiction, court lacking, 505
    power to receive evidence on oath, 505
    statement made for, 505, 506
    statutory definition, 505
  materiality, rule as to—
    admissibility, testimony, 507
    circumstantial evidence, 507
    common law, 506
    credit, testimony as to, 507, 508
    narrow construction, 506
    Perjury Act, doctrine of, 508
    relevance to proceedings, 508
    result, evidence bearing on, 506, 507
  mens rea, 509, 510
  mistake, witness sworn by, 504
  offences akin to—
    common law, at, 503
    false statements—
      births or deaths, as to, 511
      marriage, relating to, 510, 511
      oath on, 510, 511
      statutory declarations, etc., 511, 512
      vocation, registration for, 512
  opinion, statements of, 509
  statutory definition, 503
  subornation of, 510
  true, statement may be, 509
  witness lawfully sworn, 504, 505
PERMITTING,
  mens rea, whether importing, 75, 76
PERSONATION,
  juryman, of, 514
PLANTS,
  theft of, 359, 360
PLEDGE,
  theft, as, 354, 355
POACHING,
  night, by, offensive weapons, 287

MADE AND PRINTED IN GREAT BRITAIN BY
WILLIAM CLOWES AND SONS, LIMITED, LONDON AND BECCLES